ORGANIZATIONAL SYSTEMATICS

Taxonomy, Evolution, Classification

BILL McKELVEY

UNIVERSITY OF CALIFORNIA PRESS
BERKELEY   LOS ANGELES   LONDON

University of California Press
Berkeley and Los Angeles, California

University of California Press, Ltd.
London, England

Copyright © 1982 by The Regents of the University of California

Library of Congress Cataloging in Publication Data

McKelvey, Bill.
  Organizational systematics—taxonomy, evolution, classification.

  Bibliography: p. 463
  Includes index.
  1. Organization. 2. System analysis. 3. Organizational change.
4. Numerical taxonomy. I. Title. HM131.M378   302.3'5'012
82-2064
ISBN 0-520-04225-5   AACR2

Printed in the United States of America

1   2   3   4   5   6   7   8   9

CONTENTS

ACKNOWLEDGMENTS

I have been down several paths searching for explanations of why organizations are the way they are and do what they do. None of them were what Castenada called the "path with heart." I have finally found my path with heart. Many people have helped me learn along the way and many more have had a hand in the nurturing of this book by offering support, references, and critical remarks, asking questions, and offering ideas and solutions. Some deserve special mention.

First, the people of the great State of California deserve credit for unknowingly paying for my time, for allowing me the opportunity to teach a five-course load in a management school while spending the rest of my time sitting in a biology library thinking and writing about something I thought was important. It is a great honor to have had such a privilege. Little did they know that I would violate the creationist, book-burning Reagan mentality by dabbling in natural selection theory.

Whether this book is a contribution remains to be seen. That it is an example of intellectual quantum speciation there can be no doubt. Any good natural selection theorist will immediately look for the isolating mechanisms that sheltered my intellectual development from the prevailing influences in organization theory. During the past decade my two earliest research interests, long dormant, recombined to produce the new intellectual strain. At MIT my roots in studying systematics and evolution were established. On the evolutionary side, Everett Hagen, David McClelland, and the work of Max Weber stimulated the intellectual florescence of my earlier interest in the industrial development of Third World nations—an interest stemming from my ten years in India. My interest in research as a way of life was hooked by my Master's thesis on the evolution of two Indian business communities, the work of D. R. Gadgil, and the work and advice of James Abegglan. On the taxonomic side I have to thank Harry Harmon for writing a book about factor analysis and awakening me to the idea of grouping things. Factor analysis became a hobby.

Since I have not had the opportunity to put it into print before, I wish to express deep appreciation to my mentors during my MIT years—Warren Bennis, Ed Schein, Bill Evan, and the late Charles Savage. These were the most important *people* in my intellectual life. Everything else was from books. In this book much of my development builds on the shoulders of two giants of the organization theory field, Charles Perrow and the late James Thompson. For me, the subject almost begins and ends with their work.

My interest in numerical taxonomy was first stirred by the work of Deric Pugh and his colleagues at Aston and by Richard Hall and his collaborators, Eugene Haas and Norman Johnson. In scouting around the library it wasn't long before I came across the seminal work of Ernst Mayr, the leading evolutionist taxonomist in biology today. There is no book in my office that has more dog-eared pages than his *Principles of Systematic Zoology* (except one). It was and still is fascinating to me. Readers of my book and his book will see very quickly how much his approach to the subject has influenced my thinking. The exception is the equally dog-eared second edition of the classic book by Robert Sokal and Peter Sneath, *Numerical Taxonomy: The Principles and Practices of Numerical Classification*. There are many parallels between their book and mine. Both books are cited ad nauseam throughout my book, yet I mention them not only because of a special intellectual debt but also for giving me something to become excited about—a topic I hope will excite others and drive organizational science out of its doldrums.

None of my intellectual forebears can be held responsible for what I have done to their ideas. I also absolve all those who read parts of the manuscript from blame. Many of their comments I found helpful. Many others I could not or would not respond to. I accept full responsibility for what remains.

Special thanks go to Arie Lewin for giving me a much-needed boost by accepting for publication my first paper bringing a message from biology to organization theorists. I have enjoyed a close interaction with Howard Aldrich over the last few years and I want to say how much I have come to depend on his friendship, support, and contribution to my thinking. John Freeman also gave an important boost to the publication of this book as well as many insightful comments. Chuck Warriner has worked on numerical taxonomy for over a decade in the citadel of systematic zoology—Lawrence, Kansas. We finally discovered each other. He hosted the first conference on the numerical taxonomy of organizations and in many other ways helped us all in this new direction. Two other people, Marion Blute and Craig Pinder, also attended the conference and deserve special credit for helping me think more clearly about my subject. Besides being a fellow railroader, Jim Jackson is the only person besides my copy editor and my wife actually to have read the entire manuscript, a heroic effort; he made many substantive and editorial comments. Additional thanks go to Jay Barney, Marian Kostecki, Barbara Lawrence, Jim McQueen, Marshall Meyer, Jay Rounds, Dick Rumelt, Dave Ulrich, and Lynne Zucker for giving various chapters the close attention they needed. Special thanks go to Nancy Donohew and Jamie Tongue for the friendly enthusiasm, speed, and competence they brought to word processing the several drafts of the manuscript. Special thanks also go to Joe Tein for this thorough and conscientious copy editing and many helpful suggestions.

Trying to learn someone else's discipline is difficult. Stanley Burstein helped me out in learning about ancient Mesopotamia. As an outsider, being evaluated on my rendering of his discipline by someone in the discipline is downright scary. The University of California Press wanted a biologist to sprinkle holy water and otherwise bless my foray into biological systematics and evolutionary theory. Everett Olson, a vertebrate paleozoologist, recently elected to the National Academy of Sciences and current president of the Society of Systematic Zoology, graciously accepted the task. I am deeply grateful for his painstaking reading of most of the manuscript, his many comments, and his neutrality and patience in helping me through the well-heated debates over the relative virtues of evolutionist, numerical, and cladist theories of classification, not to mention the latest developments in evolutionary theory. Of course he is not to blame for what I have done to biology in applying the analogy to organizations.

I wish to thank Barry Staw for offering me the kind of retrospective logic Karl Weick is so fond of. I don't really know why I started down this path, or if there ever was a why. Much of it is blind variation, what I now call myopic purposefulness. It is tempting to say I saw some anomalies and concluded a paradigm shift was necessary—though I know that paradigm shifts, like watched pots, never boil. More likely the truth is I wanted to be less ignorant and needed something between hard covers so as to get promoted. During a symposium entitled "Inside the Research Act: How Organizational Research Actually Gets Done" at the 1980 Academy of Management meeting in Detroit, Staw offered the following observations about the process of creative research, assuming my notes are to be trusted:

Avoid the research literature!
I have already been accused of that.

Avoid practitioners' problems!
I think I'm safe here.

Never put high hopes on any study for any useful information!
If a manager finds something useful in this book I'll die.

Never plan—especially not in the long term!
Do you think I would rationally "plan" to write a book covering biological taxonomy, natural selection theory, numerical taxonomy, ancient Mesopotamia, and ending with a nonpredictive philosophy of science?

Never apply for a research grant?
Not a dime. Can you imagine the NSF bureaucrats stamping approval on compools and organizational genetics?

Never give up if everyone thinks you are wrong!
They did. I didn't.

Give up when they think you are right!
I won't hold my breath.

Finally, I dedicate this book with love to my wife and daughters—Robin, Kimberley, and Katherine—who put up with the genteel poverty of academic life, the wondering if the alleged book would ever get done, the frustration when it didn't get done, and the loneliness of family life without a husband and father around, all without ever really sharing in the adventure along my path with heart. From my heart, I thank you.

Brentwood, Los Angeles, California   Bill McKelvey
August 1981

1 INTRODUCTION

The folly of mistaking a paradox for a discovery, a metaphor for a
proof, a torrent of verbiage for a spring of capital truths, and oneself
for an oracle is inborn in us.
  [Valéry 1895, quoted in Siu 1968, p. 75, quoted in Weick 1979, p. 64]

As you can see, this quote has evolved to front-page status. I begin the
book with a warning of folly and end it with a reference to superstition. In between I write about a new direction and awakened hope in
organizational science, a 1750s body of knowledge cloaked in 1980s
garb. Stripped of its shroud, we see a paradigmless search reminiscent of
pre-Linnaean biology, ready for florescence.

Why Study Systematics?

When I say I'm interested in organizational systematics I usually draw
totally blank looks, and when I expand to say I'm interested in organizational taxonomy, sometimes the response is "Really? What kind of

animals do *you* stuff!?" The subject of this book is not well known.

Put simply, organizational systematics is the science of organizational differences: the study of differences among the forms of organizational populations, the development of taxonomic theory, the recognition and classification of important differences, and the discovery of how and why the differences came about. To learn more than that about it, you will have to read the rest of the book. But the material is rather abstract and tainted with strange biological terms, and requires a way of thinking totally at odds with orthodox views of "good" organizational sociology or organization theory; so before you get into it you should know what my motive was in learning and trying to write about organizational systematics.

In 1975 I published a paper entitled "Guidelines for the Empirical Classification of Organizations." In doing that paper I discovered and subsequently reported that two major attempts at deriving empirically based taxonomies had not turned out too well. A little more inquiry into the subject convinced me that I did not know very much about systematics either, and that if I tried to carry out a taxonomic study I probably would fare no better than those I had critiqued. More recently I have refereed a few papers on taxonomy, and they too have been stumblings in the dark. Since there seemed to be a modest growth of interest in systematic studies, the time appeared right for a book on how to conduct them.

This book is a textbook for a course that has never been taught. In it I try to set out the theory and logic of organizational systematics. I am not aware of any formal course or training program on this subject at present. There is probably not enough interest in the subject to warrant such a course. Too dull, perhaps? Systematics in biology is often seen as a rather dull subject. But I think that is because the people who think it dull have lost sight of the importance of the subject and are unaware of all the interesting problems and conflicts that are grist for the scientific mill.

The better I understand the subject the more I believe that systematic studies are crucial to the orderly progression of organizational science. Other sciences such as physics, chemistry, mineralogy, and biology all have systematic studies as a significant feature of their past, and in high-energy physics and biology the advent, respectively, of particle accelerators and electronic computers caused a reawakening of interest in classification. I would go as far as to say that the search for laws and principles in these sciences did not flourish until prerequisite work in systematics was completed. I argue in chapter 2 that systematics must play a similar prerequisite role to the successful search for laws and principles of organizational behavior. As long as they continue to use the philosophy and methods of scientific observation, analysis, and inference stemming from the physical and life sciences—methods born out of resistance to religious orthodoxy, not the peculiar nature of physical phenomena—organizational scientists will need population and sample definitions rooted in a well-established classification of organizational forms.

Systematics is not an outgrowth of sound scientific method in most sciences; it is a *prerequisite* to such methods. For reasons amplified in chapter 4, systematics has not been a central, let alone prerequisite, feature of organizational science. Systematics could be seen as a logical outgrowth of the *contingency theory* or *population ecology* schools of thought—but it is better seen as a more fundamental aspect of scientific method than that. Yet it is compatible with these schools. Underneath the normative designs of the contingency theorists is the premise that environmental differences are reflected in organizational differences. The population ecologists start more explicitly with the question: Why are there so many different kinds of organizations? (Hannan and Freeman 1977, p. 936). This question leads more naturally to taxonomy and evolution than it does to ecology. In either case, systematics is relevant.

There are many places where I am troubled by the superficiality of my treatment. I have had to learn many new things and my learning has not stopped, leading to the problem of wanting to keep researching and revising. Taking a broad view of the subjects in this book and the field of organizational science, the area of most learning pertains to what I call the POPULATION PERSPECTIVE.* This perspective encompasses the fields of systematics (taxonomy, evolution, classification) and population ecology. I now see that these subjects need to be developed concurrently, with the edge given to systematics, since we cannot really explain the regulation and growth of populations until we are agreed that there *are* different kinds, have the populations well circumscribed, and have a theory explaining the differences. You need to remember constantly that *this book is about populations of organizations, not individual organizations*, though individual organizations are frequently mentioned. This can be confusing. Since populations are fundamental to any science interested in discovering generalizable findings, I believe that pursuit of a formal population perspective is fundamental to the florescence of organizational science. This idea is taken up in more depth in chapter 13.

*Terms in capitals are defined in the Glossary.

The Biological Analogy

In casting about for ways to learn about systematics I quickly learned that the biologists were far ahead of the other sciences in the complexity and detail of their thinking. While biologists may not have been working at taxonomy longer, the immensity of the classification problem they faced far surpasses that of the other sciences. They have been seriously at work on the subject for some three hundred years, with many of the world's brightest scholars so engaged. Orthodox approaches to systematics as well as the recent cladistic and numerical applications have reached a high level of sophistication.

This is not the place to argue at length whether there are sufficient similarities between organizations and biological organisms to support a neat translation of biological thinking to organizations. The entire book responds to that. Fortunately in recent years social scientists such as Campbell (1969), Weick (1969, 1979), Aldrich (1971, 1979), Warriner (1973, 1978), Hannan and Freeman (1974, 1977), Kaufman (1975), Hill (1978), Blute (1979), and many others have all suggested that similarities between biological organisms and sociocultural and organizational systems warrant serious consideration of biological evolutionary theory and its attendant thinking. My intention has first been to get as closely as possible in touch with the most sophisticated thinking about systematics. Only then would I begin to wonder about the similarities.

In light of this, the strategy followed in this book—once a problem is identified—is to first review how the problem was handled in biology, including the points of debate, and then to draw on that experience in solving the problem in a way relevant and suitable to organizations. In each instance I have attempted to raise the biological solution to a high enough level of abstraction so that the purely biological aspects of the solution are winnowed out before its application to organizations. I have tried very hard to *not* look to biology for certain laws and then conclude that analogous laws apply in organizations. This is what Haire (1959) did when he first noted that the square-cube law explained why there were limits to the growth of biological organisms and then used that law to explain aspects of organizational growth. This use of a biological analogy is open to criticism because a law is applied without fully appreciating the presence or absence of the functional parallelisms that give rise to the operation of such a law in the first place. I *have* tried to use the sophistication of thinking in biological systematics to sensitize myself to theoretical problems and empirical variabilities pertaining to organizational differences that I might otherwise miss.

If I may be permitted to anticipate a theme raised in chapter 4, another way of looking at this is to observe that the orthodox approach to inquiry in organizational science is *reductionism*; that is, explaining the behavior of an entity by studying its constituent parts—dropping down to a lower level of analysis. The principle of enquiry underlying the evolutionary theory of classification advocated in this book is termed *rationalism* by Schwab (1960; more on this in chapter 3), where explanation comes by looking outside an entity to the environment or higher system in which it is embedded—going to a higher level of analysis. Given that biologists have been working as rationalists for over a century it seems foolish to me to ignore their experience with a principle of enquiry that is alien to organizational science, but seems necessary to explain organizational differences.

Despite the foregoing remarks, I anticipate that a defense of my drawing on biological systematics will be called for. The idea of sociocultural evolution has been met with antipathy for seventy years, as the excellent, though brief, review by Campbell (1969) described. This stems largely from a "Social Darwinist" interpretation of evolutionary theory advocated by Spencer and Sumner, among others. Campbell (1969) observed two societal trends which in combination put the knife to evolutionary theory, in the U.S. at least. First, evolutionary theory became infused with political ideology through the activities of the Social Darwinists. Second, factors in the recruitment of social scientists themselves lead them to be hostile to the existing ideology of their profession—the Social Darwinist form of evolutionary theory.

While the antipathy toward the ideologically loaded evolutionism of the Social Darwinists is excusable, the current avoidance of other less ideological variants is cause for wonder. The multilinear-progress theory of evolution (Campbell 1969, p. 70), where the embryological model advocated by Spencer is abandoned in favor of the view that diverse environmental conditions foster diverse paths of evolutionary progress; the specific evolutionary theory (Sahlins and Service 1960), where diverse environmental conditions are held to cause diverse forms but not necessarily progress—only diversity; or Campbell's own view that a proper role for social scientists is to focus not on the direction of evolution but rather on the underlying processes of variation and selective retention; *all* offer social scientists nonideological (especially the latter two) applications of evolutionary theory to sociocultural systems or organizations.

As if this general uneasiness in the face of evolutionary theory were not enough, organizational scientists often feel they have suffered from their own tilts with the biological analogy. In particular, witness McWhinney's (1965) discrediting of Haire's (1959) use of a biologically inspired geometric analogy, the critique of the organic goal-seeking model and analogies in general by Silverman (1971, pp. 26–99), the general discrediting of the machine model (Rice and Bishoprick 1971, pp. 45–48), and the disdainful reaction of those with a physics background when they encounter such things as the systems theorists' treatment of sacred terms like entropy. It seems there is always a cloud behind the silver lining of each analogy tried in organizational science. No wonder readers are suspicious!

The Nobel laureate Konrad Lorenz titled the paper he presented upon the receipt of his prize "Analogy as a Source of Knowledge" (1974), as if to remind us that despite the occasional cloud there is much to be gained by the use of analogies. In the opening section of this paper he said:

> In the course of evolution it constantly happens that, independently of each other, two different forms of life take similar, parallel paths in adapting themselves to the same external circumstances. . . . The student of evolution has good reason to assume that the abundance of different bodily structures which, by their wonderful expediency, make life possible for such amazingly different creatures under such amazingly different conditions, all owe their existence to these processes which we are wont to subsume under the concept of adaptation. . . . Whenever we find, in two forms of life that are unrelated to each other, a similarity of form or of behavior patterns which relates to more than a few minor details, we assume it to be caused by parallel adaptation to the same life-preserving function. [1974, pp. 229–230]

Lorenz's point is that wherever functional parallels are observed, analogy can be a source of knowledge. Of course the analogy applies only at a sufficiently abstract level. Lorenz used the example of bodies passing speedily through a resisting substance, bodies such as a swift, a jet fighter, a shark, a dolphin, or a torpedo. Knowing its function and what a shark looks like, we are led to suppose, at a fairly abstract level, that a streamlined sharklike shape would be something to look for in the other organisms or objects. However, we would get into trouble with the analogy if we became much less abstract and began looking for appropriately shaped muscles (which is how the shark achieves its shape) in the other bodies.

The functional parallel between organisms and organizations is obvious: both compete for survival in a changing environment. Hence analogic thinking at an appropriately abstract level is likely to be helpful, especially since the understanding of organisms in relation to their environment is highly advanced compared with parallel thinking in organizational science. The functional parallel between biological and organizational systematics is equally obvious—both attempt to theorize about, classify, and explain the origin of differences. There is also a functional parallel between biology as a science and organizational science—each faces the challenge of better understanding and perhaps predicting the behavior of phenomena composed of somewhat ambiguously diversified populations or groups of different kinds. In all three instances of parallelism, biologists must be conceded the edge in length of experience, quantity of scholars, and probably the general level of intelligence and scholarship devoted to the science. In light of these realities, arguments against trying to learn from the experience of biologists and using the biological analogy at an appropriately abstract level strike me as thoroughly foolish. This is not to say, however, that caution will not be needed in choosing an appropriate level of abstraction.

I began this inquiry bound and determined not to fall into the trap of inappropriately applying biological analogies to organizations. It is all too easy to become mesmerized by the elegant concepts of a well-established scientific field. Nevertheless I have been amazed at the number of parallels between processes causing differences among biological entities and processes seemingly at work among organizations. As you read the book I think you will come to share my sense that the biological analogy was the right one to choose. At the same time it is important to recognize that there are some very significant differences between biological processes and organizational ones. I have tried to make suitable inventions in theory and method whenever one of these differences was observed.

In sum, I have tried to immerse myself in the biological literature as a quick way to broadly learn modern thinking about systematic/evolutionary/ecological matters as they might apply to organizations. The lessons from that discipline are inescapably relevant to organizational scientists. I also firmly believe that the broad lessons may be learned in an atmosphere of caution and choice about the application of specific concepts, laws, or theories, so that excesses may be avoided.

To What End?

I have absorbed enough of the history of biological systematics to realize that I can define success for this book only in terms of conflict and debate. The most significant outcome of this book I could hope for would be recognition that the population perspective and systematic studies are important enough to be worthy of attention, conflict, and debate. This is a book of inductive theory and conjecture, not neat and tidy proofs and findings. Nothing written here should be accepted out of hand. It is meant to stimulate interest, provoke debate, and offer ideas on how to conduct sound empirical systematic studies. As these studies progress the theory will undoubtedly change. But these empirical studies need well-reasoned theory as a basis for their initial design; otherwise they will fare no better than those already attempted. Ideally, every problem with the theory may be translated into an empirical question. That makes for a fine and interesting science.

It seems to me that organizational science will remain wallowing in a swampy scientific tidal basin until significant progress in systematics is forthcoming. My attempt to shed some light on systematics takes the following path:

A general outline of systematics as a science of diversity is given in chapter 2. The three main parts of systematics—taxonomy, evolutionary inquiry, and classificatory activities—are identified and their importance to organizational science is discussed. The possibility that systematics may sometime become a viable professional activity among organizational scientists is considered.

Before we can do anything we have to have a theory of classification. This problem is explored in chapter 3. Over the years scientists have tried several kinds of principles of enquiry and several theories of classification. Not too surprisingly, these sets overlap. Of the various theories, I think empiricism and evolutionism are especially relevant to organizational systematics. In contrast to the tendency in biology to see these two theories of classification as antagonistic alternatives, I recommend that organizational science would be best served by combining empiricism and evolutionism in an inductive-deductive cycle of scientific activity.

Chapter 4 is a response to the reality that most organizational scientists seem to have questions about the relevance of systematics rather than about its substance. The chapter includes a brief review of various models of organizational variation, an important topic because natural selection theory posits a new explanation of the sources of variation in organizational populations. These, in response to environmental selection, come to have the many different kinds of forms. The review begins with a question as to why systematics was so slow in developing in organizational science, given that it was a prerequisite in all other major sciences. It ends with an attempted synthesis of autogenic, strategic-choice, or adaptive views of organizations with allogenic, natural-selection, population views.

An underlying assumption of modern systematics is that there exist naturally occurring groupings of organizations. The total universe of all organizations that actually exist (a universe presumably composed of unique individual organizations or groupings of similar organizations) I will label the protosystem. The task of the systematist is to develop a classification reflecting the groupings of the protosystem as closely as possible. Chapter 5 takes a look at environmental forces likely to produce a protosystem and how they influence sources of organizational variation, and offers some documentation that a protosystem actually exists.

At the heart of any theory of classification is a species concept. The species category holds a very special place in the hierarchical ranking of categories. In chapter 6, elements of an ideal classification and several criteria of an effective species concept are identified, drawing from the experience of biologists. The major existing typologies and empirically derived classifications of organizations are reviewed in terms of these criteria and found wanting.

All of the foregoing chapters lead up to chapter 7, which takes on the basic task of defining and evaluating an organizational species concept, or theory of differences. The theory presented here focuses on a concept of distinctive competence which includes both the primary task technology and the ability and skills of those directly responsible for managing the workplace. The species concept so defined is evaluated at some length in terms of the criteria developed in chapter 6. In the course of this evaluation another key concept, the *compool*, is defined as an analog to the "storehouse-of-information" role played by genes in the biologists' explanation of the mechanism by which the blueprint of a form is passed down from one generation to another. The compool is seen as the source of the genotype that in a population of organizations results in a polythetic grouping of phenotypes that are the individual organizational members of the population.

The development of an organizational species concept in the first seven chapters is based on scattered references to evolutionary theory. Later chapters build on this theory. In chapter 8, I draw together a number of ideas on natural selection relevant to organizational evolutionary theory, drawing mainly from the biological literature. A combined Lamarckian/Darwinian approach is taken. The chapter ends with six postulates and twenty four principles of organizational evolution embedded in a particle theory of organizational genetics which includes a concept of organizational generations.

Chapter 9 suggests operational methods for delineating the categories above the species category in a hierarchical classification. Prerequisite to this, a review of three kinds of evolution via branching is undertaken: hybridization, saltation, and gradualism. Evolution within a lineage without branching is also discussed, and evidence in support of evolution with and without branching is presented. Some assumptions and probable misconceptions about hierarchical classification are suggested. The chapter ends with a discussion of several operational principles to be applied in working up a hierarchical classification. Some preliminary illustrations of such a classification scheme applied to organizations are shown.

As a more carefully researched illustration of how an evolutionary inquiry into the development of organizational forms might unfold, I consider the case of organizational evolution in ancient Mesopotamia in chapter 10. First I review the salient environmental conditions. Five major organizational forms are found to have emerged, each having a different dominant competence. Each new form is seen to have evolved from an earlier form. A link between a salient environmental feature and the distinctive competence of each form is noted.

Chapter 11 marks a turn from evolutionary concerns to interest in classification procedures—particularly empirical, numerical ones. This chapter first focuses on selecting cases for numerical analysis. The rest of it is given over to a discussion of various issues pertaining to the selection of taxonomic characters. A review of previous lists of characters is given. The chapter concludes by offering a list of categories of taxonomic characters, recognizing that specific characters will differ for most populations. No single list of specific characters seems possible or very wise.

An overview of numerical taxonomic methods is given in chapter 12. Since many good textbooks on the subject are available, my focus is on noting the various places where subjectivity and bias may enter into seemingly objective methods. Since factor analysis and other multivariate sorting methods are relatively well known in organizational science, I have put most emphasis on agglomerative, hierarchical, joining methods. The chapter ends with a set of guidelines to follow in publishing systematic studies of organizations.

I see chapter 13 not as ending the book but rather as setting the stage for the beginning of an exciting new era in organizational science. The reconstructed logic of our field to date fits the deductive-nomological framework. The population perspective calls for a totally different way of explaining variations in organizational form, a view rooted in natural selection theory. It is a shift from the causal chains of Newtonian thinking to the explanatory but nonpredictive logic of the Darwinian paradigm. The two major contributions of the population perspective are the identification of well-circumscribed organizational populations and the shift in explanatory paradigm. Several implications for the development of the field are noted.

2 SYSTEMATICS

Systematics is at the same time the most elementary and most inclusive part of zoology, most elementary because animals cannot be discussed or treated in a scientific way until some taxonomy has been achieved, and most inclusive because [systematics] in its various branches gathers together, utilizes, summarizes and implements, everything that is known about animals, whether morphological, physiological, psychological, or ecological.

> [Simpson 1945; quoted by Mayr 1969, p. 19]

The extent to which progress in ecology depends upon accurate identification, and upon the existence of a sound systematic groundwork for all groups of animals, cannot be too much impressed upon the beginner in ecology. This is the essential basis of the whole thing; without it the ecologist is helpless, and the whole of his work may be rendered useless.

> [Elton 1947; quoted by Mayr 1969, p. 6]

Just substitute ORGANIZATIONAL FORMS (defined in section 4.3.1) for *animals* in the foregoing quotes and you will see how important I think systematics is for organizational science. If my arguments are successful, the changes in the field will be fundamental. As an indication of how absent systematics thinking is from contemporary organizational science, observe that although Elton said biological ecology was useless without systematics, Hannan and Freeman (1977), in their seminal introduction of the population ecology perspective to organizational science, never mentioned systematics or taxonomy. This even though they wondered about species and forms, why so many kinds, differences among forms, and populations of organizations which must be alike in some fashion—all topics within the purview of systematics.

This chapter sets the stage for the various topics I consider in this book by broadly defining the field of organizational systematics and some basic terms. The role of systematics in organizational science is discussed, as are the roles of two kinds of classification. The chapter ends with a review of the various roles organizational scholars may take in developing the field of systematics.

2.1 SYSTEMATICS AND FUNCTIONAL SCIENCE

There are two broad kinds of scientific investigation. One kind focuses on the study of diversity. It investigates the phenomena in question as whole entities, trying to describe them and understand the relationship among them. It tries to place all the different kinds of phenomena into some meaningful order. SYSTEMATICS is the name biologists give to this "science of diversity." The second kind of science focuses on the discovery of universal laws governing the behavior, function, and processes of a population of objects being investigated. It seeks to understand and explain how and why the objects are structured the way they are and behave the way they do. In its search for generalizable and universal laws this kind of science focuses on the uniformities within a population under study; thus it is a "science of uniformity." I have termed it FUNCTIONAL science. Hempel said:

> To be scientifically useful a concept must lend itself to the formulation of general laws or theoretical principles which reflect *uniformities* in the subject matter under study, and which thus provide a basis for explanation, prediction, and generally scientific understanding. [1965, p. 146; emphasis added]

Systematics is that aspect of scientific inquiry which, as Plato said, "cuts nature at its joints," thereby assuring that uniformities indeed are present in the phenomena to be described and explained.

The term *systematics* dates back at least to Carolus Linnaeus, who used it in the title of his book, *Systema Naturae* (tenth edition, 1758). During the intervening years, and even now, there is some confusion about the meaning of the term. Simpson (1961) and Mayr (1969) used *systematics* broadly, as is done here, to denote the study of diversity. They, along with Hempel (1965), used the term TAXONOMY to refer to the theory and practice of CLASSIFICATION, with the latter term used to refer to the actual activity of classifying objects in terms of some classificatory scheme. Though Ross (1974) used *systematics* and *tax-*

onomy as synonyms and others use *taxonomy* and *classification* as synonyms, I will follow the usage of Simpson and Mayr in this book. There have been three special concerns of systematists (Ross 1974, p. 11). Put in the context of organizational science, systematics aims to achieve better scientific understanding of the different kinds (species) of organizations and how they came into being. It includes the study of:

Taxonomy: The development of theories and methods for separating organizations into different kinds, including the understanding of the causes of the stability of organizational forms over time, as well as the mechanism by which they evolve as the result of environmental forces, or in other words a *theory* of classification.

Evolution: The study of the process of environmental and organizational evolution, the study of the emergence and decline of different organizational forms, and the development of lineages showing the emergence of new forms over time.

Classification: The actual construction of a classification scheme and the identification and assignment of organizational forms to formally designated classes.

It is important to note that while these three activities are identified separately, they nevertheless are highly interactive, with taxonomic development affecting the other two and vice versa.

Up until now systematic studies have not been a significant or very useful part of organizational science. What limited activity there has been was confined to developing typologies, which typically are simple one- or two-dimensional schemes based on a priori theorizing. Some of the better-known examples are worth mentioning. Etzioni (1975) suggested a typology of organizations based on how they obtained compliance from their members. Another idea was to classify organizations according to who benefited from what they did (Blau and Scott 1962). Parsons (1956) and Katz and Kahn (1978) grouped organizations by what function they performed for the larger society in which they were embedded. Perrow (1967) presented a typology of organizations focusing on the kinds of inputs they had and the associated problems their technology had to solve. Finally, Thompson (1967) also suggested a typology based on the kinds of technologies organizations used.

In contrast to the foregoing theoretical typologies, there have been several attempts to work out empirically derived classifications of organizations. Haas et al. (1966) used a computer cluster analysis program written by biological taxonomists to sort seventy-five organizations into groups using ninety-nine attributes. Pugh et al. (1968, 1969) used factor analysis in an attempt to group forty-six organizations according to similarities on sixteen formal structural attributes. Goronzy (1969), again using a cluster analysis approach, grouped fifty business organizations using twenty-nine attributes. Pinto and Pinder (1972) used eighteen dimensions in clustering 227 organizational subunits.

So far, neither the typologies nor the numerical approaches have had any real impact on empirical research in the field of organizational science (Kimberly 1975; McKelvey 1975; Hall 1977; Pinder and Moore 1979; Warriner 1979). Carper and Snizek recently reviewed several other theoretical and empirical classification attempts and reached the same conclusion, saying that "we have a long way to go in formulating a workable classification system for organizations" (1980, p. 74).

Also coming under the label of systematics are the many comparative analyses, some of which were included in the anthologies by Graham and Roberts (1972) and Heydebrand (1973). These studies have mostly focused on commonsense notions of organizational differences such as task, structure, size, complexity, degree of professionalization or bureaucratization, and the like. They helped uncover many differences among organizations, suggesting that an ordering of their diversity was necessary, but they did not attempt to work out a useable classification scheme. In the future, comparative studies will be an important means of identifying organizational attributes for possible use in classification.

The overwhelming majority of scientific investigations of organizations have been functional studies attempting to understand the behavior of organizations by analyzing the structure, function, and process of their various components. Often the dependent variable is organizational effectiveness, measured either in terms of success in producing a good or service or in terms of employee satisfaction and quality of working life. Many studies relate formal structural configuration, leadership style, job design, and personality to performance or satisfaction, or some variant of these. All studies of planning, organizing, staffing, directing, and controlling, the classic five functions of management, are examples of functional investigations. All investigations coming under the label of studies of organizational behavior, which are really the study of how people behave in organizations, are also inquiries into what affects the function and process of organizations. Finally, the studies pertaining to organizational change, whether through development of interpersonal processes or through changes in the design of the structural configuration, are also examples of functional science. There can be little doubt that organizational scientists have pursued functional investigations almost to the exclusion of systematic studies.

To all intents and purposes, the field of organizational systematics has been dormant, with only a rare sputtering of activity. I try to uncover why this is so in chapter 4. What is worse, the few sputterings have resulted more in confusion than in even modest development.

2.2 SPECIAL AND GENERAL CLASSIFICATIONS

I begin my discussion of systematics by pointing out two kinds of classification. Jeffrey (1968) made a distinction between SPECIAL (what he termed "special purpose") and GENERAL (what he termed "natural") classifications. Both kinds of classification are needed, and it is important to understand the role of each. Some biologists prefer the term *natural* instead of *general* because they believe that a good scientific classification should reflect the naturally occurring groupings of biological phenomena. But the distinctions reflected in the typical special classification also have their basis in nature. The terms *special* and *general* are to be preferred because they more accurately reflect what a classification does for a science.

2.2.1 Special Classifications

Special classifications group objects together on the basis of a small, selected number of attributes of particular interest. There have been numerous special classifications in biology. People interested in growing plants in different temperature zones classified them according to their hardiness or sensitivity to damage by frost. Others, interested in eating, grouped plants according to their edibility or toxicity. No doubt from the beginning of the human race fathers have told their sons and daughters, "there are two kinds of large animals—those you can eat and those that can eat you."

Special classifications focus on only one or a few attributes. All of the typologies by Etzioni, Blau and Scott, Perrow, and others mentioned earlier are good examples of special classifications. Other special classifications abound, such as: simple-complex; young-old; profit-not for profit; public-private; small-batch, mass-production, continuous-process industry; teaching, general, and chronic-care hospitals; and so forth.

Special classifications have the advantage of high predictive validity, but within a very thin slice of total organizational behavior. Such a classification is very useful for practical and scientific purposes, but only if one is narrowly interested in the one attribute. Thus, once hospitals are placed in the "teaching hospital" group one can expect that without exception they will have teaching activities. But they may vary considerably on all other organizational attributes. This latter feature means that special classifications do not allow for very good information-retrieval systems. If the scientific findings of functional studies about decentralization were grouped by big and small organizations, for example, it would be difficult to apply that knowledge to young, or complex, or bureaucratic organizations. It is almost impossible to know whether the studies of sociotechnical job design (Davis and Taylor 1979; Pasmore and Sherwood 1978) apply only to certain kinds of organizations such as small-craft, assembly, or large chemical organizations, or whether they apply to any kind of organization. It is hard to know what findings about railroads would apply to airlines or steamship companies, and so on. Do Meyer's (1979) findings about the evolution of bureaucratization in local government finance departments really apply to other government agencies, as they imply? In sum, it is difficult to assemble all that is known about a particular organization if the information is organized or "stored in publications" under a wide variety of separate special classifications.

2.2.2 General Classifications

A general classification attempts to group objects together on the basis of all their attributes (Jeffrey 1968), though some attributes may be weighted more than others. Consequently the groupings reflect the combined effects of many attributes, and the members of a group have roughly similar behavior with regard to many attributes. Since many—usually all—known attributes are taken into consideration, a general classification allows scientists to make broad predictions about the total behavior of the members of a given class. Such a classification is not as sharply predictive as a special classification with respect to any individual attribute, a compromise necessary to reflect the effects of many attributes.

Because a general classification is broadly predictive of the total behavior of the members of its classes, it serves as a good method of organizing functional studies. And because it reflects total behavior rather than specific attributes, it acts as a broadly inclusive and thus very useful information-retrieval system for scientific findings. It often will include many special classifications within it. Such a scheme is a way of organizing all findings about organizations on the basis of total behavior rather than only certain attributes.

The EVOLUTIONIST theory of classification, based on the Darwin-Wallace theory of natural selection, is an excellent example of a general classification. It is presently the dominant theory of classification in biology, though the classification approaches developed by the CLADISTS and NUMERICAL PHENETICISTS (these approaches are described in chapters 3 and 12) have gained considerable attention as an alternative method for working out a general classification. There are currently no examples of a general classification of organizations.

If available, a general classification of organizations would play several important roles. It would:

1. Offer a basis for explanation, prediction, and scientific understanding by identifying homogeneous populations of organizations about which hypotheses might be tested and general laws and principles of organizational functioning developed (Hempel 1965; Haas et al. 1966).

2. Present a conceptual framework for describing and understanding the diversity of presently existing organizational populations (Mayr 1969, p. 8).

3. Provide a very useful information-retrieval system, since information stemming from functional studies would be organized into relatively parsimonious sets of classes (Mayr 1969, p. 9).

4. Aid in the handling of complex sets of variables or attributes by identifying more parsimonious sets of constructs; in other words, allow the substitution of a few broad classification variables for many more specific attributes (Mechanic 1963).

5. Supply a classification scheme useful to other areas of organizational investigation such as studies of organizational behavior, organizational development, organizational design, and comparative studies (Mayr 1969, p. 9).

6. Be indispensable in supplying a classification of organizations about which practical management principles and guidelines might be discovered, developed, and taught.

While special classifications are important in their own right, a general classification is most important because of its ability to organize the diversity among organizations and bring order to the many scientific findings about them. The existing special typologies have been thought-provoking and useful in narrow circumstances but they have not offered an ordering of organizational diversity useful to empirical researchers. For these reasons *the purpose of this book is to develop the theory and methods of general organizational classification.* However, special classifications will continue to play an important role in organizational science. There will always be a need for highly predictive groupings, even if they are extremely narrow in scope.

2.3 THE IMPORTANCE OF SYSTEMATICS

Systematics is important because only this kind of extended inquiry will produce a general classification. In section 2.2 I observed that one of the roles of a general classification was to aid scientific understanding, explanation, and prediction. This will be underscored in this section by a more careful discussion of just why this is so. It is also true that systematics becomes a more important subject of investigation as the diversity of the phenomena in question increases, a second topic of discussion. The importance of information retrieval is discussed next. Finally, some comment will be given to the importance of systematics as a subject of inquiry in its own right.

2.3.1 Systematics and Functional Investigation

The vast majority of functional investigations are carried out by scientists using the hypothetico-deductive method (see Popper 1968; Nagel 1961; and Kaplan 1964, for an extensive treatment of the hypothetico-deductive model) and other sound scientific procedures. Even though objections are raised against the applicability of the hypothetico-deductive or "objectivist" model of inquiry to organizational science (summarized by Behling 1980), it continues to represent the mainstream of organizational inquiry. As long as scientists continue to use this method—and there is no indication to the contrary in journals such as *Administrative Science Quarterly, American Sociological Review, American Journal of Sociology, Journal of Applied Psychology, Organizational Behavior and Human Performance,* or *Academy of Management Journal**—one must conclude that anything that substantially improves the conduct of hypothetico-deductive inquiry will greatly improve functional studies of organizations. I argue here that the development of a widely accepted general classification would be one such substantial improvement.

The strength of scientific method is in its attention to the quality of knowledge. The attainment of high quality knowledge requires three acts: (1) the testing of theories by the formulation of hypotheses that are subject to falsification in specific situations; (2) careful observation and measurement of the phenomena in question; and (3) the conducting and reporting of the investigation in a public manner so that the results can be replicated by other investigators. Anything that hinders the performance of these three acts mars the scientific quality of the resulting findings.

*I do not mean to imply that these journals publish only objectivist studies, only that they still publish mostly such studies.

Systematics is prerequisite to good scientific method because it directly affects an investigator's ability to carry out all three acts—the testing of hypotheses, the discovery of patterns in the data, and the replication of findings. Let us consider each of these in turn.

The core of the hypothetico-deductive act is what has been termed the inductive-deductive cycle (Ghent 1966), as illustrated in figure 2.1. First a researcher ponders some initial discoveries about a sample of organizations. From this grounding in the objects studied, he or she induces a broad and hopefully generalizable theory—working from the particular to the general. Next the researcher tests the general theory by deducing certain specific hypotheses thought to apply to a population of organizations to which the theory is expected to generalize—working from the general to the particular—and conducting experimental or empirical tests to confirm the hypotheses. Often (but not often enough, according to Glaser and Strauss 1967), the investigator will use the data from the deductive test to inductively revise the theory, starting the inductive cycle over again and following with another deductive test on another sample from the specified population of organizations. The cycle continues until either the successive findings converge or the lack of convergence is taken as a failure of the theory.

The key to a successful completion of an inductive-deductive cycle is the existence of a homogeneous population of organizations. If the population is too heterogeneous there is a very good chance that the

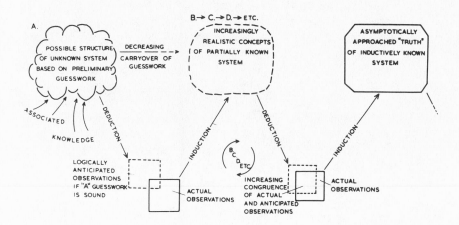

Figure 2.1. Illustration of the roles of inductive and deductive reasoning in experimental design. (From A. W. Ghent, "The Logic of Experimental Design," *Bioscience*, 16:17–22, 1966. Reprinted by permission of the American Institute of Biological Sciences.)

sample of organizations upon which the inductive step was based will differ markedly from the sample upon which the deductive test is based. This could mean weak results or, worse, no support for the theory at all. Of course, one solution to a heterogeneous population is to draw a larger sample, but this can become expensive and awkward unless one is studying a very small population. *Systematics is a necessary precursor to the effective completion of the inductive-deductive cycle because, by being sensitive to many attributes, it works toward a general classification scheme that in turn produces homogeneous groups of organizations.*

The act of discovering uniformities in a sample from a population requires that there be enough uniformity to stand out against the noise of measurement error and artifact. The clearer the uniformities in a population, the higher will be the level of explained variance by functional studies. Needless to say, one of the plagues of organizational science is the plethora of studies showing very poor levels of explained variance. The gravity of this situation was demonstrated in a recent study by Behling and Dillard (1980) showing that all the commonly used analytic methods fail to discriminate known patterns in artificially contrived data when the pattern-to-noise variance ratio is less than 80/20. *I see systematics as the main method of improving the ratio of pattern to noise by identifying more homogeneous populations of organizational forms.*

The act of replication requires that the methods of a study be publicly reported and the population of organizations defined carefully. This is so that other investigators at later times and different places can identify the population and draw an appropriate sample upon which to base their own replication of the study in question. The more homogeneous the population, the more likely it will be that a second investigator will draw a random sample that will be similar enough to the first sample to support a successful replication. Alternatively, the more heterogeneous the population of organizations identified, the larger the samples have to be to assure reasonable similarity between the first sample and those used for replication. *Systematics, by producing a classification scheme assuring the identification of homogeneous populations, also becomes a very necessary prerequisite to the act of scientific replication.*

2.3.2 Systematics and Diversity

Besides supplying much-needed homogeneous populations for functional studies, systematics becomes increasingly important as the diversity of the phenomena studied increases. As Simon (1962) pointed out so clearly, one of the most natural ways of organizing complexity is to introduce a hierarchical ordering. Because there are now thought to be on the order of five to ten million* species of living plants and animals, systematics has long been a central feature of biology. In fact, not too long ago many observers wondered if biologists would ever do anything besides systematic studies. Because of the overwhelming diversity it has been a tremendous job just to categorize and label all known plants and animals, and put them into meaningful relation with one another. Biologists now recognize that a complete classification of organisms smaller than one centimeter may never come to pass (Lewontin 1978).

The level of complexity facing organizational systematists is a function not only of diversity in kinds of phenomena, but also of the number of attributes characterizing each kind. Thus, while there may not be nearly as many different kinds of organizations as there are biological organisms, there could very well be a greater number of attributes per kind of organization because organizations may be larger and more complex than biological organisms. Sells (1964) has suggested that as many as 500 attributes may be needed to adequately characterize an organization, though early empirical attempts at classification used as few as sixteen attributes in one instance (Pugh et al. 1968, 1969).

At this point in time the true nature of the task facing organizational systematists is somewhat unknown since it is not clear just how diverse organizations are. Many management and organization textbooks give the impression that organizations are pretty much the same. In contrast, the findings of contingency theorists (collected in Kast and Rosenzweig 1973) show striking differences among organizations. And many of the comparative analyses presented in Graham and Roberts (1972) and Heydebrand (1973), for example, also point to clear differences among organizations. Further, even though they are not directly comparative, there is a host of studies of hospitals, schools, unions, voluntary organizations, business groupings, and government agencies which suggest significant differences. As long as any diversity is recognized, organizational systematics is called for.

2.3.3 Systematics and Information Retrieval

Science is like a giant picture puzzle being constructed by many investigators all around the world. The problem is that no single person can do very much of the job in his or her lifetime, and no single person has ready access to all the work of the others on a face-to-face basis. And yet each single researcher needs and wants to know what has already been completed, which parts of the puzzle are causing problems, which parts

*Everett Olson, personal communication, 1980.

need to be replicated, and which parts need the most work or are most important. Each person needs to have information about what has already been studied and what needs to be studied. This is why an information-retrieval system is so important.

Furthermore, as Hempel (1965) pointed out, science has a goal of helping people gain leverage on their environment in addition to simply satisfying curiosity. Thus a goal of organizational scientists is to help managers and employees design and manage their organizations as effectively as possible. It is well known that managers are not interested in scientific information expressed in obscure symbols, or in ideal types of organizations that have never actually existed, or in some other kind of organizational form that may make academic sense but raises practical eyebrows. Employees need to have information that looks reasonably certain to be important to them in their everyday kind of organization. A manager in charge of an automobile assembly plant will typically want high quality findings about how to run that type of organization, not some ideal type or obscure combination of several types. Imagine what mineralogy would be like if mineralogists had organized everything they know in terms of minerals and rocks that do not exist in the world today. Who could use their knowledge? Or suppose that all the relevant knowledge of researchers contributing to veterinary medicine was organized in terms of ideal animals that no practicing veterinarian would ever see. Would that person be successful in curing real live animals that differed from the ideal types?

The scheme that seems to work best in both organizing scientific information for purposes of scientific retrieval and bringing it to bear on organizational problems important to practicing managers and all other organizational members is a general classification that groups actually existing organizations into useable classes. These classes are most useful if they form homogeneous populations that researchers can use for drawing samples and generalizing knowledge and if they bring research findings to bear on organizations that members and managers recognize. Because it seeks to produce such a general classification, systematics is clearly important for information retrieval. As the biologist Gingerich said recently, "The purpose of a general formal classification of animals is to foster effective communication within and between zoological subdisciplines" (1979, p. 451).

2.3.4 Systematics and Scientific Curiosity

In biology, systematics very early became important in its own right because people were curious about all the plants and animals surrounding them. They had very practical reasons for wanting to bring some order into the diversity around them. They needed to know which plants they could eat, which made good medicinal cures, which made good thread for weaving, and so on. They needed to know which animals they could eat, which ones were dangerous, and which ones could be domesticated. But early biologists were not just satisfied with classifying plants and animals. A crude concept of organic evolution was put forth by Anaxagoras in the fifth century B.C. (Ross 1974, p. 2). Certainly one of the more emotionally involving questions over the years for biologists (and the rest of us) was the origin of life in general and the origin of the human race in particular. All of the foregoing interests were reason enough for systematics to be a central concern of biologists. Inquiry stemming from curiosity about kinds of plants and animals and the origin of different kinds of populations was well established long before the scientific methods of the functional biologists emerged and took advantage of the existing classifications as a basis for defining their populations and circumscribing the generalizability of their findings.

Biology is clearly one of the sciences most heavily engaged in systematic studies. In fact, zoology and botany are often referred to as taxonomic sciences, though now most biologists are probably more heavily engaged in functional studies. Though emphasizing systematics less, other sciences all have a systematic side and often the functional side did not progress very rapidly until the basic systematic work was completed. In physics, people struggled with a concept of matter until Dalton and Bohr worked out a concept of the atom. Even now, research in high-energy physics is focused on uncovering the diversity of particles making up the atom. It is the most glamorous part of physics for many researchers. Chemistry did not get very far until Mendeleev worked out his periodic chart of the elements. It is still used today, though in somewhat revised form, and is one of the first things students of chemistry encounter. Mineralogy comes close to being as taxonomic in emphasis as the life sciences, what with its myriad rocks and minerals. Classification is an integral part of linguistics and library science, too. In short, systematics has been an integral part of many well-established sciences. A general classification scheme produced by the systematists in each science has been the platform upon which the functional studies were formed.

2.4 BASIC TERMS

By now the reader should have a working understanding of terms such as *systematics, taxonomy, classification,* and *functional.* There are a few more terms without which it is impossible to think sensibly about classification. Other terms will be defined in later chapters, but the following ones are the foundation stones of systematics.

Population. You might think it would be easy to define POPULA-TION the most basic term in this book, but it is not. In evolutionary biology a Mendelian population is a "community of individuals of a sexually reproducing species within which matings take place" (Dobzhansky 1970, p. 130). This definition of a population is isomorphic with the definition of a biological species concept, taken up in section 3.1.5. As often as not, in the systematics literature *population* and *species* are used interchangeably. I will continue that practice here. But since a concept of organizational species is not developed until chapter 7, a temporary definition of an organizational population or SPECIES is: a group of organizations that are similar in the competence needed to produce the product or service that is essential to their continued survival. Usually members of a population are similar in observable form and behavior.

There is also the idea of a LOCAL POPULATION or what Simpson termed a *deme,* "the smallest unit of population that has evolutionary significance . . . a group of animals (of one species or subspecies) so localized they are in more or less frequent contact with each other . . ." (1961, p. 176). Warriner has recently defined an organizational DEME as "a population of similarly constituted organizations, occupying the same ecological niche, and sharing the same modeling or replication materials through interconnections among the organizations in that population" (1980, p.11). A deme is a geographical decomposition of a species population. Alternatively, a species population may be decomposed phenotypically, which is preferred by numerical pheneticists and results in *phena,* defined shortly.

Taxon (pl. = taxa). "A taxonomic group that is sufficiently distinct to be worthy of being distinguished by name and to be ranked in a definite category" (Mayr 1969, p. 413). Two points about taxa are noteworthy. First, a TAXON always refers to a real, concrete population of organizations such as foundries, hospitals, machine shops, or schools, or broader groupings such as factory, government, retail, educational, or professional organizations. It is never used to refer to an imaginary type, such as Weber's (1947) concept of *bureaucracy,* which does not exist as a population of real objects to be studied or measured. Second, a population of organizations is called a taxon only if organizational systematists have *recognized* it as something to be *formally* assigned to a definite grouping in a classificatory scheme. For example, a possible grouping such as general hospitals would not be recognized as a taxon until a study of general hospitals was made and an empirically based definition was derived which specified exactly what constituted a member of the class "general hospital." Once demes or other groupings are formally recognized as taxa they are assigned a rank category in a hierarchical classification scheme and may then be referred to as species, as higher ranks such as families or orders, as lower ranks such as subspecies or varieties, or whatever.

Phenon (pl. = phena). "A sample of phenotypically [i.e., observably] similar specimens; a phenotypically reasonably uniform sample" (Mayr 1969, p. 408). A PHENON is a group of organizations presumed to be representative of some larger grouping, the members of which all have mostly the same observable attributes. It is similar in meaning and use to a deme or local population, though not so specifically geographically local in use as these terms (Mayr 1969, p. 46). Discovering a phenon is the first step in classification. It is only after a phenon is observed that a systematist begins to think that he or she has found a population that may be considered for classification—that is, considered as a taxon. A taxon may consist of one or more phena. In North America, for example, female, male, old, and young robins are four robin phena making up one taxon, the species *Turdus migratorius.* Alternatively, other phena of different species taxa—for example, female ducks of several species— often appear to be more similar than phena of the same species taxon— for example, female and male mallard ducks, *Anas platyrhynchos.* Or young and old telephone utilities may comprise one taxon even though they may appear more different than phena such as mature, large public and private universities, which may be classified as separate taxa.

Two key questions for taxonomists are: How many attributes should be considered, and how similar do all organizations have to be in these attributes before a phenon is declared? In the definition, what is "reasonably uniform" and what is a "sample" are points of debate, and very crucial ones at that. One of the fundamental problems with systematics in organizational science is that organizational phena have not yet been thoroughly identified. For example, it is possible that large and small machine shops are two different phena making up one taxon, the "machine shop" population, or that they are two different taxa. Without a study of machine shops the answer is unclear. Whether a sample of organizations would be considered one or several phena might depend on how many attributes are measured. Organizations that appear to be similar if only a few attributes are considered may end up being quite different if many attributes are studied, and vice versa.

Category. "Designates rank or level in a hierarchic classification. It is a class, the members of which are all taxa assigned a given rank" (Mayr

1969, p. 413). For example, the genus category is composed of groupings of species taxa. It is important to emphasize that CATEGORY denotes an unspecified rank in a hierarchical classification, whereas *taxon* stands for actual measurable organizations. A category may be an abstract group of taxa. One cannot go out and measure a category such as "mass production organizations." Members of such a category exist only as differentiated taxa such as tire factories, container (cardboard) plants, automobile assembly plants, bakeries, and so forth.

It will be my practice in this book to arbitrarily accept and use the category labels used by botanists. Botanical labels are chosen over zoological ones because the former series offers more labels below the species level. It is quite possible that several ranks will be needed below the organizational species rank in order to account for meaningful, though not very stable, differentiations. There is nothing especially scientific or biological about the terms *species, genus, order,* and so forth. *Species* is the Latin word for *appearance* or *sort. Genus* is the Latin word for *race, stock, kind,* or *gender.* The other English words all have meanings quite suitable for classificatory use.

The nineteen botanical category labels most in use are:

Kingdom*
Division*
Subdivision
Class*
Subclass
Order*
Suborder
Family*
Subfamily
Tribe
Subtribe
Genus*
Subgenus
Section
Series
Species*
Subspecies
Variety
(Form)

In botany it is the rule to classify taxa using the basic ranks followed by an asterisk. In zoology it is not a formal rule but it is common practice. The remaining labels are used only if further differentiations in certain groups are called for. The use of six of the seven basic labels dates back to the time of Linnaeus (*division* was added later, as were the other labels except for *variety*, which was also used at the time of Linnaeus). It is convenient to have some neutral terms to use to refer to groupings that may be phena, taxa, or a category, but which are clearly not associated with the formal labels. I will use *group, grouping,* and *form* (a departure from the botanical list; hence *form* is shown in parentheses) informally to refer to similar kinds of organizations. Organizational scientists could dream up their own unique labels, but there is little reason not to use a set that is widely known.

Taxonomic Character. "Any attribute of a member of a taxon by which it differs or may differ from a member of a different taxon" (Mayr 1969, p. 413). Sneath and Sokal (1973, p. 71) argued for a somewhat looser definition of TAXONOMIC CHARACTERS as properties that vary from one entity to another, since one may not know in advance whether a character differs among all taxa. Cladists, who focus on branching points, insist that only apomorphic or derived characters (explained in chapters 3 and 12) be used. On one thing Mayr and Sneath and Sokal agree, that attributes remaining the same (no variance) definitely should not be used as taxonomic characters. Whether all attributes having variance are taken as characters depends on one's philosophy of classification. Generally, numerical taxonomists include all known characters with equal weighting. Other systematists prefer a more selective approach. These differences will be discussed in chapters 11 and 12. Biological characters are measures such as length, color, and texture of wings; whether the edge of a leaf is smooth or serrated; the number of teeth, the number of toes, and so forth. Organizational characters are measures such as the number of hierarchical levels, the kind of production technology, the number of policy manuals, the degree of computerized schedulization, the number and kinds of products, and so forth.

2.5 TASKS FOR THE ORGANIZATIONAL SYSTEMATIST

There are several different activities that organizational systematists will engage in. Some will probably pursue all of them, but there is also room for specialization in one or another.

2.5.1 Discovering Processes Underlying Speciation: Taxonomy

The basic unanswered question at the moment is, what is an organizational species or population? There is no general theory of organizational differences. One way of answering this question is discussed in chapter 7, but this is only a beginning. There will surely be much conjecture and debate on SPECIATION (discussed in section 6.1.2) before the question is settled. A classification must be based on real objects to be useful. The form of these objects must be constant relative to the life of the classification scheme, or else the scheme must be changed so often it loses its value as a means of ordering diversity and as an information-retrieval system. But, since organizational populations, like plants and animals, exist in an environment that causes adaptations over time, the classification scheme must also conceptualize the objects being classified in a way that allows for evolutionary change.

The biological species concept is stable for purposes of classification and also allows for gradual* long-term evolutionary change. It serves both the need for stability and the need for adaptation very well. If organizational populations are seen to maintain stability in the short term while evolving in the long term—that is, if the conceptual problem is the same—organizational scientists also will have to search for a dual-purpose species concept.

The search for an organizational species concept breaks down into several aspects. One consideration is, What are organizational entities (Freeman 1978)? Should we distinguish between organizations as legal entities and organizational forms? How do we decide when an organizational form has been adequately described? What characters should be used? Are certain characters more important than others? An organizational form is not like a lizard or rabbit that can be picked up and laid on a table for examination and measurement. Many parts of organizations, such as planning, controlling, leadership, and climate, are abstract notions. Should these be included as characters?

A second consideration is an examination of the forces causing stability in organizational forms. Many natural system theorists (Gouldner 1959; Buckley 1967) have focused on such forces that cause homeostasis in organizations. Hannan and Freeman (1977) listed a number of forces fostering organizational stability. Are there enough forces toward stability and do they maintain stability long enough for a classification to be developed without having the organizations change, thereby rendering the classification obsolete?

A third concern has to do with discovering the forces that maintain isolation among different organizational forms. If organizational populations transiently form, dissolve, and reform differently, a classification

---

*Now some evolutionary biologists believe that speciation may take place very rapidly, a point discussed in sections 6.1.2 and 8.3.

of them is impossible. What are the forces that give rise to identifiable organizational forms and maintain these forms over a period of time? What are the forces that lead to differences among organizations, or are there any differences? What happens when two different organizations merge? Are there uniformities among organizations and yet are there very important differences too?

A final consideration is of those forces emanating from the environment which lead to selection and adaptation, or reinforce stability. What are the key ties between environmental and niche characteristics and internal organizational functions like planning, controlling, differentiation, interdependencies, and work flow? How do specific changes in the environment of a certain organizational form lead to changes in its internal design and function?

2.5.2 Tracing out the Origin and Evolution of Organizations: PHYLETICS

Organizations did not always exist. Did they come into being for certain reasons? What were these reasons over the centuries? How did they result in new forms? And what were the new forms like? How is a particular form passed down through generations of organizations? Is there such a thing as an organizational generation? It is interesting to discover that there are, for example, similarities and differences between the matrix organizations in the aerospace industry and the brand management forms in commercial products organizations such as Procter and Gamble, Inc. Did they evolve independently? Do they both owe their heritage to the same earlier matrix form? Do organizational scientists know what that was? And what might have brought it into being? Questions like these may be asked about many different kinds of organizations.

Other questions are also interesting. What effect did the Middle Ages have on organizational form? What about the impact of the colonial empires on present-day organizations around the world? And what about the evolution of organizations in countries cut off from the West for long periods of time, such as China? What changes in organizational form are presently happening and will shortly emerge as newly evolved forms?

A good start in answering these questions has been made by management historians such as George (1972) and Wren (1972). But these writers focus more on management than on organizational form. It is rather difficult to tell just which organizational characteristics evolved at the time of the Industrial Revolution and which were already present, for example. While organizations do not fossilize (despite the caustic assertions to the contrary by many observers), they do leave written documents of one sort and another, so there is evidence to find and use in working out evolutionary lineages.

2.5.3 Classification

The expected outcome of inquiries into speciation and phyletics will be one of perhaps several alternative theories of classification. Several competing theories have developed in biology during the more than 2,000 years since the time of Aristotle, who suggested the first zoological classification. There is at least one example of most of these theories which has been suggested for organizational classification. These are discussed in more detail in chapter 3.

There are several kinds of questions one may ask about a classification scheme. What is the optimal size and number of groupings? Usually, the smaller the grouping, the less heterogeneous it is, but more groups are required. The more groupings, the more cumbersome the classification scheme is for purposes of information retrieval. What characters are to be used for the actual identification of organizations?

The basic work in the area of classification is the investigation of samples of organizations. Slowly, a set of standards for high-quality investigations of organizational phena will emerge. Classificatory studies will follow which will offer confirmation of an existing classification or modification of it. This kind of activity may go on indefinitely. A classification scheme, like a good theory, is seldom finished. It is only given interim acceptance with the understanding that further studies will tend to elaborate and refine it, or disconfirm it.

2.5.4 Personal Preference

With the present dominance of functional studies in organizational science, there often seems to be little room for people whose skills and interests do not fit the narrow confines of the functional side of scientific inquiry. Systematics offers a place for some of these individuals. It brings to the center of the scientific stage those interested in comparative and multivariate analysis and those interested in historical events.

Descriptive research focusing on comparisons between different organizations and on the identification of their differences is of crucial scientific interest to systematists. Functionalists tend to want to shove comparative studies aside in favor of more analytic research searching for causes of one or another function or process. They want to claim that these are more "scientific" because they are reductive-analytical rather than descriptive. But the latter are just as vital to an effective science if carried out for classificatory purposes. Systematics provides a home for those interested in the descriptive use of quantitative multivariate methods.

Organizational science has not been a very fertile field for those interested in antiquity. Other sciences, such as geology and biology, offer many opportunities for those who wish to understand the present by studying the past, with paleontology being a special synthesis of geology and biology. Phyletic inquiries about organizational evolution offer the same scientifically relevant focus for organization and management researchers who have an interest in antiquity. Systematics offers management and other historians a means of contributing directly to the development of organization science. No longer do they have to be at the margin carrying out studies that are "interesting" but not "scientific."

Some individuals interested in systematics will pursue the three aforementioned tasks with roughly equal balance. But others may find all of their interest drawn to the quantitative description of samples of potential phena and taxa. Still others with a more theoretical bent may focus solely on the processes of speciation and the theory of classification. Historians will tend to focus on phyletic inquiries. But there is another way to describe systematic studies.

Mayr (1969, p. 15) identified three stages of classification. In the first stage, called *alpha taxonomy*, the emphasis is on the description of new species and their preliminary arrangement in comprehensive groupings. The second stage, termed *beta taxonomy*, consists of a more careful working out of the relationships at the species level and eventually with higher categories. At this stage emphasis is placed on the development of an effective classification scheme. And finally the third stage, labeled *gamma taxonomy*, focuses on variations within particular species, evolutionary studies, and the causal interpretation of organizational diversity. The following chapters of this book work toward a preliminary theory and method of classification; the book is clearly an example of alpha taxonomy. Other systematists will no doubt challenge the scheme I present and will thus continue working in the first stage. Some systematists will eventually settle in at the second stage, choosing not to challenge the basic structure of an alpha taxonomist's classification, but instead trying to refine and elaborate it. Finally, those with historical and evolutionary interests will focus on gamma taxonomy, looking for the causes and lines of organizational diversity.

There can be little doubt that systematics offers a range of areas for scientific inquiry broad enough to attract almost any interest predisposition. It also offers a place where researchers with a broad range of skills can contribute directly to the advancement of organizational science. Finally, systematics is new to organizational science and consequently is a wide-open field—one can contribute from the bottom up, as it were. Some people like this; perhaps they have a high tolerance for ambiguity. Of course, as the field matures and moves toward beta taxonomy, there will be areas needing investigation that are much less ambiguous, so even researchers who shun ambiguity can find a place to contribute.

2.6 SYSTEMATICS AS A PROFESSION

In his book, Mayr (1969) had a section on systematics as a profession. He discussed the availability of positions in universities and museums, the demands of systematics for people who like wandering around jungles, who prefer laboratory work, or who prefer computers and so forth. He commented on the relative contributions of "professionals" and "amateurs." He followed this with comments about the training of taxonomists, the professional organizations, and the future of systematics. In biology there is little doubt that systematics is a profession.

Systematics is not yet a profession in organizational science. It does not even exist. There is no place where one can receive training. There are no departmental positions for taxonomists, let alone vacant ones. There is no professional organization. Should organizational systematics be a profession and should universities open up positions for members of this profession? If organizational scientists accept the idea that systematics is a necessary prerequisite of functional studies, then systematics might indeed become a profession. As with biology, it is going to need people who do not mind field trips to collect measurements about samples of organizations. It will need theoreticians and those who like computers and quantitative methods. Some will become very good at it; others will look more like amateurs.

Organized training in systematics will be difficult to obtain for some time to come. In biology, even up to a few years ago, according to Mayr (1969, p. 18), most systematists started out as apprentices to a master. To begin with, organizational systematists will not be able to receive organized training and will not find apprentice positions—there are no masters. It will perforce be a "bootstraps" operation, an exploration and learning program for each individual interested in the subject. It would seem that basic training in organization theory and multivariate methods will be unavoidable, as will exposure to biological systematics. The broader one's range of knowledge about different kinds of organizations, the better equipped one will be to make classificatory judgments. Finally, one probably would want to know something about the workplace technologies of organizations, management theory and practice, and organizational environments. Some sociology and management departments appear to be the best places in which to start at this time.

Confusion remained rampant in systematic zoology and biology until international organizations were founded which began to bring order into the methods by which taxa were recognized and named. Until this happened there was no similarity from one country to another; the same taxa were given different names, and different taxa were given the same names. It was not until 1867 in botany and 1904 in zoology that these fields had their first international codes and had an internationally recognized classification scheme and methods for identifying phena and taxa, labeling, and publishing. Organizational science will be in a similar state of confusion until there is a recognized council that can set up basic ground rules and procedures for publishing, claiming the right to name and identify taxa, and so on.

2.7 SUMMARY

A distinction is made between systematics, the science of diversity, and functional science, the study of uniformity. Organizational systematics is a search for and description of organizational populations, whereas nearly all organizational science to date has focused on functional science. The problem in the field is that organizational populations and their attendant uniformities have not yet been satisfactorily discovered or described, leading to low levels of explained variance by functional studies. Special and general classifications are identified. This book is general classification about theories and methods. Basic terms such as *population*, *deme*, *taxon*, *phenon*, and *taxonomic character* were defined. The chapter concludes with some comments about organizational systematics as a profession.

③ TOWARD A THEORY OF ORGANIZATIONAL CLASSIFICATION

The development of thought since Aristotle could, I think, be summed up by saying that every discipline as long as it used the Aristotelian method of definition has remained arrested in a state of empty verbiage and barren scholasticism, and that the degree to which the various sciences have been able to make any progress depended on the degree to which they have been able to get rid of this essentialist method.

[Popper 1950, p. 206]

The purpose of this chapter is to move toward a theory of classification which will work for organizational systematists. This theory is important because it will affect the direction taken in thinking about speciation and phyletics. Indeed, the kind of theory chosen determines whether or not the problem of trying to explain the origin of organizational diversity is even considered. One argument I make in this chapter is that up until now organizational scientists have used essentialism or typology, which, as the opening quote by Popper implies, is a barren scholastic wasteland. No wonder organizational classification has not progressed very well.

Biologists have been thinking about classification for over 200 years. During this time they have tried several alternative theories. Because their phenomena presented more of a classificatory problem, they had more difficulty coming to agreement about an acceptable theory than did the physicists, chemists, or mineralogists; hence there has been more elaboration of classificatory theories in the biological literature, and it therefore makes sense to start by drawing on the superior experience of biologists. Consequently, I begin this chapter by discussing several biological theories of classification. I conclude by suggesting a combined phyletic-phenetic approach for organizational classification.

3.1 THEORIES OF CLASSIFICATION

There is a circularity involved between a scientist's choice of a theory and the kind of data observed. On the one hand, choice of a theory focuses investigation toward certain kinds of data. On the other hand, preliminary assumptions, hunches, beliefs, and conceptions about what the data are like suggest to a scientist that one strategy of explanation might fit better than another. Often these vague, untested preconceptions are all too important because once a strategy is chosen, the range of data searched out and considered legitimate is substantially narrowed and subsequent explanation becomes inadequate. Yet many scientists seem blithesomely unaware of how critical their preconceived notions are. As Hull (1965a, p. 316) observed, " . . . even scientists have a way of not noticing what conflicts with their philosophical presuppositions."

3.1.1 Principles of Enquiry

In an excellent empirical review of what scientists actually do, Schwab (1960, p. 2) referred to those early "notions which initiate and guide the course of a line of research" as *principles of enquiry*. His review covered some 4,000 studies written by European and American physical, biological, and behavioral scientists over the past five centuries, with most papers coming from the life sciences and psychology over the last two centuries. He noted that a principle of enquiry used by a scientist may be a matter of unexamined habit or espoused doctrine. Schwab said, "A group of notions achieve the status of principle of enquiry when they succeed in *bounding* and *analyzing* a subject matter so as to make it fit for enquiry" (1960, p. 2; his emphasis). The principle of enquiry provides meaning units, terms in which to frame the problems, definitions of what are legitimate data, and guidelines for how the data are to be interpreted.

In his review Schwab found five main principles. They are listed below in grossly abstract form (I encourage the reader to consult Schwab's original paper).

Reductive Principle. The scientist searches for the explanation of the behavior of an object by studying the behavior of its constituent elements. For example, studies attempting to explain organizational effectiveness by looking at the effects of decision making, leadership, personality, organizational climate, job involvement, and job design fall into this group. A classic example of this approach was March and Simon's book (1958).

Holistic Principle. The scientist rejects the idea that the behavior of the whole can be explained solely by analyzing its parts. An object is viewed as a system of interdependencies, many of which have two-way causal flows. The focus is on the pattern of relations among the parts themselves and between the parts and the whole. The systems view of organization theory described by Buckley (1967) is an example of this principle.

Rational Principle. The scientist tries to explain the behavior of an object by looking outward to the larger system or environment in which it is embedded. The contingency theorists (Kast and Rosenzweig 1973) and organizational ecologists (Hannan and Freeman 1977; Warriner 1978; Aldrich 1979), emphasizing an organization's ties with its environment, draw on this principle.

Anti-Principle. Scientists avoid accepting and being guided by any theories or hypotheses and try to "let the facts decide." They try to observe "what is out there" as carefully as possible, trying all the while to keep presuppositions from creeping in here and there in their methods. While it is possible to avoid being biased by many presuppositions, one can never completely avoid them because even the simplest measurements assume a common language or set of meanings. Examples of studies subscribing to this approach are the attempts to empirically derive organizational taxonomies by Haas et al. (1966) and Pugh et al. (1968, 1969).

Primitive Principle. The scientist lets the existence of practical problems and norms of the scientific community be the guide to scientific inquiry. An example of this kind of study would be the investigator who goes out and interviews managers and, after hearing about problems such as low morale, high turnover, poor planning, and so forth, chooses one to investigate. Much of the traditional research about communications in organizations was a direct response to perennial requests by managers for help in solving the "communications problem." Another example would be an individual who says, "I'll study whatever the National Science Foundation will fund."   .

Before commenting further on principles of enquiry I would like to present several theories of classification. Mayr (1969), in reviewing the history of systematics in zoology, identified five theories: essentialism, nominalism, empiricism, evolutionism, and cladism. The last of these, cladism, will be seen to take the same form as evolutionism. You will see that several of the principles of enquiry are involved.

3.1.2 Essentialism, Typology

ESSENTIALISM, often termed the classical approach, dates back to the scholastic logic of Plato and Aristotle. It was subsequently adopted by the Thomists, and was the body of thought that was fundamental to Linnaeus and permeated his work (Simpson 1961, pp. 36–40). About essentialism the philosopher Popper said:

> I use the name *methodological essentialism* to characterize the view, held by Plato and many of his followers, that it is the task of pure knowledge or "science" to discover and describe the true nature of things, i.e., their hidden reality or essence. It was Plato's peculiar belief that the essence of sensible things can be found in other and more real things—in their primogenitors or Forms. Many of the later methodological essentialists, for instance Aristotle, did not altogether follow him in determining this; but they all agreed with him in determining the task of pure knowledge as the discovery of the hidden nature or Form or essence of things. All these methodological essentialists also agreed with Plato in holding that these essences may be discovered and discussed with the help of intellectual intuition; that every essence has a name proper to it, the name after which the sensible thing is called; and that it may be described in words. A description of the essence of a thing they called a "definition." [1950, p. 34; his emphasis]

Hull, the premier philosopher of the life sciences (1974), described Aristotle's view that "three things can be known about any entity—its essence, its definition, and its name. The name names the essence. The definition gives a complete and exhaustive description of the essence" (Hull 1965a, p. 318). Hull also observed, "In taxonomy this philosophical position became known as TYPOLOGY. The three essentialistic tenets of typology are (1) the ontological assertion that Forms exist; (2) the methodological assertion that the task of taxonomy as a science is to discern the essences of species; and (3) the logical assertion concerning definition" (1965a, p. 317). The essentialists adhere to a conjunctive form of definition wherein species are "explicitly defined if and only if a set of properties can be given such that each property is severally necessary and the entire set of necessary properties is jointly sufficient" (Hull 1965a, p. 323). Sneath and Sokal (1973, pp. 19–20), held that the essence gave rise to properties which were inevitable consequences of the essence or definition. For example, using Hull's (1965a) analogy, they pointed out that the essence of a triangle on a plane surface was a figure bounded by three straight sides, and an inevitable consequence was that any two sides, when added together, were longer than the third. The properties of the triangle all stemmed from its definition. It was an *analyzable entity* in the sense that all of its properties could be traced by analysis back to their roots in its definition.

When applied to biological classification, essentialism attempts to treat biological objects as analyzable entities. It starts with the premise that all the properties of a biological object can be traced back to some essence, and hence to its definition. The classification scheme is built on the essential definitions. All members of a class must have the same common patterns of shared characters. As Simpson observed:

> Every natural group of organisms, hence every natural taxon in classification, has an invariant, generalized, or idealized pattern shared by all members of the group [i.e., the archetype or ground plan]. The pattern of a lower taxon is superimposed upon that of a higher taxon to which it belongs, without essentially modifying the higher pattern. [1961, pp. 46−47]

Essentialist classification concentrates on relatively few characters. For example, of all the characters that might be chosen to describe a species, essentialists might base the definition on a few—perhaps only ten. They might then argue that only eight were common among several species taxa, only seven were common among genus taxa, only five were common at the family rank, and so on. So, as one goes up the hierarchy, fewer and fewer characters typically would be used to define the taxa. Because of the deliberate A PRIORI WEIGHTING of characters, biologists refer to classifications based on essentialism as *artificial* classifications composed of artificial groups. Essentialist classifications result in MONOTHETIC groups which are "formed by rigid and successive logical divisions so that the possession of a unique set of features is both sufficient and necessary for membership in the group thus defined" (Sneath and Sokal 1973, p. 20). *All* members of a monothetic group must possess *all* attributes used to define that group.

Mayr (1969, p. 66) reported that all but a very few biological systematists had abandoned essentialist philosophy by the mid-twentieth century. In contrast, Hull (1965a) argued that although Lamarck and Darwin and modern taxonomists have thrown out the first two of the three essentialist tenets, they still hold on to the logic of Aristotelian definition—the conjunctive form. In an excellent analysis, Hull (1965a, b) points out why this is so. His solution, a disjunctive definition, will be taken up later in section 6.1.2. Recently Olson* confirmed that in his view biological taxonomists were all essentialists where it counts—in practice. They all seem to prefer to use several species concepts, each in a conjunctive definitional form, rather than accept Hull's disjunctive definition (see Mayr 1969 and Ross 1974 for textbook usage of the multiple conjunctive form).

Most organizational scientists have been unabashed essentialists or typologists and for the most part continue to be so (see Jurkovich 1974; Filley and Aldag 1978; Meyer 1977; Mintzberg 1979; Mills and Margulies 1980, for example). Among the better-known classical ones, Etzioni (1975), in suggesting a typology based on compliance, argued that the crucial essence in differentiating organizations was how they obtained compliance from their members. The essence for Blau and Scott (1962) was who benefited from what the organization did. Parsons (1956) and Katz and Kahn (1978) both argued that the essence of organizations was the function they performed for the larger society. Perrow (1967) emphasized the amount of variability of the inputs coming into an organization and their susceptibility to being analyzed or well understood. Thompson's (1967) essence was the kind of technology organizations used. There are, of course, many many others, possibly a different typology for every person investigating organizations. For a recent review of these and some others see Carper and Snizek (1980).

The typology proposed by Mintzberg (1979) is at once the most recent, elaborate, interesting, and curious of all the essentialist approaches. I would like to believe that Mintzberg was joking when he said it is based in numerology, "the study of the occult significance of numbers" (*Webster's Seventh New Collegiate Dictionary*). He said,

> The number "five" has appeared repeatedly in our discussion. First there were five basic coordinating mechanisms, then five basic parts of the organization, later five basic types of decentralization. Five is, of course, no ordinary digit. It is the sign of union, the nuptial number according to the Pythagoreans; the *Dictionnaire des Symboles* goes on to tell us that five is the "symbol of man . . . likewise of the universe . . . the symbol of divine will that seeks only order and perfection." To the ancient writers, five was the *essence* of the universal laws, there being "five colors, five flavors, five tones, five metals, five viscera, five planets, five orients, five regions of space, of course five senses," not to mention "the five colors of the rainbow." Our modest contribution to this impressive list is five structural configurations. [1979, p. 300; emphasis added]

Mintzberg suggested five different ideal structural configurations based on the growth patterns of the five internal components which

*Everett Olson, personal communication, 1980.

grow differentially in response to "conditions" which are not specified very clearly, if at all. They are: Simple Structure, Machine Bureaucracy, Professional Bureaucracy, Divisionalized Form, and Adhocracy. Lacking solid theoretical or empirical basis, Mintzberg's typology is hard to take seriously, though the 480 pages of text in his book suggest he was not joking about fives. It does not appear to have either the predictive validity of a good special classification or the broad empirical base of an acceptable general classification.

The common approach among all of these typologies of organizations was the selection of very few characters upon which to base the classification. All other characters, even those highlighted in other typologies known at the time, were ignored. In defense of these scholars, it may be said that they were presumably working on special as opposed to general classifications. But all of them also argued or implied that their schemes were of much broader use than a special interest in function or technology. In truth their motives remain a bit obscure, as they did not make their classificatory intent very clear. In retrospect, however, it is clear that these attempts at classification resulted in special classifications and were based on essentialism.

The strength of the essentialist logic is that everything is classified into *a* or *non-a* or *b* or *non-b*, and so forth. Consequently the resulting classes are mutually exclusive and the definitional characters clearly serve as diagnostic or identifying keys. Typologies have great practicality, as few characters are involved and classifiers may quickly determine whether an object fits into a certain class. Because they treat objects as analyzable entities, essentialist classifications allow systematists to predict with great accuracy the properties of objects once their class membership is known, since the properties follow from the definition upon which the classification is based.

The weakness of essentialism is not due to any flaw in the logic itself, but lies in the fact that it may be wrongly applied to *unanalyzable entities*, those whose properties cannot be predicted from an essential definition or the pattern of a few characters. The case for essentialism in biology rested on whether or not the objects they attempted to classify were analyzable or unanalyzable entities. By the middle of the nineteenth century, and the publishing of the Darwin-Wallace theory of natural selection, most biologists had decided that biological objects were unanalyzable—there were just too many properties of species that had to be ignored to use the essentialist logic. Essentialism was based on the denial of variability. It treated most variability as trivial random differences that made the true essence just a bit harder to discover. I want to alert the reader to the reality that in practice, and in studying the classifications of botanists and zoologists, it would appear that essentialism still prevails, especially at the higher category levels. Olson* insists that *in practice* most taxonomists really are essentialists. I am more charitable, being convinced that their reconstructed logic (Kaplan's [1964] term) is not essentialistic and that their logic-in-use (also Kaplan's term) looks essentialistic because of practical or operational limitations and the practice of trying to get by with a very few characters for purposes of identification.

Organizational scientists still are undecided as to whether organizations are analyzable or unanalyzable for classification purposes. The failure of the existing typologies is probably the best evidence that organizations are unanalyzable entities. While organizational scientists have not persevered in the face of failure as long as the biological essentialists did, the record is no less consistent. It simply has not worked. In organizational science Haas et al. (1966), Burns (1967), Pugh et al. (1968, 1969), Hall (1977), and Carper and Snizek (1980) all have pointed out the uselessness of organizational typologies for empirical research. Their main theme was that these typologies ignored too much important variability among organizations. Davis and Heywood (1963) said that the essentialist approach to classification was in such disrepute among biological systematists that to mount heavy criticism against it was tantamount to flogging a dead horse. Our essentialist horse is not dead yet, but I am not going to waste more space on it. There are better alternatives.

3.1.3 Nominalism

The basic argument of NOMINALISM was that (1) only individual objects existed; (2) there was no difference between classifying living and inanimate objects; and (3) all groupings of objects were artifacts of the human mind. This approach to classification made no pretense of trying to understand why groupings might have occurred in nature; it did not even recognize the existence of such groupings. Nominalists held that the construction of classes was an activity of reason which served the purposes of classifiers in particular and of scientists in general. Perhaps understanding better than most the prerequisite importance of orderly homogeneous groupings for the population definition and sampling of functional science, the nominalists saw classification as an instrumental activity aiding functional scientists rather than as an end in itself or as an attempt to classify or explain the origin of possibly natural groupings.

*Everett Olson, personal communication, 1980.

The strength of the nominalist approach was that it did recognize the need of scientists carrying out functional studies to have homogeneous classes of objects upon which to base their inductive theorizing and to have similar homogeneous classes upon which to test their hypotheses and to generalize their findings.

But there were weaknesses, too, and because of them nominalism was never taken too seriously. Most important, most observers, upon seeing objects like snakes, birds, rabbits, people, flowers, and trees, had trouble accepting the idea that naturally occurring groupings of animals and plants did not exist. As the essentialists did, the nominalists also produced artificial groupings grounded only in the human mind. As such, they were not very stable, subject to change every time some theorist decided it would be better to see the world a little differently than before. But unlike essentialism, the artificial groupings of the nominalists were not based on a priori weighted characters in search of some essential pattern. Nominalist groupings were based strictly on a user-oriented criterion—which groupings appeared most useful for other scientific activities.

There are no examples of someone taking an explicit nominalist approach to the classification of organizations. But then, no one has explicitly said it ought not to be used, either. The view taken here is that organizational systematists should avoid nominalism because there is too much evidence (discussed in chapter 5) showing that natural groupings of organizations do exist. The goal of a user-oriented classification can be better achieved via empiricism.

3.1.4 Empiricism, Numerical Phenetics, Numerical Taxonomy

In biological systematics, the 100 years between Linnaeus's publication of his tenth edition of *Systema Naturae* in 1758 and Darwin's publication of *Origin of Species* in 1859 were marked by a steady and almost overwhelming increase in the number of known animals and plants. During this period naturalists realized that the endless variety of organic life *was* organized into natural groups and, further, that these natural groups could not be classified on the basis of some common discernible pattern composed of only a few characters. In short, the theories of essentialism and nominalism came under increasing pressure and dispute. EVOLUTIONISM took their place. Along with the rejection of essentialism and nominalism, more recently came the questioning of a priori weighting of characters, a cornerstone of evolutionism. An alternative philosophy, empiricism, came to the forefront.

In comparison to the nominalists, the fundamental premise of EMPIRICISM (and evolutionism) was that groupings of plants and animals *did* occur in nature and that a classification should follow as closely as possible the naturally occurring groupings, or what came to be called the *natural system*.* It followed that, if investigators made enough studies, these groupings would emerge. Furthermore, empiricists put their emphasis on observed similarity. Finally, they attempted to keep their observations as free as possible from a priori theories about the origin of the groupings and which characters might form an underlying essential pattern. The empiricists decoupled the task of developing a classification from the equally important, but nevertheless independent, task of explaining the origin of the natural system. They also attempted to "let the facts decide." A consequence of this was an emphasis on the EQUAL WEIGHTING of characters and an attempt to study as many characters as possible.

Because of the large numbers of characters that could be used to describe most organisms, empiricism did not make much headway before the middle of the twentieth century; the methods for comparing large numbers of variables across large samples were not available. It was replaced by evolutionism (described in section 3.1.5) after Darwin's theory gained acceptance. Empiricism has recently reemerged because the electronic computer now makes possible the study of many characters with a large sample. Now empiricism comes under the label of NUMERICAL PHENETICS, the latter term reflecting its emphasis on identifying groupings according to phenotypical similarity. The numerical pheneticists themselves seem to prefer the label NUMERICAL TAXONOMY. I should also note that it is possible to take a nonnumerical phenetic approach to classification, as was recently pointed out by McNeill (1979), who said that most phenetic studies are not numerical. Also, numerical methods are not only applicable to the phenetic approach, though this was where they were first intensively applied.

The unquestioned leaders in the field of numerical taxonomy are Sokal and Sneath, who published their first edition of *Principles of Numerical Taxonomy* in 1963. An indication of how fast the field has taken off is given by the considerable increase in the size and sophistication of their second edition (Sneath and Sokal 1973). They defined numerical taxonomy as "the grouping by numerical methods of taxonomic units into taxa on the basis of their character states" (Sneath and Sokal 1973, p. 4). They traced the origin of their basic concepts back to the French botanist Michel Adanson, who published his work on the

---

*The essentialists also searched for the natural system.

natural history of Senegal in 1757. The following principles summarize the fundamental position of the numerical pheneticists:

1. The greater the content of information in the taxa of a classification and the more characters on which it is based, the better a given classification will be.
2. A priori, every character is of equal weight in creating natural taxa.
3. Overall similarity between any two entities is a function of their individual similarities in each of the many characters by which they are being compared.
4. Distinct taxa can be recognized because correlations of characters differ in the groups of organisms under study.
5. Phylogenetic inferences can be made from the taxonomic structures of a group and from character correlations, given certain assumptions about evolutionary pathways and mechanisms.
6. Taxonomy is viewed and practiced as an empirical science.
7. Classifications are based on phenetic similarity. [Sneath and Sokal 1973, p. 5]

As can be understood from the principles, the emphasis of the numerical pheneticists is on phena, which have been defined as groupings of objects that are phenotypically "reasonably similar." Numerical pheneticists have used multivariate analytical methods, especially various forms of cluster analysis, multidimensional scaling, and factor analysis. Following the development of electronic computers, these techniques blossomed into large-scale methods for comparing large samples of objects with respect to large numbers of taxonomic characters.

Accompanying the shift from essentialism to empiricism, and later to evolutionism, was the shift from viewing taxonomic groups as monothetic to viewing them as POLYTHETIC. Bailey (1973) has also suggested that such a shift is necessary in sociology. Beckner's (1959, p. 22) definition is the standard one, being used by Mayr (1969, p. 83), Sneath and Sokal (1973, p. 21), and Bailey (1973) among others:

A class is ordinarily defined by reference to a set of properties which are both necessary and sufficient (by stipulation) for membership in the class. It is possible, however, to define a group K in terms of a set G of properties $f_1, f_2, \ldots f_n$ in a different manner. Suppose we have an aggregation of individuals (we shall not as yet call them a class) such that:
1. Each one possesses a large (but unspecified) number of the properties in G.
2. Each f in G is possessed by large numbers of these individuals and
3. No f in G is possessed by every individual in the aggregate.
   By the terms of 3, no f is necessary for membership in this aggregate; and nothing has been said to either warrant or rule out the possibility that some f in G is sufficient for membership in the aggregate.

Beckner said that a group is polythetic if the first two conditions are met, and is fully polythetic if all conditions are met.

In shifting from monothetic to polythetic groups, the status of variation took an about-face. In the former, variation was viewed as error, to be gotten rid of as much as possible. In polythetic groups variation is taken as an integral part of the concept. It is expected that the population forming a natural group will vary somewhat in taxonomic description, and the concept is defined to take this into account. For a more extended discussion of monothetic and polythetic groups from a social science perspective, see Bailey (1973).

The polythetic concept underlies all of the theoretical and methodological developments discussed in this book. It is assumed that environmental forces operate to produce groups of organizations possessing a large number of common characters, that each character is possessed by many organizations in a group, but that no character is possessed by all the organizations in the group. Much of the rest of the book is devoted to supporting this assumption directly or developing methods fostering such support in the future.

In applying the empiricist and evolutionist theories developed in biology to organizations, the term *natural system* creates some awkwardness in that nothing about organizations is really "natural" since they are all artificial—that is, created by people. Further, *natural system* has already been used by Gouldner (1959) as a way of labeling naturally or organically emerging events in organizations, and Gouldner's usage of the term also will be employed later in the book. Since throughout the rest of the book it will be convenient to have a term to use to correspond to what the biologists call the natural system, I will use the term PROTOSYSTEM to refer to groupings of organizations presumed to exist before organizational scientists decided that groupings of organizations were needed for scientific purposes, that is, needed to aid completion of the inductive-deductive cycle and thereby aid functional studies. The prefix *proto* is chosen because it means "that which comes before." It is taken as parallel in meaning to the biologists' term *natural system*.

Several examples of numerical taxonomy applied to organizational classification have appeared in the literature on organizations. Haas et al. (1966) based their analysis on a sample of seventy-five organizations from a population loosely defined as all organizations in the continental United States; they used ninety-nine characters as a basis of comparison. Their characters largely reflected the Weberian and sociological emphasis on formal structural characteristics along with other characters such as goals, differentiation, interdependency, emphasis on status, competition from other organizations, age, and financial condition. Using a computer program developed by botanists, they produced a solution composed of ten prime classes (comprised of from two to thirty organizations), with as many as four rank categories in some of the larger classes. This study did not produce a useable classification (McKelvey 1975; Hall 1977, p. 38), perhaps because the authors did not stay with and develop their data pool sufficiently but more likely because of methodological issues I will cover in chapters 11 and 12.

Goronzy's (1969) analysis was based on fifty completed returns from a sample of 500 organizations from a population of American manufacturing firms. He used twenty-nine characters, almost all of which were variations around a theme of size: total sales, sales per employee, total assets, technology-capacity index, number of production workers, number of supervisors, size of R&D department, and so forth. Goronzy concluded that his computer solution, based on correlations as similarity measures, produced four clusters approximating a four-way classification based mainly on size and technological complexity. Because of the overemphasis on size variables (which Goronzy himself noted) and a sample that would not appear to be representative of the population, the findings were of rather limited use.

Pugh et al. (1968, 1969) used factor analysis instead of cluster analysis. Their study was based on a sample of forty-six organizations from a population of work organizations from the Birmingham, England area which employed over 250 workers. They used only sixteen characters drawn directly from the Weberian tradition of organizational analysis. Their variables focused on items such as formalization, standardization, specialization, centralization, and certain aspects of structural configuration. Some of their main measures were not independent of each other* and their results consisted of somewhat arbitrary clusters based on a bifurcation at the mean of ordered rankings of three factors of a four-factor solution. This study contained a mixture of taxonomic units: independent organizations as well as subunits. Seven empirical groupings emerged, but without too much separation among groups above and below the mean on a given dimension, and rather low homogeneity within the groups. This is in part due to too few characters used and in part due to the use of factor rather than cluster analysis. The pros and cons of each approach will be taken up in chapter 12. A more detailed review of this study was given by McKelvey (1975).

---

*A careful description of their lack of independence and a replication of their factor analysis based on a reduced set of nine independent measures was prepared by McKelvey (1973).

Another cluster study (Pinto and Pinder 1972) was not really an analysis of groupings of organizations, but rather of groupings of subunits based on eighteen supervisorial ratings of subunit effectiveness. They found eight clusters, each of which was composed of subunits receiving similar ratings by supervisors. The study raises several interesting questions. Should variation in effectiveness be included as a taxonomic dimension? Or should a classification be based only on organizational forms known to be effectively adapted? Should subjective ratings be included as taxonomic characters? What is the logical unit of classification? The possibilities range from entities as small as work groups to departments, divisions, separate companies, and corporations. Like earlier ones, the Pinto and Pinder study is illustrative in an embryonic way, but many questions remain.

There are several strengths to the modern variant of empiricism, numerical phenetics. First and most important, such classification is based, at the species or population level at least, on substantial samples of organizations rather than on one or a few organizations. Thus it has a much stronger empirical base. Second, the numerical phenetic methods, while not perfect, can offer substantial improvements in objective and replicable treatment of the data, especially when they are used by knowledgeable, conservative, and conscientious systematists. They meet the scientific standards for high-quality knowledge better than the evolutionist approach. Third, numerical taxonomy is also more comprehensive, taking into account all known characters. Consequently the overall phenetic similarity of objects within a class is broadly based. This is especially good for purposes of building a general classification. Fourth, because the phenetic approach is based on many characters and lends itself to the study of much larger samples, the classification is less subject to the biases of one taxonomist, the inadvertent omission of a character, or the discovery of a new character. Because of this it also tends to be stable over a longer period of time. Finally, strictly from the perspective of classification, numerical phenetics, by decoupling the attempt to explain the origin of populations from the attempt to develop a phenetically based classification scheme, performs the latter task more adroitly, thereby serving the instrumental side of systematics more successfully.

There are also several weaknesses. First, the inclusion of many characters, usually equally weighted, while being one of its strengths, also leads to one of its weaknesses. By indiscriminately measuring all known characters a taxonomist may inadvertently weight some attributes more than others. This can happen, for example, if one includes ten characters that reflect one more fundamental attribute while only including two characters reflecting another fundamental attribute. The attribute having ten measured characters will end up having more effect on the final solution or classification. Second, critics of numerical taxonomy (Mayr 1969, for example) have argued that it has no way of discriminating trivial differences from significant ones. Since trivial differences typically are more frequent than significant ones, the resulting classification may rest mostly on trivia, even though it is scientifically objective and replicable. Third, numerical methods are not as thoroughly "objective" as their proponents are inclined to claim. Buried within the multivariate methods are numerous choice points that call for decisions by an investigator which are often arbitrary, subjective, and sometimes not widely accepted by knowledgeable colleagues. In factor analysis the choice of the number of factors to rotate, which is indeterminate, directly affects the number of factors in the solution and thus the number of cells in the classification. In cluster analysis the choice of the clustering algorithm directly affects the final configuration. Fourth, the quality of the outcome depends on how well the sector* is defined and how representative the sample is. These are age-old problems to scientists, but crucial nonetheless and still subject to questionable judgments, as the studies applying numerical taxonomy to organizations have shown (McKelvey 1975). Finally, there is the question of whether numerical phenetics can be pursued successfully without recourse to a priori theory. Many biological numerical taxonomists, but especially Sneath and Sokal (1973) and the sociologist Warriner (1977), have conveyed the impression that it can, but McKelvey (1979) has argued that decisions about sectors, characters, and taxonomic units require an a priori theory. This issue will be taken up in more detail later in the chapter.

The biological taxonomists started by first accepting existing families as a way of defining a population to study and then tried to group species into general and other intermediate-rank categories below the family rank (Sneath and Sokal 1973, p. 362). The organizational taxonomists tried to do the same thing and ran into difficulties because they did not have a foundation of well-defined species to work from. They had no basis for defining an average or exemplar member of an existing organizational grouping such as a craft organization, assembly-line operation, or school. As computers grew larger and certain technical problems were solved, the biological taxonomists began to drop their analyses

---

*Throughout the book I will use the term *population* to refer to the species groupings of organizations which are a *result* of taxonomic studies. The term SECTOR will be used to indicate the *initial* grouping from which a sample for empirical study is drawn. It could coincide with a population or contain many of them.

down to the species or population level and even below. As will be discussed later (section 3.2.3), no matter how hard they tried to avoid defining the species concept, the biological pheneticists drew on the already existing evolutionary classification when it came time to initially define sectors for analysis. They did not start from scratch by drawing a sample from, for example, a sector of all plants or animals in the United States, England, or the Los Angeles area. Their studies were much more circumscribed than that, and the evolutionary classification provided the circumscription. Generally, the biological taxonomists have "fine-tuned" the evolutionary classification rather than thrown it out and started all over.

The lesson organizational scientists can learn from this is that numerical taxonomic classifications of organizations, because of various technical problems related to the size of computers and the ability to find samples large enough to base comparisons on vast numbers of variables, cannot start from a vague sector definition such as "all business organizations in the United States." Such a sector would require many many characters for all differences to be described properly. Such a number of characters would be too large for existing computers and require an unmanageably large sample, not to mention take a long time to collect. The solution to this problem is a more circumscribed definition of a sector, and the narrower the better. Narrow sector definitions in turn require some kind of preliminary classification scheme as a point of departure. In this book, I offer such a solution in the form of an evolutionist classification, a theory of classification to which I now turn.

3.1.5 Phyletics, Evolutionism, Cladism

Ever since the Darwin-Wallace theory of natural selection and Darwin's observations about the origin of species in the mid-nineteenth century, biologists have generally agreed that the *natural groupings of biological organisms were due to their descent with modification from common ancestors.* Those pursuing the PHYLETIC approach reach for a classificatory scheme that: (1) classifies organisms according to readily delimitable groups of species and (2) explains why they came to exist in the first place and why in a particular form. They insist that character similarity alone is not the answer. Darwin said:

> Such expressions as that famous one of Linnaeus, and which we often meet with in a more or less concealed form, that the characters do not make the genus, but that the genus gives the characters, seem to imply that something more is included in our classification than mere resemblance. I believe that something more is included; and that propinquity of descent—

the only known cause of the similarity of organic beings—is the bond, hidden as it is by various degrees of modification, which is partially revealed to us by our classifications. [1859, pp. 413–414]

Phyletics is like essentialism and empiricism in that it assumes that natural groupings exist. But it is the only theory that attempts to explain the origin of groupings as well as classify them. Environmental diversity and natural selection, according to the Darwin-Wallace theory, are the means of forming natural groups. Only those organisms well adapted to their particular habitat will survive in the long run; organismic diversity reflects environmental diversity. It is a phyletic theory in the sense that it reflects the phylogenetic heritage of the presently living species. There are two hotly contested subtheories within the general phyletic approach, EVOLUTIONISM and CLADISM.

Evolutionist classification is based on what Mayr (1969, p. 25) called the BIOLOGICAL SPECIES CONCEPT. According to this concept, a species is: (1) a reproductive community, where members view each other as potential mates and have means of attracting potential mates; (2) an ecological unit, which interacts with other units of plants or animals; and (3) a genetic unit, consisting of an intercommunicating gene pool, with each member holding a small portion of the genes for a relatively short period of time. Mayr (1969, p. 26) defined biological species as "groups of interbreeding natural populations that are reproductively isolated from other such groups." The strength of this concept, according to Mayr, is that it explains why species are stable in the short run yet still provides an explanation of evolution in the long run. This concept is not without problems, however. Sneath and Sokal (1973, p. 364) noted that critics have argued that the biological species concept is nonoperational in that in practice it is often impossible to obtain biological (interbreeding) data as opposed to phenetic data (e.g., how to know whether two fossilized animals could interbreed). Ross (1974, p. 57) observed that the biological species concept preferred by zoologists such as Mayr was not acceptable, especially to botanists who were faced with many more apomictic (asexual) species, but also to some zoologists. Ross saw a need for several species concepts. Nevertheless, the biological concept fits the mainstream since most species do interbreed, and the theoretical definition is useful as a stimulus to a priori theorizing in organizational systematics, even though it does have operational difficulties. A more detailed treatment of this important concept is given in section 6.1.2.

As opposed to the empiricists, who base the affinity of group members on phenetic similarity, the phyleticists base affinity on phyletic groupings. There are two ways of defining this latter kind of affinity. One method is based on PATRISTIC AFFINITY. Here the definition of affinity is the number of similar characters that members of a given group derived from a common ancestor. The other is based on CLADISTIC AFFINITY. In this case the definition of affinity is recency of descent from a common ancestor, without taking into account the number of shared characters they might have. Patristic affinity emphasizes similarity among genes; cladism emphasizes genealogical relationship.

Ignoring cladism for the moment, the inescapable strength of the evolutionist theory of classification over numerical phenetics is that it does try to explain the origin of naturally occurring groupings. By combining classification and explanation it does two jobs at once, thereby becoming a more efficient and elegant theory. Think how cumbersome it would be to have two classification systems, one looking backward and classifying objects according to how they originated and evolved, the other looking forward and classifying objects according to what would be best for scientists ultimately using the classification. A second point, important to Mayr (who is an avowed evolutionist), is that the evolutionary classification is natural, not contrived; as he put it, "the taxonomist no longer 'makes' taxa, he becomes a 'discoverer' of groups made by evolution" (1969, p. 76). Systematists, like other scientists, are not content just to contrive or describe; they wish to explain. Because it explains the origin of species, the evolutionist theory has come to be the dominant basis of classification in biology.

The principal weakness of the evolutionist theory of classification is that often poor data are used in making judgments about phyletic descent, even where there is a strong fossil record. Fossils only offer a portion of the taxonomic characters a living organism offers, the gene structure is unavailable for true patristic determination, and of course one cannot test species by trying to see if fossils interbreed. The absence of data here and there means many judgments made by taxonomists are quite subjective. Often there is no objective way to resolve disagreements (though cladists strongly disagree on this point), and there is a tendency for each taxonomist to have his or her personal classification scheme, particularly in their areas of specialization. Second, because evolutionist classification is somewhat of a compromise based on phenetic, cladistic, and patristic affinities, the resulting classification is a compromise and consequently the classes may not be as homogeneous as to phenotype as they might be if produced by numerical phenetic methods alone. Third, an evolutionist classification tends to be unstable because of the subjectivity involved in making judgments about phyletic descent and because the taxonomists typically do not use large data bases and large numbers of characters. (The latter are the strengths of numerical phenetics.) It is more susceptible to the personal biases of individual taxonomists, and is subject to change as these biases change or as one or another taxonomist becomes an opinion leader. Finally, because of its instability, an evolutionist classification is not perfect either for scientists doing functional studies or for purposes of information retrieval. There is some risk involved in organizing scientific findings in terms of a scheme that is operationally based on not too many weighted characters that may be changed overnight because of a change in opinion or new evidence on phyletic lineages, though this could happen with any approach as a result of the discovery of new data. (The numerical phenetic method is less susceptible to this because so many equally weighted characters are used.)

Cladism, advocated principally by Hennig (1950, 1966), focuses exclusively on branching points in phylogenetic lineages. Cladists, following Hennig, like to call themselves phylogeneticists, but this is confusing since evolutionists also pay attention to phylogeny. Everyone else calls them cladists, as will I. This school is typically described as "aiming to include only information on phylogenetic kinship" (Farris 1979b, p. 483), or recency of descent (Mayr 1969, p. 70). Most of the fervor and debate in the recent biological systematics literature seem focused around cladism versus evolutionism and numerical phenetics (see recent issues of *Systematic Zoology*, for example). Instead of ignoring phylogeny as the pheneticists do, cladists go to the opposite extreme, ignoring everything but the lines of descent. Thus each grouping is MONOPHYLETIC in that membership is reserved only for species discovered to have descended from the same common ancestor. Species which cannot be linked to a specific ancestor are left in an "unknown" status (Wiley 1979). This is in direct contrast to the evolutionists, who allow both monophyletic and POLYPHYLETIC groupings. The latter are composed of species which appear to be alike phenotypically and have similar genotypic composition, though they do not share the same common immediate ancestor. The principal result of this difference is that evolutionists will group several, even many, monophyletic groups together into one polyphyletic group. This considerably reduces the number of groups in the classification scheme.

Cladists insist that every monophyletic grouping appear separately, leading to very complicated classification. Their method focuses on teasing out ancestral and derived (apomorphic) characters. Characters are designated as *ancestral* or *derived* according to the fossil record— the former are always earlier than the latter. The phylogeny is constructed more or less under the general logic that species sharing more ancestral characters are from a higher category than those having more derived characters. Thus a species having eight ancestral and four derived characters would be ranked higher than one having six ancestral and seven derived characters. It gets complicated. An introduction to this method is given by Ross (1974).

Cladists argue that the strength of cladism is that it retains more information content (Farris 1979b), where each branch of a family tree or DENDROGRAM is information (Nelson 1979). Obviously, the more branches, the more information. Cladists have conducted empirical comparisons showing that their methods produce more information content (Mickevich 1978; Presch 1979; Farris 1979b). This is a misleading comparison since neither the pheneticists nor the evolutionists try to produce a lot of branching points. In fact critics argue that producing branching points unnecessarily complicates the classification scheme and therefore is to be avoided (Gingerich 1979; Hull 1979).

Having reviewed numerical phenetic and phyletic theories, including both evolutionist and cladistic, more or less separately, a comparative perspective is a useful way to conclude this section. Evolutionism is the orthodox or traditional theory of classification. Numerical phenetics is one new approach, which holds that a classification should be totally independent of supposed phyletic (phylogenetic) groupings. Cladism, the newest theory, holds that a classification should be based exactly on branching points in phyletic lines, a belief quite the opposite of phenetics. Evolutionism falls in between. In describing it, Mayr says that, despite what the label might imply,

> it is not true that it is "the sole aim of evolutionary classification to reflect as accurately as possible the facts of evolution." Actually the most important aim of evolutionary classification is exactly the same as of all genuine classifications (in contrast to identification schemes): to combine maximal information content with maximal ease of retrieval of this information. The evolutionist believes that a classification consistent with our reconstruction of phylogeny has a better chance of meeting these objectives than any other method of classification. Taxa delimited in such a way as to coincide with phylogenetic groups (lineages) are apt not only to share the greatest number of joint attributes, but at the same time to have an explanatory basis for their existence. [1969, p. 78]

Bock (1973) captured the differences among the three theories as follows:

> *Phenetics* is based on the concept that the relationship between organisms is ascertained by their overall similarity. Greater similarity indicates closer relationship and a smaller amount of evolutionary change from the common ancestor.

> Relationship among organisms, in *cladistics*, is based upon joint posses-
> sion of derived [more recent or advanced] features. . . . Species which
> shared derived features are related, and hierarchies of taxonomic groups
> are established on hierarchies of derived characters. Thus relationships
> between organisms are strictly determined by phylogenetic branching and
> may be regarded as genealogical or kinship relationship.
>
> *Evolutionary* classification is based upon a simultaneous evaluation of
> the two variables used singly by pheneticists and cladists to ascertain
> relationships between organisms, namely:
>
> 1) Evaluation of the amount (degree) of genetical similarity between
> organisms as judged by the degree of their phenotypical similarity. Greater
> phenotypical similarity implies greater genetical similarity and hence
> closer relationship. . . .
>
> 2) Evaluation of the sequence of events in the evolution of each species
> from the common ancestor, with the evens arranged in phylogenetic order.
> This includes proper sequential arrangement of the origin and modifica-
> tions of features and of the branching sequences of each lineage. [Pp.
> 376−377; emphasis added]

Ideally evolutionists would prefer to base affinity on the GENOTYPE, looking for similarity of gene composition. Practically this is seldom directly possible because genes are unavailable (in fossils for example), or not readily available for comparative measurement. In practice evolutionists then resort to analyzing the PHENOTYPE, studying characters to ascertain their similarity or their ancestral and derived status. Evolutionists insist that *in theory*, classification should be based on genotypic (patristic) affinity, even though in practice they seldom, if ever, achieve more than phenetic or cladistic findings. For recent evolutionist views see Michener (1970, 1977, 1978), Mayr (1974), and Ashlock (1974, 1979). Pheneticists such as Sneath and Sokal (1973) argue that the evolutionary concept is in fact nonoperational. They believe that their phenetic theory (which happens to use numerical taxonomy) is better because it fits better with what is operationally possible and scientifically more objective. (See also Gingerich 1979 and McNeill 1979 for recent defenses of phenetics.) Evolutionists counter by saying that numerical phenetics is also open to subjective bias in the selection of clustering methods and is insensitive to evolutionarily important characters (Mayr 1969; Bock 1973).

At this time I am not aware of any examples of someone using the evolutionist or cladist theories to move toward a general classification of organizations, other than the preliminary suggestion by McKelvey (1978). Some of the essentialists' special classifications could be seen as attempts to explain how certain forces in an organization's environment led to its form, but a close reading of their work suggests that these authors did not have phyletic explanation as their objective. With respect to the Parsons (1956) and Katz and Kahn (1966) classifications, for example, one could view the environment—in this case the larger society—as exerting forces that led organizations to specialize in one or another of the four functions: economic, integrative, adaptative, and pattern maintenance. But they do not discuss when the society first had a need for the various functions, or when the first organization specializing in one of the functions emerged. Perrow (1967) could have added an evolutionary explanation to his classification of four kinds of organizations (decentralized, flexible-polycentralized, flexible-centralized, formal-centralized) by discussing when certain kinds of inputs first appeared in the environment and when each of the specialized forms of organization emerged in adaptation to each kind of input. But he did not. In sum, essentialist classifications could be used as a rudimentary basis for explaining how classes of organizations came into being; but none of them would be a true general classification and, in organization science at least, none of their originators seemed to be trying to explain the origin of organizational diversity.

3.1.6 Are Additional Theories of Classification Possible?

My review of the biological theories of classification has covered four major theories (the phyletic theory had two subtheories within it). Are there any other ways of thinking about classification besides these? One way to approach this question is to think in terms of the five principles of scientific enquiry identified by Schwab (1960), which were briefly described at the beginning of this section. It is possible that a theory of classification could follow from each principle of enquiry. Table 3.1 shows the relationship of the theories of classification to the principles of enquiry.

It can easily be observed that essentialism builds on the principle of reduction in that both look to the internal elements. Evolutionism, by focusing on survival within a particular environment, is clearly rooted

TABLE 3.1

THEORIES OF CLASSIFICATION RELATED TO PRINCIPLES OF ENQUIRY

Theories	Principles
Essentialism	Reductive
Evolutionalism	Rational
	Holistic
Empiricism	Anti-Principle
Nominalism	Primitive

in the rational principle. Empiricism, by eschewing preconceived notions, stems from anti-principles. Nominalism is a bit harder to place, but Schwab (1960, p. 11) gives as an example of primitive principles in operation the case where scientific studies achieve status via funding decisions, peer approval, etc. Here, as with nominal classification, the preferences of a scientific community predominate, as opposed to empirical reality.

The only principle left unaccounted for is holism. It is ironic that Schwab (1960, p. 6) said that holism is "most conspicuous in the frankly taxonomic sciences—zoology, botany, and mineralogy. . . . " Presumably he got this from the systematists interest in classifying organisms or minerals as whole entities rather than analyzing their behavior via reductionism. Yet it is clear that orthodox evolutionism in biology is based in rationalism and that all others but holism have been tried over the years. Mineralogists use an interesting mixture of essentialism based on the reductive principle with polythetic rather than monothetic grouping. As Mason and Berry observed, "most minerals are not *fixed* in composition, but they do have a *characteristic* composition, one that can be expressed by a formula" (1968, p. 67; their emphasis).

Even though holism has not been used in other taxonomic sciences, should it be tried as the foundation of a theory of classification by organizational systematists? Holism in general, via systems theory, has been broadly infused into the literature about organizations and management, but has not been much help in empirical research and has recently come under negative critical review (Melcher 1975; Pinder and Moore 1979). A further problem is that scientific methods for the pattern model (Kaplan 1964, p. 332) or compositional strategy (Wallace 1971, p. 101), which support the holism principle, are not as well developed as methods for the deductive model (Kaplan) or causal strategy (Wallace), which accompany reductionism and rationalism. Finally, holism tends to break down into reductionism or rationalism under pressures for more precise or directional explanation. So, without ruling out holism as a possibility, there are no grounds at present for viewing it very favorably as a source of an alternative theory of classification perhaps especially suited for organizational systematics.

The question remains whether pure empiricist classifications that do not try to explain organizational diversity would provide a worthwhile set of hypothetical classes to guide deductive, empiricist inquiries. The answer is probably no. How can one develop a theory of classification that produces homogeneous groupings without having a theory about how the homogeneity was produced in the first place? It will be interesting to see if, in the future, someone does work out a theory of classification, alternative to one rooted in evolutionary theory, which results in homogeneous classes and explains the cause of their homogeneity as well. My position is that the rational principle is the only basis upon which to develop a theory of classification, and that consequently phyletic theory, which follows the rational principle, is the only sound basis of inducing a general organizational classification. This idea is developed further in the following section.

3.2 ORGANIZATIONAL CLASSIFICATION: PHYLETIC *AND* PHENETIC METHODS

Despite the disputes among biological systematists, there are solid scientific reasons for preferring an organizational classification theory based on a *combined* phyletic and numerical phenetic approach. In this respect some of the parochial tendencies in biology may be avoided.

3.2.1 The Trend in Biology

In his first edition Darwin said:

> Our classifications will come to be, as far as they can be so made, genealogies; and will then truly give what may be called the plan of creation. The rules for classifying will no doubt become simpler when we have a definite object in view. [1859, p. 486]

Shortly after publication he had a somewhat different view:

> [Charles Naudin's] simile of tree and classification is like mine (and others), but he cannot, I think, have reflected much on the subject, otherwise he would see that genealogy by itself does not give classification. [Passage in a letter to J. D. Hooker, 23 December 1859, published in Darwin 1888, 2:42]

Recently Hull concluded:

> Classification should be in some vague sense "phylogenetic," but biological classifications cannot be made to reflect very much about phylogeny without frustrating other functions of scientific classification. The most systematists can hope to do is to weigh a variety of conflicting goals and produce the best possible compromise. [1979, p. 437]

While biologists have tried out all of the various theories of classification over the past several hundred years, at present only numerical phenetic, evolutionist, and cladistic theories prevail, as indicated by recent issues of *Systematic Zoology*. There are strong proponents of each theory who favor theirs to the exclusion of the others. Mayr (1969, 1974), Bock (1973), and Ashlock (1979), strong evolutionists, have little positive to say about numerical taxonomy. Leading cladists such as Nelson (1972, 1974, 1979), Farris (1979a, b), and Wiley (1975) regularly denounce all but cladism. Those pursuing phenetic theory (Sneath and Sokal 1973; Gingerich 1979; McNeil 1979) frequently defend their approach against the others. But some biological systematists take more of a compromise view. Davis and Heywood (1963) clearly took a compromise position, pointing out how both theories could be used. Olson (1964) observed that neither evolutionist nor phenetic positions, taken to the extreme, offered much help in actual classification when there was no basis for deciding whether and how to weight some characters, and too many redundant characters to blithely accept the pheneticists' equal-weighting approach. He presented a compromise method as a solution. Later Heywood said, "What is evident is that the better our phenetic groupings are, the better our chances of evolutionary interpretation will be" (1967, p. 22). In a broad view of the three theories, Michener observed that "Most workers at present use phylogenetic classifications based on a subjective amalgam of phenetic and cladistic information, modified by judgment about matters such as appropriate taxon size and equivalence of ranking to that of similar taxa" (1970, p. 33). Olson (1971, p. 178) used "whatever will work," a pragmatic theme echoed by the numerical taxonomists Clifford and Stephenson (1975). Griffiths has pointedly said all three theories need to be improved. He concluded that "It is in my opinion a wrong concept to think of the different schools of taxonomy as competitors, for the reason that there is no one optimal classification to be preferred over all others for all purposes" (1973, p. 342). Jones and Luchsinger saw a role for numerical taxonomy as "useful in creating classification for exceptionally complex groups" (1979, p. 54). Finally, in the opening quotes to this section, Darwin and Hull, about 120 years apart, both called for a pulling back from the cladists' insistence on classification as a reflection of kinship structure. Hull argued for compromise in recognition that a classification must ever reflect goals rather widely subscribed to by most systematists, no matter what their persuasion. These common goals can be seen in the following statements:

> The purpose of a general formal classification . . . is to foster communication. . . . [Gingerich 1979, p. 451; a pheneticist]

> Evolutionary systematics has always had as its goal the preparation of maximally useful classification. . . . [Ashlock 1979, p. 44; an evolutionist]

Phenetics [has a] primary, perhaps single, purpose, which is to provide a convenient general-purpose framework for accommodating . . . diversity. [McNeill 1979, p. 465; a pheneticist]

The principal schools, pheneticists, phylogeneticists, and evolutionists, agree that a general reference system for biology is necessary. [Farris 1979*b*, p. 483; a cladist]

Scientific classification . . . [has] the central theme of comprehending order. [Bock 1973, p. 375; an evolutionist]

. . . classifications are systems of words which name and group organisms in such a way that one investigation can communicate a summary of knowledge to other investigators. [Wiley 1979, p. 309; a cladist]

The evolutionist school, itself a compromise between phenetics and cladism, is still the dominant school and biologists' classification of plants and animals is still based on it. It is still the *orthodox* approach. While recognizing its weaknesses, most biologists remain satisfied with it. Even those advocating a "chemotaxonomic" approach, where chemical molecules are substituted for anatomical characters (an approach lending itself favorably to numerical methods), still draw on phylogenetic theory in developing classifications (Smith 1976).

3.2.2 A Combined Phyletic-Phenetic Approach for Organizational Science

I have come to the conclusion that using both the evolutionist and numerical phenetic theories of classification will best serve organizational systematics. This statement is at best an opening gambit to get things rolling, and echoes a plea made some years ago by Kimberly (1975). Years of debate and research will come and go before we can offer a more definitive view; nevertheless, a beginning is needed. There is the question of which principles of enquiry will best serve us and a further interest in how to speed our quest by drawing on already existing knowledge in biological systematics.

For the most part I will let developments in the rest of the book slowly accumulate comprehensive support for an evolutionist-numerical phenetic approach. Wiley (1975, p. 233) listed three basic axioms of phyletic theory:

1. Evolution occurs.
2. Only one phylogeny of all living and extinct organisms exists, and this phylogeny is the result of genealogical descent.
3. Characters may be passed from one generation to the next generation, modified or unmodified, through genealogical descent.

These axioms are embedded in evolutionary theory, which has had equally long histories in biology and the social sciences. This is not the place for a full development of evolutionary theory in biology or the social sciences, and I will have to ask the reader to accept the foregoing as axioms of organizational evolution as well. Organizational forms do change slowly over time, and each change has taken place only once in some time sequence. The idea of organizational generations may strike readers as strange, but I will argue in chapter 8 that organizational evolution does take place across generations.

I am avoiding cladism. Most importantly, I am persuaded that it will produce too complex a classification. I also do not have space in this book to develop it properly. However, I do think it may offer another way of independently corroborating the results of evolutionist or numerical phenetic methods, and therefore warrants attention in the future.

Numerical phenetics seems well suited to organizational systematics. Although some clustering methods are less familiar, other multivariate methods such as factor analysis are well known. Organizations are large and complex enough to generate the large numbers of characters needed for successful multivariate analyses. While there are difficulties of application to be overcome, such as sector definition, sampling, character selection, and choice of method, these problems are characteristic of any use of numerical methods. The problem of whether populations identified by evolutionist methods will be phenotypically similar, allowing corroboration via numerical phenetic methods, is put off until after an organizational species concept is developed in chapter 7.

3.2.3 Arguments Supporting a Combined Phyletic-Phenetic Approach

It seems that none of the proponents of the phyletic or phenetic schools give sufficient recognition to the potential symbiotic relationship between the two theories. Each method is or can be of direct support to the other and together they could produce a much sounder classification than separately.

Mutual Benefit

The role of solid theory as a prerequisite to numerical taxonomy is not as well appreciated as it should be. Nowhere is this more true than among numerical pheneticists in biology. A review of the many numerical phenetic studies in biological systematics makes it patently clear that *all* of these studies used the existing classification of species, genera, and families—all developed by evolutionist methods—as a point of departure. Though one might exist, I have not found a biological taxonomic study of a seemingly random assortment of biota from a variety of species—the random assortment that would prevail if a preconceived classification scheme were *not* used as a point of departure. There does not seem to be a study, for example, that attempts to cover a broad range of flora and fauna—say, snakes, rabbits, birds, crocodiles, flies, beetles, fungi, bacteria, mollusks, sharks, snails, large cats, worms, various flowers and trees, grains, and so on. Almost all biological numerical taxonomic studies are within families, genera, or species. A very few studies of major groupings (combining vertebrates, insects, fungi, and bacteria, for example) have been conducted, but only for subtle comparisons of proteins or cytochrome *c*, and so on, as opposed to gross anatomical differences.

The work of Sneath and Sokal (1973) is another case in point. Numerical phenetics is seen as *agglomerative clustering* or "classification from below," whereas using evolutionary theory to divide kingdoms into phyla, phyla into classes, and so on, is termed "classification from above," or *divisive clustering*. Sneath and Sokal make it quite clear, but in a very few sentences, that evolutionist theory is necessary in the selection of sectors and characters. These few sentences are quoted below:

> Classification from above therefore carries the risk that the divisions do not give "natural" taxa, yet it is a necessary practice in order to isolate a group of organisms of a manageable size for study. [1973, p. 23]

> No sharp distinction is made between the selection of specimens . . . and the selection of characters . . . since these generally proceed *pari passu*. Inasmuch as a taxonomic group is selected by "classification from above," selection is therefore necessarily based on rather few characters. [1973, p. 68]

> Should numerical taxonomy rely on the validity of prior classification for its choice of OTUs (operational taxonomic units)? . . . Operationally we have to take on faith the validity of OTUs above the rank of individuals, to "lift ourselves by our bootstraps" into a position from which it is possible to carry out classification at the intended level. . . . The employment of species as OTUs in a phenetic classification is therefore appropriate. [1973, p. 70]

In short, these six sentences pointing to the unavoidable role of a priori theory in numerical taxonomy fight for the reader's attention among 453 pages of text arguing for numerical taxonomy and criticizing approaches to classification based on evolutionary theory. Furthermore the role of a priori evolutionary theory is obvious in Sneath and Sokal's discussion of inadmissible characters as well (1973, pp. 103–106). The role of a priori taxonomic theory in general and evolutionary theory in particular has similarly been unappreciated by those pursuing organizational numerical taxonomy, such as Haas et al. (1966), Pugh et al. (1968, 1969), Goronzy (1969), Pinto and Pinder (1972), and Warriner (1977, 1979). Since there is no discussion whatsoever by Sneath and Sokal about how one might go about "classification from above," or about how one might develop solid theory upon which such classification would be based, readers may be forgiven for mistakenly concluding that a priori theory is an unnecessary prerequisite to effective numerical taxonomy.

Numerical taxonomy is only slightly more visible in the discussions by Mayr (1969), Ross (1974), and Jones and Luchsinger (1979) or orthodox classification procedures. Mayr included only rudimentary statistical treatment with only passing references to multivariate methods in his chapter on qualitative and quantitative analysis of variation, despite the fact that all of the row distinctions in his "discrimination grid" are based on morphological distinctions suitable for numerical phenetic analysis (1969, p. 146). Ross (1974, p. 162), though saying that the construction of phylogenetic dendrograms cannot commence until "the species under study have been grouped into quasi-phylogenetic units" via methods including primarily numerical phenetic methods and identification of derived characters, devoted most of his book to the latter with virtually no discussion of numerical methods or even any encouragement to the reader to consult the several textbooks on the subject available at the time. When fossil evidence is unavailable, as Ross (1974, p. 148) noted, phylogenetic analysis rests primarily on analyses of living species. In working out the higher category ranks, where *all* possible group members are reproductively isolated, lack of fossil evidence means that even in orthodox procedure the groupings are based almost solely on phenetic analysis. In short, phenetic analysis is unavoidable even in orthodox classification, meaning that numerical phenetic methods are highly relevant and clearly beneficial.

In effect, the numerical taxonomists depend on the evolutionary classification as a point of departure, and the evolutionists use phenetic methods in working up their classification. Yet neither side has given appropriate recognition to the role the opposing method played in its own preferred approach. Orthodox and numerical phenetic methods are considerably improved by each other as complements.

The argument is equally valid for organizational classification. McKelvey (1975) pointed out that two major empirical studies, Haas et al. (1966) and Pugh et al. (1968, 1969), were unable to avoid a priori theory even though they attempted to do so. A better approach would be for numerical phenetic studies of organizational forms to start with sectors defined by a well-developed evolutionist classification.

Better Science

Combined, the evolutionist and numerical phenetic approaches produce a classification of higher scientific quality than results when they are used separately. Recall that besides careful observation and replication, good scientific method depends on the completion of the inductive-deductive cycle. It is possible to set up the cycle using inductive and deductive methods of identifying and corroborating organizational populations.

Phyletic classification is inductive in the sense that it starts from observations of naturally evolving phenomena and through processes that are at once subjective, insightful, creative, and based on guesses, possibilities, and so forth, develops a broad theoretical classification from the observation of particular objects and events in the past. Thus, it is subject to all the whims, biases, and errors apt to be made by any inductive theoretician—and so needs to be put to an objective, replicable test, just like any other scientific theory.

Numerical phenetic classification is deductive in the sense that it starts from already existing, hypothesized classes and through the use of sector definition, random sampling, and careful observation and measurement, and the objective use of mutivariate statistical methods, tests the truth of the hypothesized populations. It is a powerful method, but it works best when used with sound hypotheses as a point of departure. Both kinds of classification theory are strong in their own right, but neither satisfies the standards of high-quality knowledge by itself as well as they do when allowed to play their complementary inductive and deductive roles.

Besides fitting together in an inductive-deductive cycle, another reason for combining the two theories is that the strength of each offsets the principal weakness in the other. The main criticism of the orthodox phyletic method is its subjectivity. Numerical phenetic methods add an objective means of checking the subjectively derived populations. The main objection to numerical taxonomy is its inability to separate trivial from important taxonomic characters. By focusing on evolution, phyletic theory offers suggestions about which characters are likely to be more important in distinguishing objects that became differentiated as a result of environmental diversity and evolutionary adaptation to that diversity.

For whatever reason, most biologists have yet to see the two theories as complementary for good scientific purposes. They have yet to overcome a history of parochial blindness to the opposing theory's potential contribution. Organizational scientists need not repeat this history. The view I take in this book is that *both inductive and deductive methods of science are important and both are necessary to the development of a sound general classification*. This means that *both phyletic and numerical phenetic theories will be given equal emphasis* in this book and treated as equally important elements of organizational systematics. Furthermore, the treatment will not be "separate but equal"; instead each will be taken as an integral complement of the other, a truly *combined* approach.

3.2.4 Implications of the Combined Approach

The choice to accept both the evolutionist and numerical phenetic theories of classification has several implications for theoretical and methodological inquiry. The success of the theory depends on the successful solution of these additional problems. They are discussed briefly below, since they also become the subjects of later chapters.

Implications of the Evolutionist Approach

First, the acceptance of an evolutionist theory of organizational classification means an increased need to develop conceptual models and associated empirical studies of organizational environments, niches, and organizational ecology. There has been little further inquiry into the causal texture of organizational environments since Emery and Trist (1965) and Terreberry (1968). There is not much understanding of which specific features of an environment lead to certain specific characteristics of an organization. Most empirical investigators have focused on the effects of uncertainty on elements of organizational structure and functioning (Lawrence and Lorsch 1967; Kast and Rosenzweig 1973; Lorsch and Morse 1974), without exploring the specific effects of such items as change, heterogeneity, and threat, not to mention other possibilities, though Khandwalla (1977) takes steps in this direction. The population ecology approach taken by Hannan and Freeman (1977), Warriner (1978), and Aldrich (1979) seems to offer the best chances for fruitful theoretical and empirical development. These points are discussed further in chapters 4 and 5.

Second, assuming that the protosystem is indeed composed of different kinds of organizational forms, phyletic theory requires the development of a species concept that identifies the mechanisms that have isolated species of organizations from each other so as to maintain their population distinctiveness over a long period of time. Without theoretical support and empirical confirmation of such mechanisms, a classification other than a nominal one would not be possible because there would be no reason to expect to find delimitable, homogeneous populations characteristically different from one another. Organizations would appear as one large relatively homogeneous mass. Besides the isolating mechanisms, a species concept also has to explain how organizations exist in pretty much the same form over successive generations of employees. Finally, a species concept must also explain how new forms emerge from existing ones, presumably because of changes in the environment and pressures to adapt to the new environment. One of the problems that has plagued all typological and empirical efforts to classify organizations so far has been the lack of a species concept. Surprising as it may seem, its absence has not even been noticed or missed. These issues are discussed in chapters 6 and 7.

Third, accepting evolutionary theory also leads to a hierarchical classification. Historical inquiry into the origin of distinct organizational forms will become important. The historical inquiry results in a top-down, divisive clustering of organizational forms—the inductively derived groupings subsequently put to the test via numerical phenetic methods. Hierarchical classification and the higher categories are the subject of chapters 9 and 10.

Implications of the Numerical Phenetic Approach

First, acceptance of the numerical phenetic theory of classification means that multivariate methods will become the central tools of the trade. Up until now such tools have probably been misused as much as they have been well applied. While electronic computers have made the methods readily available, they have also made it possible for researchers with little understanding of their proper use to forge ahead even to the point of publishing mistaken results. Such potential misuse accentuates the need to include multivariate methods wherever serious training in organizational systematics is made available.

Second, numerical taxonomy puts special emphasis on the measurement of organizational characters, the definition of organizational sectors, and their sampling. The population of organizational taxonomic characters is as yet relatively undefined. For example, Haas et al. (1966), Pugh et al. (1968, 1969), and Goronzy (1969) used sets of characters which very nearly did not overlap at all. Their definitions of organizational sectors were so broad that their samples were not representative. These methodological problems will not be easy to solve. Organizations cannot be put in museums for later investigators to study. They cannot be caught and measured without their permission. On the other hand, building up samples of organizations may actually be less difficult and time-consuming than Adanson's long stay in Senegal 200 years ago or Darwin's trip around the world 100 years ago. These methodological issues are discussed in chapters 11 and 12.

3.3 SUMMARY

This chapter suggested a theory of organizational classification based on the use of the evolutionist and numerical phenetic theories in combination. It began with a discussion of five theories of classification which emerged in biology over the past 200 years, with the oldest—essentialism—dating back to the time of Aristotle. Essentialists searched for the true nature of the objects they were classifying, hoping to identify a few essential characters around which classes could be formed. At present, essentialism appears in the form of typologies of one sort or another, or special classifications. The nominalists looked only for a user-oriented classification, denying the existence of naturally formed groupings. The empiricists, and most importantly the numerical pheneticists, separate the problem of classification from the explanation of why the natural groupings formed. They use multivariate methods to work up their classificatory schemes. Finally, the evolutionists integrate the explanation of the origin of species with the need to classify. Their classification forms homogeneous groupings and also explains the origin of the groupings. Evolutionary classification is the orthodox approach in biology today. An alternative phyletic school, cladism, was discussed briefly and found to be less useful than either evolutionism or phenetics.

I argued that phyletic and numerical taxonomic theories work well in combination and actually result in better scientific practice. In light of this, organizational systematists are better off to not become narrowly identified with only one of the theories, as has been the tendency among biologists. The view taken in this book is that a combined evolutionist/ numerical phenetic approach is the best theory of classification for organizational systematists to adopt.

4 ORGANIZATIONS AND SYSTEMATICS

The discovery and classification of kinds is an *early* but INDISPENS-ABLE stage in the development of systematic knowledge; and all the sciences, including physics and chemistry, assume as well as continue to refine and modify distinctions with respect to kinds that have been initially recognized in common experience. Indeed, the development of comprehensive theoretical systems seems to be possible only AFTER a *preliminary* classification of kinds has been achieved, and the history of science repeatedly confirms the view that the noting and mutual ordering of various kinds—a stage of inquiry often called "natural history"—is a PREREQUISITE for the discovery of more commonly recognized types of laws and for the construction of far-reaching theories. . . . When a system of inclusion between kinds is achieved, it is possible to explain (even if only in a *crude* fashion) why some individual thing is a member of a specified kind by showing that the individual is a member of a subordinate kind (for example, the family pet is a mammal because it is a cat and cats are mammals). Such explanations are obviously *far removed* from the sort of explanations to which the modern theoretical sciences have accustomed us; nevertheless, they are *early* steps on the road which LEADS to the latter.

[Nagel 1961, p. 31, n.2; capitalization and emphasis added]

$\mathbb{S}$ ystematics is the foundation upon which all modern natural sciences are built. Modern physics began after Dalton's and Bohr's successful conceptualizations of the atom. Much of the glamor of present-day physics still is classificatory in nature, physics being a search for high energy particles. Modern developments in chemistry awaited Mende- leev and his periodic chart of the elements. The modern life sciences are rooted in the classes fathered by Linnaeus. In mineralogy explanation of the creation of minerals and rock formation awaited the classificatory work of Berzelius and Dana. Nagel is very clear in highlighting the indispensable and prerequisite place of systematics in the development of a science. Bohm (1961, p. 15) and Hempel (1965, p. 139), among others, also located classification early in the development of a science.

The question arises, why hasn't systematics been a more central ele- ment of organizational science? This question was also asked by Kimberly (1975). We claim to be a modern science in our emphasis on compositional and causal explanatory strategies (Mackenzie and House 1978).* Despite the record in other sciences and despite what the philos- ophers say, can we have a successful modern science without a widely accepted classification of its phenomena? Or is it that, despite all its pretentions and wishful thinking, organizational science is only just now reaching the primitive stage of scientific development where classi- ficatory activity comes to the fore? Perhaps the answer is that the phenomena under study by organizational scientists are sufficiently different that classification is not necessary. Maybe, despite the asser- tions of many managers that their industry is "different," the research of policy/strategy people such as Rumelt (1974), the findings of investi- gators such as the contingency theorists Kast and Rosenzweig (1973), and the theory and discoveries of organizational ecologists such as Aldrich (1979), Warriner (1978), and Hannan and Freeman (1977), organizations really are just about all the same, meaning that classifica- tion is not necessary.

A search for the reasons why systematics has lagged in organizational science is not an idle historic venture. The most frequent questions asked about systematics do not bear at all on its technical substance. Rather they stem from the frequent belief among students and professors inclined toward the social sciences that classificatory activity is some- thing better left to the natural scientists. Systematics is thrown into the same bag as "rigorous" or "objective" scientific methods as being worthy of much suspicion, or else is seen as old-fashioned or primitive. It makes little sense to dig into the depths of the subject if readers are still thinking the whole idea may be out of place in modern organizational science.

---

*Wallace (1971, p. 106) defined compositional strategies of explanation as: "Y is composed of such and such properties, entities, or processes," and causal strategies as: "Y is caused by such and such antecedents."

The purpose of this chapter is to explore why systematics has remained in the doldrums of organizational science and at the same time confront the more frequent arguments raised against taxonomy and classification. The avoidance of systematics seems based in three elements of the science: (1) the aspirations of the theorists themselves; (2) the assumptions underlying their theories or models; and (3) the assumptions underlying their scientific methods. I explore each of these in turn. The possibility that the theoretical models we use militate against systematics needs to be reviewed carefully. It would not make sense to pursue systematics if the models are correct both in their depiction of the function and process of organizations and in their negation of systematics. Since I do not end the book after a review of the models, you may anticipate that I conclude this chapter with an attempt to reconcile the conflicting assumptions of the several models of organizations and those of systematics. A model is presented which focuses both on environmental and internal (human) causes of organizational variations. Besides being long, this chapter is complicated in that I carry on two discussions in parallel: one is an examination of why systematics has been slow to materialize and the other is the development of a model of organizations compatible with systematics and evolutionary theory. The review of various models serves both discussions.

I assume the reader is generally familiar with the material coming under the headings of organizational sociology or organization theory. The discussions of the various models are brief; the chapter is an assembly of well-known arguments and positions, not an attempt to conduct a textbooklike literature survey, present background material, or describe organizations in depth in terms of the various models or theories. There are many textbooks presently available which do these things reasonably well. What is new and deserving of close attention are my definitions of organizations, niches, environments, and organizational form, and my syntheses of several models in the literature.

4.1 ASPIRATIONS OF THEORISTS

Past management and organization theorists appear to have pursued a role for themselves which worked to negate their inquiry into differences among organizations; they therefore found little need for classification. Students of the sociology (Merton 1968; Barber 1962; Storer 1966; West 1972) and psychology (Kuhn 1970; Churchman 1971; Mitroff 1974) of science are well aware that the development of a science may depend as much or more on scientists' ideologies, norms, accepted roles, scientific communities, social psychology, motivations, egos, and commitments or beliefs in theories as it does on their careful pursuit of observation, recording, analysis, and reporting of findings. Progress depends on scientists as subjects as well as phenomena as objects. While there is reason to suspect that organizational science has been affected by sociological and psychological factors, documentation of such effects in retrospect is difficult and apt to be speculative. However, a failure to attempt to pursue this avenue of inquiry implies that the avoidance of systematics was due entirely to assumptions implicit in the theoretical models of organizations. This inference may not be entirely true either. The two main groups of theorists involved in the development of theories about organizations were the classical management theorists on the one hand, and academically positioned social psychologists and sociologists on the other. These two groups are discussed in turn.

4.1.1 Searching for Universal Principles

Though classical top management thinking seems to have begun around the turn of the century (Massie 1965), Henri Fayol, a Frenchman, is usually given credit for the first serious book on the subject, in 1916. He stated fourteen principles and five elements of administration which he very carefully qualified as not to be taken as rigid or absolute laws. Nevertheless, according to Massie, once Mooney and Reiley published their book in 1931, before Fayol's book was translated into English, the degree of similarity among the principles enunciated by these independent authors in widely separated cultures and countries—France and the U.S.—led later classicists to feel there was strong support for the principles. The later writers soon dropped Fayol's qualifications and began treating the principles as universal, unchangeable truths. This tendency even carried over into much more recent writing, illustrated particularly well by the several earlier editions of Koontz and O'Donnell's best-selling book, *Principles of Management* (1976), the best exemplar of which was probably the 1959 edition.

Specific reasons why particular later classical management theorists dropped the qualifications Fayol so carefully stated are not known. As March and Simon (1958) noted over two decades ago, there is no assemblage of empirical findings of acceptable scientific quality in support of the principles. Several of the key contributors tended to draw mainly on personal experiences: Fayol from his work in French mining companies; Mooney from his job at General Motors (though he and Reiley also drew on historical descriptions of management applications in the Roman Catholic Church and the military); Urwick from his military experience; Koontz from his days working for Howard Hughes and Convair Corporation. Possibly, to make their statements worth listening to by others they had to generalize beyond their own narrow personal work experience. Writing from personal experience without benefit of scientific procedure, their only recourse may have been simple, very abstract principles.

The consulting and teaching orientation of the classicists also may have been a factor in the trend toward simply stated universal principles. Judging from what typically appears in lay-manager oriented publications at the present time, there is considerable pressure to boil ideas about organizations and management down to simple black-or-white statements and one- or two-dimensional models. The well-known popularity of McGregor's (1960) Theory X, Theory Y formulation; Herzberg's (1966) Two-Factor Theory of Motivation; Maslow's (1954) Hierarchy of Needs; Likert's (1967) System 1-System 4; Blake and Mouton's (1964) Managerial Grid; and the two-dimensional model of leadership (Fleishman, Harris, and Burtt 1955), all attest to this.* The unpopularity of Vroom's (1964) "expectancy theory" among managers and MBA students (and many professors as well) is an indication of the fate of more complex models. Presumably the pressures toward simplicity among today's so-called sophisticated managers and students are, if anything, considerably less than they were when the classical management theorists were in their heyday. Simple principles may have been all that managers would pay attention to.

As the field of management inquiry matured there developed a more normative interest in the "science" of management as opposed to the "art" of management. This meant pressure to emulate the natural sciences in the search for fundamental truths and laws. Remember that even though statements not supported by proper sampling and data collection and analysis methods may not appear very scientific today, broad statements supported by personal experiences, anecdotal evidence, and case histories accounted for much of what went under the label of "social science" during the first half of this century. Another normative view held by many classical management theorists was the genuine belief that, at least within the higher reaches of management, there *was* a set of managerial activities that were universally characteristic of good managers no matter what kind of organization they were in or even in what culture or country it was located. Koontz, among more recent writers, reflected this view (1964) and it wasn't until the sixth edition of Koontz and O'Donnell's textbook (1976) that they grudgingly gave way to the idea of contingency theory.

---

*Bob Tannenbaum once blew the dust off an old volume and showed me his complicated, unknown 1949-vintage theory of leadership which he still thought highly of, while lamenting the tremendous popularity (number 3 on the *Harvard Business Review* reprint list) of his two-dimensional model published with Warren Schmidt (1958).

The result of these pressures was that the earliest students of organizations, the classical management theorists, had neither the inclination nor the client demand to worry about different kinds of organizations and how management activity or social behavior might differ among them. If anything, they seemed to rush to cover up or ignore bothersome organizational differences that might get in the way of generalizable principles. Perhaps their experiences in the higher management levels of organizations shielded them from environmental, technological, and structural differences showing up at lower levels—though as a community they could not have been totally immune to this exposure, since other theorists such as Taylor and Gantt were engaged at the shop-floor level.

Of course, there is some truth to the idea that if one stays at a high enough level in a set of hierarchically ranked groups, some very abstract generalizations apply universally—for instance, all mammals have hair and suckle their young. If this logic was implicit in their thinking, why did one of these theorists not attempt to move the application of the classical management approach down the organizational hierarchy and at the same time lower the level of abstraction by narrowing the principles to a smaller set of more homogeneous organizations? But in the fifty years that classical management thought was in full swing, the lowering of generality did not happen. The legacy was clearly one that avoided the possibility of more than one kind of organizational form.

4.1.2 Searching for Academic Respectability

Ever since March and Simon's well-known book (1958) was published, there has been a tendency among academically trained and based students of organizations to look askance at the classical management theorists as being prone to making "empirically vacuous" statements, as March and Simon (1958, p. 30) put it. But academicians should not don the robes of scientific smugness too quickly.

Those studying organizations have been under considerable pressure over the past two decades to bring their methods of inquiry into the mainstream of academic or scientific methodology. Whether for the "right" reason (a conscious attempt to pursue the truth in the best, most conservative, most public way) or for the wrong reason (trying to look good and gain quick academic respectability and tenure in universities dominated by the more established disciplines), organizational scientists have tried to emulate the rigor and objectivity of the natural sciences. Either way, this has led to better sampling plans, more unbiased data collection methods, more refined analyses, and more cautious reporting and generalizing.

Emulating the natural sciences has also meant a search for fundamental laws in aid of explanation and prediction (Blau and Schoenherr 1971; Mackenzie and House 1978). Perrow noted that in "... the first half of the highly respected volume by James March and Herbert Simon, *Organizations*, 160 or so propositions are stated in the course of four chapters without any indication that these truths might apply to some types of organizations but not to others" (1970, p. 27). Many researchers have emphasized prediction over explanation; hence the current emphasis on causal modeling even though philosophers such as Kaplan (1964) have pointed out that in many circumstances explanation is independent of prediction. In an excellent discussion, Marion Blute (1979) observed that social scientists, in looking at the development of different cultures and societies, invariably searched for a universal law governing the dynamic behavior of the social units under study. Never did they follow the biological evolutionists' approach and view historical development as a process of descent with modification from common ancestors. The latest example of the search for laws of historical development is Meyer's (1979) study of the process of bureaucratization.

In addition to the strong attachment to the idea of discovering natural laws, which put causal strategy in a very positive light, a more pernicious reason why organizational scientists may have avoided the study of organizational differences* lies in the interpretation of the quote from Nagel given at the outset of this chapter. Nagel makes one point very clearly: namely, that classification comes *before* the development of comprehensive theoretical systems. Observe the words *indispensable, after, prerequisite,* and *leads.* A second, more evaluative implication can be read into the quote using the words *early, preliminary, crude,* and *far removed,* which is that classification is a less sophisticated, more *primitive* kind of scientific activity. Wallace (1971, pp. 104–106), in discussing three kinds of explanatory-predictive strategies—causal, compositional, and classificatory—makes the typical interpretation of Nagel, saying that "Nagel discusses the classificatory strategy as most useful in the *primitive* stages of a science. . . ." (emphasis added).† The evaluation of classificatory activity as primitive by Wallace apparently occurs because he zeros in on classification as a logic of inquiry in and of itself. Thus the behavior of an object is explained once it is located in a class of objects already understood. Since explana-

---

*The few comparative studies, such as those collected in Graham and Roberts (1972) and Heydebrand (1973), should be noted as exceptions.

†Even though *Webster's Collegiate Dictionary* (7th ed.) gives "before" or "near the beginning" as the first definition of *early,* Wallace for some reason picked the second definition, "primitive."

tion by classification did evolve before the causal strategy, and since the classificatory strategy is not as powerful as the causal strategy as a means of understanding, it is fair to label explanation via classification as primitive.

But a more enlightened way to view classification and, more broadly, systematics, is as a very important *prerequisite* to compositional and causal strategies. This is the view of systematics taken in chapters 1 and 2 and by philosophers such as Nagel (1961) and Hempel (1965). Systematics is not primarily, and probably not at all, a good strategy for seeking understanding. I am *not* interested in it as a possible explanatory strategy. It *is* a necessary foundation to the orderly conduct of a science, especially as an information retrieval system and most importantly as an aid to the basic inductive-deductive cycle of scientific inquiry. It may be that since systematics came a long time ago for the older natural sciences, the sophistication of the logic and method in systematics in retrospect seems inferior to the present sophistication of causal theorizing in those sciences. But remember, the basic theories of classification in physics, chemistry, biology, and mineralogy were developed toward the middle of the eighteenth century when *everything* about science was primitive.

It would be a mistake to believe that systematics is a primitive activity that died off in the natural sciences once the emphasis shifted to causal theorizing, a point Nagel also made in the opening quote. In fact the development of computers has led to an entirely new approach to classification in biology, and with it increased debate and vigor among systematists. The development of vastly larger particle accelerators has meant that the search for and classification of higher energy particles continues to be a central, exciting part of modern physics.

The insight here is that causal theorizing and systematics mutually influence and help each other. Causal theorizing depends on the study of clearly defined populations and representative samples, a result of classification. Classification, on the other hand, depends on causal and compositional theorizing and on new methods for clues in identifying taxonomic characters. The more sophisticated the theories and methods, the more taxonomic characters there will likely be. Neither the science of diversity nor the science of function can reach stability if the other is still developing. In light of the continuing role and presently sophisticated logic and methods of systematics in most sciences, it is clear that writers such as Wallace (and some referees of my own papers!) do the social sciences in general and organizational science in particular a great disservice in labeling systematics as primitive.

The search for causal laws on the one hand and the negative interpretation of Nagel's thoughts about classification on the other may have been sufficient to steer most organizational scientists away from the study of differences. But accompanying their aspirations for scientific legitimacy were the theoretical models they developed and believed in along the way. Common to all of these was the reductionist principle of enquiry, perhaps the most important influence of all in leading organizational scientists to avoid systematics.

4.2 CAUSES OF ORGANIZATIONAL VARIATION

The earliest scholars who developed models of organization were either interested in making organizations more effective (Gulick and Urwick 1937; Taylor 1911; Barnard 1938) or were trying to understand and explain why organizations behaved as they did (Weber 1947; Merton 1968; Gouldner 1954). Numerous models have since been proposed. Because organizations are so different in the kind of product or service they put out, it takes a fairly abstract model to explain what they do when they are taken as one vast population. It could be said that these models attempt to picture organizational *action*, but the term *action* has a "subject acting" connotation, and in fact has been taken over by those interested in nonpositivistic, subjectivist explanations (Silverman 1971). A more neutral term is simply VARIATION, meaning "to change or alter in form, appearance, function, or substance." There are several kinds of variation in organizations to explain:

Variation in the form of a population of organizations.

Variation in the form of a single organization.

Variation in GENOTYPIC attributes (those related to the population form).

Variation in activities as opposed to form (an organization could shift market territory and related marketing activities without changing form).

The population perspective focuses primarily on variations in the population form. But in explaining this, variations in the forms of member organizations are also discussed. Although there are possible distinctions between genotype and phenotype variations, I generally will pay little attention to these. I am not interested in variations in activities, that is, changes in what organizations do, unless they bear on variations in form.

An assumption here is that organizations are *not* like machines in at least one important respect. A machine functions over its useful life without change in function or form once it has been designed to do so (barring wear and maintenance, etc.). An organization has to change to survive, for two reasons. First, variation in organizational function, process, and form is required if it is to *adapt* its overall function or form so as to respond to environmental changes. But it is also true, second, that variation is required by one or more elements of an organization if it is to *maintain homeostasis* in overall function. Breakdowns in homeostasis are largely due to variations in activities by its members or employees. Because an organization caught between environmental variation on the one hand and personnel variation on the other is unstable or intentionally changeable, the emphasis of organizational models is on picturing those elements of an organization which vary or have to vary to maintain homeostasis or to produce change. Models, then, are abstract replicas of the mechanisms of organizational variation, and organizational science attempts to explain and/or predict causes and effects of organizational variation. A focus on variation is also the approach taken by Pfeffer and Salancik (1978, p. 9).

Schemes for classifying organizational models according to their similarities and differences are not well developed. Recently Katz and Kahn (1978) discussed thirteen models more or less in list fashion, without any attempt to use a scheme for classifying them. Lacking a comprehensive scheme they left some models out—for example those by Weick (1969), Silverman (1971), Child (1972), and Georgiou (1973) among others, all of which were available before their second edition went to press. In an earlier paper the sociologist Pugh (1966) suggested six groupings, but his criteria for grouping were not consistent. Management theorists, described as unscientific, were grouped together and separated from the structuralists, who, being sociologists, were of course more scientific! The technology theorists were put together because they emphasized a particular variable. The individual theorists were grouped because they all focused on an object, people and their predispositions, and so on. Very much earlier, Gouldner (1959) identified two groupings of theorists—those focusing on rational, effectiveness-oriented activities, and natural system theorists emphasizing nonrational, unanticipated, systemic activities, mainly in reaction to the rational theorists. Another common grouping of theorists is by closed and open systems views, which largely parallels Gouldner's breakdown.

I am going to use a simple typology based on three attributes of organizational models which often appear as implicit assumptions embedded in the reductionist and rational principles of enquiry. The attributes become criteria for assigning models to the typology. The first criterion, implicit in all of the foregoing groupings, pertains to the choice of principle of enquiry concerning causes or sources of organizational variation. The theories fall into two broad categories: (1) AUTO-GENIC THEORIES, meaning that variation is self-generated or caused by forces within an organization; and (2) ALLOGENIC THEORIES, meaning that it is other-generated or caused by forces outside an organization. The many models vary on the weight put on autogenic or allogenic sources. As will be seen in the following discussion, traditional and most present models are autogenic. It is important to identify where the various models place the source of organizational variations because most of the complaints against systematics come from scholars subscribing to autogenic theories (these are discussed in section 4.2.3). But those developing allogenic models, which are compatible with systematics since they focus on organizational differences, may be too quick to reject autogenic forces, leaving both allogenic models and systematics on an unsound theoretical footing. In light of these concerns, the following review of autogenic and allogenic models is intended to aid the development of a model which includes both autogenic and allogenic forces. Organizational science and systematics are thereby put on a sounder footing because such a model would meet both the norm of interconnectivity (combining into one logical system previously separate theories) and the norm of continuity (a new theory arises from or is connected to extant theories), both discussed by Schwab (1960).

A second criterion running through previous attempts at grouping concerns the *strength of the causal coupling* inherent in the various models. There is an amazing amount of difference in the models with regard to how directly they connect autogenic or allogenic forces to organizational variation. Couplings are seen as *strong, loosely coupled* (meaning there is coupling but there also is slippage, flexibility, delay, or nonlinear movement between two coupled variables), and *weak* (or nonexistent).

A third criterion only dimly implicit in most discussions of the models, and a crucial premise to scientists, pertains to the assumption about the *amount of order* to be explained. On the one hand, actions of organizational members may be presumed to have order that eventually can be understood and perhaps even predicted. The amount of order could be posited as *simple*, to be explained by a few variables, or *complex*, meaning that the action is ordered but that it may take many variables and considerable inquiry before understanding is available. These two points on my dimension subsume the dimension of *organized simplicity, organized complexity*, and *chaotic complexity* suggested some years ago by Rapoport and Horvath (1959). I extend the dimension to include *random chaos*. At the other extreme there is presumably the end point, null or nothing to explain. Thus the behavior of people in organizations could be seen as randomly chaotic and probably quite beyond reasonable attempts to achieve understanding. On the other hand, environments could also be seen as having varying amounts of order, ranging from simple to complex sets of variables to a chaotic assemblage of forces beyond reasonable attempts at modeling and theorizing. The assumption of order dictates where most of the descriptive effort of a model goes and where the explanatory power of a theory claims to be. Most authors do not come right out and say that they are avoiding modeling people or environmental forces because they think they are chaotic, but it seems that in effect this is what happens in most discussions.

Ideally, based on these criteria and the fact that for both autogenic and allogenic causes, strong couplings and complex order are recognized by at least one model, a comprehensive, synthesized model would appear as follows unless significant portions of the literature are to be disregarded:

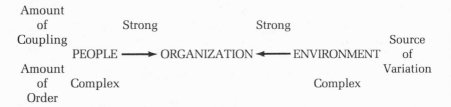

It will be seen that no present model takes this form.

Some readers will want to object to this model since its shows the arrows pointing only toward the organization. "What happened to structural influences on behavior or organizational influences on the environment?" you ask. My inquiry and the models I discuss focus on describing, in advance of theoretical explanations, only why organizations are the way they are. I am not studying people in organizations nor am I trying to explain why environments are the way they are. I will agree that my arrows may subsume a cycle of events such as:

Employees affect organizations affect employees affect organizations, and so on.

Environments affect organizations affect environments affect organizations, and so on.

It may also be true that inanimate things such as physical structures inside an organization may affect its functioning. But since these are ultimately the choice of some human decision maker I will go with the idea that autogenic sources of organizational variations are ultimately people. People acting by themselves or through organizations in an organization's environment are also a large portion of allogenic sources, but here there are also resource constraints and physical constraints or "acts of God" which cannot be attributed to people, so I will use the term *environment*. Historically environments always exist before organizations or populations of organizations; thus in the long run environments affect organizations, not the reverse. Later, in section 4.3.2, I will use a construction in which organizations do affect niches.

4.2.1 Autogenic Models

While there are occasional tendencies to reify or anthropomorphize organizations, the better-known organizational model builders manage to avoid this. The autogenic model builders have never wavered from their intent, sometimes not too conscious, to keep human actors in central position as the only true source of organizational variation. Over the years, this intent has taken many forms, some radically opposed to each other, but always the human actor has been at the nexus. The historical development of the autogenic models falls into three phases, which serve as a convenient scheme for ordering the discussion. No doubt with additional criteria and closer reading, these three stages could be further subdivided, but that is not attempted here. I do not think it is necessary given the intent of this chapter.

The Rational Model

With his usual remarkable insight, Gouldner (1959) showed that thinking up until 1959 could be split into two camps: those holding to what he termed the *rational* model and those developing the *natural system* model of organizations. Gouldner traced the roots of the rational model back to Weber (1947) and his concept of bureaucracy. Under this model an organization is seen as an *instrument* that consists of a set of people organized for the express purpose of pursuing announced goals. An organization's structure is a tool designed to facilitate goal achievement, and organizational behavior is viewed as

> consciously and rationally administered, and changes in organizational patterns are viewed as planned devices to improve the level of efficiency. The rational model assumes that decisions are made on the basis of a rational survey of the situation, utilizing certified knowledge, with a delib-

erate orientation to an expressly codified legal apparatus. The focus is, therefore, on legally prescribed structures—i.e., the formally "blueprinted" patterns. . . . Fundamentally, the rational model implies a "mechanical" model, in that it views the organization as a structure of manipulable parts, each of which is separately modifiable with a view to enhancing the efficiency of the whole. [Gouldner 1959, pp. 404−405]

Georgiou (1973) observed that under the rational model attention was almost exclusively focused on learning the extent to which organizations were effective in attaining their goals and how they could be made more effective. Burns and Stalker (1961) labeled this approach the *mechanistic model* and Katz and Kahn (1978) followed Worthy (1950) in calling it *machine theory*.

The central concern for organizational effectiveness and the goal of managers to make organizations more effective was at the core of the classical management theories of Fayol, Mooney and Reiley, and Urwick, among others, and more recently of Koontz and O'Donnell and kindred neoclassical management theorists. With the emphasis on the manager came attention to rational decision making and cognitive processes, exemplified by the work of Simon (1947), March and Simon (1958), Cyert and March (1963), and Newell and Simon (1972). Another spinoff was in the strategy and policy area, given a substantial boost by Chandler's (1962) study of how the managers of successful organizations adapted their strategy and organizational structure to changing environments. One final burst of glory for the rational model was embodied in Thompson's work, culminating in his widely cited book *Organizations In Action* (1967). Thompson worked out a set of propositions suggesting how managers under conditions of rationality would respond to conditions of environmental uncertainty via a dominant coalition, a puzzle up until then.

Most traditional definitions of organizations are rooted in the rational model because they invariably draw on the goal concept as a central element of organizations, as clearly noted by Georgiou (1973). In order to be effective, organizations must have goals appropriate for the environment they are in and must pursue them efficiently. Goals are what result from the rational deliberations of managers. Building on definitions by Weber (1947), Barnard (1938), Blau and Scott (1961), Etzioni (1964), and Scott (1964), one of the best definitions from this tradition is that given by Hall:

An organization is a collectivity with a relatively identifiable boundary, a normative order, ranks of authority, communications systems, and membership-coordinating systems; this collectivity exists on a relatively continuous basis in an environment and engages in activities that are usually related to a goal or a set of goals. [1977, pp. 22—23]

In terms of my classification criteria, the rational model takes the following form:

Coupling: Strong   Weak

Source: PEOPLE   ⟶   ORGANIZATION ◄– – – – ENVIRONMENT

Order: Simple   Simple

The prime source of variation is in the conscious, rational designs of those having the formal responsibility for designing an organization. The coupling between human behavior and organizational form is strong—organizational behavior is seen to follow without complication from the actions of managers. The elements and resultant behavior of both human actors and the environment are seen as fairly simply ordered. There is substance there to be explained, but it does not appear to be so complex that a modest set of simple propositions cannot handle it. For some rational model builders, the environment approaches being a nonentity. For others, the environment may be understood and dealt with by fairly straightforward strategies and policies that managers can work out.

The Natural System Model

Historically, the first alternative to the rational model was what Gouldner (1959) termed the *natural system* model. According to him, holders of this view consider an organization as a "natural whole" or system. The emphasis is on inherent forces toward survival, which give rise to several organizational needs, goal attainment being only one of them. In this model organizations strive to maintain homeostasis. Once the goals of rational managers or planners are created they become ends in themselves, creating additional needs and eventually additional ends that may often displace the goals originally set up by the designers. Component structures, though perhaps initially designed, take on a life of their own and develop new characteristics as a result of ends and needs felt important by their constituent members. Organizational change is seen as a cumulative, unplanned result of adaptive responses of the system as a whole. As Gouldner put it, "The focus is not on deviations from rationality but, rather, on disruptions of organizational equilibrium, and particularly on the mechanisms by which equilibrium is homeostatically maintained" (1959, p. 406). The underlying analogy is an organismic one rather than a mechanical one. Planned changes are seen as having rather considerable unintended consequences, often—if not usually—of greater import than the planned changes. "Long-range organizational development is thus regarded as an evolution, conforming to 'natural laws' rather than to the planner's designs" (Gouldner 1959, p. 406).

According to Gouldner the natural system perspective dates back to Auguste Comte and his forebears. Following Comte were Michels, Selznick, Parsons, Merton, Gouldner himself, Dalton, Blau, and Etzioni, all sociologists. Paralleling developments in sociology was a reaction against the views of Taylorism and classical management by students of organization and management in business schools, such as Mayo, Rothlisberger, Likert, Argyris, and Bennis. Still committed normatively to the idea of planned design and change, these scholars nevertheless developed their approaches with explicit attention to natural system forces and the effects of informal groups and informal patterns of organization. It should be said that in both groups there were many contributors other than those few mentioned here.

During the decade between the mid-1950s and the mid-1960s the natural system perspective was fused with ideas from Von Bertalanffy's general systems theory, some major contributors being Katz and Kahn (1978), Buckley (1967), and Miller (1978). A definition of organizations rooted in the natural system perspective was given by Katz and Kahn:

> Organizations as a special class of open systems have properties of their own [not specified but presumably including uniquely different elements such as job descriptions, plant layouts, products, people], but they share other properties in common with all open systems. These include the importation of energy from the environment, the throughput or transformation of the imported energy into some product form that is characteristic of the system, the exporting of that product into the environment, and the reenergizing of the system from sources in the environment.
>
> Open systems also share the characteristics of negative entropy, feedback, homeostasis, differentiation, coordination, and equifinality. [1978, p. 33]

Katz and Kahn specifically took issue with the goal concept as being teleological and therefore out of place in a theoretical definition. "The theoretical concepts should begin with the input, output, and functioning of the organization as a system and not with the rational purposes of its leaders" (1978, p. 20). Despite this, natural systems theorists do hold that organizations have goals and are goal-seeking systems. Georgiou (1973) argued that they are just as wedded to the goal paradigm as the developers of the rational model. But they see goals emerging over time out of the needs of subsystems and human components, as opposed to emerging from the rational designs of formally appointed planners.

Taken as a group, the natural system theorists have held to a model of the following form, although there are undoubtedly small differences among the various contributors.

Coupling:	Strong		Loose
Source:	PEOPLE ⟶	ORGANIZATION ⟵	ENVIRONMENT
Order:	Complex		Chaotic

Though natural system theorists recognize, via the "open systems" phrase, that organizations adapt to forces in the environment, the coupling is seen as loose. Environments are there to be coped with but they are not a force that directly causes organizations to take on a certain form. The root cause of action and variation is still in the behaviors of people in the organization. Natural system theorists recognize that the way in which the needs of people and the needs of subcomponents and the organization itself translate into goals, purpose, and activity are very complex. Taking Katz and Kahn (1978) as the exemplar, it is clear that the quest is to explain how the many individual and group subcomponents interact to produce organizational behavior. The assumption is that there is internal order that can be explained. Despite the open systems phrase, natural systems theorists never got hold of the environment in any substantial way. It seemed to appear as an uncertain chaotic force that had to be coped with, but how it worked or what its characteristics were, or what the specific ties between an organization and its environment were, was never spelled out.

The Market Process Model

The natural system model appears as a more complex view of organizations than the rational model, but not too different in substance, since it still holds to the goal paradigm and, as shown here, the explanation of variation still is placed squarely on the shoulders of people in organizations. In retrospect the natural system model is a significant departure from the rational model but not as radical an alternative to the rational model as its proponents think. Though containing some elements of the natural system model, the *market process* model *is* a radical departure from the rational model, though it still is autogenic.

In the market process model organizations are seen as places where people *exchange* a variety of things, thereby satisfying their own desires and in the process creating cognitive maps, perceptions of externalities, social relations, norms, values, social and organizational structure, and ultimately collective organizational goals and behavior. In the various forms of the model diverse things are exchanged, ranging from inducements, contributions, influence, views of reality, definitions of the situation, and so forth. An alternative term commonly used as a label for this model is *social construction*, since what results is constructed out of the collective social interactions of many individuals.

In the organization theory literature, the market process model appears in widely different forms, out of seemingly different traditions, and yet it is my view that underlying all of this are some common themes and roots. Though not the first to take this view of organizations, the person most clearly advocating a look at the marketplace of exchange in organizations was Georgiou: "The organization is seen not as an incentive-distributing device, abstracted from the relationships of its members, but as a marketplace in which incentives are exchanged" (1973, p. 306). In making this statement Georgiou was building on Barnard's (1938) view of organizations as incentive-distribution devices, but at the same time he was rejecting the idea that it is the organization, perhaps as some anthropomorphized being, that hands down incentives. All that is needed is the concept of a marketplace. The key idea behind the marketplace concept is that organizational substance and structure arise out of the collective interaction of people attempting to unilaterally satisfy their own individual desires.

A somewhat earlier and seemingly different view of this process was Weick's (1969) notion of "interlocked behaviors." Building on Allport's (1962) concept of collective structure, Weick viewed organizations as the result of a continuous process of organizing: "Organizing consists of the resolving of equivocality in an enacted environment by means of interlocked behaviors embedded in conditionally related processes" (1969, p. 91). The basic element is the cycled interaction between two people, not one person's behavior. In passing, Weick also noted the social exchange theories of Homans (1958, 1961) and Thibaut and Kelley (1959), among others, which specify that the behavior of one person is contingent on that of another. Drawing on Schutz's (1967) view of people as constantly exposed to an ambiguous, uncertain, ongoing stream of events, Weick argued that the main reason people interlocked their behaviors was to reduce uncertainty and thereby produce order and regularity. Through interlocking they reduce equivocality (uncertainty), especially with regard to uncertain environments, which are enacted into a form more manageable via social construction and selective perception. For historical development I have referred to Weick's 1969 book even though a revised edition (1979) has recently been published. His reliance on collective structure is still intact, though organizing and reduction of equivocality are embedded in a much more extensive reliance on the natural selection principles of enactment (variation) and selection, and consequently the discussion of these is substantially revised.

Writing almost at the same time but independently of Weick, Silverman (1971, U.S. edition) developed what he termed an "action frame of reference" rooted in prior work by Schutz (1964), Berger and Luckmann (1966), and Goffman (1959), among others. It was very much a "subjectivist" view of organizational behavior. Some key propositions in this view are:

> Sociology is concerned with understanding action rather than with observing behavior. Action arises out of meanings which define social reality.
>
> Meanings are given to men by their society. Shared orientations become institutionalized and are experienced by later generations as social facts.
>
> While society defines man, man in turn defines society. Particular constellations of meaning are only sustained by continual reaffirmation in everyday actions.
>
> Through their interaction men also modify, change, and transform social meanings.
>
> It follows that explanations of human actions must take account of the meanings which those concerned assign to their acts; the manner in which the everyday world is socially constructed yet perceived as real and routine becomes a crucial concern of sociological analysis.
>
> Positivistic explanations, which assert that action is determined by external and constraining social or nonsocial forces, are inadmissible.
> [Silverman 1971, pp. 126−127]

According to Silverman, action arises out of past experiences and perceptions of the probable reaction of others to an actor's behavior. While roles and structure may provide a framework for action, they do not determine it. Explanations of organizational behavior "are in terms of ideal-typical actors whom we take to be pursuing certain ends by choosing appropriate means on the basis of a subjective definition of the situation" (1971, p. 139). Though Silverman was not too clear on just how the subjective meanings of a group of organizational members collectively gave rise to organizational structure, form, and behavior, the marketplace concept seems implicit in the following statement:

> What actually occurs in such a situation will, therefore, be the outcome of the relative capacity of different actors to impose their definition of the situation upon others, rather than of a mechanistic relationship between an organisation's needs and the problems with which the system is faced.
> [1971, p. 165]

The relative power of the participants of a marketplace is central to the operation of the transaction or exchange. As Georgiou said,

> The possession of power is a function of the capacity of an individual to contribute incentives to one or many, or even all of the other contributors to the organization. Both the exchange of incentives and the possession of power are evident throughout the organization, every individual having some power because he contributes to the satisfaction of someone else's wants. [1973, p. 306]

Another view of the market process or social construction model was given by Benson (1977). He developed a "dialectical view," drawing on the ideas of Marx. This view, Benson said, is

> fundamentally committed to the concept of process. The social world is in a continuous state of becoming—social arrangements which seem fixed and permanent are temporary, arbitrary patterns and any observed social pattern are regarded as one among many possibilities. . . . Through their interactions with each other social patterns are gradually built and eventually a set of institutional arrangements is established. Social arrangements are created from the basically concrete, mundane tasks confronting people in their everyday life. Relationships are formed, roles are constructed, institutions are built from the encounters and confrontations of people in their daily round of life. [1977, p. 3]

Once produced, organizational structure, of course, acts as a constraint within which future social constructions take place.

There are some differences in the forebears of the views of Georgiou, Weick, Silverman, and Benson. Silverman was most strongly connected to earlier phenomenological work by Berger and Luckmann (1966), Schutz (1964, 1967), and others before them. Weick traced his development back to Schutz, but also to the psychologist Allport (1962), and to a lesser extent to social exchange theorists such as Homans (1958). Benson gave credit to Marx, recent Marxian sociologists, and the phenomenologists Berger and Luckmann. Georgiou seemed to place his foundations on the work of Barnard (1938) and Clark and Wilson (1961), though not without considerable criticism of them and everyone else.

At first reading the substantive differences among the four authors seem even more pronounced. Georgiou emphasized the market process. Benson stressed the Marxist concepts of social construction/production, totality, contradiction, and praxis, all part of the dialectical process. Weick focused on collective structure, evolutionary theory derived from Campbell (1969), and enacted environments and interlocking behavior as key elements of the organizing process. Silverman focused on subjectivity, intentionality, and action process as opposed to behavior.

Yet beneath all of these differences, all looked to the interaction, interdependence, definition of meanings, and influence of one actor over another as the root causes of social and organizational structure. The notion of process was common to all. Though they did not all use the concept as clearly as Georgiou, they uniformly saw organizations as entities whose structure and behavior were the outcome of an exchange of: incentives, inducements, and contributions (Georgiou); meanings and expectations (Silverman); power interests (Benson); or definitions of the situation and rewards (Weick)—in short, a marketplace or market process. The proponents of this model typically define organizations as settings where members interact via a market or social construction process.

The market model takes the following form:

Coupling:	Strong	Weak
Source:	PEOPLE ⟶ ORGANIZATION ◄ – – – – ENVIRONMENT	
Order:	Complex	Chaotic

The market process advocates make very little mention of environments as causes. Silverman saw environments as constraints but quickly went on to say that organizational structure resulted from the intentionalities of human actors. Weick spoke of "enacted environments" which do not *cause* anything but instead result from the interpretation of meanings by human actors. This is reinforced in his revised edition. Environments are likewise similarly disposed of by Georgiou and Benson. Expectedly, there is little order in environments to be explained and consequently no explanations of environmental causes of variation were offered. The strong coupling is on the relation between human behavior and organizational structure, function, and process. Human actors are definitely seen as complex and, like the weather perhaps, their collective behavior can be understood but not predicted because of the complexity of the market process.

There is one variant of the market model that is potentially important in the organization theory literature at present, but which differs somewhat from the main model. It is the resource-dependence model proposed by Pfeffer and Salancik (1978). Their book is somewhat misleading in that it claims to be an allogenic model focusing on the external control of organizations, while the bulk of the words and indeed the discussion of sources of variation are clearly autogenic. The reader is easily misled because in addition to titling their book *The External Control of Organizations*, the authors start out wondering why so much attention has been placed on autogenic models (pp. 6–19). They suggest that the role of managers was mainly symbolic so they could be fired, like baseball managers, but partly it was to operate on the environment—clearly an autogenic notion. They also argue that the basic concepts of a contextual view are effectiveness, environment, and constraints, all of which also figure in some of the autogenic models. The case of confusion is mild because in reality very little of the book is about allogenic causes of variation—most of it being about how managers can operate on their environment.

The true autogenic basis of the Pfeffer and Salancik book and a clear indication that it is a variant of the market model comes in a subtitle of chapter 2 (p. 24), "Interest Groups and Coalitions: Organizations as Markets for Influence and Control" (their capitals not included). Pfeffer and Salancik build on March and Simon's (1958) inducements-contributions theory and the collective structure notion of Allport (1962) and Weick (1969). In their words, "We have described organizations as settings in which groups and individuals with varying interests and preferences come together and engage in exchanges—in March and Simon's (1958) terminology, exchanging contributions for inducements" (1978, p. 26). A few pages later they say: "Organizations, then, are quasi-markets, in which influence and control are negotiated and allocated according to which organizational participants are most critical to the organization's continued survival and success" (1978, p. 36).

Surprisingly, Pfeffer and Salancik seemed unfamiliar with Georgiou's (1973) publication in which he draws on Barnard (1938), the forebear of March and Simon's inducements-contributions theory, and where he said exactly the same thing, namely, that organizations are settings where people negotiate power interests in a marketplace (see the earlier quotes from Georgiou 1973, p. 306).

Once the mixed messages are cleared away the Pfeffer and Salancik model looks just like the natural systems model, in terms of my criteria, though the substance of the models is different because it substitutes the market process for the goal paradigm underlying the natural system model:

Coupling:	Strong	Loose
Source:	PEOPLE ⟶ ORGANIZATION ⟵ ENVIRONMENT	
Order:	Complex	Complex

As can be seen, their model differs from the main market model in that environments are seen as complexly ordered and subject to eventual explanation. They are not seen as chaotic and largely ignored as in the main model. The Pfeffer and Salancik model differs from the ideal model in that the environment-organization coupling is seen as loose rather than strong. If they truly had an allogenic model the forces of the environment would undoubtedly have been seen as having a much stronger, more direct influence on organizational variation.

4.2.2 A Synthesized Autogenic Model

Remembering that there were two purposes to this chapter—to explain why systematics was so slow in developing in organizational science and to work toward a model of organizations compatible with systematics in general and evolutionary theory in particular—the foregoing discussion of kinds of autogenic models is logically followed immediately by a discussion relevant to both purposes. But, given the serial nature of writing, discussing both is impossible even though no good argument for placing one ahead of the other exists, given the priorities of the chapter. Arbitrarily then, the discussion of autogenic models will be brought to a conclusion with an attempted synthesis before continuing with the discussion about why systematics has lagged.

Ackoff (1971) suggested four kinds of systems: deterministic, goal-seeking, purposive, and purposeful. Since the usual analogs of the rational and natural system models are, respectively, mechanical and organic, it is tempting to draw on Ackoff's distinction among systems as a basis for working toward a synthesis. Since the kinds of systems are in fact ordered according to the control they have over choice of means and ends—ranging from deterministic systems that have no choice to purposeful systems that have total choice and exercise of will—one could try to order the autogenic models according to the kinds of systems they seem to fit. But the logic of such an attempt is flawed. It is clear that Ackoff's scheme does not allow a place for the market process model, since advocates of this model clearly say it is not deterministic or mechanical, not goal-seeking or organic, and does not posit that organizations as entities are purposeful over and above their members. Furthermore, even though the rational model may attempt to see organizations run as neatly as machines, it does not see the manager/designers of such organizations as without choice. All kinds of autogenic models see organizations as purposeful, though the source of choice is different—managers in the rational model, subsystems in the natural systems model, all members at large in the market process model. In short, the kinds-of-systems scheme and its implicit analogies create more confusion than clarity.

In fact there are really only two clearly stated autogenic forms, viewed in retrospect: the rational model and the market process model. The natural system model is an amorphous composite of elements of both. It has some historical relevance, but now the possibility that it might continue, and in fact does so in books such as the recent one by Katz and Kahn (1978), lies mainly in its obscurity. As Georgiou (1973) pointed out so well, the natural system model is just as wedded to the goal paradigm as the rational model, only less clear about it. And, finally, the exposition of the market process model has cleared up what was always vague in the natural system model, which was "how did all of those individual and subsystem needs get collectively worked out to the point where an observer could say an organization was a goal-seeking system?" As Silverman noted (1971, p. 31), systems theorists were always much more interested in explaining effects of system forces than causes. They never did explain exactly *how* the part determined the whole. The market process model does exactly that.

Organizations *as entities* are purposeful vicariously, through employees or members, via two very different processes: a rational-design process and a market process. The following columns of adjectives indicate the many ways these two basic processes have been referred to in the literature. Since the terms *rational* and *market* are caught up in past discussions of models often seen as antithetical if not radically conflicting views of organizations, and since irrational behavior may emanate from so-called rational managers, different terms will be used here to label the two sources:

AUTHORIZED-PREPENSIVE (Alpha)	SYSTEMIC-SPONTANEOUS (Sigma)
planned	unplanned
rational	natural system
formal	informal
top-down	bottom-up
hierarchical	nonhierarchical
managerial	nonmanagerial
strategy-driven	need-driven
anticipated	unanticipated
official	unofficial
designed	emergent
bureaucratic	organic
conscious	process
	exchange
	market

There are undoubtedly other adjectives not listed. The definitions of the binomial labels are given below (meanings drawn from *Webster's Third New International Dictionary*):

Authorized: established by authority, officially sanctioned.

Prepensive: deliberated or planned beforehand, premeditated, consciously reasoned.

Systemic: pertaining to a regularly interacting group of elements forming a unified whole.

Spontaneous: natural, without prompting, voluntary, self-acting, arising from a momentary impulse.

The position taken here is *both* Alpha and Sigma sources of vicarious organizational purposefulness are equally relevant and should be recognized as more or less equally important in explaining what happens in organizations. No doubt Alpha sources are most important in some organizations at various times. In a particular organization it may happen that variation largely results from the two sets of forces acting cyclically in opposition to each other. But in other organizations it may turn out that the two sources work in harmony.

A definition of organizations which is compatible with the foregoing autogenic view is as follows: "Organizations are purposeful systems containing one or more conditionally autonomous purposeful subsystems." This definition closely follows that of Ackoff (1971) and was first published in McKelvey and Kilmann (1975, p. 25). There are several advantages to this definition besides its simplicity and brevity:

1. Organizations are seen as having choice as well as allowing for choice among subsystems, which may be divisions, departments, groups, or individuals.

2. Implicit in the term *purposefulness* is the idea that organizational choice is rooted in two sources of variation, Alpha and Sigma. Purposefulness may appear at various levels in different groupings of individuals, formal or informal units.

3. Subsystems are seen as conditionally autonomous, after Thompson (1967, p. 58), meaning they also have choice but that it is conditioned or constrained by purposefulness emerging at a higher level or for the organization as a whole.

4. This definition sets organizations apart from any other entity. Social entities such as societies are not included because they are not purposeful as entities even though they have many purposeful subunits. Other entities such as organisms and people may be purposeful as entities but they do not have purposeful subsystems. It would be too bad if our hearts, lungs, and livers decided to set up shop as parts of our

nervous systems. Small groups act as small organizations once they become capable of exercising choice as a group entity. Families are included as organizations if they meet the conditions of the definition. Many families are highly organized. Many others approach anarchy and therefore are not considered organizations.

5. The fact that subsystems are an essential component means that organizations are only those entities that have some kind of hierarchical relation among their components, including different levels or ranks. The notion of conditional autonomy implies many other elements, listed for example in the Hall (1977) definition, such as normative order, ranks of authority, communications systems, and membership-coordination systems. Purposefulness may result in official or unofficial goals. The concepts of system and subsystem imply the additional concepts of boundary and environment. In short, all of the elements of his lengthy definition are elements of the one given here. The present definition, since it is short, has the disadvantage of not being as explicit about what is meant as those by Hall (1977) or Katz and Kahn (1978).

4.2.3 Systematics Slowed by Autogenic Models

There are two reasons why the adherence to autogenic models led to an avoidance of systematics, one stemming from the principle of enquiry and one from beliefs about methodology. First, the autogenic models clearly fit the reductionist principle of enquiry. All explanation is gained by looking to levels of analysis lower than that of the organizational whole; specifically, explanation is reduced to the level of individual human beings or sometimes molecular reduction to one level above people—specifically, aspects of institutionalization and social structure, which are social constructions. This is especially true of the rational and market process models. It could be argued that the natural system model draws on the holistic principle of enquiry, which is true as far as it goes. But I have already noted that the natural system model focuses more on effects of systems rather than on sources of variations, about which it is vague.

Reductionism need not necessarily work at odds with systematics, at least as far as classification is concerned, though it probably does create difficulties for the use of an evolutionist theory of classification. One could use an empiricist theory to classify, and simply ignore any explanation of the origins or causes of different kinds of organizations, for example. But autogenic models are not just neutral regarding the explanation of differences—they militate against it. Since in all models the coupling between organizations and environments is left in a weak or loose form, no external forces strong enough to push organizational forms toward differentiation are admitted. Without contextual forces there is nothing in the models to prevent either the rational designers or the marketplace from working toward unique solutions in every organization. Of course, exogenous forces loom in the background as constraints—members responding to economic, technological, or political aspects of the environment, and so forth; members of the same culture or educational background; members attending the same professional meetings; effects of societal norms, laws, or governmental regulations. But these forces are always posited to operate on organizational form through the purposes of employees or members. From the strict viewpoint of the models and their proponents, the reductionist principle of enquiry inevitably leads to two extreme positions: organizations are all unique or organizations are all the same. Those advocating the market process model are more inclined to see organizations as unique. Those holding to the rational model, seeing managers as often having the same goals, tend to focus on the similarities.

Another factor pushing believers in the autogenic models toward an emphasis on organizational similarities is that the reduction of levels of explanation to individuals (or to the slightly higher level of social structures arising from individual social exchanges), coupled with the assumption that individuals are by and large randomly distributed among organizations, leads to an emphasis on similarities. Thus people, no matter what kind of organization they are in, tend to have similar responses to rules, authority, rewards and sanctions, conflict, and so on. Therefore, the organizational behavior of people tends to be the same across organizations and, hence, a scientist should expect to be able to generalize across a wide variety of organizations.

The second reason for the slowdown lies in beliefs many proponents of autogenic models have about methodology. Here the arguments against systematics are the same as those against rigorous research methods, logical positivism, or objectivist philosophies in general. They are nicely summarized by Behling:

1. *Uniqueness.* Each organization, group, and person differs to some degree from all others; the development of precise general laws in organizational behavior and organization theory is thus impossible.
2. *Instability.* The phenomena of interest to researchers in organizational behavior and organization theory are transitory. Not only do the "facts" of social events change with time, but the "laws" governing them change as well. Natural science research is poorly equipped to capture these fleeting phenomena.
3. *Sensitivity.* Unlike chemical compounds and other things of interest to natural science researchers, the people who make up organizations, and thus organizations themselves, may behave differently if they become aware of researchers [sic] hypotheses about them.

4. *Lack of Realism.* Manipulating and controlling variables in organizational research changes the phenomena under study. Researchers thus cannot generalize from their studies because the phenomena inevitably differ from their real-world counterparts.
5. *Epistemological Differences.* Although understanding cause and effect through natural science research is an appropriate way of "knowing" about physical phenomena, a different kind of "knowledge" not tapped by this approach is more important in organizational behavior and organization theory. [1980, pp. 484–485]

It is not the intent here to take the space to refute these beliefs; Behling does this and so do others before him. For whatever reason, the arguments that make sense to those believing in rigorous research methods always fail to convince those believing the above propositions. Let it suffice to say that organization theorists fall into two groups, those who believe the above and those who do not. The point here is that there are many now who *do* believe in the above propositions, and four of the five have as a key element the view that organizations change far too fast for the use of rigorous methods, let alone the silly idea of trying to form them into classes. After all, why develop and publish a classification of organizations if they are all going to have changed several times before it is in print? To the extent that the belief in the foregoing propositions is widely held, it is likely that the community of organizational scientists is not going to be very quick to engage in systematics.

Even though arguments against rigorous research are not attacked here, two things can be said. First, it is important to reiterate the point made in chapter 2 that those believing in the appropriateness of rigorous "objectivist" methods should readily buy into the ideas of systematics because classification is the best way to improve population definition, the effectiveness of sampling, the levels of variance explained, and the soundness of generalizations—all near and dear to the hearts of objectivists. Second, arguments will be developed later in the book to the effect that organizational forms are not nearly as changeable and unstable as some scholars think. Strange it is that many professors of organization and management who, wearing their hats as organizational change practitioners and consultants, moan about how hard organizations are to change, are also the same people who as researchers turn around and reject rigorous methods because organizations are so changeable!

4.2.4 Allogenic Models

For the past several decades allogenic models of organizations, technological and environmental determinism, and evolutionary theory all have been unpopular among social scientists in general and organizational scientists in particular. Pfeffer and Salancik (1978, pp. 6−10) mentioned several reasons why causality has been attributed to individuals rather than external forces. First, people are much more available, convenient, easy to talk to, and easier to collect data from, than the external environment. Second, several experiments have shown that observers of individual and organizational behavior exhibit a cognitive bias toward attributing outcomes to the personal motivation and capabilities of the actors rather than to externally imposed constraints. Third, they cite Kelley (1971) as noting another human tendency, which is to attribute causality to people—who are potentially controllable—rather than to less controllable forces such as contextual factors.

For the past twenty-five years or so, students of organizations in business schools have been especially enamored of psychological need theory, popularized by Maslow (1954) and McGregor (1960) among others, which steadfastly attributes human behavior to a quest for need satisfaction. At the same time, they have equally steadfastly rejected behaviorism (Skinner 1953, 1969) or behavior modification approaches (Luthans and Kreitner 1975), though recently the latter have gained increased attention. Perrow (1970) noted that the perennial attention to leadership as the prime mover in organizations is another stone in the wall holding back allogenic ways of thinking.

Scholars have been arguing about technological determinism ever since the first yoke of oxen were hooked together. In 1904 Veblen said:

> In a sense more intimate than the inventors of the phrase seem to have appreciated, the machine has become the master of the man who works with it and an arbiter in the cultural fortunes of the community into whose life it has entered. [Quote given in Haas and Drabbek 1973, p. 73]

More recently White (1949) has become the chief proponent of technological determinism. Largely because of the influence of Parsons (1966), most sociologists have seemingly steered away from even a modest consideration of the role of technology. However, in a recent book, Lenski and Lenski (1974) base a dynamic evolutionary view of societal development on technology. But in contrast to White, they recognize that not *all* aspects of society are due to technology. (Another exception, Perrow [1970], will be discussed later.)

In some circles environmental determinism is not even allowed to exist. As recently as 1976 Starbuck wrote:

> Organizations' environments are largely invented by organizations themselves. Organizations select their environments from ranges of alternatives, then they subjectively perceive the environments they inhabit. [P. 1069]

At first glance Weick took the same position as Starbuck:

> Environments will be treated as the outcomes of organizing and as the creations of actors within the organization. [1979, p. 22]

But later in the book he says:

> Investigators who study organizations often separate environments from organizations and argue that things happen between these distinct entities. . . . But the firm partitioning of the world into the environment and the organization excludes the possibility that people *invent* rather than discover part of what they think they see.
>
> It certainly is the case that organizations bump into things and that their bruises testify to a certain tangibility in their environment. . . . [1979, p. 166; his emphasis]

In this passage, Weick does recognize that there are some hard environmental realities, though they are not featured in his analyses. If recent textbooks are taken as an indication of the "field's" view, organizational environments are definitely hard realities (Brown and Moberg 1980; Miles 1980; Osborn, Hunt, and Jauch 1980; Ullrich and Wieland 1980), but not direct determinants of organizational form.

Even though evolutionary theory and natural selection have been known to social scientists for over a hundred years (see chapter 8), they have not figured in organizational science until very recently. Campbell (1969) suggested that it was the political ideology of the social Darwinists, coupled with the personal influence and unexplained idiosyncrasy of Boas, which turned social scientists so far away from taking any element of an evolutionary paradigm seriously. No doubt the list of historical pitfalls in the way of the rational principle of enquiry could be elaborated even further.

Since the late 1960s there has been a revival in applying evolutionary, natural selection, or population ecology theories (they go by various labels) to social systems, one of the more influential papers being that of Campbell (1969). He suggested that natural selection theory offers a powerful means of explaining the differential survival and growth of many social systems. Specifically he identified three basic requirements for the natural selection model to hold: (1) the presence of *variations,* which produce changes in social units; (2) the presence of *selection forces,* which act to cull out social and organizational variations that are less effective; and (3) *retention forces,* which serve to preserve over time social or organizational forms that are most effective. The evolutionary theme has subsequently been picked up by Weick (1969, 1979), Aldrich (1971, 1979),* Warriner (1973, 1978), Hannan and Freeman (1974, 1977), Aldrich and Pfeffer (1976), Kaufman (1975), McKelvey (1978, 1980), and Blute (1979).

At this time there are only three fairly well-elaborated statements about organizations that fall clearly into the allogenic group, those by Warriner (1978), Hannan and Freeman (1977), and Aldrich (1979). All three works take what is termed the *population ecology perspective*, which draws directly on natural selection theory. In fact much of it is not strictly ecological but rather systematic; hence I call it the *population perspective*. Put very succinctly this view holds that in an environment consisting of certain levels of resources and certain imposed constraints, a population of organizations having rather similar characteristics will emerge, survive, and grow until such time that the population will no longer be able to compete effectively for additional resources, at which time it will stabilize both in size and in characteristic form. Though the three approaches all end up with the population perspective, their points of departure and arguments are different and thus worth reviewing quickly.

Warriner

In a 1978 revision of a paper originally presented in 1973, Warriner argued for a social-ecological approach as a way to overcome the problem of teleology in explaining organizational action. He defined teleology as "the attempt to account for the events and patterns of this world by references to some inherent design or purpose" (1978, p. 1), a logic drawing on the essentialist nature of Aristotelian logic. Though the social sciences all flaunt teleological thinking, according to Warriner, nowhere is this more obvious than in the study of organizations where organizational purposes, defined by managerial actions, are used to explain subsequent managerial actions—teleological thinking at its best (or worst). Parallel in time with Georgiou (1973), Warriner was also attacking the goal paradigm, but instead of looking for a solution by dropping down a level of analysis via reductionism as Georgiou did, Warriner looked to a higher plane of analysis—rationalism, specifically the population perspective.

Warriner (1978) identified five elements of the population approach as

---

*Though I give Hannan and Freeman (1977) credit for introducing the population ecology view to the organizational science literature, Aldrich should get credit for introducing the population perspective in his 1971 paper, though it has been largely ignored and undefined until now.

follows (though the headings are from Warriner, not all of the ensuing comments should be attributed to him):

1. *Organizations are explicitly treated as units of analysis.* This might seem a trivial point but it was not until around 1960 that organizations began to be treated as something more than a setting where people interact, or as more than aggregations of individual behaviors (see Meyer and Associates 1978 for confirmation of this), and even now some critics have suggested to the author that classifying organizations is a waste of time because of their apparent lack of entitivity. The main argument for entitivity is seen in the continuity of behavior which transcends the comings and going of individuals. See Freeman (1978) for an extended discussion of this issue.

2. *The focus is on populations,* not individual members of a population. In order to avoid basing explanation on idiosyncratic and random effects of individual organizations, Warriner insisted that entire populations of organizations be studied. This is the particular theme of population organizational science. However, both Hannan and Freeman (1977) and Aldrich (1979) take the position that ecological and natural selection theory can be applied to individuals as well as populations. Biological ecologists (Odum 1971; Pianka 1974) also allow that ecological methods can be used to study individual organisms as well as populations. Both arguments are correct. The point is that there are two topics of explanation: (a) the emergence, evolution, regulation, and growth of species (populations) of organizations; and (b) the life and death of individual organizations.

3. *A much broader time scale is needed for an ecological view.* Biological ecologists and evolutionists are accustomed to speaking in terms of *geological* time when they want to signal a long-term view. Organizational scientists have not developed an analogous means of distinguishing between the short time span relevant to the life and death of a particular member of a species and the long, possibly very long, time frame useful for studying the survival, growth, and death of organizational populations. Biological species may persist for hundreds of thousands of years; individual lifespans range from minutes to over 4,000 years. Most organizational species have probably existed for less than 50 to 100 years. It is hard to know, since we do not yet agree on what species are. The life spans of individual members of organizational species range from weeks or months in the case of the opening and closing of a small store to almost two thousand years, in the case of the Roman Catholic church. In this case the species is much older than the 90- to 100-year average. It is possible that the Church will be taken as a species with several individual organizations living and dying within it. The fact that the difference between the ages of species and the ages of individual members of species is much less for organizations than for most biological organisms is one apparent difference between organizational and biological populations. The pace of evolution is also much faster for organizational populations.

4. *To carry out the population perspective, similar and dissimilar organi-*

zations have to be studied in similar and dissimilar environ-ments. This means comparative research is very important. In order to discover relations between environmental forces and organizational forms, variance among environments and among organizations in the same study is necessary. The study of similarity and dissimilarity also means that classification is an essential component of population ecology studies. It is only through taxonomy and classification that organizational scientists may come to agree that organizations are or are not similar to each other.

5. Most important, as Warriner put it, the population perspective "treats the *environment as fateful* for organizations" (1978, p. 13; his emphasis). Environments have consequences for organizations whether or not managers or other members correctly perceive or enact their characteristics. This is contrary to Weick's (1979) view of environmental enactment or to the quote from Starbuck given at the beginning of the section.

While he made the role of the environment quite clear, Warriner did not discuss mechanisms whereby a population of organizations, member by member, actually adapts to a fateful environment. How a member organization comes to take on certain characteristics was not specified. The role of managers as choiceful individuals was left unclear, and there was no statement saying that they are indeed not choiceful. In short, the coupling between people and organizational form was left unspecified. Admittedly, the paper was brief and the main intent was to note the teleological problems of the goal paradigm and then discuss some concerns stemming from the ecological perspective.

Hannan and Freeman

In contrast to Warriner's focus on teleology, Hannan and Freeman (1977) started with the observation that the prevailing models of organization, both in the management and sociological literatures, emphasize organizational adaptation. The models do this by focusing on rational processes, especially decision making. Hannan and Freeman then pointed out several internal and external pressures toward inertia which suggest that adaptation may not be as easy or as frequent as the traditional models portray.

Moving into a discussion of the population ecology model, Hannan and Freeman argued that since organizational scientists have spent an inordinate amount of time on the adaptation process, it is time that someone studied how different kinds of organizations are selected out to survive and grow. They accepted the basic ecological premise that selection is owing to fitness, and defined fitness "as the probability that a given form of organization would persist in a certain environment" (1977, p. 937).

Having made a clear distinction between adaptation and selection (a similar distinction is elaborated by Starbuck 1976), Hannan and Freeman took the position that it is the environment that *optimizes* by selecting optimal combinations of organizations, given the resources available. Since the environment is not some kind of anthropomorphized being, this happens through the relative effectiveness of organizational forms in competing for resources. A population of organizations survives because it is effective in acquiring needed resources against the competition of other populations. Within a population individual organizational members are also selected out (fail to survive) as, for a variety of reasons, their individual form drifts too far off the modal form of the population. Implicit in this view is the idea that environments will support a mosaic of macro niches, in each of which lives a population of organizations of more or less similar characteristics. Otherwise there would be no reason to expect to see modal forms in populations in contrast to an infinitely varied mass of individual organizations.

Hannan and Freeman did not discuss how some organizations come to have a form that survives while others do not. There are no statements on the sources of variations in organizational form. Though they presumably agreed with Campbell (1969) that environmental variation is a basic element of natural selection theory, they do not cite his paper or make any statement directly to that effect, though they do base much of their development of niche theory on "fine-grained" and "coarse-grained" environmental variation. They do draw on the biological concept of genetic structure, recognizing that an analogous concept must be developed for organizations, to act as a blueprint to produce organizational form (a topic taken up in chapter 6). While they specify three components of an organizational blueprint (formal structure, patterns of activity, and normative order), they do not discuss *how* different blueprints come into being. In all fairness, one paper cannot be expected to accomplish everything; Hannan and Freeman make a good start on the selection process, and have continued in this vein in subsequent papers (Brittain and Freeman 1980; Hannan 1980; Freeman 1981). As noted at the outset of chapter 2, they mentioned some aspects of systematics and population definition but did not pursue the matter.

Aldrich

The point of departure taken by Aldrich (1979) was to characterize the rational or bureaucratic model as a "closed-system" approach that does not take into account differential characteristics of the environment, but does assume a thoroughly known and controllable internal structure

(1979, p. 22). But, whereas Hannan and Freeman (1977) emphasized the elements of inertia which make adaptation a less robust possibility than the rational model would admit to, Aldrich placed most attention on variations largely outside of the control of organizational members. Aldrich built mostly on the work of Campbell (1969), using natural selection theory as the basic organizing theme of his book. The majority of his chapters were devoted specifically to showing the considerable extent to which organizational variations are due to forces outside the formal decision-making procedures of organizations.*

Aldrich pictured organizations as "loosely coupled systems that are subject to change because of error, creativity, luck, and conflict, as well as through planned innovation" (1979, p. 75). The mention of planned innovation notwithstanding, Aldrich said:

> The motives of organizational entrepreneurs are important in constructing a comprehensive explanation of the creation of organizations, but I have argued in this chapter that they are much less important for a theory of organizational change than is an understanding of structural, political, and economic conditions. [1979, p. 188]

The main place where Aldrich considered the relative importance of autogenic versus allogenic forces was chapter 6, on the opportunities and constraints for what Child (1972) termed *strategic choice*. Aldrich (1979, p. 138) noted that the essence of Child's argument amounted to three points:

1. Decision makers have more autonomy than implied by those arguing for the dominance of environmental, technological, or other forces.
2. Organizations occasionally have the power to manipulate and control their environments.
3. Perceptions and evaluations of events are an important intervening link between environments and organizations' actions.

Aldrich continued his discussion by arguing "*not* that strategic choice is impossible, but rather that external constraints severely limit its impact" (1979, p. 149; his emphasis). In addition to matters of law, Aldrich noted that such economic barriers as effects of economies of scale, absolute cost of entry, and high visibility products exert considerable restraint on the freedom of an entrepreneur to enter a new environment. He argued that only the very largest organizations are really able to

---

*In his review Aldrich did not deal with the other autogenic models—natural system or market process—and neither did Warriner nor Hannan and Freeman.

manipulate their environments, whereas most organizations—which are small—are largely at the mercy of their environments. While organizational members' perceptions "play some role in their actions," Aldrich suggested that "the frequency of truly strategic choices may be quite small" (1979, p. 157). He presented some arguments to the effect that perceptual sets that may appear to reside within an individual are also largely affected by the ambient environment. Even though he ended chapter 5 with an illustration showing how both autogenic (via information flows) and allogenic (via resource dependencies) forces could be combined to explain organizational variation, and noted that "a comprehensive theory of organizational change will undoubtedly incorporate both views of the environment" (1979, p. 135), little attention was given to autogenic forces or to a theoretical synthesis that could capture elements of both in a model where strategic choice and ecological effect are treated with equal analytical importance.

Aldrich's sensitivity to both autogenic and allogenic forces, which is not resolved by an explicit satisfactory theoretical synthesis, lent an ambivalent air to his book, not unlike that in Pfeffer and Salancik (1978). He sometimes seemed to include autogenic models, but mostly the allogenic model was emphasized. The following two definitions of organizations are illustrative:

> Organizations are goal-directed, boundary-maintaining activity systems. [1979, p. 4; his emphasis not added]
>
> Organizations will be portrayed as loosely coupled systems that are subject to change because of error, creativity, luck and conflict, as well as through planned change. [1979, p. 75]

In commenting on a draft of this chapter Aldrich* said, "If there are ambivalences apparent in my book, it is in part due to the overwhelming dilemma I faced of both trying to argue strongly for a sociological and historical perspective, but at the same time paying sufficient attention to the role of individual initiative. Note that I am not retreating from my emphasis on forces much larger than any individual could control—I still feel that if our task is to explain organizational structure and organizational change, we will go much further with macro-historical and sociological explanations than we will with autogenic explanations. However, a complete explanation of particular cases, within particular eras, will always require attention to autogenic forces." The last sentence suggests the cause of the ambivalence—Aldrich's choice to take both an individual organizational *and* a population perspective—and

*Howard Aldrich, personal communication, 11 July 1979.

the cure. Autogenic models will be seen to be most useful in understanding and "curing" individual organizations, much as a physician understands a person's symptoms and then suggests a cure. Allogenic models are for understanding the organizational form and function of organizational populations. I think those taking the population perspective, including myself, would have little trouble agreeing that organizational science will ultimately focus on populations and rely on allogenic models of organizational variation.

As yet the population people have not come up with a satisfactory definition of organizations, from their point of view. Neither Warriner (1978) nor Hannan and Freeman (1977) offered any kind of definition. Aldrich's definitions, as noted above, were ambivalent. For a pure allogenic perspective taking into account Warriner's concerns for teleology, Hannan and Freeman's concerns for environmental optimality and subsequent selection of organizations rather than their adaptation, and Aldrich's focus on natural selection theory, the following definition is a possibility:

> Effective organizations are boundary-maintaining activity systems having input/output resource ratios fostering survival in environments imposing particular constraints.

Thus, organizations are selected for survival which have entitivity and have activities that allow them to compete for resources effectively in environments imposing not just any, but particular constraints or conditions. The definition does not say how organizations do these things, just that if they do them they will survive. The definition leaves open whether survival implies or requires growth—in some instances it may, in others it may not. It implies that ineffective organizations do not exist, which of course is not true in the short term. But the population approach is a long-term view.

Left unspecified so far is how, from a purely allogenic perspective, organizations actually maintain entitivity, generate activities, acquire resources, make variations either in response to or independent of environmental variations, take on a certain form, and so on. Is it possible to rise above the ambivalences apparent in Aldrich's book, the hedging in the Hannan and Freeman paper, the teleology Warriner frowns upon? Indeed it is. Organizations may be considered as "black boxes" composed of blind or random variations. Given environmental variations, working selection processes, and retention mechanisms, all that is needed in organizations is a source of variation. Randomness will do quite well.

Given the various views of organizations offered by the autogenic theorists, randomness as the source of organizational variation is not as far afield as the reader might think. Consider the description of organized anarchy offered by Cohen, March, and Olsen (1972), loose coupling in organizations by Weick (1976), the myriad elements of a market process which taken together and viewed from afar may be indistinguishable from random events (Georgiou 1973; Benson 1977), and the unpredictable course of events resulting from the interplay of rational and natural system forces described by the more traditional autogenic theorists. It may be closer to the truth—and it is certainly more expedient—to view all these happenings as random rather than try to tease out intentionality, need satisfaction, rationality, irrationality, goal seeking, or whatever.

The pure population ecology model appears to take the following form, once the ambivalence over autogenic sources of variation is cleared away:

Coupling:		Weak		Strong	
Source:	PEOPLE	----→	ORGANIZATION	◀———	ENVIRONMENT
Order:	Chaotic				Complex

The strong coupling is clearly the one between environment and organization. Environments are seen as complexly ordered objects that can be studied and explained, though perhaps with difficulty. People in organizations are viewed as chaotic, and their collective purposefulness and collective behavior taken together are essentially blind. The coupling between people and organizational form is weak, people being nothing more than a source of variation to assure that environmental forces will have different organizational forms to select.

4.3 TOWARD A SYNTHESIS OF AUTOGENIC AND ALLOGENIC MODELS

Except for the earliest writers such as Weber and Fayol, exponents of the various models of organizational variation have invariably developed their own model as a reaction or overreaction to an existing formulation. With the recent promulgation of market process or social construction models at one extreme and population models at the other, the situation has reached a curious state of affairs. On the one hand, the process models are built on the assumption of human intentionality and subjective interpretation of meanings, and on the other hand the ecological

models ignore human intentionality and take a view of external environments selecting organizations—the epitome of an objectivist perspective. Seemingly the two approaches are receding galaxies of thought.
But, and how ironic it is, if the market process model of how human
intentionality is transacted is viewed the same way that the stock market
is currently viewed—to wit, that the market indexes (similar to total
organization behavior) are random walks reflecting the path of efficient
markets, then the market process model fits in perfectly with the aforementioned notion that a strict allogenic view requires that organizational variations be randomly generated. In terms of the transaction-cost
model (Williamson 1975; Ouchi 1980a, b) autogenic sources, whether
Alpha or Sigma, are random market process walks in search of efficient
boundaries or minimal transaction costs. In this view models of organization have converged. In light of this, a synthesis of autogenic and
allogenic models cannot be far off.

There are good arguments in support of both autogenic and allogenic
models and it is time to stop developing such models in opposition to
each other. Do we have to be forced into a choice between the two? The
intent here is to suggest a synthesis that, if not fully acceptable on the
first round, will at least stimulate further synthetic developments rather
than receding arguments.

4.3.1 Environment, Organizational Variation, and Form

Before suggesting a possible synthesis, some preliminary developments
are needed. One preliminary task is to suggest a model of the essential
relation between environmental conditions, organizational variation,
and, ultimately, organizational form. An excellent development of the
main components of such a model was given by Perrow (1970) in his
attempt to answer two questions central to the theme of this book: Why
are there different kinds of organizations? and What is the basis of
organizational structure or form? Perrow saw input materials as the
prime stimulus in an organization's choice of technology. In turn, its
technology was what gave rise to different kinds of structure.

The Perrow model can be elaborated and made more general by
thinking of a stimulus-response sequence as depicted in figure 4.1. In
general, an environment is conceptualized as a set of constraints that
impose problems for an organization to solve. These could be in the form
of raw material problems, but they could also be due to other environmental conditions such as technological, economic, political, demographic, cultural, and legal factors (Hall 1977, pp. 304–311; or see
section 5.1.1), or a variety of problematic environmental characteristics

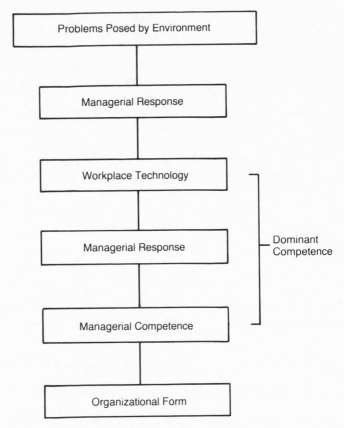

*This looks like a causal sequence; in chapter 13 I argue that it is not.

Figure 4.1. A Model of the Environment-Organizational Form Relationship.

such as resource capacity, homogeneity-heterogeneity, stability-instability, concentration-dispersion, consensus-dissensus, or turbulence (Aldrich 1979, pp. 63–70). An organization's technical competence may be seen as a direct response to environmentally imposed problems. Following Katz and Kahn (1978, pp. 136–139), there is no such thing as technological determinism; instead, organizational managers or other members select technology in response to problems they perceive. Technology, whatever kind it is, also poses problems such as planning, coordination, control efficiency, problems of interdependency, and so forth. A management competence grows up as a response to problems in running the workplace efficiently (this view reflects the thinking of

Thompson [1967] and many others). In turn, organizational structure develops partly as an element of management competence but also partly in response to problems of coordination, interdependency, human variability, and so on posed by a management competence that of necessity must be embodied in many management and staff personnel. Organizational form is the final outcome of the foregoing events.

Loosely defined for the moment, organizational FORM is taken as a concept to broadly capture the character of an organization's structure, function, and process. At this point in the development of the population perspective, I think it wise to use an intentionally broad, even vague theoretical definition of organizational form. Imagine a definition of organic form that would apply to reptiles, fish, mammals, birds, and perhaps even to flowers, bushes, and trees. As a general definition we need something to cover an equivalently broad assemblage of organizational populations. Consequently organizational form is defined as: those elements of internal structure, process, and subunit integration which contribute to the unity of the whole of an organization and to the maintenance of its characteristic activities, function, or nature. The phrasing here is different but similar in meaning to the definition of form suggested by McKelvey (1978, p. 1431). Within this broad definition other more specific operational definitions may be posed for specific populations.

Needless to say, this description of the model is brief. Aspects of its components will be elaborated in chapter 7. It is given here to acquaint the reader early with my way of thinking about what happens in organizations. It is one way to explain how environmental characteristics affect organizational workplaces, management arrangements, structure, and ultimately organizational form without disallowing purposeful human action. The external environment creates a sequence of problems, but people in organizations can, if they desire, try to solve them. A conceptualization of this set of events is one step toward a synthesis of autogenic and allogenic models. I want to alert the reader to the fact that this "sequence model" is not compatible with natural selection and evolutionary theory. The Perrow model starts with an environmental cause which is then followed by a sequence of causes inside the organization, eventually leading to a given form. Meyer and Brown (1977) and Meyer (1979) claim to demonstrate this kind of causal sequence. In chapter 13, after all developments in the book are completed, I will argue that an entirely different explanation of how Perrow's components (as elaborated here) relate to organizational form is called for by the population perspective.

4.3.2 Environments and Niches

A second preliminary task is to sort out the question of environmental versus organizational manipulation. Part of the difficulty in discussing the relative importance of autogenic and allogenic forces stems from the degree to which various authors see the environment influencing organizations or as subject to manipulation by organizations. If one sees the environment as totally beyond the influence of organizations an allogenic model is sure to follow. The reverse is true too—most theorists cannot see the environment as a causal factor and still believe in an autogenic model.

It is clear from the foregoing review that environments are seen both ways in the literature, with representative statements being given by Child (1972) in favor of organizations manipulating environments and Warriner (1978) and Hannan and Freeman (1977) in favor of environments manipulating organizations. Aldrich (1979) actually takes a compromise position in arguing that small organizations are most subject to environmental manipulation, and since there are many more small than large organizations, it is safe to conclude that *in general* environments do manipulate organizations. He narrows Child's strategic contingencies theory to apply only to very large organizations.

Rumelt (1979) disagreed with Aldrich's compromise, noting that even very large organizations are not totally immune to environmental pressures (even General Motors, the U.S. government, and the Roman Catholic church have been known to bow to environmental pressures) and that small organizations are very much involved in influencing the part of the environment closest to them (the advertising of a neighborhood store, for example). Rumelt's position is well taken. Even if one did agree with Aldrich about the effects of size, what happens to the rather large number of middle-sized organizations? They seem left out of Aldrich's position.

A solution to the problem of what manipulates what comes by following the lead of biological ecologists, introducing the term *niche*, and then following their definitions of *niche* and *environment*. From Pianka:

> The ecological niche can be defined as *the sum total of the adaptations of an organismic unit*, or as all of the various ways in which a given organismic unit conforms to its environment. . . . The difference between an organism's environment and its niche is that the latter concept includes an organism's abilities at exploiting its environment and involves the ways in which the organism actually *uses* its environment. [1974, p. 190; his emphases]

Pianka defined *environment* as:

> The sum total of all physical and biological factors impinging upon a particular organismic unit. For "organismic unit" one can substitute either "individual," "population," "species," or "community." Thus, we may speak of the environment of an individual or the environment of a population, but to be precise, a particular organismic unit should be understood or specified. The environment of an individual contains fewer elements than the environment of a population, which in turn is a subset of the environment of the species of community. [1974, p. 2; his emphasis not added]

Odum said:

> The ecological niche of an organism depends not only on where it lives but also on what it does (how it transforms energy, behaves, responds to and *modifies* its physical and biotic environment), and how it is constrained by other species. [1971, p. 234; emphasis added]

Odum did not give a specific definition for the term *environment*. However, it is clear from reading other passages in his book that the set of things organisms respond to is much larger than the set of things they are able to modify; hence, a niche is a subset of an environment defined by the more limiting conditions of what an organism is able to modify.

Note carefully that *niche is a dynamic concept* whereas *environment* is not. In this book *environment* will always be defined as *that set of external forces or characteristics that impose constraints on an individual organization or a population of organizations, and which are outside its ability to influence. The remaining forces or characteristics, which are subject to modification by an organization or a population of organizations,* are defined as *niche* attributes. In this view a niche is a *result* of organizational adaptation, not a *cause* of a particular form of adaptation. The lay usage is very apt—a niche is carved out. It is *created* by a population of organizations. The niche as a dynamic concept is an important element in Sokal's (1973, p. 369) discussion of the species concept, as it will be in my development of an organizational species concept. In some instances it will be convenient to distinguish between a *macro-niche*, created by a population of organizations, and a *micro-niche*, created within a macro-niche by a particular individual organization that is a member of the population. Usually it will be clear from the text which kind of niche is meant.

A further item to note is that it is impossible to identify the characteristics of a niche without knowing attributes of the population of organizations occupying it. Conversely, it is also true that it is not really possible to fully describe an organization without also knowing something about its micro- and macro-niches. This point is recognized by biological ecologists (Lewontin 1978) and systematists (Sokal 1973).

A question often asked is, Why not classify niches? (The word environment is typically used since the asker does not distinguish between niche and environment.) As given above, the answer is that it is impossible, since one does not know a niche without also knowing an organizational population. Strictly speaking, the reverse is also true: one cannot really classify only organizational populations. Thus, this book is really about classifying organizations and niches. It follows that attributes of organizational behavior relative to niches are eligible to be designated as taxonomic characters.

A final point is that there are large and small niches. Large animals have more widespread impact in carving out their niche than do very small or microscopic organisms. But generally the environment is very large and potent, with vast portions of it clearly beyond modification by even the largest animals. No one expects elephants to tear down mountain ranges, alter climate, temperature, or rainfall, or make oases in deserts.* It is possible that some organizational niches are much larger relative to the environment than is true among biological organisms. After the Second World War, for example, the niche of the U.S. government as a world-influencing organization may have been close to being isomorphic with its environment. The niche of General Motors is certainly closer to being isomorphic with its environment than the niche of a local ma-and-pa grocery store. It is an empirical question, but for now it is assumed that the limiting cases do not exist; nowhere is an organizational population's niche fully isomorphic with its environment, and nowhere does an organizational population exist without any niche at all, meaning it has absolutely no ability to modify any aspect of its environment.

Hopefully the foregoing distinction between niche and environment will take care of the problem of how to incorporate both autogenic and allogenic forces into one model. Environmental conditions are the true allogenic forces, and by definition, no organization can manipulate

---

*To be precise, however, it should be recognized that animals can have some long-run effect on such things as mountains, for example, by creating trails that foster erosion; by overgrazing, killing vegetation, and thus fostering erosion; by breathing out carbon dioxide that at some point enhances the life-support system for plants, and so forth. (See Odum 1971, p. 23.) In the very long term, organizational populations may have some impact on their environment. Most of the time, however, the environment is beyond influence.

them. Niches are carved out via the interaction of both autogenic and allogenic sources of variation. To understand how a certain niche was created one would have to understand the impact of both allogenic and autogenic forces. I now turn to a way of doing exactly this.

4.3.3 An Asymptotic Model of Organizational Variation

It is not easy to see how both allogenic and autogenic forces work together. There is still the nagging feeling that it would be nice to pinpoint the cause of what happens in an organization a little more precisely. Despite the distinction between niches and environments, some readers are likely to think that the environment is the prime determinant while others will think that it is still pretty well up to an organization to make of its niche whatever it wishes. Can both be correct? Yes. Think of environments as causal textures (after Emery and Trist 1965) that are composed of a network of forces. Each node in the network supports an organizational form of a certain configuration. Usually the resources available are such that a population of organizations having a modal form will exist at each node. Over time the force network changes such that the nodes change in the kinds of problems they pose for the population. Thus over time *a survival path** appears, in the sense that there is a progression in the kind of organizational form characteristics optimally required to solve the problems posed by the force node or environment. To survive, a population and the individual organizations within it must approach the form which fits the characteristics of the survival path. There may be one "true" path or, if conditions of equifinality (the general systems idea that several causal paths may lead to the same end; see Katz and Kahn 1978) prevail, two or more paths, but probably not very many. Some environments may tolerate several paths, some only one. This is an empirical question. In this view allogenic forces define the survival path. It is up to organizations in a population to find it.

How organizations go about finding the survival path of their population is explained by the autogenic forces. Environments only select. They do not cause particular organizations to search and be successful in finding the path. Autogenic forces are sources of variation—via both Alpha and Sigma processes. These variations may be purposeful or blind (in chapter 8, I will argue that in organizations both Lamarckian and Darwinian evolution takes place). As a result of the variations,

---

*Organizational SURVIVAL is defined as a long-term net importation of resources, after the general systems approach of Yuchtman and Seashore (1967).

organizations move fairly directly or wander randomly or haphazardly toward the survival path. Some do it quicker than others. Some never make it and fail. There is nothing that causes organizations to move toward the path except the behavioral variations of people in organizations. Just because one or more correct paths exist as a result of environmental conditions, an organization (via its autogenic means of variation) does not have to choose to follow the true path(s). Just as jack rabbits sometimes jump in front of trucks, or whales sometimes beach themselves, or people commit suicide, organizations do *not* have to attempt to survive and grow. Nor are they forced to be effective at surviving and growing. This is where strategic choice enters in. The degree to which autogenic forces, by choice or via random process, work to move an individual organizational member of a specific population toward the survival path is *not* influenced by allogenic forces. It is up to human intentionality or chance, or both. Take your pick.

Environments only select. They do not cause organizational variations; only autogenic forces generate variation. But given a specified environment, the wrong variations may lead to failure (to be selected). Finding the survival path may not be easy. Thus it is up to organizational members via Alpha or Sigma sources of variation to attempt to find the true path. It is up to them to perceive and enact it accurately.

Even if the survival path is perceived or enacted correctly, it is up to people in an organization to implement an appropriate course of action. It is up to them to learn whether or not their action is moving their organization toward or along the survival path. Organizational members, via Alpha or Sigma sources, may choose to stay in a particular environment and carve out a niche or they may choose to move on to another environment and perhaps a set of conditions more favorable to them.

This is sort of a "lost hiker" view of organizations and their environments. A hiker lost in a forest can survive and get out if he has the right skills and equipment, uses his experience or that of others who may be with him, and so on. He may find that rather than leave the woods it makes sense to stay and survive by finding a habitable niche. Or he can lie down and starve or freeze to death. His survival may be based on skill, luck, or both. There is a large element of self-determination—autogenic force. Nevertheless there are many features of the forest beyond his ability to modify—allogenic forces—and these ultimately determine which of all his intentional or unintentional activities prove effective.

It is likely impossible to anticipate a survival path from beginning to end. The true path can only be known retrospectively, though broad characteristics may be anticipated. We may anticipate, for example, that a desert plant species will have to solve the problem of moisture reten- tion, though we cannot know how it will accomplish this. We may know that an organizational population facing a competitive international market will have to solve the problem of low-cost transportation, but there may be several ways of doing this, some still not yet discovered. The course of a survival path is largely incremental—survival depends on something that works at the time. Given equifinality, with several workable alternatives at each step, the range of alternatives and what works at a subsequent step depends on what was tried and proved effective at the prior step; thus the path cannot be extrapolated from an awareness of allogenic forces. But it is nevertheless fully determined by them. This theme—the difference between a "causal law" explanation and a "descent with modification" explanation—will be taken up again in chapters 8 and 13.

There can be no real definition of organizational effectiveness without previously defining an allogenically created survival path, something that is usually impossible except in the very broadest terms because of the principle of descent with modification. Effectiveness is not defined in terms of an organization's goals, as is typically done (Etzioni 1964), but rather in terms of ability to gain resources from its environment (similar to how it was defined by Yuchtman and Seashore, 1967). But there can be no organizational approach toward effectiveness without autogenic forces at work.

The relation between allogenic and autogenic forces for a particular organization can be represented by an *asymptotic model* where, in a two-dimensional space, a horizontal line represents the progression of an environmentally created survival path (or more than one) and a second line, representing niche and form development, approaches it asymptotically. This is depicted in figure 4.2. It is important to under- stand what the convergence does *not* represent. It does *not* mean that the niche is becoming isomorphic with the environment in the sense that more and more environmental conditions are modifiable. It does *not* mean that the characteristics of the niche are becoming isomorphic with the characteristics of the environment. *The horizontal line represents the path that niche and form development must take if an organization is to survive and grow.* If more than one path is available then more than one niche and form configuration is possible. *The upwardly curving line represents the actual path of niche and form development an organiza- tion is taking.* The closer the actual path approaches the survival path the more effective an organization would be.

An added difficulty is that an allogenically created path cannot be assumed to be stable. This possibility is shown in figure 4.3. The

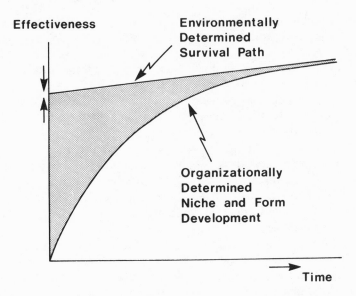

Figure 4.2. An Asymptotic Model of Environmental *and* Organizational Determination in a Stable Environment (explanation in text).

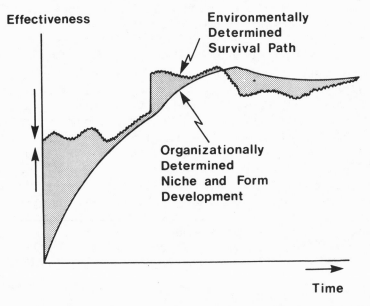

Figure 4.3. An Asymptotic Model of Environmental *and* Organizational Determination in a Changing Environment (explanation in text).

survival path is shown to make both gradual and discontinuous changes, with the niche development line lagging behind in its approach to the survival line. Again, some Alpha or Sigma sources of variation may prove more successful or luckier in approaching a changing survival path than others. An approach within a certain distance may allow survival but not growth.

As depicted, this model requires *both* allogenic and autogenic forces. Seen in this light, organizational EFFECTIVENESS cannot be pursued by an organization, or understood by organizational scientists, without knowledge of both sources of variation. Allogenic forces always define a target of niche and form development and autogenic forces are always destined to move an organization toward (or away from) the target.

Given a synthesized model, organizations are defined as follows:

> Effective organizations are myopically purposeful (boundary-maintaining) activity systems containing one or more conditionally autonomous myopically purposeful subsystems having input-output resource ratios fostering survival in environments imposing particular constraints.

This definition is a combination of the autogenic and allogenic definitions given earlier. The concepts of purposefulness and systems imply the notion of boundary maintenance just as they imply other concepts, so there is no reason why boundary maintenance should be included in the definition any more than several other concepts (though I have shown it in parentheses). Aldrich* reminds us that autogenic forces, in the form of authority, power, and the dominant coalition, are essential for preserving organizational entitivity, that is, boundary maintenance. The phrase "myopically purposeful" captures the idea that individuals, subsystems, and organizations may often (perhaps always) be purposeful in tryng to be more effective or trying to survive, but also that these variations are mostly blind in terms of what will work in the long term in an uncertain, changing environment. Many individual short-term purposeful activities do not add up to long-term collective purposefulness. The analogy I have in mind is to a bunch of prisoners escaping from a firing squad across a mine field on a black night. They are all intensely purposeful, but that will not explain why some survive and some do not. The selection process is largely outside the control of individual rationality.

When an environment is stable and understood, then rational purposefulness (e.g., goals) will probably work quite well. But we should

*Howard Aldrich, personal communication, 11 July 1979.

not let unique short-term conditions such as this mislead us into think-ing that the goal model leads to long-term selection, or explains the process. Given the allogenic component, there is, strictly speaking, no reason to include the qualifier term *effective*, since by definition ineffec-tive organizations do not exist—just as in biological ecology all biota that have survived are assumed to be fit. But, even in biology there are plants and animals "on the way out," and among organizations it appears to take some time before ineffective organizations actually fail and disappear from the scene. So, to emphasize the idea that scientific theory and propositions—and especially classification—should be focused only on effective organizations, the definition retains the term *effective*. Having said this, I do not mean to imply that one cannot learn about effective organizations by studying ineffective ones. Not at all. It just means that we should not accumulate knowledge about surviving organizations by inadvertently studying ones that are about to fail, unless this knowledge is pegged to the prior environment of the failing population when it was in fact surviving. This topic will be brought up again in chapter 6.

The advantage of the asymptotic model is that organizational scien-tists need not reject autogenic forces in order to pursue systematics and evolutionary theories of how different kinds of organizations came into being. They can retain subjective methodology as a way of learning about how organizational variations are created. They do not have to abandon human intentionality and self-determination. Alternatively they may *choose* to treat sources of organizational behavior as essen-tially blind, as observed from the outside. Thus the pursuit of system-atics need not necessarily force ideological or methodological choices. But organizational scientists *do* have to accept the idea that environ-ments impose very real constraints on organizations, whether or not their members accurately perceive, enact, or cope with them. The view here is that organization theory in general and systematics in particular will be on a much stronger footing if organizational scientists move rapidly toward acceptance of a model of organizational variation, such as the asymptotic model, which offers a way to conceptualize autogenic and allogenic forces in one overall framework. Such a model, as is the asymptotic model, should be isomorphic with the ideal model of sources of organizational variation presented in this chapter.

One final comment is that you should note that the asymptotic model is cast in terms of how an individual organization uses autogenic sources to move toward the survival path. In reality all organizations in a population are doing this. In chapter 7 it will be seen that organizations pick up ideas or variations from other organizations or produce them themselves. These ideas are distributed throughout the population via an intercommunication process that explains how a population organizational form comes into existence. Individual organizations contribute to the population form (that is, other organizations in the population pick up) those variations which aid population selection and they take from the population form those variations which aid individual organizational selection.

4.4 SUMMARY

Since systematics has been a prerequisite to the development of most modern sciences, this chapter began by trying to answer why systematics has been so slow to develop in organizational science. I first looked at the aspirations of those contributing to the subject, the classical management theorists and academically trained sociologists and social psychologists. It seems that their interest in broad generalization for practical application and academic respectability was the main factor leading them to place low priority on looking at organizational differences. Next I looked to many of the traditional models and theories about sources of variation or activity in organizations. Since these models, termed *autogenic*, were all based on the reductionist principle of enquiry, I found that they all steered thinking away from organizational differences, too. I concluded that two fundamental autogenic sources of variation in organizations exist: "authorized-prepensive" (Alpha) sources and "systemic-spontaneous" (Sigma) sources. Not wanting to reject autogenic forces out of hand, I gave an autogenic definition of organizations: Organizations are purposeful systems containing one or more conditionally autonomous purposeful subsystems. In opposition to the traditional exclusive focus on autogenic models, recently suggested *allogenic* models were discussed, all of which take a population approach to theorizing about organizations. In this view, effective organizations are defined as "boundary-maintaining activity systems having input/output resource ratios fostering survival in environments imposing particular constraints." In the pure allogenic view, internal organizational behavior is viewed as blind in consequence, and environments are seen as optimizing by selecting only organizational populations of a certain form for survival. I concluded by arguing that systematics and organization theory would be on a stronger theoretical footing if both autogenic and allogenic perspectives were synthesized. An *asymptotic* model was suggested where environmental constraints define survival paths, and organizations, via autogenic sources of variation, have the choice of carving out an adaptive niche and an organizational form which moves them toward the survival path. Populations composed of organizations of similar form which are effective in niche formation will be selected for survival by the prevailing ecological forces in the environment. In this view *effective organizations are defined as myopically purposeful activity systems containing one or more conditionally autonomous myopically purposeful subsystems having input-output resource ratios fostering survival in environments imposing particular constraints.*

5 THE PROTOSYSTEM

Organizational sociologists are quite fortunate in having environments of almost endless variation and complexity to study. The
problem is not one of finding variation, but of conceptualizing it.
[Aldrich 1979, p. 57]

In chapter 3 I pointed out that biological systematists holding to the
essentialist, empiricist, or evolutionist theories of classification posited a natural system comprised of diverse groupings of plants and
animals. An organizational equivalent was conceptualized as the
PROTOSYSTEM. Belief in the existence of the protosystem is a necessary prerequisite to belief in one of the above theories of classification.

Support for the existence of the protosystem comes via three logics:
First, is there variation in organizational environments? Campbell
noted that environmental variation, whether "heterogeneous, haphazard, 'blind,' 'chance,' [or] 'random,' " (1969, p. 73) was one of three
essential elements in evolutionary theory. Aldrich said, "Only when

variation in the environment exists, in time and space, are external conditions relevant to organizational change" (1979, p. 57). Second, do environments have an effect on organizational form? Without evidence of this effect there would be no reason to believe that organizational forms would ever become isomorphic with environments. And third, what common sense and scientific evidence is there that organizations really are different? These items are discussed in turn.

5.1 ENVIRONMENTAL VARIATION

In the last few years it has become commonplace for organization theory textbooks to include chapters about environments. Typically these discussions present environments in terms of nominal categories such as technology, culture, legal constraints, and so forth, and in terms of dimensions such as certainty-uncertainty. Usually one of the dimensions, such as stability-instability or turbulence, addresses the problem of environmental variation, but little more than that is said. In fact, variation is largely assumed and mostly taken for granted. As Aldrich said in the opening quote, "the problem is not one of finding variation, but of conceptualizing it."

5.1.1 A Concept of Organizational Environments

Recall from chapter 4 that an organizational environment was defined as that set of external forces or characteristics that impose constraints on an individual organization or a population of organizations, and which are outside its ability to influence or manipulate. Environments may be viewed as having two components, CLIMATE and TEXTURE. A definition of *climate* from Webster's dictionary is: "the prevailing temper of environmental conditions characterizing a group or period." A definition of *texture* is: "something composed of closely interwoven elements."

Climatic conditions offer a general *nonpurposeful* milieu surrounding the texture of all organizations in a particular environment. These conditions are nonpurposeful or not choiceful in that, for example, a technological or cultural condition cannot *decide* to do something for or against a particular organization. The condition, however, may be affected by an entity—for example, a church organization—that could act to make a cultural norm more pointedly relevant for a particular organization. Climatic conditions are inanimate constraints against which organizations bump. They are equivalent to factors such as rainfall, temperature, soil content and condition, bodies of water, and mountains in the biological world. My use of the term is broader than what we usually think of as climate.

Each organization is not only affected by the climatic conditions but is also embedded in a texture of causal relations composed of other (myopically) *purposeful* entities (mainly organizations but also people as individuals) and their interrelations. These are equivalent to living organisms in the biological world. It is with these entities that ecological networks and communities are formed, territorial battles fought, symbiotic relations formed, or predation pursued and avoided. Textural elements are much more subject to manipulation than are climatic ones. Niches are much more part of the adaptive defense against texture than against climate, especially as the competition for resources in a given environment becomes more severe. Ultimately, however, all members of the textural ecology are adapting and forming niches to mitigate the effects of climatic elements. Textural entities can and do *act* to strengthen or weaken the effect of climatic conditions in general, or they may act to impose their own preferences on a particular organization. Organizational niches are carved out in aid of adaptation to both textural and climatic elements.

One of the better, albeit brief, descriptions of substantive climatic conditions is given by Hall (1977, pp. 304–311). They are:

Technological

Legal

Political

Economic

Demographic

Ecological

Cultural

Some additional conditions were noted by Sethi (1970, pp. 75–86):

Physical

Social

Psychological

International

This is probably not yet a complete set of possible climatic conditions. Further, even though there is some discussion in each of the sources cited, it is quite likely that the conditions could each be further elaborated into a set of attribute dimensions. For example, technological conditions could be given attribute dimensions such as stable-dynamic, certain-uncertain, simple-complex, and so forth. Riesman (1950) described the psychological condition in terms of the attribute *inner-other directed*. Finally, climatic conditions may also be described in terms of nonsubstantive attribute dimensions directly, as has been done by Thompson (1967, p. 69), citing others before him, and more recently by Khandwalla (1977, pp. 333–341) and Aldrich (1979, pp. 63–70).

From Khandwalla:

Turbulence (dynamic, unpredictable, fluctuating)

Hostility (risky, stressful, dominating)

Diversity (heterogeneity)

Technical Complexity (high technical sophistication)

Restrictiveness (many constraints)

From Aldrich:

Resource capacity (rich-lean)

Homogeneity-heterogeneity (diversity)

Stability-instability (turbulence in Khandwalla's terms)

Resource concentration-dispersion

Domain consensus-dissensus (territorial legitimacy)

Turbulence (disturbance via increasing rate of interconnection)

There is some overlap between the Khandwalla and Aldrich lists. It could be added that a dynamic or changing environment is not necessarily an uncertain one; hence Khandwalla's concept of turbulence should be broken down. Further, textural complexity is not necessarily the same as uncertainty or heterogeneity.

Recently Miles (1980, p. 222), drawing on Jurkovich (1974), conceptualized environments as composed of:

Statics: complexity; routineness; interconnectedness; remoteness.

Dynamics: change rate; unpredictability of change.

Receptivity: resource scarcity; output receptiveness; domain choice; flexibility.

Miles (1980, p. 221) also listed attribute dimensions used by several other authors, most of which are accounted for in the foregoing conceptual framework. In any event it can be seen that there are many more environmental attributes than are typically used in present-day empirical studies. While it may be good to have even more attributes, it would be even better to begin using those already recognized as important.

Even after more than fifteen years, no one has improved on the way Emery and Trist (1965) went about describing the causal texture surrounding organizations. They started with the proposition that understanding organizational behavior required a prerequisite understanding of four kinds of interdependencies: (1) interdependencies among the several components of an organization which cause changes within it; (2) interdependencies emanating from the environment which cause changes in an organization; (3) interdependencies emanating from an organization which cause changes in its environment; and (4) interdependencies among the many components of the environment which cause the components of the environment to become related to each other. The causal texture of the environment consists of the fourth kind of interdependencies.

Emery and Trist went on to identify four ideal types or states of causal texture. They began with a limiting case and then described three other states that, in rank order, became increasingly important for managers to understand, know about, and plan for because the states were increasingly dynamic and uncertain. They were as follows:

Type I: *Placid-Randomized.* This is the limiting case where there is no interdependency among the various components of the environment. Economists have referred to this state as *perfect competition.* The behavior of one component appears totally independent of the behavior of all other components. Organizations learn to survive in this kind of environment only by trial and error. The best strategy is the tactic of dealing as best as one can on a strictly local basis. An example of this kind of environment is the one facing a peasant village. The chief and other villagers go about their daily routine, more or less recognizing that birth rates, rains, pestilence, and marauding hordes of barbarians take place independently of one another. McWhinney (1968) argued that decisions in this type of environment take place under conditions of certainty; they are arbitrary and by fiat since the strategy behind them is unrelated to what happens in the environment. Rules, regulations, myths, and beliefs are the bases of decisions, rather than knowledge about the environment and its components. Aldrich (1979, p. 72) suggested that Type I environments are "pure fantasy" since complex organizations would not likely arise in such an environment. But large organizations do not face uniform environments (Mintzberg 1979, p. 282). For example, one subenvironment a large department store faces consists of individuals working more or less as a "cottage industry" supplying art and craft objects to the store. The art and craft suppliers come and go independently, and are in perfect competition with each other. The store can treat the subenvironment as placid-randomized.

Type II: *Placid-Clustered.* This environment is still relatively simple and quite stable, but components of the environment begin to fall together in certain ways. It is composed of independent clusters, each of which is composed of interdependent components. Some of the components within a cluster may be attractive to an organization, others quite unattractive, and others very definitely hostile. Economists refer to this state as *imperfect competition.* McWhinney (1968) said that decisions in this state took place under conditions of risk. Upon encountering one component of a cluster, which may be attractive, an organization might find that this engagement leads to other contacts with members of the cluster which are not so attractive. Here strategy pays off over local tactics. It pays to learn as much as possible about each cluster. Aldrich (1979, p. 72) noted that memory of past experience becomes important. It could be that pursuing a short-term or obvious goal may lead to an unattractive long-term situation of being unable to reach less obvious but more important goals; or avoiding what appears to be an unattractive relationship might mean foregoing very rewarding engagements further along in time. An example here is a West Coast department store that decides to buy high quality furniture from a unionized East Coast supplier, and then finds that it is subject to problems caused by strikes by the furniture and railroad unions, fuel shortages, missed delivery schedules, and so forth. The local tactic of beating out other West Coast stores by selling prestigious Eastern furniture in this case turns out to have been questionable strategy because of all the other interdependent elements of the cluster. In a placid-clustered environment, organizations tend to grow in size, develop a distinctive competence, become more hierarchical, and have more centralized control and coordination.

Type III: *Disturbed-Reactive.* This environment is definitely more complex, dynamic, and uncertain than the previous two kinds. It builds on the clustering in the placid-clustered environment. In this case not only are there clusters in the environment which an organization has to contend with, but the focal organization itself is also a member of a cluster of similar, directly competing organizations. The several organizations in the cluster have the same goals and usually the same methods of reaching them. Each knows that it is not the only component aiming at a certain objective. Each knows that it could lose if a competitor gets there first. Consequently an organization cannot simply learn about the components of the cluster in its environment and act accordingly; it has to anticipate what a competitor is likely to do and counteract that activity. The best analogy here is a chess game. Each opponent has to ferret out the other's strategy, anticipate his or her several upcoming tactical moves, move to avoid being victimized by those moves, and if possible turn the tables and do in the competitor. Survival depends on developing operations consisting of a program of strategic and tactical moves designed to mislead and eventually overcome the opponent. It follows that game theory is the best approach to operating in a disturbed-reactive environment.

Since the uncertainties are so high (because the chain of possible actions and reactions can never be fully worked out), there is a pronounced tendency for organizations in this environment to collude, to agree in advance to certain prices or practices so that fierce competition is lessened. Economists refer to this kind of environment as *oligopolistic*. McWhinney (1968) pointed out that decision making in this environment takes place under conditions of uncertainty. A common example of organizations operating in such an environment is a price war between service stations on opposing corners of an intersection. In the war each one responds to the other by lowering the price. More elaborate approaches could include giveaways such as stamps, glass tumblers, and the like. Eventually the operators collude by getting together and agreeing to a price each can live with, often to the detriment of the customer. In general the most successful strategy is to do whatever it takes to reduce competition, such as merging with the competitors, running them out of business, lobbying for equally applicable laws, or colluding.

Type IV: *Turbulent Field*. This environment, like the disturbed-reactive environment, is dynamic and uncertain, even more so in fact. In the disturbed-reactive environment the dynamism stems from the action-reaction cycling of competing components. In the turbulent field, the dynamism arises outside the immediate sphere of interacting components and is beyond their power to damp down. Emery and Trist noted three sources of change: (1) Normal, but increasingly interdependent relations that at some point are so strong as to give rise to autochthonous processes; these events, for example, could be set in motion by responses to competition in the disturbed-reactive environment which are so pronounced as to cause the introduction of another reaction from a heretofore uninterested component, such as a government antitrust investigation brought about by flagrant price-fixing. (2) Deepening interdependencies among components previously in independent clusters, such as the increasing government regulation of the private sector, increasing interest in business activities by political groups such as the environmentalists and minority groups, or the decision of the Arab states in 1974 to take economic action in what was previously defined as a political altercation between Israel and Egypt. (3) The increasing background of change created by the growing emphasis on research and development activities, which has become a constant factor in modern environments. The upshot of all this is that in a turbulent field organizations may find that their actions lead to reactions from sectors they never had to consider before. Worse, they can find themselves embroiled in environmental dynamics totally independent of their own activities, totally unpredictable, and totally beyond their control. They are standing still and all of a sudden the environmental "ground" begins to move.

Several additional comments need to be made about the Emery and Trist concept of texture. First, all textures are ecological communities existing in climates of a particular character. Second, Emery and Trist treated organizations as individual isolates except in Type III. It is more likely that populations have always existed, meaning that Type III communities have always existed. Probably managers and academics have simply failed to see the prevailing disturbed reactive conditions. What we really have are two Type III environments, one under r type* conditions and one under K type† (see Levins 1968 and Hannan and Freeman 1977 for explication of r and K type situations). Thus:

> Beta texture consists of disturbed-reactive population dynamics of the r type occurring in new placid-randomized uncompetitive environments. The environment is there, but not an issue, though population dynamics exist.

> Zeta texture consists of more pronounced disturbed-reactive population dynamics of the K type occurring in an environment made much more competitive because of a larger population or a more intensely competitive one and because of larger entities or groupings of entities, often other organizational populations, making up the ecological community.

---

*r conditions are new environments containing plentiful resources and fostering r SPECIALIST organizations that are especially adapted to these conditions.

†K conditions are mature environments with scarce resources and favoring K SPECIALIST organizations that are especially adapted to competitive conditions.

A typology of organizational environments could be elaborated much further, though there is the possibility that an essentialist classification of environments might never fit reality. In my view it is probably better to avoid typologies in deference to attribute dimensions of texture such as formalization, intensity, reciprocity, and standardization (Aldrich 1979, pp. 273–278). For additional dimensions see Hall et al. (1977); Stern (1979); and Provan, Beyer, and Krytbosch (1980).

So far the difference between climatic conditions and texture has been only mildly appreciated in the literature. Furthermore there has been only sporadic development of concepts of organizational environments over the years. A slow accumulation of conditional elements has occurred but not a systematic or operational development of their attribute dimensions, though enough is known about each of the conditions mentioned earlier that an elaboration of their attributes would not be difficult. And there has been little improvement in concepts of texture over the one suggested by Emery and Trist. In view of the discussion about classification theories in chapter 3, a possible alternative might be to work toward empirically derived classes of environments. This might work for climate, since it more broadly encompasses many populations—we probably would find organizational climates of several types just as biologists have found alpine, desert, tropic, or oceanic climates. I am not saying there will be an organizational "alpine" climate—only that empirical studies could show several types of climates. This assumes that we started with a broad, well-conceived theory suggesting what to look for and studied a full range of organizational populations. Empirical studies of texture, I think, only make sense if focused on specific organizational taxa (see chapters 7 and 9).

5.1.2 Variation

Given that an organizational niche has been defined as a dynamic concept, it is clear that niches will differ. This is so because a niche is created by organizational populations as they adapt to environmental climate, and the climatic conditions impinging upon organizations may vary in the following ways. Conditions:

May vary in number; some conditions may not be relevant, or less relevant.

May vary in nature; the number might be the same but the combination might differ and the interaction effects among the conditions might vary as well.

May vary in strength or force over time.

May vary in stability and uncertainty.

The entities of texture:

May vary in number and in kind.

May vary in strength and complexity of interconnectedness among one another.

May vary in interconnectedness with the organizational members of focal populations.

May vary over time for a single population and across populations.

May vary in heterogeneity.

Given the total number of conditions and textural entities facing organizations, coupled with the possibility of variation in the conditions and entities, it seems highly unlikely that organizational populations would face the same environment over a period of time. It seems impossible that organizations would all face the same environment at the same time.

Another, less abstract, view of environmental diversity is offered by Aguilar (1967). He reported an empirical study of the kinds of environments managers think they face which found that there are four kinds: technical, economic, political, and social. The diversity of each kind is quite pronounced over the full range of organizations.

Clearly business organizations face different technical environments. What could be more different than the physical characteristics and resulting technologies of organizations running steel mills, railroads, coal mines, retail stores, law firms, and schools, to name but a few? Assembly lines entail the sequencing of multiple operations. The electronics industry faces rapid obsolescence of both ideas and technical competence. Some technologies are dangerous, some are not, and so on. The suppliers and supplies are vastly different, as are the purchasers.

Economic environments are similarly diverse. Some of them are highly competitive, some are not. Some national economies are relatively stable, some are not. Some industry economies are cyclical and uncertain, others are relatively stable and certain. Planned economies present problems different from capitalistic or "free enterprise" economies. Growing economies are different from stagnating ones and industrialized, capital-intensive economies are different from underdeveloped, capital-poor ones. What could be more different than the economies of Saudi Arabia and Bangladesh, even though they are both Muslim religious states?

At this time most managers emphasize technical and economic diversity, according to Aguilar (1967), but the political and social environments around the world are no less different. Tannenbaum et al. (1974) have shown that the management competence, skills, and knowledge by which organizations maintain control over their employees change depending on the political system of the country they are in. Organizations whose employee unions have considerable political power must operate differently than those who do not have unions. Organizations working with public employee unions seem to face different problems than those in the private sector. Business managers are very conscious of different political environments caused by the election of liberal or conservative public officials. The increased political power of consumer and environmental-protection groups has meant changes for business people.

Learning to operate within the sensibilities of differing cultures around the world has not been easy for the managers of organizations. This has been a target of understanding for many so-called cross-cultural studies, such as those reprinted by Graham and Roberts (1972). Standards of morality, such as attitudes toward bribes, differ around the world. Attitudes toward work, authority, savings and investment, the ability to trust nonfamily employees, punctuality, willingness to delegate, and so on, have all been found to differ from one social system and culture to another (Hoselitz and Moore 1960; Kerr et al. 1960). For a recent review of different environments in Sweden, Yugoslavia, and Israel see Miles (1980, pp. 390–408).

5.1.3 The Evolution of Environments

Physical environments that are closed off from energy sources are entropic, meaning that they become less differentiated and less energized as time passes; they become more homogeneous. The geographical environment surrounding biological organisms is not closed off from extraneous energy sources. During the 3.3 billion or so years (Dobzhansky et al. 1977) of biological evolution the geographical environment has cycled through many stages of change: the movement of continents via plate tectonics, the creation and leveling of mountains, the creation and filling in of lakes and seas, changes in ambient moisture and temperature, the growth and decline of predators, and the growth and decline of plants and animals as sources of nourishment. The interaction and repetition of these dynamics in the physical environment stimulated the speciation process (discussed in section 6.1.2), in which part of a species cut off from the main group evolves into a new species. There is no particular reason to believe that the physical environment "progressed" toward increased complexity and differentiation—it just changed a lot, and each change fostered speciation. Species became greater in number and more diverse as new forms successfully adapted to changed conditions.

While Emery and Trist placed their four textural states in an ordered relationship, Terreberry (1968) went further by suggesting that there was a textural evolution from Type I to Type IV. The basic mechanism fostering the evolution was the steady growth in the number of components making up the environment and the growth of interdependencies among them. Environmental diversity is a function of the number of interdependencies and their connectivity or strength. Note that the emphasis is on interdependencies, not on the number of components. The latter do not have an effect unless they are interdependent with the organization and among themselves. And the stronger the interdependencies, which is to say the greater the causal flow across the interdependencies, the more effect the interdependencies will have.

The effect of interdependencies in producing other characteristics of an environmental texture can now be understood. Textures become more differentiated as the number of components increases and as the components acquire distinctive competencies and specialized characteristics. They become more complex as the more differentiated components begin to have interactions with one another. As the number of components with similar distinctive competencies increases, the competition among them also increases. As competitors increase, the texture shifts from placid-clustered to a disturbed-reactive state. As the interdependencies among clusters and changes in technology increase, the texture moves into the turbulent-field state. Finally, increasing complexity coupled with increased dynamics leads to increased uncertainty.

As organizations become more differentiated internally they may also come to face more than one kind of texture. For example, a department store operates in a placid-randomized texture when dealing with a host of craft artisans who work individually, who are in perfect competition one with another, who have no interdependencies with each other, and who are powerless relative to the store. The store operates in a placid-clustered texture when it decides to order furniture from a distant large supplier; the prestigious furniture is coupled with possible union problems, interstate transportation problems, pressure to buy locally, and so forth. The store operates in a disturbed-reactive texture when it acts to counteract the promotional and purchasing activities of local competitors, who in turn can be expected to counteract what it does. Finally, the store operates in a turbulent field when it discovers that its ability to sell cotton, wool, or synthetic fabrics is affected by governmental changes, form, energy, export and import policies, environmental protection activities, and antipollution requirements around the world. The proportion of the store's activity in one or another texture undoubtedly changes over time, partly because of what it can do but also because of what other components of its texture are doing. I do not think Terreberry's idea of textural evolution has been satisfactorily tested empirically. In chapter 8 I take the position that evaluative or judgmental "progress" views of evolution are best avoided. They are not necessary and are problematic or easily debatable if used. In evolution, species become better adapted to specific environments. That is all. I also take the view that the climate part of organizational environments also does not evolve. It changes a lot, as does the physical environment of organisms, but there is little solid evidence, except of an evaluative judgmental type from a parochial perspective, that organizational climate progresses toward increased order, perfection, civilization, and so forth. The only exception I can see at this time is that ecological communities or environmental textures of which organizational populations are a part do seem to be evolving toward increasing complexity and interdependency.

It has been established that organizational environments vary. This is a necessary condition for the emergence of a protosystem. But it is not sufficient. A second condition is the presence of processes of adaptation in organizations. Do they respond to environmental variation?

5.2 ENVIRONMENTAL IMPACT ON ORGANIZATIONS

Organizational science is not very far along toward showing with considerable explicitness just how environments affect organizational form, either at a theoretical level or empirically. This subject of inquiry seems especially bogged down in theoretical and operational research difficulties. I am going to ignore the considerable literature on the effects of size and technology, what Jackson and Morgan (1978) said were "imperatives." The findings are equivocal and there is disagreement on the locus of the two variables—some theorists see them as contextual or part of the environment and some see them as part of organizations. My own view is that they are largely spurious and unnecessary causal variables—the true "causes" being autogenic or allogenic forces, which, as they respectively create variations or select organizational forms, also happen to affect technology and size. My attention will focus on the effects of environment on structure, the latter being one kind of operational definition of organizational form.

5.2.1 Specialization

One of the better-established theoretical views of how environments affect organizations is the model suggested by Perrow (1970). Since it was discussed in chapter 4 it will not be reviewed here. Perrow's model has influenced several recent investigations (Hage and Aiken 1969; Magnusen 1970; Grimes, Klein, and Shull 1972). Lynch (1974) pointed out that the previous studies had difficulties because of the lack of a suitable operational measure of Perrow's concept of technology. Though not able to study all of the relations shown in Perrow's model, Lynch was able to show that search strategies were related to the kind of problem (raw materials) posed by the environment. Previously, Hage and Aiken (1969) had reported that social welfare and health organizations were more centralized and formalized when routine technology prevailed, and Grimes, Klein, and Shull (1972) had found that certain managerial styles and techniques seemed to be more useful with certain technologies. These studies, though hardly definitive, give some empirical support to the idea that aspects of organizational form are isomorphic with the environment. But are we really looking for isomorphism?

Hannan and Freeman (1977) attributed the best-developed previous argument in support of the isomorphism principle to Hawley (1968), who held that in each distinguishable environmental configuration only that organizational form optimally adapted to the constraints of that configuration would appear. The idea that there is only one optimal form of organization for a particular environmental configuration is neither compatible with modern evolutionary theory—in biology or elsewhere (if there is another discipline with a modern evolutionary theory)—nor is it one that I accept. As discussed in chapter 8, the current idea is not one of "survival of the fittest" but rather of the "tolerably fit." Thus there may be several tolerably fit forms for a particular climate or texture. And if one outlasts the others, this does not mean it is optimal—only that it survived.

Hannan and Freeman expanded Hawley's views in focusing on competition and different environmental textures (they used the phrase "niche theory"). Winning the battle for resources determines which form survives. Under competitive conditions specialization is a likely outcome. Hannan and Freeman write of generalists and specialists, and I agree that both kinds exist. I would add, however, that for the discussion below, generalists are also a kind of specialization in that the form is more competitive in certain circumstances.

I see specialization as the principal means by which organizational form, and thus the protosystem, emerges. Anytime it can be shown that there are advantages for organizations to specialize and develop a distinctive competence for turning out a product or service, the seeds of a protosystem are sown. The advantages of specialization may be most clearly seen in regard to the technological climate condition. Given the two objectives of coping with any, but especially a sophisticated technology, and economies of scale, forces are set in motion for organizations respectively to reward their employees for focusing their knowledge and ability on a particular technology and to use their financial resources to acquire the technical plant capable of achieving economies of scale. Technical inventions, especially major ones, seem to be discontinuous; thus there are clear gaps between the technology of, for example, nuclear, hydroelectric, and steam power generation, or between water, rail, and air transportation technologies. Given technological gaps and the forces toward technological specialization and economies of scale, it is easy to see why there are organizational forms with gaps or discontinuities among them. Specialized technological responses, according to the Perrow model, lead to specialized organizational forms. Specialization may also take place in response to other climatic conditions, such as legal, cultural, political, and economic. Environmental texture may also act to encourage specialization. Emery and Trist (1965) noted that organizations tended to specialize as the texture changed from placid-randomized to placid-clustered.

This idea will not be developed any further here, but in chapter 7 it will be seen that technological differences are the the basis of the species concept proposed in that chapter.

5.2.2 Impact via Alpha Sources

In terms of the autogenic models, as noted in chapter 4, there are two sources of organizational variation: Alpha (Authorized-Prepensive) and Sigma (Systemic-Spontaneous). Organizations have been shown to respond to their environments through each of these processes of variation. For Alpha sources, one of the most enduring studies was Selznick's (1949) book about the Tennessee Valley Authority. He showed that the organization adapted to the values and pressures from its environment through a process he termed *cooptation*. Continuing the line of analysis started by Selznick, Sills (1957), in his study of voluntary organizations such as the National Foundation for Infantile Paralysis, noted how the organization adopted new goals and methods after the threat of polio was eradicated. The Y.M.C.A. has been the subject of two studies of organizational adaptation (Pence 1939; Zald 1970). Both were able to show how forces in the environment led to changes in the national organization (Pence) and in a particular local organization (Zald). All of these studies focused on adaptation through changes in organizational goals. Thompson and McEwen (1958) provided a conceptual analysis of how environments affect organizational goals through competition and three kinds of cooperation: bargaining, cooptation, and coalition.

Empirical support for the Thompson and McEwen view has recently been reviewed in some detail by Pfeffer and Salancik (1978, pp. 113–187) and need not be repeated here. Very briefly, they showed that organizations respond autogenically to environmental conditions and textures by merging, diversifying, growing in size, developing norms of cooperation (often leading to joint ventures), cooptation via interlocking boards of directors, forming coalitions, associations, and cartels, and finally through various means of enhancing legitimacy via public relations activities and the regulatory and licensing processes. Their entire book is a lesson in how Alpha variations can be mobilized to deal with the environment.

Regarding Alpha sources of variation, adaptation takes place when managers perceive changes in the environment surrounding them. Their perceptions of change lead them to decide to adjust the structure and processes of the organization to adapt to the new environment. In this view, an organization adapts because its managers *decide* to do so. *They* decide that the new environment is significantly different from the old one; *they* decide what changes in technology and workflow are needed; and *they* decide what kinds of structures and what changes in staffing, directing, or controlling are necessary to cope with the new environment. Alpha variations are produced when managers perceive changes, managers think about them, managers decide what to do, and managers implement the decisions. The employees, and the social system they are caught up in, are as putty in the hands of the managers, to be molded as the latter see fit.

For example, the top managers of a large organization, perhaps with the help of a planning group, might observe that the environment they operate in has become more diverse, as indicated by demands for a more differentiated set of services. They then decide to respond to the increased diversity through service diversification. If some new services are aimed at a relatively uncertain sector of the environment, or one characterized by frequent change, the managers might differentiate further the part of the organization producing these services by giving it a more organic form, hiring employees with higher tolerances for ambiguity and more flexible leadership styles, and so forth. The point is that in producing Alpha variations the managers consciously decide what to do or how to adapt.

5.2.3 Impact via Sigma Sources

Regarding Sigma sources, the classic works by Roethlisberger and Dixon (1939) and Homans (1950) gave early indication of how organizational social systems responded to their environments. The effects of the employees' social system on an organization were later described by Blau in his classic study of the dynamics of bureaucracy (1963). He found that while there were some rational system pressures leading to change in designated objectives, there were many other changes brought about by the interaction of employees with their clients and among themselves. He showed how, after competitiveness among employees had begun to interfere with service to the clients, one group of employees devised methods of working which discouraged competitiveness. He described many instances where unintended consequences of the formal objectives led to dysfunctional behavior that was in turn mitigated by adaptations on the part of the employees which led to changes in the formal system.

Besides Blau, studies by Trist and Bamforth (1951), Gouldner (1954), Sayles (1958), Dalton (1959), and Crozier (1964), among others, further established how organizations are affected by their environments, especially as these effects impinge on the organization via the social systems within them.

One of the best ways for understanding how organizations are influenced by Sigma variations is to use one of the oldest conceptual frameworks, that of Homans (1950). Since it is well known, it only needs a brief description here. Social behavior, according to Homans, may be understood in terms of three concepts: *activities*—the things people do, such as tighten bolts, sing, visit the coffee machine, leave for home, daydream, and so forth; *interactions*—the engagements people have with another person, such as verbal conversations, nonverbal communications, hitting, backslapping, or whatever; and *sentiments*—people's values and especially attitudes toward their activities, the people with whom they interact, rules and regulations, higher managers they only hear about, private enterprise, and the like. The activities, interactions, and sentiments are the basic ingredients from which social behavior emerges. People bring into the workplace what Homans called givens: their personality and needs; their education and skills; the sentiments they have about the organization, people, and life in general which were formed before they entered; their social status; and so forth.

Once in the workplace, the employees, with all of the givens, are arranged according to the physical layout of the technical system, its machines and assembly lines, and so forth. This arrangement in large part determines their activities and interactions. For example, work activities on an assembly line where workers sit close together, coupled with relative quiet, will foster interactions. Work activities where there is one worker per machine and the machines are noisy, such as in a printing and reproduction shop, will not foster interactions. The activities and especially the interactions lead to changes in sentiments. The sentiments in turn may lead to increased interaction if the employees like each other, or less interaction if they dislike each other. The interactions, coupled with needs such as needs for control, affiliation, membership, and achievement (Schutz 1958; McClelland et al. 1953), the need for a reference group, or the need to go beyond the formal system to accomplish formally assigned tasks (Schein, 1980), all lead to the formation of an informal organization, which is a naturally formed system. It is this informal system which is the source of Sigma variations, change, and adaptation. Informal organizations, especially when they are comprised of well-formed psychological groups (defined by Schein 1980), become able to make decisions, to be choiceful, or to exercise will. Thus they become purposeful (but myopically) in the same manner that organizations are myopically purposeful. They are able to change their goals and decide to deviate from the objectives assigned them by their managers. As a work unit they are able to decide to carry out the work slower, faster, or in an altered fashion.

The employees of an organization are often the first to sense changes in the environment. Their own needs may change and they, as an informal organization, may adapt to those changes. They may perceive that the inputs to the organization have changed, perhaps becoming increasingly variable or in short supply. Perhaps the employees discover ways to make the technology more efficient or less efficient and decide to do so. They may become aware of changes in the demand for their organization's outputs and respond to that. Because they can adapt and because they have considerable influence over their own behavior, members of the informal organization or natural system are able to influence what takes place in the organization. In this manner they have brought about organizational adaptation to the external environment independently and often despite the rational system of organization imposed by their managers. It should be noted, of course, that Alpha and Sigma variations are mutually causal.

The impact of environments on organizations may also be viewed from the allogenic or population perspective. As described in chapter 4, from this perspective organizations are seen to vary via autogenic sources of variation which may appear blind, and environments select certain organizational forms over others. The theory about how this works is not well developed, but Hannan and Freeman (1977), Brittain and Freeman (1980), Hannan (1980), Aldrich and Reiss (1976), and Aldrich (1979) seem furthest along, so the reader is referred to their work. Empirical support for the allogenic view is largely historical in nature and modest in quantity. While it would be most desirable to demonstrate environmental impact on organizations strictly in terms of the allogenic view, for the time being we have to look toward the autogenic view instead. This was done in this section, and the conclusion that environments *do* have an impact on organizations seems clearly warranted.

5.3 EVIDENCE OF A PROTOSYSTEM

There would appear to be two principal sources of evidence that organizations have adapted to environmental conditions through specialization and other structural configurations: (1) the observations that led many theoreticians to suggest typologies of organizations; and (2) the empirical findings of the contingency theorists. These will be dealt with in turn.

5.3.1 Observations Underlying Typologies

There are several well-known commonsense typologies of organizations which indicate specializations of one sort or another: agricultural/ industrial/service organizations; profit/not-for-profit/government organizations; American/European organizations; organizations in developed countries/organizations in underdeveloped countries; organizations handling operations/materials/information; and so forth. The *Handbook of Organizations* (March 1965) identified several institutions, each with its own specialization, such as unions, political parties, public bureaucracies, military organizations, hospitals, schools, prisons, and businesses. Within each of these institutional categories further differentiations are possible, especially among business organizations; the list could almost be endless. Each of these differentiations suggests a distinctive competence that presumably fits well with certain aspects of the environment in which the organization performs, though this hypothesis has not been tested as yet.

To bring them up once again, there are several typologies based on less commonsense dimensions. Etzioni (1975) saw that the environment legitimized three kinds of compliance: coercive, remunerative, and normative, and that organizations tended to specialize in one or another of the three. Blau and Scott (1962) noted that organizational environments contained four kinds of beneficiaries: owners, members, clients, and the public at large. Organizations specialized to focus in on the needs of one or another beneficiary. Parsons (1956) and Katz and Kahn (1978) saw the environment as demanding four basic functions from organizations: economic (production), integration (judicial, political), adaptation (R&D), and pattern maintenance (education). They noted that organizations tended to specialize in one or another of these functions. Perrow (1967) conceptualized the environment as offering organizations four kinds of inputs: uniform-analyzable, uniform-unanalyzable, nonuniform-analyzable, and nonuniform-unanalyzable. He noted further that their technologies, structures, and management practices tended to be specialized depending on what kind of input they had. Finally, Thompson (1967) pointed out that organizations specialized into three kinds of technology: long-linked (vertically integrated industries and assembly lines), mediating (banks and insurance companies), and intensive (hospitals, professional partnerships). Though he did not put it this way, the environment could be seen as sufficiently diversified to lead to such specialization.

None of these theoretical typologies was based on an empirical study where samples of organizations were actually drawn. Nevertheless, each theoretician was observing the general nature of organizations and their environments and drew his conclusions from this less formal kind of observation. In each case one has little difficulty finding examples of organizations that clearly fit each typology. There can be little doubt that each typology describes at least some portion of the range of organizational specialization.

5.3.2 Empirical Evidence

Based on a study of twenty firms, most in the electronics industry, Burns and Stalker (1961) discovered that management styles were specialized into what they termed *mechanistic* and *organic* structures. A mechanistic structure, suited to a stable environment, was defined as one where there was specialized differentiation; precise definitions of rights and obligations; hierarchic control, authority, and communication systems;

vertical communication; and behavior governed by instructions and decisions issued by superiors; and the like. An organic structure, suited to a changing environment, was defined as one where there was adjustment and redefinition of roles through communication with others; commitment to the total firm rather than to a specific task; ad hoc control and communications, depending on where the relevant expertise resides; horizontal rather than vertical communication; communications consisting of consultation and advice rather than instructions and decisions; and so forth. The authors made it clear that they saw management structure as a variable dependent on the state of the environment, in this case whether the environment is stable or changing.

One of the first large-scale empirical studies was initiated by Woodward (1965). She collected data from 100 industrial firms in the South Sussex area of England and subsequently was able to classify 92 of them into three classes: integral product systems (outputs could be counted); dimensional product systems (outputs could be measured by weight, capacity, or volume); and combined systems. The integral product systems were further subdivided into two main categories: unit and small-batch production, and large-batch and mass production. Ultimately eleven subcategories were used (see Woodward 1965, p. 39). Although Woodward did not inquire into the associated characteristics of the environment, one may reasonably presume that the organizations specialized because of advantages they saw in coping with forces emanating from their particular industrial habitat—specifically, kinds of product technology and pressure from competitors, labor, or government regulations. She went on to show that several organizational characteristics were associated with the different technological specializations, such as the span of control and the ratio of administrative to total personnel.

In 1967 Lawrence and Lorsch published the first study to directly link specifically measured environmental states with internal organizational structure. They studied six organizations in very dynamic environments and four in much more stable environments. The specific environmental attributes they measured were clarity of information, uncertainty of causal relationships, and time span of definitive feedback. These were combined into an index measuring environmental uncertainty. Very briefly, since the study is well known, they found that internal differentiation was directly affected by the kind of environment the organizations or their departments were in, with those in uncertain environments more differentiated than those in certain environments. Differentiation was defined broadly to include goal, time, structural, and interpersonal style differences. They also found that, when differentiated, the organizations or departments had to be properly integrated to function as a whole before they were effective performers.

In 1974 Lorsch and Morse published a study of organizations showing that differences in environmental uncertainty affected other organizational characteristics besides differentiation and integration. They studied four manufacturing plants and six research laboratories. Their measure of environmental uncertainty was an index comprised of time span of feedback, clarity of information about the task, and programmability of the task. They found that a high fit between employee predisposition, organizational structure, and kind of environment was associated with increased organizational effectiveness and an increased sense of competence felt by the employees. Organizations in uncertain environments had low structural formality and had employees with high integrative complexity and high tolerance for ambiguity, among other things; those in certain environments had just the opposite.

Khandwalla (1977, pp. 335-340), in his study of 109 Canadian firms, produced some specific evidence showing how various environmental conditions affect organizations. He found that as hostility increased, organizations moved from more customized to more standardized production operations and "human relations" approaches were deemphasized. As technical complexity increased, firms tended to increase reliance on management science methods. As environments become more restrictive, top management became more planning and optimization oriented. It can be seen that where such environmental conditions prevail over a period of time, organizations would slowly specialize in response to the conditions and appear different from those not facing similar conditions.

In a recent review of the research on environmental impacts, Mintzberg (1979, pp. 270-285) assembled a variety of empirical studies supporting the following propositions:

1. The more dynamic the environment, the more organic the structure.

2. The more complex the environment, the more decentralized the structure.

3. The more diversified the organization's markets, the greater the propensity to split it into market-based units [divisionalization] (given favorable economies of scale).

4. Extreme hostility in its environment drives any organization to centralize its structure temporarily.

5. Disparities in the environment encourage the organization to de-

centralize selectively to differentiated work constellations [organizations facing more than one type of environment will be composed of more than one type of structure].

There have been other studies (Dill 1958; Udy 1964; Simpson and Gulley 1962; Pugh et al. 1969) that also focused on the relation between organizational form and characteristics of the external environment, but they are not described at length here because they did not establish solid relationships. For example, the Dill study used a good set of environmental variables but the effects of these variables on the internal form of the organizations were left unclear. Udy used only institutionalized authority and rationality as measures of the institutional setting. Simpson and Gulley started with organizational goals that presumably reflected environmental demands, but they had no direct measures of the environment. Pugh et al. measured both environmental variables (history, charter, location, etc.) and internal work activity variables (workflow, control, leadership, etc.) but they did not show the ways in which the latter were affected by the external environment. Their findings, which were in the form of regression analyses, showed most of the variance in formal structure to be affected by the internal work activity variables, leaving unknown what effect the external environment had on structure or work activity. While they were not clear in establishing through empirical methods that organizational specializations followed from environmental pressures, these studies did support the idea of organizational specialization because they all presented typologies describing different forms of organizations.

Finally, the numerical taxonomic studies by Haas et al. (1966) and Goronzy (1969), while preliminary in nature and inconclusive in result, did indicate differences among organizations. Both studies used analytic methods previously demonstrated by biologists to produce demarcated classes. Haas et al.'s cluster analysis identified ten classes of organizations, with some large classes having up to three ranks of subdivisions. Goronzy found four different classes. Presumably different specializations are the root cause of these classes.

This review has touched on only a few of the more obvious studies. There are other studies, equally obvious in depicting organizational specialization and differences following four environmental conditions and texture, and many that are less obvious. The purpose of this subsection was to show that organizations are specialized and that these specializations follow from environmental pressures. The empirical data in support of this proposition are not extensive or especially strong, but it seems reasonable to conclude that a protosystem exists.

5.4 SUMMARY

An underlying assumption of modern theories of classification is the existence of an organizational *protosystem* that is a counterpart in meaning to what biological systematists have referred to as the *natural system*. There are two necessary conditions for the existence of a protosystem. First there has to be environmental variation. Environments were conceptualized in terms of *climatic conditions* such as technology, culture, political, legal and other conditions, and in terms of *causal texture*, the best view of which is still found in the four types suggested by Emery and Trist (1965): *placid-randomized, placid-clustered, disturbed-reactive*, and *turbulent field*. The evolution of texture is the result of changing levels of interdependency among entities in the environment. Second, environments have to affect organizational form. Distinctive competence based on technological specialization seems to be the most likely force creating groups or populations in the protosystem. Environmental impacts leading to specialization come about via both Alpha and Sigma sources of organizational variation. A review of some of the better-known studies supplied evidence that organizations clearly respond to environmental forces. Observations leading to typologies and other empirical studies showing organizational differences indicate that the assumption of a protosystem is warranted.

⑥ PREREQUISITES TO AN ORGANIZATIONAL SPECIES CONCEPT

Sir Skeptik did as he was told and eventually inherited the kingdom.
He and his queen, the Synthetic System, ruled long and wisely,
enjoying the approbation and acclaim of their peers and subjects.
[Stebbins 1969, p. 358]

In the population perspective the species is the basic unit of analysis. The terms *species* and *populations* are used interchangeably. Local populations, or *demes*, are potential species, the latter often composed of two or more demes. Species are the basic units of evolutionary theory. They are the basic building blocks of classification. In working up the hierarchy of classes there are three main questions: What are species? What local demes comprise a species? And how are species related to each other, which is also the question of how did they originate? It is symbolic that the two chapters devoted to species, 6 and 7, are the middle chapters of the book.

The SPECIES CONCEPT is the theoretical construct that biologists use as the central element in their theory of why one population of biota should be considered different from another. Since systematics is the science of diversity, the species concept becomes the pivotal concept in the field of biological systematics. A species concept is equally critical to the development of organizational systematics. One of the main difficulties with typological thinking to date in organizational science stems from a grossly inadequate species concept. *Given the fundamental, prerequisite role of systematics to a successful functional science of organizations, and given its pivotal status in systematics, the species concept emerges as the most important single concept in organizational science. Everything—the satisfactory definition of populations, the collecting of truly representative samples, the attainment of high levels of explained variance, and the generalization of findings to identifiable, existing, and therefore useful populations—depends on the development of an acceptable organizational species concept.*

Through custom or historical happenstance, the species rank has become the "waterline" category in the biological classification. The species is the highest-rank category of groupings of "real," "live," individual plants and animals. Above this category all classes are abstract groupings of reproductively isolated species. In terms of Mayr's (1969) biological species concept (discussed later), all the groupings below the species category are composed of individuals not fully reproductively isolated, in that if members of two different groups are brought together they are capable of interbreeding. Thus, for sexual biota, species groupings can be empirically tested by checking for interbreeding potential. No other category may be thus tested. Hence the unique waterline status of species, as illustrated in figure 6.1.

Higher categories of *groups*, each an abstract cluster.	$Rank_{10}$ $Rank_9$ $Rank_8$ $Rank_7$ $Rank_6$	

$Species_5$

	$Rank_4$ $Rank_3$ $Rank_2$ $Rank_1$	Lower categories of *individuals*, not well isolated from each other.

Figure 6.1. Illustration of the Waterline Status of the Species Category.

The organizational species category, however it is conceptualized and defined, may be expected to have a waterline status similar to that of biological species. Organizational species are composed of real, existing organizational forms that will be seen to share a common pool of elements of distinctive competence and specialization. The higher categories of organizational classification are abstract groupings of species—they do not exist as real units. Infraspecies categories are based on questionably isolated demes and more changeable characters.

The principal development of an organizational species concept is left to chapter 7. In the present chapter I discuss two prerequisite concerns: what can we learn from the biological literature about conceptual pitfalls, and what criteria might an effective species concept be expected to satisfy? In the course of this discussion I will assume that there is an evolutionary explanation to the origin of the protosystem, a topic I postpone discussing in depth until chapter 8. Second, before suggesting a new approach to a species concept, I review several existing typologies and classifications of organizations with the purpose of seeing how well they stand up to the criteria developed in the first part of the chapter.

6.1 PREREQUISITES TO A SPECIES CONCEPT

The purpose of this section is to set the stage for the development of an organizational species concept by looking to the biological species concept as a possible analog. I start by trying to uncover the concept and definition of species found most useful by biologists. It is a difficult task because even for biological systematists after all these years it is still a conceptual snake pit accompanied by much argument, disagreement, and change. My treatment will emphasize recent concerns rather than lengthy treatment of the many issues raised over the years. The anthology by Slobodchikoff (1976) offered a look at several of the classic papers but omitted a few more recent ones which are instructive. More importantly, Slobodchikoff ignored a major new concept of species as individuals rather than classes. Drawing from the biological experience, I derive some key conditions that an organizational species concept should meet to be successful in doing the following: identifying criteria useful in deciding when differences among organizations are worthy of formal classificatory recognition; explaining how and why organizations retain the same form over successive generations of employees; and explaining how and why organizations evolve into new forms over long periods of time.

6.1.1 Attributes of an Ideal Classification

Before discussing the parameters of a species concept we should find out what an effective concept should lead to. The end result is supposed to be a classification. Of course, some classifications are better than others, and therefore the attributes of an ideal classification are worth noting. It is highly unlikely that they would ever be found in practice, mainly because groupings of real objects are not always as neat and tidy as different systematists might like. Furthermore, what differences and similarities prevail are usually obscured by noisy data. For the moment, four aspects are recognized. Others will be mentioned in chapter 12.

First, an ideal classification needs *sharp discontinuities* among the objects being classified so that there can be no argument that they are different, and consequently are to be placed in different classes. The sharper these demarcations are, the easier it is for systematists to develop a classification scheme. The classification of biological objects has been much easier wherever there were gaps in the fossil record or clear gaps between the character configurations of various living species. If there are no gaps, classification is difficult and definition of the classes is arbitrary. The lack of sharp demarcations means many members of one class will be very much like members of an adjacent class. The more gaps in the protosystem, the easier an organizational classification will be.

Second, the ideal classification has *high levels of homogeneity* within classes, a condition closely coupled with the preference for discontinuity among classes. The higher the level of homogeneity within a class the more successful the classification will be because it will mean that the description of one member, or a sample of members, will apply to all members of that class. Furthermore, the greater the homogeneity the more likely scientific findings about one member, or a sample of members, will also apply to all members of that class. As was pointed out in section 2.3.1, the completion of the inductive-deductive cycle is facilitated when homogeneous populations can be defined. This condition is important to functional scientists because without homogeneous groupings they cannot pursue the inductive-deductive methods of their science.

Third, classification is to be preferred if it is composed of *groupings that are stable* over some length of time, and the longer the better. If the composition and meaning of the groupings change, the classification becomes outmoded. If the groupings change rapidly the classification will be outmoded so quickly there is no valid reason for a classification in the first place. In biology, species are stable over many generations of systematists so that the classification scheme can be refined continually with the knowledge that the objects being classified are mostly unchanging (White 1978, p. 14). Organizational forms undoubtedly speciate much faster on average than organisms, with some changing appreciably within a generation of scientists. But, as Hannan and Freeman (1977) and Behling (1980) have observed, the instability of organizations is highly overrated.

Fourth, an ideal classification scheme should have a way of showing or classifying objects that existed in the past which in some cases may have an *ancestral relationship to objects existing at present*. In other words, it should be able to show differences among objects over time as well as across all presently existing phenomena. This attribute is applicable only if the theory of classification is a phyletic one. The essentialist, nominalist, and empiricist theories of classification do not require this aspect as they do not attempt to explain the origin of the groupings. They focus only on the presently existing objects, requiring only that they be stable for some reasonable length of time. Because I have chosen to accept a combined evolutionist-phenetic theory of classification, ancestral relationship is a necessary attribute of an ideal classification.

These four ideal attributes suggest four conditions an effective species concept should meet, recognizing that the ideals may be impossible to reach in practice. But the closer the definition of a species concept is to meeting these ideals the better the classification will be.

Over the past four hundred years biologists have been searching for a species concept that initially met only the first three conditions but after Darwin the fourth condition began to be included. Several biological species concepts have been developed, some of which do not respond to the fourth criterion. None of the concepts meets all criteria. As in biology, all organizational systematists will want a concept responding to the first three criteria and some, including myself, will want to satisfy all four. As in biology, I expect we will have considerable difficulty finding a perfectly adequate concept. Despite the difficulties, an organizational species concept is a necessity.

6.1.2 The Species Concept in Biology

In the introduction to his collection of classic papers on the species concept in biology, Slobodchikoff said that "most biologists use *species concept* to refer to a theoretical construct of the role and limits of the species in biological theory, and *species definition* to refer to a rule that assigns groups of organisms to a species class" (1976, p. 1; his emphasis). Sokal (1973) said that the species problem hinged on two issues: for various ideological and historical reasons systematists *define* species differently, and there exist differences of opinion on the validity of extant explanations of the *genesis* of species, with some systematists, such as Sokal, taking the view that genesis ought to be left out of the species problem entirely. For most writers the argument is all mixed up into a general concern about the "species problem."

Between Slobodchikoff (1976, pp. 1–5) and Sokal (1973), six concepts were identified. Ghiselin (1974) introduced a seventh.

Typological species concept. This one is rooted in the essentialist theory of classification and Aristotelian logic. It is expected that a set of properties can be found to form monothetic groups, where all properties are shared by all members of a group.

Classical phenetic species concept. This concept is based on the morphological differences thought to be important in separating one species from another. It is phenetic because gaps in the phenotypes determine the boundaries, with phenetic similarity determining membership within classes. This one is, to all intents and purposes, in practice an essentialist concept, like the typological one.

Numerical phenetic species concept. This concept is based in the empiricist theory of classification, searches for polythetic rather than monothetic groupings, and is much more extensive in its selection of cases and characters. Like the concepts listed below, it emphasizes populations and variability.

Biological species concept. At present this is the orthodox view, drawing on the evolutionist theory of classification. Species are seen as forming: (1) a community of interbreeding organisms reproductively isolated from other species; (2) an ecological unit that interacts with other members of the ecological community; and (3) a genetic unit consisting of an intercommunicating gene pool (Mayr 1969, p. 26). The present classification scheme in biology is based on this concept.

Evolutionary species concept. This is the concept used by the cladists. This definition emphasizes the historical/temporal role of species (Simpson 1961) and accommodates the problem of asexual species clearly left out of the biological species concept. Drawing on Simpson (1961), Wiley defined species as "a single lineage of ancestral descendant populations of organisms which maintains its identity from other such lineages and which has its own evolutionary tendencies and historical fate" (1978, p. 18). As Wiley developed it, this concept also draws on the species-as-individuals notion of Ghiselin (1966, 1974), discussed more fully below.

Selection species concept. This concept draws on ecological selection forces as the means of determining species (Doyen and Slobodchikoff 1974; Slobodchikoff 1976). It holds that "a species is a system of genetically similar individuals maintained as a cohesive unit by a set of selection pressures that balance the disruptive forces imposed by environmental factors, mutation, or genetic recombination" (Slobodchikoff 1976, p. 4). This is a recent one and not really used to any appreciable extent by most systematists.

Reproductive competition species concept. Like the foregoing concept, this one emphasizes ecological factors. Ghiselin (1974, p. 538) defined species as "the most extensive units in the natural economy such that reproductive competition occurs among their parts." Members of a species are seen to compete for genetic resources which foster survival.

Several observers have noted that the problem arises because no single definition fits all aspects of the biological world. Sokal concluded: "I have already stated my support for the view that species and the process of speciation are highly complex and diverse phenomena and that no single theory or conceptual framework is likely to accommodate them all" (1973, p. 371). Crowson (1970) pointed out that different species concepts responded to different criteria or different forces thought to cause speciation: ecological, physiological, genetic, paleontological. The quote at the beginning of the chapter comes from a fairy tale written by Stebbins which illustrates his conclusion in favor of a synthetic system:

> The point which I would like to make is that there do not exist in nature groups of individuals which must be grouped in only one way as objective, uncontestable species. On the other hand, species are not purely subjective groupings, carved out of an amorphous welter of varying populations. What we have is an organized system of populations and groups of populations, which form an irregular variation pattern. This pattern is characterized by modes or clusters of similar variants, separated from each other by larger or smaller gaps of discontinuity. These gaps exist because various potential intermediate variants either have never been formed or have been unable to survive under existing conditions. . . . The best system for each group must be synthesized from the available data of all kinds, with due regard for the extent of agreement or divergence which this group displays from the norm. [1969, pp. 358–359]

Hull (1965a) observed some time ago that when it came to definition systematists were still stuck on the essentialist method. The clue that this is true, Hull contends, is given by Mayr's (1957) (and I could add Ross's more recent [1974]) conclusion that there is more than one general kind of species and that therefore more than one kind of species definition may be needed. "Disregarding all the talk about essences, what Aristotle was advocating in modern terms is definition by properties connected conjunctively which are severally necessary and jointly sufficient" (Hull 1965a, p. 50). More specifically, Hull distinguished between definite conjunctive and disjunctive definitions and indefinitely long disjunctive definitions. His analysis showed that definite definitions of either kind were inadequate to the task of clarifying the species problem. He proposed an indefinitely long disjunctive definition, as follows. Species are defined as populations that:

1. Consistently interbreed producing a reasonably large proportion of reasonably fertile offspring, or

2. consistently serially interbreed with synchronic populations producing a reasonably large proportion of reasonably fertile offspring, or

3. do not fulfill either of the first two conditions but have not diverged appreciably from a common ancestry that did fulfill one of them, or

4. do not fulfill any of the first three conditions because they do not apply but are analogous to populations that do fulfill at least one of the first three conditions.

Conditions 1 and 2 are based on interbreeding—the biological species concept—and conditions 3 and 4 are based on what Hull termed "morphological distance," which is the phenetic concept, numerical or nonnumerical. More elements could be added—in this sense it is indefinitely long. In a disjunctive definition, fulfilling *any one* of the conditions is sufficient, and fulfilling *at least one* is necessary.

Hull's suggestion of a disjunctive definition has not been picked up in the literature. None of the recent papers on the subject even cite Hull's paper (see the nine papers in Slobodchikoff 1976 published after Hull's paper; Sokal 1973; Ghiselin 1974; and Wiley 1978) let alone pursue the idea of a disjunctive definition. The essentialist conjunctive tradition is hard to change. In presenting his version of the evolutionary species concept (quoted earlier), Wiley (1978) had the conjunctive form in mind but could have used the disjunctive form without much difficulty. He argued that his corollaries treated the biological and phenetic concepts as special cases, which could be a disjunctive form of definition. He also stated that his definition covered the asexual species problem and the ecological aspects. If put in disjunctive form his definition would have covered all but the last of the species concepts listed earlier, it seems to me.

I do not want to belabor the biological species concept at great length, but one more issue deserves comment. Instead of taking up Hull's idea of using a disjunctive rather than a conjunctive form of definition, and thereby making more headway on the messy problem of species definition, Ghiselin (1966, 1974) suggested treating species as individuals rather than as classes. If species are treated as classes of similar things then immediately one has the problem of coming up with definitions of the classes. If species are treated as individuals one just gives a proper name to the individual, just as we give names to people and companies, with no need that the name be definitional—it is just a name. Ghiselin rightly pointed out that there should be no problem with treating an assemblage of elements as an individual rather than a collectivity. We do that all the time. People are assemblages of cells and organs—we give them proper names, not class definitions. Organizations are assemblages of people, groups, departments, and so forth (Blute* prefers to think of them as ecological communities). Yet we give them proper names, not class definitions. Recently, this idea has been strongly seconded by Hull (1976) and to a lesser extent by Mayr (1976).

Ghiselin's radical solution resolves by dismissal the problem of defining species. The debate on the species concept then becomes one of agreeing on what the role of species is. Ghiselin, and evolutionists and cladists in general, insist that species gains its importance as a concept because of its pivotal role as the unit of evolution. This view lends credence to the biological and evolutionary (including ecological) species concepts. Instead of substituting a strict phenetic concept, as Sokal and Crovello (1970) argued, where the biological species concept is eschewed due to its nonoperationality in many circumstances (it is often impossible to determine patristic affinity by testing for interbreeding or looking at genetic similarity), most biologists prefer that the evolutionary connotations be retained in the concept.

This has been an exceedingly brief review of a difficult yet very important subject. Just because the species concept is fundamental does not necessarily make it tractable. A couple of lessons are evident. First, there have been a variety of species concepts in biology and I see no reason why there will be not be a similar variety in organizational systematics. The functional parallels between the origins of the natural system in biology and the protosystem of organizations are strong grounds for expecting the argument between species as evolutionary units versus species as simply homogeneous groupings. We can expect arguments for species defined as classes versus individuals, and arguments about whether a definition, if that is preferred, should be conjunctive or disjunctive. These are all really arguments over form, not sub

---

*Marion Blute, personal communication, 13 June 1979.

stance, and they *will* materialize unless it is quickly agreed that organizations do not evolve in the context of environmental constraints—an agreement I do not think will come. Second, we should take note of the progression of thinking in biological systematics. First, a variety of species concepts was identified. Then there were arguments in favor of one at the expense of the rest. Next there were attempts to resolve the conflict by shifting to a disjunctive definition on the one hand or dismissing the definitional problem by treating species as individuals rather than classes on the other. For biologists it would appear that either of the solutions would resolve the problem, and both have sound logical support.

The lesson I have learned, which determines how I will pursue the species problem, is as follows:

1. Organizational species are units of evolution. Therefore, while phenetic methods may be necessary, we should not lose sight of the evolutionary processes the biological species concept handles.

2. In the event that an organizational species concept following the general form of the biological species concept fails to cover all possible species situations, we should set up a disjunctive definition following the form of the one suggested by Hull (1965b).

3. In pursuing a disjunctive definition we should keep in mind that genetic, phenetic, ecological, and competitive/selective similarities and differences are all important aspects of speciation.

4. We should recognize that pursuit of 3 means we are not following the biological tradition of staying with an essentialist definition of species as monothetic groupings, but rather are staying consistent with modern theories of classification in moving toward species as named individuals that are in reality polythetic assemblages of more or less similar components. Species are conceptualized in terms of a grand synthesis of aspects of speciation rather than neat, tidy, unequivocal groupings.

Working up a fully acceptable organizational species concept appears to me as a much larger agenda than I can cope with at this time. I plan to pay most attention to how the biological species concept handles some problems posed by evolutionary processes and the need to meet the criteria posed by my earlier discussion of elements of an ideal classification. The phenetic, evolutionary, and ecological aspects will be worked in somewhat more implicitly as my conceptual development progresses throughout the book.

Elements of the Biological Species Concept

There are three basic processes working in speciation. These processes operate over a period of time to cause distinct species to emerge. Readers familiar with biological evolutionary theory, ecology, and genetics will quickly see that this section grossly simplifies the difficulties, controversies, and depths of knowledge in those large subjects of inquiry. Principles of natural selection are discussed in more detail, however, in chapter 8. The intent here is to draw on those fields for systematic purposes without letting an extended discussion mar the continuity of discussion relevant to systematics.

Isolating Processes. A group of biological organisms becomes reproductively isolated when, for example, a geographic barrier* intervenes to force them into a restricted pool of available mates. The barrier might be a new mountain range, lake, sea, river, desert, and so forth. Over a period of time the organisms evolve in response to their new environment to the point where they are so different from other previously kindred organisms that they can no longer mate with them. This could be because of changed physical characteristics or changed methods of attracting mates such as scents, colored plumage, or mating dances and the like. Among biological organisms, most reproductive isolation results because the potential mates do not attract each other. In cases where members of different species do mate the offspring are most often sterile, as are mules, or do not survive in the habitat they are born into, as might be the case if a goose were to mate with a penguin in Antarctica. These processes explain how species remain different one from another. Though probably not rooted in reproduction, it seems likely that an explanation of why organizational forms remain separate will also be required for a successful organizational classification. Campbell (1969) referred to this as the retention process, a theme subsequently elaborated by Aldrich (1979). Isolation is a part of Lewontin's "principle of heredity" (1978, p. 220).

Ecological Processes. These are important because of the Darwin-Wallace theory of natural selection. If for some chance reason a new organism were formed, it would have to survive in its habitat in order to remain part of the natural system. A habitat normally includes such things as similar species competing for the same food sources, predators, symbiotic partners, and geographical features such as cold or hot, wet or

---

*White presented an in-depth discussion of other speciation stimulators that are geographic or semigeographic (1978, pp. 16–18). These actually include population structure and genetic as well as spatial factors.

dry climates, flat or rocky territory, and so forth. For example, penguins are uniquely suited for survival in extremely cold areas of the world. Marsupials evolved successfully in Australia because there were fewer significant predators for millions of years. Large African plains mammals such as rhinoceroses survive in part due to the services of tick birds, which warn them of impending danger and rid them of ticks and other parasites. In return for their services the birds are allowed to perch on the animals and feed themselves. Respectively, each of these birds or animals likely would find survival more difficult if the climate changed, if the number of predators increased, or if the symbiotic relationship broke down. The process of ecological sensitivity explains why some new forms survive and others die out. Since environments and habitats change on occasion, this process also explains why some species survive for a time and then disappear. A similar process was recognized by Campbell (1969) as a necessary element in any theory of sociocultural evolution. He saw it as environmental selection. These elements have been further developed by Hannan and Freeman (1977) and Aldrich (1979). Two of Lewontin's principles of evolution via natural selection apply here: the "principle of natural selection" and the "principle of the struggle for existence" (1978, p. 22).

Generational Processes. In biology the intercommunicating gene pool assures the existence of the species over time and through successive generations. Lewontin (1978, p. 220) referred to it as the "principle of heredity." It is the basis of propinquity. It is at once the process for maintaining the stability of the species within certain limits of variation within the population and for allowing evolutionary change in the population over a long period of environmental change. In the short term the probabilities of certain gene combinations operate to restrict the variety of forms the offspring can take. Over a very long period of time there is a higher probability that a mutant form resulting from less likely combinations of genes will emerge. As Mayr aptly put it: "The individual is merely a temporary vessel holding a small portion of the gene pool for a short period of time" (1969, p. 26). Of course, organizations do not have genes. And organizations do not mate with each other to reproduce cute little new organizations. But an organizational form does pass through successive generations of employees who act as "temporary vessels" of components of its distinctive competence; thus a generational process seems called for, an idea I bring up again in chapter 8.

The Biological Speciation Process

Based on the foregoing three processes, Mayr (1969, p. 26) gave the following definition of the biological species concept: "Species are groups of inter-breeding natural populations that are reproductively isolated from other such groups." This concept breaks down in many special instances, and hence the several other species concepts, but it covers the mainstream of organisms and therefore retains special status as a species concept. The three processes implicit in this concept explain the discontinuity of groupings in the natural system, the homogeneity of the members within the natural groupings, the stability of the groupings in the short term, and the slow change in the form of biological organisms over the long term. If any single process is missing, the biological species concept no longer depicts biological speciation.

In biology the term SPECIATION has come "to designate the genetic changes whereby new species come into existence [and to recognize] that these processes are a distinct part of the general course of evolution, and hence a legitimate field of study" (White 1978, p. 1). White's book is the most recent compilation of what is known about speciation. He presented a thirteen-step model of the speciation process (1978, p. 11), which he cautioned was an oversimplification. Since organizational science is hardly ready for a complicated model rooted in genetic processes, I take an even simpler view.

Ross presented a model of the speciation process composed of five steps, which are summarized below:

Step 1.   A parent species exists, occupying a geographical space allowing all members of the species to meet and interbreed.

Step 2.   The geographical range of the parent species is split so that two (or more) divisions result, with the effect that members in one division cannot meet and interbreed with members in the other division.

Step 3.   A *gradual* and divergent genetic change takes place in the isolated units due to the effects of accumulated small genetic differences. This process is enhanced if, as a result of the geographic split, the ecology of the two divisions is different. In this event the ecological sensitivity of the isolated groups will lead to even greater divergence as each adapts to its new ecological habitat. At this stage the groups might begin to appear different but, if brought back together again, could still interbreed. Groups at this stage are typically recognized as intraspecies variations, or subspecies.

Step 4.   The development of genetic incompatibility between the two isolated groups. If the groups are brought together for breeding at this stage, the offspring are not viable in either group's normal ecological habitat or they have reduced fertility. The different groups can still mate but the offspring do not survive or reproduce very well.

Step 5. Complete sexual isolation. The two groups cannot interbreed, or if they do, the offspring are sterile. [1974, pp. 80–84; emphasis added]

I have emphasized one word in the quote of the model from Ross: *gradual*. This model is based in the traditional view of speciation as a process composed of many small variations accumulating over a very long period of time. The discovery of a new species all at once instead of finding a slow evolution of form was explained as the result of gaps in the fossil record. In 1940 Goldschmidt had the effrontery to suggest that many evolutionary novelties did *not* occur via a long gradual development but rather occurred via SALTATION, which is to say by mutations that drastically changed an organism at a single step. He interpreted gaps as evidence of a rapid rate of change rather than as missing information. This view has become more popular in recent years (Futuyma 1979, p. 160) and is known as the QUANTUM SPECIATION or PUNCTUATED EQUILIBRIA model, the latter term suggested by Eldredge and Gould (1972). A useful description of the differences between gradual and quantum speciation is shown in figure 6.2. An excellent discussion of quantum speciation is given by Stanley (1979). In chapter 9, I will argue that both models are applicable to organizational speciation, with the advantage quite likely going to the quantum speciation model, given data by Stinchcombe (1965) and others.

6.1.3 The Unique Objectivity of the Species Category

Mayr (1969) claimed that the species category is unique because it is the only rank category in which groupings may be directly tested for interbreeding capability. Since the groupings at the species rank correspond to actually existing groups of organisms, the classification of an organism in question can generally be settled by testing to see whether it can produce nonsterile, viable offspring after mating with a known member of a species. The species rank is the only category where this test can be made. For example, an animal that looks something like a dog or a wolf can be made available for mating with known members of the dog and wolf species and, depending on which mating results in nonsterile offspring, a decision about the species of the unknown animal can be made. In some instances the differences between two species are so great as to obviate the need for the reproductive test—as between a lion, an elephant, and a small dog. In other cases, such as between horses and

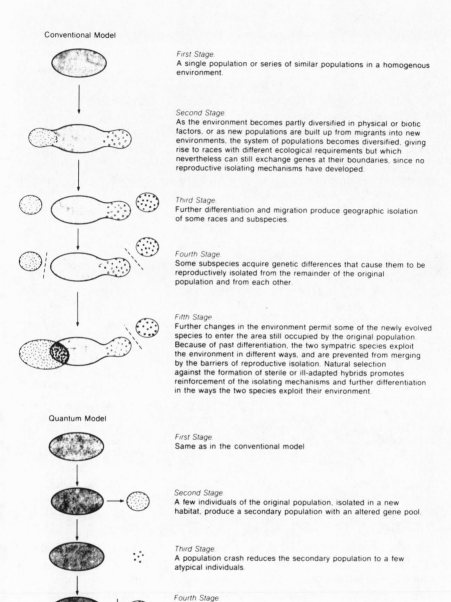

Conventional Model

First Stage.
A single population or series of similar populations in a homogenous environment.

Second Stage.
As the environment becomes partly diversified in physical or biotic factors, or as new populations are built up from migrants into new environments, the system of populations becomes diversified, giving rise to races with different ecological requirements but which nevertheless can still exchange genes at their boundaries, since no reproductive isolating mechanisms have developed.

Third Stage.
Further differentiation and migration produce geographic isolation of some races and subspecies.

Fourth Stage.
Some subspecies acquire genetic differences that cause them to be reproductively isolated from the remainder of the original population and from each other.

Fifth Stage.
Further changes in the environment permit some of the newly evolved species to enter the area still occupied by the original population. Because of past differentiation, the two sympatric species exploit the environment in different ways, and are prevented from merging by the barriers of reproductive isolation. Natural selection against the formation of sterile or ill-adapted hybrids promotes reinforcement of the isolating mechanisms and further differentiation in the ways the two species exploit their environment.

Quantum Model

First Stage.
Same as in the conventional model

Second Stage.
A few individuals of the original population, isolated in a new habitat, produce a secondary population with an altered gene pool.

Third Stage.
A population crash reduces the secondary population to a few atypical individuals.

Fourth Stage.
Recovery accompanied by new selection pressures (resulting from the altered gene pool) produces a new population reproductively isolated from the original one.

Figure 6.2. Gradual Versus Quantum Speciation Models Compared. (From *Evolution* by Th. Dobzhansky, F. J. Ayala, G. L. Stebbins, and J. W. Valentine. Copyright © 1977 by W. H. Freeman and Company. Reprinted by permission of the publisher.)

donkeys, the test may need to be made. The production of offspring in this instance may suggest that the animals are related, but since mules are sterile, horses and donkeys are considered separate species. In the case of *cryptic* species, where there are no discernible differences among the organisms, the reproductive test is absolutely required (Ross 1974, p. 97). Usually, as measures of new characters become available, cryptic species no longer remain so. For example, crickets that were first thought to be one species were later found to be many species once their voices were recorded in a way that made differences identifiable. Subsequently the voice differences were related to newly measured physical differences (Ross 1974, p. 98).

At the genus rank and higher, groupings of species or groupings of genera, and so forth, cannot be directly tested by checking for reproduction because *none* of them interbreed. Consider the problem of deciding whether a cheetah is a member of the cat family, which includes lions, tigers, jaguars, bobcats, and domestic cats, or a member of the canine family, which includes foxes, wolves, dingoes, coyotes, and dogs. The cheetah has some features of the cat family and some of the canine family. Since the cheetah does not breed with any of the species in either family, no interbreeding test is possible. Nor is such a test available to decide that the fox species is a member of the canine family, and so forth. The lack of a breeding test also means that failure to interbreed cannot be used to separate the cat and canine families. Consequently other methods must be used to arrive at groupings. Classificatory decisions at ranks higher than species are based on lineage as drawn from the fossil record, including the ancestral-derived character analyses of the cladists; and where the fossil record is obscured they are based on the genetic, molecular, and phenotypical similarity of living species.

Likewise, groupings below the species category cannot be tested by interbreeding because *all* members of the various groupings within a species can interbreed, though there may be signs of inviability or reduced fertility. These intraspecies groupings are at steps 3 or 4 of Ross's speciation model. The groupings have become isolated because of some kind of barrier and the isolated groups have begun to show genetic differences resulting in character differences and possibly reduced fertility, but have not progressed to the point of step 5 where they are sexually isolated and are termed different species. At the middle stages of speciation, if the geographical feature were to disappear and the groups allowed to mingle, they would interbreed and probably eventually evolve into a single homogeneous grouping again, as would happen with special breeds of dogs if all interbreeding barriers were removed. In some cases where the character differences between two intraspecies groups are pronounced and the geographical barrier is truly impenetrable, such as a high mountain chain, there may be little argument about the decision to form two intraspecies groupings. But if the character differences are not great and the barriers are not so strong, as in the case of the thirty-five subspecies of kangaroo rat in the southwestern part of North America (Mayr 1969, p. 39), the intraspecies groupings could be arbitrary. If two systematists disagree on how different two groups have to be before being recognized as subspecies, the method of checking through interbreeding does not supply an objective test.

Because of the possibility of testing groupings by interbreeding, classificatory decisions under evolutionary theory are most objective at the species rank and become increasingly subjective at higher or lower levels of the hierarchy. The further down the hierarchy, the more recent is the evolution toward different groupings and consequently the differences are not as pronounced. The further up the hierarchy the grouping is, the more ancient the common ancestor. Generally, the more ancient the time period the less complete the fossil evidence, increasing the subjectivity and arbitrariness of classificatory decisions. Under most circumstances the species rank is truly a waterline category having unique status. But there are some difficulties.

6.1.4 Difficulties with the Biological Species Concept

There is no difficulty in understanding how the biological species concept results in stable groupings in the short term or in evolutionary changes in the long term, and there is no difficulty in understanding how the element of ecological sensitivity causes certain species to survive or fail to survive. The difficulties occur principally when testing the separateness of tentative groupings through interbreeding is not possible. These difficulties support the case for the other species concepts and a disjunctive definition. More extended discussion of difficulties associated with the biological species concepts, and others as well, are given by Mayr (1957, 1969), Sokal and Crovello (1970), Sokal (1973), Sneath and Sokal (1973), Ross (1974), Ghiselin (1974), Hull (1976), Slobodchikoff (1976), Shvarts (1977), and Wiley (1978). I will discuss the more important problems briefly.

Lack of Sexual Reproduction. There are many biological organisms that do not reproduce by mating with a member of the opposite sex. Certain worms reproduce by breaking into sections, with each section then growing into a complete worm; certain lilies reproduce by offsetting bulbs—these lilies have flowers but they are sterile (Ross 1974, p. 64). With unisexual organisms the reproductive test is not possible. In other cases an unclassified organism will not mate with a member of a known species because it is too young or too old, resulting in an inconclusive test or erroneous separation of the organisms into new species. In the instance of fossilized organisms a reproductive test is out of the question.

Evolutionary Intermediacy. There are many instances of organisms in early stages of speciation where it is difficult to tell whether character differences simply should be recognized as another variation within an existing species or taken as an indication of a different species. At this stage it may be impossible to decide whether the production of viable, though perhaps not highly fertile, offspring is due to the fact that the organisms are in early stages of separation or is due to a chance hybridization resulting from the rare breakdown of isolating mechanisms. In some instances reproductive isolation will be attained but without any accompanying apparent morphological change.

Insufficient Information. Often there is not enough information to decide whether an organism having certain characters is a member of a separate species or a phenon within a species. Differences between sexes, differences between different ages, and variations in the characters may confuse the issue until further information is obtained. Genetic information, crucial in determining patristic affinity—which is the basis of the biological species concept—is not available to most systematists, especially in the field, because the measuring instruments are not available. The more problematic is measurement the slower is progress. In many instances, fossils especially, genetic information is unavailable and strict patristic affinity is impossible to determine.

6.1.5 Essential Elements of an Evolutionary Species Concept

There are many difficulties with the species concept. It is clear that Mayr's biological species concept does not handle all the situations that prevail. One response is to keep working toward a single concept that handles everything. An alternative is to accept the idea that a disjunctive definition may be necessary, as Hull (1976) suggested; or perhaps Ghiselin's idea of species as individuals rather than classes will prevail. Nevertheless the biological species concept seems to work for the mainstream of biological organisms that reproduce sexually. While organizations clearly do not reproduce, and there is no intent in this book to argue for that kind of biological analogy, the idea of discovering as many criteria, standards, parameters, or other guidelines that might offer clues in developing an organizational species concept seems worthwhile. We will not know what to accept or reject if we do not see it in the first place. It is also important to recognize that even though biologists have been searching for a species concept for centuries, they still are debating various issues and do not have a concept picked clean of difficulties. Yet they use it. Although there are may exceptions and these have aroused much debate among biological systematists, there are some key elements of the biological concept which form the rather stable and enduring core of orthodox biological classification. These are enumerated below as conditions worth keeping in mind if we are to develop an organizational species concept that will lead to a useful evolutionary organizational classification. A species concept probably should accommodate:

1. The operation of isolating processes.
2. Ecological processes.
3. A means of assuring reasonable stability while at the same time allowing for evolutionary change in the long term—hereditary processes.
4. Polythetic groupings (from section 3.1.4).
5. Real, existing objects as opposed to ideal or abstract objects (from section 3.1.4).

If any of these elements is missing the species concept would not fit in with the evolutionist theory of classification based on natural selection. And without the first three the species concept would not meet the conditions imposed by the goal of developing an effective classification scheme. Without the last two, the species concept would not be compatible with the goal of grounding the classification empirically to the protosystem of real, existing organizations. In fact, only the nominalist theory could exist without a species concept comprising these elements, because together they operate to produce the natural system of the biologists or the protosystem in an organizational context. Without such a system the essentialist, empiricist, and evolutionary theories have no groupings of objects to classify.

6.2 A REVIEW OF EXISTING ORGANIZATIONAL CLASSIFICATIONS

Now that some elements of an effective classification have been identified, it is possible to review existing organizational classifications to see to what extent they contain these elements. Existing classifications follow either the essentialist or empiricist theory of classification, and it will be seen that they all fail as possible approaches to a general classification scheme, but for varying reasons. It is important to emphasize that what follows is not a critique of the intentions of the authors involved, since there is little indication that these authors were offering anything more than a description of a few organizational differences, that is, special classifications. Instead, the object of the review is to determine whether any of these approaches already contains or could be adapted to contain the essential elements of an acceptable classification scheme. Presumably there is a species concept implicit within each typological or empirical approach. The classifications are discussed in turn, starting with those rooted in essentialism.

6.2.1 Inattention to Isolating Processes

The consequences of ignoring the effects of isolating processes are lack of demarcations among groups and lack of homogeneity within them.

Lack of Sharp Demarcations.   Many typologies fail because they are comprised of classes formed by splitting continuous dimensions into two or more arbitrary groupings. When this is done, members just above and below the cutoff line are very much alike. Instead of being *either-or* or *is-is not* kinds of groups, they are *more or less* of the same thing. One example was the Burns and Stalker (1961) classification breaking organizations into mechanistic and organic classes. The problem is that real organizations do not all fall cleanly into one or the other group. In fact it is quite possible that organizations are normally distributed along this dimension, with most of them falling toward the middle, in which case most organizations probably are not cleanly grouped by a two-class schema.

Lawrence and Lorsch (1967) and Lorsch and Morse (1974) have conducted empirical studies focused on the ordering dimension of environmental certainty-uncertainty. Their findings were cast in terms of a classification based on production organizations operating in certain environments and research organizations operating in uncertain environments. There is no evidence to date on how many organizations fall between the two extremes of this dimension, but probably most of them do. Another example is Perrow's (1967) scheme, which classified technologies by two dimensions, the relative uniformity of inputs and the analyzability of the exceptions in uniformity. Perrow ended up with a four-cell classification such that all those organizations having moderately nonuniform inputs that were moderately amenable to analysis fell into a nameless undifferentiated cluster in the middle. There was no indication of how large this cluster might be.

In these typologies there was no attention given to the sharpness of the demarcation between the classes. Where the classes were at the extremes of the dimension there was no attention given to what happens to all the organizations falling toward the middle of the continuum. The consequence was that many organizations either were clustered just above or below the central dividing line or were left out altogether. A scheme that leaves out many organizations is not very useful to empirical researchers. A scheme that arbitrarily separates similar organizations into two extremes tends to not produce homogeneous groupings and for this reason also is not very useful to empirical researchers.

Lack of Homogeneity. There are other typologies that do have well-demarcated boundaries between classes but do not produce homogeneous groupings. Usually this is because the groupings are too large. One example of this problem occurs in the classification offered first by Parsons (1956) and later by Katz and Kahn (1978), which grouped organizations by the function they performed for the larger society: the productive, pattern maintenance, adaptive and integrative functions. These classes were clearly demarcated in the sense that organizations that produce goods and services were different from educational, research, and legal or political organizations. Yet the groups were so large, especially the productive group, that the resulting low-level homogeneity was not sufficient to support the kind of population definition, sampling, and generalization necessary for the effective pursuit of functional studies. To date there has been little if any empirical research carried out in the context of this classification.

Another example of classes lacking in homogeneity were those proposed by Blau and Scott (1962). They were based on who was the prime beneficiary: the owners, the employees, the customers or clients, or the public at large. Again, each class was so large as to deny any meaningful level of homogeneity. The class of customer-oriented organizations included most, if not all, of those that attempted to produce goods and services, whether hotdog stands, automobile assembly plants, oil refineries, or steel mills. This scheme also has not been associated with any meaningful empirical research and most organizational scientists would probably be unwilling to concede that steel mills and hotdog stands should be classed together.

Etzioni's (1975) scheme also produced nonhomogeneous groupings. It contained only three groupings based on the type of compliance the organization depended on: coercive, utilitarian, and normative. These groupings, especially the utilitarian group, also were so large as to preclude reasonable levels of homogeneity. Each of these groupings, as did the groupings suggested by Parsons and Blau and Scott, ignored organizational variations on so many other important attributes such as technology, kind of inputs, kind of outputs, kind of environment, and structure, that they had no real meaning. Hall, Haas, and Johnson (1967) found only slight evidence that the Blau-Scott or Etzioni typologies produced differentiated homogeneous groupings. They concluded that they had "only a limited application in so far as total organizational analysis is concerned" (1967, p. 137). Not surprisingly, none of these classifications has been associated with any significant empirical research. Few empirical researchers are so naive as to try to define and sample a population as large and amorphous as any of the above.

6.2.2 Lack of Stability

Some classifications fail because they do not produce stable classes. This is because they are based on characters that can be changed, with the consequence that organizations must be reclassified as their characters change. These classifications base their groupings on characters that may be altered by the organization, either purposely or inadvertently, setting up the possibility that the organization later may be seen to be misclassified. For example, the mechanistic-organic structure of many organizations, which Burns and Stalker used as the basis of their grouping, may change as a result of changed policies brought about by a new top management. While such changes might be difficult to carry off in many circumstances, the fact that they are possible gives cause for concern if such an attribute is to be a key character for classification. The classification of organizations suggested by Filley (1962), which grouped organizations according to craft, promotional, and administrative forms, contained one form—the promotional one—which was decidedly unstable. The promotional group was a growth group, with successful organizations eventually moving into the administrative group. To include such a class in a scheme would be parallel to biologists' including separate classes for young and old members of the same species.

Another example of organizational instability is available in the Etzioni (1975) classification. Suppose that the management of a university at some point in time runs the place as a normative organization, depending mainly on scholars' interests in the university's goals of teaching and research as a basis of attracting faculty. It is possible that a new, more aggressive management may decide to compete for greater academic prestige by appealing to calculative motives in attracting faculty. At this point should the university be reclassified from the normative group to the utilitarian group? And should it be returned to the normative group once it runs out of the money necessary to pay top salaries? Characters subject to changes such as this form a poor foundation for a classification.

A further difficulty with the Etzioni scheme is that whether or not an organization is normative or utilitarian is in part related to what its management does, as has just been illustrated, but also to how its members perceive management's approach. Many professors probably do treat universities as normative organizations and are attracted on that basis. But it is also well known that many other professors travel from one place to another depending on who pays the highest salary—a distinctly utilitarian involvement. In another case, such as a mental institution, management may think of the place as a normative or therapeutic organization but the inmates may think of it as a coercive or utilitarian place. Whose view should prevail for purposes of classification?

6.2.3 Lack of Ecological Sensitivity and Explanation of Change

Some classificatory schemes fail as possible approaches to a general evolutionary classification because they do not explain how it was that organizations came to be different in the first place. In fairness it must be said that the authors may not have wanted or thought to include such an explanation. As the empiricists would argue, it may be better to keep such explanations separate from classificatory activities. But surely some earlier theorists must have wondered why the differences they observed came about.

Some schemes come fairly close to an explicit explanation because they include a process of ecological sensitivity. The schemes proposed by the contingency theorists (Burns and Stalker 1961; Lawrence and Lorsch 1967; Perrow 1967) recognized the importance of the environment as a cause of organizational differences. But they did not elaborate this view into a general theory of organizational change or into a general explanation of differences among organizations. Other schemes, especially those proposed by Parsons (1956), Katz and Kahn (1978), Etzioni (1975), Blau and Scott (1962), and Thompson (1967) did not include any discussion of ecological sensitivity nor did they attempt to explain why the various groupings existed, though it can usually be seen how they could have done so. There have been no classifications that explicitly tried to explain the origin of different kinds of organizations, though the schemes of the contingency theorists, focusing as they did on the environment, include implicit explanations.

6.2.4 Lack of Polythetic Groupings and Real Organizations

All of the theoretical typological approaches to organizational classification seem to have been based on a protosystem composed of monothetic groupings. They searched for groups all having in common an essential set of characters. This was consistent with their adherence to the essentialist theory of classification. The theoretical/typological approaches also did not develop a theory of differences which applied directly to real organizational entities such as schools, factories, or hospitals. They favored instead more abstract groupings such as "bureaucracies," "coercive organizations," "economic or productive organizations," "client-oriented organizations," and so forth. It is possible that these more abstract groupings could become higher-rank categories, as shown in figures 9.2 to 9.5. As can be seen in figure 9.3 especially, categories from the Etzioni, Thompson, Perrow, Burns and Stalker, and Woodward groupings are used. Needless to say, these groupings are preliminary and illustrative. They may well disappear after more intensive inductive and deductive research is completed.

6.2.5 Lack of A Species Concept Altogether

The organizational classifications following the empiricist theory— Haas et al. (1966), Pugh et al. (1968, 1969), Goronzy (1969), and Dodder (1969)—ignored the concept of species altogether. Presumably these investigators started with an assumed protosystem, though they did not set forth any reasons for believing in the existence of such a system. In part it would appear that these researchers were misled by their biological counterparts, who denounced the biological species concept (see Sokal and Sneath [1963] for a very strong early critique of the biological concept offered by numerical pheneticists). In fact, most of the biological empiricist studies, which existed at the time the organizational empiricists began their research, clearly made use of the biological species concept in their design except perhaps for studies classifying bacteria or asexual species—but even here species were still taken for granted.

Lacking their own species concept, and since they could not implicitly draw on a concept already in use, the organizational empiricists faced a difficult situation. The result was that their choice of characters was not very complete and their choices of populations were not guided by a theory about what the protosystem might look like (except for Dodder, who limited his study to a population of voluntary organizations).

There were also more specific inadequacies in these studies. The study by Pugh et al. used ordering dimensions and split them right at the mean, thereby maximizing the likelihood that the classes would not be sharply demarcated. Because only sixteen characters were used the resulting classes were not very homogeneous—each class included organizations that were different on all the unmeasured attributes. The Pugh et al. study did not address the issue of stability and did not comment on what might have led to the supposed protosystem, though the latter would not be expected since at the time the study was guided by the empiricist theory of classification.

The Haas et al. study ran into a different set of problems. It too did not comment on stability or ecological sensitivity, and did not say anything about the assumed protosystem. Since they had no subpopulations of the protosystem in mind they were left with an unmanageably large population (all U.S. organizations). Their sample included seventy-five organizations (neither representative of a given population nor random) and they measured ninety-nine characters. Given the wide variations among all the organizations, the ninety-nine characters probably did not control enough variance to result in a stable solution, let alone one that produced sharp demarcations among the organizations. There was no indication that the homogeneity in the resulting groupings was very high.

The Goronzy study defined a population of "American business organizations," drew a sample of 500 (the Fortune 500), and received a return of only 50. Even so, since it included only twenty-nine variables—mostly variations around a theme of size—it probably included more different kinds of organizations than it had characters to measure them by, making it virtually impossible for the solution to produce meaningful groupings. It also did not start with an assumed protosystem and so it too ended up with an untractable population.

Examination of these studies makes it clear that all empirical classificatory attempts need to start with some notion of an assumed protosystem and need to pay some attention to what the underlying species concept is. The view of the protosystem guides the choice of characters and the definition of the population. And, the protosystem cannot be conceptualized without the elaboration of a speciation process that satisfies all of the conditions enumerated in section 6.1.

The review in this section has demonstrated that all of the major typologies and empirical classifications were inadequate in terms of at least one of the essential elements of an ideal classification, most not meeting several of the conditions. The intent here was not to critique these approaches but rather to demonstrate what happens when a solid species concept is not an available prerequisite to beginning classificatory research.

6.3 SUMMARY

The species concept is the foundation stone of systematics. It is the basis of a theory of differences among many objects to be studied. The species category is the "waterline" category in any classification scheme. It is the rank where populations of individuals are most distinct and real. Below the species category distinctions among groupings blur, and above it the groupings are abstract clusters of species. The species directly reflect groupings in the protosystem. Above and below the species rank, classificatory decisions are increasingly arbitrary. A species concept is essential to any classification effort. Biologists have developed several concepts, including the typological, classical phenetic, numerical phenetic, biological, evolutionary, selection, and reproductive/competition concepts. Instead of the traditional conjunctive form, where necessary and sufficient properties of species are defined, alternatives such as a disjunctive definition or thinking of species as individuals instead of classes have been proposed. Despite various special cases, the biological species concept accommodates the majority of organisms and remains as the principal concept, with species treated as units of evolution. The difficulties with the species concept in biology and the elements of the biological species concept are instructive for organizational systematists.

There are four elements in an ideal classification scheme: *sharp demarcations among groupings, homogeneous groupings, stable groupings,* and *a means of separating ancestral groupings from those surviving effectively at present.* Experience in biology suggests that a species concept meeting the conditions of a good classification should have the following components: *isolating mechanisms, ecological mechanisms,* and *generational mechanisms.* A review of some of the major existing typologies and empirical classifications showed that none of them contained enough of the elements of an acceptable species concept to serve as a point of departure toward an acceptable general classification.

7 AN ORGANIZATIONAL SPECIES CONCEPT

The main point stressed . . . is not whether there are three or four or more types of firms, or how technology is conceptualized or measured, but that firms differ according to the kind of work they do, and thus differ in their structure.

[Perrow 1970, p. 91]

A theory of classification is really a theory of differences. In fact, it is a theory of differences *and* similarities. A classification is a compromise centered between the view that every individual organization is unique unto itself and the view that all organizations are pretty much the same. By trying to decompose organizations into populations of similar organizations that as a group appear different from other populations, classification is a *middle range theory* (Merton, 1968) between the extremes of total uniqueness and total similarity. (See Pinder and Moore [1979, 1980] for further development of middle range theory as it applies to organizations.) At the heart of any theory of differences is an implicit or explicit species concept. In the simplest language, a species concept is a means of guiding scientific observation of the differences and similarities among the phenomena to be classified.

As indicated by the review of typologies in chapter 6, species concepts are *implicit* in the thinking of the various typologists and are *explicitly avoided* by the empiricists in their organizational classifications. In the last few years, however, several authors have made much more explicit reference to the species concept. Its time may have arrived.

Taking their cue from biologists, Hannan and Freeman (1977, pp. 934−935) noted that species are defined in terms of their genetic structure, which may be thought of as a blueprint. They contended that all the *adaptive capacity* of a species is contained in the blueprint. Analogously, they saw organizational form as the blueprint for organizational action, which is transforming inputs into outputs. They suggested that the blueprint could be inferred from formal structure, patterns of activity, and the normative order. Of the three, they felt that the first and third offered the most hope for a useful species concept. McKelvey (1978) put forth the notion of *core technology* as the basis for an organizational species concept. Since it was a preliminary statement of the general message conveyed in this book it will not be reviewed further here. As an alternative to McKelvey's concept, Pinder and Moore (1979) proposed a multidimensional concept based on what they termed the *characteristic adaptation style* of an organization. In justifying their approach they said, "selection of this criterion is based on the tautological observation that all organizations at a point in time have at least one thing in common: they have adapted (more or less well) to their respective environments. Our proposed criterion of adaptation style provides an important and very meaningful sorting mechanism, since it deals with the very basis of existence of organizations" (1979, pp. 114−115). They also noted that measures of their construct would look very much like measures of organizational effectiveness. Finally, a fourth approach to the species problem was taken by Warriner (1980). Also building on the analogy of the intercommunicating gene pool, Warriner suggested the concept of *institutional culture*. He observed that this was a somewhat more generalized view of the role of knowledge in organizations than that entailed in McKelvey's notion of core technology. Warriner also focused on an organization's knowledge and ability to carry out its transformation of inputs into outputs. Warriner drew on the ethologist Dawkins (1976) for further support. Dawkins suggested the concept *meme* as the cultural analog of gene. Thus in the views of Warriner and Dawkins, cultural content is the genotype of organizational characteristics. Warriner went on to point out that while cultural content could produce a genotype for a population of organizations, the phenotypical characteristics of individual members of the population might differ for a variety of reasons. In this sense the gene pool concept is a probability statement suggesting the central tendencies of a population but seldom specifically defining the characteristics of any single member.

At first glance these four species concepts appear different, but there are similarities too. Three of the four look to the function of the inter-communicating gene pool or generational process as a central element of a species concept. Three of the four include a focus on adaptation or the ecological process as part of their concept. All of the concepts focus on what an organization does, three of the four explicitly mentioning the inputs-to-outputs conversions in the workplace. The role of isolating processes is missing in three of the four approaches, McKelvey being the exception. These concepts are all very brief preliminary suggestions. None has been carefully evaluated in terms of criteria such as those proposed in chapter 6.

With some bias no doubt, my choice is to stay with the species concept proposed by McKelvey (1978), though I will change its label. In the intervening time it has become quite evident that people are going to insist on keeping their view that technology pertains to the skills and knowledge relevant for running the machines and engineering processes of the workplace—a clanking hardware-oriented view of technology. Even though managers also have knowledge and skills, people are not willing to apply the technology label to these as well. Rather than fight, I will switch.

Instead of *core technology* I will use the term DOMINANT COMPETENCE. The French derivation of the term *competence* is "sufficiency, aptness, fitness." The Spanish derivation is "sufficiency." The Latin derivation is "meeting together, symmetry." In the sense of *compete*, the term means "to be put in rivalry with." Also in the sense of *compete* it means "to have an adequate supply, to have sufficiency." In another sense it means "a sufficiency for living comfortably, a sufficiency of qualification." All of this is from the *Oxford English Dictionary*. I conclude that *competence* is an excellent term to convey the idea that my species concept is based on differentiating organizations in terms of how they arrange their affairs so as to compete and survive. I have avoided the term *distinctive* because organizations within a population may not have different distinctive competencies—they may all be alike.* But organizations do have a variety of lesser competencies if one takes a close look, and a dominant one (Mahoney and Frost 1974). For example, universities have lesser competencies such as food service, steam plants, craft shops, street maintenance units, and so forth. But they also have a dominant competence that separates them from other

*The competencies of populations are distinct, of course.

organizations that also may have steam plants, eating places, craft shops, and the like. If appropriately and broadly interpreted, there is every indication that this concept largely overlaps the species concepts suggested by Hannan and Freeman, Pinder and Moore, and Warriner. As yet I do not see the arguments they offer in support of their concepts to be incompatible with the dominant competence concept. I will argue that it stands up under evaluation in terms of the elements of an acceptable species concept.

The dominant competence species concept offers some additional advantages as well. The operating, technical core or workplace is the largest component of most, if not all, organizations, a view that concurs with the configurational diagrams of Mintzberg (1979). The dominant competence concept focuses on the operating core as well as on the management activities directly relating to it. Furthermore, technology is the central concept of the Perrow model, which is one of the best conceptualizations of the relation between environmental attributes and organizational form. Recalling that activity systems were central to the definition of organizations given in chapter 4, it makes sense to focus on aspects of organizations directly relevant to the nature of their input-output conversion activities. And, it seems from the discussion of the protosystem in chapter 5 that environments have their greatest impact in fostering the conditions for specialization in the workplace. Finally, dominant competence is a more focused view of what Warriner (1980) termed *institutional culture*. In any event, if the view of dominant competence defined more fully below is found inadequate under future scrutiny, it may be altered to the point where it fully overlaps with the species concepts suggested by Hannan and Freeman, Pinder and Moore, Warriner, and possibly others yet to be heard from.

This chapter engages in the several tasks necessary to present a more elaborate, carefully worked out species concept. In developing it, the first task is to identify the best way to understand how environmental differences lead to different organizational forms. This is the topic of the first section. Once a species concept is defined, it needs to be evaluated in terms of the criteria suggested in chapter 6. This is carried out in the second section. In the third section some definitional questions are cleaned up, such as: What is the right taxonomic unit? How is it defined? Should the unit be a work group, a corporation, a legal entity, a structural form? Whatever the unit is, it will have some kind of form, shape, and observable, measurable status. What is it that appears, that can be measured? Finally, the isomorphism between the genotype produced via evolutionary theory and the phenotypical basis of numerical taxonomy will be discussed.

7.1 A DEFINITION OF SPECIES

Besides the questions of how objects are different or similar, another fundamental question needing an answer before classification can take place is, what objects are being classified? What the object is for biologists may be thought to be fairly straightforward—they classify living things. But it could be said that they classify ecological aggregates composed of a body plus a variety of viruses, microbes, bacteria and parasites, and in the case of large mammals, even birds. Though the body might be born, it probably would not be viable without the additional creatures. Thus, would hippopotamuses survive as a population without tick birds? Would mammals in general survive without bacteria in the digestive tract? The question of what the object is for organizational classification is problematic.

As a point of departure it is convenient to distinguish between a FUNDAMENTAL TAXONOMIC UNIT (FTU) and OPERATIONAL TAXONOMIC UNIT (OTU). An OTU is a concept originated by Sneath and Sokal and is used to refer to the *"lowest ranking taxa employed in a given study"* (1973, p. 69; emphasis added). For example, it is possible that a taxonomic study of organizations might have as its smallest unit an average of exemplar members of groupings of individual county government organizations such as sheriff's department, fire department, road repair, refuse collection, building inspection, flood control, and so forth. Another study, however, might have as its lowest ranking unit actual individual organizations. The latter are referred to as FTUs. For organizational classification purposes an FTU is an organization as defined in section 4.3.3. Alternatively, an FTU is defined as *an organizational form containing technologically interdependent subsystems whose activities are pooled toward the accomplishment of the primary task.* The key elements of this definition needing further clarification are: *organizational form, technological interdependence,* and *primary task.* The latter is taken up in this section and the former two concepts are defined in section 7.3.

7.1.1 The Concept of Primary Task/Dominant Competence

General Definition

A glass of water may be half empty or half full, depending on the observer. Analogously, many observers see organizations as composed of an infinite variety of different activities whereas others see organizations as oriented toward one kind of activity and output more than others. Neither set of observers is in error. My view is that while there is a large variety of activities making up all but the very smallest organizations, there is also a dominant activity that can be identified which differentiates one set of aggregate activites from another. Thus, both a university and a prison have security guards, food services, sleeping quarters, athletic facilities, heating plants, open spaces, wood, machine, and other craft shops, and yes, even educational and research activities on the premises. Yet few would disagree with the view that the dominant activity of a university is quite different from that of a prison, even a prison with a strong emphasis upon rehabilitation.

The idea of a dominant activity has been the basis of all the essentialist typologies. My reason for bringing typologies back into the discussion is simply to point out that many observers have concluded that organizations do seem to have a dominant activity, one that is apparent to scientific and lay observers. Noting this, it is important to also say at the outset that even though organizations are going to be viewed as having a dominant activity, there is no intention whatsoever of searching for an essential few attributes to use as a basis for classification. The dominant activity is seen as a very complex set of activities, and groupings based on differences among these activities will be polythetic.

Though they may not have been the first, the sociotechnical systems researchers Miller and Rice (1967) used the term PRIMARY TASK to describe workplace tasks that directly relate to the output of an organization's primary product or service. The primary task is defined as *that set of activities that bear directly on the conversion of inputs into those outputs critical to a population's survival.* The key words are *directly*, *critical*, and *survival*. The latter term was defined in chapter 4. Critical outputs may be defined as *those outputs that return the resources necessary for continued survival.* Outputs returning the most resources will be most critical. Thus, since teaching and research generate the resources in universities, they are usually more important than other professional activities such as university or community service.

Though there are undoubtedly exceptions, identifying activities bearing directly on the conversion process is straightforward for most organizations. For example, most would agree that the primary task of hotdog stands is to serve hotdogs to customers. An analysis of a typical hotdog stand shows that the employees are not highly trained to produce hotdogs or market them. They are trained to give service, presumably with a smile; take the customer's order accurately; and offer food that is appealing—that is, not smashed, burned, cold, soggy, or dirty, if not outrightly appetizing and nutritious. The primary task of a foundry is to produce castings by forming molds from patterns, heating metal, and pouring it into the molds properly. A foundry usually has employees who are good at performing these tasks. Its employees typically have not been trained to be patternmakers or salespersons. The primary task of an advertising firm is to market products for its clients. An elementary school has the primary task of educating children, though other tasks are carried out such as offering hot lunches, maintaining the grounds and buildings, maintaining inventories of educational materials, and so forth. But most people would be upset if it looked like a school defined its primary task as child care or serving lunches and selected its personnel on that basis. The primary task of a library is usually defined as offering information to its clients, though some might see it as simply storing books.

However, the primary task concept is not without difficulties. The library example suggests one difficulty apt to be encountered: the library personnel may be convinced that their activities offer information to the library users. The users may be equally convinced that the library is doing everything it can to make books unavailable for use, presumably so they can be kept in better condition longer and so they will not be stolen. The possibility of such disagreements about the true nature of the primary task may surface in most organizations. It is well known that operative goals—those actually leading to observable behavior—are often different from official goals (Perrow, 1961). For purposes of systematics, the best view of an organization's primary task is that of an independent outside observer such as a systematist. This view should be based on what an organization *does*—its observable behavior—not on what it intends, thinks it does, or what possibly biased users might think. Of course, systematists probably are not totally error free either. But they appear to be the most neutral of all possible observers, so their views are likely to be the least biased.

Another difficulty is that some organizations have primary tasks that seem to involve two rather separate workplaces. Many universities seem to have two primary tasks and two workplaces for their faculties. One task is teaching and the workplace is typically a classroom. There are several work activities associated with this task, such as preparing and delivering lectures, grading papers, and setting up laboratory or other exercises to involve the students more directly in the learning process. The other main task is one of creating knowledge through various intellectual and empirical research activities. These are typically carried out in a small office or laboratory. There is some overlap in the workplaces as Ph.D. students may be allowed into a professor's research laboratory and students may be counseled in his or her office. Some would probably argue that these activities remain separate and thus it would be impossible to name one primary task. Others, myself included, argue that an effective university is one that achieves synergy between its teaching and research activities and that its primary task is one of setting up conditions and encouraging or training its faculty to carry on *both* tasks synergistically. In this view the primary task of the research university population is to create knowledge *and* transmit it to its students as quickly and adroitly as possible. If it did not do both it would be a research (only) population or a college population (focusing primarily if not only on teaching).

With other organizations such as IBM and Procter and Gamble there could very well be an argument about whether the production or marketing function was the primary task. Some would argue that these companies achieve their high success rate because they define their primary task as *selling*, respectively, computers or household products. If primary task is to be the basis of classification, it might be necessary to class these companies differently from their competitors who defined the primary task as *producing* computers or soap. Again, a possible solution would be to argue that the effectiveness of the organizational populations of which IBM and P&G are exemplar members is based on the combined primary task of both producing and selling. Individual members may carve out micro niches against their competitors by emphasizing one or the other or both tasks, for example. As the populations evolve, it may turn out that member survival depends on mastering the combined primary task after the methods of IBM and P&G.

Another difficulty occurs if there is a prevailing confusion among management, users, or external observers about what a population's primary task is. Thus systematists may disagree, for example, on whether a population or member firm is in the candle making or light business, or whether another is in the horse buggy or transportation vehicle business. This does not seem a significant problem since an analysis of the workplace activities should decide the issue. If management were to change their goal from candle making to the light business, without changing activities in the workplace (assuming this were possible), the organization would not need to be reclassified, though over a period of years it might evolve into a different form because of the change in managerial intent. If, after changing goals, management tried to introduce a totally new technology such as electric light manufacturing and was successful at it, with the organization thereby ending up looking like other organizations in the electric light-making business, it would have to be reclassified. But this likely would not happen quickly, if at all, because (in this example) it is not easy to turn wax molders into glass and metal fabricators, or craft managers into effective managers of an electric light assembly line. If the entire candle-making population changed into a broader light business, reclassification would not be necessary—the population would be recognized as having evolved into a different form, an example of ANAGENESIS (defined in section 9.1.1).

The occasional debate on whether an organization's ultimate purpose is to survive, to attain a goal, or to produce a good or service is usually not problematic. For example, the workplace and directly related management activities of a foundry will continue to focus on effective molding and casting whether or not top management or shareholders see the ultimate objective as effective founding or protection of capital. Of course it is possible for top management of a maladapted and ineffective foundry organization to switch primary tasks and technology and enter a new business to survive, rather than adapt their founding technology to a changing environment. This kind of management choice may cause a particular organization to cease to exist, but it does not affect the state of the population. Management could alternatively have chosen to update their founding technology and thereby enhance their chances of survival. The character of the operations and skills of the workplace is rather enduring compared with the changeable aspirations of managers. This stabilizing aspect of the primary task and its associated activities and technology is a key attribute of the competence-oriented species concept to be introduced shortly.

In general, the working hypothesis is that most companies will have a single, readily identifiable primary task. In some cases it may be a more subtle synergistic combination of two or more equally dominant tasks. The nature of this task seems best left to determination by systematists themselves, rather than to managers, employees, users, or others. A remaining difficulty arising when a large corporation, such as a conglomerate, has several seemingly totally independent activites will be discussed later in section 7.3.1.

Dominant Competence and Unit Operations

In the previous section the concept of *primary task* was defined broadly as the conversion of inputs into outputs. Needless to say, there is more going on in an effective workplace than just conversion. The concept becomes less abstract if ways of conceptualizing primary tasks in terms of their component elements can be found. Such an array of elements will help in the identification of different primary tasks by allowing a finer analysis of workplace activities.

The basic elements of any workplace system may be described in terms of the entities and links among entities which comprise most definitions of systems. Davis and Engelstad (1966) argued that many technologies could be reduced to a set of constituent elements they termed *unit operations*, the entities of the workplace system. They felt that these were the smallest units necessary for a complete analysis and understanding of the workplace.

These units are:

1. Maintaining: keeping in operating condition or repairing the physical facilities of the unit operation.
2. Transferring: changing location or orientation of materials or information between other unit operations.
3. Transforming: changing characteristics or state of materials or information.
4. Inspecting: identifying quality or quantity characteristics of materials, information, or operation between other unit operations.
5. Storing: placing materials or information so as to be available for future use.... [Davis and Engelstad 1966, p. 5]

This conceptualization of workplace elements is what Schwab (1960) termed a molecular rather than an atomic reduction, in that they form a middle-level reduction. For example workplace activities could be broken down further into the body and material movements that industrial engineers focus on in their efficiency studies. It may be that a finer level of analysis will be needed, but for the time being the notion of unit operations seems convenient.

The unit operations change in importance depending on the primary task of an organization. They are almost always all present, but usually one is dominant in most organizations. For example, organizations that import raw materials and then perform a succession of state-changing operations have a technology in which the transformation unit operation dominates. They survive by virtue of being able to perform the necessary transformations effectively. Their ability to compete for resources depends much more on their effectiveness in the dominant unit operation than in the others. This is usually because the largest proportion of costs is associated with the dominant operation. They store, transfer, and inspect materials along the way, and they have to maintain their machines, but the dominant operation is one of transformation. In an organization such as a railroad the dominant operation is one of transferring. A railroad also stores materials and equipment and it may transform a switchyard or inspect its lines, but the dominant operation, the element its technological competence focuses on, is transferring. In libraries and large spare-parts depots such as those run by airlines and the military, the dominant unit operation is storing. They also perform the other operations, but the one their technology focuses on is storing, keeping track of what is stored, and being able to retrieve it quickly when necessary. The Rand Corporation became famous for its early studies helping the U.S. Air Force operate its parts depots more effectively. While other operations were important too, the operation that probably received most attention in the NASA Manned Space Program was the inspection operation—the goal was a zero-defect rocket flight each time, and for the most part it was achieved. A sea vessel could be launched and defects fixed up as they occurred—as long as it floated, of course. A manned rocket had to perform perfectly when its engine first fired—there were few second chances.

The unit operations concept was devised to aid the analysis of production organizations. But it generally applies to most other organizations as well. Hospitals, schools, churches, prisons, and so forth all have state changes of people as a dominant operation, although schools, hospitals, and especially prisons can be seen as storing operations as well. Political organizations attempt to change public opinion about a candidate. Service organizations can be seen as having workplaces where customers having needs for service are converted into those whose needs are satisfied. In these kinds of organizations, even though transforming may be dominant, the other operations are present as well—equipment is maintained, files are stored and transferred, performance is inspected, and so on.

The workplace technology defined by the primary task, focusing on a dominant unit operation, comprises part of the total organizational species concept. The other part consists of managerial activities that keep the workplace in operation.

7.1.2 The Workplace-Management Task

The WORKPLACE-MANAGEMENT TASK is defined as *that set of managerial activities bearing directly on the operation of the primary-task workplace which foster the continued survival of the organization.* As there is a material- or service-oriented technological competence to the workplace, there is a management-oriented competence applied to the workplace-management task. The workplace-management competence is defined as the knowledge and skills aimed at solving problems stemming *directly* from the design and technology associated with the workplace. There are at least three broad problems: the measurement of effectiveness, the coordination of interdependencies, and the mitigation of environmental forces. The solution of these three problems is directly affected by the nature of the workplace and its environment. It is probable that other workplace-management problems will be added to this set. Nevertheless, the three that will be discussed are sufficient to establish the argument that certain elements of managerial knowledge and ability are developed in the context of constraints imposed by the nature of the workplace.

Other management problems such as financing the organization, locating plants, and hiring employees are no less important, but their solution seems less specifically constrained by the nature of the workplace, so they may be less useful as differentiating attributes. Many nongovernment organizations deal with the same financial marketplaces, though in other instances different financial arrangements may help separate kinds of forms. Most governmental organizations must gain funding by taxes, but here again differences among some kinds may be significant. (The method and skill of raising money could be a significant feature separating profit organizations from other organizations, but my view is that these two groups are different more for reasons pertaining to the workplace, such as service versus production orientation, different ways of determining effectiveness, different ways of protecting against environmental forces, and so on.) While the actual location of a plant may be affected by the workplace—for example, the location of an electric-power generating plant near a coal mine, the management process of arriving at a decision about location based on where the inputs are, where the labor supply is, where the customers are, and where the best transportation is or, as is often the case, where the chief executive wants to live, seems independent of what the workplace is like. Typically a personnel department may hire employees for many specific workplaces in a large differentiated organization. The kinds of employees might differ depending on the technology in the workplace, but the process of hiring them often does not. The important management problem of directing and inducing employees to contribute their efforts to an organization's purpose is not treated separately, as it is felt that the solution to this problem is embedded in how an organization handles effectiveness, adaptation (planning), homeostasis (controlling), and structural design (differentiation and integration). The three broad problems that are affected by the nature of the workplace are discussed below.

Measurement of Effectiveness

Ever since the early work of Barnard (1938), Selznick (1948), and Merton (1968), and later Katz and Kahn (1978) and Buckley (1967), among others, organizations have been conceptualized as systems. A key element of this concept is the deviation-minimizing, negative feedback, or control process, where system outputs are evaluated in terms of system objectives and corrections in conversion processes made. The notion of control has also been a central element in the classical management literature. Of the five main elements of a deviation-minimizing process—goal specification, sensing, discrimination, action to correct, and communication (McKelvey, 1970)—the sensing process or measurement of effectiveness seems especially sensitive to the particular nature of a workplace, specifically the nature of its inputs and outputs and the degree to which they can be validly measured.

In organizations that handle concrete (nonabstract) materials such as metal extrusions, fabricated products, or plastic materials, where the quality, quantity, and cost of each item are readily measured, the effectiveness of the workplace in producing the product may be determined by comparing the net value remaining after the value of the inputs is deducted from the value of the outputs. Yuchtman and Seashore (1967) referred to this approach as the *system-resource* model of effectiveness. Ouchi (1977) termed it *output control*. It works only when the inputs and outputs can be validly measured. When this situation prevails organizations tend to focus their internal management efforts on the "bottom line" or the net profit or loss gained from the operation. This kind of management is a boundary-oriented one, basing its notion of effectiveness on the inputs and outputs to and from the workplace. Organizations may be broken down into "profit centers" so that the effectiveness of each center can be separately identified as a profit or loss. Usually the managers of each profit center are left to manage by themselves the throughput processes such as workflow and the direct planning, controlling, and organizing processes of workplace management.

In organizations that produce information and service, the value of the inputs and outputs cannot be validly measured in any straightforward manner. In schools and universities the amount of learning given the students is not easily measured. The academic prestige of a university is not easily measured. Nor can the reputation and quality of a hospital, law firm, or accounting firm easily be established. There are always opinions or survey rankings about these things but people have doubts about their validity. Universities typically have three main objectives: to produce high quality knowledge, to turn out well-educated students, and to serve their surrounding communities. There is seldom if ever a good measure of these kinds of outputs. Furthermore the inputs to an organization such as a great university—talented faculty, intelligent students, and fine textbooks and other educational materials—also cannot easily be measured.

One alternative is to develop surrogate measures that can be validly measured and thus allow an organization to continue using the system-resource model. For example, a welfare agency can measure caseloads and client contact hours instead of directly measuring "welfare." Universities may count student contact hours and number of publications instead of directly measuring learning and original contribution to knowledge. Hospitals can measure the number of patients taken in, length of stay, number of operations, number of beds filled or perhaps number of beds that are empty. The latter example dramatically illustrates the problem with surrogate measures. Should a hospital claim effectiveness for keeping its beds filled, turning out patients fast so as to empty the beds, or for increasing the number of operations so as to gain a better return on the cost of investment in expensive operating room equipment? The uncertainty over the measurement of effectiveness is a problem having wide ramifications on the legitimacy of the control system and consequently on how management goes about solving the problem of effectiveness.

An alternative approach to effectiveness was suggested by Schein (1980), in response to difficulties of the system-resource model in handling the problem of weak surrogate measures and additional problems such as multiple, possibly conflicting goals, and environmental change and uncertainty. Schein's concept, termed the *adaptive-coping* model, focuses on throughputs or the conversion process instead of comparisons of input values with output values. It views a system's effectiveness as its capacity to survive, adapt, maintain itself, and grow no matter what its product or service. In this model effectiveness is measured in terms of adaptability, sense of identity, capacity to test reality, and subunit integration (see Schein 1980 for an elaboration of these ideas). In its emphasis on conversion processes this model is similar to Ouchi's (1977) *behavior control* concept, though the latter is not specifically focused on adaptive capability.

Though control and adaptation are elements in both models, it is clear that the systems-resource model emphasizes control and stability whereas the adaptive-coping model stresses adaptation and change. The management competencies for each of these two orientations are vastly different. Managers of workplaces where good measures of the effectiveness of the workplace are available will tend to focus on comparing inputs and outputs, whereas managers of workplaces processing information or having inputs and outputs not well measured will tend to focus on throughput processes. In particular, the design and management of the control systems will differ markedly since the ability to measure workplace activities relative to the goals of the workplace is at the core of any control system. An input-ouput oriented control system would, of course, measure and offer feedback on the quantity, quality, and cost of the outputs relative to the inputs. A throughput oriented control system would set up goals for each throughput stage, whether in workflow or management processes, and measure how well each process was accomplished. This way of doing it is not flawless, as there may not be good measures for the throughput processes either; thus, how to measure effective planning or control or teaching in a university? The idea is not that there are no problems, but only that the kinds of inputs and outputs affect the way the workplace is managed. Some empirical support showing differences in managerial approaches to effectiveness stemming from differences in how effectiveness is measured was given by Mahoney and Weitzel (1969), who showed that managers of production organizations emphasized dimensions of effectiveness different from those emphasized in research and development organizations. Ouchi (1977) showed some structural differences associated with throughput as opposed to output control. These models appear to be used in some populations, and students of organizations and management have proposed their applicability to many different populations. Whether all populations with these approaches to handling effectiveness would survive is open to question. There could easily be other equally tractable solutions aiding the survival of diverse populations.

I have emphasized the sensing process. Other control system processes and associated structures may prove to have equal adaptive significance. I would recommend that attributes of these be considered as taxonomic characters also, until results show they are not related to organizational differences.

Coordination of Interdependencies

Different primary tasks and unit operations also result in different flows of the material passing through an organization. In a jet engine repair shop parts of the engine are routed to a variety of machines, depending on what is found to be in need of repair. In an automobile assembly plant hundreds of parts are supplied at various places on the line for attachment to subassemblies and the main assembly, an automobile. In a military organization men and equipment are readied and held in storage at various parts of a country or around the world. In the trust department of a bank, loan applications are processed through various individuals and committees.

These flows and operations are usually grouped into various departments or other subunit configurations. These groupings are associated with geographical, technological, and time considerations (Miller 1959) and result in various flows of material and information from one subunit to another. In some instances there is a convergent flow of inputs, as in a symphony orchestra where various sounds are combined at once to produce a symphony, or in an assembly operation where a variety of parts are brought together at one point for assembly into one output. In other cases a single input may be broken down into a variety of outputs resulting in a divergent flow, as in a petroleum-refining operation that produces a variety of fuels and chemicals. In still other instances the flow of materials is a sequence of events, each one dependent on what came just before. Finally, in many organizations there is a circular flow where ideas and plans pass back and forth among two or more departments with alterations occurring in each place.

Depending on the kind of material flow, various kinds of interdependencies among workers and departments may result. Thompson (1967) has identified three of these. *Pooled interdependency* occurs on convergent and divergent flows where the various departments of an organization work separately to produce parts that will all fit together in a final assembly, or to produce different outputs that all depend on the same input. *Sequential interdependency* occurs when the successful initiation and completion of a given step in an operation depends on the completion of a prior step according to certain standards. The material flows through a sequence of steps, with each one taking the output of a previous step as its input. Finally, *reciprocal interdependency* occurs when, for example, two departments—A and B—are in such a relationship that the outputs of A become inputs of B and the outputs of B become the inputs of A. Here A's inputs are in part dependent on B's responses to A's own outputs. This kind of interdependency occurs frequently in aerospace design operations where, for example, the design of a faster wing reduces the payload of the fuselage. Increasing the payload to its original size calls for more powerful and larger engines. The increased weight may then force alteration in the design of the wing. These changes may require larger landing gear, which again affects the design of the wing or fuselage and so on, around and around until the design stabilizes on an optimal configuration.

Thompson (1967) also discussed three kinds of coordination which were necessary to effectively manage the three kinds of interdependency. Pooled interdependency seems best managed through *standardization*, that is, by rules and regulations. Thus the autonomy of the musicians in an orchestra is conditioned by the musical rules and the beat of the conductor so the sounds of each properly come together at the same instant. Sequential interdependency seems best managed by the use of *plans* detailed in advance so that the outputs of each step in a sequence meet the input requirements of the following step. Reciprocal interdependency seems best managed by *mutual adjustment*. Representatives of the departments involved have to meet and mutually adjust until a design materializes which is optimal from all points of view. In different populations there may be alternative coordination solutions to the same interdependency problem.

The coordination of interdependencies can also be ameliorated by altering the configuration of an organization's subunits. For example, coordination costs are reduced if reciprocal interdependencies are kept within subunit boundaries, according to Thompson (1967). Too few subunits exacerbate coordination processes within each subunit because they become unmanageably large. Too many subunits create a quagmire of intersubunit coordination problems, creating a need for additional coordination of people or units.

Lawrence and Lorsch (1967), Khandwalla (1977), and Child (1977), among others, have shown that organizational differentiation (into subunits of various attributes) and integration (coordination) are key factors in organizational effectiveness and are affected by the kind of technology the organization has. Differentiation and the management of the resulting coordination problems are management problems emanating directly from the character of the workplace. The solution of these problems is a part of management competence which is directly related to the workplace.

Mitigation of Environmental Forces

Finally, managers directly involved in the workplace have to cope with the effects of the environment on the workplace. Some solutions, found in some populations, illustrate possible competencies used by managers to protect the technical workplace. By presenting these I do not mean to suggest that these are principles that are broadly applicable to many organizational populations, as Mintzberg implied with his propositions (1979, pp. 270−285).

Environmental Threat. With the exception of Khandwalla's (1977) research on the effects of hostility and Mintzberg's (1979) brief comment, this characteristic of some environments has generally been ignored in the recent literature, though earlier March and Simon (1958) also referred to the notion of hostility. Other words to convey the connotation are *crisis, noxity, dangerousness, competitiveness,* and so forth. An environment is threatening if inefficiencies and errors by an organization result in its demise. An organization can be sloppy, inefficient, and make mistakes in a benign environment and still survive, though it may not be as effective as it could be.

The Manned Space Program existed in a very threatening environment in that one mistake in space could cost the lives of its astronauts and, because of the highly publicized conditions, the mistakes would be widely known and could lead to cutbacks in funding. Note that while the industrial space hardware-producing operations that formed the technical core were highly controlled, NASA's organization was quite organic, facing the problem of protecting the technical core from the endless unpredictable problems impinging on the space program (Litzinger, Mayrinac, and Wagle 1970; Chandler and Sayles 1971). An organization having several very effective competitors cannot afford to make mistakes; otherwise it will lose its share of the market and quite possibly go bankrupt. Environments become more threatening in times of economic recession because there is less profit with which to absorb mistakes. The University of California discovered that the combination of economic recession around 1968 and a conservative Republican governor, Ronald Reagan, increased the threat level of its environment.

The possibility of environmental threat would not be important if it did not have a direct impact on the management of the workplace. Environmental threat more than anything else seems accompanied by organizations having tight and extensive control systems. Assuming an organization has the right goals (dealt with in a moment), the possibility of a threat to survival results in the wish to minimize any deviations that might prevent it from attaining its goals. At this time I am unaware of empirical studies that directly show that control systems, defined strictly as negative feedback processes, are tied to environmental threat. But several studies focus broadly on this subject. One is by Fouraker (unpublished manuscript cited in Lawrence and Lorsch 1967b, pp. 191–195). In a series of experiments he showed that threatening environments (scarcity of resources, competition) caused organizations to become more hierarchical, with more emphasis on discipline and conformity (control). A laboratory study by Hamblin (1958) found that small groups became more centralized in crisis conditions. Another study (Janowitz 1959) showed that decision making shifted up the hierarchy under conditions of military crisis. Pruitt (1961) also found that danger to objectives correlated with increased need for coordination and a shift of decision making to higher levels of authority. Pfeffer and Leblebici (1973, p. 278) found that "the extent of competitive pressure is directly related to organizational requirements for control and coordination of behavior" in a study of thirty-eight firms. Khandwalla (1977, p. 336) found that increased authoritarianism accompanied a low to moderate increase in hostility, though it diminished somewhat as hostility went higher. As might be expected, increasingly hostile environments were associated with cost cutting, an attempt to regain cost effectiveness via control. Hostility also was associated with increased standardization and fewer custom products.

Besides these studies there are many other examples of such occurrences. Most organizations instinctively tighten up their control systems during times of economic hardship. The same is true when competitors begin to get the upper hand. The University of California responded with all sorts of added controls over spending, faculty hiring, and the use of guest lecturers during the difficulties experienced in the Reagan years. Surely the Manned Space Program had one of the most elaborate and redundant control systems of all time in its attempt to assure "zero-defect" results. In short, the contention that environmental threat leads to control systems and what are known pejoratively as "bureaucracy" and "red tape" seems well founded, though more research would help.

Environmental Change. This element, and the remaining ones, have been much more frequently discussed and studied of late. One difficulty is that the dynamics of the environment have often not been separated from its uncertainty. Needless to say, many changes are not predictable. But many others are. Many organizations have learned to produce products that have a very short effective life and thus they are continually changing products; but the changes are planned and predictable— "planned obsolescence" it is often called. Other organizations operate in cyclical fashion, facing changes of considerable magnitude which are nevertheless quite predictable. The studies of Burns and Stalker (1961), Lawrence and Lorsch (1967), and Lorsch and Morse (1974), while not carefully separating out the effects of uncertainty and change, did support the idea that organizations respond to environmental change by introducing more flexible management styles. Burns (1967) found that environmental change led to more spoken rather than written communication. In a study of construction firms Stinchcombe (1959) concluded that instability decreased bureaucratization. McWhinney (1975) described one instance where an organization introduced an additional hierarchy just to cope with the problem of adapting to its changing environment. Therefore, there has been some support in the literature for the idea that environmental change favors selection of organizations having flexible systems or management capability. The purpose of flexible systems is to keep the goals and internal operating systems in a better short-term fit with forces, demands, or values emanating from the organization's environment. One of the better-developed conceptualizations of organizational response to environmental change is that by Schein (1980), referred to earlier.

Environmental Diversity. Environmental diversity not only favors selection of differentiated organizations through specialization, as discussed in chapter 4. It also causes differentiation within organizations. Organizations are divided into different product or service departments so each may specialize in producing different products demanded by customers. The classic study on this was that by Chandler (1962), who concluded that divisionalization was the direct result of a managerial response to a diversified environment. Miller (1959) argued that organizations are differentiated depending on the geographical, technological, and time diversities they face. Lawrence and Lorsch (1967) have shown that organizations are differentiated to cope with environments that have changing and uncertain components as well as stable and certain ones. Tannenbaum et al. (1974) reported findings that organizations in different countries have differentiated control system designs, depending on the kind of political and cultural environment they are in. Khandwalla (1977) found that environmental diversity was associated with divisionalization and technological diversity, as did Rumelt (1974). In general, the more different components of an environment an organization responds to, the more it is internally differentiated. Mintzberg (1979) reported a number of other studies showing how organizations responded to environmental diversity through structural differentiation.

Environmental Uncertainty. Environments are uncertain if events in them are unpredictable. The incidences of threat, diversity, and change, but especially the latter, unpredictably influence on the workplace and therefore the uncertainty has to be managed. Thompson (1967) has pointed out that uncertainty may be managed in two broad ways. One is a vertical layering where additional levels of managers result, the premise being that each level absorbs some portion of the uncertainty. Alternatively, horizontal layering occurs by introducing places or departments that buffer the workplace from rises and falls in the flow of inputs and outputs, smooth the flow of inputs by better search and selection methods, or smooth the outputs by evening out demand for the products or services. Thompson's notion of managing uncertainty through rationing affects an organization by requiring less differentiation so that fewer products are necessary. His method of managing uncertainty by increasing the flexibility of the workplace is no different from developing an adaptive response to any kind of environmental change. The general proposition is that environmental uncertainty favors selection of organizational *layering*, where the uncertainty is managed by adding vertical levels of management or horizontal pre- and post-stages to the workflow. Jelinek (1977) referred to the layering as *infrastructure technology*. Because the empirical studies do not separate uncertainty from the other elements, clean empirical findings are not available. This is reflected in Mintzberg's (1979) treatment of environmental effects, where uncertainty is not mentioned as a separate effect. He cited Duncan (1972) in support of his conclusion that uncertainty should be lumped in with environmental dynamics rather than with complexity. I think Mintzberg missed the idea that dynamics has two components—change and uncertainty. His argument for separating uncertainty from complexity/diversity was effective, however.

The foregoing remarks illustrate how some populations have survived by mitigating environmental effects on the workplace through the development of various managerial competencies. Broadly:

> Threat *favors*   Control Systems
> Change *favors*   Adaptive Systems
> Diversity *favors*   Internal Differentiation
> Uncertainty *favors*   Vertical and Horizontal Layering

There has not been a substantial amount of empirical research to draw upon in forming these illustrations, but some research, excellent theorizing, and anecdotal or other evidence were discussed. In anticipation of my later emphasis on natural selection theory and explanatory but nonpredictive understanding, I emphasize that the foregoing relations simply show that these favoring effects appear to have been found in a few limited places. I do not want to suggest in any way that I believe, for example, that threat causes control. Rather, I take the view that under conditions of environmental threat organizational populations responding by increasing control *or some alternative equally effective competence* will be favorably selected.

7.1.3 The Dominant Competence Species Concept

Taken together, the primary task and the workplace-management task may become a rather complicated set of activities that members of an organization must know how to accomplish. Their knowledge and skills comprise the main part of an organization's survival competence. To distinguish this part of the competence from other more peripheral competencies not thought to be important in classifying organizations, the primary task and workplace-management competencies will be referred to as the DOMINANT COMPETENCE.

As the discussion unfolds, *primary task, workplace,* and *technical core* will be used interchangeably to refer to the operation of the technical system and its hardware and software. The people involved will be referred to as operators. These typically include nonsupervisory personnel and first-line supervisors. The people in higher ranks of authority who handle workplace-management tasks for one or more units of the technical core will be called managers.

Dominant competence is conceptualized as the link between environmental forces and organizational form. This relationship has been aptly summarized by Perrow (1970) in his model of how environments lead to different organizational forms. A generalized view of his model was shown in figure 4.1.

Drawing on the discussion in chapter 5, environmental problems emanate from at least nineteen climatic conditions and four textural configurations, with further expansion of this list a probability. The problems posed by the environment have an immense impact on the workplace technologies that organizations develop to carry out the five unit operations of their primary tasks. The diversity in primary task technology varies as the product of climate and textural variables times the number of different products and services offered by the total populations of organizations. No doubt this number is an upper bound as not all combinations of environmental variables by different outputs would be expected to lead to primary task differences. Nevertheless, most cells in this n-dimensional configuration of problems will present the operators of the primary task workplace with a unique set of problems. According to the model this will in turn give rise to unique workplace technologies.

The Perrow model holds that the primary task technology will evolve as the operators of the technical core solve problems in converting inputs into outputs. Perrow described these problems in terms of two very general dimensions, variability in input stimuli and variation in response or search behavior. Probably each of these will be different for each unique set of environmentally imposed problems. The evolution of primary task technology follows as the operators strive to gain the technical efficiency necessary to keep the conversion process(es) competitive, given the prevailing conditions and texture. The result is that there is a probability of an n-dimensional configuration of primary task technologies largely isomorphic with the n-dimensional configuration of environmentally imposed problems. But the possibility for differences among organizations does not end here.

The design of a technical system creates organizing problems not amenable to solution within the technical core. Not all problems posed by the environment can be solved by the operators of the technical system. Furthermore, technical designs that are effective in dealing with environmental problems create, in turn, other problems in the technical system that are not amenable to solution by additional technical hardware, software, or primary task technology. For example, an assembly-line operation may be an excellent device for turning out products efficiently but it creates the need for planning and personnel training that are not part of the hardware technology. The organizing solutions to these kinds of problems are the responsibility of the managers directly responsible for the effectiveness of the primary task.

The organizing problems imposed on managers by the primary task technology have been described as largely stemming from models of effectiveness, the creation of subunits and the resultant interdependencies, and the protection of the technical core from the incursions of environmental forces. These three broad managerial functions are thought to be particularly sensitive to differences in primary task technologies or environmentally imposed problems. Further differentiations within each function are possible, but it is not expected that the n-dimensional configuration of workplace-management competencies will be isomorphic with the configuration of primary task technologies. Only two general models of effectiveness have been identified, though there could be differences in the control systems associated with each model. Only three kinds of general interdependencies were identified, but again, there could be further differences in the way they are combined with geographical, technological, and time differentiations. Only four environmental forces were seen to have direct incursions into the nature of organizational forms as managers try to protect the technical core. More forces are likely to be identified once their effect on organizational form is more clearly understood. The net effect of differences among workplace-management competencies is probably to smooth over some of the differences among the primary task technologies. Whether differences taken into account for classificatory purposes ultimately reflect the very many differences among primary task technologies, or the seemingly fewer differences among workplace-management competencies, cannot be determined until considerable classificatory research has taken place.

Primary task and workplace-management competencies together define dominant competencies. Each of the latter, according to the model, results in a unique organizational form. Form has been defined loosely as the functions, processes, and structural configuration of an organization (see section 7.3.2 for further definition of form). Each dominant competence is carried out by organizational members or employees who perform a variety of necessary functions. The combination of functions making up each dominant competence can be different from other dominant competencies. Woven in and around the people performing various functions are a variety of ongoing or continuous actions, activities, procedures, or processes, such as goal formulation and clarification, decision making, information sensing and validation, reactive and proactive action to correct deviations from intended purposes, interpretation and transmission of communications, differentiation and integration of subunits, conflict resolution, assignment of responsibility for functions to people, and so on (McKelvey 1970). In general, processes are expected to vary depending on the kind of effectiveness model used, the level of differentiation and complexity of interdependencies, and the nature of the environment and the effects of external conditions on internal political and cultural conditions—or what is referred to in the literature as "organizational climate" (Steers and Porter 1975, pp. 297– 299). Finally, structural configuration, defined in terms of variables such as workflow configuration, centralization, standardization, specialization, complexity, formalization, and so forth (see Pugh et al. 1968, for example), varies according to the effectiveness model used, the subunit differentiations at both the technical and managerial levels, the kinds of interdependencies and methods for handling them, and the various strategies managers use for protecting the technical core.

The foregoing description of the model attempts to spell out broadly how environmentally imposed problems result in organizational forms of various sorts. I think a more detailed treatment is not necessary since the various stages in the model are well understood and described in the literature. The purpose of my discussion has been to show the pivotal role of dominant competence in linking different organizational forms to different combinations of environmentally imposed problems. I have taken the Perrow model as the basic conceptualization in a theory of how organizational differences come about. While the discussion has mentioned a variety of conceptual and empirical contributions, it is clear that there are many gaps in our understanding of the entire set of events. In particular, Perrow's view offers a chainlike sequence from environment to form. In chapter 13 I offer an alternative nonsequential view, still using the same conceptual units. Nevertheless I feel that the basic units of the theory have been established. At this point in time dominant competence is the best basis for a theory of organizational differences. Therefore, the organizational species concept is defined as follows:

> Organizational species are polythetic groups of competence-sharing populations isolated from each other because their dominant competencies are not easily learned or transmitted.

The key concepts in this definition are: *polythetic, competence-sharing populations,* and *isolated.* The term *polythetic* was defined in chapter 3. The other two concepts will be defined in the course of the following discussion of the strengths and weaknesses of the dominant competence species concept.

7.2 EVALUATION OF THE DOMINANT COMPETENCE SPECIES CONCEPT

In this section the strengths of the concept will be evaluated in terms of the several criteria for an effective species concept as well as some others. Several difficulties will also be identified, though I will conclude that they are not insurmountable.

7.2.1 Strengths

In Terms of Cross-Validation with Systems Concepts

One way to get an idea of the scope of the dominant competence technology concept is to compare its elements with the generally recognized systems concepts that have emerged in general systems theory (Katz and Kahn 1978; Buckley 1967). These concepts comprise the elements of systems at many levels of analysis, whether groups, organizations, and societies, or machines or biological organisms (Miller 1978). Since they are well known and easily available in most texts on organizations, they are not discussed here. Table 7.1 shows various systems concepts in parallel with the dominant competence elements discussed in this chapter. It turns out that each concern or problem that gives rise to a competence for handling it has been recognized in general systems theory. The systems concept of throughputs is analogous to the unit operations. The measurement of effectiveness focuses on the net importation of energy after the value of inputs and outputs has been measured. Interdependence between the outputs of one subsystem and the inputs of another has been a key systems concept and is parallel to the management competence concept for coordinating interdependencies among the unit operations within a workplace or among several workplace units. Control is maintaining homeostasis, and dynamic homeostasis is the sys-

TABLE 7.1

DOMINANT COMPETENCE AND SYSTEMS CONCEPTS

Elements of Dominant Competence	Systems Concepts
Unit operations	Throughputs
Measurement of effectiveness	Importation of energy
Workplace interdependencies	Interdependencies (inputs and outputs)
Control systems	Homeostasis
Adaptive systems	Dynamic homeostasis
Internal differentiation	Negative entropy
Vertical and horizontal layering	Boundary development

tems concept covering the process of adaptation to a changing environment. Negative entropy results in internal elaboration and complexity, which is none other than internal differentiation. Vertical and horizontal layering is the same as making boundaries more or less permeable so as to protect the technical core.

In Terms of the Essential Criteria

Since the criterion most alien to present thinking about organizations is the generational mechanism, and since a new concept, the INTER-COMMUNICATING COMPOOL is required; and further since the strongest fears about the possible incursion of the biological analogy are apt to be raised over reference to the generational process, it is discussed first.

Generational Processes: the Compool. It is customary to think of a biological species as plants or animals—tangible objects. *An alternative way of conceptualizing a species is as a set of highly probable gene combinations that are passed on through time by being temporarily held in the bodies of a population.* This is an abstract conceptualization based on combinations of genes, which for a long time were themselves abstract particle concepts used by biologists to explain certain aspects of heredity. They are now seen as segments or independent nucleotide sequences of the DNA molecule which are storehouses of genetic information. The many functional DNA sequences are programs for the production of polypeptide molecules that are the components of enzymes and proteins (some sequences do not have any known function). In this sense genes are groupings of smaller units of genetic information. In this view it is not living bodies that are a species but rather the intercommunicating gene pool, with a body being just the vessel that holds one of many probable gene combinations for a while. Without getting into the myriad details of genetics and evolutionary theory and the different functions or roles of DNA molecules, chromosomes, and genes, all of which are the subject of population biology, I want to emphasize that the concept of intercommunicating genes is the way biologists conceptualize how species remain stable in the short term and slowly evolve in the long term.* Through the operation of the processes of natural selection (see chapter 8), certain combinations are more likely to produce viable offspring than others. Through these mechanisms, for example, only a minute portion of the potential variation that is possible

---

*For excellent introductions to population biology or evolutionary biology see Dobzhansky et al. (1977) or Futuyma (1979).

among human beings (approximately $10^{2,017}$ different germ cells according to Ayala [1978, p. 63], a number vastly greater than the number of atoms in the universe) can be passed down to successive generations. At the same time, slow evolutionary change results from the gradual accumulation of minor mutations (Ayala 1978, p. 59), which produce organismic forms selected favorably by the action of environmental forces, though quantum speciation is now increasingly accepted (see sections 6.1.2 and 8.3).

In the foregoing view of species, genes take on the role of *storehouses of information*, any one of which may combine with others but with varying probabilities of surviving from one generation to another. This is an *abstract* view of the process that in biology often proceeds through sexual reproduction. But that is not necessarily the only direction in which its specifics may unfold; having gone from a particular statement to a general statement, it is not necessarily true that inversely the latter generates only one kind of particular statement. Commenting on the role of analogies in producing knowledge, Lorenz (1974) noted that analogies involve similarities and not identities of traits or features. Building on this, Warriner (1980) observed that the higher the level of abstraction of the similarity highlighted in an analogy the greater the possible differences in the traits of the phenomena involved. There is nothing essentially sexual about varyingly probable combinations of storehouses of information. Thus it is possible to learn from biology and develop a concept of the generational mechanism even though it is totally devoid of the biological notion of sexual reproduction.

It is useful to think of an organization's dominant competence as composed of many elements, each of which is a storehouse of competence information. For example, one such element at the primary task level in a university could be "knowing how to write a paper suitable for a high quality journal." This element includes a considerable amount of smaller information units within it. At the workplace-management task level an element might be "control," along with all the information contained within that concept. The size of any given storehouse has yet to be determined. Certain combinations of the elements are highly probable and are more effective in a particular organizational environment than are other combinations. Each combination gives rise to a particular form of organization. These combinations are passed on through time by being held or known by the people working in an organization from generation to generation as employees come and go. An organizational species, therefore, may be further defined as *a set of highly probable combinations of dominant competence elements that are temporarily housed at any given time among the members of an organizational population.* I will refer to elements of dominant competence as COMPS. I am hardly the first to see organizations as repositories of information or ideas, as the following quote by Van de Ven implies:

> The creation of organizations is not an individual enterprise. Instead, it is a network-building enterprise that centers on the inception, diffusion, and adoption of a set of ideas among a group of people who become sufficiently committed to these ideas to transform them into "good currency" (Schon 1971). Indeed, a gnawing question is whether one should track the creation of organizations [the phenotype] or the life cycle of ideas [the genotype]. Organizations, after all, are but a structural forum in which groups of people institutionalize, harvest, and protect ideas that are in good standing. [1980, p. 131]

For purposes of classification, organizations are conceptualized as the manifestations of dominant competencies whose elements are temporarily embodied in the employees of an organization at any given time. An organization represents a certain highly probable combination of these elements. In this sense an organization is not its buildings or members or its physical manifestations. Instead it is a specific combination of comps that are constellated in slightly different ways in each member of a population of similar organizations. A compool is defined as *the total pool of comps making up the dominant competencies of all members of an organizational population.* The combination of comps forming a single member of an organizational population is a *subset* of the compool. The number of different combinations, which could be as large as the number of organizations comprising a population, may vary from population to population.

Each employee of a particular member of an organizational population holds part of the compool subset. Each employee holds one or more comps, but no employee holds a large portion of the comps, except perhaps in a very small organization. When one employee departs, a new employee replaces him or her; the new employee may already know or can learn exactly the same portion of the compool held by the departing employee, thereby having the same competence as the one leaving. Or the new employee may pick up a different portion, thereby having somewhat different knowledge and skills. Normally the new employee will know a comp or comps from the same compool as the person departing. Thus a new member of an airline typically knows or learns part of the airline compool, not part of the foundry compool or some other one. The compool concept is illustrated in figure 7.1.

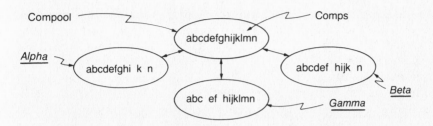

Figure 7.1. Relation Between Compool and Member Organizations.

The comps play the same genotypic role as the genetic material of biological organisms. The compool genotype materializes as a phenotype embodied in individual organizational members of the population. The phenotype is more easily observable but is not always a true representation of the genotype (a missing wing on a butterfly; an incompetent plant manager in an organization). The relation between compool, genotype, organizational form, and phenotype is shown in figure 7.2.

Within a population of organizations having the same dominant competence the intertransfer of employees from one organization to another fosters the intercommunication within the compool and creates stability in the population by preventing the competences in each organization from deviating significantly from those of other members of the population. For example, engineers transfer rather frequently among the high-technology organizations in the Boston and Los Angeles areas as contracts and layoffs come and go. Professors move from university to university, crane operators move from one company to another, and head waiters and chefs move from one restaurant to another. Similarly, within most organizational populations there are transfers of employees from one organization to another in the same population. As long as they limit their transfers to organizations of like dominant competencies,

Figure 7.2. The Genotypic and Phenotypic Roles of Compool and Organizational Form.

individuals can move from one to another without much difficulty because everyone is part of the same compool. In doing so, they provide a means for evening out differences that otherwise might emerge over a period of time.

One of the differences between organizational and biological populations is that among the former, genetic material—that is, comps—may be acquired and spread around the population without transfer of people. People in one organization may attend conferences, go back to school, spy on other population members, read books and journals, or otherwise learn comps without leaving their organization or bringing in a new member. Martilla (1973) found that word-of-mouth communication among competing firms was important in about fifty percent of adoption decisions concerning the purchase of paper. In a detailed empirical study, Czepiel (1975) discovered that knowledge about a major technological innovation in the U.S. steel industry was diffused throughout the population by an active interorganizational communication network. It may be better and faster to stimulate the local comp combination by "bringing in new blood," but it is not necessary.

Stability is also fostered by the nature of many compools. The difficulty of learning a complicated technology or management competence and the resistance to learning competencies not already known within an organization both aid stability. Examples of this are the U.S. organizations that developed aerospace technologies that were very sophisticated but almost useless once the U.S. government cut back funding for space ventures. The organizations and individuals involved faced great difficulties because the technical specialization was so narrow and the level of sophistication that made them effective could not easily be attained in any other specialized technical field. But if a form of technology is flexible in the face of environmental change, it will not have to change form just because the environment does so. Thus adaptive forms will remain stable as adaptive forms even though the environment changes, because they can absorb the changes without having to change themselves. There are undoubtedly limits to environmental change, beyond which even adaptive forms have to respond by changing form. Hannan and Freeman (1977), Brittain and Freeman (1980), and Hannan (1980) speak to this issue in terms of fine- and coarse-grained niches and r and K specialists and generalists.

As a result of the intercommunication of new ideas about competence among members of a population and as a result of the imagination and inventiveness of the employees of member organizations, elements of a competence probably emerge all the time as new ideas about how to solve technological or organizing problems are tried out. For the most part, the slow addition of useful elements develops a competence without causing a need to alter an organization's classification. Most biological species evolve slowly because those most fit for their habitat have higher chances for survival and their offspring are better able to survive. Likewise the most effective new comps will survive over the long run, and as employees transfer from one organization to another they will tend to carry the new ideas that work along with them. Thus a population of organizations may be expected to slowly improve its compool even though there are no changes in the environment. In other words, the accumulation of minor mutations moves a compool along an evolutionary trend like the slow turning of a screw (note the concept of anagenesis in section 9.1.1, and evolution via random genetic drift in section 8.3).

On rare occasions there might be a major mutant combination of comps that is very different and so much superior that it survives and must be recognized as a new form to be classified. Organizational forms that developed around major inventions like the spinning jenny, the steam engine, the steam locomotive, the airplane, and nuclear power generation would be examples of major mutant forms where previously existing dominant competencies came together and a new form eventually emerged (in the case of railroad organizations, they were canal building and transportation, wagon transportation, mining, and metal working). As Stinchcombe (1965) noted, other elements in the surrounding society also have to be present (see section 9.1). The appearance of the matrix form in the aerospace population also could be taken as such an example. Once it appeared and was found to be superior, it spread to all aerospace organizations. When a mutant form appears to branch off from an existing form it should be recognized as a new class. But generally it would seem that mutations of dominant competence are not so frequent as to undermine efforts at classification. If mutant forms appeared frequently, a classificatory scheme might be of little value because it could not keep up to date with all the new forms.

Mergers between organizations may or may not result in a new form or new combination of comps. Most frequently it appears that merged organizations whose members embody different compools are not truly merged, but stay as separate divisions under a corporate headquarters organization. For example, when Rockwell and North American Aviation merged to eventually become Rockwell International, the original automotive and aerospace divisions of each company remained as divisions under the new corporate organization—the compools were not actually merged. The only real merger was the melding of the North American headquarters organization into the Rockwell corporate organization (both probably belonging to the same "corporate headquarters" compool to begin with), with the latter being the one that survived. (The idea of a separate organizational form to cover corporation headquarters organizations will be discussed in section 7.3.1.) In other cases where a true merger takes place, the new organizations' members share the same compool to begin with, as was the case when the New York Central and Pennsylvania railroads merged. It is possible that two organizations belonging to different compools could truly merge into one new organizational form; at this time I do not know whether or not this happens. Usually an organization merges with or acquires another dominant competence not to dissolve it but to keep it intact. Thus a marketing organization such as BIC Pen buys an assembly line organization for purposes of manufacturing its own pens rather than contracting to have them made by some other organization. The purpose for doing this would be defeated if the assembly line competence of the acquired manufacturing organization were diluted by merging or mixing it with the marketing competence. On the other hand such a mixing could result in the product matrix form used by large consumer products organizations such as Procter and Gamble. If this happened BIC Pen probably would have to be reclassified, unless empirical studies showed that BIC Pen's new form was significantly different from the P&G product matrix form.

Several pages have been given to the presentation of the compool concept and a discussion of the means that assure that the organizations within a population remain similar in form in the short term. This explains how the species concept handles the problem of short-term stability across generations of employees. It was also shown that slow changes in compools were possible; thus the concept also explains the mechanism of evolutionary change over time and across generations. In my opinion the dominant competence definition of organizational species satisfies the generational mechanism of an effective species concept by allowing short-term stability while also allowing long-term evolution.

Isolating Processes. Because of the diverse problems facing those in charge of the workplace and workplace management, the compools of populations of organizations and the dominant competencies of their member organizations are complicated and highly varied. There are several factors that act to sharpen the boundaries between compools and prevent their dissolution into a common homogeneous mass.

The fact that a compool usually is complicated and extensive means that it is shared among a large number of an organization's employees. Each employee knows only a fraction of the total competence. Only in very simple forms is a single employee able to master all aspects of an organization's dominant competence, and rarely is that employee as proficient in all aspects of it as employees who can specialize in its subcomponents. The consequence is that a dominant competence is not transmitted from one organization to another simply by the transfer of a single employee, even when the individual is a very knowledgeable top manager. A recent study by Shetty and Perry (1976) showed that executives transferring from a company in one kind of industry (dominant competence) to a company in another kind were ineffective. Consider an instance where a top corporate executive moves to become the dean of a management school, as has happened on many occasions. The executive typically brings very little if any of the corporation's dominant competence of, for example, operating a canning or bottling operation with him, mainly because he probably knows very little about the specifics of the operation. Even if he knew the specifics and brought that knowledge with him, it very likely would not be picked up by the management school's faculty, who themselves engage in an entirely different dominant competence of teaching, research, and self-management. Often the new dean has considerable difficulty understanding the dominant competence of the university form of organization and learns the hard way that the dominant competence of his former corporation is not relevant. Thus there is no mixing of the elements of the compools underlying the dominant competencies.

Another factor is that while a dominant competence could be transferred by shifting *many* employees from one to another organization—so that all portions of the dominant competence are transferred—this rarely happens. Organizations are seldom in a position to hire at one time all the employees needed to move an entire dominant competence. And the more complicated and widely distributed among the employees are its components, the more difficult such a mass transfer would be. Furthermore, most organizations try to hold on to members holding key components of their competence. So, unless an organization decides on the goal of actually pursuing a radical change of its dominant competence, the chances are that it will not change significantly through the random shifting of a few, or even many, employees. In short, it is very hard for an organization to quickly learn enough of the elements of a compool to become effective without too great a loss of resources.

In the absence of a specific demand or force emanating from the environment, most members of an organization have little incentive to master a new dominant competence or even part of it. Resistance to change is a ubiquitous phenomenon among organizations. Furthermore, the well-known phrase, "not invented here," emphasizes that while organizations are open systems and can adapt, there is a tendency to draw up the boundaries and only focus on competence developments coming from within the organization. Both of these factors act to diminish the chances that the elements of a different compool will filter into an organization in the absence of a concerted effort to introduce it.

A final factor preventing an inadvertent mixing of competencies is that if an organization's present competence is already well suited to the problems of the workplace and workplace management, any new kinds of competencies are likely to be inferior. This also means there is little incentive to learn them, except in ineffective organizations that mistakenly believe that bringing in a new competence will be better than updating, or managing more effectively, the competence they already have.

A few examples should clarify how isolated different competence forms are. Imagine trying to start up and run a modern oil refinery using only employees who have never worked in other oil refining and related chemical organizations. Would you fly on an airline that had recently been staffed with nonairline employees? Would you enter a coal mine operated by hotel employees? Would you eat in a restaurant staffed by truckers? How many years of practice would you want former employees from trucking, mining, and food processing organizations to have before you thought they had fully mastered the dominant competence of a hospital? The fact you are probably thinking what a ridiculous idea that would be indicates just how different are the dominant competencies of medical, mining, trucking, and food processing organizations. In general, dominant competencies are not easily learned or transmitted. The more difficult it is to learn or transmit a competence, the more effectively it is isolated from other competencies and the greater is the isolation from other forms of an organizational form created by such a competence.

Ecological Processes. The principles of variation and selection that underlie the ecological process can be applied to organizations without the need to invent a new concept such as the compool, and the problem of a possible biological metaphor seems less of an issue. The process of variation was discussed at some length in chapter 5 and need not be repeated here. It was also shown, in chapter 4, that two sources of variation within organizations—Alpha and Sigma—are also well known. Thus the operation of the principle of variation in organizations is fairly well established. There was also considerable discussion in chapter 5 of how environments affect organizations in the sense that environmental climatic conditions and texture are forces having the potential to set the selection principle in operation.

Whether through Alpha or Sigma sources, variations in organizations continually take place. Many of these variations amount to alterations in the comps of an organization's dominant competence. Several possible consequences are worth noting. First, a particular alteration happens which could improve the effectiveness of the organization where it appeared, but the alteration is not recognized quickly enough or it is discouraged because it upsets the existing way of working. In this case a potential improvement to the compool is not even recognized in the organization of origin and never surfaces beyond the particular organization. Second, the alteration in an element of dominant competence may happen and be recognized and continued as a lasting improvement in the originating organization's dominant competence, but for some reason it is successfully or inadvertently held within the organization and never enters the compool. Perhaps the successful alteration gets out of the organization where it happened and temporarily becomes a part of the compool, but for whatever reason it is tried but never picked up by other organizations in the population and so soon ceases to be a viable part of the compool, though it continues as an idiosyncratic part of the originating organization's dominant competence. This example shows that not all elements of a particular organization's dominant competence may enter into and be carried along as part of the population's compool. Third, the successful alteration may get out of the originating organization, enter into the population's compool and be picked up by most other members of the population, all of which see it as an improvement in dominant competence. In this event the alteration lasts and affects the compool of the population and probably can be expected to have altered the organizational form of the population in some way—some changes in a comp having a more profound effect on organizational form than others. Fourth, the successful alteration could enter the population's compool, be picked up by many of the member organizations, and become a lasting element of compool; but the originating organization, for some reason, perhaps the loss of an employee or a mistaken attempt to alter its own dominant competence, does not continue to hold the altered element, even though most other members of the population do. This sets up the possibility that the originating organization will be less effective than the population in general and not survive. It is also possible that the originating organization, facing a new environment, is carving out a niche that is different enough that it has to deviate from the prevailing compool of the population. This could set the stage for the branching off of a new form from the original population.

In the foregoing four instances, forces affecting the disposition of the alteration are ecological. They could reflect environmental climatic conditions or textural forces. It would probably take a very careful analysis of all the forces prevailing before complete understanding of the fate of the alteration was possible. A couple of the best studies of the ecology of large organizations over time are those of Chandler (1962, 1977), which show how the strategy and organization structure (form) changed as a result of environmental forces. In a study of small organizations, Aldrich and Reiss (1976) showed how white-owned small businesses were replaced by state- and minority-controlled not-for-profit organizations as a result of the changing racial complexion of the area, and by minority-owned businesses that were of different organizational form than the white-owned businesses. Brittain and Freeman (1980) uncovered some aspects of population ecology in their historical study of the semiconductor industry in the United States. Hannan (1980) reported on a historical study of the ecology of national labor unions in the United States. Some other empirical studies, such as those by the contingency theorists, were cited in chapter 5. I conclude that even though there are not many empirical ecological studies, the theory is strong enough to warrant faith in the operation of ecological processes.

Polythetic Groupings. The dominant competence and compool concepts are compatible with the assumption that the protosystem is composed of polythetic groupings of organizations. The concept of polythetic groups is important because organizations are complicated and varied to the point that a small set of characters cannot reasonably be expected to differentiate the groupings. *Each* member of an organizational population or group possesses many of the same attributes as other members of the group. And *each* character is possessed by *many* members but *no* character is possessed by *all* members. Thus it is reasonable to think of aerospace organizations as having the same dominant competence even though they are not exactly alike. They possess a great many workplace and workplace-management attributes in common. Furthermore, each attribute of aerospace competence is possessed by many aerospace organizations and there may not be any single attribute possessed by all members of the aerospace group. The dominant competence species concept is compatible with modern theories of classification because it can apply to polythetic groupings.

Real Objects. Largely because they allow polythetic groupings, the dominant competence and compool concepts apply to real existing organizations as opposed to abstract or ideal types of organizations. A classification based on dominant competence is made up of populations of organizations that can be empirically studied. It results in groupings familiar to managers and nonmanagers alike. It is compatible with the way people in general are accustomed to thinking about organizations. This is mainly because the concept includes elements of the workplace where the primary task is carried out—teaching, machining, assembling, mining, and so forth, as well as the accompanying management organizing tasks.

In Terms of Empirical Validation

Besides meeting the five essential conditions of an effective species concept, the dominant competence concept gains scientific strength because it may be empirically validated. An inductive theory that does not foster deductive empirically testable propositions offers no means of scientific proof of its validity. All workplace and workplace-management competencies exist in real organizations. Populations can be defined and samples drawn. While details must be worked out, as discussed in chapter 11, the attributes of dominant competencies can be operationally measured. The species identified by dominant competencies are not ideal types that identify combinations of attributes that few if any real organizations have.

The classes of organizations resulting from an evolutionary theory of classification which are based on the dominant competence species concept can be empirically tested through use of the numerical taxonomic methods (see section 7.4.). Preliminary populations of similar organizations may be hypothesized and empirically tested for homogeneity within themselves and differences between each other. By emphasizing comps, systematists are guided away from trivial characters. This overcomes one of the principal weaknesses of the numerical phenetic theory of classification.

In Terms of Scientific Relevance

The dominant competence species concept gains its scientific relevance through the evolutionist classification that it makes feasible. Such a classification is scientifically important because it produces a general rather than a special classification and because it explains the origin of organizational groupings. Recall that a general classification is most important because it produces the homogeneous populations necessary for the proper working of the inductive-deductive cycle, and because it offers a scheme for ordering and retrieving scientific findings about organizations.

In Terms of Practical Usefulness

Focusing as it does on the workplace and the management problems directly associated with the functioning of the workplace, the dominant competence concept receives high marks for its centrality to the everyday concerns of practicing managers and their subordinates. It fits in very well with typical commonsense notions about why one organization is different from another. It also fits in well with the prevalent clustering of training programs and skills into professional and trade groupings. It does not require a wholesale change of the way people are accustomed to thinking about organizational groupings. Most managers and employees can be expected to like the idea of finding scientific knowledge organized around groupings they recognize and can readily apply to the organizations they are responsible for or work in.

7.2.2 Difficulties

The dominant competence species concept is not without difficulties, just as the biological species concept has its problems.

Lack of Operationality

The biological species concept is strong because it offers the objective test of reproduction at the species level. Its weakness is that there are many circumstances and species where the reproductive test cannot be applied: for example, when fossils and asexual species are concerned. And there are other circumstances where it does not hold, such as when hybridization occurs. Similarly the dominant competence concept is strong because many dominant competencies are clearly isolated from each other because of the difficulty of learning and transferring them. But no doubt there are going to be situations where dominant competencies appear to be distinct but are not so complicated as to prevent relatively easy sharing and mixing.

The biological species concept generally gets into more difficulties as the organisms become simpler because these are more likely to be asexual. The same may also hold for organizations—as they become simpler their competencies will be more easily learned and transmitted and so the isolating process implicit in the dominant competence species concept no longer applies. It may be that very simple organizational forms will have to be classed as one kind somewhat less homogeneous than other classes. Thus, even though the workplaces of gas stations, day care centers, roadside fruit stands, and new entrepreneurial or inventors' garage shops are different, they may all have the same simple—possibly the primitive—*Hunters* organizational form (see chapter 10). Alternatively, it may be that more than one species concept will emerge to handle special situations, as has happened in biology, or that a disjunctive definition of species will be used. The dominant competence concept could very well apply to the mainstream of complicated organizations with other concepts being used for special cases.

Insufficient Information

I expect that in organizational science, as in biology, there will never be sufficient information to allow an evolutionary classification to fully escape from subjective judgments. This will be especially true in trying to understand the origins of present organizational forms. Whereas biologists rely on fossil records for clues about the past, organizational systematists will have to rely on documentary reports of past organizational forms. Since old documents were never planned in light of the future needs of systematists, they will never be perfect data for systematic judgments. But, as with fossils, they will probably provide good clues to those with enough insight to put them into proper perspective. No doubt some organizational forms will be better documented than others, just as some biological organisms leave better fossils than others. Consequently insights into the formation of some forms will undoubtedly be more complete than knowledge about others.

Insufficient information may also be a problem in the identification of organizational species. It is virtually certain that not all the relevant characters for all species are known at this time. While the dominant competence concept has been defined at some length, it is possible that some time will pass before valid measures are available for all known characters, and there probably will be debate over which characters are relevant. In some instances it may prove difficult to measure enough characters of the organizations included in a study of certain populations to allow stable numerical solutions.

Fortunately the problem of insufficient information diminishes as more experience accumulates. Measurement techniques will improve and the development of new methods expressly for purposes of systematic studies will bring more information to bear.

Evolutionary Intermediacy

As in biology, organizational systematists should assume that they will discover some organizational populations in early stages of speciation. This means that their dominant competencies are somewhat different from the population they are closest to but that their competencies are not effectively isolated from the parent compool. These forms are in the intermediate steps of speciation (see the discussion of Ross's model of speciation in section 6.1.2). The environmental change causing the speciation may have been so recent that the organizations have not had time to fully adapt. Possibly a "shake-out" has not yet occurred in that slack resources have worked to protect a population from the kinds of environmental pressures that would select for or against members of the population. It may be that the dominant competencies—that is, the comps—are quite different but as yet these differences have not shown up as phenotypic differences in the more obvious aspects of form. In the case of evolutionary convergence, it is possible that two different organizational forms may have moved toward similar dominant competencies but, because of the recency of the move, differences in some aspects of form still prevail.

The main cause of evolutionary intermediacy is a recent change in a population's environment. Belief that an organizational form is on the way to becoming a new species would be strengthened if corroborative forces were identified in its environment. Without such forces it could be that a population or member has been inappropriately moved in the direction of a new form by managers or consultants who have an incorrect view of an environment. Or in the case of some consultants, the organization is being changed following some preconceived notion of what an effective organization should look like. Thus, in the mid-sixties it was popular for some academic experts on planned change to imply that the democratic universitylike organizational form should be the model of all future organizations (Bennis 1966). Such statements are suspect as they assume that all organizations exist in the same environment as universities.

Rapid Evolutionary Pace

Many biological organisms evolve so slowly that at any given time they appear to be quite stable. Furthermore their evolution has been going on for so long that only effective forms have survived. Those remaining can generally be assumed to be effectively adapted to their environment, though there are now many species not surviving because of the rapid environmental changes brought about by the human race. It seems that organizations have evolved at a much faster pace than biological organisms and that some present populations are not effectively adapted, the U.S. automobile and steel populations being good examples. If they survive, their present form will be considerably altered. Because of the fast rate of environmental change and fast pace of evolution, systematists will have to pay close attention to measuring both environmental and organizational attributes so as to ascertain which forms are adaptive in which environments.

Biological systematists recognize different rates of evolution as *tachytelic* (rapid), *horotelic* (moderate), and *bradytelic* (slow "living fossils") (Simpson's terms, cited in Sneath and Sokal 1973, p. 313). They have even developed a system for measuring different rates of evolution. Interestingly, much of the initial thrust toward numerical taxonomy came from systematists studying bacteria that evolve so fast that orthodox classificatory methods were inadequate. The important point to note here is that fast evolutionary rate is not sufficient reason for eschewing systematic inquiry.

The implication of fast environmental change is that organizational forms cannot be expected to remain stable for great periods of time and, further, that new organizational forms may emerge more rapidly than new biological forms. Thus, while there are not nearly as many organizational forms as biological forms, organizational systematists may have more difficulty in keeping their classification up to date.

The legitimacy of expecting new organizational forms rather frequently will tend to result in many false claims that new forms have been found. There will be difficulty in identifying new forms that are genuine species amid other organizational changes that can be expected to come and go as managers or management fads change. This problem can be alleviated somewhat, if not completely, by emphasizing characters that change only in response to true and significant environmental changes. Only experience will help systematists understand which of all the characters are useful in this respect.

7.2.3 Strengths and Difficulties in Perspective

The identification of the foregoing difficulties does not negate the validity of the organizational species concept any more than similar difficulties negate the validity of the biological species concept. These difficulties will clearly be the basis of much debate among organizational taxonomists, just as they have been among biologists. This is as it should be. Fortunately the organizational species concept posed here does lend itself to empirical testing, and therefore the application of numerical taxonomic methods will allow it to be put to an empirical test. However, there may be some forms that for various reasons do not lend themselves to numerical methods, and so subjective judgments will continue to exist in organizational classification and the difficulties will continue.

The dominant competence concept meets all the essential conditions required of a species concept fitting under the evolutionist theory of classification. It accommodates isolating, ecological, and generational processes, and produces polythetic, real organizational forms. The concept achieves scientific relevance and practical usefulness as well. However, it mainly applies to the mainstream of organizational forms, leaving to other means the handling of special situations.

The dominant competence species concept may not turn out to be the only concept that meets all the conditions. As experience accumulates, other conditions of an effective concept may be identified which will influence the final choice of a species concept. It is possible that an alternative species concept will meet the criteria set forth in chapter 6 better than does the dominant competence concept. However, it seems to be a suitable concept for the moment.

7.3 DEFINITIONAL NOTES

Two key concepts in the definition of fundamental taxonomic units (section 7.1) not yet elaborated upon are technological interdependence and organizational form. These are discussed in this section with further comment on the operationality of the dominant competence concept.

7.3.1 Technological Interdependence and Organizational Entitivity

Technological interdependence is present when, in the accomplishment of the primary task, the successful performance of one element of an organization's dominant competence requires the successful performance of other elements of its competence. Since "successful performance" is itself difficult to define, a more operational means of identifying technologically interdependent units is needed. A recent paper by Freeman (1978) offered help on this. He concluded that, "In general when changes in the dependent variable occur simultaneously, and result from changes in the same independent variable(s), the subunits can be treated as a macro unit. It is this simultaneity of change and the operation of correlated causes that produce the unified pattern of action that we generally use to infer unitary properties" (1978, p. 349). In terms of this definition, *a fundamental taxonomic unit is one in which it can be determined that changes in technologically interdependent subunits took place simultaneously as the result of changes in one or more independent variables.* This definition is operational in that key elements in the definition, "simultaneous change among the parts" and "response to independent variables" can be empirically tested, though not necessarily without difficulty. Thus at least some attributes that indicate the competencies of the units in question are expected to vary unitarily in response to the same environmental variables. Otherwise the units would not be considered technologically interdependent. Those not varying unitarily would not be considered part of that organization's dominant competence. The meaning of the phrase "at least some" is necessarily vague. Unless all possible environmental elements are changed at the same time—an impossibility—it does not seem possible that all attributes of the technologically interdependent units in question would vary unitarily. It is possible that only one attribute would fulfill the test. Further speculation on this seems fruitless until a specific study is underway.

The idea of technological interdependence raises the question of organizational entitivity in two respects: (1) Are organizations organismic entities or ecological aggregates? (2) How to handle a case where an organization seems to have two or more primary tasks?

Over the years there has been considerable discussion of whether organizations are entities in and of themselves or whether they are just aggregates of subunits. Operationally the problem has been whether measures based on aggregating employees or members were all that was possible or whether true measures of organizations as "macro" or non-aggregated entities could be found (Lazarsfeld and Menzel 1969). Much of this discussion was reviewed by Freeman (1978) and need not be repeated here. Recently there has been a discussion of this issue in the context of taxonomy and evolutionary theory. Warriner (1980) raised the issue in an argument aimed at demonstrating that the biological analogy of a species concept is appropriate to organizational taxonomy. His question was whether organizations were "organismic" (an organism is defined by Webster's dictionary as "a complex structure of interdependent and subordinate elements whose relations and properties are largely determined by their function in the whole") enough to warrant the species analogy. As he noted, "In the biological case, organisms are systems in which the traits or features are interrelated and interconnected so that any given part or organ must fit with and be adapted to other parts, organs, and characteristics" (1980, p. 15). Thus the adaptation of birds to flight meant a beak instead of massive teeth and jaws, porous instead of dense bones, feathers instead of hair, and so forth. There is coherency to the adaptation of a constellation of attributes, which is characteristic of organismic status. "If organizations are merely assemblages of generally autonomous parts or traits whose characteristics are each independently and externally determined, then our problem is unlike that of the biologist and it would be possible to conclude that a similar environmental feature would evoke the same response or would be adapted to in the same way by quite diverse kinds of organizations" (Warriner 1980, p. 16). He concluded that the argument for an organizational species concept could only go forward under the assumption that organizations had organismic qualities.

In personal communications to Warriner and McKelvey, Blute* raised two questions. First, are organizations really organismic in nature? In organisms, she supposed, the subunits are never in conflict with the purposes of the whole. In this sense they are altruistic, though it is not clear that subunits such as the heart or lungs, which operate homeostatically, are really altruistic. Organizations, in contrast, often have subunits that operate in direct conflict with the purposes of the whole, or in general there seem to be many more conflicts and cross purposes among organizational employees and subunits than among organismic subunits. Blute wondered if a better approach might be to see organizations as ecological aggregates in which all the subunits compete for survival, with the whole representing some sort of ecosystem. Second, is Warriner's assumption warranted that the organismic status of organizations is necessary for evolutionary theory to apply? The questions are highly relevant and definitive answers are hardly in the offing. And yet they cannot be left dangling. My own view is that organizations, like organisms, are *not* ecological systems. In contrast to Blute, I think that in each case there are numerous subsystems potentially at odds with each other, but in each case there are other "executive" systems that keep the subordinate antithetical but equally necessary subsystems contained in support of the entity as a whole. An example of possibly antithetical subsystems with which I have personal experience is the secretion of acid in the stomach. If the executive balancing system works properly the normally functional flow of acid is controlled. In my case it was not for a time and I ended up with an ulcer; yet I am still an organism. The point is that entitivity does not depend on the presence of altruistic subcomponents.

The degree to which the genotypical form is correctly embodied in individual organizations is one of the determinants of their effectiveness. The correct embodiment of the form depends on the people in the individual organization. Some employees will consistently make decisions compatible with the form that has proven effective in the environmental conditions confronting the population of which their organization is a member. Other employees, perhaps because of their interests or incompetence, will not. Presumably a form that is so alien to the interests of the people working in organizations will not really exist, or certainly not exist for long, because it would never be correctly em-

*Marion Blute, personal communication, 13 June 1979.

bodied in any real organizations. A possible example of this is the "democratic," "Theory Y," "T-Group," "open, authentic," or "high commitment" organizational form advocated by Argyris (1962), Schein and Bennis (1965), Margulies and Raia (1978), Walton (1980), or other "Organizational Development" proponents. This form, so far as is known, has never achieved more than temporary "life" in organizations. The genotype of the "O.D." form does not appear to exist in the compool of any real population of U.S. organizations. One could say it is a test-tube hybrid form that so far has not found a viable host of real organizations.

The idea of technological interdependence is also important in resolving the problem of what to do when an organization, as a legal entity, has more than one dominant competence. This occurs most obviously among organizations known as *conglomerates*, though vertically integrated corporations whose various divisions all contribute to a final product, such as an automobile, also may have many divisions that have nothing in common from a technological perspective. Even some large divisions of corporations may have subunits that are technologically independent. A large corporation thus may have both horizontal differentiation (several technologically independent divisions) and vertical differentiation (headquarters, division, craft shop) of forms. A solution to this problem is to accept the idea that an organization as a legal entity may include more than one organizational form. Take the University of California, for example. It has a "headquarters" form that has the workplace and workplace-management competence of integrating nine campuses and interfacing with the legislature, the governor's office, and the public. It has nine campus organizations that have the "university" form in which teaching and research activities are pursued, presumably in a synergistic fashion (for most effectiveness). Finally, each of the several campuses has different subunits that probably follow a form different from that of the university form, examples being the craft shops on most campuses—painting, printing and reproduction, cabinet making, machine shops, and so on. Additional forms could be the hospital form, the hotel form (dorms), and food service forms, large to small. In short, a variety of forms exist in the one legal entity. The subordinate forms may be classed separately or considered as parts of the dominant competence. Systematists may try out both possibilities. Whatever happens, similarities among subordinate forms should not be allowed to obscure differences among dominant competencies.

A remaining problem occurs around possible differences between a form that is embodied in a subunit versus one that is embodied in an independent legal unit. For example, do printing and reproduction organizations on a university campus, at a private business, and those that operate as independently owned shops all have the same organizational form? Fortunately, this question can be resolved empirically. It could turn out that they will be of the same species but represent infraspecies variations. My position is that an organizational classification will be one of forms, not of organizations as legal entities.

7.3.2 Organizational Form

Hannan and Freeman (1977, p. 935) defined organizational form as "a blueprint for organizational action, for transforming inputs into outputs." The blueprint included formal structure (organization charts, written policy manuals, and so forth), patterns of activity (who does what), and normative order (what is defined as legitimate). In section 4.3.1 I took a broader view, saying that form is defined as those elements of internal structure, process, and subunit integration which contribute to the unity of the whole of an organization and to the maintenance of its characteristic activities, function, or nature. The problem here is to work toward some idea of what an organizational form might look like without going too quickly toward a narrow definition that might prematurely preclude important aspects of form. Warriner (1977), McKelvey (1978), and Blute (1979) all agreed that the single greatest flaw in systematic thinking among organization scientists so far (except for Sells, 1964) was to make a much too narrow definition of form and use far too few characters to measure it.

It does seem to make sense to limit organizational form to what is observable and measurable. Form can be measured via morphological, physiological, ecological, behavioral, and geographic characters. This is discussed in more detail in chapter 11. In this view, form includes shape, appearance, and displacement as well as both function and process behavior. It is doubtful that a more precise definition of organizational form can be had except by working up specific definitions for a particular population of organizations. Again, note that form is a population concept, for classification purposes. The problem is to sift through all the "noisy" phenotypic forms of individual organizational members of the population to find the true generic form.

The best preliminary and most operational approach is to say that *organizational form is "that which is measured by taxonomic characters."* In turn, the best strategy for selecting taxonomic characters is to measure everything possible, with the further note that where one is in any way inclined to depart from the dictum of equal weighting, one should emphasize characters associated with dominant competence and evolutionary/ecological importance.

7.3.3 Dominant Competence Operationally Defined

Throughout this book organizations have been viewed as surviving because they were effective in gaining needed resources under conditions of competition against other entities in their ecological community. Organizations gain resources by introducing outputs (products and services) into the environment which have value, thereby allowing the organization to get resources in return. In this view, what is important is not what an organization thought it did or what it intends to do with respect to its environment. Only its actual outputs are important. Therefore, it follows that any operational definition of dominant competence has to be tied directly to the nature of the outputs. Hence the emphasis on the workplace technology of the primary task. Several management organizing tasks were also defined which had direct relevance to the effective operation of the primary task.

An organization's dominant competence is operationally defined as including any aspect of the primary task or workplace-management task that directly affects the nature of its outputs or the level of resources necessary to produce them. There will never be a perfectly clean definition of *directly*. Some workplace tasks will seem obviously relevant, like painting automobile bodies or talking to clients; others will be somewhat less direct but surely relevant, such as maintaining critical machines or storing necessary files. But other activities, such as sweeping floors, may be of more marginal relevance. The latter could be important if dirty or oily and slippery floors lead to accidents which raise the cost of the output, or they could be less important if they are carried out for less obvious aesthetic or marginal long-term health reasons. Similarly, at the management level, decisions regarding the pricing of the product may be directly relevant, whereas decisions regarding the architectural quality of a new factory building may not. It would seem that in any population of organizations, if a broad definition of form and relevant taxonomic characters is taken, there will be enough aspects of the primary task and the workplace-management task to offer up the necessary number of taxonomic characters for solid numerical solutions. Again, it is impossible to offer precise definitions of *directly relevant* without having in mind a specific population of organizations. Once a population is chosen, the identification of directly relevant task competencies is not expected to be overly difficult or contentious. Here too, it is better to err on the side of selecting possibly less relevant characters than to run the risk of omitting truly relevant characters. As experience in the classification of particular populations builds up, there will probably be a parallel development of consensus about what is directly relevant and what is not.

7.4 ORGANIZATIONAL PROPINQUITY AND NUMERICAL PHENETICS

I have suggested the dominant competence species concept as the basis of organizational propinquity and diversity. Since a phyletic classification is largely based on subjective judgments, I have argued that numerical taxonomic methods are necessary to provide an objective test of the resulting classes of organizations. But numerical phenetics will not work unless organizations whose members share the same intercommunicating compool are phenotypically reasonably similar. (An alternative is to do what some biological systematists have done, which is to focus numerical taxonomic studies directly on the underlying genetic material. For organizations this would mean classifying according to similarities among compool elements rather than similarities among attributes of organizational form. As in biology, working with organizational genetic material, the compool, may be very difficult because of a lack of readily measurable information.) Further, it also needs to be established that as the compool becomes more broadly shared as the population of organizations multiplies from its ancestor form (that is, the form that first emerged as a result of a new environment), the phenotypical similarity will not break down. The applicability of numerical methods will be demonstrated best by empirical findings showing that inductively derived classes are confirmed by the numerical studies.

As I pointed out in section 3.1.4, much of the debate among biologists as to the relative superiority of evolutionist or numerical phenetic approaches focused on the significance of character weighting. Sneath and Sokal (1973, pp. 18–30) argued unequivocally for equal weighting. Their main thesis was that numerical phenetics, coupled with the equal weighting of characters, was the best way to identify the groupings present in the natural system. They also recognized, however, that some parts of plants and animals, because they were more complex and needed more characters for complete description, had more influence in multivariate solutions than simple parts. Biologists generally agree that evolution tends to result in increased complexity; hence it turns out that numerical methods, by including more characters from complex parts, inadvertently give extra weight in their solutions to evolutionarily important features—they weight the function, not the individual characters used to measure it. Mayr's (1969) principal objection to numerical phenetics was that it did not weight characters that experience showed were especially important in reflecting evolutionary heritage. He noted that since evolution tended to produce elaboration and complexity, orthodox systematists placed extra weight on characters associated with complex parts such as genitalia, eating parts, and parts used for locomotion. In fact, both biological evolutionists and pheneticists give extra weight to the more complex and evolutionarily important parts of organisms, in the former case by including more evolutionarily important characters in the numerical solution and in the latter case by weighting the characters more heavily.

My view is that in the vast majority of instances groupings based on phyletic and phenetic approaches will identify the same protosystem groupings and thus closely overlap. This is because organizational evolution and specialization tend to result in increased elaboration, so that highly evolved portions of an organization will be more complex than less evolved parts. Therefore the more complex parts will be described phenetically by more taxonomic characters and, even if all characters are equally weighted in multivariate solutions, evolutionarily important features of organizations will receive extra weight. This is no different in effect than what results when orthodox evolutionists give more weight to evolutionarily important characters.

In biology the only instances when the two methods produce clearly conflicting results occur when there are *sibling species* and *sexual dimorphism*, the two extreme cases. Sibling species are pairs or groups of species that are reproductively isolated but which have great phenotypical similarity, which is approximately the case with female ducks of various species. Phyletically they would be placed in totally different groups; phenetically they would be placed in the same group. With sexual dimorphism the two phena sexually mate and reproduce but look dramatically different, as in the case of birds of paradise, where the male is remarkably plumaged and highly colored and the female is smaller, drab, and has rather ordinary feathers. In this case phyletic methods would place them in the same group and phenetic methods would place them in different groups.

At this point there is no way of knowing just how much of a problem these extreme cases will be in organizational classification. An organizational parallel to sibling species would occur if two populations of organizations were phenotypically alike even though their compools remained dissimilar. An analog of sexual dimorphism would materialize where two populations have different forms but the same underlying compool. Neither of these possibilities seems very likely but there will doubtless be instances where evolutionary theory via divisive phyletic clustering will produce groupings not isomorphic with numerical phenetic (agglomerative) results (see chapter 12 for further comment on divisive and agglomerative clustering). In any event, organizational systematists will probably find, as did the biologists, that while there are numerous exceptions where the theory falters and needs further elaborations or even stopgap measures, the vast majority of cases will be adequately taken care of.

7.5 SUMMARY

The purpose of this chapter was to introduce and discuss a species concept to serve as the foundation of an evolutionary organizational classification. A *fundamental taxonomic unit* is defined as an organizational form in which the activities of technologically interdependent subsystems are pooled toward the accomplishment of the primary task. The *primary task* is that set of activities that bear directly on the conversion of inputs into those outputs critical to an organization's survival. An additional concept, the *workplace-management task*, is introduced and defined as that set of managerial activities that bear directly on the operation of the primary task workplace in such a manner as to foster the continued survival of the organization. Of special relevance are the measurement of effectiveness, coordination of interdependencies, and mitigation of environmental forces. Taken together the primary task and workplace-management task define an organization's *dominant competence*. The scope of the dominant competence concept is similar to that of the basic concepts of general systems theory. Building on the competence concepts, *organizational species* are defined as polythetic groups of competence-sharing populations isolated from one another because their dominant competencies are not easily learned or transmitted. The species concept holds up under evaluation in terms of criteria such as the need for isolating, ecological, and generational processes. Genes are abstractly defined as storehouses of information as a bridge to the compool concept, which is defined as the total pool of competence elements, *comps* (storehouses of knowledge and skill), making up the dominant competencies of all members of an organizational population. The evaluation shows that the organizational species concept has scientific and practical strengths as well. Several difficulties are also identified. My conclusion is that the dominant competence concept will apply to the mainstream of organizational forms but that special cases may have to be handled by additional species concepts or by a disjunctive definition. Some operational definitions for technological interdependence, organizational form, and dominant competence are presented. Finally, it is argued that reasonable phenotypical similarity will prevail among organizations belonging to the same compool. This is necessary to allow the use of numerical taxonomic methods in testing the validity of the groupings identified by evolutionary theory.

⑧ AN EVOLUTIONARY PERSPECTIVE

Nothing in biology makes sense except in the light of evolution.
[Dobzhansky 1973, p. 125]

I have come to the conclusion that this model—which I summarize
as "blind-variation-and-selective-retention"—is the only and all-
purpose explanation for the achievement of fit between systems and
for the achievement and maintenance of counterentropic form and
order.
[Campbell 1975, p. 1105]

The previous seven chapters have developed an evolutionary-
empiricist theory of organizational classification. Passing references
to evolutionary theory were made throughout, though no substantial
development of the theory was undertaken. I realize that references to an
undeveloped subject have made comprehension of some points difficult. Nevertheless, since taxonomy is a rather separate topic and since
some organizational systematists will prefer a straight numerical phenetic approach, the separation of taxonomy and evolutionary theory
seems warranted. My position is that the development of the higher
categories should broadly reflect the evolutionary paths of the protosystem and not simply phenotypic similarity. The reader should note,
however, that I also believe that phenetic similarity is a dominant indi-

cation that organizations are of the same population. Therefore, I develop the numerical phenetic method of classification in chapter 12.

Readers should attend to this chapter for reasons beyond trying to understand my theory of classification. Evolutionary theory holds a fundamental position in biology, as illustrated by Dobzhansky's statement above. The quote from Campbell clearly announces his view of the coming centrality of natural selection in the social sciences. Kaufman, a leading contributor to the literature on public administration, has observed that "the [biological evolutionary] metaphor fits remarkably well and explains why human institutions ostensibly created and controlled by people seem to be governed by a momentum of their own" (1975, p. 131). In Weick's (1979) revision of his highly cited 1969 book, natural selection theory, a la Campbell, has been elevated to a more central position. Natural selection is pivotal in Aldrich's (1979) book and underlies the work of Hannan and Freeman (1977) and Freeman (1981). Whether evolutionary theory will ultimately be selected is impossible to say, but it is presently a variation attracting the attention of influential scholars. However, evolutionary theory is more than natural selection, Lamarckian theory may be more relevant to organizational science than the strict Darwinian view in biology, and Campbell's version ignores the population and heredity concepts that are inescapable components of the biological version.

A fuller development of evolutionary theory in organizational science is required. In this chapter, I present a somewhat extended alternative view to that presented by Campbell and subsequently taken up by Weick and Aldrich. I do not offer an extended critique of the many fine points of interpretative differences—space precludes this. Nor will I offer a comprehensive statement on why I view evolutionary theory as a central element of future organizational science, other than to observe that Weick (1979) inserts it as the central theory in his treatment of the internal microcosm of individual organizations (Micro Organizational Behavior) and I have inserted it as the central element of a general theory explaining how organizations survive in their external environments (Macro Organizational Behavior), thus making much of the book witness to the point. The purpose of this chapter is to present some basic postulates and principles of evolutionary theory uncluttered by social scientists' misinterpretations and moralisms.

Evolutionary theory is a tough subject to expound in a short space. Recent biological treatments run 500 pages and more (Løvtrup 1974; Mayr 1976; Dobzhansky et al. 1977; Futuyma 1979). Evolutionary theory has a long and involved history in the social sciences as well as in biology. My decision has been to largely ignore most of the literature and argument in the social sciences and draw directly from the biologists. This is not necessarily because biologists have been working on the theory longer. Anthropologists had an evolutionary view before Darwin, and Herbert Spencer's voluminous sociological writings were concurrent with Darwin's work. The biologist Lamarck (1809) had the earliest complete theory of evolution. It has since been discredited in biology, as have been the ideas of Spencer in sociology.*

Darwin's 1859 book, *Origin of Species*, was distinguished for its comprehensiveness and its synthesis of all available information. But it was its basis in careful observation and experiment that especially set his work apart from the subjective, rhetorical, untestable speculations of Lamarck, Spencer, and the rest. Following Darwin's lead, evolutionary theory in biology developed in the context of an inescapable hard empirical reality. In contrast to its fate in the social sciences, its essence has been honed constantly under the scrutiny of replicable experiments. This is especially true since Fisher (1930), Wright (1931), Haldane (1932), Dobzhansky (1937), and Huxley (1942) spawned the *Modern Synthesis* of the 1930s, which drew together the works of geneticists, systematists, and paleontologists.† The truth of evolutionary theory is clearly evident in the incontrovertible evidence of slow change in the genetic structure of populations—termed *microevolution*.

In contrast, social scientists have tended to load up their evolutionary views with moralisms such as order, direction, progress, and perfectibility (see Campbell 1969 for a brief review), though biologists also have not been totally immune to this. These additions are questionable, unnecessary, and clutter up the basic theory. Furthermore, the social science literature is given over more to arguments about their various interpretations or similar excess baggage than to constructive theory development, the latest example of this being a paper by Quadagno (1979) which draws on a muddy interpretation of evolutionary theory in attacking sociobiology. Later in this chapter I will draw on papers by Campbell (1969), Blute (1979), Langton (1979), and to some extent a book edited by Sahlins and Service (1960), which are exceptions.

Finally, and most important, I favor the biologists' perspective because their theory is phrased in population terms—a view fundamental to this book and totally missing in the social science literature. The population perspective is especially compatible with taxonomy and

---

*Brief reviews of the history of evolutionary thought are given by Dobzhansky (1977) and Futuyma (1979); longer treatments are given by Eiseley (1958) and Greene et al. (1959).

†This synthesis of these disciplines is a distinguishing feature still evident in the book by Dobzhansky et al. written forty years later. Whereas Futuyma's (1979) book is rooted more in modern genetics and is somewhat less Darwinian in tone.

classification, which as a matter of course also focus on populations. Organizations, as opposed to other kinds of sociocultural phenomena, also seem to fit the population perspective more readily.

8.1 DEFINITION

Evolution is a world view that has existed since at least the beginning of the nineteenth century. There is a tendency among some social scientists to confuse evolution the world view with evolution a theory or body of specific falsifiable propositions. As Quadagno (1979) put it:

> Evolution is a world view which embodies many principles, not all of which are admitted in its various uses. Even those concerned with organic evolution, which is its most commonly known form, are unable to agree on the essence of evolution (Lewontin 1968, p. 202). In the evolutionary world view as a general paradigm, a hierarchy of principles can be identified. These include change, order, direction, progress and perfectibility, with each principle being present in some but not all theories of evolution. [P. 101]

EVOLUTIONARY THEORY can be and is stated without reference to any of the foregoing principles except change. "The essential tenets of evolutionary theory entail no value judgments, nor any sense of purpose or direction" (Futuyma 1979, p. 7). Futuyma quotes Schoon in defining evolution to mean "a continuous process of change in temporal perspective long enough to produce a series of transformations" (p. 7). "Evolutionary changes are those that are inheritable from one generation to the next. . . . Evolutionary changes can be almost immeasurably slight, or they can be dramatic. . . ." (Futuyma 1979, p. 7). It is easy to be misled into thinking that biologists do take a moralistic view, however. Dobzhansky et al. do refer to progress (irreversibility) and complexity in their definition of evolution:

> Organic evolution is a series of partial or complete and irreversible transformations of the genetic composition of populations, based principally upon altered interactions with their environment. It consists chiefly of adaptive radiations into new environments, adjustments to environmental changes that take place in a particular habitat, and the origin of new ways for exploiting existing habitats. These adaptive changes occasionally give rise to greater complexity of developmental pattern, of physiological reactions, and of interactions between populations and their environment. [1977, p. 8; emphasis not included]

They define progress as "systematic change in a feature belonging to all members of a sequence in such a way that posterior members of the sequence exhibit an improvement of that feature" (1977, p. 509). They take pains to point out that while "improvement" or "better" is evaluative, they do not use it in any moral sense such as good or evil, right or wrong. *Improvement* simply means "more efficient, or abundant, or more complex" (1977, p. 509). Evolutionary progress may follow several criteria such as dominance, invasion of new environments, replacement, improvement in adaptation, adaptability and possible further progress, increased structural complexity, increased vital processes, or increased range and variety of adjustments to the environment (Simpson 1949). This concept of progress is very much keyed to specific criteria and specific features, for organisms in specific environments. There is no general view that evolution implies progress in any grand sense of the term or for any group of organisms broadly defined. In this sense the view of Dobzhansky et al. is not much different from Futuyma's.

Returning to the quote by Quadagno, I wish to point out one other insidious tendency of some social scientists and most "creationists," which is to interpret the lively debate among biological evolutionists as evidence that evolutionary theory is wrong, untested, unproved, and so forth. A reading of books by Løvetrup (1974), Mayr (1976), Dobzhansky et al. (1977), and Futuyma (1979), to name but a few recent ones, should convince the reader that there is a vast amount of material upon which there *is* agreement. It is agreed that biological evolution is an incontrovertible empirical fact. *Whether* there is evolution is not at issue. The debate is in the *how*, what mechanisms are responsible. Of course biologists are quick to point out that evolutionary theory has not been proven directly in the sense of actually proving an alternate hypothesis, H_1. No biologist has actually seen a new species emerge! Rather, biologists subscribe to the Popperian (1934) notion of falsifiability as the demarcation between science and other forms of knowledge, where a theory is corroborated by rejecting a set of logically derived null hypotheses, H_0. As Dobzhansky et al. say, "the hypothesis of evolution, that new organisms come about by descent with modification from dissimilar ancestors, is an example of a hypothesis corroborated beyond reasonable doubt. This is what is claimed by biologists who state that evolution is a fact rather than a theory or hypothesis" (1977, p. 481).

8.2 THE SOCIAL SCIENCE EXPERIENCE

Using the book edited by Sahlins and Service (1960) and the classic paper by Campbell (1969) as a starting point, an insight into the course of evolutionary theory in the social sciences may be obtained from the following sources: Gerard, Kluckhohn, and Rapoport (1956); White (1959); Rouse (1964); Parsons (1966); Lewontin (1968); Campbell (1970,

1975); Carneiro (1973); Dole (1973); Ruse (1974); Alexander (1975); Kaufman (1975); Service (1975); Wispe and Thompson (1976); Lenski (1976), and Hill (1978). A brief classification of some of the applications of evolutionary theory in the social sciences was offered by Campbell (1969). I have taken his headings verbatim.

1. Interaction of culture and social organization with man's biological evolution.

   1a.   Genetic influence upon culture.

Biological advancement leads to cultural advancement; thus "advanced" cultures are seen as genetically superior to primitive cultures; upper classes are biologically superior to lower classes. Sociobiology (Wilson 1975) is a modern variant of this approach that holds that genes provide the basis of human behavior, though sociobiology is much more explanatory in tone as compared to the evaluative and moral connotations of the older variants. The evaluative form has been discredited and sociobiology is strongly debated (for example, see Caplan 1978; Quadagno 1979).

   1b.   Cultural influence upon genetics.

Takes the view that social customs and policies influence the nature of the genetic stock. The Social Darwinists' (Spencer, Sumner) stand against social welfare and immigration policies argued that these would encourage the unfit to reproduce and thereby weaken the genetic stock of, in this case, American society. This position has been thoroughly rejected, so much so that much of social scientists' enthusiasm for evolutionary theory virtually disappeared along with it.

2. Sociocultural evolution of sociocultural forms independent of changes in genetic stock.

This view holds that the evolution of competence, language, culture, and so forth may take place independently of changes in genetic stock.

   2a.   Theories descriptive of the fact and course of sociocultural evolution.

As did Futuyma (1979, p. 10), Campbell noted that these theories predated Darwin, the Greeks having had an evolutionary view of their emergence from a barbarian past, and linguists having had the concept at least by 1788. There are three subtypes:

2a$_1$. Nonvaluational transformational theories.

The emphasis is on continuity or gradualism in change and the effects of isolation and the passage of time. There is no commitment to differentiating cultures with regard to superiority.

2a$_2$. Unilinear progress theories.

In extreme form this position is: "(a) that all changes in specific cultures or societies represent progress (e.g., advances in complexity of organization, division of labor, size, and energy utilization); (b) that all societies, in the course of their advance, go through the same stages; and hence, (c) that the less advanced societies in the contemporary world are similar to earlier stages of the more advanced peoples." This view, based in large part on Spencer's embryological development analogy, predated Darwin and has since been rejected along with Social Darwinism. Thus, the general idea of sociocultural evolution taken independently of Social Darwinism was beaten down even further among social scientists.

2a$_3$. Multilinear progress theories.

In these theories biological species formation is the analog rather than embryological development. Cultures having a common origin are expected to diverge in response to diverging environmental conditions. Parallel environmental conditions would produce parallel sociocultural evolution. Each line is seen as progressing toward increased adaptive adequacy but only in terms of its own peculiar environment—a view similar to that of Dobzhansky et al. (1977) discussed earlier in this chapter.

2b. Theory descriptive of the process of evolution: variation and selective retention.

Campbell argued that the foregoing kinds of theories all focused on describing the course of sociocultural evolution, either with or without evaluative and moralistic overtones, as opposed to describing the *process* by which evolution might take place. In an attempt to remedy the gap, Campbell devoted the rest of his paper to a discussion of variation and selective retention in sociocultural evolution.

In addition to the classification by Campbell, the characterization of evolution by Sahlins (1960) as being either specific or general should be noted. Specific evolution is based on the phylogenetic model of the biologists. It explains how one culture grows out of another, the historical relation of one culture to another, the environmental conditions equated with various cultures, and so forth. The idea of progress is akin to that of Dobzhansky et al. described earlier, that progress is always relative to adaptive optimality with respect to specific environmental conditions and specific characters. General evolution is based on the biological notion of *grades*; that is, that fish are further advanced than invertebrates, amphibians are advanced relative to fish, reptiles are advanced relative to amphibians, and mammals are more advanced than reptiles. Aside from Huxley (1942), who thought progressive general evolution more important than divergent or specific evolution, biologists now focus exclusively on the latter. Sahlins argued that anthropologists ought to use both. His view was that much of the argument about evolution would be cleared up if the distinction between the two kinds were recognized. He concluded that cultures undoubtedly exhibit specific evolution and also felt that certain stages in the development of general cultural systems could be identified. He felt that feudalism was a less advanced stage than the Roman or Chinese states of earlier times and that some modern primitive cultures are similar in advancement to other extinct cultures. Note that while there are stages of cultural advancement, they are not necessarily arranged in a historical time sequence from less to more advanced. This chapter is about specific or multilinear progress evolutionary theory.

Evolutionary theory has lain on fallow ground in the social sciences for many years. Campbell suggested that the major reason was "the early contamination of the evolutionary perspective with the reactionary political viewpoints of the privileged classes and racial supremacist apologists for colonialism, exclusionist immigration laws, etc." (1969, p. 71). Social Darwinism was equated with political conservatism. Why social scientists, who might be expected to judge the theory for its own sake and not attribute "guilt by association," did not do so could have been due to the lower-class ethnic minority backgrounds and liberal persuasions of many of those ending up in positions of influence, suggested Campbell.

How were social scientists to explain the history of sociocultural systems if not with evolutionary theory? Blute (1979) observed that instead of the "descent with modification from common ancestors" theme of organic evolutionary theory, social scientists espoused "causal laws" purporting to explain historical developments. She listed several of these:

From despotism through monarchism to republicanism (Montesquieu);

From theological through the metaphysical to the scientific (Compte);

From primitive through feudal through capitalist to socialist (Marx);

From savagery through barbarism to civilization (Morgan);

From *gemeinschaft* to *gesellschaft* (Toennies);

From the ideational through the idealistic to the sensate (Sorokin);

From folk through feudal to industrial (Redfield);

From mechanical to organic solidarity (Durkheim).

Blute concluded, first, that sociocultural developmentalists searched for a universal law governing the dynamic behavior of social systems or cultures whereas biological evolutionists viewed organic history as descent with modification; and second, that social developmentalists arranged their groups in a serial array, supposing that the series represented the developmental sequence of each group, whereas the biological evolutionists constructed hierarchical classifications revealing the degree of affinity among groups. She further noted that social scientists are developmentalists because they draw on the embryological rather than the phylogenetic analogy. Shades of Spencer again. She quoted Parsons, for example, as saying that his own theory is "most closely analogous to the process of growth in the organism" (Blute 1979, p. 50).

This short section has given only the briefest view of evolutionary (really developmental) theory in the social sciences. The interested reader should quickly go and study the papers by Campbell, Sahlins, Blute, and others to obtain a much deeper understanding of the arguments and points of view they present. They are excellent and interesting works.

I would like to retain the distinction between evolution and development. It is possible to use evolutionary theory to explain both processes in the social sciences. Campbell (1969) and Weick (1980) used it to understand the development of individual social systems or organizations throughout their life span. Biologists do not do this. They—and I—apply evolutionary theory to change by populations across generations. Looking at organizations, the former is a micro-organizational behavior, short-run view. My perspective is a macro-organizational behavior, long-run view. Aldrich (1979) took both approaches. Since

Campbell and Weick did not focus on the strict sociocultural or organizational counterpart of the biological focus, that is, populations and heredity, their reliance on the biological analogy is much less than mine, though even a mild parallel is too much for many social scientists to take—witness the war of words critiquing Campbell's 1975 paper published in *American Psychologist* (Wispe and Thompson 1976, pp. 341–384). In light of this, I fear my use of the analogy will really upset them.

8.3 BIOLOGICAL NATURAL SELECTION THEORY AND RECENT CHALLENGES

There are four basic principles of natural selection theory (Lewontin 1978, p. 220). The first three are:

1. THE PRINCIPLE OF VARIATION.   There have to be variations among the members of a species or population. These variations may be "heterogeneous," "haphazard," "blind," "chance," or "random," as Campbell (1969, p. 73) put it, or they may be purposive, as Corning (1974) insisted. In biology it is now agreed that variations are strictly random—they do not occur in response to adaptive need. For natural selection theory to work, however, it does not really matter whether they are random or purposive—they just need to occur. Most genetic variation in organisms is slight, but sometimes it is dramatic. Most changes in cultural norms or organizational practices are slight but here too some are dramatic. Campbell (1974) preferred the term *blind* to avoid the modern statistical implications of "random"; variations are not equiprobable—they are independent of each other, they are separate from the environment, they are uncorrelated with the solution, and later variations are not corrections of former ones. Following the development in section 4.3.3, variations by human actors in organizations are treated as myopically purposeful at best and usually quite blind. Because human variations, though blind, may be patterned and not random, I will follow Campbell and refer to them as blind variations rather than random ones.

2. THE PRINCIPLE OF HEREDITY.   The principle of heredity is that offspring on average have to resemble their parents more than they resemble other members of their species. Obviously, if heredity were perfect there would never be any variations. And if offspring did not resemble their parents more than by chance there would be little likelihood that the gene combinationof a particularly fit pair of parents would be passed on. Campbell (1969) termed this RETENTION. He seems to

have avoided reference to heredity or generations, though in his 1975 paper he mentioned retention by children of their parents' culture (p. 1107). But, as noted in section 8.1, biologists define evolutionary theory in terms of changes across generations. Analogously, this refers to generations of successive cultural units carrying along the genotype of a sociocultural form, as opposed to generations of people who, like cells perhaps, carry along the genotype of one cultural unit during their life span. By not recognizing generations, Campbell ends up doing what most social scientists have done, which is to address development throughout the life span of a single sociocultural system rather than across generations as biologists have done. These problems are addressed later in the chapter. My emphasis on populations and evolution across units of culture or different organizations does not preclude, however, the application of natural selection to explain how a culture changes over its lifetime (Campbell 1969) or how an organization changes during its lifetime (Weick 1979). The application of evolutionary theory to developmental processes during the life of a social entity *in addition* to successive generations of units sets social science apart from biology. Clearly organizational and other social sciences need to be more cognizant of developmental processes in contradistinction to evolutionary processes.

3. THE PRINCIPLE OF NATURAL SELECTION. Better-adapted organisms leave increased numbers of offspring either immediately or in the future. For biologists, selection is in terms of surviving offspring or individuals, not in terms of their attributes. Over successive generations, if individuals having certain traits have a higher chance of survival and slowly increase in number relative to the total size of their species, the frequency distribution of the traits in question will change. As will be seen in section 8.6.2, biologists measure evolutionary change in terms of changes in the frequency distributions of traits.

Lewontin (1978) observed that the foregoing three principles are necessary and sufficient to explain the process of evolutionary change but they do not account for adaptation. Darwin introduced a fourth principle dealing expressly with adaptation.

4. THE PRINCIPLE OF THE STRUGGLE FOR EXISTENCE. The variations or gene combinations that are preserved are those giving an individual added advantage in competing for resources against other organisms, staying alive, avoiding being eaten, or enduring stress imposed by the ecological habitat. Only in understanding the ecological context can one understand why species of certain character come into being and survive.

As Darwin said:

> Owing to the struggle [for existence], variations, however slight and from whatever cause proceeding, if they be in any degree profitable to the individuals of a species, in their infinitely complex relations to other organic beings and to their physical conditions of life, will tend to the preservation of such individuals, and will generally be inherited by the offspring. The offspring, also, will thus have a better chance of surviving, for, of the many individuals of any species which are periodically born, but a small number can survive. I have called this principle, by which slight variation, if useful, is preserved, by the term Natural Selection, in order to mark its relation to man's power of selection. But the expression often used by Mr. Herbert Spencer of the Survival of the Fittest is more accurate, and is sometimes equally convenient. [Quoted in Futuyma 1979, p. 291]

Three comments about this quote are in order. First, the struggle for existence does not refer only to an aggressive nature "red in tooth and claw." It also refers to a plant struggling quietly against the drought in a desert or to the mutual help and cooperation of a symbiotic pair.

Second, according to Dobzhansky et al. (1977, p. 98), Darwin did not use the Spencerian phrase "survival of the fittest" in his earlier editions. They point out that natural selection does not lead to the superlative *fittest*, only the *tolerably fit*. Species that survive are just that—survivors. Whether they are the fittest form possible is an evaluative element that is not necessary to natural selection theory.

The third point focuses on GRADUALISM. Darwin and most biologists up until recently have believed in gradualism, the idea that divergence among species was the result of accumulative, ever-so-slight changes over millions of years. Great differences are only the magnifications of minute variations over a long time span. A continuing embarrassment for gradualists were the gaps in the fossil record, though they are handy for taxonomists. In 1940 Goldschmidt proposed an alternative, very unpopular at the time. He argued that some mutations can transform a phenotype drastically in a single step, thus leading to "evolutionary novelties" very quickly. Simpson (1953) proposed that in contrast to the conventional gradualistic speciation model described earlier in this book (section 6.1.2), QUANTUM SPECIATION could occur over a few generations. The process is that a chance new character may develop very rapidly in a small population isolated from the main population. Eldredge and Gould (1972) referred to this process as evolution via PUNCTUATED EQUILIBRIA. Quantum speciation may be a much more useful model for organizational speciation than the traditional model since it will be argued (section 9.1) that organizational forms diverge very quickly after a major invention such as the steam locomotive, airplane, telephone, and so forth, but do not diverge very rapidly afterward. The difference between gradual and quantum speciation was shown in figure 6.2.

Two criticisms are often leveled at natural selection theory, as illustrated in the following passages:

> For what good is a theory that is guaranteed by its internal logical structure to agree with all conceivable observations, irrespective of the real structure of the world? If scientists are going to use logically unbeatable theories about the world, they might as well give up natural science and take up religion. [Lewontin 1972a]

> Natural selection, which was at first considered as though it were a hypothesis that was in need of experimental or observational confirmation turns out on closer inspection to be a tautology, a statement of an inevitable although previously unrecognized relation. It states that the fittest individuals in a population (defined as those which leave most offspring) will leave most offspring. [Waddington 1960]

These are quoted in a recent iconoclastic review by Rosen (1978), who wants to send natural selection theory off to join the ether and phlogiston.

The essence of these criticisms is that natural selection theory is not falsifiable and circular. The first of these criticisms was refuted by Williams (1973), who identified a number of falsifiable predictions following from natural selection theory which were in opposition to known facts and accepted theory current to the time before Darwin or Wallace proposed it. She concluded by observing that many falsifiable predictions have been successfully tested, but that even to biologists they do not look like predictions because the natural science gestalt trains us all to look for predictions about *human-sized* events or individuals rather than about ratios, patterns, and frequencies in sets or populations. The criticism about lack of falsifiability also may be countered by a recent development in evolutionary biology indicated by Futuyma (1979, p. 447).

At the microevolutionary level of genetic variation within populations it has been shown that some characteristics of species may be the result of random genetic drift. Random changes in the genotype are retained over successive generations. These retained variations occur outside the ecological context and do not show any selective response to ecological forces. Thus natural selection is no longer universally applicable and therefore may be falsifiable. It is falsifiable because changes may also be explained by the random drift process. Since the random drift idea may be more pronounced in organizations than in organisms (see section 9.1.1), falsifiability of natural selection theory should be less of an issue for us than for biologists.

With respect to the circularity criticism, Dobzhansky et al. offered two rebuttals. Their first argument referred back to the genetic drift finding. They said that critics erroneously equate fitness with changes in gene frequencies. While fitness differences lead to changes in gene frequencies, not all changes in gene frequencies are due to fitness differences. Some are due to random genetic drift. The second argument reminds us that natural selection theory is postulated to explain divergence of species through *adaptation*. This is why the fourth principle (left out of Campbell's 1969 presentation) is so important and why Dobzhansky et al. felt that Darwin erred when he added Spencer's "survival of the fittest" phrase in his later editions. Instead of Waddington's caricature in his quote, natural selection theory should be restated as: *The gene frequencies of better-adapted offspring will increase in a population due to the enhanced survival chances of these offspring.* Now the circularity disappears. But, you ask, How do you determine which offspring are better adapted? The usual response is, Those that have more offspring! The circularity enters in not because of the way the theory is stated but because of how part of it is operationally measured. The problem is not with the theory but with the operational definition of "better adapted."

Ideally the operational measure of "better adapted" should focus on what it takes to win the struggle for existence. Some way of operationally measuring the extent to which certain traits help an organism survive in its particular ecological habitat is required. This assumes that the evolutionist knows which attributes of the habitat are pertinent to the organism's survival and which traits of the organism are responding to the habitat, and furthermore has measures sensitive enough to detect small differences between members of a population.

Lewontin (1978) discussed at some length the difficulties associated with this approach. Defining an ecological niche without knowing the adaptive predilections of an organism or organization is problematic. Oppositely, identifying attributes that are "units of adaptation" for a given entity is difficult if not impossible without knowledge of the niche. These problems face organizational evolutionists just as much as they face biologists. The question of which environmental problem is solved by each attribute is truly difficult. Lewontin (1978, p. 228) asked, "If the adaptionist program is so fraught with difficulties and if there are so many alternative explanations of evolutionary change, why do biologists not abandon the program altogether?" He offered two reasons:

> On the one hand, even if the assertion of universal adaptation is difficult to test because simplifying assumptions and ingenious explanations can almost always result in an ad hoc adaptive explanation, at least in principle some of the assumptions can be tested in some cases. . . . On the other hand, to abandon the notion of adaptation entirely, to simply observe historical change and describe its mechanisms wholly in terms of the different reproductive success of different types, with no functional explanation, would be to throw out the baby with the bathwater. [1978, p. 230]

Tough or not, like it or not, "the role of the evolutionary biologist is then to construct a plausible argument about how each part functions as an adaptive device" (Lewontin 1978, p. 217). And so for the organizational evolutionist.

Given these difficulties it is no wonder biologists take the easy way out and simply measure "better adapted" by counting the number of surviving offspring. The point of all this is that there *is* circularity in the simple way "better adapted" is typically operationally measured; hence natural selection theory is assumed, not really tested, when this measure is used. But the *theory* is not circular, and it can be tested in a nontautological way.* I do not know that it is fortunate, but "better adapted" for organizations may not be measurable simply by counting offspring since they do not exist in the biological sense. So right away we do not have this kind of operational circularity, but we do have a problem in that a simple way out is not readily available.

Having said this I wish to propose that, based on a definition of an organizational generation appearing later in this chapter (section 8.6.2), a proxy for the measurement of quantity of surviving offspring may be the number of employees in good standing leaving an organization to join other members of the population. This could be an adequate measure of the adaptive viability of the combination of comps held in total by the employees of the organization in question, and recognition of such by other members of the population. For example, the ability to place students in universities is often taken as a measure of the quality of a graduate training program. The luring away of top quality faculty by other departments is also an indication that the comps of the department

---

*After having written this section I discovered the excellent article by the philosopher Brady (1979). He also observed that the *theory* of natural selection is not tautological although it is in the typical operational form. He concluded that because of the vast indeterminacy that clouds organism-environment relations, the theory is untestable. I agree that a direct test of the general principle of the theory is untestable, but as Williams (1973) has shown, many subordinate propositions that were unknown before the theory was suggested and which have since been proven add up to a broad corroboration of natural selection theory.

(held by some or all of its faculty) are highly regarded. Some companies are well known as training grounds for top quality executives. The possibility that good recent arrivals might represent the viability of their previous organization is not a problem since high quality employees usually may be presumed to search out better quality organizations. Though a single employee probably holds much less of the total compool than a biological offspring holds of its gene pool, the fact that even a portion of the combination of comps held by an organization is valued is a modest indication of its viability. The broader the skills and the greater the number of employees getting offers or being hired away, the more viable the organization is likely to be.

8.4 ORGANISMS VERSUS ORGANIZATIONS: EVOLUTIONARY COMPARISONS

There are many ways in which the slow change and evolution of organizations are similar to those of organisms, as well as some key differences. First the similarities.

Considerable attention has been given to the applicability of the basic principles of natural selection to sociocultural systems, including organizations. Several authors (Teilhard de Chardin 1959; McLuhan 1962; Thorson 1970; Masters 1970; Samuels 1972) have commented on the analogy between biological evolution and the evolution of language. Blute (1979) discussed the ways in which variations occur in language, how they are selected, and how they are retained. Whether there is a language population and whether it struggles for existence is problematic. Alland (1967) and Campbell (1969) carried out the discussion of similarity in terms of learning theory and human behavior, where again the processes of variation, selection, and retention may be observed. Rapoport (quoted in Miller 1978, p. 855) concluded that "there is little doubt that the principles operating in the evolution of societies are very much like the principles of organization evolution. . . . Natural selection is a simple, extremely 'prosaic' principle, and it acts without distinction on biological, technological, and social phenomena." Table 8.1 shows a list of correspondences between organic and sociocultural evolution recognized by Gerard, Kluckhohn, and Rapoport (1956).

An extended list of similarities and differences was suggested by Miller (1978, pp. 856–858). Corning (1974) took a Lamarckian view of political events, in which variations are seen to arise in response to adaptive needs. Kaufman (1975) considered the strictly biological elements of evolutionary theory such as offspring, generations, birth, proliferation, and mortality, and concluded that there is an equivalent

TABLE 8.1

CORRESPONDENCES BETWEEN BIOLOGICAL AND CULTURAL EVOLUTION*

Biological evolution	Cultural evolution
Distinct species and varieties	Distinct cultures and subcultures
Morphology, structural organization	Directly observable artifacts and customs distinctive of cultures
Physiology, functional attributes	Functional properties attributable to directly observable cultural characteristics
Genetic complex determining structures and functions	"Implicit culture," i.e., the inferred cultural structure of "cultural genotype"
Preservation of species but replacement of individuals	Preservation of cultures but replacement of individuals and artifacts
Hereditary transmission of genetic complex, generating particular species	"Hereditary" transmission of idea-custom-artifact complexes, generating particular cultures
Modification of genetic complex by mutations, selection, migration, and "genetic drift"	Culture change through invention and discovery; adaptation; diffusion and other forms of culture contact; "cultural drift"
Natural selection of genetic complexes generally leading to adaptation to environment	Adaptive and "accidental" (i.e., historically determined) selection of ideas, customs, and artifacts
Extinction of maladapted and maladjusted species	Extinction of maladapted and maladjusted cultures

*Reprinted from *Behavioral Science*, Vol. 1, No. 1, 1956, by permission of James Grier Miller, M.D., Ph.D., Editor.

natural history of organizations of which natural selection theory is a powerful explanation. Most relevant here is the seminal book by Aldrich (1979) entitled *Organizations and Environments*. Aldrich devoted entire chapters to demonstrating how variations in organizational practices arise, the many ways in which selective criteria operate to preserve some variations and eradicate others, and how selected variations persist in organizational populations. His book offered many historical developments showing very carefully how variations arise, are selected, and come to persist. I think that after reading his book the reader will join me in believing that there is strong evidence that natural selection takes place in organizational populations and that it can be explained at least in part by the variation, selection, and retention processes.

The fact that I focus only on organizations gives me several advantages in applying evolutionary theory. One of the most significant differences between the biological and social science literatures on evolution is that the former is cast in population terms whereas the latter is not. It should be obvious to the reader by now that the subject of this book is organizational populations, not individual organizations or other kinds of socio-

cultural systems. Since biological evolutionary theory is clearly successful as formulated in terms of populations, it is possible that one of the
main weaknesses of social science attempts at evolutionary theory may
be their failure to look at sociocultural systems from a population perspective. The theory simply may not work in nonpopulation terms. An
added difficulty is a failure to distinguish between the evolution of
groups of entities and the life cycle development or growth of a single
entity. Perhaps this is not possible in all cases; I am not ready to say
whether or not there are populations of languages, primitive or advanced societies, or cultures. But there are populations of organizations,
and I can very easily pose evolutionary questions in terms of population
tendencies and look at how changes in individual members of organizational populations do or do not spread throughout the population.

A second advantage of attending only to organizations is that the
recent challenges to traditional Darwinian evolutionary theory seem to
apply with even less difficulty to organizations than to organisms. In
section 9.1.1 I discuss the idea of drift within lines where no branching
takes place. There is clearly evidence of changes in organizations which
have no adaptive significance and do not result in branching. This is
akin to random genetic drift. And organizations, seemingly more obviously than organisms, follow the quantum speciation model, as I also
have argued in section 9.1.1. I have no trouble at all therefore in accepting the latest advances in biological evolutionary theory.

Third, the struggle for existence is a concept that applies as well to
organizations as it does to anything else. I am not willing to say whether
societies, cultures, or languages struggle for existence. But surely organizations do. Admittedly some organizations exist in environments so
full of resources and having so few competitors that the struggle seems
rather phlegmatic. But the annual incidence of failures (Aldrich 1979,
pp. 36−37) indicates that for many other organizations, even large ones,
the struggle is very much a reality.

And fourth, the existence of isolating mechanisms seems more of a
reality among different kinds of organizations than among cultures. As
presented in chapters 4 and 7, organizations develop different technologies in responding to environmentally imposed problems. These workplace and management competencies are usually so different, complicated, and known by people with such different training, that there are
clear barriers preventing an organization knowing one kind of competence from easily or successfully crossing the barrier to accomplish a
different competence.

A major difference between organic and organizational evolution is
that LAMARCKIAN EVOLUTIONARY THEORY seems to apply to orga-

nizations whereas it has now been proven that it does not apply to organisms. First, consider the Lamarckian notion of the heritability of acquired characteristics. Organizations appear to be able to pass competencies (or incompetencies) acquired by present-generation organizational members who hold the phenotype of a particular organization directly to subsequent generations of employees even though these phenotype characteristics are unique to the organization and more importantly are not present in the population's compool. By "acquired" in an organizational sense I mean attributes not present in the compool which are brought into an organization by bringing in people with new knowledge and skills or by existing employees learning new competencies. This is opposed to the more hereditary idea of passing on to subsequent generations only variations of elements already part of the compool. In short, for organizations there is a blurring of the distinction between hereditary and acquired characteristics. Second, consider the Lamarckian idea that variations arise in response to adaptive needs. That is, variations are produced by needs, not by chance, as in Darwinian theory. In the Darwinian view variations arise only by chance but it is selection that responds to adaptive needs. I strongly agree with Campbell, Aldrich, and Blute in attending to the role of blind variations and the role of selection in responding to adaptive needs to favor or disfavor certain variations in applying Darwinian theory to organizations. But it also seems likely that a certain portion of organizational variations may in fact be directly responsive to adaptive needs. This is the view taken by Corning (1974) and Goldschmidt (1976). Organizational systematists should be prepared to accept the possibility, therefore, that our evolutionary theory may be a joint Lamarckian-Darwinian construction. This clearly differentiates our evolutionary theory from that of the biologists.

A second key difference is that the pace of organizational evolution is magnitudes faster than the geological time span of biological evolution. A new variation undoubtedly diffuses through an organizational population at a vastly faster rate than gene flow through a biological population. This is partly because organizational populations, on average, are smaller but also because the shortest time for the diffusion of genetic variations is in the order of decades (as little as two or three), whereas an organizational variation such as microcomputers or a curriculum development could sweep through a population in a few years or perhaps even faster. Furthermore, organizational environments probably change at a much faster rate than biological environments, thereby providing a strong stimulus toward faster evolutionary response in populations. Organizational isolating mechanisms, though they clearly exist, are not as strong as the reproductive isolation of biological species. They probably can be set up faster, leading to a faster pace of divergence. The increased possibility that the barriers can be broken also probably means an increased pace of convergent evolution. The Lamarckian element of variation in response to adaptive pressure and the passing on of acquired characteristics also speeds up the pace of organizational evolution. Finally, the modern challenge to gradualism, quantum speciation, recognizes that evolution in both biological and organizational entities may progress faster than the gradualists had thought. Since this modern variant of Darwinian theory seems appropriate to organizations, our evolutionary theory probably will be different from traditional gradualistic evolutionary theory, though not necessarily from the modern challenge if that becomes widely accepted by biologists.

A third difference, which usually is the first one mentioned by the uninitiated but which may not be too much of a problem, pertains to the general idea that organizations do not produce offspring, either sexually or asexually. Since heredity is a basic principle of natural selection theory, this could be a fundamental difference and indeed a real problem. This question breaks into two parts: What is inherited and how?

In chapter 7 I discussed at some length, drawing on Mayr's (1969) idea of organismic bodies as temporary vessels holding highly probable gene combinations, the compool concept and the idea that organizational members are the temporary vessels holding highly probable combinations of comps of workplace and management competence. What is passed on are the technological comps important to an organizational population's adaptation. How these comps are passed on is by one employee learning from another or learning the comps via formal education or other training. This explains how comps are passed from one generation of employees to another during the life span of a single organization. This is not unlike the passage of DNA code from one generation of cells to the next. The technical variations and selections of the several members of an organizational population are mixed around by the comings and goings of employees from one member of the population to another, by bringing in trainees from professional schools influenced in turn by the compool, by industrial spy or other intelligence networks, or by attendance at professional associations.

Organizational births and deaths within a population seem different from those of biological organisms but they are not if we think in terms of dissemination of comps rather than of organizational bodies and the patter of little organizational feet. New organizations may "inherit" comps of the population's compool when one or more employees of an existing organizational member leave to start up their own new organization. This is nicely illustrated in the study of the evolution of the semiconductor industry by Brittain and Freeman (1980). Or new organizations may "acquire" comps of the compool of a population by retraining their existing employees or bringing in employees with different training. When an organization dies those of its employees having what are judged to be adaptively relevant comps of the population's compool are hired on by other organizational members of the population. Thus the viable comps of the dying organization's combination of comps are passed down and mixed in with other members of the population. These processes offer one explanation of how "heredity" takes place in an organizational population. Other ways of viewing organizational heredity may arise in the future, but this one seems to respond to the problem and fits in with what is known about how organizations and their employees behave during the birth, life, and death of organizations.

8.5 THE GENETICS OF ORGANIZATIONAL FORM

Organizational scientists have a choice of trying to develop a natural selection-based evolutionary theory with or without the notion of heredity. The former case requires the creation of an analog to heredity, which I have tried to do in chapter 7 and in this chapter. In the latter case we might dispense with the principle of heredity and attempt to come up with a new formulation of evolutionary theory. No doubt there will be some organizational scientists so upset with my drawing on the biological analogy that including a counterpart to biological heredity will be the straw that breaks the camel's back and drive them to work out a nonhereditary evolutionary theory, if that is possible. Good luck to them. I think a much easier, more fruitful, and better-fitting idea is to set out the basics of the compool concept and organizational heredity.

GENETICS is the science of heredity. Futuyma (1979, p. 33) mentioned two basic principles of modern genetics: (1) "that the hereditary factors are particles"; and (2) "that the flow of information from genotype to phenotype is unidirectional." The latter principle is simply modern biologists' rejection of the Lamarckian theory that traits acquired by a phenotype could be passed into the genotype. The PARTICLE THEORY expresses the idea that, for example, a pink-feathered bird produced by red- and white-feathered parents does not pass on a new pink-producing gene form. Instead the underlying gene forms (alleles) remain the same, barring mutation. In the next generation they combine anew to produce red- or white-feathered offspring or pink ones. Now, I am not at all interested in the rules geneticists have formulated about the replication and alteration of biological genetic material. However, I do think that describing organizational forms in terms of the compool comps (particles) may be useful and quite possibly fairly accurate as well.

Anything I write here is highly speculative, since organizational scientists have not yet taken the trouble to attempt to describe organizational forms in any but very gross ways, such as loose-coupled educational systems or tight bureaucratically structured government agencies or mechanistic industrial forms, and so forth. In fact we already know in an informal way that the competence or method by which, for example, a university gets its job done is not some kind of undecomposable, monolithic, global knowledge unit that all members of universities know about. Instead there are many comps or particles, such as registration, test preparation, hiring faculty, making tenure decisions, controlling costs, producing credible research findings and papers, training doctoral students, and so on. These are fairly well bounded "particles" in that, for example, the competence for getting a paper published in a top journal is well focused and does not do much to help a university handle all of the other things it does. As with genes, which can appear in a variety of forms (alleles), comps, such as the one bearing on paper publishing, also appear in several forms. Some of these forms are more useful for successful adaptation and some less so.

Variations may appear in several ways. First there are variations over time in what is acceptable form and substance in, for example, a published paper. Empirical papers published in *American Sociological Review* or *Administrative Science Quarterly* twenty years ago would probably not be published today. Thus each comp may vary over time. Some of these variations are selected favorably and some negatively. Second, there are variations in how the many comps are combined to make up the total competence of a given university. Some of these variations in combinations of comps are selected favorably and some negatively. This affects the continuation of various university forms in the population. Thus there is the Stanford line, the Simon Fraser or other more experimental lines, the church-related line, the nonpublishing line, the Oxford line, and so forth. These particular lines may persist or die out. Finally, there is variation at the population level in that the total compool varies as it reflects the variations of members of the population. A good example of this is the case study method taken over from law schools by the Harvard Business School and subsequently passed on into the population compool of business and management schools. The variation of the population compool level also is passed on into individual organizational members. The population variations are also selected favorably or negatively.

Biologists still rely largely on morphological descriptions for taxonomic and other descriptive purposes, even though much is known about the underlying genotype descriptive characteristics. But not enough is known for genotypic descriptions to be widely used as substitutes for morphological, physiological, or ecological categories of characters, though the trend is in this direction, as indicated by chemotaxonomy and related methods. Organizational scientists are probably a long way from describing organizations in terms of the frequencies of their comps. We can only wonder if there will ever be a formal particle theory of organizational birth, life, and death. I should think, though, that such a theory would enhance our understanding of how organizations evolve. I also believe that evaluations of organizational populations in terms of comp frequencies would benefit both research and practical management activities.

8.6 BASIC ELEMENTS OF AN EVOLUTIONARY THEORY OF ORGANIZATIONAL FORMS

8.6.1 Postulates

Before stating some basic principles of organizational evolution, I should like to identify several postulates. They have to be accepted as a point of departure for the principles to make sense.

1. *Organizational competence appears as a mixture of more or less irreducible units or particles, termed comps.* In this chapter and in chapter 7 I have offered some arguments that such comps exist. Atomic reductionists (Schwab 1960) will no doubt hold that the so-called comps can be reduced right down to the minute language symbols used to describe them. I have taken a molecular reductionist view, arguing that the particles or comps are convenient, if not readily apparent, units of analysis. It remains to be determined how operational this concept is and just where in the continuum from a global concept of organizational competence to an atomic view the proper molecular level is.

2. *Each population of organizations shares an intercommunicating compool of comps which is fairly well isolated from the compools of other populations.* I have made arguments in favor of isolating processes in chapter 7 and need not repeat them here.

3. *There is some concept of heredity applicable to organizations.* I

have defined the concept in terms of the average length of time holders of comps (employees) stay in member organizations of a particular population. This view requires getting used to the idea that what is inherited is not an "organizational body" but rather a combination of comps held by a collectivity of employees. A new generation is not necessarily the birth of a new organization but rather the passing of the comps from one organization to another. As with many biological organisms, the parent does not have to die to create a new generation. Even when a new form is born, such as railroad organizations or the pony express, there is no drawing of comps out of thin air. Instead they are drawn from preexisting organizational forms, as argued in chapter 9. New organizational forms may have several parent forms, as was the case for railroads, which emerged from the compools of mining, canal, wagon, and metalworking forms.

4. *Organizations do actually evolve in that they exhibit slow change over successive generations.* It is true that individual members of organizational populations are subject to short-term instabilities* and wildly fluctuating changes, perhaps related to the personalities of influential members, unusual decisions good or bad, or strange environmental quirks that offer much more or less in resources. These are analogous to sudden changes that may afflict individual organisms. People grow obese or thin, thereby grossly changing, but the population form is not affected. Wolves grow lean or fat depending on the size of the rabbit population, but in the short term the wolf population form is not affected, though the size of the population may rise or fall. Rabbits decide to run across roads and get killed by vehicles but the population is not affected, unless only dumb rabbits run in front of trucks. Likewise a particular organization may suffer from poor decisions or may bask in the ease of slack resources or absence of competitors in the short term. While many short-term changes may be observed, Hannan and Freeman (1977) have also noted just how much inertia exists in organizations. Even so, I know of no student of organizations willing to take the view that slow change does not take place—total instability does not exist any more than total inertia. I think most would agree that slow change is an inescapable fact. Organizational evolution exists—it is just a matter of explaining how it takes place.

5. *Organizations exist in environments and are responsive to environmental forces.* As described in chapter 4, organizations adapt, in

*A useful discussion of instabilities and reasons why they should not be allowed to undermine objective methods of organizational investigation was published by Behling (1980).

part, by carving out niches. A niche and an organizational form are definable only in reference to each other. An environment consists of immutable external factors whereas a niche consists of factors subject to the influence of the members of an organizational population. I do not think any serious student would argue that organizational environments do not exist, nor would they argue that organizations are totally independent of their environments. But the exact relation between organizations and their environments is not well understood. I suppose that the prevailing view would be to want to search for causal relations between environmental attributes and attributes of organizational form. This would follow from the long-standing tradition among social scientists of searching for causal laws to explain historical change, as Blute (1979) observed. A modern example of this approach is the work of Meyer (see Meyer and 3rown 1977, for example). My position, following Blute (1979), is to eschew causal laws in favor of a combined Lamarckian/ Darwinian view of descent with modification from common ancestors. Following Campbell (1969) and Aldrich (1979), I think natural selection will turn out to be the best way to explain the relation of organizations to their environments. I follow Corning (1974) and Goldschmidt (1976) in also recognizing that Lamarckian processes seem to obtain in organizational evolution as well.

6. *Organizational environments change.* This premise was developed in chapter 5 and need not be further discussed here.

The entire inductive generalization comprising this book is built on these postulates. I suppose that some people might debate them, but I assume that most organizational scientists would accept them as self-evident truths. The first three are apt to be most contentious but even here one surely has to accept the idea that competence can be decomposed, that groups of organizations share certain aspects of competence among themselves much more than they share the competence of other kinds of organizations, and that a large proportion of organizational competence is passed on by former employees or mixed into different organizations by employee transfers.

8.6.2 Basic Principles of Organizational Evolution

The following principles broadly summarize much of the discussion in the book to this point. They are couched more or less in terms of both a genetic particle theory and a combined Lamarckian-Darwinian view of evolution. These are very freely adapted from a set of twenty-three principles of evolutionary theory presented by Futuyma (1979, pp. 19–31).

1. *Every attribute or comp element of organizations has a frequency distribution.* Each distribution has a mean value and variance across all organizations in all populations. Where the distributions have high variance and when they have more than one mode, partitioning may occur, which is the basis for forming the higher categories (distinct populations), as described in chapter 9. Evolution may be defined broadly as any change in the frequency distribution of one or more attributes that persists for one or more organizational generations. An *ORGANIZATIONAL GENERATION is defined as the average length of time holders of comps (employees) stay in member organizations of a particular population.* This definition captures the idea that a generation is simply the transfer of a particle combination from one holder (body or group of employees) to another. I am sure that r-type populations will be found to have shorter generations than K types (see Hannan and Freeman 1977 for a description of r and K types), as is true among similar biological populations.

2. *The frequency distribution of comps will remain constant unless: (a) there is change in the comps held by employees; (b) the comps held by (usually) young employees entering a population differ in frequency from those held by (usually) elderly employees who leave; (c) the flow of people out of some organizations into a population is higher than from other organizations,* meaning that the comps and combinations of comps held by these organizations will have a greater impact on a population as a whole. Point *a* is essentially Lamarckian in that acquired characteristics can be passed on into the population compool. The other points are Darwinian in that employees do not change the nature of the comps they hold but rather change their frequency in a population by moving in or out. To the extent that a variant form held by a particular member organization is not passed into the population by transferring employees or acquired by employees in other members, that form will not persist in the population.

3. *Variations in organizational form exist because organizational heredity is not perfect.* Organizational forms may come to differ because the organizations possess different genetic material in the form of different distributions of comps, which leads to different phenotypes, or because exposure to different environmental forces leads to Lamarckian acquisition of new characteristics (new or altered comps) or to Darwinian selection of some comps (or the employees holding them) over others.

4. *The more mutable a comp is the more evanescent a new variant in organizational form will be.* A mutation in the university compool such as the invention of tenure, which turns out to be fairly immutable, will

lead to a long-lasting change in form whereas a highly changeable element such as a shift from authoritarian to democratic leadership in, say, the steel industry, may not. As much as possible taxonomic characters should reflect less mutable attributes at any given time.

5. *All evolutionary changes depend upon changes in the population frequencies of comps held by member organizations.* There are presumably forces that stabilize or destabilize the frequencies of comps.

6. *One factor affecting evolution is the rate of mutation of comps.* Compared to biology this rate is presumed to be fairly high in organizations.

7. *Another factor is the rate of acquisition of comps.* This Lamarckian process is considered totally absent in biological evolution.

8. *Another factor is random drift.* In this instance there is a purposeful or accidental change in the frequency of comps from one generation to the next, quite independent of selection processes connected with environmental forces. A purposeful change could be totally independent because, in Weick's (1979) language, managerial or employee *enactments* (his term for variations) are oblivious to, out of tune with, uncoupled from, or misguided with respect to environmental constraints and adaptive need. Note that an uncoupled or misguided change that is purposeful from a manager's perspective will probably appear as blind from an organizational and especially an evolutionary perspective. This is why I expect that, in total, Campbell's blind variation view (Darwinian) will fit a larger portion of organizational variations than Corning's or Goldschmidt's Lamarckian views, but not all of them.

9. *Often the phenotype forms in an organizational population and the underlying comp frequencies differ consistently in their ability to survive*, as indicated by the degree to which employees holding the comps are seen as attractive (in the sense that they will foster adaptation) candidates for hire by other organizations. If one form were to be replicated faster than all the others the population would end up being *monomorphic*, in that the same comps would exist in the same frequency among all members. This is highly unlikely. Organizational populations are most likely to be *polymorphic* in that there may be several genotypes stabilized at intermediate comp frequencies. For example, among universities there may be a private university form and a public university form. These would not be separate species or populations since employees would shift back and forth and none of the training or professional-association isolating processes would obtain. But persistent differences might be observed.

10. *The statements concerning variation and selection apply to each level of analysis as long as there is some kind of heredity.* Thus variation

and selection can occur among comp frequencies, phenotype frequencies, or compool combinations, within populations or species, or over entire populations.

11. *A drastic mutation of one comp probably will not have a lasting effect on an organizational form because the highly changed element will be incompatible with the other comps.* Thus an organization producing a drastic change in its locus of decision making (centralization) probably has a form that will not survive because the new decision-making procedure is incompatible with other comps such as information flow, kinds of sensing control systems, career paths, and the like. The gradual change of several or many comps more or less concurrently will likely produce more lasting change.

12. *Variations may have positive or negative effects on an organizational form's or population's ability to adapt.* It is likely that a particular variation will not be advantageous or deleterious for all organizational forms at one time or for one population at different times in different environments.

13. *The advantage of a particular comp may be determined only in the context of a specific environment.* Furthermore, each comp functions in the internal environment of an organization composed of many other comps. Thus while a comp by itself may render some advantage to an organization, it may function at a disadvantage due to the constellation of other comps surrounding it, and vice versa. By way of example, a comp such as a fast-paced, highly controlling assembly line may be very advantageous for an organization's adaptation to its larger environment, but it is often incompatible with other comps such as motivation plans or frequent production design or schedule changes associated with the functioning of the surrounding social or technical system, as sociotechnical systems observers have noted over and over again.

14. *Because comps need to be co-adapted to each other, the pace of evolution is necessarily slowed.* The needed variations will not all likely occur among a constellation of comps at the same time. Even in the Lamarckian case where variations are created purposively or new comps are acquired, it may not be possible to move the entire constellation of associated comps in a particular adaptive direction, as the many failures in so-called "organizational development" experiments would indicate.

15. *The incidence of most variations is not affected by the advantage or disadvantage they confer toward adaptation.* In organizations some variations are Lamarckian in that they do occur in response to an adaptive need. We do not know at this time what the ratio between purposeful and random variations is. Though variations are (probably) mostly random, selection is nonrandom; it *is* driven by adaptive needs.

16. *"Natural selection is simply differential survival . . . not Provi-dence,"* as Futuyma put it (1979, p. 28). Attribute variations selected at one particular time are not the best of all possible attributes—they simply aid adaptation at the time selected. Attributes evolved to foster adaptation to one environment may be irrelevant or deleterious in later changed environments. A prior path of evolution may not leave an organizational form well positioned to adapt to a changed environment. Attributes that were adaptive in an earlier environment may be retained to the disadvantage of the population in a later environment. For exam-ple, some people, especially administrators, would argue that tenure for high school teachers (or university professors) inhibits the ability of these populations of organizations to adapt to current environments.

17. *Not all attributes of organizations have necessarily evolved be-cause of adaptive pressure.* Some may be the result of random drift in the nature or combination of comps. Other comps may have appeared or changed due to movement in a constellation of comps. Thus some comps in the constellation may have responded to environmental pres-sure while others may have changed simply to remain compatible with the adaptive comps. These former comps may be irrelevant or even deleterious. It would certainly be foolish to look for adaptive reasons for their presence. This principle uncovers one of the flaws in the old structural-functional argument that all aspects of structure are or were functional. One of the great difficulties is in trying to fathom why one or more attributes are present, knowing that probably not all of them were directly responsive to adaptive needs. An added difficulty is that a retained element produced via the random drift process may be PRE-ADAPTIVE in that it turns out to be a small variation that is carried along until at some future time, in a changed environment, a quantum specia-tion process begins in which there is rapid adaptation. In retrospect it may appear that the initial variation was a purposeful anticipation of a future need to adapt and so was selected before the need actually arose. In fact it was random retention and just happened to be adaptive in a later environment.

18. *The development of diversity among organizational forms re-quires barriers to the exchange of comps.* These barriers or isolating processes were discussed in chapters 6 and 7. In organizations the main barriers appear to be technical complexity, difficulty of learning and training, professional association membership, and interorganizational patterns of personnel flows. Geographical separation may also be a factor.

19. *When the barriers to the mixing of comps among organizations are so strong as to prevent intercommunication, speciation has taken*

place. For organizations this means that when the flow of personnel between organizations is high among some organizations (A) and low between these organizations and others, the former group is said to be a species. The high flow of comps among organizations within group A creates a homogenizing effect whereas the low flow between group A and other organizations creates a diverging effect.

20. *Once speciation has taken place, evolutionary changes in one species are usually not transmitted to the other.* Among organizations the Lamarckian capacity to pass on acquired attributes means that evolutionary paths may have some similarities even after speciation. Since the ratio between Lamarckian and Darwinian processes is unknown, it is also unknown how much similarity in evolutionary paths will prevail. It is true that if the environments of two organizational species take on many of the same characteristics, there will be convergent evolution such that the two species will become more alike. A key difference between biological and organizational evolution occurs here. Biological species, once reproductively isolated, will usually not interbreed sexually, even after a period of strong convergent evolution. Organizations, however, may very well start intermixing comps after convergent evolution. Organizational systematists would probably collapse the converging lines into one species again, whereas biological systematists would not collapse converging lines. One of the main complaints orthodox systematists have against numerical pheneticists is that the latter's methods do not keep converging lines separated because the phenotypes may be more or less alike. This should not be an issue for organizational systematists.

21. *The course of evolution is determined by the nature of organizational environments.* Where environments are similar, parallel evolution may take place. When environments become increasingly different, divergent evolution occurs. The faster the rate of change in the environment of an organizational population the faster its pace of evolution. If the general organizational environment becomes increasingly heterogeneous one may expect an increase in the number of different kinds of organizational populations. Environmental effects are more pronounced when resources are scarce. As the environment faced by a particular population of organizations becomes more complex or heterogeneous, the organizational form of that population can be expected to become more complex. If a fringe element of this population begins a faster-paced adaptation to a particular sector of the environment, an instance of evolution via quantum speciation may take place. After the split the parent population may become somewhat less complex since it presumably would be driven out of the sector of the environment taken

over by the new species, and therefore face a smaller and less complex environment.

22. *Organizational populations vary considerably in the life span of their members and in the rate of speciation and extinction of the populations themselves.* One of the reasons Hannan and Freeman began their empirical study of organizational ecological processes with restaurants is because these, like fruit flies, have short life spans. In contrast, life spans in the oil or automobile industries may be quite long. People are inclined to look at General Motors or the Roman Catholic church and say that organizational evolution does not happen because organizations do not die. Well, over the years most automobile organizations have died and the Roman Catholic church is still less than half the age of the oldest bristlecone pine in the White Mountains. Organizational populations also have varying spans of existence. One of the best-known but shortest-lived new forms was the Pony Express organizational form. It existed from April 1860 to October 1861, when the telegraph offered an even faster means of sending messages. This was also a very small population, having only one member before it became extinct. A good example of an organizational form that, as a population, grew very quickly and became extinct equally suddenly was the one composed of interurban trolley car transportation organizations. It flourished between the years 1899 and 1908 and was a fairly large population until it rapidly became extinct by 1931 because of the rise in intercity automobile traffic.

23. *The evolution of organizational forms takes place in the context of an ecological community.* The course of evolution of one form is determined by ecological pressures created in part by the evolution of other species in the same community. The evolution of a particular form may stabilize or destabilize the community. Obvious examples are the ecological consequences of the growth of the automobile industry in Detroit, electronics around Boston, and aerospace companies in the Los Angeles area. The evolution and survival of these populations affects many other populations of organizations, ranging from founding, machining, and fabricating shops to restaurants and schools and universities. A recent ecological study of these forces at work among fast-food restaurants along a commercial strip was published by Kangas and Risser (1979).

24. *The principles of intraspecific evolution apply to the full range of organizational attributes,* such as those listed in table 11.6. Species can also evolve in the speed with which they can respond to adaptive pressure, and they may increase or decrease in adaptive capability by becoming more specialized or more generalized. The capacity for generalized behavior cannot be construed as more adaptive, more advanced,

or better or more progressive. Depending on the course of change among organizational environments, specialized or generalized forms may each come under severe environmental pressure and succumb. Organizational applications of biological population ecological concepts are progressing rapidly under the leadership of Hannan and Freeman (1977), Brittain and Freeman (1980), Hannan (1980), and Freeman (1981).

These principles are, strictly speaking, close to the form of refutable hypotheses. I believe they have a strong inductive logical basis. Of course they are a first, preliminary formulation. I think that organizational science is now positioned to take advantage of their specificity, though the specificity and some of the implicit concepts may come as a surprise to some readers. Nevertheless, there has been an increased tendency of late for social scientists to apply the genetic particle theory to social phenomena. Langton (1979) has recently argued that social scientists are in as good a position with respect to prevailing knowledge to make the evolution of sociocultural systems comprehensible as was Darwin when he explicated the evolution of biological species. He concluded that

> the social sciences know, nomologically and factually, at least as much about innovation and enculturation as Darwin knew about heredity and variation; that they know at least as much about the struggle for reinforcement as Darwin knew about the struggle for existence; that they know at least as much about sociocultural selection as Darwin knew about natural selection; and that they know at least as much about the relationships among these components of sociocultural evolution as Darwin knew about the relationships among the components of organic evolution. [Langton 1979, pp. 288–289]

Langton made his case in terms of behavioral theory, as did Alland (1967) and Campbell (1969). I argued earlier in this chapter that the case for organizations is even stronger than it is for other sociocultural phenomena.

Evolutionary biology has come to be split into micro- and macroevolutionary levels. Microevolutionary theory comprises the study of the variation, selection, and random drift of genetic material. At this level experiments are possible and have been conducted. Futuyma (1979) concluded that there is no doubt that evolutionary processes have been shown to work at the micro level. Macroevolutionary theory consists of all of the work focusing on the origin, divergence, and extinction of major species or populations over the course of geologic time. Here the poor fossil record makes the task of testing the theory difficult. The slow pace of evolution of major species relative to the life spans of scientists makes direct tests impossible. Therefore evolutionary processes are experimentally tested at the microevolutionary level and historically unraveled at the macro level.

Organizational scientists may have about an equal chance of testing the theory at either level. Conducting microevolutionary experiments on organizations may prove more difficult than conducting genetic experiments. On the other hand, since the history of organizations is relatively short and much of it is seemingly well documented, testing the theory at the macro level may be easier for us than for biologists. Most, if not all, of the principles can be stated in refutable terms and so put to scientific test. This is the task that lies ahead.

8.7 SUMMARY

Evolutionary changes are those that are inheritable from one generation to the next. Evolution is defined without reference to moralisms such as order, direction, progress, or perfectibility. Organizational evolution is a fact. The problem is to explain how it occurs. Social science applications have been tainted with moralistic or political overtones in the manner of Spencer. To avoid this and to gain the advantage of the population perspective, organizational evolutionary theory is adapted directly from the biological literature. Four basic principles of natural selection theory are discussed: (1) the principle of variation, (2) the principle of heredity, (3) the principle of natural selection, and (4) the principle of the struggle for existence. Recent challenges to traditional Darwinian emphasis on gradualism are noted. The modern version of evolutionary theory seems to apply to organizations as well as or better than it applies to organisms. Though natural selection theory is often criticized as tautological, this is because of a method of operationalizing better adaptation rather than the form of the theory itself. Major parallels between biological and organizational evolutionary processes are described, including the principles of natural selection, the population concept, and the applicability of recent challenges to traditional evolutionary theory. Two key differences are that organizational evolution is Lamarckian (acquired attributes may be inherited, variations may be purposive) as well as Darwinian, and the pace of organizational evolution is much faster than biological evolution. A concept of heredity or organizational form is developed which is clearly different from biological heredity but equally essential to evolutionary theory. I have chosen to stay with an evolutionary theory that requires a concept of heredity rather than try to develop a new nonhereditary theory of evolution. Twenty-four principles of evolution are stated in terms of a particle theory of organizational genetics, based on two key concepts: comps and an intercommunicating compool. Underlying these principles are six postulates that are assumed without positive evidence of their truth; I think they are self-evident truths. They form the foundation for my combined evolutionary/phenetic approach to organizational classification.

⑨ ORGANIZATIONAL EVOLUTION AND THE HIGHER CATEGORIES

Maturity in an organization is signaled by its ability to reproduce. It reaches this point when it exhibits historicity and control; that is, when its values and ideals, which serve as templates for interpreting experiences and taking action, can be passed down through successive generations so that the organization "exists" independently of those who currently embody it.

[Lodahl and Mitchell 1980, p. 184]

Chapter 7 presented a concept of organizational speciation based on comps and the compool. With this concept an understanding of organizational differences becomes possible. The present chapter is based on two interrelated premises. The first one is that organizational populations making up the protosystem share varying numbers of similar attributes. This offers the possibility of arranging them in a hierarchy of ranks, each composed of groupings of decreasing similarity. The second premise is that the idea of descent with modification holds for organizational forms as it does for biological organisms, as outlined in chapter 8. A brief empirical demonstration of the descent with modification idea will be given in chapter 10, through an analysis of the evolution of organizational forms in ancient Mesopotamia. Though I argue in this chapter that there are a variety of ways in which new forms emerge, the underlying theory is that new forms always originate and follow to a varying extent those organizational forms already existing.

The pressure toward descent with modification is provided by ever-changing environments, as depicted in the model of speciation presented in section 6.1.2. As the environments of various historical populations of organizational forms became more differentiated, these groups splintered into subgroups that in turn divided into still smaller groups, and so on down to the present wide range of organizations. The division and redivison of organizational groups as time passed provides the basis for a hierarchical classification of organizations. Each higher level in the hierarchy groups forms with successively fewer shared characters stemming from an increasingly ancient ancestor form. The successive division of organizations into increasingly specialized forms makes a phyletic classification possible, in which existing lines of organizational form are traced back to their ancestor forms.

One may debate whether any useful purpose is served by demonstrating, for example, that commercial profit-oriented forms are different from normatively oriented political organizations because the former branched off from the latter around 2100−1750 B.C. (see chapter 10). This is really the debate between evolutionists and empiricists. The numerical pheneticists argue that while the question of branching might be interesting, it is better left out of the classification problem, the preferred solution being to base the higher categories strictly on relative similarity. The view pursued here is the evolutionist one. As discussed earlier in the book, the reasons are twofold: (1) the question of origin *is* interesting and it *is* more elegant to have a classification theory that both explains and classifies; and (2) the tracing of lineage is the best way of suggesting hypothetical groupings that can then be used as a much-needed point of departure and subsequently tested by numerical taxonomic methods. If, as was pointed out in section 7.4, it is likely that most of the time both approaches will produce the same answer, the debate becomes less relevant.

The objectives in developing the higher categories are, therefore, to: (1) order the many species of organizations into ever more broadly encompassing groupings, forming a hierarchical classification scheme; and (2) explain the evolution of the groupings since the beginning of collective organized activity among human beings. Accordingly, this chapter includes a discussion of how new organizational lineages emerge, some basic premises of higher classification, some anticipated misconceptions, and some key operational principles that guide the development of a classification scheme.

9.1 THE FORMATION OF ORGANIZATIONAL LINEAGES

In the following discussion it will be convenient to focus on populations (compools) rather than on individual organizations. As developed in chapter 7, a compool is the set of all the competence elements, held by the employees, of the population of organizations comprising the compool. In this view, organizations to be classified are temporary vessels embodying the combinations of comps making up a particular compool. The combinations of comps embodied by various members of a class of organizations are very similar, though not exactly alike, and they are quite different from combinations reflecting other compools. Thus a theory about organizational evolution is really a theory about the evolution of new combinations of the comps comprising compools. A corollary to this theory is that the dominant competence and form of one member of a population of organizations are very much like those of another member because they draw from the same compool. Accordingly, for the most part, the effective members of the population evolve at the same rate, in the same way, and toward the same end state.

For example, an inquiry into the evolution of effective airline organizations would not focus on any one organization, which might somewhat imperfectly reflect the compool genotype, but rather on the evolution of all comps making up the dominant competence of airline organizations as a group. It is the very similar combinations of comps which give rise to forms of organization phenotypes which may be studied, measured, and classified. In working up descriptions and identification keys, systematists will presumably focus on *both* the genotypic combinations of comps which directly comprise the airline compool, and the phenotypic form of the organizations embodying the compool, although, as in biology, the initial attention will undoubtedly be on the phenotype. They might record as taxonomic characters the nature of the various unit operations in the primary workplace, the organizing solutions with which the workplace operators and managers reduce their management problems, as well as aspects of form such as workplace layout, employee relations, hierarchical configuration, and the like. Perhaps later, after operational concepts of the genotypical compool elements are developed, attention may shift toward basing groupings directly on measures of the genotype. This would require a concept of what units of information comprise a comp—following the view that comps are storehouses of information that combine in certain ways. Drawing on the experience in biology, I expect that most early classification will be based on phenotype analysis, and if and when more direct analysis of compool elements become possible, the changes in the classification scheme will not be substantial.

9.1.1 How New Compools Form

New organizational forms may evolve in two fundamental ways. In the first case, because of a significant event leading to speciation, a new form *branches* off from one already existing. The branching kind of evolution is called CLADOGENESIS. In the second instance there is no branching; instead, a slow movement toward a new form within a lineage or species takes place. This is known as ANAGENESIS. These two kinds of evolution are illustrated in figure 9.1. In Environment Two, time t_1, an organizational compool exists which has characters a, b, c, d, e. In time t_2 a new compool is seen to branch off which has characters a, b,),/, (, \$, which in combination are considerably different from those of the form in time t_1. Hence a new branch is depicted, an example of cladogenesis. An illustration of anagenesis is also given in Environment Two in times t_2 and later, where the compool slowly adds a new character in each time period and also drops a character in each time period. Needless to say, real populations would have many more characters and more than one might be added or dropped in successive time periods. The kinds of evolution are discussed at length in later sections, but first it is helpful to the discussion to introduce some illustrative dendrograms showing how organizational evolution *may* have taken place.

Illustrative Dendrograms

In biology there is a clear separation of the results of classification from a discussion of the theory and methods of classification. Books on systematics do not typically include a presentation of descriptions of all the infraspecies, species, genera, families, and all the other classes that have been discovered and described. Given the approximately five to ten million types of species, one can see that such a book would probably be too big to lift, let alone buy. The descriptions of higher categories are sometimes given in the appendixes of basic biology books. More detailed descriptions of various groupings are given in volumes specializing in those groupings, such as books on reptiles or insects, or families such as bees, cats, and so forth. In mineralogy, given about 2,500 species of minerals, the tendency is to present both theory and methods of classification (which are not very extensive) along with descriptions of all the minerals in the same book.

In organizational systematics the problem is that an acceptable classification does not exist, so even if it were not too large it cannot be

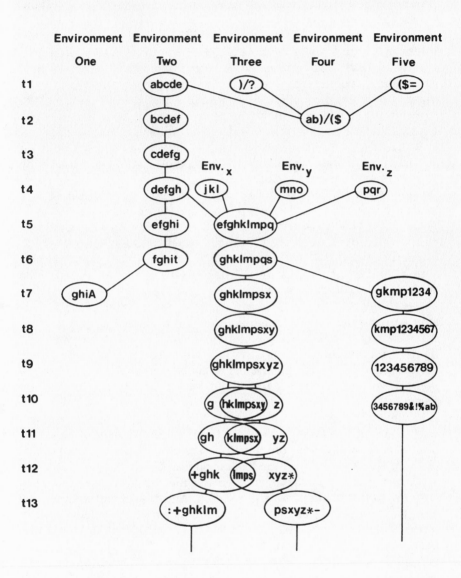

Figure 9.1. Kinds of Evolution. Vertical distance represents time; horizontal distance represents amount of difference.

presented along with the theory and methods of organizational systematics. Yet there is no question that a discussion of how higher and infraspecies categories have formed would take on more life and explicitness if an actual classification based on the theory being presented were available to draw examples from. The discussion of basic classificatory theory in books on biological systematics is brought alive (and made more difficult for the reader who is not a biologist) by the richness of the many examples about such things as Geospizinae, Anthracomys, Equidae, Musophagidae, Saturniidae, and so forth.

At this juncture the development of a delineation of organizational evolution would be a heroic task. It would involve a careful tracing of the history of environmenal change and accompanying changes in organizational form from as far back as 8500 b.c. At least one paper, and probably several if the data were fuzzy and debate emerged, could be written about each branching point. Even if this were done it would still be an inductive development, not yet tested by empirical, numerical phenetic, or cladistic methods. Clearly we are without any such classification. And of course it is equally obvious that any attempt to present such a classification must be taken as highly speculative.

Nevertheless, the need for examples to use in the course of the discussion is important to bring meaning to the rather abstract level that the discussion could take. One possibility would be to follow the pattern of figure 9.1 and base examples strictly on very abstract illustrations. But the reader still may not grasp some of the issues, problems, and excitement involved in wondering about the questions needing to be answered.

In view of these concerns, figures 9.2, 9.3, 9.4, and 9.5 are presented with considerable qualification and trepidation. *The dendrograms are preliminary illustrations only;* their substance will be explained as the chapter develops. At this time there is no reason to believe that they are at all correct. In many instances even an educated guess is not possible without considerable historical research. And please understand that, except in the case of ancient Mesopotamia, I have not carried out such research. However, I have not tried to be incorrect, either. The main disadvantage of making such a presentation of preliminary dendrograms is that if they are picked up by subsequent readers and authors, the latter may not be sufficiently careful to note the qualifications. This was seen in chapter 4, where I observed that all of Fayol's qualifications about his functional areas were later dropped by people picking up his ideas.

But there are some advantages to even preliminary dendrograms. The discussion will be much less abstract. At times even questionable exam-

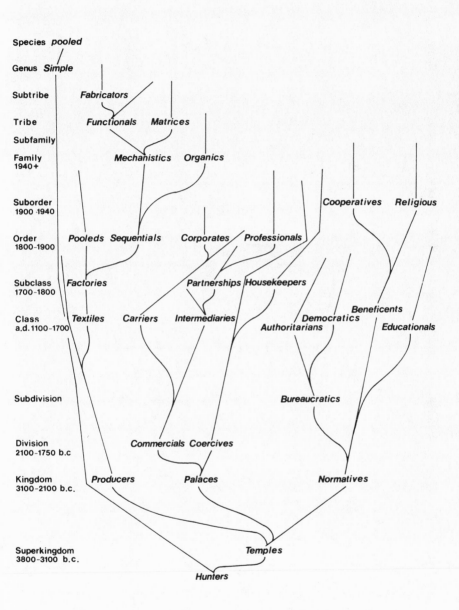

Figure 9.2. The Higher Categories (a preliminary illustration only).

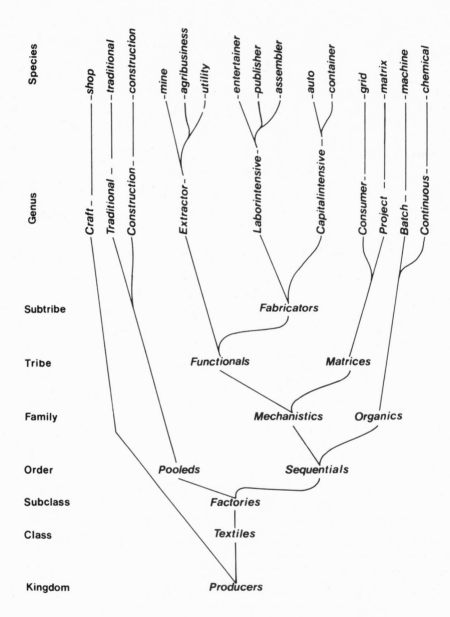

Figure 9.3. The Producers Kingdom (a preliminary illustration only).

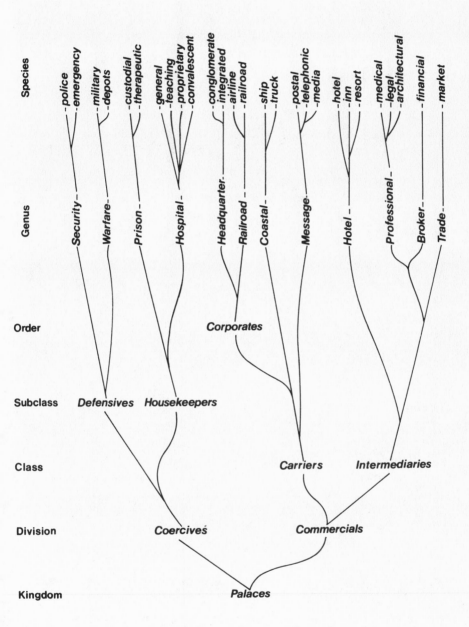

Figure 9.4. The *Palaces* Kingdom (a preliminary illustration only).

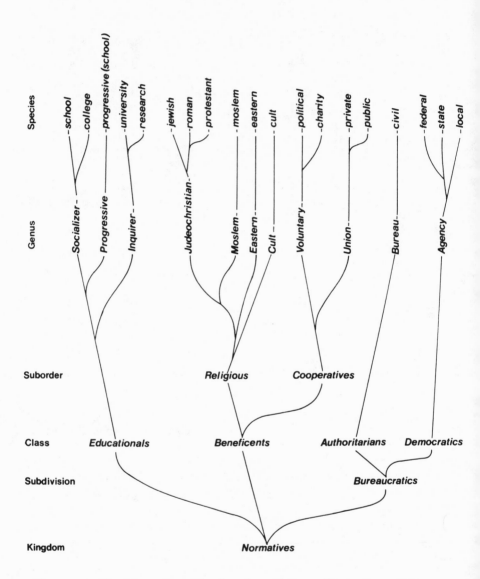

Figure 9.5. The *Normatives* Kingdom (a preliminary illustration only).

ples will help bring meaning to the discussion. The dendrograms will offer a visual picture much better than words of what an evolutionary classification and its higher categories might be like. Hopefully readers will become intrigued or incensed enough at the research questions underlying each branching point or decision to portray anagenesis rather than cladogenesis that they will want to do the kind of research necessary to put the evolutionary delineation on a better footing. The dendrograms, better than anything else, give readers an understanding of how the basic idea of descent with modification might unfold in a hierarchy of ranks composed, as one moves up the hierarchy, of groups sharing fewer characters and having an increasingly older common-ancestor form of organization.

In the dendrograms the lineage of the ancestral form that continues after a new form branches off is indicated by a straight line. The new branch is indicated by a curved line. Thus in figure 9.2 the *Normatives* form is shown to be a continuation of the older *Temples* form via a straight line. In this figure the lines that do not point to a label are shown in the subsequent dendrograms to end in a genus. For the most part the dates are approximate and the dates of the branching points are not well worked out at all. The dendrograms are composed of elements of many of the typologies reviewed in section 6.2, which are combined into a hierarchical framework according to the time when the particular element emerged as a dominant (but not an essential or only) characteristic of a population of organizations.

Cladogenesis

Evolution by branching occurs when a new organizational form or lineage is observed which emerged from a form already existing (an observation that may never be thoroughly confirmed), and the ancestor form continues to exist for some time after the new form has emerged. In this instance the new form is *in addition to* the ancestor form; a new form has been added to the total number of organizational forms. The ancestor form may survive into the present along with the new form, it may evolve into a new form via anagenesis, or the ancestor form may die out some time after the new form has emerged. For example, in figure 9.1, the new branch forming in Environment Four is depicted as dying in time t_3, whereas the branch forming in Environment Five, time t_7, continues through time t_{13}. In the latter case a new form would be recognized whereas in the former case the new form may have died off so quickly that it would not be recognized as a viable new form. In order to keep cladogenesis separate from anagenesis it is necessary that the continuance of the ancestor form be observed or that the new form be distinctly different. If not, a new form is not added, but rather the old form simply evolves into a newer form. Thus the branch at time t_6 which moves into Environment Five clearly results in a new form because the ancestor form in Environment Three continues. But the shift of the form in Environment Two into Environment One, in retrospect, could be an example of anagenetic movement into a new environment (even though it took place fairly rapidly) because the older form does not continue. Or it could be taken as a branching, even though the older form died out, because the combination of characters in the new form is viewed as substantially different from those of the ancestor form. This possible difference in interpretation may not be subject to review by numerical methods because the form that has died out may not be measurable.

In figure 9.2 many branches are shown. The long vertical lines without any branching, depicted better in figures 9.3, 9.4, and 9.5, are examples of anagenesis. Where cladogenesis does take place, at least three different ways of branching may be identified.

Hybridization. One form of branching is by the mixture of several existing forms to create a new hybrid organizational form to handle a newly invented product or service. My use of hybridization seems parallel to Sarason's (1972) "confronting history" or Kimberly and Miles's (1980) "prehistory." As a result of the new invention, a new workplace is needed, meaning new primary and workplace-management tasks. Since the requisite competence does not exist in any existing organizational form it has to be created from what already exists. Usually this happens by the collecting together of people who have somewhat related skills and interests. Because it is new, the new product or service exists in a new environment. The competition is different; the markets are different; the environmental problems management must mitigate to be successful are different; the materials, workflow, and workplace operations are different. The result is that the accumulation of environmental forces gives rise to a new dominant competence that in turn means a new organizational form. The new members of the organization draw on competence they knew from their previous occupations and by working together they combine it in a new way to form a new compool. Miles and Randolph (1980) referred to the development of competence by drawing on knowledge and experience brought from prior settings as *proactive* learning. Competence developed in the new setting based on new behavioral experiences, which is part of the anagenetic process, they termed *enactive* learning. Branching by hybridizing is illustrated in two places in figure 9.1. The hybrid form at time t_2 in Environment Four does not survive, whereas the one at time t_5 in Environment Three does. In each case some but not all of the characters from the previous forms combine in the new form. In the first case, elements from forms in Environments Two, Three and Five combined to make a form which does not survive in Environment Four. In the second case elements from forms in Environments Two, x, y, and z combine to make a form that is very successful in Environment Three.

Examples of evolution by hybridization are common. Inventions such as the steam engine, the steam locomotive, the gasoline engine, the automobile, the radio, the telephone, the electronic computer, the airplane, petroleum refining, microcircuitry, and so forth, all forced the mixing of elements from already existing compools formed around older products. The identification of needs for services such as research, psychotherapy, physical health, and social welfare, among other things, also led to new competencies through the mixing of people with different technical backgrounds. In the case of the early railroads in the United States, for example, there was a mixture of people who knew something about the wagon trade, mining tramways, iron works, and canal building and operation (Comstock, 1971). As a result of changing technical, economic, and political forces, these people combined to form the first railroad companies and in doing so set the stage for the development of the intercommunicating compool of railroad organizations; a new lineage was formed. In figure 9.4 the evolution of the railroad form is shown in the *Carriers* class, where a branching of the railroad form off the ancestral *Coastals* form consisting of the old wagon and sea shipping organizations occurs. The old line is seen to branch recently into modern ocean shipping and trucking organizations as separate species. It is possible, however, that shipping and wagon organizations became separate species two or three centuries ago and thus the dendrogram would be in error.

Saltation. In contrast to the mixing of different combinations of comps as a result of a totally new product or service, saltation, quantum speciation, or rapid cladogenesis takes place when an organizational form mutates suddenly in the absence of a new invention or need for a service. Mutation occurs when significant innovations in the existing competence of the primary or workplace-management tasks take place and prove effective in the existing environment. This might be an invention in production methods in the workplace, such as the assembly line or automated machine tools, or enough changes in the environment of an existing product or service may have occurred so as to confront the existing workplace-management competence with different problems to handle. These problems may have led to many different innovations in the dominant competence, some of which were unsuccessful and some of which may have been relatively successful. A saltation in dominant competence and subsequently in organizational form occurs when one of these many innovations is of such striking superiority that it immediately takes hold, survives, is accompanied by other changes in interdependent comps, and relatively quickly is observed to be considerably superior to the existing compool. For systematists to recognize such an innovation as the cause of a new compool and organizational form it must be of some magnitude and significance. In figure 9.1 saltation is illustrated in the formation of the branch into Environment Five. The new form is composed in part of characters g, k, m, p from the ancestor form, but also of characters 1, 2, 3, 4, which are mutant elements heretofore not seen.

The matrix form of organization (Litterer 1963; Cleland and King 1968; Kingdon 1973; Davis and Lawrence 1977) may be a good example of saltation. Its origin does not appear to have been associated with the invention of a particular product or service. The organizations in which it originated were already producing aerospace equipment (see figure 9.3) or, later, consumer products. They did not change their product mix appreciably just before the new form emerged and in these instances the primary task and workplace did not change very much either. But many aspects of their environment did change, such as the competition, the rate of change in product obsolescence, and the need for finding and promoting new products. The workplace-management competence for mitigating environmental forces bore the brunt of these changes. Consequently, once the idea of the matrix form was identified it quickly took hold and spread to other members of the compool. The development of the compool of which these organizations were a part took a quantum leap forward in evolution and the result was that the matrix form of organization became a new lineage split off from the older functional form. Note that the variations inherent in the matrix form may have occurred frequently before the post-World War II period, but because of an inappropriate environment they did not aid survival and hence were not retained. The corporate form of organization was invented some thirty years before the environment faced by the U.S. railroads made corporate form an important adaptive character.

Gradualism. This kind of cladogenesis takes place so slowly that it is only after some considerable passage of time that a branching can be recognized as having taken place. It may be that no clear branching point, and thus no sharp discontinuity between the new and old forms, can be identified. Yet in retrospect it may seem that a new form of organization has emerged and therefore ought to be classed separately from the ancestor form. In contrast to the other kinds of branching, gradual speciation occurs when environmental change is slow. This is illustrated in figure 9.1 after time t_9 in Environment Three. Here there is a slow addition of different characters that eventually leads to a clear branching at time t_{13}.

For example, it is clear at this time that there are at least two kinds of major automobile manufacture and assembly: the standardized high-production lines operated by General Motors, Ford, Volkswagen, Fiat, Toyota, and the like; and customized, much more handcrafted lines such as those run by Rolls Royce, Jensen, and Lamborghini. The lines operated by Jaguar and Porsche are probably somewhere in between. Although all lines have evolved over the years and now are much different from the production methods of the early twentieth century, the big standardized lines are much more automated and less hand-crafted than the customized lines. Yet there is probably no clear point in time when the two lines branched. (This is of course an empirical question that can be investigated.) They just drifted apart over the years. Each began to respond to slightly different portions of the total environment of automobile manufacturing. As the environment differentiated into two or more kinds of customers and demand forces, the manufacturing compools followed, each specializing in one or the other set of demands. At some point in time they may have become different enough to warrant separate classification. Note that in this example it may be that the differences between the two major groupings still are not sufficient to warrant classification as different species. This decision would have to await empirical study and the development of standards of minimum differentiation before branching could be recognized.

Anagenesis

Evolution also occurs under conditions where no branching is ever recognized. In the face of an environment that slowly changes but which does not become further differentiated, or in which further differentiations are ignored by the organizations, there are pressures for adaptation but not for further division and specialization. Thus there is no pressure for branching, just slow adaptation as the environment changes. In this case the grouping of organizations may already be recognized as different from others and as the environment changes it continues to remain different. Here the organizational form evolves toward a new form but there is no branching and no addition to the number of different kinds of organizations. This form of evolution is known as anagenesis. Thus in figure 9.1 the form in Environment Two evolves slowly within the line over six time periods (though three branches also take place). The result is that in time t_6 none of the original characters are still present.

For example, over the past century the railroad form of organization has developed slowly toward a more modern form—not as modern as some would like, perhaps, but nevertheless more sophisticated than in the beginning. Yet there probably are no additional specializations within railroads that would warrant splitting them into subdivisions. Wyckoff (1976) mentioned two possibly significant differences among railroad organizations, though the nontraditional form has not burgeoned into a population yet. Railroads have evolved by drifting slowly without branching. There are other long-lasting examples where the compool has evolved within the lineage but no branching has occurred, such as the shipping organizational form beginning in 1600 with the British East India Company, and various educational, government, and religious organizations.

9.1.2 Evidence of Cladogenesis

Existing studies and histories are vague on the origin of organizational lineages. The empirical studies mentioned in chapter 5, showing that organizations specialize, do not give an indication of the origins of the different specialties. No doubt much specific evidence of the origins of various compools or industries is recorded in histories of these industries. Because of a personal interest, I was able to use railroads as an example of evolution by hybridization. Histories of other industries probably indicate much the same pattern of early development, but a broad study of the origins of many industries would provide more convincing evidence of branching by hybridization. Needless to say, little attention has been given to distinguishing between kinds of origins, such as hybridization, saltation, gradualism, or whatever. Management historians such as Wren (1972) give some accounts of the origin of other significant elements of the workplace-management task part of the dominant competence, but since they were written without any conceptual framework about the origin of organizations, these accounts do not give much specific evidence of branching. Several authors—Kimberly (1980), Miles and Randolph (1980), and Van de Ven (1980)—recently discussed the organizational creation process in individual organizations; but none of them focused specifically on kinds of cladogenesis or anagenesis, or the distinction between them specifically in population terms. The discussions on transformations by Tichy (1980), Lodahl and Mitchell (1980), and Walton (1980), though about individual organizations, could be extrapolated into an understanding of the anagenetic process in part. Insight about the anagenesis of a population relative to that of its members would still be missing, however.

Two notable exceptions are Stinchcombe (1965) and Aldrich (1979). Stinchcombe's inquiry was into the relation between social structure and the tendency to organize. A key argument he made was that some societies contain conditions necessary for new organizational forms to emerge and others do not. The discussion below follows Stinchcombe's presentation closely.

Motives to organize. According to Stinchcombe, new organizational forms emerge when:

1. There is the discovery of new ways of doing things that are not easily done under the existing social arrangements.
2. There is reason to believe that the new organization will survive long enough to be worth the trouble of building it and the resources invested.
3. There is the belief and presumably evidence that the group building the new organization, or some other group they are strongly identified with, will receive some of the benefits from the new way of doing things.
4. The new organizers can lay hold of the wealth, power, and legitimacy necessary to start the new organization.
5. The organizers can defeat or avoid being defeated by those with vested interests in the old ways of doing things.

Stinchcombe discussed how these elements of individual motivation are affected by the social structure. Important mitigating factors are such things as well-developed innovative roles, the existence of people skilled in performing innovative roles, the existence of rational and stable governments, and money economies.

The liability of newness. Stinchcombe continued by identifying several conditions that affect the chances of a new organizational form's survival:

1. The more difficult new organizational roles are to learn the poorer the chances of survival. To be efficient a new organization's members must learn new specialized roles. If generalized role skills are not available in the larger society, if it is difficult to recruit people holding these skills into the organization, and if people generally have a low ability to learn new roles, the chances of survival are considerably diminished.
2. If standardized methods of running the daily affairs of the new organization are not available, and therefore it has to make up new organizational methods as it goes along, methods such as cost-account-

ing, control, and coordination systems, standardized forms, and the like, the startup costs are much greater and consequently the chances of survival are diminished. On the other hand, if members coming into the new organization bring with them basic elements of dominant competence developed elsewhere, and if these can be quickly adapted to the new situation, survival is enhanced.

3. A new organization's chances of survival are greatly diminished if it is difficult to build social relations and satisfactory levels of trust among strangers. This is probably more true for organizations starting off at a relatively large size where family and kin are not sufficient to fill all the needed roles. The building of social relations among strangers is enhanced if universalistic religions, legal contractual systems, and methods for evaluating competence are available. Thus while bureaucracy is much maligned, it is also an example of a universalistic system that makes the building of new organizations much easier.

4. The strength of the interdependence between producer and consumers also affects a new organization's chances for survival. Where old interdependencies are numerous and strong it may be very difficult for the new organization to pry its suppliers and potential consumers away from their ties to the old organizations. The more particularistic these ties, the more they are based on friendship and kinship, the harder they will be to break up. Here again universalistic relations help the new organization where it has something better to offer.

Variables affecting organizing capacity. There is reason to believe that some societies support or even cause much faster evolution and branching of organizational forms than others. Stinchcombe identified five factors that affect the pace of new branchings in different societies:

1. He identified the basic literacy level of a society as probably the most fundamental factor in the pace of organizational evolution. Literacy aids in learning and the diffusion of new ideas. Universalism is much more likely to function where written codes, laws, and procedures are possible. Stinchcombe goes so far as to argue that it was literacy, not the Protestant ethic, which spurred the rise of early capitalism and industrialization.

2. A second factor is the level of urbanization. Because urban areas force interaction among strangers, there is a quicker and more sophisticated development of the social means necessary to regulate such interactions. These means, and the tendency of people to conform to them, are generalized skills that new organizations may draw upon. It is

also true that literacy rates tend to be higher in cities, and people with new ideas—artists, writers, and inventors—seem to gravitate toward large urban areas.

3. A money economy makes the movement of resources from one place to another and from one form of investment to another much easier. It simplifies the calculation of the relative advantage of the new versus the old.

4. Political disruptions such as revolutions (Stinchcombe mentions the Meiji Restoration in Japan, the Russian Revolution, and Nazi Germany as examples) are prime instances where the relative advantage of vested interests is often lost so that new organizations have a better chance of survival. Though Stinchcombe does not explicitly mention them, international wars also seem to be political disruptions that may change the internal social structure of a nation enough to allow faster development of new ideas and organizations.

5. The level of organizational experience within a population is also a main factor affecting the organizing capacity of a society. The best way to learn how to start up new organizations is to have already tried it previously. The chance of finding people who have relevant technical and organizational skills is greater if there are many of them who already have experience working in organizations.

In the terms of this book, Stinchcombe was working on a theory of how and why new compools and the organizations embodying them come into being. Although he wrote in terms of "new organizations" and did not distinguish between the ways a new population might form, it seems clear that he was writing about branchings, and since the new organizations often multiplied, he was writing about the formation of new compools comprised of several or many organizations. Therefore, his ideas about motivation to organize, liabilities, and the organizing abilities of different societies may be applied to compools as well.

A second key idea introduced by Stinchcombe was that new organizational forms tended to remain stable over time. Thus at the time a new form branched off from its ancestor form, according to Stinchcombe, it quickly became differentiated from the ancestor form. However, once having branched, the new form tended to develop very slowly and, in fact, remained rather stable despite other advances in the larger society of which it was a part. He presented rough data showing that as new industries emerged from pre-factory to modern times, the older forms did not change to reflect the characteristics of the new forms. Thus, the older industries tended to have higher numbers of self-employed and family workers to begin with and these levels remained high in these industries right into modern times. Stinchcombe found that the trend over the years was for a decline in the number of self-employed and family workers and for a swelling in the number of professionals, but that these increases took place incrementally with each new industry. In general, each new industry had higher levels of professional and administrative employees, but the older industries stayed at their original levels. Stinchcombe argued that the effects of institutionalization locked organizations into the competencies and forms they had shortly after they first came into being, their compools and forms showing little further evolution.

The implication of these data is that organizational evolution occurs much more through the emergence of new lineages (industries) via cladogenesis than by anagenesis. Presumably these kinds of branchings and new lineages have occurred throughout the history of organized activity. Since the phyletic approach to classification and its hierarchy of categories is based on the existence of branchings, empirical evidence such as Stinchcombe's is crucial. Nevertheless, his data are preliminary and further investigation is necessary before it is possible to have complete confidence in evolution by cladogenesis. He only looked at the percentage of unpaid family workers, percentage of self-employed and family workers, clerical workers as a percentage of administrative workers, and professionals as a percentage of top management or high-status officials. These measures of ratios among different sets of employees are only the grossest measures of underlying competence differences among organizations.

Aldrich's (1979) extensive discussion of factors leading to the creation of new forms of organizations and new organizations fleshes out Stinchcombe's earlier analysis by reviewing recent literature in considerable detail. One significant difference is that Aldrich put his discussion in the context of natural selection theory. Thus, rather than refer to the motives of entrepreneurs, Aldrich focused on environmental conditions that foster more incentives leading people to found new organizations. The role of the state assumes greater importance in Aldrich's analysis. He noted that the "world-state" may be a more relevant unit of analysis than individual sovereign nation-states, which were the focus of attention for Stinchcombe. Nevertheless, nation-states are still very important in that they exercise considerable influence over the origin of new forms via the degree of political stability they offer, the degree to which they support "ideologies of management," and the extent to which the state overtly protects new organizations through the use of import quotas and subsidies or through investments of public resources in the educational, technological, and communications (one could add transportation) infrastructures that support organizations.

Aldrich identified three elements especially important to the branching of new forms of organizations. First, there is the incidence of technological invention and the extent to which a society or state provides the kind of support that might increase the incidence of new inventions. He cited Germany's early support of technological innovation via universities, which allowed that country to overtake England in industrial development. The development of laboratories in industrial organizations also was a contributing factor. Second, there is access to wealth and power and the degree to which a society fosters this. Thus, even though the corporate form of organization was invented in England, it wasn't until three decades later in the U.S. that the social/legal conditions allowed the railroads to use it to gain the size necessary to attract the financial support they needed. Likewise, Aldrich noted, the financial institutions in England were oriented toward the landed mercantile class and held the new industrialists at bay, whereas in the U.S. the financial institutions grew up at the same time as the railroads and large industrial organizations, thereby giving them easier access to financial support. And, finally, there is the availability of a productive labor force. Educational and immigration policies in the U.S. provided organizations a disciplined, competent, and motivated work force.

The rise in new organizational forms not only requires conditions of support for initial branching but also for the survival of the new form once it has branched off into a new environment. Aldrich discussed three items in some detail. Workers have to learn or already know the technology required to operate the new form. The kind of technical training, attitudes and values, personality, and tolerance of change and diversity are some of the characteristics often associated with the shift from traditional to more modern organizational forms. In the terms of this book, if workers cannot learn the comps, the new compool will not survive. The market characteristics and barriers to entry are also important to the survival of new forms. Entry is very difficult into highly concentrated oligopolistic settings due to the probable existence of agreements between buyers and sellers, the ability to control prices, or other cartellike practices. In a setting where one firm dominates, predatory pricing is possible, along with the use of profits from one product line to offset selling another product at a loss to undercut a newcomer. Finally government regulation, Aldrich showed, is a significant factor in lowering the incidence of survival, though this is more by preventing entry than by reducing viability of a form once created. Generally the factors that affect new creation also affect viability after creation.

The analyses by Stinchcombe and Aldrich are fairly global in nature. Stinchcombe does not distinguish between organizations and organizational forms. Organizations may be created and fail to survive even though the population remains viable. Thus in an oligopolistic situation the population of organizations having a particular form may be exceedingly stable yet at the same time new organizations may find it very difficult to survive and remain members of the population. Aldrich *does* distinguish between the population form and individual organizations but his analysis for the most part is carried on in terms of organizations rather than population forms. Hence, as written, his analysis leads the reader to think more of the birth and death of organizations as legal entities rather than the creation and survival of species. Thus, his discussion of the role of the state and his historical discussion of environmental variability and niche generation apply more to the creation and survival of species while his analysis of the constraints on viability applies more to individual organizations, though the section on work force characteristics seems relevant to both populations and individual organizations. Neither analysis is sensitive to the distinctions made here between kinds of branching. Presumably their analyses apply equally well to branching by hybridization, saltation, and gradualism.

Pennings (1980) pursued the population perspective in the framework of natural selection. He emphasized the ecological communities in urban areas and their effects on the creation of new organizations. He also focused on the size and life-cycle stage of organizational populations. Pennings then considered the economic and social resourcefulness or carrying capacity of urban environments. His analysis focused on the creation of new organizations within populations, not on the creation of new populations, and hence does not bear on cladogenesis per se, though it is an instructive analysis of some difficulties to be expected in applying the population perspective to organizations.

Perhaps the best recent treatment of both cladogenesis and anagenesis is the work of Brittain and Freeman (1980) on the development of the U.S. semiconductor industry. They carefully traced out technical novelties in the industry and the changes in organizational forms, all in a population perspective. Their findings offer convincing evidence of evolutionary developments within at least one population. It is an exciting piece of work.

At this point it is possible to conclude that branchings do occur and that we have a general idea of how and when new forms will emerge and remain viable. But more precise conceptualizations of kinds of origins, clearer distinctions between organizations and species, and better separation of environmental factors that increase the incidence of new branchings from those that foster viability after branching are called for.

9.1.3 Evidence of Anagenesis

The evidence in support of organizational evolution by anagenesis is not straightforward. The most pertinent study (Stinchcombe 1965) suggested that new forms occur via new branches and that these branches, once formed, tend to persist relatively unchanged. Stinchcombe suggested three reasons for such persistence: (1) the original form may be the most efficient (implying that the environment has not changed); (2) the original form may have been permanently institutionalized via the forces of tradition, vested interest, or ideological legitimization; or (3) the original form may have no competitors, meaning that even though the environment has changed the population is not under pressure to become more efficient by adopting a new form. Aldrich (1979, pp. 195–197) built on this, but in terms of natural selection theory. He observed three conditions under which the organizational form of a population might persist: (1) natural selection operates freely and the new form continues unchanged because it remains more efficient than contending forms; (2) natural selection operates freely but factors inhibiting variation prevent new forms from emerging even though the requisite environmental changes are present; and (3) natural selection does not operate because the population is insulated from environmental pressures.

Despite these factors fostering persistence, there is also evidence of enough evolution within lineages to suggest that in many of the industries mentioned by Stinchcombe, modern dominant competencies are different from their original form. In a footnote, Stinchcombe (1965, p. 159) noted that there was some evidence of anagenesis in the space of a decade, and he only looked at professionalization of authority and the ratio of clerical to administrative employees. A broader look suggests more evidence. Multinational divisionalized organizations have gone through various organization design approaches over the years (Allen 1978). Assembly line oriented manufacturing organizations have shifted to computerized planning and scheduling, though many still use a noncomputerized form. There have been tremendous changes in the workplace and primary tasks of many industries due to technological developments in energy production; computer-based scheduling, inventory control, and billing; solid-state components; microcircuitry; antipollution measures; antitrust measures; and energy conservation, to name but a few major events. The professionalized perspective of MBA degree holders has altered the management practices of many companies. The MPA and the Educational Administration master's and doctoral degrees may have had a similar effect in government and educational organizations. The spread of the "industrial democracy" orientation toward the operation of the workplace has also brought about change in the workplace (Davis and Taylor 1979, Walton 1980). Even the railroads operate in a much more modern fashion than they did a few decades ago. These changes in dominant competence suggest that their compools have changed over the years (Wyckoff 1976).

I have little doubt that anagenesis is an important piece of the total puzzle. It seems inconceivable that there have not been important changes within various organizational lineages in response to environmental pressures. At this point there is no clearly established relationship between the kind of employee ratio indicators used by Stinchcombe and attributes of dominant competence, so there could have been many significant changes in dominant competence which would not show up in the employee ratios. Only careful empirical study with sophisticated conceptual notions of the evolutionarily significant elements of dominant competencies will resolve this issue.

It may be, however, that many technological changes affect relatively insignificant elements of the total dominant competencies of the various populations and therefore such changes may not indicate much real organizational evolution. This would be evidence that organizational evolution did not take place by anagenesis. Thus, it could be that while there have been numerous small changes in the dominant competencies of populations, there have been few significant changes in organizational form measured at a higher level of abstraction. It is possible that Stinchcombe's data reflects this. Once sets of characters are developed for each population of organizations, along the lines suggested in chapter 11, a better indication of the relative importance of changes in some characters will be possible.

In summary, there is broad evidence that new forms emerge, but specific evidence of how and why the evolution of compools takes one of several kinds of cladogenesis is not available. Common sense suggests that populations of organizations have evolved by anagenesis, though the tendency of academicians such as Stinchcombe and Aldrich has been to emphasize persistence rather than change once a new branch is formed. Full understanding of evolutionary change awaits the development of more complete sets of taxonomic characters.

9.2 BASIC ASSUMPTIONS OF HIGHER CLASSIFICATION

Given the probability of evolution via both cladogenesis and anagenesis, the many centuries since the first organizational forms appeared, and the many kinds of organizational species apparently existing at present, the task of developing an evolutionary classification is not straightforward. Any sensible approach to this task involves several assumptions and many operational procedures. As with previously discussed aspects of systematics, the biologists have already tilled this field and it makes sense to draw from their experience.

Several basic assumptions upon which the phyletic approach to higher classification rests are important. Some of these have been discussed specifically as part of the development of the theory of organizational speciation. Others have not yet been discussed but they too follow from the evolutionary theory of classification. All of them are drawn from Ross's (1974, pp. 144–147) discussion of the basic assumptions underlying biological phyletics. In a couple of instances it seems too early to decide one way or another whether the biological experience translates to an organizational context. In any event I caution the reader that these are *starting assumptions*, not incontrovertible facts. They are offered because some set of starting assumptions is necessary and it seems that, just as much of the richness of biological experience applied to the development of a theory of organizational speciation, so much of it also applies to the theory of higher organizational classification.

1. It should be eminently clear by now that the most fundamental assumption is that, through a succession of branchings and developments within lines, organizations have evolved from the simplest primeval form to the many different lines of the present. If so, then there is a correct "family tree" or dendrogram for all groups of organizations that exist now or existed in the past, and with investigation these trees can be identified, except where the historical record is totally obscured.

2. Because these events took place in the past, the correct tree can only be inferred from whatever evidence is available. In some instances this evidence will be relatively complete and the image of the tree will be fairly accurate. In other instances the trees will approximate rough guesses due to poor evidence. Consequently a phyletic classification can never be more than a scientific inference, a hypothetical construct or model of what actually took place in the past. Like all scientific statements, it is subject to change as new data come to light. Evidence from

the past will be mainly documentary in form; additional evidence, and the only evidence when documents are not available, will come from studies of present species of organizations, often by numerical phenetic methods. The preliminary illustrations given in figures 9.2 to 9.5 are at best only rough models of what actually happened.

3. Fairly complete documentary evidence about some family trees will be found. About these, accurate models can be developed of how branchings came about in the past and what environmental factors affected specific dominant competence configurations. Armed with this knowledge, systematists can extrapolate what probably happened in organizational lines less well documented. Their interests will probably focus on some kinds of organizations more than others, as has happened among biologists. Economically important organizations, those especially interesting or numerous, and those that are more complex and larger will no doubt receive most attention, just as biologists tend to focus more on medically or economically important species such as people, apes, monkeys, pets, farm animals, and laboratory rats and mice. Furthermore, public and private sources of research funds will probably have as much influence as systematists about which lines shown in figure 9.2 are thoroughly studied.

4. Intraspecific variation within past organizational species probably and usually resembled the level of variation in present species; hence past as well as present groupings are polythetic and no group has had members that were identical. The limits of variation allowed in defining and classifying present species generally will be applied to past ones. Broader variations will have to be taken as evidence of incipient or already developed subspecies. Thus it is assumed that the *Producers* group around 3100−2100 B.C. (figure 9.2) was no more or less polythetic than presently existing species (shown in figures 9.3 to 9.5). The same guidelines for identifying species are expected to apply to past and present species.

5. Each phyletic line is composed of one or more species thought to have descended from two or more immediate ancestors, though ultimately from a common ancestor. This is the concept of polyphyletic lines used by the evolutionists. Cladists, such as Ross, insist that each line comprise one species, the concept of monophyletic lines. Since I have followed evolutionist rather than cladist theory, I take the position of polyphyly rather than monophyly; this results in a simpler classification. When variation in the genotypic compool exceeds a certain limit (to be determined by future experience and the establishment of acceptable criteria) it will have to be assumed that a branching took place and that two or more lines subsequently exist. However, where it can be

reasonably argued or demonstrated that a modern compool contains a considerably greater number of elements than past compools, assumptions 4 and 5 probably no longer apply. Ross (1974, p. 145) said that species variations have stayed roughly the same because the store of genetic variability for any given species has remained the same. He might have added, however, that variability did increase as the number of genes increased from single-cell organisms to the larger mammals. Where the potential for greater compool variability is present, the acceptable levels of intraspecific variation will likely have to be raised. The latter should be expected of organizational populations.

6. The more complex an organizational form, the less likely it is that it evolved independently more than once. This seems like a risky statement in view of people's tendency to reinvent the wheel, but consider the forces involved. Such an independent evolution could only happen where it was impossible for the combination of competence elements characterizing the first evolved form to have been disseminated. This means that the cultures and political environments would likely be quite different where the form supposedly had its second incarnation. The economic and technical environments most likely would be different too. These differences would probably be sufficient to prevent the form from taking hold in the second situation, if indeed it were even required. There is the remote possibility that the same form could have been invented at the same time in two difference places. The odds of this happening are not high, as it would require highly similar habitats, but it deserves investigation. One obvious possibility, the development of early irrigation societies in ancient Mesopotamia, Egypt, and the Indus River valley on the the one hand and the rise of irrigation civilizations in Peru and central Mexico on the other, is an example of the independent rise of ancient organizational forms, but whether they were similar enough to be taken as an example of independent evolution of the same form remains in doubt. Their independence is proven but their similarity is in question. I think it is possible that primitive "acquisitional" technologies, or *Hunters* forms (see chapter 10), are quite simple and are invented independently. But even here it could be argued that no one starts a new organization and subsequently a population without some prior exposure to other organizational forms.

7. Within a given organizational lineage, some characters may evolve at a faster pace than others. For example, workplace technology has often far outpaced management competence. Control systems in many organizations have developed faster than the adaptive systems. The guidance or control of machines is more sophisticated than the guidance of employees, where in some instances nineteenth-century

views prevail. In some organizations the handling of one unit operation, such as transforming, has outdistanced other elements of the dominant competence, such as inspecting or maintenance. In figure 9.2, as illustrated, it appears that the *Producers* kingdom has evolved faster (more category ranks) than either the *Palaces* or *Normatives* kingdoms. Again, as illustrated, the latter two kingdoms seem to have evolved faster between the end of the Middle Ages and the Industrial Revolution. Some observers may be inclined to suggest that the evolution of recent forms in the *Normatives* kingdom has speeded up in the last twenty years. But it is not necessarily true that growth in size and the ease with which individual members of a population (the *Agency-* genus, for example) survive is accompanied by a faster pace of evolution.

8. In different lineages, the same character may evolve at different rates. Thus technical systems are often more sophisticated in many profit organizations than they are in not-for-profit schools and hospitals. Adaptive technologies are seemingly more sophisticated in consumer product organizations and drug companies than they are in New England shoe companies or the railroads. The workplace technologies of government agencies, schools, and universities have changed little in decades as compared with changes in the workplaces of textile mills or food processors.

9. Different lineages may evolve at different rates, taking all their characters into account. Profit organizations seem more highly evolved, differentiated, and complex than not-for-profit organizations or government agencies. The American aircraft industry seems to have evolved faster than the shipbuilding industry. Universities have gone through more changes than elementary schools. German automobile manufacturers evolved faster than their English counterparts. It will be interesting to see if the current economic crises in England will work to speed up the evolutionary pace of English dominant competencies and even give rise to totally new forms uniquely suited to their present economic and political environment.

Two further assumptions, true in biology, may not apply to organizations:

10. According to Ross (1974, p. 145), complex biological structures once lost are never regained in the same form. At present there seems to be no way of knowing whether organizations follow this pattern or not. There is not enough accumulated evidence of past forms to ascertain whether they have died out and reemerged. But there is some reason to think that such an assumption might be justified. For example, there

apparently were rather complex organizations for the construction of the early canal networks in the Mesopotamian valley and the Egyptian pyramids, and for the great early Persian, Greek, and Roman armies. These sophisticated organizations died out to a considerable extent during the Middle Ages, though the early military sophistication may have been carried along by the Byzantine Empire. As the civilizations of Europe and the Mideast came out of the Middle Ages the organizational sophistication of the earlier periods may have been regained. However, it is also possible that the cultural, economic, and political environments after the Middle Ages were sufficiently different as to have caused the new organizations to emerge in significantly altered form. These conjectures may never be resolved for lack of evidence.

11. Ross also stated that biological characters are lost more often than new ones emerge. Whether this is true for organizations is impossible to say. Much of the biological evidence in support of this seems to stem from the fact that the organisms losing characters also diminished in size, though this is not true in the case of stamen loss among flowering plants. Since organizational forms tend to become larger and more complex rather than smaller and simpler, it seems more likely that organizations have generally added characters over the years. This is an empirical question, though it may be harder to answer for organizations than for biological organisms. Those who prepared whatever documents are now available may not have paid much attention to recording all the relevant characters.

A final corollary to assumptions 7, 8, and 9, which is not uniformly true for biological organisms or organizations, is that characters evolve at the same rate as the environment. This may be true for some organizations and not true for others. For example, in a slowly but continually changing environment, character changes may be at discrete intervals. It could also be that primary task technologies (and their measurable characters) stay more in tune with the environment than the workplace-management task competencies. It is an empirical question that may or may not be answerable, though the chances are better for more recent times.

9.3 SOME MISCONCEPTIONS

On the basis of what has happened in biology, some misconceptions about organizational phyletics can be anticipated. Those mentioned below are drawn from Ross (1974, pp. 147–148). Since organizational systematics has not yet emerged as a field of study, it is impossible to determine what misconceptions unique to it will be forthcoming. Undoubtedly there will be some.

1. It is not true that organizational family trees have to be charted against historical time. The family tree is first meant only to trace out the supposed pattern of branching from early to later forms. If it is possible to locate when branchings happened and in terms of other parallel events in their respective environments, so much the better. Usually the tree will come first, and then as further study takes place the time dimension will be filled in. In the illustrations of family trees in figure 9.2, dates have been attached to the various rank categories. While I have done some research on events in ancient Mesopotamia (chapter 10) and therefore feel more confident of the approximate dates of the forms before the Middle Ages, in general the dates are only the most preliminary indication of the era of each category. The dates are included mainly to indicate that the protosystem evolved over many years and that the categories should ultimately be placed in their proper time context. It is quite likely that many lines will be suggested and branchings indicated long before they can be placed accurately in time. This is even more true of the dendrograms in figures 9.3 to 9.5.

2. It is not true that an organizational tree must be based solely on documentary evidence from the past. Where such evidence exists it must be used, of course. But there will be many instances where such evidence will be limited or totally unavailable. In these cases considerable emphasis must be placed on phenetic comparisons of presently existing organizations, usually via numerical phenetic methods or, as the possibility develops, on numerical comparisons of the underlying genetic material of the compools. With careful measuring of characters, inclusion of as many characters as possible, and by studying the relation between organizational groupings and the assembly of characters identifying each group, considerable insight as to the probable cladogenesis and anagenesis of the various groups may be gained. Once it is known which competence characters are more recently evolved, it can be determined which organizations are probably more recent in origin. Ross's (1974, pp. 162–191) discussion of cladistic procedures for constructing family trees based on identifying ancestral and derived character states seems especially relevant here. Specifically those with a greater proportion of more recent characters are likely to be more recently evolved. An ideal situation would be one where both kinds of evidence may be used. The use of documents will always be a problem because not all elements of past dominant competencies will have been equally well documented. Likewise, phenetic methods will have difficulties where char-

acters are not easily measured in ways that lend themselves to computer analysis.

3. Finally, it is also not true, where organizations go through distinct metamorphic stages, such as the craft, promotional, and administrative forms identified by Filley (Filley, House, and Kerr 1976, chap. 22), that systematists have to be content with two separate trees, one based on the young stage and one based on the older stage. Some investigators, not wanting to try to merge the two trees, might want to argue which one is correct. A better practice will be to work toward a single tree, drawing on information from any and all metamorphic stages. This will be easier if we remember that classificatory data are not facts that automatically indicate the true tree. Instead they are clues that, if used with some skill and imagination, will contribute toward the construction of a concept of past organizational evolution. It is important to note that most metamorphic differences and other more transient variations are best left as infraspecies variations rather than used as formal classificatory characters.

9.4 SOME OPERATIONAL PRINCIPLES OF ORGANIZATIONAL PHYLETICS

There are several operational principles that need to be generally agreed upon before creating an evolutionary hierarchical classification. The ideas discussed below are drawn from the biological texts on systematics and adapted to an organizational context. They are proposed only as a point of departure. Whether they will be altered, partially replaced, or totally replaced remains to be seen. These principles were applied as far as possible in working up the family trees illustrated in figures 9.2 to 9.5. The main exception is that the ecological features accompanying each new branching are not presented except for the *Producers* kingdom (see chapter 10)—the needed research has not occurred.

9.4.1 Patristic Groupings

In initially presenting the evolutionary theory of classification (section 3.1.5), I noted that biologists leaned either toward patristic or cladistic affinity in working out their hierarchical classification, with the former being by far the most orthodox. Using cladistic affinity, only branching points would be used to determine a classification. With patristic affinity both branching and pace of evolution within lines are taken into account. The difference is best understood by looking at the dendrogram in figure 9.6.

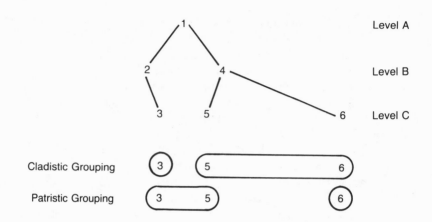

Figure 9.6*. Comparison of Patristic and Cladistic Groupings.

---

*The following terms will be used eventually and the figure also aids in seeing how they apply.

A grouping at 2 would be *monotypic* because it contains only one lower-level taxon.

Groupings at 1 and 4 would be *polytypic* because they contain 2 (or more) lower-level taxa.

A grouping of 5 and 6 together would be *monophyletic* because it includes descendants of one founder species, 4.

A grouping of 3 and 5 together would be *polyphyletic* because it includes descendants of two founder species, 2 and 4.

Cladistic grouping is based solely on recency of branching. Thus lines 5 and 6 are grouped together and line 3 is grouped by itself. Because the branching at 4 was most recent, 5 and 6 are grouped together even though 6 is shown to have evolved in such a fashion as to be very different from 5. This difference is represented in the diagram by the large horizontal separation between 5 and 6. The result is that, even though lines 3 and 5 evolved rather directly from lines 2 and 4 and have even converged a bit, since 5 is shown to have moved closer to 3 than 4 was to 2, they are *not* grouped together.

In contrast, patristic grouping is based on the supposed similarity of the underlying gene composition, which is not always accurately reflected in phenotypical similarity. So 3 and 5 are grouped together to reflect their common descent from ancestor 1, with 6 grouped by itself, even though 5 and 6 came from the same more recent ancestor. The reason for doing so draws upon the basic purposes of a general classification scheme—to set up homogeneous populations in support of the inductive-deductive cycle and to offer a means for information retrieval. It is clear from the way the groups in the diagram have evolved that the total behavior of 5 is probably more like that of 3 than of 6.

In practice it is often difficult for biologists to point to differences between the schemes of cladists and evolutionists using the patristic approach. The branchings in the dim past may be so obscured that it is impossible to know what really happened. For example, in the diagram it may be impossible to know whether the branch at 1 came before or after the branch at 4. Or, in figure 9.4, it is quite possible that the branching of *Housekeepers* from the *Coercives* line happened *after* the *Warfare-* line separated from the *Security-* line, not before as shown in the figure. Hopefully in this instance further research would clarify the issue. Furthermore, it is often difficult to infer the gene composition of dead species except via phenotypical similarity, and with fossils there may be little of even that kind of evidence available. The argument usually is made in terms of extreme cases. Most often the example of classifying snakes, crocodilians, and birds is used. As it happened, again using the diagram in figure 9.6, crocodilians and snakes evolved from the same reptilian ancestor, 1. Later birds evolved from crocodilians, at 4, and then because they took to the air, birds (at 6) evolved at a much faster pace and became totally different from crocodilians (at 5) because their new environment was so different. Cladists, arguing that birds evolved from crocodilians, say that birds and crocodilians should be grouped together, at Level C in the diagram, though of course they *are* separated at a lower category level. Those following the patristic method, and this includes modern biologists, say that since crocodilians have many characters in common with snakes, they ought to be grouped with snakes, with birds grouped separately. And this is the way it is presently done.

It makes sense to follow the method of patristic affinity in grouping organizations. Past organizational or compool branching points are no doubt obscured by lack of solid evidence concerning their timing, making the cladistic method difficult to apply. The purposes of a general classification are also desired by organizational scientists and so the patristic method is preferrable for grouping organizations for the same reason biologists used it, that is, it results in homogeneous classes. The operational principle is that: *Organizational species having the greatest overall similarity between their compools will be grouped together.* The patristic approach in grouping organizations is based on the same logic and methods as are patristic groupings of biological organisms. Fortunately, differences between cladistic and patristic grouping methods will be small most of the time because the pace of evolution within lines will be roughly the same and the dates of the branchings somewhat obscured and thus movable forward or backward in time.

The reader may wonder what the difference is in grouping according to patristic affinity as opposed to phenotypical similarity. Usually the latter results because of patristic affinity, and for the most part there is little difference in the resulting groupings. In biology the principal difference is that patristic groupings include several identifiable phena such as male, female, old, and young members of the same species, which are not always phenotypically similar—for instance, male and female birds, nymph and adult flies. With organizations different phena within the same species may also be recognized, as with young promotional and old administrative organizations, autonomous organizations versus those which are subsidiaries of a larger corporation, or possibly, publicly and privately owned hospitals, profit and not-for-profit hospitals, public and private mail and parcel services, and so forth. The point is that patristic affinity results in groupings that reflect the underlying similarity of combinations of comps, not just on more overt phenotypical similarities. Note however, that as phenotypical classification methods move closer to measuring directly the combinations of comps in organizations, the differences between patristic groupings and phenotypically similar groupings may mostly disappear.

Once a suitable set of characters for describing dominant competencies is identified the patristic approach will produce organizational groupings that are homogeneous within groups with respect to all important competence characters, with competence differences among groups being as large as possible. Needless to say, the actual levels of propinquity and diversity will depend on how the protosystem has evolved.

9.4.2 Higher Taxa

Mayr (1969, p. 88) defined a higher taxon as "an aggregate of related species, separated from others by a discontinuity." Although the ideal is to have each higher taxon composed of several lower-level groupings, there are occasions when this is not possible. What are termed *monotypic* taxa sometimes occur where the "aggregate of related species" consists of only one group. This is illustrated in figure 9.5 with the *Authoritarians* line. As classification studies advance it is possible that more forms besides the *Bureau-* form will be identified, but it could also happen that all bureaus or offices in authoritarian governments have the same form. It is an empirical question. The opposite difficulty is also to be avoided, of having so many groupings under a single higher-level grouping that it becomes so heterogeneous as to be useless and impossible to label and describe besides. No examples of this possibility are shown in the figures. The operational principle becomes: *Avoid the extreme of either too small or too large an aggregation of groupings at the higher levels, unless the evidence clearly indicates that one of the extremes is closest to reflecting the true nature of the protosystem.* In other words, work toward some semblance of horizontal balance across the various groupings.

In practice this is difficult to achieve for two reasons. First, in organizational systematics at least, there is no present indication of what the modal size of groupings might be. With accumulated experience this should become clearer. Second, the two main goals of a general classification, homogeneous groupings and an information-retrieval system, tend to work at cross purposes. Pursuing only homogeneous groupings produces a very tall hierarchy with many levels, with each grouping composed of very few highly similar members, or perhaps only one member. The cladistic dendrograms of biologists illustrate this. Pursuing only the goal of information retrieval produces a flat hierarchy with few levels, since the goal is best served if there are fewer groups and thus fewer labels and things to remember, locate, and retrieve. Mayr (1969, pp. 238–241) referred to systematists leaning toward the goal of achieving homogeneity as *splitters* and to the others as *lumpers*, including himself in the latter group.

If the true nature of the protosystem were always fully reflected in the evidence available to systematists, there would be no issue. Where the protoysystem was composed of monotypic groups, monotypic taxa would be recognized; and where they were many members of a single group that also would be recognized. The more the various groupings in the protosystem are characterized by sharp discontinuities the easier the task of finding the higher taxa becomes. Where the evidence is lacking, or where the discontinuities are not so sharp, the phyletic decisions become more arbitrary and subject to the tendencies of systematists to be lumpers or splitters.

In general it is also good practice (Mayr 1969, pp. 241–242) to keep the classification relatively balanced vertically as well. Most biological systematists have specialized in particular parts of the plant or animal kingdoms and it seems likely that organizational systematists will also specialize in, for example, educational or manufacturing or other kinds of organizations. The tendency is for systematists to do more splitting within their own area of specialty and to tolerate more lumping elsewhere. For example, sociologists, who tend to specialize in the public sector, will probably look at the *Normatives* kingdom (figure 9.5) and complain that it is not nearly as differentiated as it should be, whereas they may feel relatively more comfortable with the delineation of the other kingdoms. Researchers in business schools, in contrast, will probably want more splitting in the *Producers* and *Palaces* kingdoms and perhaps more lumping in the *Normatives* kingdom. When this happens, groups in the same category level will not have the same equivalence or significance across the full width of the classification. Generally a family-level grouping of one kind of organizational form should have roughly the same equivalence as any other family grouping. In anticipation of such a problem, however, the following operational principle is suggested: *All groupings across all vertical levels of the classification should be roughly equivalent, where equivalence is defined as equal degrees of overall similarity among the groupings comprising the category under investigation.*

9.4.3 Ecological Significance

In biology, according to Mayr (1969, p. 88), "most well-defined higher taxa, particularly at the genus and family level, occupy a well-defined niche or adaptive zone." The discussion in chapter 5 suggests that this holds true for organizations as well, though there is not yet as much sound empirical evidence supporting this assertion as one might like. A founder organization moves into a new environment, or its old environment changes, thrusting the organization into a new ecological habitat. To survive, it adapts; and as its form succeeds in the new environment a population forms and multiplies as the form is copied and used by other managements operating in the same zone. An effective dominant competence is therefore most likely associated with a unique habitat.

There are two specific reasons for emphasizing the ecological significance of the higher taxa (after Mayr 1969, p. 88). First, different species of organizations occupying the same well-defined habitat may very well have evolved from the same founder species that first invaded that habitat. This would clearly qualify them as members of the same grouping. Second, since the organizational species occupy the same ecological habitat, they would presumably share many elements of their compools in common. This too would qualify them as members of the same grouping.

In light of these considerations it seems clear that an identified phenon should not be formally recognized as a taxon until its ecological habitat has been defined and the effects of environmental forces on the dominant competence explained. Table 10.2 illustrates my attempt to identify the dominant environmental feature and the competence arising to cope with that feature for the various rank categories of the *Producers* kingdom. In some instances a new phenon might be identified and then a search for the changes in the ecological habitat of the phenon undertaken. Once the ecological forces are identified which could have favored the selection of the new phenon, then the phenon may be formally recognized as a taxon. Alternatively a newly discovered organizational environment may prompt a search for an organizational phenon particularly adapted to that ecology, again eventually leading to formal recognition of a taxon. In sum, the operational principle is: *Formal recognition of a taxon must, if at all possible, be accompanied by the identification and definition of its ecological habitat.* In some instances a phenon may be so different from adjacent forms that the definition of habitat may be waived.

In biological systematics attention to environmental habitat, and more specifically attention to the particular forces causing the adaptation, has not seemed to have been a uniformly necessary requirement for formal recognition. Often the habitat is taken for granted, usually because it is so different and is clearly reflected in some of the characters—the white fur or feathers of some arctic mammals and birds, for example. In other cases the rise of a mountain chain causing a rain forest on one side and an arid plain on the other clearly creates new classes as the plants and animals adapt to the changed climate. In many instances the branching took place so long ago that there is no way of identifying the specific environmental causes.

The most probable reason for biological systematists' lack of attention to ecology (until recently) may be that the chance of a species evolving a new character over successive generations is so rare, given the incredible number of matings and births within a species, that the event was tantamount to formal recognition of a new class. In other words, the normal process of gene combination keeps such a tight rein on the limits of variation that when an event occurs outside those limits, such as a new character or the loss of one, it is usually safe to conclude that a new species has been produced. In the face of the minimal chance of its happening, the gain or loss of a character forces recognition of a new class even though the specific ecological forces may not have been identified.

With organizations, there does not seem to be such tight limits on variation within the compool. Consequently there is the probability of a much larger range of variation within an organizational species. In order to begin higher classification with some caution, it would seem a good idea to insist on having an investigator corroborate the identification of a new class of organizations by identifying specific forces leading to the adaptation. Whether this will be any easier for organizational ecologies than for biological ones remains to be seen. Although organizational evolution does not date back anywhere near as far as biological evolution, the record of changes in organizational ecologies may be equally well obscured.

The application of this operational principle will force a better understanding of the ties between specific environmental forces and internal organizational functioning. This will be good for the science even if it is not always needed to corroborate the identification of new classes.

9.4.4 Number of Species Considered

All higher organizational taxa are based on an analysis of known species. Since more species may be identified at any time, a classification is always a temporary statement, just as is any theory. A higher taxon that is presently monotypic may become polytypic if more related species are discovered. Or a monotypic taxon may be merged with another if their compools or character sets are enlarged. All taxa are subject to change as new species emerge or are discovered. Nevertheless, the closer a sample of species is to representing the known world population of organizational species, the more likely the classification will reflect the true protosystem.

Frequently it is impractical to obtain or measure all possible species at the time of a particular classification analysis. Even if there were dogmatic insistence on analyzing all known species, another one might be discovered subsequently. The key question is how to select a small sample, if doing a numerical phenetic analysis, or how to focus on a portion of all potentially important lineages, if doing a phyletic analysis. The answer seems to be to work out from the mainstream of a branch or lineage of interest. The further up the hierarchy the interest lies, the more subordinate lines will be included or alternatively the more lines will have to be arbitrarily excluded. In other words, the operational principle is: *Start with those lineages that have the sharpest discontinuities, are most clearly defined, are most easily measured, have the most clearly defined ecological habitats, or are most interesting and significant from a scientific or practical perspective.* If all of these guidelines are followed the resulting initial classification will be sound and useful even though it may be incomplete.

9.4.5 Nomenclatural Preliminaries

In chapter 2 I announced that the plan of this book would be to use the botanical labels for labeling classes of organizations (see section 2.4 for a listing of these). I further noted that of all these levels there were seven major ones: Kingdom, Division, Class, Order, Family, Genus, and Species. In botany it is the rule to assign taxa to all of these ranks; in zoology it is common practice but not a formal rule. If the lines in question have a sufficient number of branches there is no problem in finding the ancestor forms necessary to fill in the hierarchy. With organizations there may not always be the number of branching points to fill each level; hence it seems more fitting to follow the zoological practice of assigning taxa only to those categories that are needed to represent the natural hierarchy in the development of the protosystem. The operational principle is: *Assign category labels only as needed, not to arbitrarily fill all seven levels.* In the classification presented in figures 9.2 to 9.5, all seven or more categories were needed in some places. In other places all the categories were not needed, but this does not preclude their use in the future as the scheme becomes more elaborate.

Ever since Linnaeus, the binomial labeling method has been used in which all species are given two names, a genus label and a species label. These are in Latin, as are all other labels, though at the higher levels the English (in English textbooks at least) translations are frequently used. The binomial labeling method has stood the test of time and experience and so I will adopt it too. For the most part the bionomial system works very well, especially if the number of objects to be classified is not expected to be tremendously large (most of the concerns about the binomial system in biology arise because of the vast numbers of plants and animals now known). I should note that there have been various complaints lodged against the binomial label and that the numerical taxonomists have suggested a substitute system that is based on labels that more clearly indicate the relative phenotypical similarity at the category level in question. In mineralogy Dana used the binomial scheme in his first and second editions but dropped it in his third and later editions as it was not universally accepted, especially in Europe (Mason and Berry 1968, p. 198). In most instances the genus label (the first one, capitalized) differs from the species label, as in *Turda merula* (blackbird), *Cyprinus carpio* (carp), or *Crotalus horridus* (timber rattlesnake). In other instances they are the same or nearly the same: *Vulpes vulpes* (red fox), *Lynx lynx* (lynx), *Hydrochoerus hydrochoeris* (capybara). Some Latin names reflect the common name, some the name of the discoverer, and some the animal's habitat; some are descriptive, some are obscure, and some are very imaginative; and so on. The advantage of Latin is that it is a dead or neutral language. Thus at the time the convention was laid down no living language was moved in or out of scientific centrality. All biologists used the formal scientific language, and often the common or vernacular name of his or her own language was used as well. But it was the Latin label that kept things from getting confused.

It seems premature to suggest using Latin as the scientific language for labeling organizations. But no arguments are offered against doing so, either. The operational principle followed will be: *Use an italicized, hyphenated binomial name, with the genus name coming first with a capital first letter and the species name second, such as Corporate-conglomerate; if either label is used separately, its formal status may be signified by following the genus label with a hyphen, as in Corporate-, or by preceding the species label with a hyphen, as in -conglomerate.* For the time being at least this convention will work to separate formal labels from common names, which may or may not be the same as the formal name. A second principle is: *All genus-species labels will be in the singular. All higher category labels will begin with a capital letter and will be given in the plural. They will be italicized.*

Mayr (1969, p. 88) pointed out the tendency to think of members of a higher taxon as carrying a single identifying character. Thus carnivores eat meat, mammals suckle their young, birds fly, and reptiles have cold blood. Some may also be inclined to think that these characters are essences explaining much of the specialization of the class, after the essentialist theory of classification. The truth of the matter is that mammals, for example, are different from reptiles on many characters and it is too awkward to use a labeling term that includes all the relevant differentiating characters. The label most likely will reflect a dominant differentiating character, and this serves as a useful mnemonic for information retrieval purposes; but even the dominant character may not always apply to all members of the class. For example, some birds do not fly. The same can be expected to hold for organizations. The labels will probably reflect a dominant character, but that should not be taken to mean that an essentialist logic is being used. Thus even though a particular competence feature is highlighted in table 10.2 and in some cases one aspect of the competence represented in the label (many instances in figures 9.2 to 9.5), under no circumstances should the reader conclude that an essentialist theory of classification is implied. Empirical investigation will undoubtedly show that the dominant character is accompanied by many other differentiating characters. The operational principle is: *Label a higher class after a dominant character differentiating that class from others at the same category rank.*

The several operational principles of phyletic classification are collected together in table 9.1.

TABLE 9.1

OPERATIONAL PRINCIPLES OF PHYLETIC CLASSIFICATION

1. Organizations having the greatest overall similarity between their compools should be grouped together.

2. Avoid the extreme of either too small or too large an aggregation of groupings at the higher levels, unless the evidence clearly indicates that one of the extremes is closest to reflecting the true nature of the protosystem.

3. All groupings across all vertical levels of the classification should be roughly equivalent, where equivalence is defined as equal degrees of overall similarity among groupings comprising the category level under investigation.

4. Formal recognition of a taxon must, if at all possible, be accompanied by the identification and definition of its ecological habitat.

5. Start with those lineages that have the sharpest discontinuities, are most clearly defined, are most easily measured, have the most clearly defined ecological habitat, or are most interesting and significant from a scientific or practical perspective.

6. Assign category labels only as needed, not to arbitrarily fill in all seven levels.

7. Use an italicized, hyphenated binomial name, with the genus name coming first and capitalized and the species name second, such as *Corporate-conglomerate*; if either label is used separately, its formal status may be signified by following the genus label with a hyphen, as in *Corporate-*, or by preceding the species label with a hyphen, as in *-conglomerate*.

8. All genus-species labels should be in the singular and all higher-category labels should be capitalized, given in the plural, and italicized, as in *Producers*.

9. Label a higher class after a dominant character differentiating that class from others at the same category rank.

9.4.6 Miscellaneous Additional Operational Principles

In addition to the operational principles identified previously there are several others that, if followed, will make the resulting classification better from a variety of views. To some extent these are further practical interpretations of the foregoing principles, but for the most part they draw on themes developed elsewhere in the book. Most of them do not need much additional explanation but it is useful to have them assembled in one place.

1. Where ambiguity in the true nature of the protosystem prevails, develop categories that define populations useful in the empirical investigations of functional organizational science. If the classes can incorporate or not depart too much from popular or more or less accepted populations used in past functional studies, so much the better.

2. Where ambiguity leaves room for more arbitrary choices by the systematist, work toward categories that would make sense to people

concerned about the organizations in question and offer a way of organizing knowledge about organizational problems.

3. Focus on characters central to dominant competence.

4. Arrange the higher categories so that the family tree of organizational forms reflects the path of their evolutionary development from past to present.

5. Recognize that some classes of organizations have evolved faster than others, and hence more levels will be needed in these lines to account for the increased levels of specialization and diversity.

6. Arrange the dendrogram (family tree) so that, as much as possible, similar organizational forms are adjacent to each other, with different forms separated horizontally according to the amount of difference.

7. Leave room in the use of categories for further elaboration in the future.

9.5 SUMMARY

The intent of this chapter was to discuss a theory of the origins of branches in the evolution of organizations. Three kinds of evolution by branching, termed *cladogenesis*, were identified: *hybridization, saltation,* and *gradualism.* I also noted that evolution without branching may take place, labeled *anagenesis.* There is some evidence in support of cladogenesis and anagenesis, though it is rudimentary. Following this, some basic assumptions of higher classification were discussed. These were drawn from biological phyletics and I concluded that most of them would be necessary starting assumptions for organizational phyletics as well. Some misconceptions, also drawn from past experience in biological systematics, were then noted. Finally I discussed several operational principles; following these will expedite the development of organizational classifications at the higher category levels. They offer a practical point of departure and were followed as closely as possible in working up the dendrograms in figures 9.2 to 9.5.

10 THE EVOLUTION OF ORGANIZATIONAL FORM IN ANCIENT MESOPOTAMIA

Of what relevance is it to know what happened 3,000 years ago, let alone 300,000 years ago? . . . We must never, as Arnold Toynbee has reminded us, allow transient economic and political power to obscure the fact that Western Civilization is only one of the many civilizations that have existed, only one of the handful that now exist. Archaeology surely helps us take a genuinely world view of man and his past history. It helps us see the literate, history-recording civilizations as branches from a common trunk that is rooted in prehistoric antiquity.

[Lamberg-Karlovsky 1972]

The more parochial of us are inclined to think that management technology is a modern phenomenon. We forget that its roots go back to the first organizations of antiquity, even though they were severely attenuated during the Middle Ages. We stand in awe at the base of the Great Pyramid of Cheops outside Cairo and marvel at the engineering and management skills associated with its creation. The building of elaborate burial monuments in Egypt began around 3000 B.C., the same time that the Sumerians in ancient Mesopotamia invented writing in cuneiform script. Management historians (George 1972; Wren 1972) point to these monuments as evidence that complex organizations and management skills existed in ancient times.* We do not understand how they could have accomplished such feats. In fact, simple organizations evolved several thousand years earlier and complex organizations evolved over one thousand years earlier. So, by the time the Great Pyramid was built, around 2575 B.C., Cheops and his staff had the benefit of many centuries of prior experience in managing complex organizations.

In this chapter I try to unravel the first family tree of organizational lineage—in other words, model the course of early organizational evolution. My purpose is to illustrate the basic idea of a lineage of organizational forms as well as to demonstrate some of the mechanics of creating such a tree. I have also tried to follow as much as possible the guidelines for developing the higher categories shown in chapter 9.

10.1 MODELING AND HISTORICAL ANALYSIS

10.1.1 Evolutionary Theory and a Model: The Family Tree

The difference between a theory and a model is not always understood. For example, Dubin observed, "There has come increasingly into current usage the term *model* as a synonym of *theory*" (1978, pp. 17–18; his emphasis). He continued by saying that he, too, would use the terms *theory* and *model* interchangeably. I think there is a very important difference.† A model depicts more or less accurately some structure or behavior that is of interest; it is a representation, a facsimile. For example, one may build a model of an airplane. The model usually has wings. The model offers no explanation of why the wings are there—it just represents them more or less accurately. The theory of flight or one of several theories of correct airplane design explains the role of the wings. A model may be used to depict structural relationships or help generate behavior that in turn leads to better theoretical explanation, but the model by itself does not explain.

A family tree, or dendrogram, is a model. It is a more or less accurate representation of the path of evolution. It typically starts with a main trunk and has branches. It simply represents; it does not explain. The explanation of what is modeled by a dendrogram is held in evolutionary theory. I have come to understand this theory as consisting essentially of

---

*The dates used by George (1972, pp. 3–5) in the text of his book are accurate; the corresponding dates in the continuum on page vii should both be 3000 B.C., not 5000 and 4000 B.C.

†Kaplan (1964) offered a useful discussion of theories and models.

six postulates and twenty-four principles, as developed in chapter 8. I also developed it in a more taxonomically useful form as elements of a species concept elaborated in chapters 6 and 7. The most observable components of a family tree of organizational evolution are lineages, branchings, and divergence.

Evolutionary theory is a general framework of explanation and, where the conditions admit, it prescribes a set of forces necessary and sufficient to generate behavior modeled in general by a family tree. Thus the tree depiction is seen to represent evolutionary sequences among all kinds of organisms and at different times. The theory is general in that the tree model is an accurate representation across a wide variety of organisms and across many different time frames. It is my thesis that the generality includes organizational evolutionary sequences. In this sense the theory is *nomothetic* in that it holds "for indefinitely repeatable events and processes" (Nagel 1961, p. 547). Although the tree model is very general at a sufficiently abstract level, it is not at all general in particular. There is no law developed by biological evolutionists and no law developed here for organizations which explains or predicts the particular form of descent illustrated by a tree model. The only law involved here is that of descent with modification from common ancestors. Where this law applies it predicts that a family tree model will represent what unfolds. It does not predict what organism or organization will branch from what, nor which lines will survive. It simply says that there will be branchings and some lines will survive and some will not. In this sense the theory is *idiographic* in that it explains "the unique and the nonrecurrent" (Nagel 1961, p. 547).

10.1.2 Induction, Falsifiability, and History

My review of ancient Mesopotamian history affords two possibilities regarding a theory of organizational evolution. First, it offers a weak preliminary test of the theory in its nomothetic form. If the historical review shows that the family tree model of lineages, branches, and divergings describes what has happened during the course of organizational evolution, the generality of evolutionary theory is enhanced and its applicability to organizations weakly corroborated. The test is weak because with all my biases I might squeeze events to fit the model when other observers might not see any fit with the model. Also, there could be other explanations of why the events fit a family tree model, not just evolutionary theory. But at least the worst will not have happened— which is that even I, with all my biases, could not find events fitting the model.

Second, this historical analysis will offer a first inductive development of the idiographic form of the theory. I will try to lay out as best I can the unique and nonrecurrent pattern of descent with modification from common ancestors of the several major organizational forms in ancient Mesopotamia. This inquiry will set up hypothetical classes of organizations. When these classes are extended into modern times they serve as a point of departure for numerical taxonomic studies. If the hypothetical classes are corroborated by the deductive numerical findings of like homogeneous groupings, a stronger test of organizational evolutionary theory will be at hand.

The historical record therefore offers two bases of falsifiability. On the one hand the generalization of evolutionary theory to an organizational context is falsifiable and will be so if events fitting the model are not found. Lineages, branchings, and divergences are relatively firm, hard, observable facts, Although uncovering an old record might be difficult and fraught with false conclusions along the way, nevertheless the facts are there; they are not subject to change and eventually the truth of the matter may be unraveled. On the other hand, the actual creation of the many organizational forms is also a matter of historical record, much of it quite recent. This record unquestionably allows the tracing of new compool formations and the arrangement of organizations into hierarchically related classes of differing phenetic similarity. Classes formed through historical analysis which are supposed to be homogeneous should be corroborated via numerical phenetic analysis of modern species. If they are not, there is reason to believe that organizational evolutionary theory has been falsified.

10.1.3 Historical Analysis

To date no general histories of organizational form have been written,* so immediately the problem is that the documentary record of organizations is still scattered. Of course there are many histories of different kinds of organizations—hospitals, schools, prisons, labor unions, bureaucracies, factories during the Industrial Revolution, medieval guilds, businesses, and the like. There are some histories of management thought (George 1972; Wren 1972) that give a solid introduction to many aspects of the development of organizational forms. But these histories generally do not make specific connections between a new management idea or dominant competence element and other attributes of the domi-

---

*I should note, however, that a recent manuscript by Aldrich and Mueller (1980) about the evolution of mercantile and industrial organizational forms in the U.S. during the past 150 years is an excellent beginning toward correcting this problem.

nant competence present at the time. No do they relate a new technology to specific surrounding ecological forces, though in some instances they do mention roughly why the new idea was needed at the time. Generally the record of how key environmental attributes have related to the development of the dominant competence of organizational forms over the years is vague. Quite possibly it will always remain so, but I assume that the documentary record is available in more detail than present knowledge would indicate. Usually, going through old information from a new perspective turns up new insights, and there is little reason to believe such will not be the case here.

With careful reading one can pick up clues about organizational form, even from secondary sources as presently written. For example, Wren (1972, p. 43) gives the impression that around A.D. 1800 English industrial organizations could not rely on dogma and rigid disciplines as the church and military organizations could, and industrial managers thus had to find new methods for handling labor problems. Increasing competition had led to larger factories to gain economies of scale, which in turn led to increased problems in training and inducing the employees to work harder. Wren noted that one response was to deskill jobs (increased specialization). While this is an example about new organizational technologies that do exist, it also illustrates a related problem, namely that there is no record given of whether, in this case, specialization was a new technological element introduced at this time or whether it was taken over from church or military organizations that had introduced it earlier. Presumably there are records of how specialized church and military organizations were at the time, but the reader can begin to see how laborious the task of finding the likely sources is going to be.

The archaeologist Braidwood (1972) suggested there have been two principal *economic* revolutions in human history since the earliest times when men and women first began using tools, circa 500,000 B.C. The first revolution came many thousands of years later, around 6000 B.C., when there was a shift from hunting and gathering food to producing it by planting and cultivating. The second revolution occurred with the invention of the steam engine, around A.D. 1770,* and ultimately brought about factories, mass production, and consumer-oriented economies. It is not surprising to discover in retrospect that the two

---

*Strictly speaking, the first economically useful steam engine was invented in 1705 by the Englishman Thomas Newcomen, though enough critical improvements were made around 1770 by James Watt and a Frenchman, Nicholas Cugnot, that this date is typically used.

florescent ages of organizational evolution were spawned by these two revolutions. The discussion in this chapter centers on organizational developments in the first of these ages. I had planned to pursue developments just before and subsequent to the steam engine, but the scope of this task and time and space limitations prohibited this. This does not imply that I think the intervening period, which included the Greek, Roman, and Byzantine periods as well as the Middle Ages, is unimportant or uninteresting in general. But from a strict taxonomic view toward classifying modern organizations, it is less important. Of all of the elaborations in form which emerged before the end of the Middle Ages, only the most ancient ones stemming from prior to the 2500 B.C. date seem to have survived the ravages of the barbarians during the Middle Ages. Consequently most of the elaborations in the intervening period probably had little impact on the evolution of modern organizational forms as we know and can study them today. Given space and time limitations it makes sense to focus first on evolutionary happenings that might more directly help present-day investigators form groupings for empirical research.

Another consequence of attending only to past elaborations that seem to have impact on modern forms is that developments in ancient Egypt, the ancient Harappan civilizations of the Indus River valley, the ancient Far East and China, and the Inca and Mayan civilizations of the New World are also ignored. Archaeologists and historians (Hallo and Simpson 1971; Lamberg-Karlovsky 1972, various selections; Oppenheim 1977) are of a mind that developments in ancient Egypt came after and were influenced by those in Mesopotamia. Since the Harappan civilization was totally wiped out it seems to have had little discernible impact on organizational form and besides it, too, appears to have developed later and to have been influenced by events in Mesopotamia. Though there is reason to believe that the rice cultures of the Far East, specifically Ban Chiang in Thailand, arose much earlier than the culture of Mesopotamia, they seem to have had little impact on the development of present-day organizational forms. They apparently did influence events in China, but again Chinese developments seem to have had little impact on modern forms. More substantial historical findings may ultimately prove this view to be in error, especially as to developments in ancient Thailand and China. Organizational developments in the New World transpired very much like those of ancient Mesopotamia even though there was no apparent communication. (See Steward 1955 for comparisons of Mesopotamia and New World developments.) But since the New World civilizations later died out it is doubtful they had any impact except possibly via the Spaniard conquerors, and there is little reason to

believe this. The dominant Inca and Mayan forms at the time the Span-
iards arrived were dynastic empires run by palace organizations based
on religious or military legitimacy. These forms were hardly new to the
people of the Old World at that time.

10.1.4 Limitations

The application of evolutionary theory presented in this chapter is
unusual enough in perspective and method as to need some special
words of qualification to avoid misunderstandings and falsely raised
hopes. The classification scheme presented in this part is illustrative and
suggestive. Though there is reason to believe that the archaeological/
historical record about ancient times is available, it is a record that is vast
and scattered about in archaeological, anthropological, and historical
data of various time periods. Tracing the full development of specific
forms at particular times would be a laborious and time-consuming
effort, one beyond the scope of this chapter. Yet it did not make sense to
dodge the question of the origins of organizational forms totally, and an
illustration of how such research might unfold is desirable. Consequently a limited treatment is attempted.

Such a treatment is necessarily time-bound and subject to numerous
alterations, if not total replacement, as knowledge accumulates. Organizational science now seems to be roughly where biology was around the
beginning of the eighteenth century. Few paradigms, as Kuhn (1970)
used the term, exist and those that do are not widely accepted; certainly
no classificatory paradigms are accepted. Linnaeus brought some order
to the field of biological systematics with his book of 1758, but it wasn't
until Darwin's book of 1859 that there began to be widespread acceptance of a particular theory of biological classification. Possibly biology
is a much more difficult field for systematists to work in than is organizational science, but on the other hand there have been many more biologists over the years, too. And the time span between Linnaeus and
Darwin was 100 years! Now, over 100 years later, biologists are still
debating, with the evolutionist theory of classification facing a significant challenge from the numerical taxonomists and cladists. The labels I
have used are temporary or "throwaway" terms that have to be used here
because no others exist. Where possible labels having as much mnemonic value as possible are used. Note that some concepts suggested in
previous typologies are embedded in the scheme to be presented and the
mnemonics reflect this heritage. If and when nomenclatural rules
governing the formal recognition of taxa and the adoption of labels are
agreed upon, investigators whose empirical work suggests certain

groupings presumably will have the privilege of naming them. These qualifying statements apply even more to the tentative schemes presented in figures 9.2 to 9.5.

10.2 ENVIRONMENTAL EVENTS IN ANCIENT MESOPOTAMIA

My search through ancient records starts with an inquiry about the nature of ancient environments. Only with this foundation can an understanding of ancient organizational ecology be gained. An overview of ancient environmental events and associated time periods is presented in table 10.1. The evidence upon which this view is based is drawn from two sources. Historians limit history to the study of things written or otherwise explicitly recorded by past men and women. Consequently, history only goes back in time to the point where symbols of some kind were first placed on objects for the express purpose of conveying meaning. This is generally thought to have happened around 3000 B.C. with the invention of the early precursors to the cuneiform script of ancient Sumer. Before 3000 B.C., the evidence comes from inferences drawn from archaeological diggings at various ancient settlements. These inferences are based largely on kinds and quantities of tools found, symbols on potsherds that may indicate their uses, other materials such as food remains (bones), clothing, and so forth that tell something of the lifestyles of the ancient inhabitants; and finally the architecture of the buildings and towns, which gives indications of social hierarchy, wealth, values, and necessities, among other things.

For the most part the dates, periods, and labels shown in table 10.1 are after Hallo and Simpson's (1971) text on ancient Mesopotamia. Not surprisingly the dates and periods given by paleontologists, anthropologists, archaeologists, and historians, who all study ancient environments, do not totally agree. The dating problem is exacerbated by recent discoveries that the carbon dating methods of the 1950s and 1960s are incorrect (Renfrew 1973). Fortunately this latter problem is ameliorated somewhat by a table prepared by Suess (in Renfrew 1972, pp. 204-205). Unless expressly noted, I use uncorrected dates. Nevertheless, Hallo and Simpson's dates seem to agree with those suggested by others such as Oppenheim (1977) and the various authors whose works are collected in the anthologies by Steward (1955) and Lamberg-Karlovsky (1972). For several of the early periods, the archaeological site that provided the first and often the most thorough information about the period is also included in the table.

TABLE 10.1

ENVIRONMENTAL EVENTS IN ANCIENT MESOPOTAMIA

−10,000 B.C.	*Upper Paleolithic Age.* End of Neanderthal Man; rise of *Homo sapiens*.
10,000−7000 B.C.	*Mesolithic Period.* Mobile bands of hunters, fishermen, food gatherers; cave dwelling; miniaturization of stone tools; early settlements such as at Mallaha in northern Israel.
7000−5500 B.C.	*Neolithic Revolution.* Domestication of plants and animals; emergence of farming villages; reliance on stone pottery to the exclusion of clay; later a shift from temporary to permanent shelter; settlements in rain-watered forested mountains (Jarmo, Karim Shahir) or near springs (Jericho).
6000−3500 B.C.	*Chalcolithic Period.* Development of clay pottery; development of specializations such as plowman, baker, herdsman, leatherworker, lapidary, smith, brewer, etc.; spinning of flax; trade in luxuries such as precious stones and copper; development of cylinder seals (meaning obligations and contracts); food surpluses (Hassuna, Halaf, early Ubaid).
3800−3000 B.C.	*Protoliterate Period.* Migration into Mesopotamia of Subarians from central Turkey; movement out of mountain villages onto alluvial plains; increased dependence on irrigation; market towns, temple building; incipient urbanization via development of social and political aspects of culture and village governing assemblies (developed Ubaid, Warka).
3100−2900 B.C.	*Urban Revolution.* Mastery of irrigation under difficult circumstances; invention of bronze followed by development of a tool and weapon industry; increased monument building and fortification; increased population density and economic growth; accumulation of capital; invention of writing (Jamdet Nasr).
2900 B.C.	*The Flood.* A somewhat localized Mesopotamian occurrence as indicated by excavations at Shuruppak and Kish.
2900−2300 B.C.	*Early Dynastic Period.* Grouping of Sumerian city-states in loose hegemony under the "King of Kish"; ad hoc kingship, legitimized by priests at Nippur, which was rotated among the eleven city-states involved (the first of which was at Kish); increased accumulation of capital, increased specialization; increased wealth and productivity went into building and furnishing vast temples that were also the residences of the earliest kings; in the last third of the period the kingship was institutionalized, with a system of royal succession adopted; kings claimed rule by divine right; a firm alliance between royal and religious interests; gradual redistribution of wealth, increased social stratification and class struggle; land ownership shifted into hands of royalty, priests, and nobles—commoners became serfs of palaces, temples, and large estates, where they subsisted on rations of food and clothing; some became slaves; banking and trade shifted from temple to royal monopoly.
2300−2100 B.C.	*Akkadian Empire.* Sargon of Akkad established first true empire; brought internal stability, numerous social, religious, and artistic innovations and new political organization; empire building went far beyond the borders of Sumer and Akkad.
2100−1800 B.C.	*Ur III-Isin Dynasties.* With the fading of the Akkadian empire and increased inter-city-state warfare in the south (Sumer), Assur (far to

TABLE 10.1 (Continued)

ENVIRONMENTAL EVENTS IN ANCIENT MESOPOTAMIA

2100—1800 B.C. (Continued)	the north) gained independence; a highly organized Assyrian trade developed with Kanish (in Cappadocia in the southeastern part of Anatolia, Turkey), dominated by a number of commercial families who followed the discipline of the Assyrian *Karum* (a sort of board of trade) and the *Wabartum* (a trade association); mainly traded cloth and tin for gold, silver, and other metals; overland travel on donkey back.
1800—1600 B.C.	*Age of Hammurapi.* Reunification of Mesopotamia almost to the old Sargonic borders; development of the famous "code of laws."

The following overview of ancient prehistory and history is probably one of the shortest ever attempted. Needless to say, the reader may want to exercise some caution in accepting such a boiled-down view of several thousands of years. Yet such a view is a necessary precondition to understanding how organizations came to evolve as they did. A more detailed treatment would expose more nuances but might not necessarily present a more accurate global view.

Upper Paleolithic Age

The climax of the fourth glaciation, around 11,000 B.C., has been defined as the turning point between the Middle Paleolithic Age and the Upper Paleolithic Age (*paleolithic* literally means "old stone"). During the former period Neanderthal Man (*Homo sapiens neanderthalensis*), now thought to be one of several of the hominid species *Homo sapiens* (Dobzhansky et al. 1977), appears to have been the dominant species in Europe. During the thousand or so years after the end of the fourth glacial period another subspecies, *Homo sapiens sapiens*, competing with Neanderthal Man for the same territory, seems to have survived while Neanderthal Man became extinct. Most of the evidence about the human spirit during the Upper Paleolithic Age comes from the remarkable cave paintings in France south of the Loire River and to a lesser extent in Spain (Leroi-Gourhan 1972). Though this is speculative, it is possible that the religious and magical impulses shown in the paintings are the roots of shamanistic elements in the later Sumerian religion (Hallo and Simpson 1971, p. 9).

Mesolithic Period

During the Mesolithic Period, roughly from 10,000 to 7000 B.C., there was a notable population increase among *Homo sapiens sapiens*. Cave dwelling still persisted but there was a change to more mobile bands of hunters, quite possibly due to overhunting near the most popular dwelling caves. The economic activity of the period consisted of hunting by men and gathering of wild plants by women. Two other remarkable events took place besides the increasing mobility. Stone tools were miniaturized. Being more portable, perhaps these smaller tools (termed *microliths*) aided mobility. The other event was that the first manmade housings and settlements appeared, such as the ones in Mallaha in northern Israel, dated around 9000 B.C. (Cambel and Braidwood 1972). For a long time it had been thought that settlements came only with food production. But evidence from Mallaha shows that while it definitely was a settlement there was no evidence of food production. Other settlements of hunting peoples have also been found (Perkins and Daly 1972).

Neolithic Revolution

The Mesolithic Period is considered an intervening time useful for placing times and events that did not clearly fall into either Upper Paleolithic or Neolithic times. The Neolithic label has been applied to a site whenever there was evidence that it had a localized culture; usually it has not been applied indiscriminately to broad geographical areas. Hallo and Simpson referred to the period from 7000 to 5500 B.C. as the Neolithic Revolution. This was the time when plants and animals were first domesticated—specifically wheat, barley, sheep, goats, pigs, and the ancestor of the modern cow. The dog, though not an economically important animal, had been domesticated some time earlier. Another key event of this time was the emergence of farming villages. These settlements, such as Jarmo and Karim Shajir, were located principally in hilly regions of the Near East where there was considerable rainfall, an area known as the Fertile Crescent, and in places where there were unfailing springs the year around, such as Jericho. During this time there was no evidence of defensive or offensive weapons, suggesting that there was little difficulty with aggressive neighbors or mobile bands of nomads. Reliance was still on stone pottery, flint for sharp tools, and obsidian (imported from the Anatolian Plateau of Turkey [Dixon, Cann, and Renfrew 1972]), which was in rare supply but especially valuable for sharpness and beauty. Two basic trends seem to have started during this time—increased population density and freedom from total preoccupation with subsistence. Adams (1972) commented that priests were probably the first specialists to be freed somewhat from food production to spend time on some other activity.

Chalcolithic Period

Hallo and Simpson gave the label *Chalcolithic Period* to the next time frame, from 6000 to 3500 B.C. This was principally due to the development of clay pottery during this time. Clay pottery meant a much easier and less time-consuming process of making pots. It meant that many more of them could be made, and in a much greater variety of shapes. Perhaps most important from an economic perspective, clay pots became available not just for day-to-day living but as storage vessels. Now, for the first time, people could take advantage of food surpluses by storing them for the winter or for the times of low rainfall and poor growing seasons. For the first time, some freedom from total dependence on the vagaries of changing weather patterns and uncertain food availability was possible. Clay pots were indeed a key step along the way to civilization*.

Prehistorians believe that increasing food surpluses brought about more freedom for some people to begin specializations in various crafts. Words from the Chalcolithic Period incorporated later into the Sumerian language suggest this. Specializations so indicated are: plowman, baker, herdsman, leatherworker, lapidary, smith, and brewer. The earliest, probably woolen, textiles were found at the 6500 B.C. level in Catal Huyuk on the Anatolian Plateau (Mellaart 1972). People also spun flax and traded for luxuries such as precious and semiprecious stones and copper. Obsidian trade, which can be clearly traced, extended all over the Near East by this period (Dixon, Cann, and Renfrew 1972). There was the development of cylinder seals that were rolled onto soft clay to make an imprint unique to the owner of the cylinder. The cylinder seals suggest that obligations and contracts existed, requiring a person's "signature," just as contracts require one now.

The increase in population, food surpluses, and often valuable craft artifacts meant that settlements now contained many valuable items that were tempting to surrounding nomads or other settled people less well off. Settlements even in the early Chalcolithic Period, such as Jericho and Catal Huyuk, had defensive walls. Weapons such as daggers and spears have been found, though it is not clear whether these were only for killing animals or for fighting other people as well.

Protoliterate Period

The Protoliterate Period extended roughly from 3800 to 3000 B.C. The key feature of this time was incipient urbanization. People began to move down from the mountains on the north and east of the two great rivers of Mesopotamia, the Tigris and the Euphrates. Slowly settlements

---

*An insight into the importance of clay pottery is given by one of the most amazing artifacts of the latter part of this period. It is an eight-inch pot made out of obsidian, with a spout even (pictured in Dixon, Cann, and Renfrew 1972). I have a piece of obsidian on my desk—it is a black, glassy, brittle, very hard rock. Think how important a pot must have been some 6,000 years ago for someone to make that pot by a slow process of chipping and polishing: an immensely difficult, time-consuming task.

extended to the piedmont and out onto the alluvial plains. Whereas early farming had depended on rainfall, as the settlements moved down the valleys they began to take advantage of the downward sloping valleys to move flowing water directly onto the fields further away from the streams. As they moved out onto the hot plains where no rain fell, the settlements began to depend entirely on irrigation to water the fields. The fertility of the plains brought about increasing food surpluses, increasing population densities, and increased time to devote to arts and crafts. Small agricultural settlements turned into market-oriented towns where considerable trading took place of agriculturally derived goods such as food and textiles and for things unavailable on the plains, such as wood, stone, and metals. There was increased attention to architecture, especially the building of temples; the structure of the latter began to take on a relatively fixed form that was to extend into the future for many centuries. Incipient urbanization was marked by the development of social structures and political entities such as the early village assemblies that elected ad hoc warlords when needed and dealt with other governmental matters. The increase in the number of pots covered with ceremonial decorations suggests that temples at this time were able to command the efforts of the artisans—either through the strength of their devotion, by being wealthy enough to pay for the objects, or by managing their own workshops and craftsmen.

The early part of this period was marked by the migration of the Sabarians into Mesopotamia from the Anatolian Plateau. Presumably they brought with them many of the advanced cultural developments found around Catal Huyuk, which around 6000 B.C. seems to have been a large, wealthy community of 50,000 people with more advanced crafts, as indicated by the kind of pottery and textiles found. Wheat and barley grains found in the town suggest a more advanced and much older level of farming (Mellaart 1972). Presumably the Sabarians mixed with the fisher folk of the lowlands and the peoples living in the mountain valleys. Toward the end of the Protoliterate Period the migration of the Sumerians from the south, up the Persian Gulf, and into the southern part of Mesopotamia took place. Indications from their own language suggest they subjected the Sabarians, who were the dominant people of Mesopotamia by that time, to a lower social position. The word *Sabarian* became a synonym for *slave* in the Sumerian language (Hallo and Simpson 1971, p. 24).

Urban Revolution

Hallo and Simpson called the period of 3100 to 2900 B.C. the *Urban Revolution*. Urbanization and the beginning of civilizations are synonymous. Even the word *civilization* reflects the root Greek word *civitas*, indicating the life and times of the city dweller. Lamberg-Karlovsky (1972, p. 133) cited Adams as listing three social institutions that, when functionally interdependent, comprise civilization:

1. Class stratification, each stratum marked by a highly different degree of ownership or control of the main productive resources.

2. Political and religious hierarchies complementing each other in the administration of territorially organized states.

3. Complex division of labor, with full-time craftsmen, servants, soldiers, and officials existing alongside the great mass of primary peasant producers (Lamberg-Karlovsky 1972, pp. 133–134).

A key question is what conditions gave rise to urbanization at this particular point in time. Depending on the author, several ingredients are highlighted. Adams (1972) suggested three things:

1. Productivity, specifically food surpluses, due to irrigation. Food surpluses gave people freedom from the uncertainities of weather and allowed them to stay in one place even though the rains did not come that year. Surpluses also gave them freedom to become specialists in something other than food production, which in turn gave rise to craft goods and the need of one specialist to trade his product for something else. This created a need for a marketplace, which happened most easily in a larger settlement.

2. The practice of irrigation itself. For a long while it was thought that the need to organize extensive irrigation was probably the root cause of urbanization (Steward 1955). In Mesopotamia, irrigation was not easy and required continual attention and considerable effort. The water table was high, especially in southern Mesopotamia, creating a constant problem of poor drainage and resultant soil salinity. Therefore dikes and channels promoting drainage had to be created and maintained. Furthermore, unlike Egypt where the river flood came well before the growing season, deposited its rich mud, and subsided so the crops could be planted, the Mesopotamian rivers reached the crest of their flood during the growing season, which began in the fall. This meant that green fields had to be protected from the floodwaters by dikes. As if that were not enough, the Mesopotamian rivers flowed much faster and carried more silt than the Nile. This meant irrigation channels clogged up faster and had to be maintained much more often than they did in Egypt. (See Oppenheim 1977, pp. 40–41 for further discussion of these points.) Though it is recognized that irrigation created a need for rather sophisticated organization of many people, Adams states that irrigation

does not appear to have led to urban growth. Urbanization was already present before the extensive irrigation systems came into being, suggesting that urban growth led to a need for better irrigation. But even though irrigation may not have been the direct cause of urbanization, Adams noted that it prompted the gathering together of people into larger settlements because the food surpluses and craft products increased the need to collectively defend against warring neighbors seeking wealth through thievery. Also, by creating differences in land productivity (land with good drainage and near water sources prospered more than other land), irrigation produced different levels of prosperity for the owners and ultimately the stratified society that is one of the elements of civilization.

3. Finally Adams noted that the increased complexity of economic life on the plains may have produced social institutions to mediate conflicts of interest such as those between herdsman and cultivator, sailor and fisherman, plowman and plowmaker, and so forth, and to settle disputes about land rights and water rights, and rights to stored surpluses. And, whether through a market system or rationing administered by the temple or palace, the city provided a convenient place for the storage, exchange, and redistribution of surpluses.

Hallo and Simpson (1971, pp. 29–34) emphasized the invention of bronze rather than the role of irrigation. The Sumerians seem to have been the first ones to alloy copper with other metals, especially tin. Perhaps this was because, in southern Mesopotamia, they were situated right where the tin trade from the northern mountains met with the copper trade from the Persian Gulf. Bronze was not only malleable like copper but it could also be cast from molds. Bronze was much more workable than either tin or copper by themselves. With bronze, a tool and weapon industry quickly developed, producing items vastly superior to those already in use. Hallo and Simpson noted that bronze was not a sufficient cause of urbanization by itself. But bronze greatly facilitated two other developments that were more central to urban growth: monument building and fortification. Bronze tools made the former easier. Bronze weapons made the latter more necessary. The monuments, mainly temples, were attractions in times of peace; the walls in times of war. Hallo and Simpson's thesis was that bronze eased the difficulties of life and thus led to population growth. This in turn led to increased need for efficient farming and irrigation. Farms or manors were managed efficiently by absentee landlords living in the cities. They argued that the resulting accumulation of capital was a key ingredient to urbanization. The final element was the invention of writing, which seems to have been a direct outgrowth of the need to keep track of economic goods. The earliest writing discovered was given over exclusively to record keeping—who was tending whose herd, and so on.

Oppenheim took a somewhat different view from either Adams or Hallo and Simpson. He ventured the following hypothesis:

> The community of citizens was originally made up of owners of landed property, fields, gardens, and manorial estates situated along natural canals and depressions, that could be easily improved by simple irrigation methods and on which a labor force of family members, serfs, and slaves produced food and the few essential goods necessary to supply the lord of the manor, whose status may have been that of a conqueror, his family, and retainers. With growing prosperity, and also for prestige purposes, the landed owners began to maintain "town houses" at nearby sanctuaries and eventually moved their main residence into the agglomeration of dwellings that grew up around the temple complex. [1977, p. 113]

Oppenheim saw the Sumerian city dwellers as equal-status people: engaging in little trade among themselves since each was self-sufficient, having high solidarity and valuing the idea of living in a stable community as opposed to the tendency to value nomadic life seen in the Bible; centering their activities around the management of their rural holdings; and keeping intercity trade separate from activities within the city by housing it in a "harbor" outside the city walls. He based this hypothesis on later better-documented discoveries of the origins of Greek cities of the fourth and fifth centuries B.C. and the Italian city-states of the early Renaissance.

Taken together, the views of Adams, Hallo and Simpson, and Oppenheim suggest that a set of interacting causal processes—principally increased food surpluses, specialization, trade, inventions of bronze and writing, capital formation and wealth, plundering, monument building and fortification, irrigation, and last but not least a positive attitude toward communal solidarity—worked together to eventually produce cities in southern Mesopotamia.

The Flood

The Flood story has occurred often enough in early myths that archaeologists have sought archaeological confirmation of it. Hallo and Simpson (1971, pp. 35–36) noted that evidence has been found of a considerable flood around 2900 B.C. in the cities of Shuruppak and Kish, both in southern Mesopotamia. (See figure 10.1 for the location of ancient Sumerian cities.) But the evidence does not yet indicate that it was a particularly widespread deluge. The Flood takes on importance because the Sumerians themselves attribute the origins of their own civilization to eight to ten semidivine antediluvian sages, who quite possibly came from the island of Dilmun in the Persian Gulf (see Hallo and Simpson 1971, p. 29; Glob and Bibby 1972). These sages are paralleled in the biblical account of the sages from Adam to Noah. The Flood does not appear to have had a significant impact on the development of civilization, despite the implications of the biblical account. It does serve to mark the shift from the dominance of the temple as the first of what Oppenheim (1977) referred to as the "great organizations" to the dominance of the palace as the second great organization. The semidivine status of the antediluvian sages and the dominance of the temple before the Flood as the leading socioeconomic and political organization should not go unnoticed.

Early Dynastic Period

After the Flood the character of the environment began to take on a rather different nature. These times have been referred to as the Early Dynastic Period, from 2900 to 2300 B.C. Generally the change was from passive manorial-based city-states having at most defensive fortifications to outright empire building and offensive war making. The eleven city-states of Sumer came together in a loose hegemony under the "King of Kish." The kingship was of an ad hoc nature that passed from city-state to city-state on a turn-by-turn basis. Sometimes the hegemony was more in name than in fact. During these times, however, there was increased wealth and capital formation and increased specialization. The increased wealth went into building vast and splendid temples. These were also the residences of the earliest kings. Note that during the Protolithic Period political leaders, specifically warlords, were picked on an ad hoc basis by village assemblies. During the hegemony of Kish the political leaders were more permanent but still were rotated from city to city, with no one person or family becoming permanent kings.

During the Early Dynastic Period the king gained legitimacy only from the priests. Once the kingship was institutionalized with royal succession in the last third of the period, the stage was set for the rise to power of the palace organizations. During these times kings claimed to rule by divine right; there was a strong alliance between royal court and temple. There was a gradual redistribution of land and wealth into the hands of the palace. This brought about increased social stratification and class struggle. Commoners became serfs of the palace, temples, and large estates on which they lived. This process came about mainly because the commoners traditionally assigned their land, children, or themselves over to the great organizations in return for subsistence during times of

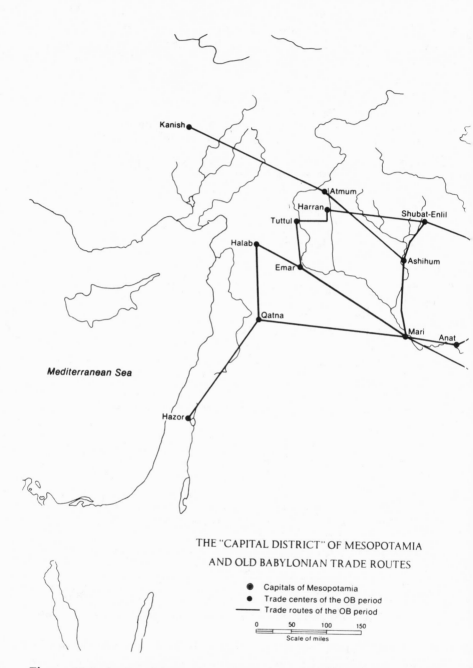

THE "CAPITAL DISTRICT" OF MESOPOTAMIA
AND OLD BABYLONIAN TRADE ROUTES

● Capitals of Mesopotamia
● Trade centers of the OB period
— Trade routes of the OB period

0   50   100   150
Scale of miles

Figure 10.1. Ancient Mesopotamia, Showing the "Capital District" and the Trade Routes. (From *The Ancient Near East: A History* by W. W. Hallo and W. K.

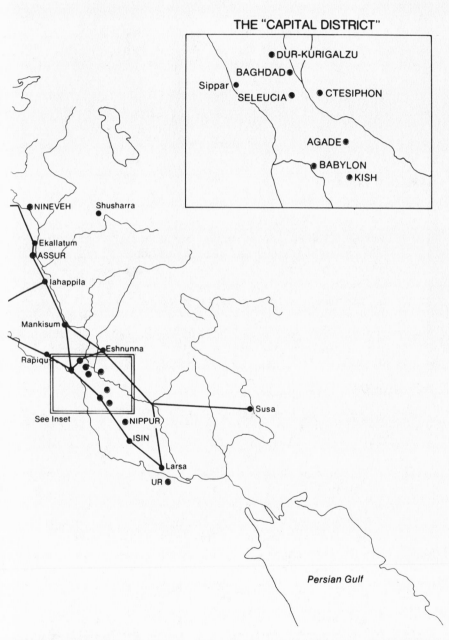

THE "CAPITAL DISTRICT"

DUR-KURIGALZU
BAGHDAD
Sippar
SELEUCIA
CTESIPHON

AGADE

BABYLON
KISH

NINEVEH   Shusharra

Ekallatum
ASSUR

lahappila

Mankisum

Eshnunna
Rapiqu

See Inset   NIPPUR
ISIN

Susa

Larsa
UR

Persian Gulf

famine; some became slaves, though slavery was never a dominant economic factor in Mesopotamia. Banking and trade shifted from temple to royal monopoly. Generally, the more success the king had on the battlefield the more power he acquired at home. In the large successful empires the palace organizations came to dominate virtually all political and economic activities. It is possible that the idea of kingship came from outside Sumer. Semitic peoples migrated into the Akkadian area to the north of Sumer about the time of the Flood. Kish, the city-state of the first king of Kish, was in the middle of the Akkadian area. Also, some of the early kings, according to Oppenheim (1977, p. 104), had Semitic names.

Akkadian Empire

Since the region of Akkad* gave Mesopotamia the idea of kings, it is not too surprising to discover that the first real empire was also an Akkadian idea. Sargon of Akkad, a man of apparent humble origins,† eventually took over the kindom of Kish, waged war on neighboring city-states, and during a fifty-year reign put together an empire that extended over much of Mesopotamia and whose influence was felt far beyond Mesopotamia. Sargon brought about internal stability and was responsible for numerous social, religious, artistic, and political innovations that greatly solidified the political power of the king and made it more possible for the power to pass on to succeeding generations. The time of Sargon and his dynasty, from 2300 to 2100 B.C., is labeled the Akkadian Empire.

Ur III-Isin Dynasties

The period following the Akkadian Empire is important mainly because it gave rise to the first large-scale private commercial organizations. During the period of 2100 to 1800 B.C. the power of the Akkadian Empire declined and there was increased fighting between the southern Mesopotamian city-states of Ur and Isin, each of which gave its name to dynasties in the Sumerian King List. The political instability of the latter two dynasties was such that even at the height of their power and stability the region of Sumer and Akkad to the north was never securely held. This gave the Assyrians, in the city of Assur some 375 miles to the north of Ur, an opportunity to assert their independence. They established remarkable trade relations with the peoples of the Anatolian

---

*Akkad is in the "Capital District" (see Figure 10.1) near the cities of Kish and Babylon, but its actual site has not been discovered.

†Myth has it that he was the illicit son of a high priestess who left him in a reed basket on the Euphrates to be discovered by a commoner, an interesting turnabout from Moses, who was left in a reed basket by a commoner and found by a princess! Sargon, perhaps, was the prototype of the Horatio Alger rags-to-riches hero.

Plateau at Kanish, not far from Catal Huyuk. The political environment was such that the king of Assur could protect the caravans and help them maintain their autonomy from the neighboring princes.

Age of Hammurapi

This short review of Mesopotamian history ends with the Age of Hammurapi of Babylon, from 1800 to 1600 B.C. Babylon was an ancient city in what Hallo and Simpson referred to as the "Capital District," near modern Baghdad. The district included, within a fifty-mile radius, many ancient capitals, among them Kish and Akkad. Hammurapi, who is most famous for his development of a code of laws, reunified the empire almost to the old Sargonic borders.

10.3 THE *HUNTERS* FORM

Given the general description of ancient Mesopotamian developments in the previous section, it is now possible to discuss more specifically the main organizational forms that appear to have originated during those times. In doing so I will use the framework developed earlier in chapter 4; which was based on Perrow's (1970) scheme for understanding the relation between environmentally posed problems and organizational form. In reaching back into ancient Mesopotamia I find that many of the details about environments and organizational technology and form have been lost. The image is necessarily one of salient aspects. In my discussion, therefore, I will tend to focus on the *salient* environmental characteristic of a certain time period and associated *salient* aspects of organizational technology and form.

Table 10.2 lists the salient features of five different environments existing in ancient Mesopotamia. Each feature presented an organization existing at the time with a problem that required a particular dominant technology. This technology in turn resulted in certain management problems and an attendant organizational form, also listed in the table. Undoubtedly there were other elements of environments, dominant competence, and form besides those shown in the table. Nevertheless, until a more complex understanding of the ecology of organizations is available, a view based on salient features seems worthwhile as a point of departure. In doing this I want to make it clear that I am *not* adopting an essentialist view by assuming that only a few attributes are all that is necessary. Not at all. I believe that many environmental problems lead to the selection of a rich set of adaptive characters. I just do not think that I can uncover them all in this initial try. Going after an association of salient characteristics is not what I would prefer,

TABLE 10.2

SALIENT ENVIRONMENTAL FEATURES, DOMINANT COMPETENCE,
AND ORGANIZATIONAL FORM

Time Period	Salient Environmental Feature	Dominant Competence	Organizational Form*
Late Mesolithic 8500–7000 B.C.	Scarcity; marginal subsistence	Acquisitional, pooled inter-dependency	*Hunters*
Proto-literate 3800–3000 B.C.	Increased population density, interdependence, and conflict	Mediating-normative	*Temples*
Urban Revolution 3100–2900 B.C.	Increased dependence on crafts as basis of military security and foreign trade	Complex-acquisitional and pooled	*Producers*
Early Dynastic 2900–2300 B.C.	Increased threat of intercity warfare	Mediating-coercive; discipline- and control-based effectiveness	*Palaces*
Ur III-Isin 2100–1750 B.C.	Dynastic weakness	Mediating-utilitarian; input-output-based effectiveness	*Commercials*

*Following preliminary nomenclatural procedures suggested in section 9.4.5, the labels of higher categories (older forms) are italicized, capitalized, and given in the plural.

but it is better than nothing at all and it may be all that is possible after so many years have passed.

The dominant feature of the primordial environment probably was one of scarcity. Subsistence was a full-time occupation based on hunting, fishing, or gathering wild foods. These foods typically were not so plentiful that people could devote significant amounts of time to other activities. Of course danger from wild animals existed; but the technologies of primitive tribes today seem more oriented toward subsistence than fighting off dangerous animals and presumably this was true in ancient times as well. In Paleolithic times people lived in caves and moved out during the day to search for food. Probably, as the population around the cave area grew, it became more difficult to find food. The local area might have been picked clean at some time and consequently small bands of people moved to another area. By the time of the Mesolithic Period most people, from what evidence can be discovered, lived in caves and foraged the surrounding area or else were in mobile bands that may have moved over a wide area in search of food or may have followed migrating herds of animals.

For most of the time this environment does not appear to have given rise to a form of purposeful organization. The groups of cave dwellers or small bands of nomads probably had some kind of social organization, but probably did not have an organization fitting the definitions of an organization given in chapter 4. The existence of a settlement does not necessarily imply the existence of a purposeful organization. While the settlement may have had a social organization, with its norms and means of applying positive and negative sanctions to those conforming to or violating the norms, this does not mean that the people were collectively organized to attain specific goals and make the associated decisions.

In the later Mesolithic Period there is evidence that hunting and gathering peoples did begin to live in settlements and organize purposefully to hunt. Perkins and Daly (1972), by studying the bones of animals found around the site of Suberde in Neolithic Turkey (about 6500 B.C., uncorrected), were able to conclude that 70 percent of the meat consumed in the settlement came from hunting tactics requiring group activity. Based on the behavior of present-day primitive hunting parties, it is possible to speculate that the Suberde hunting parties probably had some specialization—some individuals may have been good at imitating animal calls, some may have flushed the game and driven it toward others who waited in ambush, and so forth. They obviously had specific goals and presumably could change them from hunting oxen to hunting herds of red deer, for example. They probably did not have much of a hierarchy. They could have had only one level—the hunters sharing leadership responsibility—or they may have had a leader, the tribal chief for example. But with the latter there is no reason to think they had a "middle management" level between the chief and the hunters. In Jericho, evidence of defensive walls around 5500 B.C. suggests the existence of a simple organizational form for building rather than hunting (Kenyon 1972).

Using Thompson's (1967) typology of organizational interdependencies, it seems clear that the primordial form illustrated above was essentially the *pooled* variety. Surely there was no *reciprocal* interdependency; and while one could note that a hunting activity was *sequential* in the sense that the hunters first located the game, then stalked it, flushed it, killed it, dressed it, and finally packed the meat home, the dominant competence of a successful hunting party probably focused on the pooling of effort. After all, an individual hunter also went through the sequence from locating game to packing the meat home. The technology of the organization was not necessary to facilitate that.

Thompson also discussed three kinds of technology: *mediating, long-linked*, and *intensive*. None of these resemble the dominant competence of early hunting organizations such as the one at Suberde. A fourth basic concept, that of *acquisitive* technology, is needed to reasonably characterize this simple form and perhaps more complicated ones in later times, which are designed to generally acquire things or keep other people from taking things. These technologies did not mediate between clients or customers, link several different technologies in a sequence, or assemble an array of technologies for intensive application to a particular client as needed. That Thompson did not feel the need to include the acquisitive form may have been because most private-sector organizations are profit-making and thus acquisitive; his intent was presumably to provide a further differentiation within this group. Though this primitive technology may nowadays be pervasive and taken for granted, it is still worthwhile to identify it.

The acquisitive dominant competence seems to have remained the only organizational technology for many hundreds of years. During the Neolithic Revolution and the Chalcolithic Period there do not seem to have been any organizational developments that differed in significant ways from the simple technology of acquiring things or defending taking by others. The things acquired and the means of acquiring them changed, from only acquiring food from hunting to getting it from farming. And in the latter part of the Chalcolithic Period specialists may have pooled their efforts to acquire the items needed for their craft, such as in a tin-mining expedition. But there is little reason to believe that these simple organizations ever amounted to more than the pooling of a few people for the purpose of mining metal, farming, building irrigation dikes and canals, and so forth.

Some prehistorians, for example Melaart (1972), suggest that a large settlement such as Catal Huyuk (which may have had 50,000 people living within its walls and which was wealthy mainly due to its trade in obsidian) indicates rather sophisticated organizing ability. This need not be the case. Walls could be built with very little organization, once there was agreement that without walls all were in danger.* This was mainly a pooled interdependency, perhaps with a leader and probably with specialization as different people made bricks, carried them, laid them, and so forth. One might conclude that the obsidian trade, which resulted in the finding of obsidian as far away from Catal Huyuk as Jericho (Dixon, Cann, and Renfrew 1972), might imply a rather sophisticated organization, given the distance, probable danger, and the fact that donkeys—the first beasts of burden—had not yet been domesticated. But Burstein† observed that there were two kinds of trade that could explain such activity without any organization at all. One form is known as *down-the-line* trade, in which objects were traded by members of one settlement to members of an adjacent settlement. The latter in turn traded the objects with members of another settlement further down the supposed trade route. In this way objects eventually crossed considerable distances even though the traders never went further than villages nearest to their own. A second form is known as *dumb* trade. Here members of one group took the things they wanted to trade to a point where their territory met someone else's. They placed the goods they wanted to trade on the ground along with the amount and kind of goods they wanted in return; then they retreated into the bush. The neighbors came out and, upon seeing the items, placed what they wished to trade along with other items they wanted in payment, and then they retreated. This continued until there was balance between the items each group wanted to trade (or substitutes they were willing to settle for) and what the other group would give in return. Then each group picked up the items they wanted and the trade was finished. All of this could take place without a word being spoken and certainly without any organization.

In retrospect it should come as no surprise to conclude that the technological root cause of organizational form was the need or desire to acquire things and the root form was the pooling of individual efforts. The acquisition of food and other things seems to be a basic need of human and other animal organisms. The acquisition of resources continues to be the basic concern of all organizations: businesses, not-for-profit hospitals, universities, cities, states, national governments, and the like. And pooled interdependency, Thompson noted, was the fundamental

---

*At Catal Huyuk the walls around the town were the same as the outside walls of the houses. Each family built its own house in such a way that the wall toward the outside of the town was solid. Entrance to the home was from the roof. In this way the defense of the town was the accumulation of individual effort—the outside "wall" got larger as the town expanded, as each new home was built.

†Stanley Burstein, personal communication, April 1977.

kind of interdependency present in all organizations. Perhaps as the salinity of blood in all animals points to their common origin in the sea, the acquisitiveness and pooled interdependency in all organizations points to the acquisitive primordial organizational form! Though the lineage may not be passed on quite as neatly as the genes do it for biological organisms, nevertheless the initial organizational features seem to have passed down through all the generations of employees who have worked in organizations and either consciously or otherwise passed on the basic dominant technology to their replacements.

In table 10.2 these earliest organizations are given the label *Hunters*. In figure 10.2 they are shown to be the wellspring of all subsequent organizational forms. Since there was no differentiation at this time, a formal category rank is unnecessary. The line branched into the *Temples* form. The *Hunters* form still exists today in the form of what may be termed the *Simple-pooled* genus and species. This class includes all simple, basically acquisitive organizations—ma-and-pa grocery stores, mountaineering teams, small student organizations—where there is pooled interdependency, a few rules, some specialization, and a possible two-level hierarchy. These organizations adopt a form probably little different from the one hunters adopted some 8,000 years ago. This form seems to be quickly learned from other people familiar with the problems an environment poses on a new organization. Its dominant competence

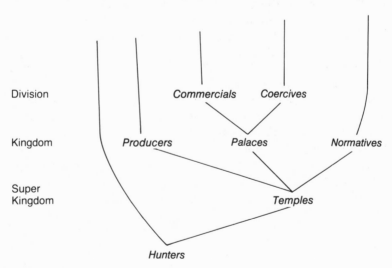

Figure 10.2. Dendrogram of Ancient Organizational Forms.

may be created anew by people unfamiliar with previous examples of the form, but probably is learned from other people. Unlike in biology, the circumstances of initial organizational form creation may still be present here and there, leading to both new creation and recombination of the primitive form. I suspect, however, that instances of true creation of the *Hunters* form in isolation from other people already familiar with it are very rare. As forms become more complex, evolution through generational lineages outweighs new creation, probably almost completely.

10.4 The *TEMPLES* FORM

During the Neolithic and Chalcolithic times life became more complicated. Craft specialities developed. Specialists had to trade what they made for goods made by others and so became dependent on them. Farming slowly moved from the valleys onto the plains, ultimately to become totally dependent on irrigation. Because of the surpluses the population grew. There were increasing numbers of trading settlements, each surrounded by a circle of farms. It was probably inevitable that differences of opinion and squabbles would break out as the population grew, the distances between neighbors diminished, trading among people increased, and dependency on common water sources, canals, and dikes increased. Though prehistorians now largely agree that irrigation projects, via their need for organization, were not the root cause of urbanization and the growth of the temple organizations, dependency on irrigation considerably increased the potential for conflict among people. There probably were altercations over who had access to the water in a particular canal; who had to maintain it; who had rights to the land nearest the canal; and who had rights to build a canal across a certain stretch of land. As some lands lost their fertility, and as other lands became more fertile, there probably were disagreements over land rights. As population densities increased, there may have been arguments over where the herds could pasture and along what parts of the land they could be driven on their way from one pasture to another. And what happened when one person's herd ate a farmer's grain crop along the way to a new pasture? A further problem was noted by Adams (1972, p. 138). During the hot summers all vegetation withered except right along the watercourses. To get through this period, fodder had to be grown during the wet time of the year and then stored and distributed during dry spells. The people with the herds came to depend on the farmers growing fodder and there were probably arguments over who got the fodder in times of shortage and at what price.

The accumulated effect of these changes was that the dominant feature of organizational environments changed. Instead of widely scattered bands of people struggling for subsistence in a land of scarcity, Sumer now could be characterized as a land of increasing agricultural resources but accompanied by growing interdependencies, differences of opinion, and conflict. The basic problem posed by the environment seems to have changed from one of how to find scarce resources to how to resolve conflict. Rather than depending only on the surrounding environment for sustenance, the Sumerians now increasingly depended on each other.

Adams (1972) has already been cited as suggesting that priests were probably the first specialists released from full-time preoccupation with growing food. As the spiritual world of the Sumerians grew in sophistication, the priests increasingly were either placed in the role of mediating between the gods and the people or were forced into the role by demands for the appeasement of the gods. This role is still characteristic of shamans or witch doctors in primitive tribes. Presumably some or all priests came to understand how to ply what Thompson (1967) labeled *mediating* technology and often used it to their own advantage. Again, the power and advantages of the shaman are seen in primitive tribes existing to the present time.

Although there is no evidence remaining which shows directly that priests became the mediators among squabbling Sumerians, indirect evidence appears in the slow ritualization of the mediating role of the priests and the institutionalization of that role in the temple competence. That the power and legitimacy of the priests had grown is indicated from before the Protoliterate Period by ceremonial markings on pot-sherds and because there are many more ceremonial pots than other pots from that time. Adams (1972) indicated that the ritual activities of priests were also depicted in seals and stone carvings from the Protoliterate Period. During this period the priests also became economic administrators, as indicated by the ration and wage lists among the earliest known writings. The management of herds also rapidly became the responsibility of people associated with the temples. The activities of the priests eventually required temples of considerable size.

Well before the Flood, temples had become "great organizations." Adams (1972) noted that before the Protoliterate Period, before 4000 B.C. in fact (often referred to as the Early Ubaid Period), there was evidence that the temples had lost their original fluidity of plan and had adopted architectural features characteristic of the later monumental temple edifices. Presumably along with architectural continuity came a continuity in the function and processes of the temple organization as structured by the building. Archaeological sites show that temples were easily the largest buildings in a city, containing workshops, and store-houses; later on in the beginning of the Early Dynastic Period the tem-ples even housed the kings (both gods and kings were treated in much the same manner at that time). According to the clay tablets, temple organizations were quite large and had hierarchies and specialized staffs. Their responsibilities included the management of herds, the collection, storing, and redistribution of surpluses, and the management of temple workshops where pottery, textiles, and other crafts were pur-sued. Their wealth put them in the position of largely controlling foreign trade since the temples controlled agricultural produce and agricul-turally derived materials such as textiles, which were traded for luxuries such as precious and semiprecious stones and valuable metals. The ability to store surpluses in times of plenty and distribute them in time of need was an important key to their wealth. During times of famine the traditional response of the commoners was to turn over to the temple their land if they still owned some, their children, and finally their wives and themselves, in return for food, clothing, and the settlement of debts. Over the course of many years' supluses and famines the temples ended up owning most of the land and controlling most of the commoners as serfs. Though the temples took the land during hard times, they did not give it back in good times. They did allow the former owner to work the land as a serf, however.*

The temple organizations mastered the mediating technology very well. They became the first examples of complex organizations having hierarchies, middle management, specialized staffs and workers, writ-ten rules and regulations, and so forth (Hall 1977). Though they, too, were acquisitive and very good at it, the thing that gave them their success and differentiated them from the *Hunters* form was the dis-covery of mediating technology.

I think it is not unwarranted to conclude that the environment posed a problem that only an effective mediating technology could solve. In Williamson's terms, the market clearly failed. The conditions of market failure—bounded rationality, opportunism, environmental uncertainty and small-numbers bargaining (Williamson 1975; Ouchi 1980b)—seem to have been present in ancient Sumer. Some evidence has been men-tioned showing how the temple organizations managed the problem by running an extensive mediating technology. Some details as to organi-zational form could also be surmised—hierarchy, specialization, staffs,

---

*See Sterba (1976) for a similar description of ancient Mesopotamian temple organization.

standardization through rules, and so forth. But beyond this, little detail remains as to what else might have characterized the temple organizations. Even so, recognition is given to this form in table 10.2 as the *Temples* form of organization. In figure 10.2 the *Temples* form is placed at the Super Kingdom category level, leaving the Kingdom rank for the first branching of complex organizations.

Toward the end of the era of the Urban Revolution (2900 B.C.) the general environment of Sumer began to undergo a change. Up until this time the distinctive feature of the environment was growing interdependency among people. The temples were clearly effective in this kind of environment. Why was this so? The answer to this question could very well rest on the basis of the legitimacy of the temples. Etzioni (1975) suggested a typology of organizations based on how their members become involved and how the organization gains compliance from its members. *Normative* organizations are composed largely of members who are morally involved with their goals and purposes. The authority to gain compliance from their members rests on their ability to deliver normative rewards based on the values of their members. *Utilitarian* organizations depend on a rational-legal basis of authority and the members become involved on a calculative basis if the wage or price is right. *Coercive* organizations, which depend on coercive power and authority, have employees or members who are alienatively involved.

It would appear that the temples gained their effectiveness in the prevailing environment because they never lost their legitimacy as normative organizations. A large part of their basis of legitimacy was due to their cult activities. They and they alone could mediate between the people and the gods, or so the people believed. Presumably this basis of legitimacy spilled over, giving them legitimacy to mediate difficulties among people. Even though the temples had considerable economic power toward the end of the antediluvian times, the basis of this power seems to have been their ability to mediate effectively. At all times the people vastly outnumbered the temple personnel and by sheer force could have gone in and just taken what food they wanted. They never did as far as the written record indicates; and even in hard times the temples had the power to coerce people into giving up their land, their children, and their freedom. The organizations never appeared to have been threatened by a mass revolt. By contrast, resistance to coercion by the palace organizations did become a problem, as indicated in the Epic of Gilgamesh (Adams 1972, p. 142).

The environment surrounding the temple organizations never appears to have been threatening or hostile to them. Their basis of legitimacy was never threatened. Their wealth was never under attack, so far as it is known. In short, the environment as far as the organizations were concerned was essentially benign, just as the environment of the *Hunters* form was benign, and as long as the environment remained so the organizations' mediating dominant competence continued to be effective. But once significant outside forces began to threaten the security of the cities of which the temple was the center, the environment was no longer benign and the stage was set for the evolution of a new organizational form. But before discussing the *Palaces* form, comment on the *Producers* form, which evolved within the temples, is necessary.

10.5 THE *PRODUCERS* FORM

For the most part, early production of art and craft objects such as ornaments, weapons, textiles, and tools appears to have been carried out by families, presumably using the *Hunters* form. Generally the historical literature is considerably less detailed in its coverage of producer organizations than it is of either the temple or palace forms, seemingly because early producer organizations of a more complex and larger size evolved as subsystems of the temple and palace organizations. So, findings about them occur only as a subset of findings about temples and palaces.

Two forces suggest that the elaboration and rationalization of craft industry took place under the control of the temples. First, at the time of the Urban Revolution, the temples were the only entities wealthy enough to import luxuries—mainly precious and semiprecious stones and metals. To pay for these items they traded what Sumer could produce, which was textiles and bronze tools and weapons (Oppenheim 1977, pp. 90–91). Accordingly the temples had considerable incentive to make sure that the craft goods they needed for trade were available. This need in itself could easily have led them to organize their own production. The second force was that during times of famine the general populace was in the habit of turning its autonomy over to the temple as previously mentioned, and subsequently was largely controlled by its managers. After a time the temple undoubtedly had craft and arts personnel as well as farmers under its control as serfs. The joint effect of needing craft production and acquiring craftsmen as serfs meant that the temples ended up organizing a substantial production operation.

Archaeological evidence indicates that craft workshops were a standard feature of temple complexes during the time of the Urban Revolution (3100–2900 b.c.) (Adams 1972). Adams (1955, p. 13) cited other archaeological sources as indicating that craft guilds existed at Shuruppak and that a temple at Lagash employed 200 slave girls in the production of textiles. Oppenheim (1977, p. 80) noted that even later during the Babylonian dynasty of Hammurapi, craft guilds were organized under a palace overseer and that such guilds were organized to function as part of the temple or palace.

The decreased isolation of Sumer, which eventually created a need for warlords, also meant increased awareness of foreign cultures and their crafts and luxuries, and ultimately a desire for them. The acquisition of foreign luxuries depended on having craft items to trade. Craft production shifted from fostering aesthetic values or making life easier by producing ornamental, tool, and cloth items, to being the basis of military success via the production of highly prized bronze weapons and the basis of wealth and splendor via trade for imported luxuries. It is little wonder that the great organizations became interested in production and eventually took much of it into their own control.

The dominant competence of the production organizations differed both from the acquisitive technology of the *Hunters* form and the mediating technology of the *Temples* form. Unfortunately little seems to be known about how such large production operations were managed. Undoubtedly the pooled technology of the *Hunters* was present, as it is a basic element of all organizations. It is unlikely that what Thompson (1967) termed a *long-linked* technology was present; each craftsperson made a complete object from start to finish. Specialization was obviously present as there were weavers, bronze workers, ornament and weapons makers and the like. Whether there were formalized rules and regulations is unknown, but given the ritualization, regularity, and writing down of procedures which characterized the cult activities of the temples it is quite possible that the priest/managers also formalized their production operations. Being quite large and having several specializations, the production organizations probably had a hierarchy that merged with the general temple hierarchy at some level. (See organization chart in Sterba [1976].)

In contrast to the other forms discussed in this chapter, which all evolved in separate organizational entities, the *Producers* form evolved as part of the temple and later the palace organizations. This is an early example of two forms in one legal organizational entity, something that becomes much more frequent many hundreds of years later in the large corporations of present times. As shown in table 10.2, the *Producers* form can be identified as early as the Urban Revolution and therefore deserves labeling. The dendrogram in figure 10.2 shows the *Producers* evolving from the *Temples* form.

10.6 THE *PALACES* FORM

By the time of the Early Dynastic Period the plains of Sumer were ruled by several relatively large city-states; these consisted of a walled city crowned with a spectacular temple and ringed with fertile fields, and contained considerable wealth. Not surprisingly, the cities became increasingly popular targets of plunder by hostile nomads and later by the ambitious warlords of neighboring city-states.

The first response of cities to increasing hostility was to build defensive walls. Such walls date back to around 5500 B.C. in some cities like Jericho, but generally they did not appear frequently until around the Urban Revolution. Oppenheim (1977, p. 127) noted that from about 3000 B.C. on the distinguishing mark of all cities, with the possible exception of those in Egypt, was a wall or rampart. Before the Flood the political organization took the form of village assemblies whose principal duty was to elect an ad hoc warlord when the village or nascent city seemed to be coming under attack from hostile nomadic people. Initially these warlords seem to have been defensively oriented—they did not purposefully go out and attack another city-state. As attacks became more frequent (the time is not clear), the ad hoc warlord gave way to a more permanent warlord who was constantly preoccupied with defensive and offensive warfare and the maintenance of a standing army. Sometimes these new leaders emerged from within the priestly community and sometimes outside it.

Oppenheim (1977, p. 104) noted, "As for its origin, it is difficult to determine whether the palace organization developed solely from manorial roots, whether it is to be considered, in certain respects, as an offshoot of the early Sumerian, if not pre-Sumerian, temple organization, or whether it is to be related to alien, non-Mesopotamian political concepts." The view taken here is that though there is some reason to believe that the *idea* of kingship came from outside Sumer, it is difficult to argue that the palace organizational form did not evolve from the *Temples* form. Sumer was invaded by Semites from the west around the time of the Flood with the result that some of the names of the first postdiluvian kings who ruled at Kish bore Semitic names. Since the idea of kingship had not appeared before this, it may be reasonable to presume that the Semites brought the idea with them.

Despite the possible outside origin of the idea of kingship, it would take much more convincing evidence than the appearance of the idea to believe that the palace form did not evolve from the *Temples* form. Consider the degree to which the early political rules were embedded in the temple organization. The temples were well established before there was any evidence of kings or palaces. In fact it was the priests at Nippur (the religious center) who gave the early kings at Kish and elsewhere in Sumer their legitimacy. According to Hallo and Simpson (1971, p. 37) the schools at Nippur transmitted the belief that the early Sumerian King List was lowered from heaven. The following statement by Hallo and Simpson supports the idea that the palace organization evolved from the temple:

> Since no clear traces of royal palaces before ED III [2500 B.C.] times have been found by excavations except at Kish . . . , it would seem that the earliest city-state rulers resided in a part of the temple complex. The myths list en-ship (that is, the high priest-hood) first and well ahead of kingship among the norms of civilization. In fact, the first inscriptionally attested royal title is not king (etymologically "big man" in Sumerian) but lord (etymologically "high priest" in Sumerian). [Hallo and Simpson 1971, p. 44]

When palace organizations first became separate from temples there were many similarities, as noted by Oppenheim (1977, pp. 95–97). Both received their principal income from agricultural holdings (either directly through payment of rent or indirectly through taxes), what the workshops produced, gifts from pious worshippers to the god, or gifts from respectful or fearful citizens to the king. Both organizations redistributed part of their income as food rations, clothing allowances, and other benefits to all their "managerial" personnel and other temple or palace employees. Much of the similarity may be attributed to the Sumerian conception of both organizations as "households." The god was thought to reside in the *cella* (the principal enclosed structure of the classical temple), to be fed, clothed, and attended to as the king was fed, clothed, and attended to while on the throne. The similarity in style was enhanced by the emphasis early kings placed on the idea that they had a family relationship with the god. With either organization much of the wealth went into building and furnishing the temple or palace.

Toward the middle of the Early Dynastic Period (around 2500 B.C.) the kingship was institutionalized, with the practice of royal succession begun. Kings began to see themselves as ruling by divine right. Also at this time the first palaces separate from the temples began to appear. The palace oganization became chiefly occupied with the activity of preparing for and waging war, which included raising and supplying its army, maintaining large retinues of servants and entertainers, and building walls around the city. One significant difference that became apparent, according to Oppenheim (1977, p. 97), was that the level at which the temple could display the wealth of the deity became relatively fixed according to the rank of the deity, the temple's agricultural holdings, and the piousness of its worshippers. The only chance at increasing wealth came via the largesse of the king. But the size and lavishness of the palace were directly related to the political and military effectiveness of the king. In short, the temple organization seems to have remained relatively more stable whereas the palace organization became large or small, weak or powerful depending on how successful the king was. When the king was strong most of the economic power shifted to the palace. When the king was weak the power shifted to the temple or to private interests. As the tendency toward states of war increased in the later part of the Early Dynastic Period, the need to maintain large palace retinues and armies took a heavy toll on the populace. In the Epic of Gilgamesh, for example, there are records of complaints over forced labor to build walls (Adams 1972, p. 142).

The dominant competence of the palace organizations was military activity. In this they differed distinctly from the temples. The temples always seemed to maintain cult activities as top priority, even though they had considerable economic power. The rather remarkable result was that the temple organizations let the economic power shift to the palace without any record of significant complaint or conflict. Presumably if the temples had come to define their dominant competence differently and their basis of legitimacy had shifted to coercive or utilitarian rather than normative authority, they would have resisted the coercive authority of the palace when it took over control of economic activity, taking away whatever basis of coercive or utilitarian authority the temples had. In return, the palace organizations do not seem to have questioned the normative authority of the temples. In fact, when times were good the kings seem to have given the temples rather luxurious support.

Successful palace organizations seldom seem to have lost sight of the primacy of warfare as the cornerstone of their existence and war making as their dominant competence, even though they also were motivated by wealth, economic power, and foreign relations and trade. The historical record suggests that if in fact the king did become interested in artistic and economic florescence in disregard of military might and actual conquests, the dynasty came to an end. The following cycle seems characteristic of both ancient Mesopotamia and ancient Egypt: The empire and dynasty were established by an enterprising, strong, autocratic, often brutal empire builder. He was followed by successors who for the most part maintained the empire but who were less brutal and more tolerant. The end of the dynasty often came during the reign of a king who favored relative freedom for the people, artistic and economic florescence, and general well-being. The dynasty crumbled into smaller entities such as city-states or was conquered by an outside empire builder. The palace organizations were at their greatest strength when they kept their attentions on the dominant feature of the environment facing them and wielded their dominant competence to advantage in military operations.

Like that of the temples, the dominant competence of the palace organizations, in terms of Thompson's (1967) typology, was a mediating one. But it differed from that of the temples in that its legitimacy was coercive rather than normative. It was a technology born as the prevailing environment shifted from a benign character to a threatening one. The shift was caused by threat to the cities and the temples as the then-dominant organizations of the cities. The threat was thus from other organizations in the environment and this is the dominant feature that was significantly different from the dominant characteristic of the environment the temple organizations faced. Consequently a new form evolved. In table 10.2 it is listed as the *Palaces* form since that is the label typically used in the historical literature. In figure 10.2 the Kingdom level of classification is thus composed of three members: *Palaces*, *Producers*, and *Normatives*. The latter are given the *Normatives* label in recognition of their reversion to a clearer example of Etzioni's (1975) concept of normative organizations after the *Palaces* branched off. As was illustrated in figure 9.5 *Normatives* are seen as the ancestor form to modern religious organizations, political parties, colleges and universities, government bureaucracies and agencies, voluntary associations, and the like, all of which have a dominant technology rooted in mediation and normative legitimacy.

10.7 THE *COMMERCIALS* FORM

The earliest commercial organizations operated with the *Hunters* form of organization. They used an acquisitive technology to gain whatever wealth they could through the trading and fabrication of art and craft materials: trade in obsidian, metals, stone, wood, and other materials not found in the local area; fabrication of pots, ceremonial objects, weapons, weaving of textiles, and so forth. They were probably simple family-run enterprises—a husband, wife, sons, and daughters combining to produce things that, when traded or sold, would offer them a livelihood. Rooted in the *Hunters* form, organizations such as these have continued into the present time.

It is possible that a more complex form of commercial organization evolved directly from the *Hunters* form. Indications are, however, that a complex commercial form evolved from the *Palaces* form instead, but only after a significant environmental change.

Historians agree that most economic power between the Protoliterate Period (3800–3000 B.C.) and the Ur III-Isin Period (2100–1600 B.C.) lay first in the hands of the temple organizations and then the palace organizations. During this time trade with other ethnic groups around the Near East was under the monopoly of the great organizations. Early on this was because they were the only ones with the wealth to command the luxury of imported goods. Later, during the dynastic times, the kings had enough power and control over the countryside to prevent trading that was not under their purview. During this time Sumer evolved into a two-level society. Those on top controlling the wealth were directly connected to the temple and palace organizations. Successive land purchases by temple, palace, and nobility (the latter often living in or closely associated with and dependent for their status on the king) reduced most of the populace to the role of serfs (Adams 1972, p. 142; Hallo and Simpson 1971, p. 49). As noted before, these land transfers were hastened in times of famine when the people traded their land for food and clothing. Consequently, though there was considerable economic activity, it was all controlled by the temple or by the palace and its courtiers. If such activity required an organizational form more complex than that of the *Hunters* form, it presumably drew on the organizational experience developed in the temples and palaces. In sum, it is likely that large-scale economic activity before 2100 B.C. was managed by the technologies typical of the great organizations at that time.

The key environmental change began when conflicts arose between the city-states of Ur and Isin, respectively in Sumer and Akkad. The Akkadian Empire built up by Sargon eventually fell to the Sumerians of Ur, who formed the Ur III dynasty. After about 100 years the power shifted to a non-Sumerian from Mari named Ishibi-Irra who moved the seat of power to Isin. After several generations the descendants of Ishibi-Irra lost control to the Amorites, who established their own dynasty in Larsa and eventually took over Ur (see Hallo and Simpson 1971, pp. 84–93 for more detail about this period). The breakdown of the Akkadian Empire into fighting among the three southern city-states of Ur, Isin, and Larsa, each with its own ethnic background, meant that other city-states were free to reassert their independence and establish their own rulers and dynasties.

A principal beneficiary was Assur, some 375 miles north of Ur. Having gained their independence from the southern dynasties, the Assyrians, under their own ruler, began very extensive trade relations with the people of Cappadocia, on the Anatolian Plateau of eastern Turkey. Eventually they established a large trading settlement, or *Karum*, just outside the ancient Cappadocian town of Kanish, roughly 525 miles northwest of Assur. This Karum controlled eight other smaller ones at other major cities of the indigenous Hatti people. This trade was under the control of a few commercial families at Assur. The Karum was a kind of board of trade which controlled the activities of the traders. Quite a bit is known about the Assyrian trade because they left numerous clay tablets covered with cuneiform script which described their day-to-day activities. Gold and silver were the main exports of Assur; tin, textiles, hides, fleeces, and rugs were the principal imports. There were extensive credit arrangements available with various kinds of collateral possible, including wives and children. The records indicate that though the Assyrians lived outside the city of Kanish, they entered into many relationships with the people of Kanish, including marriage (for further details see Özgüc 1972).

Indications are that the commercial families of Assur had considerable organizational skill. There were most likely great difficulties in running donkey caravans over hundreds of miles of roads through country that was dangerous from wild animals, thieves, and runaway slaves, even during times of political stability. Treaties had to be negotiated with the autonomous prince controlling each city. Trade was controlled by local councils at each city made up of officials appointed from Assur and other members elected locally. All local councils were subordinate to the one at Kanish, which had direct ties to "the City," as Assur was referred to in the clay tablets (Özgüc 1972, pp. 244–249). The management hierarchy consisted of the family owners at the top, the appointed officials at Assur, then officials at Kanish, then officials at the other eight cities, with journeyman traders and craftsmen at the bottom—five ranks in all.

It seems probable that the commercial families got their organizational skills from exposure to the Assyrian palace. The Assyrians in turn would likely have picked up the organizational knowledge of the Sumerian and Akkadian palaces just as they picked up other cultural practices of Sumer and Akkad such as writing in cuneiform. Özgüc (1972) observed that the tablets at Kanish showed that this process also worked there. The Hatti princes learned the cuneiform writing from the Assyrian traders, as well as their administrative skills and taste for fashions and luxuries from Babylon. Özgüc suggested that the provincial Anatolian peoples—both Hatti and the later Hittites—probably picked up the empire idea from the Assyrians.

The historical record suggests that sophisticated and extensive commercial activity by private interests was always a latent possibility at any time from the Protoliterate Period on. But when the temple and later the palace organizations were strong, they dominated economic activity. There seems to be little record of complex commercial organizational forms until the Cappadocian trade of the Assyrians. It is possible that complex commercial organizations evolved before those of the Assyrians, as there were trading settlements outside many cities in Sumer (Oppenheim 1977, p. 116). But the archaeological and historical records do not yet offer the amount of evidence that was available at Kanish, even though clay tablets were found in the Karum outside the city of Ur. All indications are that complex commercial organizations on a scale comparable to those at Assur and Kanish did not exist elsewhere.

It would appear that the kind of environment most suitable for the development of private commerce was one where neither of two extreme possibilities prevailed. Private commercial organizations did not seem to develop, for obvious reasons, when there was no political control at all and the towns, cities, and countryside were left unprotected from the ambitions of wandering nomads, migrants, or other kinds of thieves and plunderers. Oppenheim (1977, p. 120) observed that travel by private persons in Mesopotamia was too dangerous most of the time and therefore did not occur. Only armies, large donkey caravans, and special persons with military escort were able to travel from city to city. Private commercial organizations also did not seem to prosper when a strong king was on the throne—one who was building an empire, building up a power base, accumulating the spoils of war and other wealth. The empire builders and other strong kings typically also controlled all important economic activity. The evidence from ancient times suggests that the more complex private organizations, such as those of the Assyrian traders, developed mainly, if not only, during times of political moderation. Judging from the account of Mesopotamian history given by Hallo and Simpson (1971), such a moderate supportive environment did not occur very frequently in Mesopotamia. The large complex trading organizations operating between Assur and Kanish may have been quite unique.

During the Middle Babylonian times, after the sack of the Hammurapi Empire, the long succession of weak kings resulted in the development of a feudal system and the emergence of guilds, grouped into real or fictitious clans identified by a common family name. These guilds were successful in maintaining discipline and self-government and thereby filled a serious governmental vacuum. They survived until the end of cuneiform times—about the first century B.C. Given the pervasiveness of the Mesopotamian civilization centered in Babylon, even during the times when Babylon was just one province in another king's empire (such as those of the great Persian kings, Cyrus and Darius I), the guilds, as representatives of the commercial organizational form, probably served as models for the development of commercial organization all around the rest of the Near East and the Greek and Roman Empires.

The dominant competence of the first commercial organizations was a mediating technology, like that of the temple and palace organizations, so some of the technological developments of the commercial organizations were not too much different from those of their predecessors. But their basis of legitimacy was different and the model of effectiveness applicable to them also was different. The difference in the basis of legitimacy has been thoroughly discussed by Etzioni (1975), though his discussion was not cast in terms of ancient organizations. In contrast to the normative authority of the *Temples* form and the coercive authority of the *Palaces* form, the commercial organizations probably relied on what Etzioni termed a *utilitarian* basis of authority and compliance. Employees became involved in the organization because they could see some calculable gain to themselves. Although employees of the temples and palaces probably also had a calculative involvement at times, either organization could fall back on the strength of its normative or coercive basis of legitimacy when necessary and gain involvement on those grounds. No so for the commercial organizations. They could only draw on the utilitarian basis of legitimacy, though in some cases some employees may have been serfs or slaves, whereupon the coercive basis of authority might have applied.

In order to remain effective on a calculative basis, the organizations probably became much more sophisticated in another aspect of dominant competence which differentiated them even further from the temples and palaces—the measurement of the value of their inputs and outputs. Private trading organizations would have survived on a long-term basis only if they were clever at buying items at a price they could make a profit on. These were the first "bottom-line" oriented organizations, with the control systems necessary to assure a return on their investment. The inputs and outputs were measurable on a continuous day-to-day basis in a way that the effectiveness of the cult activities of the temples or the military preparedness of the palaces were not. Employees could be motivated and controlled on a more specific basis in terms of whether they were successful or not in adding value to the organization.

Military organizations were intermediate in their ability to use an "input-output" model of effectiveness. Generals who lose wars could be fired or otherwise removed, if they hadn't already been killed in battle. Thus there would appear to be an evolution from temple to palace to commercial organization paralleling their ability to base effectiveness on the "input-output" model of effectiveness. With the temples and other normative organizations that subsequently evolved from them, effectiveness was probably based more on the care with which they carried out the religious rituals and processes rather than on a direct measure of how well they appeased the gods. They depended more on a process or "throughput" model of effectiveness. Yuchtman and Seashore (1967) have described in some detail what they termed a "system resource" model that is the same as the bottom-line or input-output model. Schein (1980) described an "adaptive-coping" model of effectiveness which is the same as the throughput model. McKelvey (1974) discussed the differences in some detail.

In table 10.2 the commercial form is given the label *Commercials*, and in figure 10.2 it is shown to have evolved from the *Palaces* form. The main argument here is that the *Commercials* form evolved because of a unique environmental development and that it developed a dominant technology different from that of the temples and palaces in its basis of legitimacy and model of effectiveness. Of course there were probably other differentiating features as the commercial organizations became more differentiated and specialized, just as there are many differentiating features between churches and businesses today.

10.8 SUMMARY

The review of organizational evolution in ancient Mesopotamia affords an opportunity to accomplish two things: (1) test whether the events fit the general model of a family tree, which they appear to do; and (2) induce a set of specific organizational forms that, if elaborated into modern times, would identify a set of hypothetical classes useful as a point of departure for numerical phenetic clustering and which, if the induced groupings were corroborated by the numerically produced groupings, would offer a test of evolutionary theory. These two items offer some basis for testing the falsifiability of organizational evolutionary theory. A review of dominant environmental events in ancient Mesopotamia was undertaken; eleven time periods were noted, as shown in table 10.1. Five organizational forms were identified having different dominant technological features and forms: *Hunters, Temples, Producers, Palaces*, and *Commercials* (shown in fig. 10.2). In each case the new form appears to have evolved slowly and branched from a previous form. Each new form appeared after significant changes in the environment. The dominant competence of the new form in all instances seems to have been a direct outgrowth from the dominant competence of an ancestor form of organization.

11 TAXONOMIC CASES AND CHARACTERS

A major bar to the cumulation of knowledge about organizations, to effective theory construction, and to the accumulation of data collected by different research teams lies in the fact that each investigator uses a different set of variables, and thus, organizations of the same type and even the same organizations are described in quite different ways (cf. Kostecki and Mrela 1979).

[Warriner, Hall, and McKelvey 1981, p. 173]

The principal advantage numerical methods have over orthodox methods is that they allow many more taxonomic characters to be taken into account in forming groupings. If desired, they also allow the classificatory results to be based on more than just one or a very few representative organizations of each potential grouping. But these advantages come to nought if poor judgment is used in choosing organizational cases and measuring taxonomic characters. After a definition of taxonomic units, my discussion about cases breaks down into a consideration of population selection and, once populations are chosen, the selection of a sampling plan. I follow this with a lengthy section on selecting characters.

11.1 OPERATIONAL TAXONOMIC UNITS

Organizational systematists may wish to use numerical methods to classify several kinds of entities in addition to individual organizations. This is not to say that sorting individual organizations into groups is not an important, if not the principal, activity of systematists. But on many occasions systematists will want to work with higher rank categories. In the latter instance the cases to be sorted will be *groups* of organizations, not individual organizations. In other instances systematists taking an ecological rather than a taxonomic approach will be using numerical methods to classify environmental sites or locations, using the kinds of organizations populating such sites as variables. In still other circumstances systematists will be comparing the internal structures of organizations via numerical methods so as to ascertain whether the organizations are homologous—more on this in section 11.4.2. Because of these different kinds of case inputs to numerical computer programs, a generalized term to cover them all is useful. Over the years the term OPERATIONAL TAXONOMIC UNIT (OTU) has become the conventional one, largely due to Sneath and Sokal and their colleagues. Sneath and Sokal (1973, p. 69) define OTUs as "the lowest ranking taxa employed in a given study."

Until recently numerical taxonomists in biology have given most of their attention to classifying at category levels higher than species, for a couple of reasons (Sneath and Sokal 1973, p. 362). First, it was felt that classificatory decisions using orthodox methods at the higher levels were more subjective and arbitrary than classificatory decisions at the species level and hence needed review soonest. The typical numerical systematist would take for granted that plants and animals were fairly accurately differentiated into appropriate species, especially those that propagated via sexual mating, and therefore concentrated on sorting out genera, families, and higher ranks. Second, the limited capacity and slow running of early computer programs meant that only a limited number of OTUs could be studied at one time. Since there were fewer taxa to be sorted at higher levels than at the lower levels, this again led to a concentration on the higher rank categories.

As organizational systematists begin their studies, the situation is quite different. First, there are no well-accepted organizational species categories. Thus it is not reasonable to assume that we can begin numerical taxonomic studies by taking single representatives or EXEMPLARS (this term will be explained in section 11.3.2) of organizational species and then focus on discovering genera, families, and the like. Second, after two decades of development, modern computers have very fast processing speeds, and the classification algorithms and computer programs have been developed to the point where large numbers of OTUs can be processed at one time. Therefore, there is no sensible reason at all why organizational systematists could not start at the species level. Since they are presently undefined, the first order of business has to be the identification of organizational species. Fortunately, given the size of modern numerical taxonomic programs and their hierarchical clustering algorithms, systematists can also classify some higher ranks at the same time even though the OTUs are individual organizations thought to represent species. In fact, some cluster programs do this automatically. So, just because the OTUs are members of organizational species, systematists are not going to be precluded from also classifying organizations into the higher rank categories. Bearing in mind the needed priority for first classifying species, however, the following discussion of population selection is devoted entirely to choosing OTUs applicable to species rather than to supposed higher categories.

11.2 POPULATION SELECTION

While present-day numerical taxonomic computer programs are large, they are not large enough, nor are sufficient time and funds available, to allow systematists to study a proper sampling of *all* potential organizational species. Therefore a dilemma of the following kind arises: numerical taxonomic methods are the best way of first identifying populations of different kinds of organizations, yet the best way to begin a numerical taxonomic study is to start with a relatively intensive study of a few previously identified populations of organizations. Inherent in the quality of population definitions is the quality of the species concept implicitly used, and arguments may be made for starting with or without a species concept.

11.2.1 Starting Without a Species Concept

The main argument for beginning a numerical taxonomic study without any attempt to define a species concept follows the empiricist theory of classification, which in turn is based on the anti-principles principle of enquiry. Since the pros and cons of this approach were discussed at some length in sections 3.1.1 and 3.1.4, further discussion is unnecessary. While my approach is definitely one of advocating starting with an a priori theory, specifically a species concept, it is nevertheless possible that some readers will feel so uncomfortable with any theory or species concept that might be developed that they would still prefer the anti-principles basis of enquiry.

As I noted some time ago (McKelvey 1975), it is often difficult to pursue a truly anti-principles approach. It is very easy to inadvertently let preconceived notions about organizational differences slip into a study, as happened in the Pugh et al. (1968, 1969) and Haas et al. (1966) studies. I argued that the only way to avoid preconceived notions was to totally avoid any decisions about what kinds of organizations or kinds of characters to include in a numerical study. The best way to accomplish this is to make sure that all organizations considered have an equal chance of being included in the study, which is to say that the broadest possible probability sampling plan for selecting organizations should be used, after defining as inclusive a population of organizations as possible. This was the intention of guidelines 1 and 2 in McKelvey (1975, pp. 512–514). These are:

Guideline 1: "Define the broadest possible population of organizations, or, if a delimitation is unavoidable, base it on a significant cultural unit." In practice researchers will be unable to avoid some kind of delimitation since to do otherwise would mean sampling from a world-wide population of all known organizations. In general the best kind of delimitation is one made on any basis other than an attribute apt to distinguish one kind of organization from another. The problem is that almost any delimitation could probably be seen to have some grouping or differentiating effect making organizations within the delimitation somewhat different from those outside it. Although McKelvey (1975) suggested that cultural delimitations would be acceptable, caution is warranted since many aspects of dominant competence, the main basis of the species concept presented in this book, may be affected by cultural and even language differences. For example, workplace management competence could be affected by culturally based ideologies for or against democracy or communism, attitudes of managers toward workers, attitudes toward manual labor, machinery, automation, capital intensity, and so forth. This is borne out by the research findings of Tannenbaum et al. (1974), among others. Geographical delimitations are an alternative, but would be suspect where it could be shown that organizational environments differed in significant characteristics, especially resources and levels of competition, culture or language.

However, there is a bright side to the coincident cultural/language/ geographical delimitation in that the link between systematists working on classifications and those apt to use them—other scientists, managers, and management or other schools training people how to manage or work in organizations more effectively—is likely highest where the same language and culture prevail. Since most scientists and practitioners live and work within the same culture, the possible consequences of intercultural differences making a classification within one culture different from that in another are not too worrisome. For those who will insist on worrying about cross-cultural differences, a noncultural delimitation would be necessary, perhaps one based on transportation or trade routes. Or, preferably, cross-cultural studies should be put off until species populations and higher ranks within cultural/geographical units are better identified.

Guideline 2: "Use a probability sampling plan without any stratification for selecting a sample of organizations." Stratification might be called for when organizations are grouped in some way such that one group may be represented more or less than another group unless a stratified random sample is used to even them out. To avoid as much as possible inadvertent groupings based on preconceived notions there is no substitute for a simple random sampling. While any individual study may include a seemingly unrepresentative sample, an accumulation of random samples would eventually even up the representation. Larger samples would also reduce this problem. While there may always be significant holes in random samples of a broadly defined population of organizations, and while it may not be possible to conduct as many studies as might be necessary to fill in all the gaps on a random basis, beginning with a random sampling approach and using it to make initial population definitions seems warranted. Such an approach would undoubtedly define broad subgroupings of organizations within the initial cultural delimitation. These broad subgroupings could then each be more intensively studied via the random sampling method, or the systematist might switch principles of enquiry and develop a species concept for the smaller, more delimited subpopulation.

To be consistent with the probability sampling approach, a systematist taking the anti-principles approach should also define the broadest possible sample of characters and if the computer program will not handle all of them, randomly select those to be included (guidelines 3 and 4 from McKelvey 1975). An alternative is to use factor analysis to reduce the number of characters by combining some of them, but this raises problems in that the relative weighting of the characters may be inadvertently altered. Further discussion of this is put off until section 11.4.4.

11.2.2 Starting With a Species Concept

The principal argument in favor of a species concept is that it aids in selecting populations when the total population at hand is too large for a single study. Since this argument is given at length earlier in the book it is not pursued any further here. The stronger or more credible the species concept available, the more logical it is to begin a numerical study by using the species concept to give preliminary definitions of the populations to be studied. Even though numerical taxonomists such as Sneath and Sokal (1973, p. 70) suggested on the one hand that the biological species concept is nonoperational, they noted on the other hand that most numerical taxonomists take species population definitions as a point of departure in their analyses of the higher categories. Relative to the poor-to-nonexistent definition of species in organizational science, the strength of definition in biology makes it logical for biological systematists to use species in choosing populations.

It is not clear just how poorly defined or theoretically unsubstantiated a species concept must be before there is no recourse but to take the empiricist anti-principles approach described in the previous section. Organizational systematists are bound to have widely and strongly differing views on this, each with considerable justification. For better or worse, my view is that a species concept is helpful and that the dominant competence concept of organizational differences meets a solid enough set of criteria to be worth using as a preliminary basis of selecting populations. The relative quality and contribution of studies based on one or the other approach will be the final arbiter.

Any species concept used will offer a way of breaking down the population of organizations into subpopulations. One possibility would be commonsense notions most people have about different kinds of organizations—schools, businesses, hospitals, amusement parks, government agencies, and so forth. Another approach would be to use one or more of the existing typologies of organizations. The more sophisticated and comprehensive the species concept, the greater the probability that it will produce preliminary subpopulations likely to be substantiated by subsequent numerical taxonomic studies. The subpopulations identified in figures 9.2 to 9.5 are based on the dominant competence species concept and a careful study of the evolution of organizational forms in ancient Mesopotamia, but with a more cursory delineation of evolution since that time, drawing on subpopulation concepts offered by several existing typologies as described briefly in chapter 9. Though preliminary, these figures offer a more complex hierarchical view of possible subpopulations, one that has its roots in evolutionary history.

No matter what species concept is used, some groups of organizations are going to be more clearly differentiated than other groups, which is to say that the gaps between the groups are going to be larger or more obvious. The question then becomes, Should we begin a numerical taxonomic inquiry by including organizations that are clearly separated by large gaps, presumably making it easier for the numerical solution to depict taxonomic groups, or should we focus on subtle differentiations where the gaps are almost nonexistent, thereby using the power of the numerical approach to clarify subtle distinctions in groupings? In orthodox biological systematics the size of the gap is the first of five criteria for delineating species and higher ranks (Mayr 1969, p. 233). Recently some organizational systematists (Hall 1979; Pinder 1979) have also taken the view that the way to begin is by studying the more obviously different groupings of organizations. However, the pattern among biological numerical taxonomists is clearly that of using the power of numerical methods to tease out subtle distinctions; in other words, to fine-tune taxonomic groupings. This strategy is not an arbitrary one. What is the point of taking a very powerful tool to uncover differences among such obviously different groupings as turnips and trees or minnows and mastodons? It is like using a sledgehammer to pound tacks. Likewise, since in this day and age numerical methods seem most appropriate, taking the trouble to carry out a sophisticated numerical study for the purpose of showing that aerospace organizations are different from small restaurants seems questionable.

The most fruitful way to begin, therefore, appears to be to select subpopulations that appear marginally different—organizations that probably would belong to the same family or genus if we already had such groupings. For example, a numerical study of hospitals, including teaching, general, and proprietary hospitals, those for the chronically ill, and even nursing or convalescent homes, would be a likely possibility. Or take the supposed genus of continuous-process organizations shown in figure 9.3—petroleum refineries, chemical plants, modern continuous smelting and pouring aluminum plants, food canning plants, and so forth. Do these organizations use the same form or not? And if not, how do they differ?

The initial focus on subtleties does not mean that the more obviously different groupings will be ignored. Their time will come as early work on classifying adjacent species is completed. As more and more genera and families are put on a sound taxonomic foundation, numerical solutions will logically be shifted from a concentration on the species level to the higher categories. As this happens it is likely that the groupings separated by the larger gaps will be included in the same analyses.

11.2.3 Kinds of Populations to Begin With

Both the plans of starting at the species level and of looking at subtle differentiations among related species rather than grossly unrelated ones somewhat narrow the selection of populations to study initially. But given the large number of organizational populations, further narrowing seems warranted. Other considerations pointing toward the selection of some populations over others are as follows:

1. Following the general dictum that it is best to try out new methods on well-known theory and data, organizational systematists should start with populations where their theory of classification seems to work best. Since an evolutionary approach is taken in this book, it follows that the place to begin is where the evolutionary lineages and resultant relatedness among species are clearest. Where the evolutionary developments are clearly supported by an understanding of the ecology, so much the better. Rather than start out with just any organizational species, this means developing theoretical rationales for identifying potential species making up a genus or family of related organizations and putting these to the numerical test. For example, my colleagues Bill Ouchi, Jay Barney, and Dave Ulrich have recently chosen to define an initial sector consisting of all U.S. and Japanese electronics firms, a grouping defined by the industry itself. A taxonomic study based on published data concerning products, internal structure, and financial data will lead to the definition of subpopulations for detailed analysis.

2. A corollary to the above is to choose populations where the species concept is most clearly defined, straightforwardly applicable, or least contentious. In the case of the dominant competence species concept this might mean starting with populations where the workplace and management competencies are fairly simple, thoroughly understood, and where general consensus as to their nature prevails. Small businesses such as retail stores and restaurants, schools, hospitals, fabrication and assembly manufacturing operations, and materials producers such as mines, smelters, lumber mills, and farms are ideal examples. Multinationals and government organizations may be more questionable because of complexities or vagueness about what the competence is. If there is more than one species concept in the literature, start with the one that is more "mainstream." The latter idea may not be helpful in the very beginning because there could well be several, if not a plethora, of species concepts to choose from, none of which has any substantial following.

3. Given roughly equally well worked out theory for several potential families of organizational populations, choose the better known, more easily available for measurement, more interesting, more economically or culturally important populations. Also select a potential family or genus that seems to be separated from other families or genera by a large gap. A crasser way to put this is to go where the research funding is.

4. Select populations blessed with more easily measured, numerous, stable, widely recognized taxonomic characters. If possible, pick populations that may be described by characters having well-known, unquestionable measures rather than those needing new ones.

A final comment has to do with balancing the inputs to a numerical study with sets of related and unrelated species in order to keep the lumping and splitting in perspective. It would be expected that closely related species in each genus or family would be lumped together in the solution. By including one or more families or genera that are expected to be clearly differentiated from other families or genera, one could also look for clearly expected gaps in the solution. Without the inclusion of both related and unrelated species in the solution at the same time there might be a tendency to force splits where they are not likely or, conversely, to force lumping of species when they might better fit in different groupings. In other words, since cluster programs are designed to produce hierarchically arrayed groupings, it is best to include as inputs kinds of organizations that probably will, when grouped, form a nested hierarchy of clusters.

11.3 SAMPLING OTUs

As yet biological systematists do not have any definitive answers for the question of how many OTUs should be sampled or included in a study (Sneath and Sokal 1973; Clifford and Stephenson 1975; Moss, Peterson, and Atyeo 1977). Usually they have avoided this problem by staying away from the study of species-level populations. Instead, by studying higher categories such as genera or families, they could: (1) Delimit a study by including only OTUs comprising a category as defined by orthodox methods. Thus Moss, Peterson, and Atyeo studied all sixty-one species of mites already identified as members of the feather mite family *Eustathiidae* by traditional methods. (2) Select exemplars of species of higher categories rather than take a random sample of members of each species to be studied. Thus only one or two (one of each sex) members of a species are selected. The use of exemplars in biology was condoned because it was thought that there was relatively little variation in character states within a species as opposed to the wide variations among different species. However, results from studies accounting for, instead of ignoring, variance within a species, such as use and nonuse of Mahalanobis's D^2 statistic, are different, suggesting that using exemplars and thereby suppressing evidence of within variance is not a good idea.*

Even though Sneath and Sokal (1973) do offer one chapter on numerical approaches to population (as opposed to exemplar) studies, they do not offer any guidelines on sampling. The biggest sample size they

---

*Everett Olson, personal communication, 15 July 1980.

mention was a study of 119 galls (which are parasitically induced swellings of plant tissue) caused by a kind of aphid (Sneath and Sokal 1973, p. 369). Ideally the upper bound to sampling is set either by the size of the program being used or the amount of computing time available. In cluster programs the computing time goes up roughly according to the square of the number of OTUs included. In practice, size is often determined by the availability of cases.

In organizational systematics the approaches to sampling OTUs so far do not fall cleanly into either the method of exemplars or population sampling. Since populations have not been clearly defined they have neither been appropriately sampled on a random basis nor represented by exemplars that could be taken to represent a species validly. Haas et al. (1966) drew a sample that amounted to seventy-five very diverse organizations. Pugh et al. (1969) sampled fifty-two broadly different organizations, and Goronzy (1969) sampled fifty manufacturing organizations—all groupings probably larger and more diverse than the family rank. Dodder (1969) studied what may well be a family of organizations, namely one hundred voluntary associations, probably the largest sample drawn to date. Dodder's study is also a good example of using a numerical approach to study closely related rather than widely differing organizations. Whether the Dodder study is a study of exemplars or a sampling at the population level is somewhat unclear—this would depend on how species of voluntary organizations are defined.

Though it seems likely that organizational systematists will begin at the population level, it is possible that the method of exemplars will be used as well; hence both are discussed below.

11.3.1 Sampling Populations

Studies at the species level or lower are primarily concerned with ascertaining the level of homogeneity of a preliminarily defined population, what I have termed a SECTOR. The results of such studies may help define species, identify groupings within species which may be labeled subspecies, or identify even lower-ranked categories. Often in biology such studies focus on the geographical dispersion of species or discover how a single species might differ from one geographical location to another. The same is likely in studies of organizational populations, though the primary concern will be to define species, since such definitions do not really exist now.

There are clearly no hard and fast rules for determining the number of OTUs representing sectors to be sampled. Generally in multivariate analyses, in the social sciences at least, the preference is to have at least three times as many cases as there are variables to be analyzed, whether via regression analysis, factor analysis, or some other method.* Translated into taxonomic terms, this norm suggests that at least three times as many taxonomic characters are needed in comparison to OTUs. Whether such a ratio is used among biological systematists is unclear. It is not mentioned in such standard works as Sneath and Sokal (1973) or Clifford and Stephenson (1975). Table 11.1 shows ratios from six recent numerical phenetic studies published in *Systematic Zoology*, one archeological study from *American Antiquity*, and four organizational classification studies. The archeological study has an excellent ratio. The biological studies have an average ratio of characters to OTUs of about 2.2 to one. The organizational studies average less than one to one. If these examples are a fair indication, the upper bound on the number of OTUs will be determined mainly by the number of characters and the degree of adherence to the three-to-one ratio. It can be seen that even though Sneath and Sokal (1973, p. 106) suggested that at least 60 characters should be used, and Dodder (1979) suggested that for organizations at least 100 characters seem necessary, one could easily wish for even more characters so that the number of OTUs entered into a solution at one time may be larger.

The lower bound on sampling is dictated by the number of subpopulations apparent within the species being studied. To the extent that subpopulations are clearly evident, a straight random sample may be thought unsatisfactory as it could easily leave out or overselect certain groups. Most likely the systematist will want to use a stratified random sampling plan where representatives of each presumed subpopulation are randomly sampled. Following this logic it can be seen that, for example, if ten related species are to be studied, and it is felt that there are about seven subpopulations within each species, and further that three representatives are needed per subpopulation, the total number of OTUs needed would amount to 210. With a three-to-one ratio of characters to OTUs, about 630 characters would need to be measured. Even the hardest-working systematist will blanch at such a large number of characters. And of course it may not be possible to find that many characters to measure for many organizations.

The best solution to the problem of overly large numbers of characters is to more carefully delimit the number of populations considered at one time. Several analyses may be used, each including different sets of OTUs, until a picture of all OTUs in relation to each other is built up. It may take many different computer runs before it is clear that all appropriately related OTUs have been included in the same solution.

*Nunnally (1978) recommended a ten-to-one ratio.

TABLE 11.1

CHARACTER-TO-CASE RATIOS FOR RECENT NUMERICAL TAXONOMIC STUDIES

Study	Characters	Cases	Ratio	Discipline
Moss, Peterson, and Atyeo (1977)	111	61	1.8/1	Biology*
Schnell, Best, and Kennedy (1978)	82	24	3.4/1	
Lidicker (1973)	64	28	2.3/1	
Ciochon and Corruccini (1977)	10	18	.55/1	
Baum and Lefkovitch (1978)	36	16	2.3/1	
Moulton (1978)	74	23	3.2/1	
Christenson and Read (1977)	64	9	7.1/1	Archeology
Haas, Hall, and Johnson (1966)	99	75	1.3/1	Organizations
Pugh *et al.* (1968)	16	52	.31/1	
Goronzy (1969)	29	50	.58/1	
Dodder (1969)	101	100	1.01/1	

Average ratio from biology = 2.4/1 (not including the Ciochon and Corruccini study, in which the number of characters was severely limited by the main case in the study—the fossilized shoulder joint of a European Miocene primate).

Average ratio from the organizational studies = .88/1.

*All the biological studies are from recent issues of *Systematic Zoology* and include the total population published from 1973.

11.3.2 The Exemplar Method

When a group is well known, biological systematists often alleviate the problem of sample size by arbitrarily selecting one member (or two when each sex needs to be represented) to represent the group. Sneath and Sokal (1973, p. 183) have termed this the method of exemplars. This method works best when the level of homogeneity within the group is exceedingly high. In any event the method of exemplars requires that the systematist be satisfied that the variation within groups is considerably less than between groups. In biology, since most species are well identified by orthodox methods, systematists may readily take advantage of the exemplar method knowing that variations within species are very much less than variations between species. The exemplar method is of dubious value even in biology and I cannot recommend it for organizational systematists since the definition of species is so vague and variations in character states are so high.

There are two general ways the exemplar method may be used in practice, if it is used. First, one actual member is chosen to represent a group. Of course, the member chosen must represent the central tendency of a group as much as possible. The second way is to construct an artificial representative by taking an average score for each character across all members of a group. This may be either the arithmetic mean or, if outliers are a problem, the mode or median of each character may be used.

To keep the number of OTUs to a manageable size most studies of higher categories may use exemplars to represent species. Needless to say, the quality of these studies directly depends on how well the species were clustered and defined and how well the exemplar represents the group. It is also possible that some studies of higher categories will start with genera or families or some other higher category as OTUs, whereupon the exemplars would be selected to represent the higher group.

Fortunately, organizational systematists are getting started on numerical taxonomic methods at a time when the advent of fourth- and fifth-generation computers offers tremendous increases in size and computational speed. These developments mean that program constraints on numbers of characters and OTUs are less of a problem. Eventually, however, the upper bound on size will depend much more on the availability of characters to measure and limitations of time and money, rather than on the size limitations of computers. Rather than worrying about the minimum, systematists will be looking for more independent characters so as to be able to process more OTUs. It is the subject of taxonomic characters that is taken up next.

11.4 TAXONOMIC CHARACTERS

Nothing is more fundamental to valid classification than the taxonomic characters used. Thinking about the subject by organizational systematists has yet to approach a level of sophistication commensurate with the complexity of the problem of identifying suitable characters for numerical analyses, or for orthodox methods for that matter. The legacy of essentialism has focused attention on the selection of a few "essential" characters rather than on selecting as many independent characters as possible.

11.4.1 Definition of Taxonomic Characters

According to Mayr (1969, p. 122), taxonomic characters perform two functions:

1. They have a diagnostic aspect uniquely specifying a given taxon; an emphasis on the differentiating properties of taxa is particularly strong at the level of the lower categories.
2. They function as indicators of relationship; this property makes them especially useful in the study of the higher taxa.

For the past couple of centuries orthodox taxonomists have taken the view that a taxonomic character is an attribute that differentiates taxon A from taxon B (Mayr 1969, p. 122). Mayr offered the following definition: "A taxonomic character is any attribute of a member of a taxon by which it differs or may differ from a member of a different taxon" (1969, p. 121). This orthodox view has been criticized by Sneath and Sokal as suffering from a circularity in which "characters are restricted to differences between members of taxa, but the taxa cannot be recognized without the characters themselves being first known" (1973, p. 71). Michener and Sokal (1957) proposed a way around the problem by distinguishing between characters and character states. Characters were defined as a "feature which varies from one kind of organism to another." The kind of variation a character takes for a given organism was defined as its state. Thus for organizations a character is an attribute such as number of hierarchical levels or ratio of staff to production workers, whereas the respective character states for a hypothetical organization might be 4 and 15/73. As you can see, the numerical taxonomist's character state is similar to the orthodox systematist's character definition. Therefore, for organizations, the definition of characters given by Michener and Sokal should be modified to read: *a taxonomic character is a feature that varies from one organization to another.* In this way characters may be defined without any prior suppositions about what kinds or organizations or species or any other groupings may or may not exist. The revised definition immediately above is the one that will be used here.*

Now that it has been established that a character is an attribute that varies, the question arises as to the size or comprehensiveness of an organizational character. As an example, consider the often-used categorization of organizations suggested by Burns and Stalker (1961) into mechanistic versus organic. This could be a character since organizations seem to vary along this scale. But should systematists accept this attribute as one rather all-encompassing character, or should they break it up into narrower characters such as specialized differentiation of functions, abstractness of tasks, level of precision of definition of rights and obligations, use of lateral in addition to vertical information channels, and so on? Burns and Stalker break down the mechanistic-organic scale into some twenty-two lesser attributes. It is possible that some of the lesser attributes could themselves be subdivided on down into infinitesimally narrow characters. Clearly, having too broad a set of

---

*I should note that for cladists useful characters are all those having states that may be identified as being ancestral (plesiomorphic) or derived (apomorphic). The ancestral or derived status is determined from the fossil record.

characters leaves out valuable information, may collapse into one character attributes that vary independently, and makes it harder to achieve a large enough set of characters to retain a healthy ratio between characters and OTUs. However, a vast number of extremely narrow characters would create problems in finding independent measures and would be far beyond the capabilities of most computer programs to process or for systematists to interpret and use.

Ideally there should be some agreement among organizational systematists about just where on the continuum from huge to tiny the most useful organizational characters should lie. This agreement is not at hand and may never be. Of more concern is a single systematist's level of consistency within his or her own study. There is little to be gained by having some characters very narrow while others are broad in scope; the part of the organization measured by several narrow characters would have more weight in determining the grouping than the parts measured by one broad character.

Sneath and Sokal (1973, pp. 72−75) used the concept of *unit character* to refer to the smallest level of information captured by the characters. They defined it as "*a taxonomic character of two or more states, which within the study at hand cannot be subdivided logically except for subdivisions brought about by the method of coding*" (Sneath and Sokal 1973, p. 74; their emphasis). Note that the unit character is defined only in reference to a particular study. Other systematists may define their unit characters differently, though of course the field would move along faster if widespread consistency in definition were achieved fairly rapidly. The above meaning of unit character is parallel to the concept of *unit technological operations* used by Davis and Engelstad (1966) in that both search for indivisible elements. With the concept of unit characters there seems little likelihood, given the complexity of all but the smallest organizations, that systematists will have difficulty building up large pools of characters. Rather the problem will be assuring independence among them and avoiding too many obviously trivial ones.

11.4.2 Homologous Characters in Organizations

One of the more perplexing problems facing taxonomists is that of making sure that comparisons are based on the same parts. A biologist would not want to make the mistake of comparing the front legs of one lizard with the hind legs of another and then concluding that the lizards are not of the same species. Similarly an organizational systematist would not want to compare the attributes of the Management Department at UCLA with those of the History Department at U.C. Berkeley and then conclude that the two universities are not members of the same species. Most of the time it is fairly obvious which parts are the same, but sometimes there are difficulties. Suppose one is comparing an assembly line organization with no automation to a place where the line is automated to the point where there are no laborers at all. Now, should one consider the bottom rank of employees in the automated plant similar to the laborers in the nonautomated plant or to its first-line supervisors?

Are parts the same because they look the same, function the same, are the same relation to other parts, from the same part in an ancestor firm, or all of the above? Traditionally, biological systematists have distinguished between *homologous* parts, defined as those derived from a common ancestor, and *analogous* parts, defined as those which have similar looks or function but cannot be traced back to a common ancestor (Mayr 1969, p. 85). This definition of homology became caught in a circularity in that one of the purposes of orthodox systematics was to delineate organisms according to common ancestry, yet before taxonomic comparisons could be made the systematist had to ascertain which parts were related to a common ancestor. An alternative approach, suggested by Sneath and Sokal (1973, p. 97), is to recognize that there is a continuum from greater to lesser resemblance among the parts of objects being compared, with homologous parts at the extreme of very high similarity, with analogous parts toward the middle having moderate similarity, and with other parts having no similarity at all. Evolutionists and cladists would object to this approach on the grounds that great similarity is not always a good test of homology. I do not have a pat resolution of this conflict. All I can suggest is that one be aware of both possibilities and exercise good judgment. For the time being I will lean toward the approach of Sneath and Sokal. All organizational parts will be viewed as more or less homologous based on similarity, as discussed below.

The problem of homology, in principle, is greater for numerical than for orthodox taxonomists simply because the number of characters used is greater. Presumably the problem will be even greater for organizational systematists because of an anticipated even greater number of characters. Whether homology is more of a problem as unit characters become more narrowly defined remains to be seen. Sneath and Sokal (1973, pp. 82–90) offered an extended discussion of quantitative approaches to ascertaining the level of homology via measures of structural correspondence or phenetic similarity. The suggested approaches are imaginative, thoroughly objective, complicated, and involve considerable effort. They appear to be largely in the experimental phase so far. A more reasonable approach for organizational systematists, at this time at least, is what Sneath and Sokal termed *operational homology*. Characters are operationally homologous "when they are very much alike in general and in particular" (1973, p. 79).

There are three methods of determining whether things are alike or not: external, compositional, and structural. The *external* method of determining homology, whether for a unit character, a set of unit characters, a small or large part, or the organization as a whole, is based on some measure of an attribute which does not depend on knowing what the part is composed of or what its relation to other parts is. The size, inputs, outputs, formalization, flexibility, and so forth of an organization's parts are examples of externally determined homology. Thus subunits of two organizations might be considered homologous because they are geographically remote from the headquarters, score high on measures of bureaucratic structure, are financially controlled by headquarters, send in similar reports and sales orders, and so forth.

The *compositional* method consists of taking two parts and looking very carefully at what they are composed of (their subparts) as a way of determining whether they are homologous. For example, in comparing universities one would identify the major subunits—say, departments. Then for each department one would compare competencies, perhaps by comparing course content and laboratory research activities. One could keep breaking down the part at each level into smaller parts almost indefinitely. Clearly one has to make a cutoff at some point to avoid a ridiculous amount of work. One of the more obvious ways of making a quantitative determination of the level of homology is to apply numerical phenetic methods to the task of determining homology. Thus one could, for some level of parts of organizations, conduct a numerical phenetic analysis of all of their respective subcomponents and then define as homologous all parts clustered together.

The *structural* method looks to the structural relationship or systemic position of parts relative to other parts within the objects being compared. Thus in lizards the pair of legs furthest from the head are termed hind legs and they are compared. Staff groups in organizations are in a certain relationship to line managers. Middle managers are, perhaps, defined as those two levels below the president and two levels above the bottom-level employees. Case workers in social welfare agencies are those who work directly with clients and therefore should be compared with workers in other organizations who deal directly with clients. The main difficulty with the structural method in general is that in comparing parts relative to other parts one has to be sure that the other parts are themselves homologous. To take the poor lizard again, defining the hind legs as those furthest from the head assumes that one has identified the heads of two lizards and that they are homologous parts, and similarly for the backbone, tail, and so on. In comparing two matrix organizations one might want to compare the relation of a particular product unit with various functional units. This would only make sense if one had already ascertained the homology of the various functional units.

The advantage of the external method is that it alone does not require some kind of a "bootstraps" operation. Both the compositional and structural methods at some point in the analysis require an assumption that, respectively, lower-level components are homologous or that other structural units are homologous. Fortunately systematists can use all three, especially for grouping components where the various subparts are taken as characters and similarity coefficients are developed for each pair of components based on the overall similarity of their subparts. But how to determine objectively if subparts in each of two components are truly homologous? Treat the sub-subparts as characters and compute similarity coefficients for each pair of subparts. Those having the highest overall similarity would then be considered homologous and would be compared to determine whether the components were similar. Now it can be seen why, if pursued rigorously, the quantitative approach is almost unusable. One either makes a quantitative determination of simi-larity coefficients at *all* levels in the hierarchy of components, subparts, sub-subparts, and so on to the very smallest part possible (what Schwab [1960] called *atomistic reductionism*), or one arbitrarily stops at some level, judges subjectively that the lower-level subparts are homologous, and compares the parts above this level quantitatively (what Schwab termed *molecular reductionism*). There is no reasonable way to avoid subjective judgments by systematists about homologous parts—the only question is which is the best level in an organization at which to shift from an objective comparison to a subjective one.

11.4.3 Kinds of Characters

Though it is not necessarily obvious in print, a good many organiza-tional systematists seem to be looking for "the list" of characters they can use for classification. Somewhere lurking out there, they feel, is the perfect list that, presumably, all systematists should use, and if used will provide the best possible classification scheme. This is a pipe dream. There is no all-encompassing list, except perhaps for classification at the highest rank categories, where the OTUs are divisions or classes. In-stead, as in biology, many if not most characters useful in one genus or family will differ substantially from those most central to characterizing other groupings. For example, most characters essential in helping differentiate large matrix forms would be useless in classifying small businesses, schools, or voluntary associations. Furthermore, if a very large generalized list including many characters irrelevant for certain organizations is used, the organizations will be grouped together not according to characters they have in common but rather because of the many more characters they do not possess.

Therefore, while the purpose of this section is to develop a categorization of major kinds of characters, there is no intent whatever to offer any suggestion of specific characters to be used in any given study. It is likely but not a certainty that most classification studies will include characters reflecting all of the major categories, but each category may be represented by nonoverlapping sets of measurements. In principle a systematist's first priority should be to define as taxonomic characters all attributes that show independent variation for the species studied. Lists of categories should not be used as constraints about what to include or what not to include, but rather as guidelines about where to look in the event that all possible attributes are not already well known.

One of the earliest lists of categories of characters was suggested by Sells (1964). It is shown in table 11.2. Perhaps reflecting the state of the field, it first lists categories of attributes of people working in organizations, such as abilities, traits, and demographic characteristics. Hall (1979) also began his comments about characters with the mention of personnel characteristics. In contrast, McKelvey (1979) omitted such attributes in his category list. To the extent that individuals in organizations are randomly distributed as to personal attributes, the inclusion of such characters would not aid the grouping of organizations. But if there are indications of considerable self-selection of employees of certain characteristics into particular organizations, or if there is reason to believe that organizations as a matter of practice, say for purposes of enhancing survival, recruited certain kinds of people, or if it became apparent that some organizational forms were inherently associated with certain kinds of people, then the avoidance of personnel characteristics could decrease the efficacy of an organizational classification. Sells estimated that, if elaborated, the full list of individual difference variables could reach at least 500. If so, not only would this be cumbersome but individual differences would probably outweigh organizational differences. An added problem with using measures of individuals is that organizational systematists will routinely have to collect survey samples of organizational employees, greatly raising the difficulties of gaining resources to conduct studies of many organizations, not to mention the increased resistance to participation by many organizations. In short, a decision to include individual difference measures will

TABLE 11.2

THE SELLS CATEGORIZATION OF TAXONOMIC CHARACTERS*

A. Personnel Characters

    1. Abilities (aptitudes and acquired skills).

    2. Motivational traits.

    3. Stylistic personality traits.

    4. Biologic and constitutional factors: age; sex; height; weight; coloring; somatotype; appearance; ethnic origins; physical handicaps; genetic factors.

    5. Social and demographic factors: education; social class; economic status; geographic-culture exposures; family background; siblings; family relations; marital status; citizenship; legal status (military service, voting, parole, etc.); occupational experience and status; responsibilities and dependencies; possessions; religious background and practice; linguistic background; group memberships; reference groups; roles.

    6. Motivations related to participation in the situation: relations of individuals' goals to those of the organization; identification with the organization; identification with other organizations and groups; identification with role in organization, problem, or task with other participants; attitudes re locale, situation, and conditions of participation.

    7. Relationships among participants: previous interactions among participants; role relationships in organization and their stability; dependencies among participants; social and cultural normative characteristics of participants (distribution).

B. Group and Organizational Characters

    1. Characteristics of group task or problem, situation, and setting. Factors defined by the primary task (for each separate task group):

        Area and level of knowledge and skills required.

        Hazards and risks involved.

        Novelty of situation to participants.

        Procedures permitted.

        Information required and available.

        Number of participants, required, permitted, or available.

        Material and facilities.

        Degree of personal contact involved.

        Role expectations regarding participants.

    2. Group structure.

        Stability of reciprocal expectations achieved by group; time in operation; reorganization, turnover.

        Formal structure: intragroup patterns.

        Group goals: definiteness; clarity; relation to basic objectives; relations to personnel capabilities and facilities; unusual aspects.

        Membership patterns: requirements of experience; training; special qualifications; restrictive requirements (age, sex, race, religion, etc.); permeability of entrance and exit conditions; voluntary nature; time commitments.

        Control of group members: freedom of movement, goals, expression, dress, schedules; regulations re conduct, work, living arrangements; rituals, ceremonies, standard operating procedures; regulation of group procedures; work controls; regulation of participation in activities; communication channels and practices.

        Stratification; status hierarchy; power structure.

        Modus operandi, including methods of communication, supervisory methods, procedures, decision-making, training.

        Responsibility structure: organization and relationships of roles; departmentalization, division of labor among subgroups; role responsibilities (for what, to whom),

TABLE 11.2 (Continued)

The Sells Categorization of Taxonomic Characters*

B. Group and Organizational Characters (Continued)

power, privilege, prestige; requirements re individual qualifications; space and facility requirements; status mobility provisions.

Rewards; compensation; welfare; provision for individual and group satisfaction; incentives, recreation; benefits.

3. Formal structure: intergroup patterns.

Autonomy of organization and subgroups.

Pattern of centralization-decentralization.

Social status of organization and subgroups ("league standing").

Patterns of dependency, cooperation, competition in relation to other organizations.

Requirements concerning communication and transactions with other organizations.

Operating patterns, including conformity to formal patterns.

Goals.

Membership patterns.

Control.

Stratification, status hierarchy, power structure.

Modus operandi.

Responsibility structure.

Rewards, compensation, welfare, etc.

Intergroup patterns.

Superior-subordinate behavior patterns.

C. Environmental Characters

1. Physical aspects of the environment:

Gravity.

Radiations and radioactive fallout.

Climate and weather: temperature; humidity; atmospheric pressure; oxygen tension; atmospheric changes (winds, storms); rainfall; snow; ice and related phenomena.

Terrain: rivers, lakes, mountains, valleys, deserts, forests, swamps, coastal plains; elevation, erosion; earthquakes, etc.

Natural resources: sources of food (fish, game, vegetation, crops), shelter, clothing; minerals; timber; water.

Culture products: facilities and technology related to transportation, power, communication, construction, manufacturing, distribution, agriculture, housing, habitability, warfare; characteristics and location of centers of population industry, government, education, research, entertainment, recreation, arts.

2. Social aspects of the environment:

Nonmaterial culture: ascriptive solidarities (family, kinship, relationship systems; ethnic solidarities; primary groups; territorial community); occupation and economy (economic institutions, organization of the economy, units of the economy, economic trends); stratification and mobility of the population (class, occupation, social stratification); political organization and authority (political power, political organizations); religion and society; linguistic patterns; education; law; the arts, recreation, and entertainment; technology; science, value systems, beliefs, symbolic systems, health and welfare.

Social and economic states: level of the economy, health, education, crime, morality, morale, intergroup tensions, cold war, strikes, disasters, etc.

Factors defined by locales and geographic setting of the organization: physical and social factors peculiar to locales, remoteness, physical restraints (communication,

TABLE 11.2 (Continued)

THE SELLS CATEGORIZATION OF TAXONOMIC CHARACTERS*

C. Environmental Characters (Continued)

travel, mobility), parameters of nonmaterial culture, social and economic states applicable to sites and locales of operation.

Relations with other organizations: hierarchical relations with parent and subordinate organizations, sources of support, competitive organizations, sources of threat and conflict; relations with unions, clients, regulatory agencies, trade associations, community groups, eleemosynary agencies, etc.

*From S. B. Sells, "Toward a Taxonomy of Organizations," in *New Perspectives in Organization Research*, ed. by W. W. Cooper, H. J. Leavitt, and M. W. Shelly II. New York: Wiley. 1964. Reprinted by permission of the publisher.

have far-reaching consequences in the design and implementation of classification studies.

Since the increased difficulties of carrying out studies that include individual difference measures outweigh the uncertain benefit of possibly accounting for added bases of organizational differences, the most prudent course for the time being is to avoid individual difference variables. They should not be included just "because they are there." However, it is possible that a limited number of individual measures will be important bases of differences in organizational form. For example it may be that police organizations are most effective as a form when tall, beefy, somewhat authoritarian individuals are hired, or that universities are distinguished from teaching-oriented colleges, in part, because the former hire "prima donna" professors with strong egos and Ph.D. degrees.

The foregoing examples may also show the way out of having to include individual difference measures. Most likely, if an organization seems to have a nonrandom selection of employees, there will be complementary differences between other measures that are not personnel differences. Thus, police departments probably will possess dominant competence characteristics in their structure, function, and process which have developed over the years in consequence to the same environmental constraints that led to the selection of large, beefy officers. Consequently the approach advocated here is to avoid individual difference measures until it is apparent that they offer a significant basis of organizational differences not reflected in any other categories of characters. While experience may demonstrate otherwise, it is expected that individual difference measures of employees will prove unnecessary. Needless to say, despite the view taken here, this is an empirical question and will undoubtedly be put to the test.

Concurrent in time with Sells's thinking about taxonomy, Pugh and his colleagues at Aston began a major study of organizations. Part of their study was devoted to developing a seemingly exhaustive set of dimensions of organizational structure. These were published in Pugh et al. (1968) and are shown in table 11.3. The dimensions were all designed to be measured via one or a few interviews with key members of an organization and thus avoided the problem of conducting a large survey to learn about individual differences between employees. In their approach they measured what top managers "officially expected" should be done, not what actually was done. They chose measures that as much as possible avoided employees' perceptions of organizational structure, instead concentrating on objective measures. They began with a huge number of items and refined these down to sixty four characters, though only sixteen of these were used in the subsequent factor analysis (Pugh et al. 1969).

While Sells's categorization is fairly well balanced over most aspects of organizations, including dominant competence (showing up in the group characters), the Aston categories are largely limited to the main Weberian variables traditionally thought to comprise formal organizational structure: specialization, standardization, formalization, and centralization. Extras are a set of workflow configuration variables and traditionalism. The focus was on the organization as a whole.

Separated geographically, though not in time, from the Aston study, the empirical, numerical taxonomic approach of Haas et al. (1966) was the first cluster analysis of organizational groupings. Their initial catalog of characters amounted to 210 relatively discrete attributes, which were reduced to a list containing 36 categories of characters. All individual-difference variables that would have required a survey of employees were omitted. They distinguished between the "official" or formal structure and the "performance" structure as described by top executives; the latter was the one ostensibly tapped by their measures.*
Their 36 categories, shown in table 11.4, emphasized structural attributes of organizations as wholes, though via different measures than the Aston group, with very little emphasis on ecological measures or subcomponent characteristics.

---

*However, it should be noted that while both Pugh et al. and Haas et al. interviewed top managers, the former felt they were getting the official view while the latter thought they were getting information about actual performance. It is possible that executives—at least some, anyway—could give an interviewer a fairly clearly demarcated view of either official or actual practice if the interview context fostered a discussion and comparison of both. Given an evolutionary/ecological approach, where organizational survival depends on performance rather than official dogma, systematists should logically emphasize actual practice, what Perrow (1961) termed *operative* goals.

TABLE 11.3*

THE ASTON CATEGORIZATION OF TAXONOMIC CHARACTERS

Scale number of dimension	Scale title
Specialization	
51.01	Functional specialization
51.02–51.17	Specializations no. 1–16
51.18	Qualifications
51.19	Overall role specialization (51.02–51.15, and 51.17)
Standardization	
52.00	Overall standardization
52.01	Procedures defining task and image
52.02	Procedures controlling selection, advancement, etc.
Formalization	
53.00	Overall formalization
53.01	Role definition
53.02	Information passing
53.03	Recording of role performance
Centralization	
54.00	Overall centralization of decisions
	Criteria to evaluate performance:
54.01	Finance
54.02	Costs
54.03	Time
54.04	Quality
54.05	Labor relations
54.06	Output volume
54.07	Decisions affecting whole organization
54.08	Decisions affecting subunits of organization
54.09	Decisions affecting individual
54.10	Autonomy of organization to make decisions
Configuration	
55.08	Chief executive's span of control
55.09	Subordinate ratio
55.42	Status of specializations
55.43	Vertical span (height) of workflow hierarchy
55.44	Direct workers (%)
55.46	Female direct workers (%)
55.47	Workflow superordinates (%)
55.48	Non-workflow personnel (%)
55.49	Clerks (%)
55.50–55.65	Size of specializations (%)
Traditionalism	
56.00	

*From D. S. Pugh, D. J. Hickson, C. R. Hinings, and C. Turner, "Dimensions of Organizational Structure," *Administrative Science Quarterly*, 13:65–105, (© 1968). Reprinted by permission of the *Administrative Science Quarterly*.

TABLE 11.4*

THE HAAS *et al.* CATEGORIZATION OF TAXONOMIC CHARACTERS

1. Organizational goals and objectives
2. Major activities of the organization
3. Basic organizational character or orientation
4. General levels of workers (members)
5. Major divisions or departments (horizontal differentiation)
6. Vertical and horizontal complexity (combined index)
7. Geographical dispersion of personnel and facilities
8. Interdependency of departments
9. Concreteness of positional descriptions
10. Committees and boards
11. Organizational control (source of major policy decisions)
12. Centralization of authority
13. Formalization of authority structure
14. Communication structure
15. Dependence on written rules and policies
16. Penalties for rule violation
17. Emphasis on status distinctions
18. Manner in which new members enter the organization
19. Orientation program
20. In-service training program
21. Distinctions regarding types of organizational members (non-hierarchical)
22. Number of members, with extent of variation in size of departments
23. Turnover of membership, by level (per year)
24. Planned limit on size
25. Restrictions on membership
26. Dependency on other organizations
27. Other organizations dependent on one studied
28. Competition with other organizations
29. Governmental control and regulation
30. Supply of potential members
31. Share of potential customer market
32. Geographic factors as a handicap
33. Primary sources of income
34. Financial condition of the organization
35. Age of organization
36. Shifts in major activities throughout history of the organization

*From J. E. Haas, R. H. Hall, N. J. Johnson, "Toward an Empirically Derived Taxonomy of Organizations," in *Studies on Behavior in Organizations*, ed. by R. V. Bowers. Athens: University of Georgia Press. 1966. Reprinted by permission of the publisher.

The most elaborate and comprehensive categorization of taxonomic characters to date is the one suggested by Warriner (1979, p. 35), which is a revision of his earlier list (Warriner 1977). He said that "from the array of current approaches we can extract four basic definitions of organizations according to whether they are viewed as (a) technical (purposeful) systems, (b) social systems (human organizations), (c) administered or power systems, or (d) cultural (belief) systems." He argued that all of these definitions should be accounted for in any character list. He defined the *technical* system as

> a set of recurrent, organized, and interrelated (purposeful, technical, or work) *activities* through which *raw materials* (physical, human, or symbolic) taken from the environment are *transformed* into *values* (products, services) that are (directly or indirectly) *exchanged* with the environment (i.e., other actors) for the *resources* (personnel, facilities, tools, capital, etc.) needed to maintain the activities. [1979, p. 35; his emphasis]

Major attributes of the technical system included:

1. Activity system characteristics (kinds of activities, nature of their articulation, multiplicity of activity systems, etc.).
2. The character and quantities of raw materials used and values produced.
3. Character and quantity of resources (e.g., capital or labor intensity, mechanization, employee skill, variety and levels used, etc.).
4. Frequency and character of the transactions (input-output relations) through which flow the raw materials, values, and resources. [1979, pp. 35–36]

Warriner defined the *social* system as

> a set of *social positions* (offices, statuses, task positions, departments, divisions) occupied by *human beings* and interconnected by patterns of *relationship* (roles) through which (among other things) technical activities are organized, articulated, allocated to positions, and performed. [1979, p. 36; his emphasis]

Major attributes included

1. Structural characteristics (number and kinds of positions, structuring principles used, their interconnections, etc.).
2. The processes and criteria used by which persons are allocated to positions and move from and to positions.
3. Modes and patterns of relationships.
4. Division of labor (relation of social system to technical system). [1979, p. 36]

He defined the *power* system as:

> [a set] of explicit and implicit directives (orders, instructions, rules, etc.) through which actors in certain positions define the actions desired of those in other positions, along with *inducements* (rewards and punish-

ments whether coercive, instrumental, or normative) that are differentially allocated to persons and positions according to recurrent procedures and criteria. [1979, p. 36]

Major attributes included:

1. The authority (directives) structure and the power (inducements alloca-tion) structure and their interconnections.
2. The character of the directive system (degree centralized, scope, "tight-ness" of control through feedback reports, etc.).
3. The inducement allocation structure and procedures.
4. The relation of each to the technical activity system.
5. Transactions with environment through which directives flow to and from organizations. [1979, p. 36]

The *cultural* system was defined as

several sets of "*collective representations*" (sensu Durkheim), that is, be-liefs, ideas, conceptions in the form of "facts," norms, and values that are accepted as true, pertinent, and operative by virtue of participation in the organization and . . . the activity, power, and social structure through "logics" (sensu Warner) of application and use. [1979, p. 36]

Major attributes included:

1. The techn*ology* (in the strict sense of the word)—the facts, norms, and values which constitute the beliefs related to the technical system activities, the raw materials and values produced.
2. The psych*ology* or beliefs that concern persons (participants, clients, consumers, others).
3. The soci*ology* or beliefs about the structure including those which legitimate the power and authority systems.
4. These various belief systems are often derived from external sources; hence we need to be concerned with the transactions through which such ideologies flow. [1979, p. 37]

Table 11.5 shows Warriner's categorization of characters as presented in his 1979 paper. Warriner recognized the difficulties in measuring indi-vidual as opposed to organizational characters but felt that they "may be worth including especially if a theoretical argument justifies each" (1979, p. 38).

McKelvey (1978) suggested a set of categories, shown in table 11.6, built around major headings drawn from Mayr (1969). The second head-ings are organizationally rather than biologically relevant. No doubt each second heading could be broken down into still further categories,

TABLE 11.5*

THE WARRINER CATEGORIZATION OF TAXONOMIC CHARACTERS

1. *Activity System Characteristics.* (a) "purpose(s)" (interpreted as defined by the nature of the work-flow activities and raw materials, e.g., "teaching-primary," "retailing-grocer," "processing-steel," "counselling-marriage," etc.) characteristics including "goal diversity," (b) degree of differentiation of tertiary (administrative), and secondary (supervisory) activities from those who perform primary (work flow) activities, (c) degree and nature of division of labor, (d) forms of interconnection or contingency of work flow activities, (e) etc.

2. *Epiphysial Environment.* I introduce this term (from the Greek *epiphysis*, for "a growth upon") to refer to those kinds of materials that are not activity, social organization, power, authority or culture, but which are necessary adjuncts to most activity systems, viz: facilities used, tools and machines employed and personnel (as contrasted with participant—see #9) characteristics (gender, age, prior training, skill attainment, etc.)

3. *Transactions with Environment.* 3.1 *directives* (a) presence, absence, scope of directives from parent or sponsoring organization, from licensing and accreditation organizations, from governmental agencies (IRS, OSHA, FDA, etc.), from peer organization associations, from labor or employee associations, etc. 3.2 *input-output transactions.* (b) measures which define the rates, frequency, etc. of flows of raw materials, personnel, capital and loans, tools and machine acquisition, etc. and which define the rates, calendarity, and "demand" for output values, and (c) measures which define the contingency between value user (client, consumer) populations and resource suppliers, etc.

4. *Structural features.* Those descriptive of the social structure as described in the structure definition above, including measures describing the "morphology" of the structure, the degree of differentiation of administrative, supervisory, and work force components, etc.

5. *Internal Process ("metabolic") features.* (a) technical processes—forms of structuring of technical ("throughput") activities, (b) authority and control forms and processes—flow of directives and reports, resource allocation processes, (c) reward system processes, (d) personnel flow processes, (e) decision making processes, (f) information and culture flow processes.

6. *Cultural characteristics.* Measures which describe the nature of the belief systems as indicated in the cultural definition above including classification as to external reference systems ("free enterprise," "science," etc.).

7. *Scale of operations.* Includes the various indicators of "size" such as (a) number of participants, (b) area scope of market or clients served, (c) net worth, (d) processing capacity (number of units of raw materials that can be handled), etc. Although such measures are not directly suggested by the definitions, they lie back of such definitions. Two problems are particularly relevant to this category: (a) it is difficult to find operational definitions for some measures that are comparable across different types of organizations (e.g., how to compare number of beds, tons of raw materials, student-teacher ratio?); and (b) some measures may be direct functions of others so that there is a danger of redundancy and consequent "loading" on a single dimension.

8. *Origin and Life History Characteristics.* Some hypotheses (e.g., Stinchcombe) suggest that date of origin becomes a crucial fact in the effect of larger social facts on organizational design; similarly, age (maturity) or length of time since last major structural or technical reorganization have been suggested as important factors in the character of organizations. Others have suggested that organizations go through cyclical stages. A number of characters representing these kinds of hypotheses but not suggested by the four basic definitions might be considered.

9. *Participant Characteristics.* (Compare with "personnel" characteristics described under 2). Hypotheses from various sources (human relations school in particular, but also

TABLE 11.5* (Continued)

The Warriner Categorization of Taxonomic Characters

many psychological theories) suggest that organizations must adapt to or are constrained by the state of (variable) participant characteristics, especially attitudinal ones, such as "morale," "loyalty" and "professional commitment," "job satisfaction," and the like. In addition, certain structural theories suggest that social positions have accompanying "persona" characteristics which constrain the kinds of personality characteristics presented by their occupants (for example, salesman, waitress, or flight attendant character in different companies). Many of these characteristics present special difficulties in measurement, but may be worth including especially if a theoretical argument justifies each.

10. *Environmental Characteristics.* There is a theoretical question about the appropriateness of including environmental variables per se in taxonomic studies. However, certain environmental variables measure (a) the degree of dependency of an organization upon its environment (for raw materials, training of personnel, etc.), and (b) the degree of autonomy-heteronomy of the organization with respect to directives from environmental agents. These may be more indicative of the organization than of the particular environment and thus might be included. Other environmental features might include (c) measures of environmental complexity, whether fine or coarse grained, and stable-chaotic character. Similarly, (d) we might wish to include measures of the number of peer organizations (competitors), and (e) actual share of client-consumer, activity-purpose, activity-mode, personnel, raw material or other domains.

Finally, as in any only partially deductive listing we should include a category 11. *Other Features* to encompass other characters that may be suggested.

*From C. K. Warriner, "Empirical Taxonomies of Organizations: Problematics in Their Development," presented at the American Sociological Association (Roundtable Discussion), Boston, 1979. Reprinted by permission of the author.

with specific characters and character states still to follow. Thus there are at least 22 fairly broad or abstract character categories that are relevant in measuring organizations, each multiplying into several specific characters and states. It does not take much imagination to see that such categories as general formal structural, internal morphology, variance characteristics, metabolic flow, workplace throughput processes, environmental characters, and input-output characteristics can be readily expanded into 20 or 30 characters each, easily bringing the total set of characters above the 200 to 300 mark.

The character category lists suggested by Pugh et al. and Haas et al. offered evidence that some, if not most, categories in the Sells, Warriner, or McKelvey lists can be greatly expanded, depending on the level of detail a systematist is interested in and the resources available. The broad scope of the latter lists indicates that many categories are available to be expanded. The problem facing systematists is not one of struggling to find characters, as Warriner (1979) also observed, but rather one of either mounting the effort and finding resources to handle a large number of characters or else finding ways to reduce the set without damaging the overall validity of the resultant descriptions of organizations.

TABLE 11.6

THE MCKELVEY CATEGORIZATION OF TAXONOMIC CHARACTERS*

1. Morphological Characters
   a. General formal structural (formalization, specialization, levels, etc.)
   b. Special structures (technical, accounting, control, planning systems, etc.)
   c. Internal morphology (workflow configuration, div. of labor, staff groups, etc.)
   d. Subunit characteristics (kinds of subunits, formal-informal nature, etc.)
   e. Variance characteristics (variance in subunit size, formality, etc.) (Pinder and Moore 1979)
   f. Interdependency networks (coordination structures, etc.)
2. Physiological (process and functional) Characters
   a. Metabolic flows (personnel, communications, workflow rates, etc.) (Warriner 1977)
   b. Managerial functions and processes (decision making, conflict handling, etc.)
   c. Adaptation and change characteristics (managerial succession, changes in influence postures, etc.)
   d. Workplace throughput and conversion processes (assembly lines, work stages, etc.)
3. Ecological Characters
   a. Environmental (physical, cultural, economic, social, technical, etc.)
   b. Epiphysical (buildings, layouts, personnel characteristics, etc.) (Warriner 1977)
   c. Dependency networks (on others, by subcontractors, etc.)
   d. Environmental variances (diversity, dynamism, uncertainty changes, etc.)
   e. Input-output characteristics (supplies, products, information, energy, etc.)
4. Behavioral Characteristics (nontransient)
   a. Attacker, avoider, achiever styles, etc. (Bell 1974)
   b. Competitive posture (monopolistic, oligarchic, etc.)
   c. Human resource posture (conserver, user, developer of people, etc.)
5. Geographic Characters
   a. Location patterns (local, national, multinational, etc.)
   b. Product distribution patterns
   c. Employee recruitment patterns
   d. Variance in cultural-social forms dealt with

*From Bill McKelvey, "Organizational Systematics: Taxonomic Lessons from Biology," *Management Science*, 24: 1428–1440, 1978. Reprinted by permission of the editor.

11.4.4 Selection and Weighting of Characters

Each organizational form has sets of phenotypic and genotypic attributes. The task of systematists is to find a parsimonious set of taxonomic characters that come as close as possible to a perfect image of one or both of these attribute sets. One way of finding the ideal set is to rather exhaustively identify the total population of characters available for measuring each organizational form. Besides being a practical impossibility, such a set may (1) contain many trivial characters, (2) contain many that more or less overlap others, (3) give too little weighting to some important characters, or (4) include characters that inadvertently lead to measuring some attributes more than others, thus overly weighting their influence on the final outcome. The problem reduces to, first, finding a set of characters that can be measured in a manageable way for all organizations to be studied and, second, deciding whether or not some characters should be weighted more than others. Since the organizations to be classified probably have not as yet been thoroughly described, the problem is how to decide what selection and weighting approach will produce an image closest to an organizational form's attributes while we still have only a very fuzzy view of what those attributes might be.

Character Selection

In the classification of phenomena where both genotypic and phenotypic attributes are known to exist and where it cannot be readily assumed that they are isomorphic, there is the choice of attempting to have character sets reflect either the genotype, the phenotype, or both. In biology numerical taxonomists have mostly settled on phenotypic characters, though recently there has been increasing interest in chemotaxonomy (classification based on genetic material such as protein sequence studies, serology, and nucleic acid pairing). Early numerical systematists felt that numerical phenetics could help discover genotypic factors differentiating species, and later chemotaxonomists have felt that chemotaxonomy would result in better classifications because its focus was on characters related more closely to the genotype (see Sokal and Sneath [1963] and Sneath and Sokal [1973] for a fuller discussion of these issues). This hope has not proven false, but neither has there been much progress toward broad-scale genotypically based classifications. The relation between genotype and phenotype has proved to be very complex.

Given that the relation between genotype and phenotype is still not fully understood in biology, a well worked out science compared to organizational science, it probably does not make sense at this time for organizational systematists to worry about just where along the dimension of genotypic to phenotypic attributes characters are selected. It could be, however, that the relation between genotype and phenotype among organizational forms is fairly clear compared to the case in biology, but since this is not yet known we still cannot worry too much about whether to pick genotypic or phenotypic characters. Some characters may be closer to reflecting attributes of the underlying compool than others, but until a theory of organizational differences is established more soundly, and with it the concept of the compool and the distinction of compool elements from phenotypical attributes of organizations, it seems prudent to ignore such fine distinctions.

If organizational systematists eschew the distinction between genotype and phenotype, what is left is the task of cutting a possibly too-large total population of characters down to a more practical size. The problem is, how to do this without inadvertently over- or underselecting certain characters and thereby over- or underrepresenting certain organizational attributes? The best advice, very simply, is *don't*. While certain analytical methods, most obviously factor analysis, seem like they might offer a way out, remember that to reduce the rank of a data matrix by factor analysis one still has to collect measures on all of the characters as inputs to the factor solution; thus none of the effort in collecting data is really avoided.

If you must have fewer characters, the best answer is Guideline 4 from McKelvey (1975): "Use a probability sampling plan for selecting a sample of organizational attributes [characters]" (p. 516). Actually this guideline can be improved upon if a broad, theoretically sound set of categories is available, perhaps such as those suggested by Warriner or McKelvey. Rather than take a random sample of the total population of characters and run the risk of leaving out some categories, a better idea would be to take a stratified random sample, making sure that each category is represented, with the number of characters taken within each category proportionate to the total number of characters in each category.

The *nexus hypothesis* in biological systematics assumes that every phenetic character offers information about several underlying genetic factors and, conversely, that most genes affect several characters (Sneath and Sokal 1973, p. 96). The implication of the hypothesis is that there exists a redundancy such that the genetic differences that have evolved are each reflected in more than one character. This means that the underlying differences among species can be tapped accurately even though some phenotypic attributes are not actually measured by characters. If the same hypothesis holds true for organizations, then each underlying cause of organizational differentiation—that is, each compool element—will be redundantly reflected in more than one phenotypic character. Consequently, a random selection of characters within each subcategory, or within an even finer partitioning of categories, is not likely to miss any significant attributes.

There is even the possibility that leaving out some categories will not have too much of an effect on the validity of the end result. Another proposition from biological systematics, the *hypothesis of non-specificity*, assumes that there are no distinct groupings of genes that exclusively affect one category of characters. Translated into organizational terms, this means that there is no grouping of compool elements that affect exclusively one category. If this hypothesis is true for organizations it would mean that, for example, a study based on formal structural characteristics, such as the one by Pugh et al. (1968) or Haas et al. (1966), would produce a classification very similar to one based on a total sample of all categories. But some categories are apt to produce solutions closer to ones based on the total sample of characters than are other categories. Caution is warranted here. Even in biology, where there is presumably a much tighter relation between genotype and phenotype than we have reason to believe prevails for organizations at this time, the similarity coefficients of comparisons between categories range from .17 to .79 (Sneath and Sokal 1973, pp. 101–103).

In conclusion, the best bet for character selection is, first, to try to avoid it by using all but the most obviously trivial characters; second, to spend time developing as elaborate and comprehensive a categorization of characters as possible; and third, to take a stratified random sampling of as many characters within each category as can be managed.

Character Weighting

One of the more heated debates between orthodox and numerical systematists in biology has to do with character weighting. Since these arguments will not be presented in detail here, the interested reader should be sure to read the discussions of the subject by Mayr (1969), Sneath and Sokal (1973), and others. There is an inescapable logic in favor of both sides of the debate, a point often seemingly missed by the major contenders.

The main point *in favor* of weighting is that once a classification of species is worked out it is quite clear that some characters are very important while others are trivial and unreliable. The main point *against* weighting is that until a classification is known it is impossible to know which characters are most important, and therefore it is premature to weight characters before entering them into a numerical analysis. In biological systematics both points of view are justifiable. There have been some 200 years of experience in orthodox classification; classifications are well accepted and it is known which characters are important and which are trivial. To traditionalists such as Mayr it would seem to be a mistake to ignore all of this experience. However, the numerical taxonomists started with the premise that numerical solutions offered an alternative to the more subjective side of orthodox systematics and they felt it did not make sense to begin by running the risk of biasing the more "objective" numerical solutions with possibly mistaken traditional weightings.

The situation is different in organizational systematics. There is no accepted orthodoxy and no accepted classification. We are very much at the beginning. We do not know which characters might eventually be more important; thus we have virtually no grounds at all for weighting some characters more than others at this time. Even if one accepts an evolutionary theory of organizations and therefore believes that evolutionarily important characters should be given more weight (a basic argument of Mayr's and one which in principle I subscribe to) it is impossible to know at this time which characters are evolutionarily more important. The only recourse now seems to be equal weighting.

Fortunately, the supposed discrepancy between solutions based on weighted versus unweighted characters is not likely to be too large for at least two reasons. First, as is true in biology, evolutionarily important organizational subcomponents, being more highly evolved, also tend to be more complex and have more characters available to measure. This trend of "negative entropy" is a central element of general systems theory as applied to organizations (Katz and Kahn 1978, p. 25). Thus subcomponents described by relatively more characters will have more influence on the total numerical solution. As Sneath and Sokal (1973, p. 109) noted, just because *unit characters* are given equal weight does not mean that complexes of characters, such as those describing particular organs or organizational subcomponents, do not have more impact. Second, as the total pool of characters used increases, the impact of a single character diminishes; hence whether or not it is weighted has less bearing on the outcome.

It is conceivable that *trivial* characters, those which have little evolutionary importance and thus have little constructive role in differentiating organizational forms, can obscure a numerical solution if there are too many of them. For example, if a product-moment correlation is used as a coefficient to show the similarity between two very much alike organizations, it is possible that the twenty really important characters that would form an upward sloping linear plot might be obscured by the fuzzy rounded pattern of many more randomly varying trivial characters. Thus the similarity coefficient could be lowered.

What are the chances that a systematist would end up with a damaging number of trivial characters? It would be very hard to say at this time. While not important, trivial characters are not totally meaningless (they are discussed in the next section and consist of attributes such as the number of steps up to the front door or the height of the smokestack), and therefore are not always easily avoided by a systematist even though he or she is reasonably knowledgeable about the structure, function and process of organizations. In the absence of careful tracing of the evolutionary development of a particular group of organizational forms, coupled with no prior attempts at classification, one would have little basis to separate evolutionarily important from trivial characters. Once a thorough numerical analysis is completed, a systematist should have little trouble identifying characters having no impact on the solution and dropping them. If it appeared that a large number of characters were candidates to be dropped, one would proceed with caution, leaving randomly chosen trivial characters out of one or more computer runs on a test basis until it is clear that the role of other characters and the form of the solution are not affected by the characters targeted to be dropped.

11.4.5 Inadmissible Characters

There are some kinds of characters that numerical taxonomists have clearly identified as appropriately left out of numerical solutions. The following list is adapted from Sneath and Sokal (1973, pp. 103–106).

Meaningless Characters. Some attributes of organizations clearly have nothing to do with the structure, function, or process of organizations. Nor do they warrant attention because of some role in evolutionary development, present-day indication of such developments, ecological relevance, or ability to discriminate between different kinds of organizational forms even if their evolutionary relevance is not yet fathomable. Characters such as the color of pencils used, the number of rollers on assembly-line racks, the location of water fountains, the number of potted plants, and the hair styles of secretaries would seem to have no bearing on grouping organizations. However, the latter character—hair style—might achieve trivial status if there was reason to think that hair style reflected a broader management style or attitude toward employees. Characters that are so closely tied to environmental fluctuations that their evolutionary role cannot be determined are also useless. Thus for universities, the number of lecturers probably depends on changing student preferences, the number of regular faculty on leave, the availability of interesting guests, and so forth, making it a useless character for taxonomic purposes.

Theoretically Related Characters. If two characters are available which are just different ways of measuring the same underlying attribute, one of them should not be selected. A variable that is simply the sum or product of two others already selected should not be included. If two theoretically distinct but usually highly associated variables are identified, such as level of trust and openness of communications, or centralized decision making and lack of autonomy, one of the pair should be dropped. In general, one should try to base each character chosen on a theoretically independent and unique attribute.

Partially Theoretically Related Characters. Suppose that character B, about to be selected, is thought to be in part logically dependent on character A, already included. Should B be selected? The answer is yes, if there are factors leading to the variation of B (in addition to those affecting A) which are thought to reflect evolutionary developments apt to be important in differentiating one organization from another. If these reflect error or other measurement factors then B should not be included. Thus the number of managers (B) in an organization is due in part to the number of hierarchical levels (A). But in this case B is also affected by the span of control, which could reflect evolutionary trends, so B should be included—unless, of course, the empirical correlation between A and' B was so high (say, 0.7 or higher) as to lead to problems of multicollinearity.

Invariant Characters. Characters that are invariant over the entire sample should not be included since they would add nothing to the solution. Metric computer programs cannot handle such variables anyway since they mean dividing through by zero at some point, and they automatically delete them, come to a halt, or show an error.

Highly Correlated Characters. To what extent should characters that are empirically known to be highly correlated be included in the same numerical solution? Sneath and Sokal (1973, pp. 106–107) take the position of assuming that there are some independent sources of variation in any empirical correlation, unless there is specific information to the contrary. They say that "when we have evidence that more than one factor affects two correlated characters within a study, regardless of whether this evidence comes from within the study or from outside, we would include both characters; otherwise we employ only one" (1973, pp. 105–106). For practical purposes in organizational systematics this probably means that highly correlated characters would always be included, since in organizations there almost always seems to be more than one factor affecting every variable imaginable. The danger is that although the characters actually measured may almost always be shown to have some direct sources of independent variation, there is the risk that the underlying attribute, which presumably is the principal cause of the high correlation, will end up being overrepresented in the final solution if more than one of a highly correlated pair or group of characters is included. In the case of variance-based measures of similarity such as the product-moment correlation, the convention in the social sciences is to avoid the problem of multicollinearity by not including one of a pair of correlated variables if that correlation coefficient reaches the .7 level (or more conservatively, the .6 level). Here, for reasons of statistical calculations, the high correlations are avoided. But for many other measures of similarity or association there is no computational problem caused by including even perfectly correlated characters; the problem becomes one of exercising good judgment by systematists. In conclusion, my view would be that the disadvantage of inadvertently weighting some underlying attributes more than others is worse than the disadvantage of including redundant characters resulting from trying to include all possible characters. Fortunately, organizations being the way they are, the problem of highly correlated empirical measures is usually not too great.

11.5 SUMMARY

The focus of this chapter has been on organizational taxonomic cases and characters. Recognizing that classification studies may not always focus on the classification of individual organizations, *Operational Taxonomic Units* (OTUs) were defined, following Sneath and Sokal (1973), as "the lowest-ranking taxa employed in a given study." While the general approach of this book is to use a species concept as a point of departure, it is possible to begin classification studies without a species concept; probability sampling is clearly the least biased method in this regard. Given a species concept that allows initial identification of subpopulations, the best approach seems to be to use numerical methods to study subtly differing kinds of organizations rather than obviously different ones. Also, an initial focus at the species or population rank category rather than higher categories is suggested, since widely accepted, empirically based species of organizations are not yet identified. The upper limit on a sample of a population is determined by the norm of a three-to-one ratio between characters and cases generally required in the social sciences. The lower limit is determined by the number of different kinds of organizational forms expected to be included in the study. Once species have been identified the *method of exemplars* may be used to reduce the number of cases needed by letting central tendencies represent a species. A *taxonomic character* is defined as "a feature that varies from one organization to another." The concepts of *unit character* and *character state* are also defined. Comparisons of organizations can only be based on *homologous characters*—that is, characters that are the same. The degree of alikeness is determined by one or more of three methods: *external*, *compositional*, and *structural*. There is no such thing as a single character list good for all kinds of organizational forms. However, it is likely that a widely applicable list of broader, more abstract *categories* of characters will be discovered. Several preliminary categorizations of taxonomic characters are presented for use as guidelines in building up populations of characters for organizational species. At this time it does not seem to make sense to distinguish between genotypic and phenotypic characters in making selections. Also, since organizational systematists are just beginning, it does not make sense to weight characters. Since evolutionarily important aspects of organizations are likely to be more complex and therefore involve more characters, these aspects are weighted more in numerical solutions even though all characters are equally weighted. It is important to note that some characters are inadmissible because they are meaningless, invariant, or lack theoretical or empirical independence.

12 NUMERICAL TAXONOMIC METHODS

I hardly want to argue against methodological rigor in science, but I also do not want to see scientific progress sacrificed to it. Invariably methodological rigor is a retrospective exercise, carried on long after all the Nobel prizes have been won.

[Hull 1979, p. 420]

The numerical taxonomists Sneath and Sokal (1973) traced the heritage of their approach back to Michel Adanson, who published his major work on Senegal in 1749, right in the middle of the two decades separating Linnaeus's early work and the publication of his tenth edition of *Systema Naturae* in 1758. Numerical phenetics did not come to full flower, however, until the advent of the electronic computer in the mid-1950s. By this time, 200 years of orthodox taxonomy, rooted in evolutionary theory, had developed a comprehensive classification scheme that the numerical taxonomists have barely chipped at, let alone significantly changed. Modern numerical taxonomy in biology cannot be fully appreciated, therefore, without an understanding of the context provided by the orthodox approach. Its emergence was a case of a brand-new method being started up in the face of a well-entrenched, successful, orthodox approach.

Numerical phenetic methods in organizational systematics begin in a totally different context. At present there is no established taxonomic method or classification scheme in our field, and by contrast numerical methods are relatively well developed, though hardly mature. Consequently this chapter is based on the presumption that organizational systematists will want to place most emphasis on numerical taxonomic methods for the development of actual classification schemes. I also recognize that orthodox and cladistic methods may offer important insights, and I have noted previously that a priori theory and resultant hypothetical classes needed as a point of departure for numerical methods may best be developed via these latter methods. To offer an appropriate context for the development of and emphasis on numerical methods, brief descriptions of orthodox and cladistic methods are given below. (See chapter 3 for further description of orthodox, cladistic, and numerical phenetic theories of classification.)

Mayr (1969) made it quite clear that the orthodox approach to biological systematics has focused on a posteriori weighting of characters. "The weighting of similarities as evidence for relationship is the key operation in this approach" (Mayr 1969, p. 217). Evolutionary theory is used to justify the approach. "Different characters contain very different amounts of information concerning the ancestry of their bearers. WEIGHTING, then, can be defined as a method for determining *the phyletic information content of a character*" (p. 218; his emphasis). Perhaps rebelling a bit against the inroads of the numerical method, Mayr continues, saying that "it is neither necessary nor even possible to give a precise numerical value to the relative weight of each character. Qualitative statements are usually more important than quantitative ones. In order to assign a species to the correct phylum, to know that it has a chorda is more important than a thousand measurements" (p. 218). The basic principles of evolutionist orthodoxy are difficult to elucidate, as even Mayr admitted: "The scientific basis of a posteriori weighting is not entirely clear, but difference in weight somehow results from the complexity of the relationship between genotype and phenotype" (p. 218). A bit later he observed, "No overall treatment of this subject has yet been published, and it is still cloaked in uncertainty" (p. 219). Mayr continued by saying that the orthodox approach works backwards from classifications of natural groupings by identifying the characters delimiting such groupings, but he did not say how such groupings were identified in the first place. While owning up to the trial-and-error flavor of the orthodox method, Mayr, highly critical of cladistic and phenetic methods, sees no alternative. In fairness, the orthodox method appears to have worked so well that the numerical taxonomists seem to have been unable to do more than offer "fine-tuning" alternatives. Few, if any, gross changes seem attributable to their contributions or to those of the cladists. Of the relatively recent books in the field, Simpson's (1961) and Mayr's (1969) appear to offer the best idea for how traditional classification is carried out. The method is as rich and complex as it is uncertain and subjective. For recent discussions of the orthodox, "evolutionary" method see Bock (1973), Mayr (1974), and Ashlock (1979). Organizational systematists probably can learn much from it, especially for working up a priori or "top-down" divisive classificatory schemes.

Cladists eschew overall similarity, whether achieved by the character-weighting methods of the traditionalists or the equal-weighting methods of the numerical pheneticists. The general goal of the cladists is to give primacy to branching patterns. The emphasis is on reconstructing the sequence of phylogenetic branchings. Where a branching has occurred a new group is recognized. As noted in chapter 3, according to Olson cladists are nominalists in that they do not really expect to successfully ground the time of past branchings in empirical reality because of the dimness of the empirical record. Though the time of branchings is nominal, branchings do occur, and the sequence can be extended into the past with perhaps mostly nominal branching times but some that are reasonably well pinpointed. This method is actually rather complex as it is aimed at sorting out unchanging ANCESTRAL characters from DERIVED characters that have changed considerably. The cladistic approach owes much of its development to Hennig (1966). Though Ross (1974) did not label himself a cladist, his book presented a well-developed scheme for separating ancestral from derived characters. It is a good place to learn the basics of this approach. Cladistic methods are complicated and well beyond the scope of this brief description of cladism. For recent discussions of the cladistic, "phylogenetic" method see Farris (1979a,b), Gingerich (1979), Hull (1979), and Nelson (1979). As an analytical approach it deserves serious attention by organizational systematists. It is more "objective" than the orthodox method and should play a useful counter role to the numerical method.

Upon reading Mayr's own admission of the obscure, uncertain, trial-and-error flavor of orthodox systematics, it is easy to understand Sokal and Sneath's unbridled enthusiasm for the apparent objectivity of numerical methods in their first book (1963), dimmed only slightly in their later edition (Sneath and Sokal 1973). But the early dream of true objectivity has been only partially fulfilled. While Sneath and Sokal's work (1973) is an excellent textbook introduction to the mechanics of numerical methods, it is not always the best place to learn about the many places where arbitrary and subjective decisions intrude, largely because of their perhaps overenthusiastic advocacy of their method in place of the orthodox method. In preparing this chapter, therefore, I have tried to highlight places where systematists may markedly influence the results via choice of technique.

Since the various techniques of numerical taxonomy are now well known and generally well detailed in several textbooks—most notably Sneath and Sokal (1973), Hartigan (1975), and Clifford and Stephenson (1975)—there is no need to offer yet another technical treatment showing formulae, derivations, and nuances of several approaches to the same techniques. Jardine and Sibson (1971) offer an excellent treatment of the mathematical underpinnings of the approach. Sneath and Sokal's second edition (1973) is the unquestioned "bible" of the field. It is the most comprehensive and is an absolute necessity for any serious organizational systematist. Bailey (1975) gave an excellent comprehensive review of many of the clustering methods, aimed at sociologists. Recent comment on numerical phenetics was given by McNeill (1979) and Presch (1979). An excellent comparative analysis of several quantitative clustering approaches in behavioral science was recently published by Mezzich and Solomon (1980).

Instead of classifying species, ecologists use numerical taxonomic methods to classify different ecological sites. While the techniques are largely the same, many of the problems emphasized by Clifford and Stephenson (1975) are different. Their book, reflecting much of the work of G. N. Lance and W. T. Williams, did for numerical methods in ecology what Sneath and Sokal did for taxonomy. However, the Clifford and Stephenson book is simpler to understand and offers many insights not available in the other books. While species play opposite roles in taxonomic and ecological classification and therefore it is easy to become confused, Clifford and Stephenson's book is a better introduction to the field than the more compendious tome of Sneath and Sokal.

This chapter will emphasize various choices available to organizational systematists using numerical methods. I have especially tried to highlight choices that have a material impact on the form of a classificatory solution. Rather than giving equal exposure to both popular and less-popular techniques, the former are unabashedly emphasized. In twenty-five years of use, some techniques have proven obsolete or unnecessarily complicated, or just different but not better. These will be ignored, as will unproven recent developments. The concern here is on choices in application rather than technical intricacies. Despite the twenty-five years of experience, patience is still required. Different clustering methods can produce rather different results, and in organizational systematics no solid external criteria exist for choosing one solution over another. Presch (1979) recently concluded, after comparing twenty-four phenograms produced by different methods, that phenetic analysis ought to be rejected as a tool for determining classifications with phylogenetic content. Yet, equally strong criticisms have been leveled against orthodox evolutionism (Sneath and Sokal 1973) and cladism (Gingerich 1979; Hull 1979). Classificatory rigor is not yet in place; but, as Hull's statement at the beginning of this chapter suggests, we are too new at the game to be overly daunted by a lack of rigor at this point.

A final introductory remark is that this chapter does not make a distinction between phenetic and phyletic applications of numerical methods. As developed in earlier chapters (3 and 9), my view is that for organizational classification phenetic and patristic affinities are likely to result in similar classes. These are both synchronic approaches and thus fit my synchronic treatment of numerical methods. (Cladistic method, though diachronic, is probably compatible with my approach as well. I argued in chapter 3 that it probably is a less useful method for classifying organizations, but I could be mistaken.) At the moment I assume that numerical phenetic methods of ascertaining similarity among organizational forms will work no matter whether the ultimate goal of the systematist is to simply identify groupings or to work toward an evolution-based classification, though it is possible that this distinction may be forced upon us as the field develops. It should be noted, though, that Sneath and Sokal (1973) do make such a distinction and offer techniques especially useful for phyletic as opposed to phenetic classification. The interested reader should pursue the matter in their book.

12.1 CODING AND SCALING DATA

Taxonomic characters come in a variety of states, some having only two states, others having almost an infinite number. Since much of the concern in chapter 11 and in this chapter is on finding ways to avoid bias in the selection of characters or clustering methods, it would be senseless to let the number of states a character has affect either its inclusion or weighting in the final solution. While some resemblance coefficients tolerate mixed kinds of data, others do not; so unless recoding takes place, some characters might have to be excluded. In other instances gross differences in variance lead to different weightings unless the characters are rescaled.

Taxonomists tend to work in terms of the following four kinds of data, though Clifford and Stephenson (1975, pp. 34–35) felt a finer typology was needed:

1. *Binary*—comprised of two states, such as present-absent, and usually coded 0 or 1. For example, industrial organizations may be coded as having functional form or not, or organizational ownership might be coded as private or public. Note that in the latter code, both the 0 and the 1 stand for something specific, but that in the former, 1 stands for functional while 0 could mean anything other than functional; this kind of ambiguity, and how it should be handled in the formulas for matching coefficients, will be shown to be a major consideration in their selection.

2. *Nominal*—comprised of three or more unordered or equally ranked states. For instance, schools might be coded as public, private, or parochial.

3. *Ordinal*—comprised of a number of ranked states. Thus organizations might be coded as regional, national, or international (rank based on geographical dispersion); or organizational environments coded, after Emery and Trist (1965), as placid-randomized, placid-clustered, disturbed-reactive, or turbulent field (rank based on level of uncertainty). These first three kinds of data are often termed *qualitative*.

4. *Continuous*—comprised of states separated by the smallest interval the coding scheme will allow. Clifford and Stephenson (1975, pp. 45–46) broke out a separate category, *meristic*, for states that take the form of whole numbers, such as the number of hierarchical levels or number of departments in an organization. True continuous data are produced when averages, square roots, or other statistical quantities are used. Continuous data are often assumed to have metric properties such as equal intervals and zero points, though this is not always valid. These are also termed *quantitative* data.

Often systematists have little choice over the dominant form the character states will take. Fortunately some resemblance coefficients tolerate mixed data so that choice of characters based on kind of data is avoided. But these may not be the best algorithms to use, so a systematist will often want to head for either all-binary or all-continuous data, usually the former since recoding is almost always a one-way trip—toward binary states. Sneath and Sokal still seem to prefer binary coding: "We favor more strongly now than we did when we wrote *Principles of Numerical Taxonomy* (Sokal and Sneath, 1963) a similarity coefficient based on binary coding of the data not only because of its simplicity and possible relationship to information theory but also because, if the coding is done correctly, there is the hope that similarity between fundamental units of variation is being estimated" (1973, p. 147). But before you take quick solace in this it should be noted that thirty-one pages later, after discussing the meaning of phenetic resemblance, they said: "We would recommend r (product-moment correlation coefficient) as the most useful similarity coefficient in that it is the purest measure of shape of the commonly used resemblance measures, and since we believe that distinctiveness is the resemblance component most useful to taxonomists, correlations on standardized characters are to be recommended for general use" (1973, p. 178). Since both can be recommended (setting aside for the moment the fact that they produce somewhat different results) the choice comes down to the preponderance of data. As there is considerable loss of information or increase in unequal weighting if continuous data are coded into binary data (discussed below), the former should probably be used unless almost all of the data are naturally in binary form.

12.1.1 Coding

Nominal to Binary. First consider the problem of changing nominal (qualitative, unordered, multistate) character states into binary form. Take for example a character reflecting Etzioni's (1975) differentiation of organizations by dominant form of authority: coercive, utilitarian, or normative. One possibility is simply to use one character having different symbols to represent the three states, but this often is not an accepted form of input to the resemblance programs. The usual solution is to substitute several binary characters for the one nominal character, as shown in table 12.1. But there are several difficulties with this approach. First, the character *kind of authority* now has the weight of three characters rather than one. It could be said that because authority comes in several states there is more underlying compool complexity represented and therefore the extra weighting is necessary to give a true equal weighting of the underlying component. But suppose that the system-

TABLE 12.1

MULTISTATE CHARACTER RECODED AS BINARY CHARACTERS

Kind of Organization	Binary Characters		
	1	2	3
Coercive	1	0	0
Utilitarian	0	1	0
Normative	0	0	1

atist wanted to have the character reflect the nine nominal states of Etzioni's full-compliance typology? It would take nine binary characters to represent that; is kind of authority now worth a weighting of nine characters? Who can say at this point? Many systematists would want to avoid such a priori judgments. With the nine binary characters, another problem becomes evident: two voluntary cancer research foundations would probably match on all of the nine characters yet only one, *normative-moral*, would be a match based on common substance. The other eight would be what are called CONJOINT ABSENCES: they match 0s or common absences. Recognizing this, it can be seen that a comparison of a hospital with a prison would show mismatches on two characters, *coercive-alienative* and *normative-moral*, and matches (pairs of 0s) on seven characters, for a net result of a match—clearly the wrong conclusion. A third problem is that the three or nine binary characters used to measure "kind of authority" are not independent. For example, once a pair of hospitals are scored 1,1 on the character *normative-moral* they have to be scored 0,0 on the other eight characters. As was discussed in section 11.4.5, theoretically related characters are to be avoided.

Lack of independence can often be ameliorated by converting a nominal-state character into one or more other independent characters. Thus in the case of Etzioni's nine typological categories, one could substitute three continuous-state characters labeled something like *degree of coercive-alienative congruence*, *degree of utilitarian-remunerative congruence*, and so forth. This still ends up with three characters for kind of authority, but given the attention in the literature and the fundamental importance of the attribute to organizational functioning, the argument that authority is an evolutionarily important and complex variable and therefore should be reflected by several equally weighted characters may well be the most valid one.

Continuous to Binary. Next, the problem of transforming continuous data into binary form warrants attention. The simplest solution is to *bifurcate* the range of continuous data at the mean. Even at best, when the distribution is clearly bimodal, this usually means considerable loss of information. In the more likely case, a more-or-less normal distribution around one mode, a bifurcation is unacceptable because the furcation is drawn right at or near the mode where the most organizations are least different.

A better solution to this problem is known as *additive binary coding*. Here, for example, a multistate character or a continuous-state character collapsed into four ranked states, *m*, can be transformed into *m*-1 binary characters as shown in table 12.2. It is additive in the sense that the third

TABLE 12.2

RECODING A MULTISTATE CHARACTER INTO ADDITIVE BINARY CHARACTERS

Multistate Character (number of hierarchical ranks)		Binary Characters		
		1	2	3
State One	(1−3 ranks)	0	0	0
State Two	(4−5 ranks)	1	0	0
State Three	(6−7 ranks)	1	1	0
State Four	(8 or more ranks)	1	1	1

or generally the *n*th character includes the accummulated positive scores of characters 1, 2, . . . ,*n*. Sneath and Sokal (1973, pp. 150−151) discussed this approach in more detail and considered an alternative, *nonadditive binary coding*, which has also appeared in the taxometric literature. Since in most cases the methods give similar results, and since additive coding is simpler, only it is mentioned here. Inasmuch as both approaches change the weighting of the initial character somewhat, a better approach might be to avoid this kind of recoding by using a resemblance coefficient not requiring binary coding.

Missing Components. A third problem in coding occurs when some organizations have a subcomponent of some complexity which is missing in other organizations. A likely example would occur when comparing organizations having only what Thompson (1967) called "pooled interdependency" against those having pooled and "sequential" interdependency, where the latter organizations also have several attributes of sequential interdependency totally absent from organizations having only pooled interdependency. Under normal procedure the coding scheme might look something like that shown in table 12.3A. Taxa A and C are alike on the primary character in that they both have sequential interdependency, but they both differ from taxon B, which has not. But three kinds of secondary characters of the organizations having sequential interdependency are shown: sequential work stations not connected by an assembly line* versus an assembly line of some kind; informal planning methods* versus formal planning methods; and computer-aided scheduling* versus computer-controlled scheduling. (Note that the latter character only occurs if formal planning methods are used; therefore it is itself secondary to its "primary" character—presence of formal planning—and thus it could be given the "tertiary" label; I have ignored this for purposes of simplicity.) As can be seen from table 12.3A, under normal procedure taxon C looks more like taxon B than taxon A,

*The starred half of each dimension is left off table 12.3 because of space limitations.

TABLE 12.3

METHODS OF CODING SECONDARY CHARACTERS

A. CHARACTERS NOT WEIGHTED, NOT TREATED AS MISSING

	Characters	Taxon A	Taxon B	Taxon C
Primary:	Sequential Interdependence	1	0	1
Secondary:	Assembly Line	1	0	0
	Formal Planning	1	0	0
	Computer Scheduling	1	0	0

B. PRIMARY CHARACTER WEIGHTED ACCORDING TO NUMBER OF SECONDARY CHARACTERS

	Characters	Taxon A	Taxon B	Taxon C
Primary:	Sequential Interdependence	111	000	111
Secondary:	Assembly Line	1	0	0
	Formal Planning	1	0	0
	Computer Scheduling	1	0	0

C. SECONDARY CHARACTERS TREATED AS MISSING

	Characters	Taxon A	Taxon B	Taxon C
Primary:	Sequential Interdependence	1	0	1
Secondary:	Assembly Line	1	NC	0
	Formal Planning	1	NC	0
	Computer Scheduling	1	NC	0

D. METHODS B AND C COMBINED

	Characters	Taxon A	Taxon B	Taxon C
Primary:	Sequential Interdependence	111	000	111
Secondary:	Assembly Line	1	NC	0
	Formal Planning	1	NC	0
	Computer Scheduling	1	NC	0

which is probably not true. An alternative method of coding is to weight the primary character more than the secondary characters. The coding for this approach is shown in table 12.3B, where the higher-level character is weighted by the number of characters secondary to it. Thus the primary character, *presence of sequential interdependency*, is given a weight of three. In this coding scheme taxa B and C are matched on three weights and mismatched on three weights and the same is true between taxa A and C.

Another alternative is to treat the lower characters as missing information when the primary (higher-level) character is scored 0, as shown in table 12.3C. In this arrangement taxa A and C are more nearly alike. A fourth alternative, table 12.3D, combines the approaches of tables 12.3B and 12.3C. In this example, at least, it is probably the best one. One can easily see that there is no straightforward solution. The systematist is put in the position of trying to guess which coding scheme most closely fits reality.

The general problem of how to code characters representing components missing in some organizations occurs whether the data are binary or some other kind. As with binary data, if multistate or continuous characters denoting the missing attributes are all scored zero, then a match or high resemblance will be recorded for pairs of missing characters, thus producing an artificially high resemblance between the two organizations being compared. The best procedure appears to be one of treating missing components as missing information, coding them NC, and using a program having a pair-wise method of deleting missing information from the calculations.

12.1.2 Size Reduction

While a systematist may with good reason want to avoid any a priori deletion of characters, there may be a need for reduction in the size of the data pool before beginning computations. Clifford and Stephenson (1975) recognized three reasons for wanting to reduce the data pool. First, since the cost of computer computations goes up geometrically in relation to the increase in characters even though the program may be dimensioned large enough to handle the pool, the cost of running several kinds of analyses can be prohibitive. Second, some methods take up more computer memory space than others for a given size of data pool; therefore, even though cluster analysis is possible with the larger pool, the systematist may be precluded from using some methods. In both of these cases one option is to use a cheaper-running method to find preliminary clusters and then eliminate characters that do not figure in the formation of these clusters. Then more expensive and presumably more sophisticated methods can be used on the smaller data pool. Another alternative is to break character sets into subsets and run preliminary analyses on each subset, dropping characters not figuring in the subsets. A more conservative approach to subset analysis is to use overlapping subsets to get at least partially around the possibility that a character not important on one subset may be very important in a cluster appearing in an adjacent subset.

Third, some characters may have positive scores with only a few OTUs, meaning that most of the row in the data matrix is filled with zeros. Many such characters contribute to an unjustifiably high resemblance. Clifford and Stephenson (1975, pp. 85−89) did not mention any guidelines for how many characters can be deleted without damaging the pattern of the data matrix, but any number greater than two percent would appear excessive unless a visual inspection shows that no patterns in the data would be disrupted by dropping a higher number.

12.1.3 Scaling

The general equal weighting of characters can be inadvertently affected by differences in variance. In a comparison of organizations ranging from less than 25 to over 250,000 employees, the larger organizations will contribute far more variance than the former. In the case of capital investment the extremes could range between thousands to billions of dollars. These effects should be rescaled, either by using log transformations or by substituting a rank order for the continuous data. Another possibility is to take square or cube roots to diminish the impact of huge ranges in the data.

While on the subject of size, we need to ask to what extent size effects should be allowed to affect the cluster solutions. The assumption here, as is usually the case in biological systematics, is that size in and of itself is not important. In organizations it seems likely that the impact of size on the organization will be picked up by other characters that more directly measure technological and other managerial competence attributes. Thus, including characters that directly measure size more than likely gives a less important attribute extra weighting. If in fact size does not have any direct impact on organizational form and functioning, nothing is lost by deleting the size effect. Needless to say, the final story of the effects of size is not in yet. For a recent review of this subject see Kimberly (1976) and Jackson and Morgan (1978). Much of the effect of size can be reduced by the several scaling transformations just discussed. Leaving out direct size characters is an even better approach. Sneath and Sokal (1973, pp. 169−171), following Penrose (1954), offered further discussion and an approach to separating the effects of size and shape.

In addition to treating a few characters that may have huge variances in comparison to others, *standardization* of the entire data matrix was recommended by Sneath and Sokal (1973) and Clifford and Stephenson (1975), but only for continuous data. Standardization is typically not carried out on binary data because, for example, to do so gives inordinate weight to the few 0s of a character scoring mainly 1s.

Standardization—setting all character (column) means to zero and standard deviations to unity—is usually done by character across all

OTUs (rows). It can also be done by OTU across all characters (columns) but this is done much less frequently, though it should be done when the product-moment correlation is used as the resemblance coefficient, as the effects of outliers are thereby reduced. A full discussion of the effect of row and column standardization and the interaction effects was presented by Cattell (1966, pp. 115—119).

The reader should note one anomaly. In the section on size reduction it was suggested that characters positively scored so infrequently as to have virtually no impact on the clustering, which is to say they have little variance, should be deleted. But in the discussion of standardization the object of the exercise is not to delete characters with low variance but rather to enhance it. Obviously, the level of variance is one clue used to determine whether a character is important enough to be included in a data matrix, but other theoretical reasons should also be taken into account and possibly be given more credence than the sampled level of variance. Once a conclusion is reached that a character is important and therefore should be included, it should be weighted equally—which includes giving it equal variance.

12.2 RESEMBLANCE COEFFICIENTS

Once the data are collected and coded and scaled, the next step is the creation of resemblance coefficients that offer a numerical indication of the overall resemblance or similarity between all possible pairs of organizations. In the literature the terms *resemblance* and *similarity* are used interchangeably; the former will be used here. Somewhat more confusing is the frequent reference to measures of DISSIMILARITY, such as distance measures, as RESEMBLANCE or SIMILARITY measures. This practice will be continued here since one is really just the reciprocal of the other and the full range of similarity-dissimilarity is implied no matter which extreme is referred to. Thus:

$$R = S = (1 - D)$$

where R is the general resemblance coefficient, S is a similarity measure and D is a dissimilarity or distance measure.

12.2.1 Numerical Taxonomic Resemblance

The overall differences or similarities among organizations to be classified are translated into numerical form through the use of a *data matrix* in which rows are formed by OTUs and columns by characters, as shown in table 12.4. Organizational scientists familiar with factor analysis will

TABLE 12.4

AN EXAMPLE OF AN OTU BY CHARACTER DATA MATRIX

OTUs	Characters					
1	X_{11}	X_{12}	X_{13}	.	.	X_{1t}
2	X_{21}	X_{22}	X_{23}	.	.	X_{2t}
3	X_{31}	X_{32}	X_{33}	.	.	X_{3t}
4	X_{41}	X_{42}	X_{43}	.	.	X_{4t}
.	.	.	.	.	.	.
.	.	.	.	.	.	.
n	X_{n1}	X_{n2}	X_{n3}	.	.	X_{nt}

recognize immediately that two forms of analysis may be pursued. The most common is clustering of variables (columns) using cases (rows) as sources of variance, termed R MODE by Cattell (1966, pp. 69, 142, 228–230). A method less frequently used by social scientists, based on a transposed matrix and labeled Q MODE by Cattell, sorts cases using variables as sources of variance. Most taxonomic clustering and factoring uses Q mode in which OTUs (rows) are grouped using characters (columns) as sources of variance or discrimination. Although these terms are not used frequently in what follows, at one point factor analysis will be suggested in both Q and R modes, so the distinction should be kept in mind. Unless specifically mentioned, the reader may assume that Q mode is involved.

The RESEMBLANCE COEFFICIENT is defined as a quantified estimate of the similarity or dissimilarity between two elements of the data matrix. Almost as many coefficients have been suggested over the years as there have been researchers. Most of these will be ignored in favor of a few most popular ones. It would be desirable if the remaining popular ones held the property of *joint monotonicity*, but they do not. This is to say, if the resemblance coefficients obtained by one method are ranked in order of size, they will not usually be in perfect correlation with the ranked coefficients produced by another formula. In short, it makes a difference which coefficient is used.

What does it mean to say that one rock resembles another, one animal resembles another, one organization resembles another? Is it same size? same shape? same kind of macro or micro detail? same level of vigor? same complexity? These are some of the components of phenetic resemblance discussed by Sneath and Sokal (1973, pp. 168–178). The psychological meaning of resemblance is unclear to systematists, to say the least. To be unaware of the full range of what resemblance means is to run the risk of being sensitive only to one meaning, as Goronzy (1969) was in limiting his characters mainly to measures of size. For organizations, it is impossible to say at this time whether even the several components listed by Sneath and Sokal cover the full range of what organizational systematists might mean by resemblance. Sneath and Sokal placed most emphasis on shape, but what that concept means for organizations is obscure. Seemingly the best approach at this time is to take cognizance of the full range of categories of characters such as those suggested in table 11.6. This list includes several concepts of resemblance.

Of those mentioned by Sneath and Sokal, overall size seems least important, especially with respect to the dominant technology species concept elaborated in this book. But relative size of subcomponents may be more important since that might indicate technological differences. Organizational shape may be the result of number, relative size, and arrangement of subcomponents. Pinder and Moore (1979) emphasized the importance for resemblance of the concepts of vigor, change, metabolic rate, and internal dynamism. They introduced a new one, dispersion or variance, where the resemblance lies in the degree to which homologous subcomponents in the same organization differ. For example, different kinds of organizations might depend on different levels of variety of specific workplace technologies in pursuing their dominant competence. For Sneath and Sokal, resemblance was a function of human senses—OTUs look, sound, or feel the same. All of their components in one way or another seem to depend on the seeing, hearing, or feeling ability of systematists. This may be a reflection of the historical limitations of field situations where there was little else to "sense" with. Recently the normal senses have been augmented by laboratory equipment, but the implied meanings of resemblance are the same. Organizational systematists should remain sensitive to the possibility that for organizations additional meanings of resemblance may be forthcoming. Organizational structure, processes, abilities, and so forth may show resemblances in myth, ideology, or intentional or behavioral meaning. These resemblances may not be directly seen or felt but rather are interpreted meanings. That these may lead systematists into interpreting rather than just recording what is present is a problem for objectivity, but the notion of symbolic resemblance should not be quickly dismissed because of possible method difficulties.

12.2.2 Kinds of Resemblance Coefficients

Besides lacking in joint monotonicity, resemblance coefficients differ in other important respects and users need to be careful in selecting them. Three kinds are discussed briefly here: MATCHING, DISTANCE, and CORRELATION coefficients. Others, such as probabilistic and information-theory based measures, are more complicated (not necessarily better) and not yet in the mainstream of numerical taxonomy; thus they are passed over. They are discussed at some length by Jardine and Sibson (1971), Sneath and Sokal (1973), Clifford and Stephenson (1975), and Hartigan (1975).

Matching Coefficients

A matching coefficient is a ratio between the number of matched binary scores occurring between two OTUs and the total number of such characters. Often termed *similarity* or *association coefficients*, matching coefficients are the simplest and the oldest of the resemblance measures and appear in the most variants. While Sokal and Sneath attempted to review all those in use at the time in 1963, in their 1973 book they gave up the attempt. Of all the variations, most have been used only by the authors proposing them, some are of historical interest, and few remain popular. The latter are of interest here.

An appreciation of the formulations of matching coefficients is aided by figure 12.1, where the possible matches or mismatches between a pair of OTUs are shown. The matches 1,1 and 0,0 are represented by the letters a and d and the mismatches 1,0 and 0,1 are indicated by the letters b and c. The concern underlying the many variations in the formulation of the matching coefficients largely pertains to the relative weighting of the four cells in the table, and especially there has been concern over cell d, where the CONJOINT ABSENCES occur. Does it make sense, for example, to conclude that organizations as widely different as a small job shop, a large assembly line plant, and an advertising agency are similar because they share the absence of a continuous-process technol-

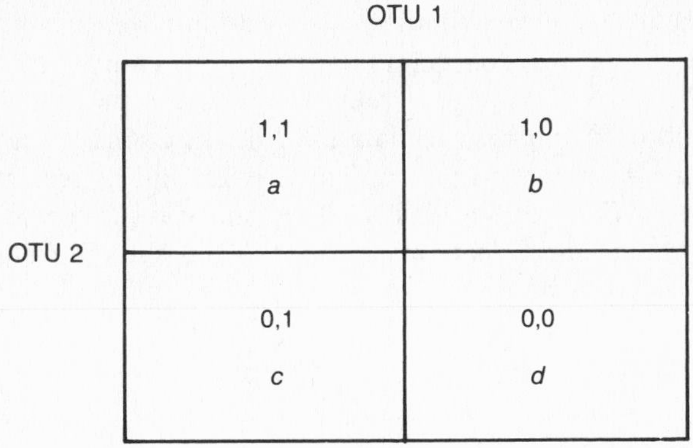

OTU 1

	1,1 a	1,0 b
OTU 2		
	0,1 c	0,0 d

Figure 12.1. Representation of Matches and Mismatches of a Character for a Pair of OTUs.

ogy? Perhaps not. Consequently matching coefficients are split into two groups, those including conjoint absences and those ignoring them.

Without Conjoint Absences. Both Sneath and Sokal (1973) and Clifford and Stephenson (1975) placed most faith in a formula proposed a long time ago by Jaccard (1908):

$$R_m = \frac{a}{a + b + c}$$

where R_m denotes resemblance and a, b, c, d represent the boxes of figure 12.1. A variant of this which double-weights a so as to have the matches balance the two kinds of mismatches is the formula by Czekanowski (1913):

$$R_m = \frac{2a}{2a + b + c}$$

While the Jaccard form has had more use, the Czekanowski form has also been used. Clifford and Stephenson (1975, p. 56) showed that Jaccard is preferable when the number of matches is high relative to the number of mismatches. Conversely, they showed that Czekanowski is preferable when a is smaller relative to b and c. Obviously, variations in weighting are limitless. Another variant that is worth noting is that of Ochiai (1957):

$$R_m = \frac{a}{(a + b)\,(a + c)}$$

With all three of these formulas the coefficients range between zero and unity. In situations where there are a considerable number of conjoint absences the foregoing coefficients are much to be preferred.

With Conjoint Absences. In data matrices containing very few conjoint absences the following formulas are examples of preferred matching coefficients. One of the oldest, and the one most preferred by Jardine and Sibson (1971) and Sneath and Sokal (1973), is the Simple Matching Coefficient:

$$R_m = \frac{a + d}{a + b + c + d}$$

A variety of different weightings have been proposed over the years. Russell and Rao (1940) dropped d from the numerator:

$$R_m = \frac{a}{a + b + c + d}$$

Rogers and Tanimoto (1960) doubled the effect of the mismatches:

$$R_m = \frac{a}{a + d + 2(b + c)}$$

Sokal and Sneath (1963) doubled the weight of matches, altering the simple matching coefficient the same way Czekanowski altered Jaccard's coefficient:

$$R_m = \frac{2(a + d)}{2(a + d) + b + c}$$

As can be seen, all these variations have relevance depending on the relative occurrence of a, b, c, or d. The intent has been to maintain some kind of balance in the weighting of the four elements. Whether or not this should be done is problematic. Except in rather extreme circumstances it would appear best to stay with the simple matching coefficient. In biology the systematists had some externally valid reason for adjusting the weighting because in many instances they had a well-established classification via orthodox methods to use as a basis of comparison. Coefficients were adjusted so as to obtain a good match between orthodox and numerical groupings. Since organizational systematists have no solid groupings against which to compare numerical results, there is the danger that the results will be inappropriately "engineered" by shifting the weightings of a, b, c, or d around.

Distance Coefficients

An alternative to assessing the similarity of two OTUs by determining some form of ratio of character matches and mismatches is to locate them in terms of the Cartesian coordinates of a hypercube, then find the Euclidean distance between each pair. For the case of two organizations compared in terms of two characters, figure 12.2 offers an illustration. Two OTUs, $A_{(1,2)}$ and $B_{(3,3)}$, are plotted and the average distance calculated according to the general formula:*

$$R_{d_{jk}} = \frac{1}{n}\left[\sum_{i=1}^{n}(X_{ij} - X_{ik})^2\right]^{1/2}$$

*As given in Sneath and Sokal (1973) though it was first defined for numerical taxonomy by Sokal (1961).

where $R_{d_{jk}}$ is resemblance based on the distance between two OTUs, **j** and **k**, X_i is the state of the *i*th character and *n* is the number of characters. For OTUs A and B in figure 12.2 this works out as shown in the figure for two characters X_1 and X_2. More detail about the calculation of distance and the expansion of the notion into a multicharacter hypercube is given in Sneath and Sokal (1973, pp. 121–128).

The principal advantage of distance coefficients, other than the rather easy intuitive grasp of the notion, is that they handle mixed data—that is, both binary and continuous scores. There are a variety of other distance coefficients, several of which are reviewed by Sneath and Sokal (1973, pp. 124–128) and Clifford and Stephenson (1975, pp 57–61). Most of these add in a denominator generally similar in form to that in the Canberra metric:

$$R_{d\text{(Canb.)}jk} = \sum_{i=1}^{n} \frac{|X_{ij} - X_{ik}|}{(X_{ij} + X_{ik})}$$

(where *n* is the number of characters and X is the state of the *i*th character of any pair of OTUs, **j** and **k**), as well as other variations in how the elements are summated and whether it is squares or nonsquares that are summed.

One disadvantage is that the coefficient does not discriminate between the two instances of zero distance when, for example, both organizations in figure 12.2 are scored $A_{(0,0)}$ and $B_{(0,0)}$ (attributes missing) or $A_{(2,2)}$ and $B_{(2,2)}$. A circumstance may arise where two organizations might share a very low distance score across many characters simply because of many conjoint absences. This is especially likely if a large number of binary character states occur. In such a situation it might be best to drop the distinction between conjoint absences and missing information and use NC rather than 0 as the score. Then, using an average distance measure, resemblance coefficients can be calculated using pairwise deletion of missing information (coded as NC).

There is occasionally a complaint about the use of distance coefficients: that the distance is often between very unlike characters. For example, suppose that two organizations are located in space in terms of gross sales (A = \$1 million; B = \$500 million) and presence or absence of matrix organization (A = 0; B = 1). The difference in the scale factor is significant. In this case $R_d = \sqrt{(1 - 500)^2 + (0 - 1)^2}$. Obviously the sales character completely overwhelms the effect of whether or not a matrix form is used. Several leading authors (Sneath and Sokal 1973, p. 122; Clifford and Stephenson 1975, p. 67; Hartigan 1975, pp. 59–61;

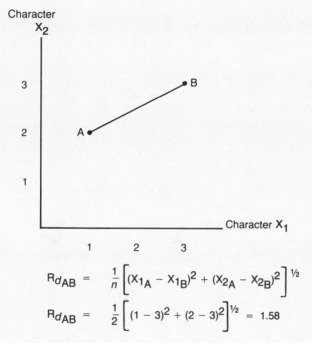

$$R_{d_{AB}} = \frac{1}{n}\left[(X_{1A} - X_{1B})^2 + (X_{2A} - X_{2B})^2\right]^{1/2}$$

$$R_{d_{AB}} = \frac{1}{2}\left[(1 - 3)^2 + (2 - 3)^2\right]^{1/2} = 1.58$$

Figure 12.2. Location of Two OTUs in a Two-Dimensional Space Based on Two Characters.

Jardine and Sibson 1971, p. 32) agree that the distance measure becomes acceptable if all characters are standardized to unit variance and zero (or at least a common) mean, though Jardine and Sibson add the further qualification that the distributions should have about the same dispersion, a rarity in taxonomic studies.

Correlation Coefficients

A third approach frequently used in taxonomic studies is to calculate Pearson product-moment correlation coefficients (r), which conveniently summarize the relation between two OTUs across all their characters. This according to the following formula:

$$R_{r_{jk}} = \frac{\displaystyle\sum_{i=1}^{n} (X_{ij} - \bar{X}_j)(X_{ik} - \bar{X}_k)}{\sqrt{\displaystyle\sum_{i=1}^{n} (X_{ij} - \bar{X}_j)^2 \sum_{i=1}^{n} (X_{ik} - \bar{X}_k)^2}}$$

where *n* is the number of characters measured, X_i is the state of the *i*th character for a pair of OTUs **j** and **k**, and $\bar{X}_j$ and $\bar{X}_k$ are the means across all characters for each OTU. For ordinal data the Pearson or Kendall rank correlation coefficients could be used. As can be seen in figure 12.3, if both OTUs have the same score across all characters the plot of the deviations from the means will form a positively sloped straight line and the correlation will be +1. Thus the coefficient is simply an averaging statistic indicating how well matched, on average, the character scores are for a pair of OTUs. Jardine and Sibson (1971, p. 31) objected to the correlation coefficient because the statistic is an "average" of scores for different characters and hence has no meaning. They called it absurd. In fact, their criticism is absurd because the coefficient really reflects the distance of the plotted point of each pair of similar characters from the line of perfect correlation. The distances all have the same meaning. A comparison of figures 12.2 and 12.3 shows that both the distance and correlation coefficients are projections in space described by Cartesian

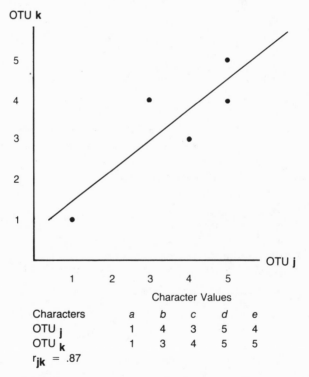

Characters	a	b	c	d	e
OTU $_j$	1	4	3	5	4
OTU $_k$	1	3	4	5	5

$r_{jk} = .87$

Figure 12.3. Plot of Two OTUs Using Five Characters, Illustrating the Correlation Coefficient.

coordinates. Hartigan (1975, p. 64) correctly referred to the correlation coefficients as a "disguised Euclidean distance."

A positive attribute of the correlation coefficient is that it accepts both binary and continuous data. But the effects of the mixing are not always straightforward. Normal practice calls for standardization of character scores across all OTUs. The effect of this is to assure that characters are not differentially weighted due to differences in variance. When binary characters are included, however, the effect of standardizing on them is to increase their weighting relative to continuous characters since all the binary characters take on the extreme values whereas most of the continuous characters will not. This effect holds true for the distance coefficient as well. Note that the effect is the opposite when continuous characters are recoded for use in the matching coefficient—the recoding increases the number of characters representing the continuous character, thereby increasing its relative weight.

An undesirable property of the correlation coefficient, as pointed out by Eades (1965), is that when few characters are involved the direction of coding can easily affect the value of the coefficient. For example, if character a in figure 12.3 had been reverse-coded so that the OTUs each scored 5 on it, $r_{jk} = 0.53$, a considerable difference in numerical resemblance even though nothing has changed but the coding scheme. This property was the only relevant basis for Jardine and Sibson's (1971, p. 31) criticism of the correlation coefficient. Since two like OTUs are correlated across all characters, most variance and hence the greatest chance of a high positive correlation will occur if the OTUs match all along the full range of the scale. As in figure 12.2, they should match at both the (1,1) end and the (7,7) end. If by some chance the characters were all arranged so that two perfectly alike OTUs always scored (6,6) or (7,7), the variance would be very attenuated, leaving room for error and other anomalies to reduce the correlation toward the zero mark. So, in coding the best procedure is, for example, to pay special attention to two OTUs that are expected to be highly similar and code the characters so that the full range of the scale will be used.

The correlation coefficient, like the other coefficients, also has the problem of conjoint absences. In this case they will have considerable weight since conjoint absences lead to zero scores that are at one extreme in distance from the mean scores across all characters for the pair of OTUs involved. If many characters were absent, the zero scores would have considerable weight toward producing a high positive correlation, much more weight in fact than a group of similar OTU scores toward the middle of the scale. The only way around this is to treat such absences as missing information and use the pairwise deletion option available in most correlation programs. This could create problems in assessing statistical significance, but since that is problematic in numerical taxonomy anyway, not too much is lost.

Another difficulty to watch out for is that two OTUs may show a perfect positive correlation even though they are systematically different on all characters. It could be possible, for example, that a small organization might score 1, 2, 3, 4, 5, 6 across six characters while a larger organization would score 2, 3, 4, 5, 6, 7 across the same characters. A correlation coefficient would not show this difference whereas the other coefficients would. Since the likelihood of such a systematic difference between two organizations across many characters is negligible, this limitation of the correlation coefficient is something to keep in mind and check for, but not to worry about.

The Resemblance Coefficient in Perspective

There is no consensus that one coefficient is better than another. Williams, Lambert, and Lance (1966) and Clifford and Stephenson (1975) preferred their own information statistic coefficient, which they say is better than the others. Jardine and Sibson (1971) also suggested one of their own, the K-dissimilarity measure, which they said avoids all the problems they see in the others. But neither of these measures has seen much empirical use. As noted before, Sneath and Sokal (1973, p. 147) concluded that a matching coefficient based on binary data was the best, but elsewhere (p. 187) they concluded that the product-moment correlation was the best measure of shape, the dominant aspect of phenetic resemblance.

Clifford and Stephenson (1975, pp. 77−82), following Kelley (1955) and Williams and Dale (1965), suggested that coefficients be tested for their *metric* quality, which depends on their satisfying the following four criteria:

1. *Symmetry*. That the distance between two OTUs be independent of the direction of measurement and positive, provided the taxa are not coincident. Thus, if $d(x, y)$ is the distance between two OTUs, x and y, then

$$d(x, y) = d(y, x) > 0.$$

2. *Triangular Inequality*. That the length of any one side of a triangle of differences formed by three OTUs be less than the sum of the other two sides. Thus, if x, y, and z are OTUs, then

$$d(x, y) < d(x, z) + d(y, z).$$

This property may be lost when distances are squared as in the squared Euclidean distance coefficient and perhaps the correlation coefficient, but not necessarily; it should therefore be checked.

3. *Distinguishability of Nonidenticals.* For two OTUs, x and y, if

$$d(x, y) \neq 0, \text{ then x is not like y.}$$

4. *Indistinguishability of Identicals.* Given two identical OTUs, x and y,

$$d(x, y) = 0$$

If the nonsquare Euclidean distance coefficient is used, it is metric. The simple matching coefficient and the Canberra metric are both metric. The correlation coefficient is probably metric most of the time— it may falter on the third criterion as mentioned in the discussion of the coefficient, and possibly on the second. Nonparametric correlation coefficients such as Kendall's Tau surely meet the first, second, and fourth criteria and for organizations having characters that are not all correlates of some global property such as size or age they also meet the third criterion. For further details, consult Williams and Dale (1965) and Clifford and Stephenson (1975).

There is no doubt that phenetic resemblance is described a bit differently by each of the coefficients. Since there is no straightforward view on which one is best, organizational taxonomists are left with the prospect of trying out several in order to discover which one works best. Over the years biological systematists have usually followed the path of comparing numerical with orthodox groupings until they felt the best sense was made. Since organizational taxonomists do not have a well-established orthodox set of classes, what are we to do? The only answer I have is to compare the numerically derived groupings with groupings derived by other methods, principally hypothetical groupings suggested by a priori theoretical, top-down divisive, inductive methods. Hence, again we see the need for a strong a priori theory of organizational speciation and an accompanying set of hypothetical groupings. From this a process of iterative comparison of theoretically and empirically derived groupings coupled with a juggling of groupings and methods may be used until the results of each approach compare favorably. Sneath and Sokal said in defense of the correlation coefficient that "it has in fact been the experience of numerical taxonomists that when the interpretation of taxonomic structure is made on the basis of pheno-grams, correlation coefficients are usually the most suitable measure when the results are evaluated by conventional taxonomists" (1973, p. 140). In their comparative study, Mezzich and Solomon (1980, p. 141) found that the Euclidean distance coefficient ranked first, though not consistently so, over the correlation coefficient and a third, termed the "city-block" distance coefficient. Until a wealth of comparative results are available, our best choice may be to stay with the correlation co-efficient. It seems to receive the best marks when strong measures of external validity have been available.

12.3 STRUCTURAL ANALYSIS

The information about the relative similarities among the OTUs under consideration is assembled into a *resemblance matrix*, as shown in table 12.5. Each element in the array is a resemblance coefficient representing the resemblance between a pair of OTUs. Since with all acceptable resemblance coefficients there is the requirement of symmetry, which is that the similarity of x to y be the same as the similarity of y to x, only the lower left half of the table is typically used.

Sneath and Sokal (1973, pp. 202–214) presented a classification of structural analysis methods which in terms of the development in chap-ter 2 might better be described as an essentialist typology based on eight dimensions. For a full discussion the reader is advised to consult their presentation. The dimensions are presented here very briefly so as to provide a broad context in which the few clustering methods to be described may be understood.

1. *Hierarchic versus Nonhierarchic Methods.* Nonhierarchic meth-ods, what Blashfield and Aldenderfer (1978) referred to as "iterative partition methods," break a set of t OTUs into substantially less than t groups or partitions. ORDINATION methods such as factor analysis and nonmetric multidimensional scaling are examples of this approach, as is the k-means approach of MacQueen (1967) and others. Nonhierarchic methods traditionally have been popular in the social and behavioral sciences. In hierarchic clustering a set of ranked groupings results with all OTUs formed into one group at the top and broken into the greatest number of groups at the bottom. The intervening layers are arranged so that each layer has more groups than the layer above it and fewer groups than the layer below it. There is no implied constraint against overlap-ping. An OTU may or may not be a member of more than one higher-

TABLE 12.5

EXAMPLE OF A RESEMBLANCE MATRIX

OTUs			OTUs			
	1	2	3	4	.....	t
1	—					
2	S_{21}	—				
3	S_{31}	S_{32}	—			
4	S_{41}	S_{42}	S_{43}	—		
.	.	.	.	.		
.	.	.	.	.		
.	.	.	.	.		
t	S_{t1}	S_{t2}	S_{t3}	S_{t4}	.....	—

ranked group. As Blashfield and Aldenderfer showed in table 4 of their paper (1978, p. 280), hierarchical methods are far and away the most popular—of 162 uses of clustering in 1973 some 100 were hierarchical.

2. *Agglomerative versus Divisive Methods.* There are two kinds of hierarchical clustering. Agglomerative methods combine a set of t OTUs into a smaller number of w_0 groups. The set of w_0 groups is then combined into a smaller set of w_1 groups and so on, until the final combination results in one group composed of all OTUs. Agglomerative methods are used most frequently by numerical taxonomists. Divisive methods work in just the opposite fashion. They take the total group of t OTUs and divide it into two or more groups. Each of these groups is then divided into two or more groups, and so on. Divisive methods tend to produce monothetic groupings. Thus they are seldom used—Blashfield and Aldenderfer (1978) found that only 5 of the 162 uses of clustering in 1973 involved divisive clustering methods.

3. *Nonoverlapping versus Overlapping Methods.* In the nonoverlapping method, OTUs may belong to only one group for any given rank; thus groupings are mutually exclusive and a hierarchy is composed of nested groupings. The clustering approaches used by most taxonomists are of the nonoverlapping sort. Overlapping methods produce groups having overlapping membership. Common examples of these are ordination methods such as factor analysis and multidimensional scaling when Q mode is used. Thus when characters are used to sort OTUs into groups (factors), OTUs may load onto more than one factor—unless, of course, a pure case of simple structure is achieved.

4. *Sequential versus Simultaneous Methods.* Most hierarchical clustering methods are sequential in that they operate to produce one rank of the hierarchy at a time and then sequentially work toward the top

(agglomerative) or the bottom (divisive) of the hierarchy. Simultaneous methods of developing a hierarchic cluster have not been adopted and little attention has been given to this possibility. All iterative partitioning or nonhierarchical methods are, of course, simultaneous. Ordination methods are good examples of simultaneous methods.

5. *Local versus Global Criteria.* Sneath and Sokal (1973, p. 208) cited Rohlf (1970) in saying that clustering methods are not equally effective at all levels of a taxonomic hierarchy. Ordination methods tend to be better at the global upper reaches of a hierarchy, whereas clustering methods tend to work better in grouping local similarities between the OTUs at the bottom of the hierarchy.

6. *Direct versus Iterative Solutions.* The most popular hierarchical methods are of the type where calculations by which groups are formed proceed directly from optima local to each level of the hierarchy. Once the criteria at a given rank are satisfied the program moves to the next stage or rank and produces those groups to satisfy criteria at that level. Once a level of analysis is left it is not altered because of findings at later stages of analysis. Iterative approaches work through the hierarchy according to some initially set criteria, and on the basis of some global measure of optimality return to the earlier stages, alter the criteria applying to those stages, and then rework the solution. This is continued until the global optima are reached. Sneath and Sokal (1973) described several attempts at iterative solutions; these have not achieved any popularity, according to the Blashfield and Aldenderfer (1978) study.

7. *Weighted versus Unweighted Clustering.* Perhaps the most frequent use of weighting in clustering is to assure that large groupings of OTUs do not have a disproportionate impact on later steps in the sequence of forming agglomerative hierarchically arranged clusters. Thus, stems having few OTUs are weighted to bring their impact on the solution into balance with stems having a large number of OTUs. Another type of weighting occurs when the effects of OTUs along the major axis of an elliptically shaped cluster are scaled down so these OTUs will have no more effect than OTUs along the minor axis.

8. *Nonadaptive versus Adaptive Clustering.* Virtually all cluster methods in use are nonadaptive in that they do not alter their algorithm to account for particular characteristics of the taxa under study. Adaptive methods are those that alter their algorithms after "learning" about special attributes in the data. A learning program would have a variety of algorithms at hand and would switch from one to another in search of the best-fitting one. Attempts at modest learning methods have been tried, as described in Sneath and Sokal (1973, p. 213), but these are largely experimental.

In the main, the most frequently used numerical taxonomic structural analyses fall into two groups: (1) hierarchical, sequential, agglomerative, nonoverlapping methods; and (2) nonhierarchical, nonsequential, overlapping methods, often called ORDINATION methods. Bailey (1975) assembled an additional eight dimensions from the clustering literature used at one time or another to describe the first group. Of these eight, he concluded that only two, form of linkage and whether similarity levels were objectively or subjectively set, were necessary to fully classify most nonordination methods. Since an investigator may make all similarity levels "objective" by setting them in advance according to prevailing custom, I think this dimension is not a very compelling one. Thus it is most useful to think of the nonordination methods as falling into three classes—SINGLE, AVERAGE, and COMPLETE LINKAGE—in addition to being hierarchical, sequential, agglomerative, and nonoverlapping. Consequently my discussion of these methods will focus on the three kinds of linkage (defined in the next section).

Hartigan (1975, pp. 11–12) referred to the first group as JOINING methods, because after finding the closest pairs of OTUs they successively join other OTUs to these pairs until all OTUs are clustered. He called the second group SORTING methods because OTUs are partitioned according to value taken on by a few important OTUs. Hartigan's terms, which are based on method of search, will be used here instead of acronyms or other cumbersome labels.

Joining methods have the advantage of being easily represented on a two-dimensional page and can be readily described. Their disadvantage is that the two-dimensional hierarchical structure may not fit the true pattern in the data. To overcome this problem, sorting methods are often used in addition. These methods are multidimensional, and their advantage is that they better fit the dimensionality inherent in the data. Their disadvantage is that they have to represent three- or four-dimensional solutions on a two-dimensional page. Because of this they are usually limited to two or three dimensions, thus robbing them of much of their real advantage over the joining methods. Highlights of these methods are briefly reviewed below with an eye to the application and selection of the best approaches.

12.3.1 Joining Methods

Nearest Neighbor Method

The oldest method of clustering was labeled the NEAREST NEIGHBOR method by Lance and Williams (1967) as well as the *single linkage method* (Sneath and Sokal 1973) and a host of other names, as indicated by Blashfield and Aldenderfer (1978). In the 1973 survey of usage by Blashfield and Aldenderfer (1978), this method ranked first in popularity. It is also a logical algorithm to begin with since the first step of the nearest neighbor method is also the first step in other methods described below.

Suppose that six OTUs—*a, b, c, d, e, f*—are plotted in a two-dimensional space as shown in figure 12.4. This circumstance is highly idealized and quite unlikely to ever appear in reality, but it offers a clear illustration of the differences in joining methods. The OTUs are separated by an increasing number of units of distance ranging from one unit between *a* and *b* to five units between *e* and *f*. The numbers between each OTU pair actually indicate the sequence of joining steps, though in this case they also coincide with the distances. In the first step the method identifies one or more pairs that are most similar or, alternatively, are separated by the smallest distance. In figure 12.4 there is only one pair, *ab*, separated by only one unit of distance. In the nearest neighbor method, the OTU nearest to *a* or *b* is then selected to join the group on the second step. In figure 12.4 it is *c*. If there had been another OTU, x (not shown), which was less than two units from *a*, it would have joined before *c*. If another OTU, y (not shown), were two units away from *a*, it would have joined at the same time as *c*. If *c* were less than two units away from some other OTU, z (not shown), it would have joined the latter to start a second cluster. The nearest neighbor method increases the odds that at subsequent steps OTUs will join an existing cluster

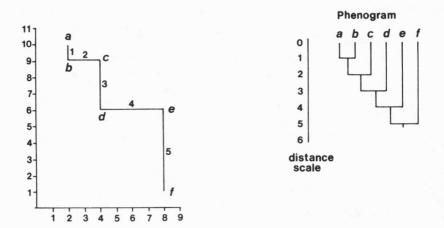

Figure 12.4. Illustrates How Five OTUs, *a* to *f*, Are Joined by the Nearest Neighbor Method and are Represented by a Phenogram.

rather than form a new one. This feature, termed SPACE-CON-TRACTING by Lance and Williams (1967), means that the nearest neighbor method represents OTUs and resultant clusters as more similar than is really true. The result is a phenogram similar to the one in figure 12.4, where more distant OTUs are typically joined to the initial pair in the familiar "chaining" effect. Even though it received mathematical support from Jardine and Sibson (1968), the nearest neighbor method has been characterized as "least useful" by Pritchard and Anderson (1971) and "obsolete" by Clifford and Stephenson (1975). The latter argue that rather than mathematical elegance the criterion should be how well it works (1975, p. 109). In fact, the nearest neighbor method does not work very well—unless, of course, the OTUs really are chained.

Farthest Neighbor Method

The most opposite to the nearest neighbor is the FARTHEST NEIGHBOR method, so labeled by Lance and Williams (1967), and called the *complete linkage* method by Sneath and Sokal (1973). See Blashfield and Aldenderfer (1978) for other labels. The clustering by this method is shown in figure 12.5 for the same plot of six OTUs as in figure 12.4; hence the results of the nearest and farthest neighbor methods can be directly compared. The methods are the same in the first step in that the nearest pairs are identified. But in the second step of the farthest neighbor method the relevant distance determining which OTU will join the cluster next is the distance between a prospective joiner and the member of an extant cluster that is farthest away from it. In figure 12.5 this distance is ab. Since there is no other OTU nearer to c than a, the member of cluster ac farthest from c, c joins ab. If another OTU, x (not shown), were nearer to c and a, c would have joined x. In this case the distance would have to be less than the Euclidean distance between a and c, which is $\sqrt{ab^2 + bc^2} = \sqrt{1^2 + 4^2} = 2.236$. On the third step there is a clear difference between the two methods. OTU d joins with e since the distance de is less than that between d or e and their farthest neighbor in the abc cluster, which is a. That is, $de = 4.00$; $da = \sqrt{16 + 4} = 4.47$; $ea = 16 + 36 = 7.21$. On the fourth step f joins the cluster de since f is nearer to the farthest neighbor of that cluster, d, than it is to the farthest neighbor, a, of the abc cluster. Finally, on step five the two clusters are joined, with the difference between farthest neighbors, f and a, being $\sqrt{81 + 36} = 10.82$. The distances determine the locations of the horizontal bars in the phenogram. In contrast to the nearest neighbor method, the farthest neighbor method tends to represent OTUs and clusters as less similar than is really the case. Rather than one large chained cluster, the tendency is for several small tightly knit clusters to form and stay separate at

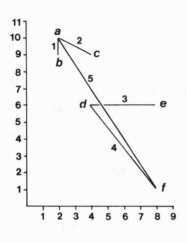

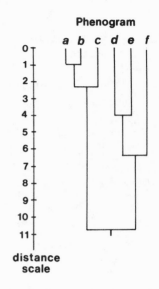

Figure 12.5. Illustrates How Five OTUs, *a* to *f*, Are Joined by the Farthest Neighbor Method and are Represented by a Phenogram.

lower levels of the hierarchy. Because of this feature it is a SPACE-DILATING strategy according to Lance and Williams (1967).

While the illustrations in figures 12.4 and 12.5 are helpful in following *how* the phenograms are produced, figure 12.6, though produced by Lance and Williams (1967) using their "flexible clustering" approach, more clearly illustrates the differences in the phenograms produced by the nearest and farthest neighbor methods. The upper left phenogram, produced when $\beta = 0.98$, is a classic depiction of the chaining effect of the nearest neighbor method. The lower right phenogram, produced when $\beta = -1.00$, is a good example of the intense clustering effect of the farthest neighbor method. The farthest neighbor method has not been used much (Clifford and Stephenson 1975, p. 110; Blashfield and Aldenderfer 1978) mainly because better alternatives to the nearest neighbor method exist.

Group Average Method

A logical outcome of many taxonomists' wish to avoid the extremes of the nearest or farthest neighbor methods was to search for methods producing phenograms that would have neither the chaining effect nor the intense clustering effect of these two methods. Two of these, the *centroid* and *median* methods (labels used by Lance and Williams 1967)

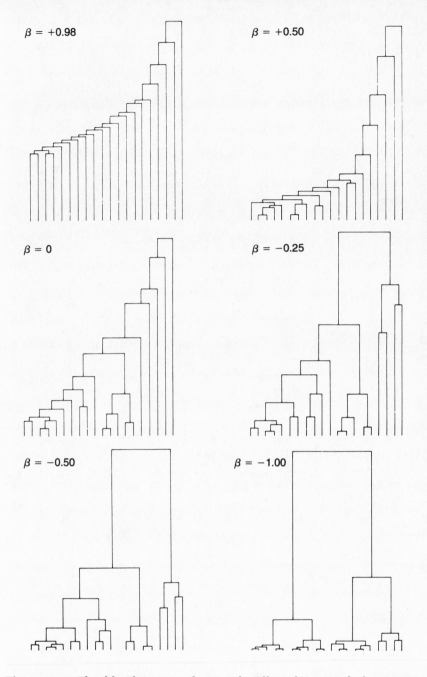

Figure 12.6. Flexible Clustering, Showing the Effect of Varying β; the 20 OTUs are specified by 76 characters. The resemblance measure is Euclidean distance. (From G. N. Lance and W. T. Williams, "A General Theory of Classificatory Sorting Strategies. I. Hierarchical Systems," *The Computer Journal* 9:373–380, 1967. Reprinted by permission of the editor.)

are considered obsolete because they produce what are called *reversals*. These occur when a joining of clusters takes place at a distance level less than that characterizing a fusion at an earlier step in the process. This is illustrated in figure 12.7. The method given best marks by both Sneath and Sokal (1973) and Clifford and Stephenson (1975) is what Lance and Williams (1967) labeled the GROUP AVERAGE method. Sneath and Sokal (1973, p. 230) referred to it as the UPGMA method, an acronym for "unweighted pair-group method using arithmetic averages."

The joining algorithm for the group average method at *all* steps is the same as the first step of the nearest neighbor method; that is, the nearest OTUs are joined. What is different is that some distances are recalculated after a cluster forms. For the plot of OTUs in figure 12.4, the successive recalculated matrices are shown in table 12.6. Since there is no obvious geometric interpretation of the group-average method, none is shown. In step one, the nearest distance is between a and b; and since there are no ties, only one cluster—ab—is formed. In preparation for step two, the distances between ab and the other OTUs are recalculated by taking the unweighted average distance between *each* member of an existing cluster and a prospective new member. For example, the distance between the cluster ab and c is $\frac{1}{2}(ac + bc) = \frac{1}{2}(2.24 + 2.00) = 2.12$. In step two, since the distance between ab and c is less than the other distances, c joins with ab at a fusion level of 2.12. In step three, the distances between each member of the cluster abc and the other OTUs are recalculated. The distances between OTUs remaining unjoined are simply carried along unchanged. Thus the distance between abc and f is $\frac{1}{3}(af + bf + cf) = \frac{1}{3}(10.82 + 10.00 + 8.94) = 9.92$. At step four, e joins with f at a fusion level of 5.00, since this distance is less than the average distance between e or f and the members of cluster $abcd$. Finally, in step five, the two groups $abcd$ and ef are joined at a fusion level of 7.33.

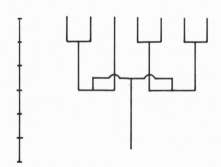

Figure 12.7. Illustration of the Tendency of the Centroid and Median Methods to Produce Phenograms Having Reversals.

TABLE 12.6

EUCLIDEAN DISTANCES USED TO FORM CLUSTERS BY GROUP AVERAGE METHOD

	a	b	c	d	e	f
a	—					
b	1.00	—				
c	2.24	2.00	—			
d	4.47	3.61	3.00	—		
e	7.21	6.71	4.58	4.00	—	
f	10.82	10.00	8.94	6.40	5.00	—

Step One: a joins b; fusion level = 1.00

	ab	c	d	e	f
ab	—				
c	2.12	—			
d	4.04	3.00	—		
e	6.96	4.58	4.00	—	
f	10.41	8.94	6.40	5.00	—

Step Two: c joins ab; fusion level = 2.12

	abc	d	e	f
abc	—			
d	3.69	—		
e	6.17	4.00	—	
f	9.92	6.40	5.00	—

Step Three: d joins abc; fusion level = 3.69

	abcd	e	f
abcd	—		
e	5.63	—	
f	9.04	5.00	—

Step Four: e joins f; fusion level = 5.00

	abcd	ef
abcd	—	
ef	7.33	—

Step Five: ef joins abcd; fusion level = 7.33

Sneath and Sokal (1973, pp. 230–234) offered a detailed account of the group average method. It can also be used with correlations and other similarity or difference measures. Lance and Williams (1967) suggested a linear combinatorial method that simplified computing.

As can be seen by comparing the phenogram in figure 12.8 with those in figures 12.4 and 12.5, the group average method produces a somewhat different grouping. A better illustration of the group average method in

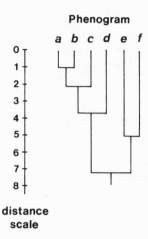

Figure 12.8. Phenogram Produced by the Group Average Method, Based on Data in Table 12.6.

comparison to the nearest and farthest neighbor methods is seen in figure 12.6. The group average method is equivalent to $\beta = 0$. The centroid method produces a phenogram equivalent to $\beta = -0.25$. Lance and Williams (1967) concluded that unless special circumstances, such as are sometimes found in ecological site classification studies, warrant an extreme space-dilating method such as $\beta = -0.50$ or -1.00 or the farthest neighbor method, β of a slightly negative value is best. If the data allow the use of $\beta = -0.25$ or the centroid solution because reversals do not materialize, they recommend this first. Otherwise the group average method, or $\beta = 0$ is recommended.

I have mentioned the Lance and Williams (1967) flexible combinatorial method mainly to offer interpretive perspective to the three better-known methods. If a systematist has access to their computer program he should by all means use it. The danger with their flexible clustering strategy is that taxonomists will tend to pick a β which produces results they like rather than results based on some a priori criterion. It would appear to be a better practice to use their combinatorial method without the flexibility—just pick $\beta = 0.00$ to -0.25 or thereabouts and stay with it. As long as the coefficients in the combinatorial formula are set so that it is monotonic, the Lance and Williams combinatorial strategy with $\beta = -0.25$ is the method to use for most circumstances, or at least until it is clear that the data better fit some other β value. When the Lance and Williams formula is not available (programmed), the group average method is the best one to choose. This conclusion is supported by Lance and Williams (1967), Sneath and Sokal (1973, p. 303), and Clifford and Stephenson (1975, p. 113, p. 116). Blashfield and Aldenderfer found, in their 1973 review of usage, that the group average method ranked second to the nearest neighbor method in popularity. Very recently the group average method has proved best in comparative studies involving a variety of joining methods in biological systematics (Astolfi, Kidd, and Cavalli-Sforza 1981) and in behavioral science (Mezzich and Solomon 1980).

There are many other methods, some described by Sneath and Sokal (1973) and Bailey (1975). Most seem to offer little advantage over the group average or Lance and Williams formula, especially for the early stages of analysis or for taxonomists not well versed in all the details, advantages, and disadvantages of the many methods. Once some level of sophistication is achieved and more is known about the real structure of the data, the less popular methods may be worth pursuing. If one has to buy or write a program for use in one's local computer center, he or she should be sure to end up with a program offering one or the other of the two better methods. The Biomedical Computer Programs (BMD) published by the University of California Press include the better-known methods.

Joining methods—that is, those that are hierarchical, sequential, agglomerative, and nonoverlapping—have two obvious strengths. First, they produce phenograms that are easily depicted on a two-dimensional page of paper; second, they produce clear-cut clusters arranged in a hierarchy—a pattern closely mirroring the way systematists like to go about their work. Generally, joining methods work best at identifying the relatively tighter, more numerous clusters furthest away from the main trunk of the tree. But they also tend to produce neat tidy clusters even when these do not exist, as when random data are used. Hence the need for ways of evaluating the results, a topic taken up briefly in section 12.5.

12.3.2 Sorting Methods

Factor Analysis

Perhaps unknowingly following the old adage that the grass always looks greener on the other side of the fence, it seems that biological taxonomists are reaching out for sorting methods such as factor analysis as answers to problems they see with joining methods at the same time that social or organizational scientists are reaching out for joining methods after many years of frustration with that black art, factor analysis. Since the basic factor analysis algorithms are probably better known to organizational scientists than are the joining algorithms, no discussion of what factor analysis is or how eigenvectors are extracted will be offered here. Readers can easily consult the classic in the field, Harman (1967), or the more recent excellent discussion by Gorsuch (1974).

Several kinds of factor analysis, such as maximum likelihood, image, and alpha, have been proposed over the years. Gorsuch (1974, pp. 122–123) presented a table comparing them; he concluded that, except for very small data matrices, none of them offered any real improvement over the more popular methods. The traditional factor analysis algorithm has been applied in two different situations. In one the principal diagonal is left with unities, following the assumption that all of the variance in the variables at hand is to be explained by the factors; this was labeled the PRINCIPAL COMPONENT method by both Harman and Gorsuch. In the other application, the unities in the principal diagonal are replaced by communality estimates, often by an iterative procedure, under the assumption that both *common* and *unique* factors exist. The former represent common variance among a group of variables and the latter the variance of a specific variable. Harman labeled this approach the MULTIPLE FACTOR method, whereas Gorsuch called it the COMMON FACTOR or PRINCIPAL AXES method. The common factor label seems to have a clearer mnemonic value and so it will be used here.

The main advantage of the principal component solution is that it is the best way to fully represent the variance in the original correlation matrix. This only happens to full extent if the number of factors equals the number of variables, whereupon the practical advantage of factor analysis in reducing the number of dimensions necessary to represent the variance in the correlation matrix is lost. In practice a truncated form is used in which trivial and error factors are ignored. But as Gorsuch (1974, p. 95) noted, a truncated principal component solution is a "back-door" approach to a common factor solution in that even though unities are used in the principal diagonal as initial communality estimates, the effect if only some of the factors are retained is about the same as if the common factor method were used to begin with. Since taxonomists are interested in grouping and therefore are interested in common variance, not specific variance, it makes sense to avoid some of the traditional arguments for or against one or the other factoring methods and get right to a use of the common factor method. Fortunately, the effects of the elements in the principal diagonal are diminished with large matrices; thus it makes little difference which method is used.

Once extracted, factors may be rotated so the factor axes line up better with extant clusters in the data. Rotations may be orthogonal, where independence among axes is preserved, or oblique, where axes are allowed to be correlated if the result is that the axes pass more closely through the cluster centers. The advantage of rotation is that interpretation of the factors is often improved because the factors more clearly separate the variables at the center of a cluster from more peripheral ones. Rotation schemes are well known and need not be described here. See Gorsuch (1974) for a full discussion of rotation procedures.

More important to taxonomists than the choice of principal component or common factor analysis or whether to rotate axes is the number of factors to be extracted. When R mode factor analysis is used the number of factors is not too important since the two-dimensional limitations of the printed page impose the main limitation of two or three factors. In R mode analysis OTUs are plotted in terms of the two or three character factors explaining the largest portion of variance among OTUs. The number of factors does not directly determine the number of clusters, though more factors may lead to the identification of more clusters. The resulting clusters can be compared with the clusters represented by the main stems of a joining method. When Q mode analysis is used the OTUs themselves are factored into groups. Here the number of factors selected directly determines the number of groups identified. These groups would also typically be compared with groups identified by a joining method, so the number is of critical importance.

Gorsuch (1974, pp. 130–160) gave an excellent discussion of how the number of factors might best be determined. Three methods are available: statistical, mathematical, and direct identification of trivial factors. The statistical method tends to include a fair number of trivial factors as significant, especially in matrices based on large samples. For organizational taxonomy, where samples are going to be small, the statistical approach may make more sense, but it will have to be tried out. Experience would indicate that it will not be found very useful.

The mathematical approach used most frequently is to accept all factors whose characteristic roots or eigenvalues are greater than or equal to unity. As Gorsuch (1974, p. 147) noted, this is based on Guttman's (1954) classic paper on lower bounds. Gorsuch also noted that many users of factor analysis forget that the eigenvalue $\geq$ unity criterion is a lower bound, not a cutoff point. It only indicates that no fewer than those with a root $\geq$ unity should be taken, but the rank of the correlation matrix and thus the number of acceptable factors may be greater. In practice this criterion seems almost universally misinterpreted. When the common factor method is used with estimated communalities, the lower bound occurs when the characteristic root becomes negative. But here again the number typically indicated by the lower bound still includes what many analysts would consider trivial factors.

Of the methods for directly identifying trivial factors, Cattell's (1966) *scree test* appears to be the best, though it too is not without difficulties in some circumstances. In this test the value of the root is plotted on a vertical axis with the factor number plotted on a horizontal axis, as shown in figure 12.9. In most cases it will be possible to draw a line through the moderately sloped "scree" of the trivial factors. The plots of the significant factors form a much steeper "cliff." In this case the three factors falling above the scree line are taken as significant. This test runs into difficulty when there is no sharp break between cliff and scree, as tends to happen with an insignificant or random correlation matrix (Gorsuch 1974, p. 154). Another problem occurs when more than one break in the points occurs, which is to say that more than one scree line is possible. In this case additional evidence is necessary.

Another way of trying to identify significant factors is to extract more than the expected number of factors, or all that are possible if no specific expectation is forthcoming. This set is then rotated and factors having only one or two variables loading at very modest levels (say 0.3 or lower) are considered trivial and dropped from later solutions. This approach is open to considerable arbitrariness on the part of the investigator. A more objective criterion has been suggested by McKelvey (1969). Briefly, this approach identifies an optimal number of factors by calculating the closeness to "simple structure" obtained by rotating various numbers of factors. A perfect simple structure obtains when all variables achieve factor loadings of ones or zeros. The degree of simple structure can be tested for by computing Chronbach's (1951) *Alpha* coefficient for the variables loading high on only one factor and correlation coefficients

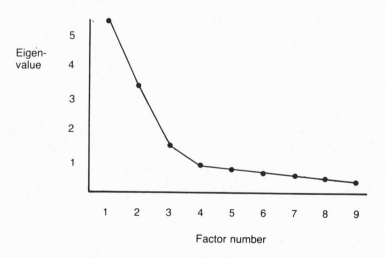

Figure 12.9. Illustration of the Scree Test for Identifying Trivial Factors.

between the clusters of high-loading variables. The number of rotated factors producing the highest alphas and lowest intercluster correlations is probably the best one to use. If oblique factors or groups are desired the low correlation component of this approach cannot be used.

A final method is simply to rotate different numbers of extracted factors, picking factor clusters that are relatively stable no matter how many factors are selected. In this method it would not make sense to select a number less than that indicated by the scree test or the eigenvalue ≥ unity test. As the reader can see, there are no elegant or foolproof methods for selecting the number of factors.

* * * * *

Several other sorting methods were discussed by Sneath and Sokal (1973), Clifford and Stephenson (1975), and Hartigan (1975), including principal coordinate analysis, canonical variate analysis, canonical correlation analysis, nonmetric multidimensional scaling, seriation, and the variance components algorithm. A discussion of these is beyond the scope of this chapter, but the sophisticated reader will want to consider them, especially the multidimensional scaling method, which has seen increased popularity recently (see Moss, Peterson, and Atyeo 1977, for example).

Sorting methods tend to be of most use to taxonomists as a comparison check on the groupings identified by joining methods. Clifford and Stephenson (1975, p. 187) cite instances where as many as twenty factors were needed before all groupings were identified in the factor solution. Obviously the full advantage of a twenty-dimensional R mode solution is lost because of our inability to graphically depict and interpret such a solution. Generally, sorting methods are most useful when a fairly high level of variance is explained by the first two or three factors, say 75 to 80 percent. Then one can display the solution with ease on a two-dimensional page and groupings of OTUs can be plotted in terms of the axes defined by an R mode analysis. In this regard it is also true that sorting methods are most helpful in cross-checking the major branches or groupings. If the first two or three factors do not account for a large portion of the variance, a better choice might be Q mode, where an analysis of characters is used to load OTUs onto factors. The resulting groupings can be compared with those produced by a joining method.

12.3.3 Rank Considerations

A final note on structural analysis pertains to decisions regarding the rank of groupings identified by one or more cluster programs. Rank determination becomes a special problem when a classification scheme is being developed on the basis of several independent cluster studies. For example, are the third-level fusions across several phenograms of the same classificatory rank comparable? And if rank is not to be directly determined by the fusion levels of a joining method, how is it to be determined?

A general discussion of principles for developing the higher categories and deciding upon rank is presented in chapter 8 and thus needs not be repeated here. Considerations such as internal diversity, number of taxa, gaps between them, and so forth were discussed. Orthodox biological taxonomists such as Simpson (1961), Davis and Heywood (1963), and Mayr (1969) included these as well as stability and tradition. Sneath and Sokal (1973, p. 291) object to all of these except the criterion of internal diversity.

Numerical taxonomists are interested in a numerical criterion of rank which is as objective as possible. This is a necessity if numerical methods are to be used as a deductive test of groupings stemming from a more theoretical, divisive approach. Sneath and Sokal (1973, pp. 292–294) suggested that the rank of a superior taxon be defined as the standard deviation of all OTUs in all groups included about a common centroid. They discussed a model that accommodates several special circumstances. By using their model one is assured that the rank of the superior taxon will be higher no matter how broad the diversity of a subordinate group. Sneath and Sokal also noted that the fusion levels of most joining methods, and especially the group average method, are good approximations of the foregoing model since the fusion levels are based on average distances.

Most numerical taxonomic studies do not seem to publish data giving an indication of rank independent of the particular fusion criteria of the program being used. They just accept the ranks as they appear. Ideally one should use one of the several models offered by Sneath and Sokal (1973, pp. 292–293) for identifying rank via the root mean square of the distances from the centroid. This would lead to consistency in establishing a numerical basis for cluster ranks independent of the various cluster algorithyms typically used. This is especially true if the nearest or farthest neighbor methods are used.

12.4 METHODS OF VISUAL REPRESENTATION

After many years of experimentation with different methods of illustrating taxonomic schemes such as stick and ball models, shaded similarity matrices, graphs, skyline plots, or contour diagrams (see Sneath and

Sokal 1973, pp. 259–277) two methods prevail: dendrograms and multi-dimensional plots. These are reviewed in turn.

12.4.1 Dendrograms

Dendrograms typically appear in two forms: PHENOGRAMS, which represent clusterings based on an analysis of phenotypic similarity, and CLADOGRAMS, which depict clusterings based on evolutionary branching points. In this book the discussion of numerical aspects bears only on phenograms. Numerical approaches to cladistic analysis are ignored.

Dendrograms have traditionally been placed so that the branches go upwards. Recent studies involving large numbers of species have presented the dendrograms horizontally, with branches going to the right, as shown in figures 12.10 and 12.11, because of space limitations. The abscissa is graduated in a scale of similarity or dissimilarity coefficients. In figure 12.10 the scale illustrates the use of the product-moment correlation as the measure of resemblance, whereas in figure 12.11 the scale represents a distance measure. Both dendrograms are from Goronzy's (1969) study of business organizations and are based on the same data. Though they both use the group averaging method (Goronzy noted that the nearest neighbor methods led to the familiar chaining effect), observe that the results of the correlations are quite different from those of the distance measure. The level of resemblance (dissimilarity) between two clusters is indicated by where the branching point falls on the abscissa. This was illustrated in more detail in figures 12.4 and 12.5. The branches are labeled by OTU codes or mnemonics.

There is the problem of how to show the labels of the higher groupings. Biological taxonomists have generally not bothered to add anything more than the OTU labels to their phenograms. It is hard to know just why this is so, but possibly it is because there typically is not enough space on the dendrogram on the one hand, and possibly because they do not appear to have tackled the problem of formally altering the traditional higher category groupings and associated labels on the other. One possible way of labeling higher categories on a crowded dendrogram is to add numbers to each fusion stem with a separate table relating numbers to labels.

The ordinate has no special significance. Branches can be switched around as desired. Usually clusters that are the most different from each other are placed at the top and bottom of a horizontal dendrogram if at all possible. The intervening clusters are juggled around as much as possible to place similar clusters adjacent to each other, recognizing that

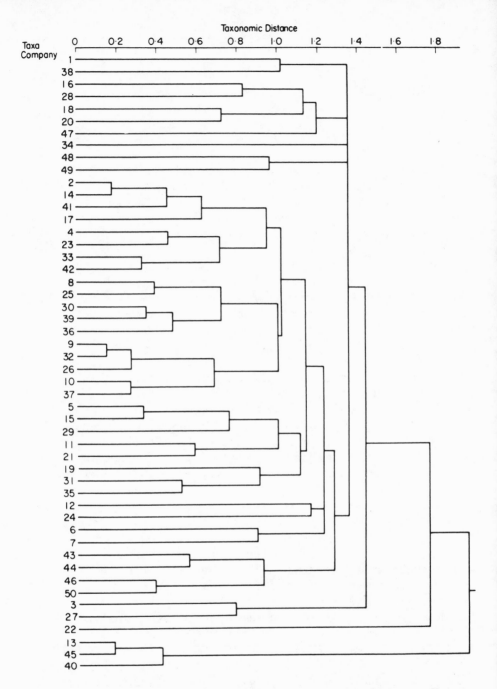

Figure 12.10. Phenogram Based on Product-Moment Resemblance Coefficient and Group Average Clustering Method; data consisted of 50 organizations and 29 characters. (From F. Goronzy, "A Numerical Taxonomy of Business Enterprize," in *Numerical Taxonomy*, ed. by A. J. Cole. London: Academic Press. 1969. Reprinted by permission of the publisher.)

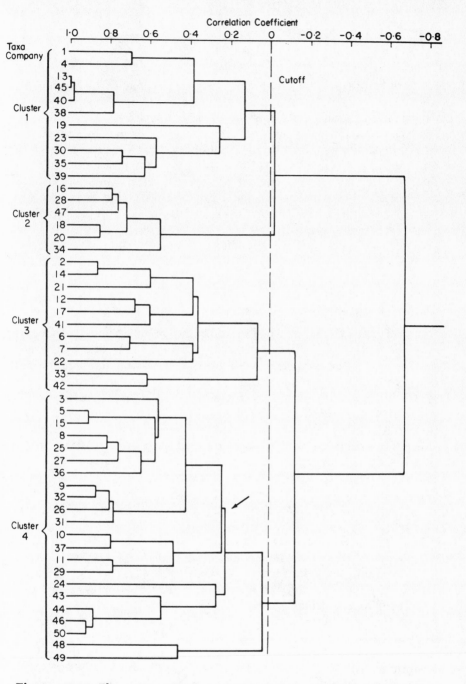

Figure 12.11. Phenogram Based on Distance Resemblance Coefficient and Group Average Clustering Method; data consisted of 50 organizations and 29 characters. (From F. Goronzy, "A Numerical Taxonomy of Business Enterprize," in *Numerical Taxonomy*, ed. by A. J. Cole, London: Academic Press. 1969. Reprinted by permission of the publisher.)

clusters that fuse together at the next higher rank have to be adjacent to each other. In other words, a pair of clusters may be relocated only by rotating them around their fusion or branching point.

As can be seen in figures 12.10 and 12.11, the usual joining method works by finding pairs at each branching point. This, of course, is an arbitrary imposition of pair structure on data that may naturally split up into three or more groups at a particular point. In actual effect this is not particularly problematic since the fusion of a third cluster to an existing pair of clusters at a similarity level almost the same as the existing cluster has the same effect. This is illustrated in figure 12.11 in cluster 4 at the 0.24 fusion level on the similarity scale (marked by the little arrow).

12.4.2 Multidimensional Plots

Often a systematist is interested in confirming the major branches shown in a dendrogram or in discovering the extent to which data have been warped by the imposed structure of a two-dimensional dendrogram. In this event a partitioning method is used such as factor analysis or multidimensional scaling, or as in a recent study by Moss, Peterson, and Atyeo (1977), a complicated multistep combination of these two ordination methods may be used. Figure 12.12 shows one of the multidimensional plots reported in their study. (A suitable multidimensional plotting of organizations was not available.). This plot resulted after the following analytical steps were taken:

1. An R mode Principal Component Analysis (PCA) resulted in three factors.

2. A transposed matrix of the three largest factors was post-multipled by the standardized data matrix to yield a matrix of OTU projections.

3. The OTU projections in three-dimensional PCA space were used as a starting point for nonmetric multidimensional scaling (MDS) placement of Q mode distances among OTUs.

4. A PCA was performed on the variance-covariance matrix obtained from MDS coordinates.

5. The Q and R mode results were superimposed with the use of minimum spanning trees (see Clifford and Stephenson 1975, p. 123, for a description of minimum spanning trees), which are groupings indicated by lines drawn between OTUs and circles around various subsets.

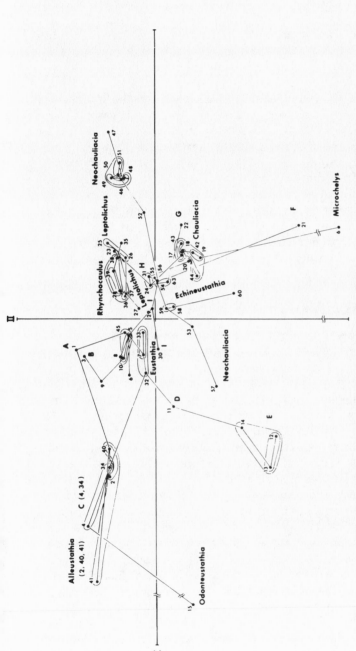

Figure 12.12. Species and Genera of Eustathiidae, 61-Species Study. Ordination by principal component analysis of character correlations, component I vs. II, followed by multidimensional scaling of taxonomic distances. Minimum spanning tree and subsets superimposed. Matrix correlation between 61-species taxonomic distances and distances between species in the 2-space = .907. (From W. W. Moss, P. C. Peterson, and W. T. Atyeo, "A Multivariate Assessment of Phenetic Relationships Within the Feather Mite family Eustathiidae [Acari]," *Systematic Zoology* 26:386−409, 1977. Reprinted by permission of the editor.)

It should be noted that the Moss, Peterson, and Atyeo procedure is considerably more complicated than that used by most biological numerical taxonomists. It is mentioned here to illustrate the level of numerical sophistication currently being applied by some systematists.

Figure 12.12 shows a plotting of OTUs in terms of the first and second factors of a three-factor ordination solution. In this case an R mode analysis of characters was used to find factors. Such a plot is most useful in determining how tightly knit the clusters are, how they relate in space one to another, how distinctive they are relative to one another, and how individual OTUs compare with one another. Such a plot often resolves uncertainties found in a phenogram or when two different joining methods produce rather different cluster structures. Such plots can be quite illuminating, but also cumbersome when three factors are involved and impossibly so with more factors. Even so, present-day practice tends to use sorting and joining methods and their respective plots and dendrograms in combination.

12.5 EVALUATION OF RESULTS

The evaluation of a numerical taxonomic solution may be pursued from two perspectives: *external* and *internal validity*. In the former case a set of clusters is compared to groupings in the protosystem determined in some other way, probably via an evolutionary/historical analysis of trends in the development of groupings drawing on one or more theories of how such processes might have come about. There seems little doubt that in biological taxonomy numerical solutions have universally been evaluated in reference to the traditional orthodox classification scheme. It is impossible to understate the advantage that biological systematists have had in being able to take the first steps toward a numerical method while having at hand essentially uncontested orthodox solutions to use as bases for testing external validity. For example, Moss, Peterson, and Atyeo (1977, p. 388) observed that "the genera [previously] recognized in the monograph were present in the correlation and distance phenograms for the most part, although distortions (species displaced from nearest relatives) were evident at the lower levels of clustering." Such a statement is possible only if a well-accepted orthodox classification was already known—in this case, Moss is a well-known expert in the study of mites, and feather mites were the subject of the investigation. Numerical solutions in biology have generally had such high external validity in the sense that they corresponded so well with the orthodox solutions that they have had more or less only a "fine-tuning" impact on biological classifications. Again using the Moss, Peterson, and Atyeo

(1977, p. 400) study as a typical example (though it does use a much more sophisticated method than most), observe their conclusion: "In general, the numerical findings confirmed the existence of the nine new and nine described genera recognized earlier by conventional means."

While numerical methods may not have altered biological classification very much, they have offered a more objective deductive confirmation of the orthodox results. The rest of us interested in classification may offer thanks that the numerical methods have been developed to the point where they do have high external validity in a field where the existing classification has been thoroughly worked over via orthodox methods and subsequently confirmed to a considerable extent for many families and genera by numerical methods. Though there are still many difficulties with numerical methods, organizational systematists may begin their inquiry with the knowledge that where there is a substantial disagreement between numerical and nonnumerical findings about organizational groupings, the trouble probably lies more with the latter than the former methods. For us, numerical phenetic methods are relatively more highly developed than nonnumerical evolutionary/historical methods focusing on homotechnical (patristic) or cladistic affinity. Nevertheless, the problem of the external validity of either numerical or nonnumerical clusterings cannot be ignored by organizational systematists. The reader is cautioned to note that "better" here is a long way from being *definitive*, since nonnumerical evolutionist methods are almost unknown in our field and the problem of selecting significant characters is unresolved.

12.5.1 Phyletic Validity

Given the combined evolutionist/empiricist approach advocated in this book, it is clear that an essential criterion is that of external or phyletic validity. I have observed previously that numerical methods offer a deductive test of solutions produced via evolutionary/historical studies of the origins of different kinds of organizations. At the same time, these latter solutions offer the possibility of an external evaluation of numerical solutions. As the solutions converge, both the deductive test and external validity are achieved.

In section 12.5.2, notions of internal validity are discussed. These test how well the numerical clustering solution captures the group structure implicit in the data collected. The internal test operates only within the constraints imposed by the quality of the data actually collected. It does not test the adequacy of the population definition, the sampling plan, the scope of the taxonomic characters selected, or the quality of the coding and scaling procedures. The adequacy of these several fundamental components of numerical methods can only be tested via external validity—a comparison of numerical solutions with a representation via other methods of the actual groupings present in the protosystem. In this sense phyletic validity is the fundamental test of the quality of a clustering solution. For reasons not clear to me, this aspect of evaluation is not discussed by Sneath and Sokal (1973) nor by the authors of the other principal books on numerical taxonomy. This despite the obvious advantage biological systematists have in drawing on their well-developed orthodox classification scheme.

Whereas external validity is objectively testable in numerical taxonomic studies of biological phenomena, comparisons of numerical clusters with traditional classificatory groupings are largely informal, as in the example given earlier by Moss, Peterson, and Atyeo (1977). In biology this appears to have been acceptable, presumably because the fits between most numerical solutions and the orthodox classification were so good that the fits were obvious except for a few minor exceptions. One may anticipate that in organizational systematics the fit between a numerical solution and a set of hypothetical groupings proposed by a phyletic analysis will often be quite poor and in some cases virtually nonexistent.

Since a systematist is likely to have only one or two phyletic clustering dendrograms and only one or two numerical phenograms to compare, the application of statistics is problematic. This is complicated by the fact that finite populations are involved. Clifford and Stephenson (1975, pp. 138–142) presented two approaches to comparing dendrograms, one based on counting the number of nodes separating each of all possible pairs of OTU groupings, and the other based on comparing the composition of groupings. Neither approach is accompanied by a statistical test. Take the node-counting approach: most statistical tests are inappropriate either because the distribution is unknown or because of the relatively small sample size—the sample in this case being the number of pairs of OTU groups. However, the Kolomogorov-Smirnov one-sample test, as described in Siegel (1956) or Gibbons (1976), seems appropriate if the following steps are taken:

1. The number of nodes separating each of all possible pairs of OTUs are counted. For example, in figure 12.10 the number of nodes separating OTU (company) #1 from OTU #30 (in Cluster 1) is seven. The number separating OTU #30 from OTU #35 is one.

2. Following some arbitrary replicable order, such as comparing OTU #1 with all others from left to right, OTU #2 with all others from left to

right, and so forth, the node counts in the phyletic cluster scheme are arranged in the theoretical cumulative frequency distribution, where the denominator is the sum total of all counts and the numerator is the cumulative frequency count progressing through all possible pairs of OTUs.

3. Following the same counting order, the node counts of the numerical clustering solution are arranged into the observed cumulative frequency distribution.

4. It is likely that the sum totals of the phyletic and observed numerical node counts will not agree because the solutions have differing numbers of OTU clusters, the probability being that the numerical solution will be more detailed (have more clusters) than the phyletic one. In this case it seems best to collapse OTU clusters in the numerical solution until the totals agree. I also think that it would be best to arrange the collapsing to progress in a direction toward as much compatibility between the two solutions as possible. In other words, if a genus in the phyletic solution contains one species, collapse the species in the numerical solution for the corresponding genus into one. To collapse in such a way as to increase the mismatch between corresponding categories within the two solutions seems to work at cross-purposes with our objectives.

5. Calculate the K-S statistic and make the test as outlined by Siegel (1956) or Gibbons (1976).

One reservation I have about putting too much emphasis on external validity stems from the possibility of highly subjective, poorly thought-out, poorly researched phyletic clusterings based on an inferior theory of organizational differences. Alternatively, some theoreticians might also be worried about the test of their historically derived groupings by a decidedly inferior numerical solution. The best that can be hoped for is that in the event that there is not a good fit between a phyletic and numerical solution, *both* solutions are considered suspect until further investigation or replication by other investigators shifts the benefit of the doubt in favor of one or the other.

12.5.2 Cophenetic Optimality

A test of the internal validity of a numerical solution is best conceived as the ability of a clustering solution or dendrogram to reproduce the original similarity matrix. This is similar in concept to the approach long taken by the factor analysts of testing a factor structure by its ability to reproduce the original correlation matrix. The approach most frequently used by numerical taxonomists is that of cophenetic optimality, based on a correlational method developed by Sokal and Rohlf (1962). It takes the following steps:

1. Start with the resemblance matrix.
2. Construct a cophenetic matrix corresponding to all pairs of values in the resemblance matrix, as illustrated in table 12.7 for the nearest neighbor, farthest neighbor, and group average dendrograms shown in figures 12.4, 12.5 and 12.8. The cophenetic resemblance between two OTUs is taken as the *highest* fusion level by which they are joined. Thus in figure 12.8, which shows the group average dendrogram, the fusion level between OTUs a and d is 3.69 (the same as the fusion level in Step Three in table 12.6) and the fusion level between OTUs c and f is 7.33 (Step Five in the table). For large clustering jobs done on a computer it is best to have the computer produce the cophenetic matrices directly using the phenetic values (fusion levels) as they are calculated.
3. Using the elements of the matrices as data points, a product-moment correlation coefficient, called the cophenetic correlation, r_{mm}, is calculated. These matrices are shown in table 12.7 for the three clustering methods.

For further details on the cophenetic correlation method and other less frequently used methods, the reader should consult Sneath and Sokal (1973, pp. 277–284). Experience to date suggests that the group average method is most likely to produce the highest cophenetic correlation, although in the especially contrived example used here, which exhibits the chained cluster pattern to begin with, it is no surprise that the nearest neighbor method produces the highest correlation. Farris (1969) has shown that the measures can be maximized by clustering methods producing "reversals," but since these are not used this is of little consequence.

The cophenetic correlation method can also be used to compare the cophenetic matrices of different clustering methods directly with each other (assuming they are all based on the same sample) in additon to comparing them with their original similarity matrices. Thus for the dendrograms in figures 12.4 and 12.5 and table 12.8, the cophenetic correlations between the three pairs of dendrograms are:

$R_{nearest-farthest} = 0.58$

$R_{nearest-group} = 0.89$

$R_{farthest-group} = 0.69$

TABLE 12.7

COPHENETIC MATRICES AND CORRELATIONS FOR PHENOGRAMS IN FIGURES 12.4, 12.5, AND 12.8.*

Similarity Matrix

	a	b	c	d	e	f
a	—					
b	1.00	—				
c	2.24	2.00	—			
d	4.47	3.61	3.00	—		
e	7.21	6.71	4.58	4.00	—	
f	10.82	10.00	8.94	6.40	5.00	—

Nearest Neighbor Cophenetic Matrix $r_{SN} = 0.85$

	a	b	c	d	e	f
a	—					
b	1.00	—				
c	2.00	2.00	—			
d	3.00	3.00	3.00	—		
e	4.00	4.00	4.00	4.00	—	
f	5.00	5.00	5.00	5.00	5.00	—

Farthest Neighbor Cophenetic Matrix $r_{SF} = 0.65$

	a	b	c	d	e	f
a	—					
b	1.00	—				
c	2.24	2.24	—			
d	10.82	10.82	10.82	—		
e	10.82	10.82	10.82	4.00	—	
f	10.82	10.82	10.82	6.40	6.40	—

Group Average Cophenetic Matrix $r_{SG} = 0.81$

	a	b	c	d	e	f
a	—					
b	1.00	—				
c	2.12	2.12	—			
d	3.69	3.69	3.69	—		
e	7.33	7.33	7.33	7.33	—	
f	7.33	7.33	7.33	7.33	7.33	—

*The similarity matrix contains the original distance values underlying all three phenograms. The cophenetic values in the other matrices are based on fusion levels in the respective phenograms.

In this example the nearest neighbor and group average methods are most alike because of the special nature of the illustration. Typically, it has been found elsewhere (Sneath and Sokal 1973, p. 280) that the farthest neighbor and group average clusters are closer to each other than either is to the nearest neighbor results. An alternative approach to comparing two numerical phenograms based on the same population is given by Boorman and Olivier (1973).

12.5.3 Significance of Clusters

Hartigan (1975) lamented the lack of a sound statistical basis for any of the clustering methods. The tendency has been to use what seems to work rather than to use methods having statistical credibility. The fact that statisticians have largely ignored clustering and taxonomists have seemed to find the comments of statisticians and mathematicians irrelevant has not helped.

One of the main problems is that most assumptions about multivariate normal distributions do not apply. This means that an obvious statistic like Hotelling's T^2, which might otherwise be used to test for the significance of differences across the centroid of the several clusters, cannot be used. A variety of other methods based on Mahalanobis's D^2 or some other statistic also suffer the same fate.

One approach has been to explore the likelihood that a clustering solution could have emerged from a random data set. Rohlf and Fisher (1968) looked into this possibility and found, using the group average method on a random data set, that the cophenetic correlation coefficient decreased as both the number of OTUs and characters was increased, reaching as low as 0.3 for a correlation matrix and 0.6 for a distance matrix. Presumably r_{SG} would have to be significantly higher than either of these levels to warrant a conclusion that the clusters were significant. Since the cophenetic correlation varies by the number of OTUs and characters, the ideal approach would be to construct an OTU-by-OTU resemblance matrix the same size as the organizational resemblance matrix in question, using random normal deviates to give distributions, for the same number of characters used in the organizational study. Since a clustering method will invariably produce some kind of cluster dendrogram even when there is no cluster structure in the data, the cophenetic correlation becomes a measure of the degree to which a cluster structure may be arbitrarily imposed on the resemblance matrix. To be accepted, the cophenetic correlation of the organizational clustering would have to be significantly higher than the one based on random data.

A second rather cumbersome approach reduces the characters to a few well-established independent sets, perhaps via factor analysis. Then the mean of each of these sets is calculated for each of a pair of OTU clusters. The differences between each character set for a pair of groups can be tested via nonparametric methods (see Gibbons 1976, for example). This is really feasible only if several OTUs comprise each cluster; otherwise the statistic is based on exemplars that are Ns of 1. All possible pairs of groups can be compared in this fashion.

Other attempts at some kind of statistical determination are discussed by Sneath and Sokal (1973), Clifford and Stephenson (1975), Hartigan (1975), and Jardine and Sibson (1971). They do not offer much that is either well accepted, well worked out, or specific. The problem of statistical substantiation is largely unsolved at this time. In this vacuum the tendency has been to take the view, as do Clifford and Stephenson (1975, p. 109), of "How well does it work?" This question takes us back to external validity.

12.6 IDENTIFICATION

As defined in this book, classification is the term used to refer to the general set of procedures by which one develops the clusters of OTUs and higher categories making up a classification scheme. IDENTIFICATION is the procedure for placing an organization into a particular class. Although most available taxonomic characters are typically used to construct a classification scheme, only a relatively few diagnostic characters are used to make up KEYS by which particular organizations are placed into a class. Mayr (1969, p. 405) defined a key as follows: "A tabulation of diagnostic characters of species (genera, etc.) in dichotomous couplets facilitating rapid identification." In other words, keys are used to rapidly answer the question, I wonder what kind of, or what class of organization this is? As Davis and Heywood (1963) noted in their classic work, the objective of any identification approach is ease and certainty of identification.

The number of characters needed for identification is always less than the number of characters desirable for establishing a classification scheme in the first place. Sneath and Sokal (1973, p. 386) observed that the theoretical minimum number needed to separate as many as ten million species was 24 binary characters. In practice many more than this are needed. For biology, Munroe (1964) has suggested that some 500 characters may be needed; Sneath and Sokal think this is an underestimate; they think that about as many keys will be required as there are branches. It seems likely that for identifying organizations a sizable number of keys will be needed.

A discussion of the actual procedures for developing keys is extensive and complicated, and well beyond the scope of this book. Both Mayr's (1969) and Sneath and Sokal's (1973) books are good places to check for further discussion of this subject, though obviously the content is biological. The traditional approach results in SEQUENTIAL KEYS inasmuch as they are developed to apply sequentially with the single trunk as the starting point. There are two kinds of sequential keys:

MONOTHETIC KEYS occur when one diagnostic character will do the job of separating OTUs at a particular branching point. Thus all organizations having one state would fall into one class and all those having the other state would fall into the other class. (This assumes that the dendrogram consists of two-cluster branches.) Multistate keys are possible, though the tendency is toward dichotomous keys, following the tendency to use clustering methods producing pairs at each node. Monothetic keys are the simplest and easiest to use, but they are vulnerable to many exceptions.

POLYTHETIC KEYS are those in which at some branching point several diagnostic characters are needed to sort all the organizations into one or the other class. A decision for a particular organization is based on a "majority vote," as Sneath and Sokal (1973, p. 391) termed it, of the several characters involved. These keys are more difficult to use, but fewer exceptions or misplaced OTUs result.

Another approach focuses on SIMULTANEOUS KEYS. Here all characters are used. Usually a matrix of all characters by typical values for all known taxa is constructed. Thus it might be that ten kinds of assembly line organization are known and described by ninety-five characters. The matrix would be ninety-five rows by ten columns. Each column would contain the typical (mean, median, modal) value of the taxa making up each kind of organization. The unknown organization would then be compared across all characters until the closest match was found, whereupon it would be classed as a member of that group. Since a large table, such as the one in the example with ninety-five characters, is hard to comprehend all at one time, the comparison can often be done sequentially, with an unclassed organization first identified with respect to major classes of taxa and subsequently with individual taxa within a major class. This ends up essentially a sequential polythetic approach as described earlier. Alternatively one could use a correlation coefficient to ascertain the overall relation between the unknown organization and each of the known columns of character values. This assumes that the characters are independent and equally weighted.

A third approach is based on the use of *discriminant functions.* A multiple discriminant analysis may be used to develop functions composed of weighted characters that most clearly separate OTUs. Obviously it would take several analyses to develop functions to discriminate all groupings in a larger classification scheme. Discriminant analysis is well known to organizational scientists and need not be discussed here. A difficulty with this method is that the number of OTUs making up each of two or more groups for which a function is developed is very small, making the needed assumption of multivariate normality problematic. Without the use of an F test it is hard to know whether the function is significant, not to mention the related problem of deciding which characters in the function are the significant ones.

The ultimate payoff in organizational systematics rests on the development of efficacious identification keys. Otherwise researchers interested in studying the function and process of certain kinds of organizations will have great difficulty placing the organizations into the general classification scheme. If organizations are not easily placed into known populations the generalizability of the findings to those populations is questionable. Furthermore the location of the findings in the information retrieval scheme that the classification represents is also problematic. In short, the identification keys make a classification usable for those doing nonsystematic kinds of studies.

12.7 PRESENTATION OF RESULTS (SUMMARY)

To date one of the most sophisticated approaches to numerical taxonomy is that undertaken by Moss, Peterson, and Atyeo (1977), the details of which will appear in a monograph. A study such as this offers an excellent guide to conducting an outstanding numerical taxonomic investigation. Readers are strongly encouraged to study this and other reports carefully before starting and publishing research of their own. Since the methods and reasoning behind the use of combinations of methods are now fairly well known there is little excuse (except for time and money, perhaps!) to conduct an inferior study. By way of summarizing the ideas in this chapter and offering a guide to the main steps in carrying out a numerical taxonomic study, I will present some points that all organizational systematists should be cognizant of in designing a study and preparing a published report. They follow fairly closely a similar set of points listed by Sneath and Sokal (1973, pp. 303–305):

1. The theoretical and classificatory considerations supporting the selection of the population studied should be adequately considered and discussed. This is fundamental—no amount of technical virtuosity will overcome a lack of attention to initial population selection (section 11.2).

2. The selection of exemplar OTUs or sampling of OTUs from a population warrants careful attention (section 11.3).

3. Some justification of the decisions regarding the number and kinds of taxonomic characters selected is important (section 11.4).

4. Methods of transforming and coding the data should be discussed briefly (section 12.1).

5. Considerations leading to the choice of resemblance coefficients should be presented (section 12.2).

6. It would seem that group averaging is the best joining method and factor analysis the most likely sorting method, though special situations may call for other methods. In any event, readers should be offered some discussion of the subjective or arbitrary decisions made in using these methods. They are not objective in the sense of being totally free from personal bias. While such decisions cannot be avoided, readers can be suitably informed (section 12.3).

7. Good current practice suggests presenting one or more dendrograms based on different clustering methods, complete with cophenetic correlations, followed by factor or other multivariate analyses of major clusters. Both R and Q modes may be used. Nonmetric multidimensional plots are also often employed (section 12.4).

8. Evaluative comments, with or without statistics, should be made (section 12.5). If factor analysis is used, special attention to the method for determining the number of factors should be noted (section 12.3).

9. The general relation between phyletic or evolutionary/historical and numerical solutions—that is, the question of external validity—should be discussed (section 12.5).

10. If an identification key is presented (and if not presented it should be available from the author), information on how well it actually classes organizations not used to develop the classification should be presented.

11. Since official bodies for approving nomenclature do not exist in the field of organizational science, formal nomenclatural procedure, assuming it is necessary, remains problematic. In the interim a simple scheme such as the one mentioned in section 9.4.5 may be helpful. Labels should probably have mnemonic value, hold as much continuity as possible with names already in use either in the organizational science literature or in the lay community and, following recent moves by

the international communities of biologists and physicists, avoid personalisms such as family or other personally meaningful names.

12. Data should be made available to anyone wishing to replicate, critique, or otherwise analyze it. In general, taxonometric methods should be described in enough detail—with names of computer programs, kinds of computers, and so forth—that replications are possible.

13. Inasmuch as organizations cannot be stuffed, pressed, dried, or mounted and placed in museums, organizational systematists will have to find other ways to make data about organizations they have studied available to others. Hopefully studies will be designed with an eye toward improving the chances that other systematists studying other organizations will be able to include the data along with their own. At least data should be stored in a form readily usable by others.

13 THE POPULATION PERSPECTIVE

An age of superstition is a time when people imagine that they know more than they do.

[Hayek 1978, p. 31]

In place of the social scientists' favorite Myth of the Second Coming (of Newton), we should recognize the Reality of the Already-Arrived (Darwin): the paradigm of the explanatory but non-predictive scientist.

[Scriven 1959, p. 477]

Starbuck (1974) reported a casual (very casual, I think) census suggesting that there are about 6.7 paradigms per organization theorist. Even if this is a gross exaggeration, paradigms are truly legion in our field. In light of this, the prospect of characterizing what Kaplan (1964) termed *reconstructed logic* and *logic-in-use* for organizational science seems impossible.* A philosophy of organizational science has yet to be reconstructed. In saying this I mean to separate the philosophy of *organizational* science from the philosophy of other social or behavioral sciences, as I suspect there may be significant differences. A clear com-

---

*Logic-in-use refers to the more or less logical practices scientists actually use in carrying out scientific investigations. Reconstructed logic is the explicit formulation of the philosophy of science or other formal statements about proper research methods.

pendium of the logic-in-use of organizational scientists also does not exist—though the *Administrative Science Quarterly* amounts to a rather lengthy surrogate. Since either of these compilations would be a considerable task, I cannot undertake it here. But I will offer very brief notes on our apparent reconstructed logic and logic-in-use as a point of departure for this chapter. I will then move on to the main thrusts of the chapter— first, toward a new compromise model of the organizational world, and second, toward an explanatory but nonpredictive paradigm of organizational science. The new paradigm is an alternative to both the traditional objectivists, predictive reconstruction and the more recent subjectivist, phenomenological one.

The field is in such a state of paradigmatic confusion that a clear, widely accepted description of the reconstructed logic is impossible. By and large the natural science model, logical positivism, the hypothetico-deductive method, or what Hempel (1965) termed *deductive-nomological* thinking, still seems to drive the designs of most empirical studies.* Briefly, the key elements of the natural science method are (Behling 1980):

1. Public procedures.
2. Precise definitions.
3. Objective phenomena (in that they exist independently of the human mind).
4. Replicable findings.
5. The method is systematic and cumulative.
6. The purpose is understanding via explanation and prediction.

True, there have been constant attacks against it.† These were summarized by Behling (1980) into five main objections (which he went on to refute):

1. *Uniquess:* each organization differs to some extent from all others.
2. *Instability:* organizational "facts" are transitory, with the governing laws changing also.
3. *Sensitivity:* organizational behavior may change once researchers' hypotheses or findings become known to members of an organization.
4. *Lack of Realism:* the manipulated and controlled findings of experiments cannot reasonably be generalized to their real-world counterparts.
5. *Epistemological Difference:* the process of "knowing" about human behavior is different from knowing about physical facts.

*For example, see Berelson and Steiner (1964), Campbell and Stanley (1966), Blalock and Blalock (1968), Borgatta and Bohrnstedt (1970), Kerlinger (1973), Filley, House, and Kerr (1976), Cook and Campbell (1976), Jackson and Morgan (1978), among many others.

†For instance, Bailey (1970), Argyris (1972), Phillips (1973), Lundberg (1976), Pondy and Mitroff (1979), Aldrich (1979), Blute (1979), Weick (1980), among others.

I doubt whether very many organizational scientists thus far have really been convinced by the critics—certainly not the number crunchers. Some active people in the field have definitely not been convinced.

No one has sat astride the methodological horse of organizational science over the past two decades more comfortably than Peter Blau. He is a firm believer in Hempel's *deductive-nomological explanation* (Hempel 1965, pp. 335–347). In this form of explanation the "explanadum," or what is to be explained, or the set of specific hypotheses that are empirically tested, is a logical consequence of the "explanans," which consists of statements describing the phenomena and general laws. Blau (1970, p. 202; Blau and Schoenherr 1971, p. 295) was fond of quoting Braithwaite:

> A scientific theory is a deductive system in which observable consequences logically follow from the conjunction of observed facts with the set of fundamental hypotheses in the system. [Braithwaite 1953, p. 22]

Kaplan described this form of explanation as a *hierarchical* theory because its "component laws are presented as deductions from a small set of basic principles" (1964, p. 298). In this form, the general laws are accepted as valid if they explain a set of deduced, empirically confirmed propositions of more specific nature. As Blau said, following Braithwaite:

> Strange as it may seem, the higher-level hypotheses that explain the lower-level propositions are accepted as valid purely on the basis that they do explain them, in the specific sense that they logically imply them, and without independent empirical evidence; whereas acceptance of the lower-level propositions that need to be explained is contingent on empirical evidence. [Blau 1970, p. 202]

Blau is very explicit about what he believes. Others are less so, but I think it is fair to say that most organizational scientists would subscribe to a reconstructed logic they might loosely characterize as the hypothetico-deductive method. What Blau was not so explicit about was whether or not he really accepted a fundamental requirement of deductive-nomological explanation, which is that the laws are universally true, laws that Hempel and Oppenheim (1965, p. 250) said "are customarily called causal, or deterministic." Hempel and Oppenheim (1965) and especially Hempel (1965) are unmistakably clear in distinguishing between deductive-nomological explanations and *inductive-statistical* explanations that attempt to explain individual events occurring according to some statistical frequency. Since Blau cited the

Hempel and Oppenheim paper, one would think he was also indicating acceptance of the universal predictive requirement of their reconstructed logic. I note, however, that in Blau and Schoenherr the evidence of statistical treatments suggests a logic-in-use more in tune with the inductive-statistical form. So, in the work of a respected leader in the field, one who has been more careful and explicit than most in enunciating the reconstructed logic he was following, there seems to be an inconsistency between reconstructed logic and logic-in-use.

Blau is not the only one falling prey to such an inconsistency. A recent paper by Mackenzie and House (1978) began by pledging allegiance to deductive-nomological explanation. They also cited Hempel and Oppenheim (1965) and a more recent work by Hempel (1966). But they were in some disagreement about the requirement of universality. In footnote #1 it seems that Mackenzie was more inclined to hold out for universals, subject to measurement error, whereas House clearly accepted statistical significance as adequate. Later in the paper they cited Minor's work as an example of strong inference, and it is clear that his work involved statistical procedures such as "significant correlations." Again it would appear that leading organization theorists have taken a reconstructed logic from natural science which is fundamentally inconsistent with the logic-in-use. It is a case of misapplying Hempel's deductive-nomological explanation to phenomena calling for his inductive-statistical form.

I have referred to Blau and Mackenzie and House largely because they were quite explicit in grounding their views in Hempel's deductive-nomological form of explanation. More importantly, they were formulating a reconstructed logic they presumably hoped others would follow. Though probably not because of the direct influence of Blau or Mackenzie and House, the logic-in-use of most researchers whose work appears in journals publishing pieces about organizations, such as *American Sociological Review, American Journal of Sociology, British Journal of Sociology, Sociology, Administrative Science Quarterly, Academy of Management Journal, Academy of Management Review*, and *Human Relations*, to name but a few, generally follows the natural science model.

As a more specific example of logic-in-use I would like to cite a recent study by Meyer and Brown (1977) published in the *American Journal of Sociology*, a very well-respected journal. This piece is part of a major study recently reported in a book by Meyer (1979). Meyer has to be considered a major contributor to the field at this time, having published many papers and books about organizations (especially 1972, 1977). The Meyer and Brown piece was a study of the process of bureaucratization among government finance agencies. The study reported longitudinal historical data taken in the years 1966 and 1972. The main hypothesis was that the process of bureaucratization begins with environmental pressures, which give rise to formalization that in turn gives rise to decentralization. In their conclusion they said:

> An increase in formalization, it was shown, gives rise to multitier hierarchies, and hierarchical differentiation in turn gives rise to the delegation of personnel decisions to lower levels. A causal chain from origins and the environment to formalization to hierarchy to decentralization was thus posited. . . .
> Several implictions arise from these results. First, the patterns described here need not be peculiar to finance agencies or to the history of the civil service movement in the United States. Effects of origins and the environment and the discontinuous pattern of change should be evident for diverse institutional sectors. [Meyer and Brown 1977, pp. 383–384]

Though people might argue about some of the particulars of the Meyer and Brown study, I believe that many would have no difficulty accepting the form of the quoted conclusions as exemplars of the hypothetico-deductive method. It is possible that Meyer would not go so far as to fully accept the implication of universals in the deductive-nomological form. Nevertheless, I suspect that he and others would view his research as a good example of the logic-in-use to which many, if not most, organizational scientists aspire today.

The population perspective that I develop in this chapter conflicts with the Meyer and Brown logic-in-use, and the reconstructed logic behind it (with or without universals), on two points. First, it can be seen that Meyer and Brown offer no theoretical or empirical taxonomy of differences and similarities between organizations as a basis for asserting that their results are generalizable to organizational form beyond that represented by the local government finance agencies that they studied. In fact they have no basis, other than conventional wisdom or commonsense notions, for believing that the finance agencies they studied are representative of any homogeneous, delimited population about which general statements or laws might be phrased. Second, the population perspective offers an alternative explanatory logic for a general theory of organizational variation. In light of this it cannot be assumed, just because some specific lower-level propositions are empirically confirmed, that the more general, higher-level explanation is valid. Specifically, there is nothing in the testing of the lower-level statements to support the assertion that a causal law is the only applicable higher-level explanation. Because the natural selection explanation is available, it calls into question the conclusion that Meyer and Brown's findings support the validity of the causal law form of explanation.

It is time for organizational scientists to move toward a reconstructed logic that is compatible with organizational phenomena. Our logic-in-use at present is wallowing somewhere in never-never land. Running through this book is a fundamental theme calling for a switch from the Myth of the Second Coming of Newton and causal law to the Reality of the Already-Arrived Darwin and explanatory but nonpredictive explanation. The purpose of this chapter is not to offer a definitive statement in support of the explanatory nonpredictive paradigm, but rather to let you know that this is what is implied by my discourse.

13.1 ORGANIZATIONAL POPULATIONS

Conventional inquiry about organizations breaks down into two subject areas. One is the study of people in organizations. This field is often called micro organizational behavior. A second traditional field is usually labeled organization theory or organizational sociology. Recently it has also come to be called macro organizational behavior. This field inquires about organizations taken as entities. Each field is well represented by textbooks* that offer extended definitional statements, so I need not define them further here. A view of the population perspective in relation to the conventional view is shown in figure 13.1. In the conventional view there are three main subjects: people, organizations, and environments. In the populationist perspective a fourth subject is added: organizational populations, as shown in the upper row of blocks.

There are four main subcomponents to the population view. These are shown in figure 13.2. I have set taxonomy up at the top because it is fundamental to the other three, though, as the arrows suggest, they are all interrelated. Organizational taxonomy has the principal task of developing a theory of differences as well as a related theory of classification. One of the more important criticisms of the population ecology of organizations as it has been developed to date is simply that no effort has gone to defining and discovering organizational populations in any but a commonsense fashion. The principal need for evolutionary theory is to

---

*For example, recent micro organizational behavior books are: Cummings and Dunham (1980), Szilagi and Wallace (1980), and Steers (1981). Some recent organization theory books are: Hall (1977), Jackson and Morgan (1978), Mintzberg (1979), Connor (1980), Hage (1980), and Scott (1981).

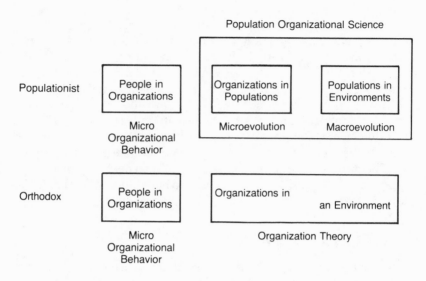

Figure 13.1. The Population Perspective Compared to Conventional Organization Theory.

explain how there come to be so many kinds of organizations. Explaining the origin of many kinds does not make much sense if there is no formal theory of kinds in the first place, or no theoretically substantiated belief that different kinds exist and ought to be taken seriously by organizational scientists. Hence taxonomy is more fundamental.

I suspect that Hannan and Freeman (1977) ended up at the wrong place, given the "Why so many kinds?" question they began with. This is a question calling for systematic and evolutionist analysis. Population ecology, as the field is usually thought of, focuses not on the origin of kinds but rather on the regulation and growth of a particular kind once it has been recognized as existing. I am tempted to say that population ecology cannot be satisfactorily pursued as a field of inquiry until the other three fields are established. However, the line of inquiry into organization-niche-environment dynamics is one of the best ways to begin to appreciate the forces at work in the evolutionary process. So, the fields should really be pursued all at once.

For conventional organization theorists, studying organizational form in the context of natural selection in a fateful environment raises an apparent fundamental conflict with the prevailing tendency of social scientists to see people as purposeful and solely causal in determining

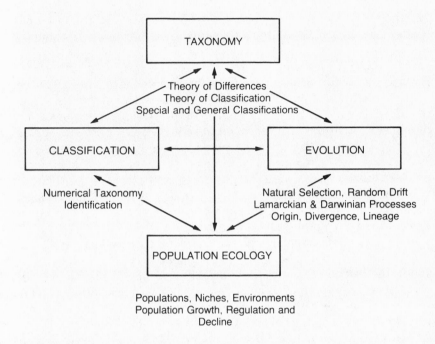

Figure 13.2. Major Components of the Population Perspective.

organizational form.* A theory of different organizational populations makes little sense to theorists who think that people either are (1) a fairly homogeneous population more or less randomly distributed among organizations and having similar responses to contextual forces, causing organizations to be pretty much alike and thus constituting one large all-encompassing population about which generalizable statements may be made, or (2) a set of unique individuals responding idiosyncratically to their interpreted phenomenal world, appearing in a unique combination in each organization, with the result that all organizations are individually different. Two points are to be made here. First, the population perspective offers a compromise between the extremes of "all organizations are the same" and "all organizations are different." I

---

*Even sociologists, such as Blau and Meyer, who do not include people as explicit entities in their models, do so implicitly; otherwise they are in the awkward position of saying, for example, that formalization—defined as things written in a policy manual—causes hierarchy, without managers ever reading the manual and acting in some way. A policy manual sitting closed, unread, and not acted upon does nothing but collect dust.

take the view that some organizations resemble each other and form a homogeneous population that differs from other homogeneous populations. Taxonomy, as a field, develops the theory that explains why this can be so. Second, the population perspective, by shifting attention from human purposefulness as the major determinant of organizational form to natural selection processes as the major determinant, offers an explanatory way out of the bind of having to think of organizations as all the same or all different. Once people are removed as the principal cause of organizational form, their supposed similarities or idiosyncrasies cease to be the driving force. Now that environments, defined as external nonmanipulable forces, are set in place as the ultimate long-term driving force, there is a logic for the appearance of organizational populations. The principal arguments in this book, about taxonomy and evolution, support these two points.

Imagine the field of chemistry as a search for fundamental predictive laws concerning the behavior of ad hoc, poorly described mixtures of chemicals instead of the existing successful science that is the study of elements and compounds as homogeneous populations. I think that this is an apt characterization of present-day organizational science. What we actually have going on most of the time (there are exceptions, of course) are studies of single organizations or loose mixtures of several organizations carried on under a reconstructed logic that is loosely scientific but incompatible with both the phenomena in question and the actual logic-in-use. Studying individual organizations is interesting, just as biographies of famous people are interesting. Such studies are also interesting in the way a physician's study of a patient is interesting—it could mean life or death to the patient. Studying General Motors is interesting because GM is GM. But who in science cares about Amalgamated Pea, Inc.? There are no generalizable statements possible in either case, strictly speaking. Yes, inductive theory development is possible from studying individual cases, but there is still the question as to what objects the theory is applicable to. There is only one GM, one Amalgamated Pea, Inc. Any theory induced could be expected to miss other organizations unless they were like GM or API; the induction would likely have to be repeated before the theory would be worth testing. Loose mixtures of organizations based on commonsense notions of their similarity, or worse, based on personal contacts or willingness to participate in a study, are not scientifically acceptable populations. Loose mixtures that are populations only in the heads of investigators have no real meaning to any other scientist. It is impossible to see why a scientific community would want to be bothered with knowledge about a fantasized population. Unless a population is found empirically in the protosystem (natural system) according to scientifically acceptable definitions and methods, and unless there is some acceptable theory explaining why such a population should exist, knowledge allegedly found is not scientifically useful. Instead it is confusing and possibly misleading. Since much of what we think we know comes from studies of ill-defined populations, our textbooks describe knowledge that does not apply to anything that really exists. In this sense we think we know more than we do and thus can only be described as superstitious, as suggested by the first quote at the beginning of the chapter.

One point I have tried to stress throughout this book is that the study of populations of organizational forms should constitute a central target of inquiry for organizational scientists. Only by defining a population of homogeneous organizations and identifyng the population's form can we rise above the idiosyncrasies of particular organizations.* Studies of function and process may then be carried on in the context of the population form with the knowledge that samples are representative of the same population and generalizable statements apply to the population and to its members. Future inquiry should turn to such questions as:

How to define, theoretically and operationally, organizational form?

How to classify various forms?

How to identify different forms and thus different populations?

How to explain the regulation and growth of various forms?

How to explain the persistence of some forms and the extinction of others?

How to operationally distinguish organizational niches from organizational environments?

How to study forms in relation to niches and environments?

What are the organizational functions and processes attendant to each form and how do they differ from functions and processes in other populations?

What are the microevolutionary dynamics associated with the genetics of new or changing forms?

---

*The study of a single organization is still useful, however, for purposes of improving its health, just as it is useful for a physician to study the symptoms of illness of a particular patient. Just as the life sciences study populations and physicians study individuals, organizational scientists should also study well-defined populations and leave the study of single organizations to consultants.

Once tradition gives way to population organizational science, a new research strategy and new basic issues emerge. Any list of questions is only a prologue to the development underway.

13.2 EXPLANATORY BUT NONPREDICTIVE SCIENCE

Most philosophers of science and researchers take for granted that prediction is the test of an adequate explanation. Hempel and Oppenheim said: "An explanation of a particular event is not fully adequate unless its explanans [what is doing the explaining], if taken account of in time, could have served as a basis for predicting the phenomenon under consideration" (1965, p. 249). Blau and Schoenherr (1971, p. 337) also referred to a theory's ability to predict accurately, and Mackenzie and House (1978, p. 9) said: "The requirements for explanation are those appropriate for prediction." These and other leading organizational scientists also take it for granted in studying organizations. Blute (1979) has pointed out social scientists' proclivity to look for causal laws in explaining historical developments. The interest in path analysis is an example of an equally strong tendency to look for causality in single-point-in-time correlational studies (Land 1969; Heise 1969). Perhaps the most logical and straightforward application of the causal-law approach is in longitudinal studies, Meyer's studies of government finance agencies at two time periods being a good example.

In fairness it should be said that predictability is the only practical objective test for quality of knowledge available for logic-in-use under the deductive model of reconstructed logic, what Kaplan termed *hierarchical* theory.* Kaplan does offer an alternative, which fits the pattern model of reconstructed logic, what he labeled *concatenated* theory.† Thus, "objectivity consists essentially in this, that the pattern can be indefinitely filled in and extended: as we obtain more and more knowledge it continues to fall into place in this pattern, and the pattern itself has a place in a larger whole" (1964, p. 335). As a practical test this falls short—too much left undefined. But would it not make sense to develop a better test of quality for the pattern model than to stay with an ill-suited deductive logic just because the latter's test is more straightforward?

Meyer (Meyer and Brown 1978) claimed to have discovered a causal

*Hierarchical theory "is one whose component laws are presented as deductions from a small set of basic principles" (Kaplan 1964, p. 298).

†Concatenated theory "is one whose component laws enter into a network of relations so as to constitute an identifiable configuration or pattern" (Kaplan 1964, p. 298).

chain, which is depicted in figure 13.3. Meyer's chain consists of an environmental stimulus followed by a structural response where formalization leads to hierarchy leads to decentralization. Meyer's model leaves out a key element present in Perrow's model: search behavior by managers, which leads to kinds of technology, which then leads to a structural response. In the figure I also compare the Meyer and Perrow models with the model that underlies the developments in this book. The main difference is the addition of boxes signifying human choices between environmentally posed problems and technological solutions, and between the latter and organizing solutions to technologically posed problems. Technological and organizing solutions together make up an organization's dominant competence, which materializes as its form. Form elements of the organizations comprising a population are intercommunicated to produce a population form. At the right end there is the box showing the intercommunicating comps and finally the organizational form of the population. All three models are embedded in the rational principle of enquiry (Schwab 1960). Choice of a principle of enquiry is independent of whether one follows the natural selection or natural science framework.

Throughout the book I have more or less left my model in the sequential or chain form of Perrow's development. I am now going to propose a model that retains all of the boxes or theoretical conceptual units but gets rid of the causal chain. I think the notion of causal chains rests in the heads of organizational sociologists like Perrow and Meyer but in fact has nothing to do with what causes variations in organizational form. Figure 13.4 depicts a model that I think comes much closer to organizational reality. As you might guess, it is rooted in natural selection theory.

This model draws on Weick's (1979) view of natural selection explanations of micro organizational behavior. You can read his book to figure out how that works—it is much too well worked-out and complicated for me to attempt to describe it here. Judging from the frequency of citation, perhaps everyone knows it well already! The circles depict people in organizations, so you can see I am consistent with my synthesis of chapter 4. Weick used the term *enactments* as a substitute for variations. People in organizations create enactments of the environment or environmental forces. These enactments may be more or less accurate or inaccurate, conscious or unconscious. People create variations in the form of behaviors in organizations. Enactments and behavioral variations are shown in the model as the arrows emanating from the circles. Forces from the environment are not seen as affecting organizations except through the enactments and variations of people, be they employees, members, or managers. Some things, which I will call ele-

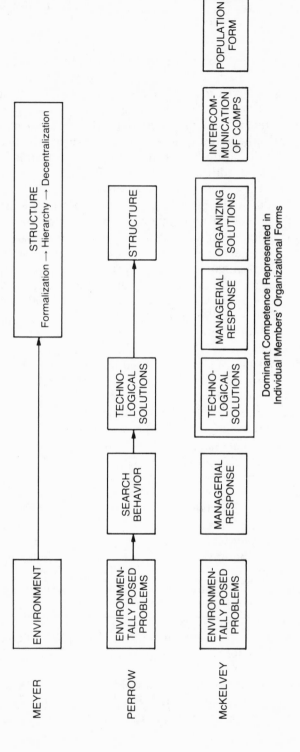

Figure 13.3. Meyer's Chain Overlaid on Perrow's and McKelvey's Models. These models display the causal-law form of explanatory path characteristic of deductive-nomological explanatory form, excepting McKelvey's.

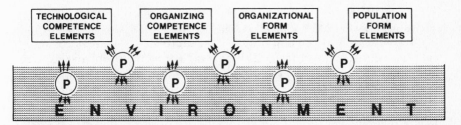

P = PEOPLE

Figure 13.4. A Natural Selection Model of Organizational Form (see text for explanation).

ments of organizational form (technology and organizing solutions), happen as a result of Alpha sources of variation, conscious official activities, and so forth, or they may happen because of Sigma sources, the marketplace model, spontaneous, systemic, informal, less-planned variations, and so on. Organizational form continues to be broadly defined as including aspects of structure, function, process, internal and ecological behavior, and so forth. In specific studies, operational definitions will be much narrower than this. As a consequence of continuing environmental pressures and ongoing selection and retention of certain variations, an organization takes on a certain form. Aspects of a given organization's form which meet adaptive needs tend to be retained by the organization and acquired by others facing similar environmental pressures. A set of organizations facing similar environmental pressures tend to acquire similar aspects of form and come to form a homogeneous population. The homogeneity is enhanced by the intercommunication of elements of dominant competence relative to the impinging environmental pressures. Populations are different in form due to isolating processes. In the course of its adaptation a population carves out a macro niche in its environment. The macro niche is paired with the population form, and niche and form are seen as a coupled pair in the adaptation process.

Since we are accustomed to reading in an implied sequence from left to right, I offer you figure 13.5 as a means of jarring loose any vestiges of sequence. It is a perforated version of the Garbage Can model proposed by Cohen, March, and Olsen (1972). In this model the units are still the same—people and elements of organizational form (I have thrown in some unknown boxes in the spirit of further inquiry)—but they are arranged in a jumbled bunch in a perforated circle depicting the side of the can. The impression I want to convey is that I see no basis at all for sequence in the development of form in a particular individual organization. "The garbage can process is one in which problems, solutions, and participants move from one choice opportunity to another in such a way that the nature of the choice, the time it takes, and the problems it solves all depend on a relatively complicated intermeshing of elements. These include the mix of choices available at any one time, the mix of problems that have access to the organization, the mix of solutions looking for problems, and the outside demands on the decision makers" (Cohen, March, and Olsen 1972, p. 16).* It could happen according to the sequence in figure 13.4, but it could just as easily not happen that way. It could turn out, for example, that in a particular organization in a population, some people notice that the population form of structure is more bureaucratic and mechanistic than what exists in their organization. They have influence with the dominant coalition and a change in formal structure is made. Then someone else discovers that technological and/ or managerial organizing competence elements can also be brought more in line with the population form. And so on for virtually any combination of form elements. The population perspective does hold, however, that nonmanipulable elements of the external environment form a constant pressure on a population and its members, and that the natural selection process is ever present and continually operating. The population view holds that the form of a particular organization is framed between what is learned about the environment and what is learned about the population form. The explanatory path flows from environment to individual organizations and thence to and from the population. In this view the "cause" is the environment. The result is a population form and macro niche, and within the population, individual member forms and micro niches. People do not cause a particular form but they are the means by which variations (enactments and behavioral variations) arise. The model does not work without people to play the role of sources of variation.

The idea of explaining organizational variations by natural selection theory rather than by human purposefulness stimulates a common reaction in those who believe that people cause organizational form. They see population proponents as subjugating organizational members to a role of helpless, alienated symbols (Van de Ven 1979, 1980b; Pfeffer and Salancik 1978; for other arguments in favor of purposive rather than blind variation see Boehm 1976; Goldschmidt 1976). Nothing could be

---

*In a recent review of J.G. Miller's book, *Living Systems* (1978), Kuhn went even further, saying "Even within their decider subsystems, I am convinced that courses of action adopted by formal organizations are more often occurrences than decisions" (1980, p. 43).

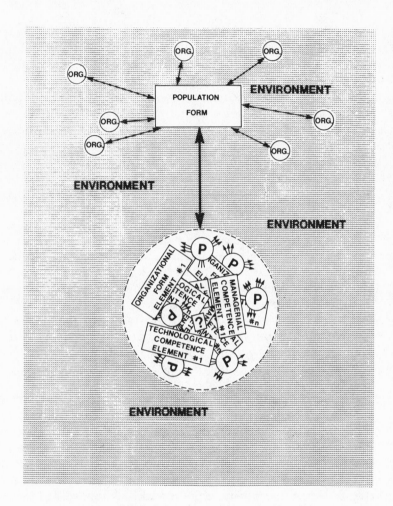

Figure 13.5. A Perforated Garbage Can Natural Selection Model (end view!).

further from the truth. By way of illustration I would like to pass on a comment about downhill ski racing. Anyone who follows the sport will remember the fantastic run of Franz Klammer in the Men's Downhill in the 1976 Winter Olympics. He seemed "out of control" for the entire run, which in skiing language means he was on the verge of falling and in fact looked as though he surely would fall throughout the entire run. He did not fall and won the Olympic Gold Medal. Up until Klammer's run the prevailing thinking among downhill racers was that the winner of a race would be the one who was in the best condition, had the best technique, and skied just this side of the edge of losing control. By the time the 1980 Winter Olympics came the thinking had changed.* Now, the thinking is that to win a race one has to ski on the other side of the edge of losing control—that is, one must ski out of control and hope to avoid a fall by recovering from being too much out of control. In 1976 Klammer was the only one (of the truly world-class skiers) who skied out of control, and since every other top skier was trying to ski just short of losing control, Klammer won easily. Now all top skiers, perhaps fifteen or twenty, are skiing out of control and on any given day it is largely natural selection stemming from factors beyond the skier's control which determines who wins. During any run there are many blind variations in the form of ruts, bumps, mistakes, and so forth, which are all beyond the control of the skiers at the speed they are now going. The skier who skis most out of control and is luckiest in avoiding falling will win. Each skier knows that he cannot determine his winning just by training, good technique, and skiing at the edge of control. But skiing out of control only guarantees he will have to make numerous miraculous recoveries from near falls. The skier who takes the most risks and makes the most miraculous recoveries wins. The skier who skis in control does have control over his destiny and guarantees only one thing—losing. Since there are so many good skiers skiing out of control the odds are excellent that one of them will always take enough risks and manage enough miraculous recoveries to beat the under-control skier.

So it is with organizations, in the logic of the population perspective. Managers, or other people in organizations, do not have much if any direct control of organizational success—they essentially generate variations, some of which are selected favorably, and a selected organizational form is an accumulation of favorably selected variations. In this sense managers are like the skier out of control. They have to take a lot of risks in an uncertain environment and it is impossible to know which of their variations will ultimately lead to an effective organizational form. On the other hand, if managers did not perform up to the best of their ability, which includes learning appropriate areas of competence and acting with purposefulness (even though it is myopic) in pursuing what appear to be the best strategies, they *will* be guaranteed one thing—some other competitor will be selected instead. Managers have to be purposeful, highly talented, hard-working, and all of those other good things associated with nonalienated, useful people just to

---

*I learned this from a television interview with Ken Read in January, 1980. Read was a leading contender for the World Cup and was favored to win the Gold Medal in the Olympics.

avoid being selected against. Managers who feel alienated, useless, and lacking in purpose will end up losers just like downhill skiers who, thinking the race is won only by luck, give up practicing and working to stay at the very peak of their competence.

Modern downhill skiers look to the World Cup as a better indication of who the best skier is, since they believe that external factors cannot repeatedly favor an individual in many races whereas they might in a single race. I admit that there may be some managers who are more prescient than most in the creation of variations that end up being favorably selected. This is why I have held to the possibility that organizational evolution is a combined Lamarckian/Darwinian process. Not all variations are blind, as Darwinians would expect. Some may very well be purposeful—they are genuine responses to adaptive demands imposed by an environment. Some managers or people in organizations may be more able to create these kinds of variations.

I should note that most variations are purposeful or intentional from the point of view of the individual making them. This is why it is so important that we avoid the notion that the natural selection form of explanation breeds alienation. But under conditions of bounded rationality, impaired information, market exchange processes, and environmental change, complexity, and uncertainty, *human intentionality is surely myopic.* From a long-term retrospective view it will appear as quite blind in terms of what actually led to long-term survival of an organizational form. Human activities in organizations are, therefore, necessary but not sufficient determinants of organizational form.

The full implications of studying and understanding organizations are vague at this time. The significant research questions are not well understood, let alone properly framed. Some that come to mind are:

How to study micro organizational behavior under an explanatory logic consistent with evolutionary theory and natural selection?

What are the practical normative messages to employees and managers under conditions of the natural selection framework as opposed to the rational/goal model?

What are the implications of evolutionary theory and natural selection for planned organizational change or organizational development?

What is scientific method under the explanatory but nonpredictive paradigm?

How to assure high quality knowledge under the Darwinian paradigm?

13.3 MAJOR IMPLICATIONS

The implications of the population perspective follow in part from the roles that a general classification plays for a scientific field.

1. *The population perspective and its taxonomy and classification methodology will produce better-defined and more homogeneous populations for scientists engaged in studies of organizational function and process.* This will make the sampling problem easier. Taken to an extreme it might mean that exemplar organizations can be identified which fairly well reflect the central tendencies of a population, with the result that only one organization would have to be studied—at least for inductive theory generation, which requires more in-depth, rich, subjective, participant-observation, ethnographic, or other qualitative methods. For deductive, more objective tests of theory, a sampling would be preferred but its size might be substantially reduced. The odds of favorable replication would be improved with a population perspective, again because samples spaced over time or collected by different investigators would not have to be so large and would stand a better chance of being similar and fully representative of the population.

2. *The population approach will enhance the retrieval of information about organizations.* For many systematists this is the primary goal of a classification. By organizing the phenomena studied into logical homogeneous groupings, the findings of studies carried on by those doing functional science are also more logically ordered. Once population definitions are widely agreed upon, studies that are diverse in geographical location, substantive interest, and methodology will be organized in terms of well-specified groupings of organizations. Knowledge about each population will be accumulated in terms of that population, labeled in terms of that population, passed on to students and managers in terms of that population, and be retrievable in terms of that population. The classification scheme is the key to it all. Other fields of organizational study, such as micro organizational behavior, organizational development, organization design, comparative studies, industrial and labor relations, economics, career studies, and the like will all be enhanced if organizational populations are more clearly and acceptably delineated.

3. *The population perspective embeds its four components—taxonomy, ecology, evolution, and classification—in an integrated framework that aids the study of any one of them independently.* Each of these is essential to the successful pursuit of the others. The already-developed interest in the field of population ecology will be aided by more careful delineation of populations. Taxonomy and classification

are aided by evolutionary theory, especially for character selection. Ecological studies offer insight into the dynamics of the evolution of species and in turn macroevolutionary theory provides the explanation of the origin of groupings and is a source of external validation of numerical taxonomic solutions; microevolutionary theory explains the dynamics of population homogeneity and underlying change in population genetics resulting from ecological effects.

4. *The population view also offers an integrated framework for organization theory in general.* Some of the taxonomic and classificatory implications have already been noted. Population ecology will offer significant new insights to our understanding of the birth, growth, and failure of organizational populations in relation to the broader ecological community of organizations. It will also offer important underlying analytical strength to the study of competitive strategy as defined by Rumelt (1974) and Porter (1980). Historical analyses will be aided by evolutionary theory and by ecological studies offering underlying theory and development of the concepts and variables discussed in the historical studies.

* * * * *

One final remark. Our field is not totally without a population perspective already. We do have schools oriented toward educational administration, public administration, hospital administration, hotel administration, unions, and the like. Much of our knowledge about organizations is also organized in terms of these populations. But the boundaries of these populations are vague. For example, are there significant differences between public and private universities, between universities and colleges or junior colleges? Do these forms make up one population or several? Are general, chronic-care, teaching, and proprietary hospitals one population? What about local and national unions? Do Meyer's findings about government finance agencies generalize to other agencies, nongovernmental organizations, and so forth? Do steel companies around the world form one population irrespective of their nation's culture, or are steel companies in each country a separate population? What useful information can German steel company managers expect to learn from studies of American steel company organizational forms? Are all continuous process organizations members of the same population? What about mass-production organizations? (See also Lammers and Hickson 1979.)

Our present populations seem like loose mixtures of nuts. It is time to get beyond chain-headed theorists and nutty populations. We do not know nearly as much about organizations as all the brand-new textbooks would lead us to believe. To return to the quote at the beginning of the chapter, we are superstitious in that we imagine we know more about organizations than we do. We have tried to skip a prerequisite step in science—systematics—and consequently we are superstitious. The causal-law god that many believe in does not exist.

> According to my lights, a last chapter should resemble a primitive orgy after harvest. The work may have come to an end, but the worker cannot let go all at once. He is still full of energy that will fester if it cannot find an outlet. Accordingly he is allowed a time of license, when he may say all sorts of things he would think twice before saying in more sober moments, when he is no longer bound by logic and evidence but free to speculate about what he has done. [Homans 1961, p. 378]

GLOSSARY

Allogenic theories. Theories that attribute organizational form to exogenous causes.

Alpha sources. Same as Authorized-Prepensive.

Anagenesis. Evolutionary change that consists of slow movement toward a new form within a line, without branching.

Ancestral characters. Characters that have remained unchanged from ancestral states.

Anti-principles. A strategy for conducting research which eschews a priori theory in favor of an empirical, "let the facts decide" approach (Schwab).

A priori weighting. Same as Weighting.

Authorized-Prepensive. Sources of variation that are premeditated and officially sanctioned.

Autogenic theories. Theories that attribute organizational form to endogenous causes.

Average linkage clustering. Same as Group average method.

Biological species concept. States that a species is (1) a reproductive community; (2) an ecological community; and (3) a genetic unit consisting of an intercommunicating gene pool (Mayr).

Category. The rank or level in a hierarchical classification scheme (Mayr).

Cladism. A theory of classification which groups entities strictly according to lines of descent. The emphasis is on recency of branching points. Members of a group all have the same immediate ancestor species.

Cladistic affinity. Affinity is based on recency of descent from a common ancestor species without taking into account the number of shared characters. It emphasizes genealogical relationship and branching points.

Cladogenesis. Evolutionary change that occurs when a new form branches off from an existing form, which continues in existence.

Cladograms. Dendrograms based on evolutionary branching points, typically the result of cladistic analysis.

Classification. The actual construction of a classification scheme and the identification and assignment of organizational forms to formally recognized classes.

Climate. The prevailing nonpurposeful, inanimate conditions impinging on organizations, such as technological, legal, economic, or cultural factors.

Common factor method. A method of factor analysis in which the unities in the principal diagonal of the correlation matrix are replaced by estimated communalities, the assumption being that only variance common to two or more variables is explained by the factors.

Competence elements. Same as Comps.

Complete linkage clustering. Same as Farthest neighbor clustering.

Compool. The total pool of competence elements (comps) making up the dominant competencies of all members of an organizational population.

Comps. Elements of knowledge and skill that in total comprise the dominant competence of an organization.

Conjoint absences. Two entities appear to be matched because the same character state is absent from both.

Cophenetic correlation coefficient. A coefficient used to find cophenetic optimality and to compare the relative similarity of different clustering methods (Sneath and Sokal).

Cophenetic optimality. A measure of internal validity defined as the ability of a clustering solution to reproduce the original resemblance matrix (Sneath and Sokal).

Darwinian evolutionary theory. Darwin, and others since, have held that variations are not purposive but blind, that acquired phenotypic characteristics are not inherited, and that changes in species occur only on a very gradual incremental basis over a very long period of time.

Deme.   A population of similarly constituted organizations, occupying the same ecological niche, and sharing the same modeling or replication materials through interconnections among each other (Warriner).

Dendrogram.   A family tree showing paths of descent from ancestor forms of organization.

Derived characters.   Characters that have changed considerably since ancestral times.

Dissimilarity coefficient.   Same as Distance coefficient.

Distance coefficient.   A means of determining the resemblance between two OTUs by locating character scores in terms of the Cartesian coordinates of a hypercube and finding the Euclidean distance between them.

Dominant competence.   The combined workplace (technical) and managerial knowledge and skills that together are most important or salient in determining an organization's ability to survive.

Ecological processes.   Attributes or forces in a species' habitat which materially affect its ability to survive.

Effectiveness.   Same as Survival.

Empiricism.   An approach to classification which posits the existence of naturally occurring groupings, tries to keep classificatory decisions as free from a priori theories as possible, weights all possible attributes equally, and assumes that repeated empirical studies using numerical clustering methods will ultimately define a classificatory framework. See Numerical phenetics.

Environment.   That set of external forces that impose constraints on an individual organization or a population of organizations and are outside its ability to influence.

Equal weighting.   The practice of giving all characters equal weight in classificatory analyses.

Essentialism.   A theory of classification holding that groups of entities exist, each group being composed of members who share a few essential attributes; it is the basis of typological groupings of organizations.

Evolutionary inquiry.   The study of the history of organizations and the emergence and decline of diverse organizational forms, and the discovery of different lineages of forms in historical time and space.

Evolutionary significance.   Refers to characters that are observed to enhance an organization's ability to survive; they result from its adaptation to new environmental conditions.

Evolutionary theory.   An explanation in which differences among species are attributed to a continuous process of slight or dramatic change over a long period of time.

Evolutionism. A theory of classification which groups entities according to their overall ancestral (genetic) affinities.

Exemplar method. The practice of selecting only one typical member to represent a group in a numerical taxonomic study (Sneath and Sokal).

Farthest neighbor clustering. A clustering method in which the decision to join an OTU to an existing cluster (as opposed to pairing the OTU with another single OTU to start a new cluster) is made by comparing its resemblance to the least similar member of the existing cluster.

Functional science. The study of uniformities within a population of objects.

Fundamental taxonomic unit (FTU). An organizational entity containing technologically interdependent subsystems whose activities are pooled toward the accomplishment of the primary task; an entity where it can be determined that changes in technologically interdependent subunits took place simultaneously as the result of changes in one or more independent variables; a specific organizational form. An FTU is not necessarily a legal entity such as a corporation, company, or partnership; it may be a subunit.

General classifications. These are attempts to group entities together by taking into account most if not all of their important attributes (Jeffrey). They result in polythetic groupings.

General evolution. The view that evolution results in higher-order forms of sociocultural systems such that the systems can be grouped into general categories (called grades) characterized by lower or higher degrees of progress (Sahlins).

Generational processes. These processes assure that characters proving favorable for survival are passed down through successive generations and also spread more or less throughout all members of a species. An intercommunicating gene pool is a central feature of such processes in biology.

Genetics. The science of heredity. In biology it is based on two principles: (1) that hereditary factors are particles; and (2) that the flow of information from genotype to phenotype is unidirectional (Futuyma).

Genotype. The genetic constitution of an organization or a group of organisms. For organizations, the pattern of competence elements shared by the entire population.

Gradualism. The theory that new species, or major changes in species, are the result of slowly accumulated, very small incremental changes.

Group average method. A clustering method in which the decision to join an OTU to an existing cluster (as opposed to pairing the OTU with another single OTU to start a new cluster) is made by comparing its resemblance to an average of the characteristics of the OTUs in the existing cluster.

Heredity, principle of. In biology, this says that offspring resemble their parents more than they resemble other members of their species. For organizations, it implies that successive generations of organizational members retain the competencies held by previous members more than they acquire competences from other members of their organizational species.

Holistic principle, holism. States that the behavior of an entity is to be explained by studying the pattern of relations among the parts together with their relation to the whole (Schwab).

Hybridization. The combining of several existing organizational forms to create a new one.

Identification. The procedure for placing an organization into a particular class.

Isolating processes. The processes that keep species that have separated from merging back and thereby losing their distinctness relative to each other.

Joining methods. Methods that find pairs of OTUs closest in resemblance and successively join other OTUs to these pairs until all OTUs are clustered (Hartigan). These include hierarchical, sequential, agglomerative, and nonoverlapping methods.

Keys. An assemblage of diagnostic characters in dichotomous pairs to facilitate rapid identification of an organism or organization (Mayr).

K specialists. Organisms or organizations that are especially suited for survival in mature environments characterized by scarce resources.

Lamarckian evolutionary theory. Lamarck held that acquired phenotypic characteristics could be passed to the next generation and that variations were purposive.

Local population. Same as Deme.

Macro niche. A niche created by a population of organizations.

Matching coefficient. The ratio between the number of matched binary scores occurring between two OTUs and the total number of such characters.

Micro niche. A niche created by a single organization.

Monophyletic groups. Groups whose membership is restricted to species discovered to have descended from the same common ancestor.

Monothetic keys.   Identification keys that use only one diagnostic character to separate OTUs into the correct classes at a branching point.

Monothetic groups.   Groups whose members must possess all of the attributes used to define that group.

Monotypic.   A group that only contains one lower-level taxon.

Multilinear progress theories.   Hold that sociocultural systems are all progressing in their evolutionary development but each one progresses in a unique fashion in response to diverging environmental conditions.

Multiple factor method.   Same as Common factor method.

Natural selection, principle of.   States that attributes that aid the survival of a species in a particular environment will increase in frequency among members of that species.

Nearest neighbor clustering.   A clustering method in which the decision to join an OTU to an existing cluster (as opposed to pairing the OTU with another single OTU to start a new cluster) is made by comparing its resemblance to the most similar member of the existing cluster.

Niche.   That set of external forces that impose constraints on an individual organization or a population of organizations that are subject to its influence. *See* Micro niche, Macro niche.

Nominalism.   A theory of classification which ignores the possible existence of naturally occurring groupings, choosing instead to form groupings that serve the needs of the scientific community to have homogeneous classes.

Numerical phenetics.   A theory of classification that groups entities on the basis of most, if not all, known attributes, using numerical coefficients of resemblance and clustering or other grouping algorithms.

Numerical taxonomy.   Same as Numerical phenetics.

Operational taxonomic unit (OTU).   The lowest ranking taxa employed in a particular study (Sneath and Sokal).

Ordination methods.   Grouping approaches such as factor analysis or multidimensional scaling which use an iterative partitioning method to break a set of *t* OTUs into substantially less than *t* groups.

Organizational form.   The internal structure and process of an organization and the interrelation of its subunits which contribute to the unity of the whole of the organization and to the maintenance of its characteristic activities, function, or nature. *See* Fundamental taxonomic unit.

Organizational generation.   The average length of time that holders of competence elements (employees) stay in member organizations of a particular population.

Organizational species.   A set of highly probable combinations of dominant competence elements that are temporarily housed at any given time among the members of an organizational population.

Particle theory. The idea that genetic stock is composed of discrete nonchanging (except for mutation) units that are mixed together in different ways among members of a species, as opposed to the idea that each member of a species has a single unit of stock that differs from the unit in another member.

Patristic affinity. Based on the number of similar genes that members of a group have in common, often estimated by looking at the similarity among phenotypic characters.

Phenograms. Dendrograms representing clusterings based on the similarity of phenotypic characters, typically the result of numerical phenetic analysis.

Phenon (pl. *phena*). A sample of phenotypically similar entities (Mayr).

Phenotype. The observable attributes of a particular organism or organization resulting from the interaction of the genotype and the environment.

Phyletics, phylogenetics. The study of evolutionary lines of descent of entities from their ancestors for the purpose of discovering delimitable groupings and explaining their origin.

Phyletic validity. A measure of external validity in which clusters produced by numerical phenetic methods are tested for correspondence with clusters produced by an evolutionist or cladist method.

Polyphyletic groups. Groups whose members are not from the same common ancestor but do appear to be alike phenotypically and have similar genotypic composition; groups that contain members of two or more founder species.

Polythetic groups. Groups whose members share most attributes in common; each attribute used to help define the group is held by many members but no attribute is held by all members (Beckner).

Polythetic keys. Identification keys that use several diagnostic characters to sort organizations into one or another class at a branching point.

Polytypic group. A group that contains two or more lower-level taxa.

Population. A species.

Preadaptive. A character present as the result of random genetic drift that later turns out to be adaptive because of a subsequent environmental change.

Primary task. That set of activities that bear directly on the conversion of inputs into those outputs that are critical to an organization's survival (Miller and Rice).

Primitive principles. Principles that guide scientific inquiry in accordance with practical problems and the norms of the scientific community (Schwab).

Principal axes method. Same as Common factor method.

Principal component method. A method of factor analysis in which the principal diagonal of the correlation matrix is left with unities, the assumption being that all variance in the variables is to be explained by the factors.

Principle of heredity. Same as Heredity, principle of.

Principle of natural selection. Same as Natural selection, principle of.

Principle of the struggle for existence. Same as Struggle for existence, principle of.

Principle of variation. Same as Variation, principle of.

Progress. A kind of evolutionary change in which later members of a sequence exhibit improvements over earlier members.

Protosystem. A label that refers to the universe of organizations within which organizational groupings are assumed to exist. It is equivalent to the "natural system" in biology.

Punctuated equilibria. Same as Quantum speciation.

Q Mode. A factor analysis of OTUs (cases) in columns using characters (variables) in rows as sources of variance.

Quantum speciation. A drastic change in a species in a very short period of time.

R Mode. A factor analysis of characters (variables) in columns using OTUs (cases) in rows as sources of variance.

r specialists. Organisms or organizations that are especially suited for survival in new environments characterized by plentiful resources.

Random genetic drift. A process whereby random variations in the attributes of species may be retained over successive generations, as opposed to the idea that only variations aiding in the survival of the species are passed down.

Rational principle, rationalism. An approach to explaining the behavior of an entity by looking outward and studying the impact of the larger system or environment upon it (Schwab).

Reductive principle, reductionism. An approach to explaining the behavior of an entity by studying the behavior of its constituent parts (Schwab).

Resemblance coefficient. A quantified estimate of the similarity or dissimilarity between two elements of an OTU-by-character data matrix.

Saltation. The rapid formation of a new organizational form due to significant innovations in dominant competence. *See* Quantum speciation.

Sector. The initial space from which a sample for empirical classificatory study is drawn. It may include one population, part of one, or several.

Sequential keys. Identification keys that use diagnostic characters in sequence, one at a time.

Sigma sources. *See* Systemic-spontaneous.

Similarity coefficient. *See* Matching coefficient.

Simultaneous keys. Identification keys that use all characters at the same time to separate organizations into the proper classes.

Single-linkage clustering. Same as Nearest neighbor clustering.

Social Darwinists. People who argued, among other things, that the genetic stock of a society would be weakened if permissive immigration or welfare policies were adopted.

Sorting methods. Methods that partition OTUs according to the value taken on by a few important OTUs. These include both ordination and nonhierarchical, nonsequential, or overlapping methods.

Space-conserving. A clustering method that does not represent OTUs and resultant clusters as either more similar or less similar than they really are.

Space-contracting. A clustering method that represents OTUs and resultant clusters as more similar than they really are.

Space-dilating. A clustering method that represents OTUs and resultant clusters as less similar than they really are.

Special classifications. Groupings of forms based on only one or a few attributes (Jeffrey).

Speciation. The process of genetic change whereby a new species comes into existence (White).

Species concept. A theoretical construct at the center of any theory of differences between populations of entities.

Specific evolution. The view that sociocultural systems evolve from one state to another in response to changes in the environment specifically affecting them (Sahlins). *See* Multilinear progress theories.

Struggle for existence, principle of. States that members of a biological or organizational species have to struggle to gain resources from the environment, but recognizes that for some periods of time the resource availability is so high that "struggle" may be almost unnecessary.

Survival. The net importation over the long term of resources into an organization from its niche or environment.

Systematics. The science given over to the study of the diversity of form (Mayr).

Systemic-Spontaneous. Sources of variation which occur naturally, impulsively, voluntarily, or without prompting among a regularly interacting set of organizational members.

Taxon (pl. *taxa*). A taxonomic group distinct enough to be formally recognized and named as a definite category (Mayr).

Taxonomic character. A property or attribute that varies from one entity to another and has discriminatory power (Sneath and Sokal, Mayr).

Taxonomy. The development of theories and methods for classifying organizations; the theory and practice of classification (Hempel).

Texture. The ecological community of purposeful, animate organizations or people whose activities may affect an organization.

Typology. Same as Essentialism.

Unilinear progress theories. Theories based on the view that all changes in a sociocultural system represent progress; that all societies go through the same stages of evolution; and that less advanced societies in the contemporary world are similar to earlier stages of more advanced societies.

Variation. A change in form, appearance, function, or substance, but not pertaining to changes in day-to-day activities, which may change independently of the above.

Variation, principle of. States that variation in attributes occurs among members of a species. In biology these variations are blind, random, or haphazard. In organizations they may be blind or the result of purposive human behavior.

Weighting. The practice of making classificatory decisions by giving some characters more weight than others on the basis of their discriminatory power or phyletic information content.

Workplace-management task. That set of managerial activities bearing directly on the operation of the primary task workplace which foster the continued survival of an organization.

BIBLIOGRAPHY

Ackoff, R. L. 1971. "Towards a system of systems concepts." *Management Science* 17:661–671.

Adams, R. M. 1955. "Developmental stages in ancient Mesopotamia." In *Irrigation Civilizations*. Ed. J. H. Steward, pp. 6–18. Social Science Monographs, vol. 1. Washington: Pan American Union, Social Science Section, Department of Cultural Affairs.

———. 1972. "The origin of cities." In *Old World Archaeology*. Ed. C. C. Lamberg-Karlovsky, pp. 137–144. San Francisco: Freeman.

Adanson, M. 1757. *Histoire Naturelle du Senegal*. Paris: Bauche.

Aguiler, F. 1967. *Scanning the Business Environment*. New York: Macmillan Co.

Aldrich, H. E. 1971. "Organizational boundaries and inter-organizational conflict." *Human Relations* 24:279–293.

———. 1979. *Organizations and Environments*. Englewood Cliffs, N. J.: Prentice-Hall.

Aldrich, H. E., and S. Mueller. 1980. "The evolution of organizational forms: technology, coordination, and control." Mimeographed. Ithaca, N. Y.: School of Industrial and Labor Relations. Forthcoming in *Research in Organizational Behavior* IV. Ed. B. Staw and L. L. Cummings. Greenwich, Conn.: JAI.

Aldrich, H. E., and J. Pfeffer. 1976. "Environments of organizations." *Annual Review of Sociology* 2:79–105.

Aldrich, H. E., and A. J. Reiss, Jr. 1976. "Continuities in the study of ecological succession: Changes in the race compositions of neighborhoods and their businesses." *American Journal of Sociology* 81:846–866.

Alexander, R. D. 1975. "The search for a general theory of behavior." *Behavioral Science* 20:77–100.

Alland, A. 1967. *Evolution and Human Behavior.* New York: Natural History Press.

Allen, S. A., III. 1978. "Organizational choices and general management influence networks in divisionalized companies." *Academy of Management Journal* 21:341–365.

Allport, F. H. 1962. "A structuronomic conception of behavior: Individual and collective." *Journal of Abnormal and Social Psychology* 64:3–30.

Argyris, C. 1962. *Interpersonal Competence and Organizational Effectiveness.* Homewood, Ill.: Dorsey.

––––––. 1972. *The Applicability of Organizational Sociology.* Cambridge: Cambridge University Press.

––––––. 1980. *Inner Contradictions of Rigorous Research.* New York: Academic Press.

Ashlock, P. D. 1974. "The uses of cladistics." *Annual Review of Ecology and Systematics* 5:81–99.

––––––. 1979. "An evolutionary systematist's view of classification." *Systematic Zoology* 28:441–450.

Astolfi, P., K. K. Kidd, and L. L. Cavalli-Sforza. 1981. "A comparison of methods for reconstructing evolutionary trees." *Systematic Zoology* 30:156–169.

Ayala, F. J. 1978. "The mechanisms of evolution." *Scientific American* 239:56–69.

Bailey, K. D. 1970. "Evaluating axiomatic theories." In *Sociological Methodology 1970.* Ed. E. F. Borgatta and G. W. Bohrnstaedt, pp. 48–71. San Francisco: Jossey-Bass.

––––––. 1973. "Monothetic and polythetic typologies and their relation to conceptualization, measurement, and scaling." *American Sociological Review* 38:18–33.

––––––. 1975. "Cluster analysis." In *Sociological Methodology 1975.* Ed. D. R. Heise, pp. 59–128. San Francisco: Jossey-Bass.

Barber, B. 1962. *Science and the Social Order.* New York: Collier.

Barnard, C. 1938. *The Functions of the Executive.* Cambridge, Mass.: Harvard University Press.

Baum, B. R., and L. P. Lefkovitch. 1978. "A numerical taxonomic study of phylogenetic and phenetic relationships in some cultivated oats, using known pedigrees." *Systematic Zoology* 27:118–131.

Beckner, M. 1959. *The Biological Way of Thought.* New York: Columbia University Press.

Behling, O. 1980. "The case for the natural science model of research in organizational behavior and organization theory." *Academy of*

Management Review 5:483–490.

Behling, O., and J. F. Dillard. 1980. "The limits of theory in organizational science." Mimeographed. Columbus: The Ohio State University.

Bell, G.D. 1974. "Organizations and the External Environment." In *Contemporary Management*. Ed. J. W. McGuire, pp. 259–282. Englewood, Cliffs, N.J.: Prentice-Hall.

Bennis, W. G. 1966. *Changing Organizations*. New York: McGraw-Hill.

Benson, J. K. 1977. "Organizations: A dialectical view." *Administrative Science Quarterly* 22:1–21.

Berelson, B., and G. A. Steiner. 1964. *Human Behavior*. New York: Harcourt, Brace & World.

Berger, P. L., and T. Luckmann. 1966. *The Social Construction of Reality: A Treatise in the Sociology of Knowledge*. New York: Doubleday.

Blake, R. R., and J. S. Mouton. 1964. *The Managerial Grid*. Houston: Gulf.

Blalock, H. M., Jr., and A. B. Blalock. 1968. *Methodology in Social Research*. New York: McGraw-Hill.

Blashfield, R. K., and M. S. Aldenderfer. 1978. "The literature on cluster analysis." *Multivariate Behavioral Research* 13:271–295.

Blau, P. M. 1963. *The Dynamics of Bureaucracy*. Rev. ed. Chicago: University of Chicago Press.

———. 1970. "A formal theory of differentiation in organizations." *American Sociological Review* 35:201–218.

Blau, P. M., and R. A. Schoenherr. 1971. *The Structure of Organizations*. New York: Basic Books.

Blau, P. M., and W. R. Scott. 1962. *Formal Organizations*. San Francisco: Chandler.

Blute, M. 1979. "Sociocultural evolutionism: An untried theory." *Behavioral Science* 24:46–59.

Bock, W. J. 1973. "Philosophical foundations of classical evolutionary classification." *Systematic Zoology* 22:375–392.

Boehm, C. 1976. "Biological versus social evolution." *American Psychologist* 31:348–351.

Bohm, D. 1961. *Causality and Chance in Modern Physics*. London: Routledge and Kegan Paul, 1957. Reprint. New York: First Harper Torchbook Edition.

Boorman, S. A., and D. C. Olivier, 1973. "Metrics on space of finite trees." *Journal of Mathematical Psychology* 10:26–59.

Borgatta, E. F., and G. W. Bohrnstedt, eds. 1970. *Sociological Methodology 1970*. San Francisco: Jossey-Bass.

Brady, R. H. 1979. "Natural selection and the criteria by which a theory is judged." *Systematic Zoology* 28:600–621.

Braidwood, R. J. 1972. "The agricultural revolution." In *Old World Archaeology*. Ed. C. C. Lamberg-Karlovsky, pp. 71–79. San Francisco: Freeman.

Braithwaite, R. B. 1953. *Scientific Explanation*. Cambridge: Cambridge University Press.

Brittain, J. W., and J. H. Freeman. 1980. "Organizational proliferation and density-dependent selection: Organizational evolution in the semiconductor industry." In *The Organizational Life Cycle*. Ed. J. R. Kimberly, R. H. Miles, and Associates, pp. 291–338. San Francisco: Jossey-Bass.

Brown, W. B., and D. J. Moberg. 1980. *Organization Theory and Management*. New York: Wiley.

Buckley, W. 1967. *Sociology and Modern Systems Theory*. Englewood Cliffs, N. J.: Prentice-Hall.

Burns, T. 1967. "The comparative study of organizations." In *Methods of Organizational Research*. Ed. V. Vroom, pp. 113–170. Pittsburgh: University of Pennsylvania Press.

Burns, T., and G. M. Stalker. 1961. *The Management of Innovation*. London: Tavistock.

Campbel, H., and R. J. Braidwood. 1972. "An early farming village in Turkey." In *Old World Archaeology*. Ed. C. C. Lamberg-Karlovsky, pp. 113–119. San Francisco: Freeman.

Campbell, D. T. 1969. "Variation and selective retention in sociocultural evolution." *General Systems* 14:69–85. Reprinted from *Social Change in Developing Areas: A Reinterpretation of Evolutionary Theory*. Ed. H. R. Barringer, G. I. Blanksten, and R. W. Mack. Cambridge, Mass.: Schenkman, 1965.

———. 1974. "Evolutionary epistemology." In *The Philosophy of Karl Popper* (Vol. 14, I & II). *The Library of Living Philosophers*. Ed. P. A. Schilpp, pp. 413–463. La Salle, Ill.: Open Court.

———. 1975. "On the conflicts between biological and social evolution and between psychology and moral tradition." *American Psychologist* 30:1103–1126.

Campbell, D. T., and J. C. Stanley. 1966. *Experimental and Quasi-Experimental Designs for Research*. Chicago: Rand McNally.

Caplan, A. L., ed. 1978. *The Sociobiology Debate*. New York: Harper & Row.

Carper, W. B., and W. E. Snizek. 1980. "The nature and types of organizational taxonomies: An overview." *Academy of Management Review* 5:65–75.

Carneiro, R. L. 1973. "Classical evolution." In *Main Currents in Cultural Anthropology*. Ed. R. Naroll, pp. 57–121. New York: Appleton-Century-Crofts.

Cattell, R. B., ed. 1966. *Handbook of Multivariate Experimental Psychology*. Chicago: Rand McNally.

Chandler, A. 1962. *Strategy and Structure*. Cambridge, Mass.: The MIT Press.

———. 1977. *The Visible Hand*. Cambridge, Mass.: Belknap.

Chandler, M. K., and L. R. Sayles. 1971. *Managing Large Systems*. New York: Harper & Row.

Child, J. 1972. "Organization structure, environment, and performance: The role of strategic choice." *Sociology* 6:1–22.

———. 1977. "Organization design and performance: Contingency theory and behavior." *Organization and Administrative Sciences* 8:169–183.

Christenson, A. L., and D. W. Read. 1977. "Numerical taxonomy, R-mode factor analysis, and archaeological classification." *American Antiquity* 42:163–179.

Chronbach, L. J. 1951. "Coefficient alpha and the internal structure of tests." *Psychometrika* 16:297–334.

Churchman, C. W. 1971. *The Design of Inquiring Systems*. New York: Basic Books.

Ciochon, R. L., and R. S. Corruccini. 1977. "The phenetic position of *Pliopithecus* and its phylogenetic relationship to the *Hominoidea*." *Systematic Zoology* 26:290–299.

Clark, P. B., and J. Q. Wilson. 1961. "Incentive systems: A theory of organizations." *Administrative Science Quarterly* 6:129–166.

Cleland, D. I., and W. R. King. 1980. *Systems Analysis and Project Management*. New York: McGraw-Hill.

Clifford, H. T., and W. Stephenson. 1975. *An Introduction to Numerical Classification*. New York: Academic Press.

Cohen, M. D., J. G. March, and J. P. Olsen. 1972. "A garbage can model of organizational choice." *Administrative Science Quarterly* 17:1–25.

Comstock, H. B. 1971. *The Iron Horse*. New York: T. Y. Crowell.

Connor, P. E. 1980. *Organizations: Theory and Design*. Chicago: SRA.

Cook, T. D., and Campbell, D. T. 1976. "The design and conduct of quasi-experiments and true experiments in field settings." In *Handbook of Industrial and Organizational Psychology*. Ed. M. D. Dunnette, pp. 223–326. Chicago: Rand McNally.

Corning, P. A. 1974. "Politics and the evolutionary process." *Evolutionary Biology* 7:253–294.

Crowson, R. A. 1970. *Classification and Biology*. New York: Atherton.

Crozier, M. 1964. *The Bureaucratic Phenomenon*. Chicago: University of Chicago Press.

Cummings, L. L., and Dunham, R. B. 1980. *Introduction to Organizational Behavior*. Homewood, Ill.: Irwin.

Cyert, R. M., and J. G. March. 1963. *A Behavioral Theory of the Firm*. Englewood Cliffs, N. J.: Prentice-Hall.

Czekanowski, J. 1913. *Zarys Metod Staystycznck*. Warsaw: E. Wendego.

Czepiel, J. A. 1975, "Patterns of interorganizational communications and the diffusion of a major technological innovation in a competitive industrial community." *Academy of Management Journal* 18:6–24.

Dalton, M. 1959. *Men Who Manage*. New York: Wiley.

Darwin, C. 1859. *On the Origin of Species by Means of Natural Selection*. London: Murray. (A Facsimile of the First Edition with an Introduction by Ernst Mayr [Cambridge, Mass.: Harvard University Press, 1964].)

Darwin, F. 1888. *The Life and Letters of Charles Darwin*. New York: D. Appleton.

Davis, L. E., and P. H. Englestad. 1966. "Unit operations in socio-technical systems: Analysis and design." Mimeographed working paper No. T-894. London: Tavistock Institute of Human Relations.

Davis, L. E., and J. C. Taylor, eds. 1979. *Design of Jobs*. 2d ed. Santa Monica, Calif.: Goodyear.

Davis, P. H., and V. H. Heywood. 1963. *Principles of Angiosperm Taxonomy*. Edinburgh: Oliver and Boyd.

Davis, S. M., and P. R. Lawrence. 1977. *Matrix*. Reading, Mass.: Addison-Wesley.

Dawkins, R. 1976. *The Selfish Gene*. New York: Oxford University Press.

Dill, W. R. 1958. "Environment as an influence on managerial autonomy." *Administrative Science Quarterly* 2:409–443.

Dixon, J. E., J. R. Cann, and C. Renfrew. 1972. "Obsidian and the origins of trade." In *Old World Archaeology*. Ed. C. C. Lamberg-Karlovsky, pp. 80–88. San Francisco: Freeman.

Dobzhansky, Th. 1937. *Genetics and the Origin of Species*. New York: Columbia University Press.

———. 1970. *Genetics of the Evolutionary Process*. New York: Columbia University Press.

———. 1973. "Nothing in biology makes sense except in the light of evolution." *American Biology Teacher* 35:125–129.

Dobzhansky, Th., F. J. Ayala, G. L. Stebbins, and J. W. Valentine. 1977. *Evolution*. San Francisco: Freeman.

Dodder, R. A. 1969. "A numerical taxonomy of voluntary associations." Ph.D. dissertation, University of Kansas.

Dole. G. E. 1973. "Foundations of contemporary evolutionism." In *Main Currents in Cultural Anthropology*. Ed. R. Naroll, pp. 247–279. New York: Appleton-Century-Crofts.

Doyen, J. T., and C. N. Slobodchikoff. 1974. "An operational approach to species classification." *Systematic Zoology* 23:239–247.

Dubin, R. 1978. *Theory Building*. Rev. ed. New York: Free Press.

Duncan, R. B. 1972. "Characteristics of organizational environments and perceived environmental uncertainty." *Administrative Science Quarterly* 17:313–327.

Eades, D. C. 1965. "The inappropriateness of the correlation coefficient as a measure of taxonomic resemblance." *Systematic Zoology* 14:98–100.

Eiseley, L. 1958. *Darwin's Century*. New York: Doubleday.

Eldredge, N., and S. J. Gould. 1972. "Punctuated equilibria: An alternative to phyletic gradualism." In *Models in Paleobiology*. Ed. T. J. M. Schopf, pp. 82–115. San Francisco: Freeman, Cooper.

Emery, F. E., and E. L. Trist. 1965. "The causal texture of organizational environments." *Human Relations* 18:21–32.

Etzioni, A. 1964. *Modern Organizations*. Englewood Cliffs, N. J.: Prentice-Hall.

———. 1975. *A Comparative Analysis of Complex Organizations*. Rev. ed. New York: Free Press.

Farris, J. S. 1969. "On the cophenetic correlation coefficient." *Systematic Zoology* 18:279–285.

———. 1979a. "On the naturalness of phylogenetic classification." *Systematic Zoology* 28:200–214.

———. 1979b. "The information content of the phylogenetic system." *Systematic Zoology* 28:483–519.

Filley, A. C., and R. J. Aldag. 1978. "Characteristics and measurement of an organizational typology." *Academy of Management Journal* 21:578–591.

Filley, A. C., R. J. House, and S. Kerr. 1976. *Managerial Process and Organizational Behavior*. 2d ed. Glenview, Ill.: Scott, Foresman.

Fisher, R. A. 1930. *The Genetical Theory of Natural Selection*. Oxford: Clarendon.

Fleishman, E. A., E. F. Harris, and H. W. Burtt. 1955. *Leadership and Supervision in Industry*. Research monograph No. 33. Columbus: Ohio State University, Bureau of Educational Research.

Freeman, J. H. 1978. "The unit of analysis in organizational research." In *Environments and Organizations*. Ed. M. W. Meyer and Associates, pp. 335–351. San Francisco: Jossey-Bass.

———. 1981. "Organizational life cycles and natural selection processes." Mimeographed. Berkeley: University of California.

Futuyma, D. J. 1979. *Evolutionary Biology*. Sunderland, Mass.: Sinauer.

Galbraith, J. 1973. *Designing Complex Organizations*. Reading, Mass.: Addison-Wesley.

George, C. S. 1972. *The History of Management Thought*. 2d ed. Englewood Cliffs, N. J.: Prentice-Hall.

Georgiou, P. 1973. "The goal paradigm and notes toward a counter paradigm." *Administrative Science Quarterly* 18:291–310.

Gerard, R. W., C. Kluckhohn, and A. Rapoport. 1956. "Biological and cultural evolution: Some analogies and explorations." *Behavioral Science* 1:6–42.

Ghent, A. W. 1966. "The logic of experimental design in the biological sciences." *Bioscience* 16:17–22.

Ghiselin, M. T. 1966. "On psychologism in the logic of taxonomic controversies." *Systematic Zoology* 26:207–215.

————. 1974. "A radical solution to the species problem." *Systematic Zoology* 23:536–544.

Gibbons, J. D. 1976. *Nonparametric Methods for Quantitative Analysis.* New York: Holt, Rinehart, and Winston.

Gingerich, P. D. 1979. "Paleontology, phylogeny, and classification: An example from the mammalian fossil record." *Systematic Zoology* 28:451–464.

Glaser, B. G., and A. L. Strauss. 1967. *The Discovery of Grounded Theory.* Chicago: Aldine.

Glob, P. V., and T. G. Bibby. 1972. "A forgotten civilization of the Persian Gulf." In *Old World Archaeology.* Ed. C. C. Lamberg-Karlovsky, pp. 165–173. San Francisco: Freeman.

Goffman, E. 1959. *The Presentation of Self in Everyday Life.* New York: Doubleday.

Goldschmidt, R. 1940. *The Material Basis of Evolution.* New Haven, Conn.: Yale University Press.

Goldschmidt, W. 1976. "Biological versus social evolution." *American Psychologist* 31:355–357.

Goronzy, F. 1969. "A numerical taxonomy of business enterprise." In *Numerical Taxonomy.* Ed. A. J. Cole, pp. 42–52. London: Academic Press.

Gorsuch, R. L. 1974. *Factor Analysis.* Philadelphia: Saunders.

Gouldner, A. W. 1954. *Patterns of Industrial Bureaucracy.* New York: Free Press.

————. 1959. "Organizational analysis." In *Sociology Today.* Ed. R. K. Merton, L. Brown, and L. S. Cottrell, Jr., pp. 400–428. New York: Basic Books.

Graham, W. K., and K. H. Roberts, eds. 1972. *Comparative Studies in Organizational Behavior.* New York: Holt, Rinehart, and Winston.

Greene, J. C. 1959. *The Death of Adam: Evolution and Its Impact on Western Thought.* Ames, Iowa: Iowa State University Press.

Griffiths, G. C. D. 1973. "Some fundamental problems in biological classification." *Systematic Zoology* 22:338–343.

Grimes, A. J., S. M. Klein, and F. A. Shull. 1972. "Matrix model: A selective empirical test." *Academy of Management Journal* 15:9–31.

Gulick, L., and L. Urwick, eds. 1937. *Papers on the Science of Administration.* New York: Columbia University, Institute of Public Administration.

Guttman, L. 1954. "Some necessary conditions for common-factor analysis." *Psychometrika* 19: 149–161.

Haas, J. E., and T. E. Drabek. 1973. *Complex Organizations.* New York: Macmillan Co.

Haas, J. E., R. H. Hall, and N. J. Johnson. 1966. "Toward an empirically derived taxonomy of organizations." In *Studies on Behavior in*

Organizations. Ed. R. V. Bowers, pp. 157–180. Athens, Ga.: University of Georgia Press.

Hage, J. 1980. *Theories of Organizations: Form, Process, and Transformation*. New York: Wiley Interscience.

Hage, J., and M. Aiken. 1967. "Relationship of centralization to other structural properties." *Administrative Science Quarterly* 12: 72–92.

————. 1969. "Routine technology, social structure and organizational goals." *Administrative Science Quarterly* 14:366–376.

Haire, M. 1959. "Biological models and empirical histories of the growth of organizations." In *Modern Organization Theory*. Ed. M. Haire, pp. 272–306. New York: Wiley.

Haldane, J. B. S. 1932. *The Causes of Evolution*. New York: Harper & Row.

Hall, R. H. 1977. *Organizations: Structure and Process*. 2d ed. Englewood Cliffs, N.J.: Prentice-Hall.

————. 1979. "Empirical taxonomies of organizations." In *Empirical Taxonomies of Organizations: Problematics in their Development*. Ed. C. K. Warriner, pp. 14–16. Presented at Roundtable Discussion, Annual Meeting of the American Sociological Association, Boston.

Hall, R. H., J. P. Clark, P. C. Giordano, P. V. Johnson, and M. Van Roekel. 1977. "Patterns of interorganizational relationships." *Administrative Science Quarterly* 22:457–474.

Hallo, W. W., and W. K. Simpson. 1971. *The Ancient Near East*. New York: Harcourt Brace Jovanovich.

Hamblin, R. L. 1958. "Leadership and crisis." *Sociometry* 21:322–335.

Hannan, M. T. 1980. "Notes on the ecology of national labor unions." Mimeographed. Palo Alto, Calif. Stanford University.

Hannan, M. T., and J. Freeman. 1974. "Environment and the structure of organizations." Presented at the Annual Meeting of the American Sociological Association, Montreal.

————. 1977. "The population ecology of organizations." *American Journal of Sociology* 82:929–964.

Harman, H. H. 1967. *Modern Factor Analysis*. 2d ed. Chicago: University of Chicago Press.

Hartigan, J. A. 1975. *Clustering Algorithms*. New York: Wiley.

Hawley, A. H. 1968. "Human ecology." In *International Encyclopedia of the Social Sciences*. Ed. D. L. Sills, pp. 328–337. New York: Macmillan Co.

Hayek, F. A. 1978. "The three sources of human values." Mimeographed. Hobhouse Lecture, London School of Economics, London.

Heise, D. R. 1969. "Problems in path analysis and causal inference." In *Sociological Methodology 1969*. Ed. E. F. Borgatta, pp. 38–73. San Francisco: Jossey-Bass.

Hempel, C. G., ed. 1965. *Aspects of Scientific Explanation*. New York: Free Press.

————. 1966. *Philosophy of Natural Science*. Englewood Cliffs, N.J.: Prentice-Hall.

Hempel, C. G., and P. Oppenheim. 1965. "Studies in the logic of explanation." In *Aspects of Scientific Explanation*. Ed. C. G. Hempel, pp. 245–290. New York: Free Press.

Hennig, W. 1950. *Grundzüge einer Theorie der phylogenetischen Systematik*. Berlin: Deutscher Zentralverlag.

————. 1966. *Phylogenetic Systematics*. Urbana: University of Illinois Press.

Herzberg, F. 1966. *Work and the Nature of Man*. Cleveland: World.

Heydebrand, W. V., ed. 1973. *Comparative Organizations*. Englewood Cliffs, N. J.: Prentice-Hall

Heywood, V. H. 1967. *Plant Taxonomy*. London: Edward Arnold.

Hill, J. 1978. "The origin of sociocultural evolution." *Journal of Social and Biological Structures* 1:377–386.

Homans, G. C. 1950. *The Human Group*. New York: Harcourt, Brace.

————. 1958. "Social behavior as exchange." *American Journal of Sociology* 63:597–606.

————. 1961. *Social Behavior: Its Elementary Forms*. New York: Harcourt, Brace & World.

Hoselitz, B. F., and W. E. Moore. 1960. *Industrialization and Society*. New York: UNESCO-Mouton.

Hull, D. L. 1965a. "The effect of essentialism on taxonomy—two thousand years of stasis (I)." *British Journal of the Philosophy of Science* 15:314–326.

————. 1965b. "The effect of essentialism on taxonomy—two thousand years of stasis (II)." *British Journal of the Philosophy of Science* 16:1–18.

————. 1974. *Philosophy of Biological Science*. Englewood Cliffs, N. J.: Prentice-Hall.

————. 1976. "Are species really individuals?" *Systematic Zoology* 25:174–191.

————. 1979. "The limits of cladism." *Systematic Zoology* 28:416–440.

Huxley, J. S. 1942. *Evolution: The Modern Syntheses*. New York: Harper.

Jaccard, P. 1908. "Nouvelles recherches sur la distribution florale." *Bulletin de la Societé Vaudoise des Sciences Naturelles* 44:223–270.

Jackson, J. H., and C. P. Morgan. 1978. *Organization Theory*. Englewood Cliffs, N. J.: Prentice-Hall.

Janowitz, M. 1959. "Changing patterns of organizational authority: The military establishment." *Administrative Science Quarterly* 3:473–493.

Jardine, N., and R. Sibson. 1968. "The construction of hierarchic and non-hierarchic classifications." *Computer Journal* 11:177–184.

————. 1971. *Mathematical Taxonomy*. London: Wiley.

Jeffrey, C. 1968. *An Introduction to Plant Taxonomy*. London: J. & A. Churchill.

Jelinek, M. 1977. "Technology, organizations, and contingency." *Academy of Management Review* 2:17–26.

Jones, S. B., and A. G. Luchsinger. 1979. *Plant Systematics*. New York: McGraw-Hill.

Jurkovich, R. 1974. "A core typology of organizational environments." *Administrative Science Quarterly* 19:380–394.

Kangas, P. C., and P. G. Risser. 1979. "Species packing in the fast-food restaurant guild." *Bulletin of the Ecological Society of America* 60:143–148.

Kaplan, A. 1964. *The Conduct of Inquiry*. San Francisco: Chandler.

Kast, 'F. E., and J. E. Rosenzweig, eds. 1973. *Contingency Views of Organization and Management*. Chicago: SRA.

Katz, D., and R. L. Kahn. 1978. *The Social Psychology of Organizations*. 2d ed. New York: Wiley.

Kaufman, H. 1975. "The natural history of organizations." *Administration and Society* 7:131–149.

Kelley, H. H. 1971. *Attribution in Social Interaction*. Morristown, N.J.: General Learning Press.

Kelley, J. L. 1955. *General Topology*. New York: Van Nostrand.

Kenyon, K. 1972. "Ancient Jericho." In *Old World Archaeology*. Ed. C. C. Lamberg-Karlovsky, pp. 89–94. San Francisco: Freeman.

Kerlinger, F. N. 1973. *Foundations of Behavioral Research*. 2d ed. New York: Holt, Rinehart, and Winston.

Kerr, C., J. T. Dunlop, F. H. Harbison, and C. A. Myers. 1960. *Industrialism and Industrial Man*. Cambridge, Mass.: Harvard University Press.

Khandwalla, P. N. 1977. *The Design of Organizations*. New York: Harcourt Brace Jovanovich.

Kimberly, J. R. 1975. "Classification and organizational analysis: The case of rehabilitation organizations." *Western Sociological Review* 6:47–60.

———. 1976. "Organizational size and the structuralist perspective: A review, critique and proposal." *Administrative Science Quarterly* 21:571–597.

———. 1980. "Initiation, innovation, and institutionalization in the creation process." In *The Organizational Life Cycle*. Ed. J. R. Kimberly, R. H. Miles, and Associates, pp. 18–43. San Francisco: Jossey-Bass.

Kimberly, J. R., R. H. Miles, and Associates, eds. 1980. *The Organizational Life Cycle*. San Francisco: Jossey-Bass.

Kingdon, D. R. 1973. *Matrix Organization*. London: Tavistock.

Koontz, H. 1964. *Toward a Unified Theory of Management*. New York: McGraw-Hill.

Koontz, H., and C. J. O'Donnell. 1976. *Management.* 6th ed. New York: McGraw-Hill.

Kuhn, A. 1980. "Differences vs. similarities in living systems." *Behavioral Science* 25:40–45.

Kuhn, T. S. 1970. *The Structure of Scientific Revolutions.* 2d ed. Chicago: University of Chicago Press.

Lamarck, J. B. 1809. *Zoological Philosophy.* Translated by H. Elliot. Reprint. New York: Hafner, 1963.

Lamberg-Karlovsky, C. C., ed. 1972. *Old World Archaeology.* San Francisco: Freeman.

Lammers, C. J., and D. J. Hickson, eds. 1979. *Organizations Alike and Unalike.* London: Routledge & Kegan Paul.

Lance, G. N., and W. T. Williams. 1967. "A general theory of classificatory sorting strategies. I. Hierarchical systems." *Computer Journal* 9:373–380.

Land, K. C. 1969. "Principles of path analysis." In *Sociological Methodology 1969.* Ed. E. F. Borgatta, pp. 3–37. San Francisco: Jossey-Bass.

Langton, J. 1979. "Darwinism and the behavioral theory of sociocultural evolution: An analysis." *American Journal of Sociology* 85: 288–309.

Lawrence, P. R., and J. W. Lorsch. 1967a. "Differentiation and integration in complex organizations." *Administrative Science Quarterly* 12:1–47.

———. 1967b. *Organization and Environment.* Boston: Harvard University Press.

Lazarsfeld, P. F., and H. Menzel. 1966. "On the relation between individual and collective properties." In *A Sociological Reader on Complex Organizations.* 2d ed. Ed. A. Etzioni, pp. 499–516. New York: Holt, Rinehart, and Winston.

Lenski, G. 1976. "History and social change." *American Journal of Sociology* 83:548–565.

Lenski, G., and J. Lenski. 1974. *Human Societies.* New York: McGraw-Hill.

Leroi-Gourhan, A. 1972. "The evolution of paleolithic art." In *Old World Archaeology.* Ed. C. C. Lamberg-Karlovsky, pp. 13–23. San Francisco: Freeman.

Levins, R. 1968. *Evolution in Changing Environments.* Princeton, N.J.: Princeton University Press.

Lewontin, R. C. 1968. "The concept of evolution." In *International Encyclopedia of Social Sciences.* Ed. D. L. Sills, 5:202–210. New York: Macmillan.

———. 1972a. "Testing the theory of natural selection." *Nature* 236: 181–182.

———. 1972b. *The Genetic Basis of Evolutionary Change.* New York: Columbia University Press.

———. 1978. "Adaptation." *Scientific American* 239:212–230.

Lidicker, W. Z., Jr. 1973. "A phenetic analysis of some New Guinea rodents." *Systematic Zoology* 22:36–45.

Likert, R. 1967. *The Human Organization*. New York: McGraw-Hill.

Linnaeus, C. 1758. *Systema Naturae* (editio decima, reformata). Tom. I. Laurentii Salvii, Holmiae.

Litterer, J. A. 1963. "Program management: Organizing for stability and flexibility." *Personnel* 40:25–34.

Litzinger, W., A. Mayrinac, and J. Wagle. 1970. "The manned spacecraft center in Houston: The practice of matrix management." *International Review of Administrative Sciences* 36:1–8.

Lodahl, T. M., and S. M. Mitchell. 1980. "Drift in the development of innovative organizations." In *The Organizational Life Cycle*. Ed. J. R. Kimberly, R. H. Miles, and Associates, pp. 184–207. San Francisco: Jossey-Bass.

Lorenz, K. Z. 1974. "Analogy as a source of knowledge." *Science* 185:229–234.

Lorsch, J. W., and J. J. Morse. 1974. *Organizations and Their Members: A Contingency Approach*. New York: Harper & Row.

Løvtrup, S. 1974. *Epigenetics: A Treatise on Theoretical Biology*. New York: Wiley.

Lundberg, C. C. 1976. "Hypothesis creation in organizational research." *Academy of Management Review* 1:5–12.

Luthans, F., and R. Kreitner. 1975. *Organizational Behavior Modification*. Glenview, Ill.: Scott, Foresman.

Lynch, B. P. 1974. "An empirical assessment of Perrow's technology construct." *Administrative Science Quarterly* 19:338–356.

McClelland, D. C., J. W. Atkinson, R. A. Clark, and E. L. Lowell. 1953. *The Achievement Motive*. New York: Appleton-Century-Crofts.

McGregor, D. 1960. *The Human Side of Enterprise*. New York: McGraw-Hill.

McKelvey, B. 1969. "On developing efficient statistically significant measuring instruments by factor analytic technique." Mimeographed. Los Angeles: Graduate School of Management, UCLA.

———. 1970. "Toward a holistic morphology of organizations." Mimeographed. Santa Monica: RAND Corp.

———. 1973. "Dimensions of organizational classification: A replication of the Aston study." Mimeographed. Los Angeles: Graduate School of Management, UCLA.

———. 1974. "Organizational effectiveness I & II." Videotape. New York: Edutronics/McGraw-Hill.

———. 1975. "Guidelines for the empirical classification of organizations." *Administrative Science Quarterly* 20:509–525.

———. 1978. "Organizational systematics: Taxonomic lessons from biology." *Management Science* 24:1428–1440.

————. 1979. "Issues in the numerical taxonomy of organizations." In *Empirical Taxonomies of Organizations: Problematics in Their Development.* Ed. C. K. Warriner, pp. 17–25. Presented at Roundtable Discussion, Annual Meeting of the American Sociological Association, Boston.

————. 1980. "Organizational speciation." In *Middle Range Theory and the Study of Organizations.* Ed. C. C. Pinder and L. F. Moore. Leiden, The Netherlands: Martinus Nijhoff.

McKelvey, B., and R. H. Kilmann. 1975. "Organization design: A participative multivariate approach." *Administrative Science Quarterly* 20:24–36.

Mackenzie, K. D., and R. House. 1978. "Paradigm development in the social sciences: A proposed research strategy." *Academy of Management Review* 3:7–23.

McLuhan, M. 1962. *The Gutenberg Galaxy.* Toronto: University of Toronto Press.

McNeill, J. 1979. "Purposeful phenetics." *Systematic Zoology* 28: 465–482.

MacQueen, J. 1967. "Some methods for classification and analysis of multivariate observations." In *Proceedings of the Fifth Berkeley Symposium on Mathematical Statistics and Probability.* Ed. L. M. LeCam and J. Newman, 1:281–297. Berkeley and Los Angeles: University of California Press.

McWhinney, W. H. 1965. "On the geometry of organizations." *Administrative Science Quarterly* 10:347–363.

————. 1968. "Organizational form, decision modalities, and the environment." *Human Relations* 21:269–281.

————. 1975. "Dual hierarchies on a path to self management." Mimeographed. Los Angeles: Graduate School of Management, UCLA.

Magnusen, K. O. 1970. "Technology and organizational differentiation: A field study of manufacturing corporations." Ph.D. dissertation, University of Wisconsin.

Mahoney, T. A., and P. J. Frost. 1974. "The role of technology in models of organizational effectiveness." *Organizational Behavior and Human Performance* 11:122–138.

Mahoney, T. A., and W. Weitzel. 1969. "Managerial models of organizational effectiveness." *Administrative Science Quarterly* 14: 357–365.

March, J. G. 1965. *Handbook of Organizations.* Chicago: Rand McNally.

March, J. G., and H. A. Simon. 1958. *Organizations.* New York: Wiley.

Margulies, N., and A. P. Raia, eds. 1978. *Conceptual Foundations of Organizational Development.* New York: McGraw-Hill.

Martilla, J. A. 1971." Word-of-mouth communication in the industrial adoption process." *Journal of Marketing Research* 8:173–178.

Maslow, A. H. 1954. *Motivation and Personality.* New York: Harper.

Mason, B. H., and L. G. Berry. 1968. *Elements of Mineralogy.* San Francisco: Freeman.

Massie, J. L. 1965. "Management theory." In *Handbook of Organizations*. Ed. J. G. March, pp. 387–422. Chicago: Rand McNally.

Masters, R. D. 1970. "Genes, language and evolution." *Semiotica* 2:295–320.

Mayr, E. 1957. "Difficulties and importance of the biological species concept." In *The Species Problem*. Ed. E. Mayr, pp. 371–388. American Association for the Advancement of Science Publication No. 50.

———. 1969. *Principles of Systematic Zoology*. New York: McGraw-Hill.

———. 1974. "Cladistic analysis or cladistic classification." *Zeitschrift für zoologische Systematik und Evolutionsforschung* 12: 94–128.

———. 1976. *Evolution and the Diversity of Life: Selected Essays*. Cambridge, Mass.: Harvard University Press.

Mechanic, D. 1963. "Some considerations in the methodology of organizational studies." In *The Social Science of Organizations*. Ed. H. J. Leavitt, pp. 137–182. Englewood Cliffs, N.J.: Prentice-Hall.

Melcher, A. J. 1975. "Theory and application of systems theory: Its promises, problems, and realizations." *Organization and Administrative Sciences* 6:3–10.

Mellaart, J. 1965. *Earliest Civilizations of the Near East*. London: Thames & Hudson.

Merton, R. K. 1968. *Social Theory and Social Structure*. 3d ed. Glencoe, Ill.: Free Press.

Meyer, M. W. 1972. *Bureaucratic Structure and Authority*. New York: Harper & Row.

———. 1977. *Theory of Organizational Structure*. Indianapolis: Bobbs-Merrill.

———. 1979. *Change in Public Bureaucracies*. London: Cambridge University Press.

Meyer, M. W., and Associates. 1978. *Environments and Organizations*. San Francisco: Jossey-Bass.

Meyer, M. W., and M. C. Brown. 1977. "The process of bureaucratization." *American Journal of Sociology* 83:363–385.

Mezzich, J. E., and H. Solomon. 1980. *Taxonomy and Behavioral Science*. New York: Academic Press.

Michener, C. D. 1970. "Diverse approaches to systematics." *Evolutionary Biology* 4:1–37.

———. 1977. "Discordant evolution and the classification of allodapine bees." *Systematic Zoology* 26:32–56.

———. 1978. "Dr. Nelson on taxonomic methods." *Systematic Zoology* 27:112–118.

Michener, C. D., and R. R. Sokal. 1957. "A quantitative approach to a problem in classification." *Evolution* 11:130–162.

Mickevich, M. F. 1978. "Taxonomic congruence." *Systematic Zoology* 27:143–158.

Miles, R. H. 1980. *Macro Organizational Behavior*. Santa Monica, Calif.: Goodyear.

Miles, R. H., and W. A. Randolph. 1980. "Influence of organizational learning styles on early development." In *The Organizational Life Cycle*. Ed. J. R. Kimberly, R. H. Miles, and Associates, pp. 44–82. San Francisco: Jossey-Bass.

Miller, E. J. 1959. "Technology, territory, and time: The internal differentiation of complex production systems." *Human Relations* 12:243–272.

Miller, E. J., and A. K. Rice. 1967. *Systems of Organization*. London: Tavistock Institute.

Miller, J. G. 1978. *Living Systems*. New York: McGraw-Hill.

Mills, P. K., and N. Margulies. 1980. "Toward a core typology of service organizations." *Academy of Management Review* 5:255–265.

Mintzberg, H. 1979. *The Structure of Organizations*. Englewood Cliffs, N.J.: Prentice-Hall.

Mitroff, I. I. 1974. *The Subjective Side of Science*. New York: American Elsevier.

Moss. W. W., P. C. Peterson, and W. T. Atyeo. 1977. "A multivariate assessment of phenetic relationships within the Feather Mite family Eustathiidae (Acari)." *Systematic Zoology* 26:386–409.

Moulton, T. P. 1978. "Principal component analysis of variation in form within *Oncaea Conifera* Gisbrech, 1891, a species of copepod (Crustacea)." *Systematic Zoology* 27:141–156.

Munroe, E. 1964. "Problems and trends in systematics." *Canadian Entomologist* 96:368–377.

Nagel, E. 1961. *The Structure of Science*. New York: Harcourt, Brace & World.

Nelson, G. J. 1972. "Phylogenetic relationship and classification." *Systematic Zoology* 21:227–231.

———. 1974. "Classification as an expression of phylogenetic relationships." *Systematic Zoology* 22:344–359.

———. 1979. "Cladistic analysis and synthesis: Principles and definitions, with a historical note on Adanson's *Familles des Plantes* (1736–1764)." *Systematic Zoology* 28:1–21.

Newell, A., and H. A. Simon. 1972. *Human Problem Solving*. Englewood Cliffs, N.J.: Prentice-Hall.

Nunnally, J. C. 1978. *Psychometric Theory*. 2d ed. New York: McGraw-Hill.

Ochiai, A. 1957. "Zoogeographic studies on the soleoid fishes found in Japan and its neighboring regions." *Bulletin of the Japanese Society of Scientific Fisheries* 22:526–530.

Odum, E. P. 1971. *Fundamentals of Ecology*. 3d ed. Philadelphia: Saunders.

Olson, E. C. 1964." Morphological integration and the meaning of characters in classification systems." In *Phenetic and Phylogenetic Classification*. Ed. V. H. Heywood and J. McNeill, pp. 123–156. London: Systematics Association. Publication No. 6.

———. 1971. *Vertebrate Paleozoology*. New York: Wiley-Interscience.

Oppenheim, A. L. 1977. *Ancient Mesopotamia*. Rev. ed. completed by Erica Reiner. Chicago: University of Chicago Press.

Osborn, R. N., J. G. Hunt, and L. R. Jauch. 1980. *Organization Theory*. New York: Wiley.

Ouchi, W. G. 1977. "The relationship between organizational structure and organizational control." *Administrative Science Quarterly* 22:95–113.

———. 1980a. "Efficient boundaries." Mimeographed. Los Angeles: Graduate School of Management, UCLA.

———. 1980b. "Markets, bureaucracies, and clans." *Administrative Science Quarterly* 25:129–141.

Özgüc, T. 1972. "An Assyrian trading outpost." In *Old World Archaeology*. Ed. C. C. Lamberg-Karlovsky, pp. 243–250. San Francisco: Freeman.

Parsons, T. 1956. "A sociological approach to the theory of organizations." *Administrative Science Quarterly* 1:63–85 and 2:225–239.

———. 1966. *Societies: Evolutionary and Comparative Perspectives*. Englewood Cliffs, N.J.: Prentice-Hall.

Pasmore, W. A., and J. J. Sherwood, eds. 1978. *Sociotechnical Systems: A Sourcebook*. La Jolla, Calif.: University Associates.

Pence, O. E. 1939. *The Y.M.C.A. and Social Need: A Study of Institutional Adaptation*. New York: Association Press.

Pennings, J. M. 1975. "The relevance of the structural-contingency model for organizational effectiveness." *Administrative Science Quarterly* 20:393–410.

———. 1980. "Environmental influences on the creation process." In *The Organizational Life Cycle*. Ed. J. R. Kimberly, R. H. Miles, and Associates, pp. 134–160. San Francisco: Jossey-Bass.

Penrose, L. S. 1954. "Distance, size, and shape." *Annals of Eugenics* 18:337–343.

Perkins, D., Jr., and P. Daly. 1972. "A hunter's village in Neolithic Turkey." In *Old World Archaeology*. Ed. C. C. Lamberg-Karlovsky, pp. 105–112. San Francisco: Freeman.

Perrow, C. 1961. "Goals in complex organizations." *American Sociological Review* 26:854–865.

———. 1967. "A framework for the comparative analysis of organizations." *American Sociological Review* 32:194–208.

———. 1970. *Organizational Analysis: A Sociological View*. Belmont, Calif.: Brooks/Cole.

Pfeffer, J., and G. R. Salancik. 1978. *The External Control of Organizations.* New York: Harper & Row.

Pfeffer, J., and H. Leblebici. 1973. "The effect of competition on some dimensions of organizational structure." *Social Forces* 52: 268–279.

Phillips, D. L. 1973. *Abandoning Method.* San Francisco: Jossey-Bass.

Pianka, E. R. 1974. *Evolutionary Ecology.* New York: Harper & Row.

Pinder, C. C. 1979. "Empirical taxonomies of organizations." In *Empirical Taxonomies of Organizations: Problematics in their Development.* Ed. C. K. Warriner, pp. 26–29. Presented at Roundtable Discussion, Annual Meeting of the American Sociological Association, Boston.

Pinder, C. C., and L. F. Moore. 1979. "The resurrection of taxonomy to aid the development of middle range theories of organizational behavior." *Administrative Science Quarterly* 24:99–118.

––––––, eds. 1980. *Middle Range Theory and the Study of Organizations.* Leiden, The Netherlands: Martinus Nijhoff.

Pinto, P. R., and C. C. Pinder. 1972. "A cluster-analytic approach to the study of organizations." *Organizational Behavior and Human Performance* 18:408–422.

Pondy, L. R., and I. I. Mitroff. 1979. "Beyond open system models of organization." In *Research in Organizational Behavior.* Ed. B. M. Staw, 1:3–39. Greenwich, Conn.: JAI.

Popper, K. R. 1950. *The Open Society and Its Enemies.* Princeton, N.J.: Princeton University Press.

––––––. 1968. *The Logic of Scientific Discovery.* 2d English ed. New York: Harper & Row.

Porter, M. 1980. *Competitive Strategy.* New York: Free Press.

Presch, W. 1979. "Phenetic analysis of a single data set: Phylogenetic implications." *Systematic Zoology* 28:366–371.

Pritchard, N. M., and A. J. B. Anderson. 1971. "Observations on the use of cluster analysis in botany with an ecological example." *Journal of Ecology* 59:727–747.

Provan, K. G., J. M. Beyer, and C. Krytbosch. 1980. "Environmental linkages and power resource-dependence relations between organizations." *Administrative Science Quarterly* 25:200–225.

Pruitt, D. G. 1961. "Problem Solving in the Department of State." Cited in P. N. Khandwalla. *The Design of Organizations.* New York: Harcourt Brace Jovanovich.

Pugh, D. S. 1966. "Modern organization theory: A psychological and sociological approach." *Psychological Bulletin* 66:235–251.

Pugh, D. S., D. J. Hickson, and C. R. Hinings. 1969. "An empirical taxonomy of structures of work organizations." *Administrative Science Quarterly* 14:115–126.

Pugh, D. S., D. J. Hickson, C. R. Hinings, and C. Turner. 1968. "Dimensions of organizational structure." *Administrative Science Quarterly* 13:65–105.

Quadagno, J. S. 1979. "Paradigms in evolutionary theory: The socio-biological model of natural selection." *American Sociological Review* 44:100–109.

Rapoport, A., and W. J. Horvath. 1959. "Thoughts on organization theory." In *Modern Systems Theory for the Behavioral Scientist.* Ed. W. Buckley, pp. 71–75. Chicago: Aldine.

Renfrew, C. 1972. "Carbon 14 and the prehistory of Europe." In *Old World Archaeology.* Ed. C. C. Lamberg-Karlovsky, pp. 201–209. San Francisco: Freeman.

———. 1973. *Before Civilization.* New York: Knopf.

Rice, G. H., Jr., and D. W. Bishoprick. 1971. *Conceptual Models of Organizations.* New York: Appleton-Century-Crofts.

Riesman, D., with N. Glazer and R. Denny. 1950. *The Lonely Crowd.* New Haven, Conn.: Yale University Press.

Roethlisberger, F. J., and W. J. Dickson. 1939. *Management and the Worker.* Cambridge, Mass.: Harvard University Press.

Rogers, D. J., and Tanimoto, T. T. 1960. "A computer program for classifying plants." *Science* 132:1115-1118.

Rohlf, F. J. 1970. "Adaptive hierarchical clustering schemes." *Systematic Zoology* 19:58–82.

Rohlf, F. J., and D. R. Fisher. 1968. "Tests for hierarchical structure in random data sets." *Systematic Zoology* 17:407–412.

Rosen, D. E. 1978. "Darwin's demon." *Systematic Zoology* 27:370–373.

Ross, H. H. 1974. *Biological Systematics.* Reading, Mass.: Addison-Wesley.

Rouse, I. 1964. "Archaeological approaches to cultural evolution." In *Explorations in Cultural Anthropology.* Ed. W. H. Goodenough, pp. 455–468. New York: McGraw-Hill.

Rumelt, R. P. 1974. *Strategy, Structure, and Economic Performance.* Cambridge, Mass.: Division of Research, Graduate School of Business Administration, Harvard University.

———. 1979. "Strategic fit and the organization-environment debate." Paper presented at the Annual Meeting of the Western Region, Academy of Management, Portland, Oregon.

Ruse, M. 1974. "Cultural evolution." *Theory and Decision* 5:413–440.

Russell, P. F., and T. R. Rao. 1940. "On habitat and association of species of Anopheline larvae in southeastern Madras." *Journal of the Malaria Institute of India* 3:153–178.

Sahlins, M. D. 1960. "Evolution: Specific and general." In *Evolution and Culture.* Ed. M. D. Sahlins and E. R. Service, pp. 12–44. Ann Arbor: University of Michigan Press.

Sahlins, M. D., and E. R. Service, eds. 1960. *Evolution and Culture.* Ann Arbor: University of Michigan Press.

Samuels, M. I. 1972. *Linguistic Evolution.* New York: Columbia University Press.

Sarason, S. B. 1972. *The Creation of Settings and the Future of Societies.* San Francisco: Jossey-Bass.

Sayles, L. 1958. *Behavior of Industrial Work Groups: Prediction and Control.* New York: Wiley.

Schein, E. H. 1980. *Organizational Psychology.* 3d ed. Englewood Cliffs, N.J.: Prentice-Hall.

Schein, E. H., and W. G. Bennis. 1965. *Personal and Organizational Change Through Group Methods.* New York: Wiley.

Schnell, G. D., T. L. Best, and M. L. Kennedy. 1978. "Interspecific morphologic variation in kangaroo rats (*Dipodomys*): Degree of concordance with genic variation." *Systematic Zoology* 27:34–48.

Schon, D. A. 1971. *Beyond the Stable State.* New York: Norton.

Schutz, A. 1964. *Collected Papers.* 2 vols. Ed. Maurice Natanson. The Hague: Nijhoff.

———. 1967. *The Phenomenology of the Social World.* Evanston, Ill.: Northwestern University Press.

Schutz, W. C. 1958. *FIRO: A Three-Dimensional Theory of Interpersonal Behavior.* New York: Holt, Rinehart, and Winston.

Schwab, J. J. 1960. "What do scientists do?" *Behavioral Science* 5:1–27.

Scott, W. R. 1964. "Theory of organizations." In *Handbook of Modern Sociology.* Ed. R. E. L. Farris. Chicago: Rand McNally.

———. 1981. *Organizations:* Rational, Natural, and Open Systems. Englewood Cliffs, N.J.: Prentice-Hall.

Scriven, M. 1959. "Explanation and prediction in evolutionary theory." *Science* 130:477–482.

Sells, S. B. 1964. "Toward a taxonomy of organizations." In *New Perspectives in Organizational Research.* Ed. W. W. Cooper, H. J. Leavitt, and M. W. Shelly II, pp. 515–532. New York: Wiley.

Selznick, P. 1948. "Foundations of the theory of organization." *American Sociological Review* 13:25–35.

———. 1949. *TVA and the Grass Roots.* Berkeley and Los Angeles: University of California Press.

Service, E. R. 1975. *Origins of the State and Civilization: The Process of Cultural Evolution.* New York: Norton.

Sethi, N. K. 1970. "A research model to study the environmental factors in management." *Management International Review* 10:75–86.

Shetty, Y. K., and N. W. Perry, Jr. 1976. "Are top executives transferable across companies?" *Business Horizons* 19:23–28.

Shvarts, S. S. 1977. *The Evolutionary Ecology of Animals.* Trans. and ed. A. E. Gill. New York: Consultants Bureau.

Siegel, S. 1956. *Nonparametric Statistics.* New York: McGraw-Hill.

Sills, D. L. 1957. *The Volunteers.* Glencoe, Ill.: Free Press.

Silverman, D. 1971. *The Theory of Organizations.* New York: Basic Books.

Simon, H. A. 1947. *Administrative Behavior.* New York: Free Press.

———. 1962. "The architecture of complexity." *Proceedings of the American Philosophical Society* 106:467–482.

Simpson, G. G. 1949. *The Meaning of Evolution.* New Haven, Conn.: Yale University Press.

———. 1953. *The Major Features of Evolution.* New York: Columbia University Press.

———. 1961. *Principles of Animal Taxonomy.* New York: Columbia University Press.

Simpson, R. L., and W. H. Gulley. 1962. "Goals, environmental pressures, and organizational characteristics." *American Sociological Review* 27:344–351.

Siu, R. G. H. 1968. *The Man of Many Qualities.* Cambridge: MIT Press.

Skinner, B. F. 1953. *Science and Human Behavior.* New York: Macmillan Co.

———. 1969. *Contingencies of Reinforcement.* New York: Appleton-Century-Crofts.

Slobodchikoff, C. N. 1976. *Concepts of Species.* Stroudsburg, Pa.: Dowden, Hutchinson & Ross.

Smith, P. M. 1976. *The Chemotaxonomy of Plants.* London: Arnold.

Sneath, P. H. A., and R. R. Sokal. 1973. *Numerical Taxonomy.* San Francisco: Freeman.

Sokal, R. R. 1961. "Distance as a measure of taxonometric similarity." *Systematic Zoology* 10:70–79.

Sokal, R. R. 1973. "The species problem reconsidered." *Systematic Zoology* 22:360–374.

Sokal, R. R., and T. J. Crovello. 1970. "The biological species concept: A critical evaluation." *American Naturalist* 104:127–153.

Sokal, R. R., and F. J. Rohlf. 1962. "The comparison of dendrograms by objective methods." *Taxon* 11:33–40.

Sokal, R. R., and P. H. A. Sneath. 1963. *Principles of Numerical Taxonomy.* San Francisco: Freeman.

Stanley, S. M. 1979. *Macroevolution: Pattern and Process.* San Francisco: Freeman.

Starbuck, W. H. 1974. "The current state of organization theory." In *Contemporary Management.* Ed. J. McGuire, pp. 123–139. Englewood Cliffs, N.J.: Prentice-Hall.

———. 1976. "Organizations and their environments." In *Handbook of Industrial and Organizational Psychology.* Ed. M. D. Dunnette, pp. 1069–1123. Chicago: Rand McNally.

Stebbins, G. L. 1969. "Comments on the search for a 'perfect system.' " *Taxon* 18:357–359.

Steers, R. M. 1981. *Introduction to Organizational Behavior.* Santa Monica, Calif.: Goodyear.

Steers, R. M., and L. W. Porter. 1975. *Motivation and Work Behavior.* New York: McGraw-Hill.

Sterba, R. L. A. 1976. "The organization and management of the temple corporations in Ancient Mesopotamia." *Academy of Management Review* 1:16–26.

Stern, R. N. 1979. "The development of an interorganizational control network: The case of intercollegiate athletics." *Administrative Science Quarterly* 24:242–266.

Steward, J. H., ed. 1955. *Irrigation Civilizations*. Social Science Monographs, vol. 1. Washington: Pan American Union, Social Sciences Section, Department of Cultural Affairs.

Stinchcombe, A. L. 1959. "Bureaucratic and craft administration of production: A comparative study." *Administrative Science Quarterly* 4:168–187.

———. 1965. "Social structure and organizations." In *Handbook of Organizations*. Ed. J. G. March, pp. 142–193. Chicago: Rand McNally.

Storer, N. W. 1966. *The Social System of Science*. New York: Holt, Rinehart, and Winston.

Szilagyi, A. D. Jr., and M. J. Wallace, Jr. 1980. *Organizational Behavior and Performance*. 2d ed. Santa Monica, Calif.: Goodyear.

Tannenbaum, A. S., B. Kavcic, M. Rosner, M. Viannello, and G. Wieser. 1974. *Hierarchy in Organizations*. San Francisco: Jossey-Bass.

Tannenbaum, R., and W. Schmidt. 1958. "How to choose a leadership pattern." *Harvard Business Review* 36:95–102.

Taylor, F. W. 1911. *Scientific Management*. New York: Harper.

Thibaut, J. W., and Kelley, H. H. 1959. *The Social Psychology of Groups*. New York: Wiley.

Teilhard de Chardin, P. 1959. *The Phenomenon of Man*. New York: Harper and Row.

Terreberry, S. 1968. "The evolution of organizational environments." *Administrative Science Quarterly* 12:590–613.

Thompson, J. D. 1967. *Organizations in Action*. New York: McGraw-Hill.

Thompson, J. D., and W. J. McEwen. 1958. "Organizational goals and environment: Goal setting as an interaction process." *American Sociological Review* 23:23–31.

Thorson, T. L. 1970. *Biopolitics*. New York: Holt, Rinehart, and Winston.

Tichy, N. M. 1980. "Problem cycles in organizations and the management of change." In *The Organizational Life Cycle*. Ed. J. R. Kimberly, R. H. Miles, and Associates, pp. 164–183. San Francisco: Jossey-Bass.

Trist, E. L., and K. W. Bamforth. 1951. "Some social and psychological consequences of the longwall method of coal-getting." *Human Relations* 4:3–38.

Udy, S. 1964. "Administrative rationality, social setting, and organizational development." In *New Perspectives in Organization Research*. Ed. W. W. Cooper, H. J. Leavitt, and M. W. Shelley II, pp. 173–192. New York: Wiley.

Ullrich, R. A., and G. F. Wieland. 1980. *Organization Theory and Design*. Rev. ed. Homewood, Ill.: Irwin.

Van de Ven, A. H. 1976. "A framework for organization assessment." *Academy of Management Review* 1:64–78.

———. 1979. "Review of *Organizations and Environments* by H. E. Aldrich." *Administrative Science Quarterly* 24:320–326.

———. 1980a. "Early planning, implementation, and performance of new organizations." In *The Organizational Life Cycle*. Ed. J. R. Kimberly, R. H. Miles, and Associates, pp. 83–133. San Francisco: Jossey-Bass.

———. 1980b. Presentation to the doctoral consortium. Academy of Management Meeting, Detroit, Michigan.

Vroom, V. H. 1964. *Work and Motivation*. New York: Wiley.

Waddington, C. H. 1960. "Evolutionary adaptations." In *The Evolution of Life*. Ed. S. Tax, pp. 381–402. Chicago: University of Chicago Press.

Wallace, W. L. 1971. *The Logic of Science in Sociology*. Chicago: Aldine Atherton.

Walton, R. E. 1980. "Establishing and maintaining high-commitment work systems." In *The Organizational Life Cycle*. Ed. J. R. Kimberly, R. H. Miles, and Associates, pp. 208–290. San Francisco: Jossey-Bass.

Warriner, C. K. 1973. "Teleology, ecology, and organizations." Presented at the Annual Meeting of the Midwest Sociological Society, Milwaukee, Wisconsin.

———. 1977. "Empirical taxonomies and the comparative study of organizations." Presented at the Annual Meeting of the American Sociological Association, Chicago, Ill.

———. 1978. "Teleology, ecology, and organizations." (Revision of 1973 paper.) Mimeographed. Lawrence: University of Kansas.

———, ed. 1979. *Empirical taxonomies of organizations: Problematics in Their Development*. Presented at Roundtable Discussion, Annual Meeting of the American Sociological Association, Boston.

———. 1980. "Organizational types: Notes on the organizational species concept." Mimeographed. Lawrence: University of Kansas.

Warriner, C. K., R. H. Hall, and B. McKelvey. 1981. "The comparative description of organizations: A research note and invitation." *Organization Studies* 2:173–180.

Weber, M. 1947. *The Theory of Social and Economic Organization*. Trans. A. M. Henderson and T. Parsons. Ed. T. Parsons. New York: Free Press.

Weick, K. E. 1969. *The Social Psychology of Organizing*. 2d ed., 1979. Reading, Mass.: Addison-Wesley.

West, S. S. 1972. "The ideology of academic scientists." *Institute of Radio Engineers Transactions in Engineering Management*. EM7:54–62.

White, L. A. 1949. *The Science of Culture*. New York: Farrar Strauss. Paperbound edition 1958, Grove Press.

————. 1959. *The Evolution of Culture*. New York: McGraw-Hill.

White, M. J. D. 1978. *Modes of Speciation*. San Francisco: Freeman.

Wiley, E. O. 1975. "Karl R. Popper, systematics, and classification: A reply to Walter Bock and other evolutionary taxonomists." *Systematic Zoology* 24:233–243.

————. 1978. "The evolutionary species concept reconsidered." *Systematic Zoology* 27:17–26.

————. 1979. "An annotated Linnaean hierarchy, with comments on natural taxa and competing systems." *Systematic Zoology* 28:308–337.

Williams, M. B. 1973. "Falsifiable predictions of evolutionary theory." *Philosophy of Science* 40:518–537.

Williams, W. T., and M. B. Dale. 1965. "Fundamental problems in numerical taxonomy." *Advances in Botanical Research* 2:35–68.

Williams, W. T., J. M. Lambert, and G. N. Lance. 1966. "Multivariate methods in plant ecology. V. Similarity analyses and information analysis." *Journal of Ecology* 54:427–445.

Williamson, O. E. 1975. *Markets and hierarchies: Analysis and antitrust implications*. New York: Free Press.

Wilson, E. O. 1975. *Sociobiology: The New Synthesis*. Cambridge, Mass.: Belknap.

Wispe, L. G., and J. N. Thompson, Jr. 1976. "The war between the words: Biological versus social evolution and some related issues." *American Psychologist* 31:341–384.

Woodward, J. 1965. *Industrial Organization: Theory and Practice*. London: Oxford University Press.

Worthy, J. C. 1950. "Organizational structure and employee morale." *American Sociological Review* 15:169–179.

Wren, D. A. 1972. *The Evolution of Management Thought*. New York: Ronald.

Wright, S. 1931. "Evolution in Mendelian populations." *Genetics* 16:97–159.

Wyckoff, D. D. 1976. *Railroad Management*. Lexington, Mass.: Heath.

Yuchtman, E., and S. Seashore. 1967. "A system resource approach to organizational effectiveness." *American Sociological Review* 32:891–903.

Zald, M. N. 1970. *Organizational Change: The Political Economy of the YMCA*. Chicago: University of Chicago Press.

INDEX

Designer: Michael Sheridan and Gayle Birrell
Compositor: Trend Western
Printer: Braun-Brumfield
Binder: Braun-Brumfield
Text: 10 pt. Melior
Display: Melior Bold